MARRIAGES & FAMILIES

IN THE 21ST CENTURY

MARRIAGES & FAMILIES

IN THE 21ST CENTURY

A BIOECOLOGICAL APPROACH

TASHA R. HOWE

WILEY-BLACKWELL

A John Wiley & Sons, Ltd., Publication

This edition first published 2012
© 2012 Tasha R. Howe

Blackwell Publishing was acquired by John Wiley & Sons in February 2007. Blackwell's publishing program has been merged with Wiley's global Scientific, Technical, and Medical business to form Wiley-Blackwell.

Registered Office
John Wiley & Sons Ltd, The Atrium, Southern Gate, Chichester, West Sussex, PO19 8SQ, UK

Editorial Offices
350 Main Street, Malden, MA 02148–5020, USA
9600 Garsington Road, Oxford, OX4 2DQ, UK
The Atrium, Southern Gate, Chichester, West Sussex, PO19 8SQ, UK

For details of our global editorial offices, for customer services, and for information about how to apply for permission to reuse the copyright material in this book please see our website at www.wiley.com/wiley-blackwell.

The right of Tasha R. Howe to be identified as the author of this work has been asserted in accordance with the UK Copyright, Designs and Patents Act 1988.

Wiley also publishes its books in a variety of electronic formats. Some content that appears in print may not be available in electronic books.

Designations used by companies to distinguish their products are often claimed as trademarks. All brand names and product names used in this book are trade names, service marks, trademarks or registered trademarks of their respective owners. The publisher is not associated with any product or vendor mentioned in this book. This publication is designed to provide accurate and authoritative information in regard to the subject matter covered. It is sold on the understanding that the publisher is not engaged in rendering professional services. If professional advice or other expert assistance is required, the services of a competent professional should be sought.

Library of Congress Cataloging-in-Publication Data

Howe, Tasha R.
  Marriages and families in the 21st century : a bioecological approach / Tasha R. Howe.
     p.   cm.
  Includes bibliographical references and index.
  ISBN 978-1-4051-9501-0 (hardback)
1. Families–United States.   2. Families.   3. Marriage–United States.   I. Title.
  HQ536.H69 2012
  306.8750973'09051–dc23

                                        2011019726

A catalogue record for this book is available from the British Library.

This book is published in the following electronic formats: ePDF: 9781444344684; epub: 9781444344691; mobi: 9781444344707; oISBN: 9781444344714

Set in 10/12pt Minion by SPi Publisher Services, Pondicherry, India

1   2012

For my grandparents, Louise and Charles Kent,
For nurturing my faith in the potential of all families

BRIEF CONTENTS

CONTENTS

PREFACE

Dear Instructors and Students

I am thrilled to be able to bring a fresh new approach to a topic near and dear to my heart: family relationships. Over the decade or so that I have taught the marriages and families course at my university, I have struggled each year to find an adequate textbook/reader/journal article combination that would truly reflect the diverse and dynamic families in which we all live. I found this such a difficult task that I decided to write a book myself, which would reflect the complexities of individuals, families, and cultures, while also being fun to read and interesting for students. My student test-pilots have given the book a resounding "thumbs up" and have said that when they read this book, it feels like they're having a conversation instead of trudging through dense text. And professional reviewers have commented on the lively, engaging writing style, combined with its multi-disciplinary focus and depth of analysis, which encourage students to think critically. I was delighted by the reviews and feel that I have been able to accomplish my main goals in writing a textbook unlike any other on the market. It covers all the topics instructors are used to examining in marriage and family courses (e.g., divorce, mate selection) yet it explores them in a way no other book does, from a bioecological approach. Key terms are given in bold, listed at the end of each chapter, and defined in a glossary at the end of the book.

I believe that we can only understand how families function if we take the time to examine them within the multiple contexts in which they live. We are all biological beings, with brains that have been organized to reflect our social and cultural milieu. The inner workings of our nervous systems, hormones, and neurotransmitters are not laid down solely through some genetic blueprint, however, but are intimately linked to the environments that shape us. Biology and context work bi-directionally to impact our family's functioning, whether it be healthy, safe, and stable, or in some way challenged or less than optimal. The bioecological approach easily integrates social ecologies with individual developmental influences like personality, coping skills, and neurophysiology.

Every topic in the book is explored using research from many disciplines, which may include cutting edge discoveries in neuroscience, medicine, sociology, social work, nursing, psychology, economics, psychiatry, and anthropology. Each chapter includes a *How Would You Measure That?* box which presents the details of an innovative research study and encourages students to build their abilities to approach research findings analytically. Because the book sets up this complex framework at the outset, students immediately begin to assimilate ways to critically think about research. I have used this framework in my classes for years and have found that within the first month of instruction, students become well versed in the bioecological model and can use it to understand their own and other people's families. They know, for example, that something like "love" is not simply a feeling but is a concept affected by everything from neurotransmitters to religion to culture. Indeed, the bioecological approach makes intuitive sense right away and students easily apply its principles to every topic we study. My intent in writing this text was for students to gain a deeper understanding of the complexities of families and no longer endorse statements like "his mother made him that way," or "she's that way because it's in the genes." The bioecological approach makes it patently clear that all things we are and all things we do are multiply determined.

In addition to the bioecological framework, other aspects of this text also make it unique and effective at eliciting deep structure learning, analysis, critical thinking, and personal insight. The limitations of stereotyped family forms such as the Standard North American Family (SNAF) are explored throughout the book, and it becomes evident that very few people live in SNAFs. SNAFs consist of a working white heterosexual middle-class father, his stay-at-home legal wife, and their small number of biological children. The SNAF ideology emerged from media images and biased memories of the 1950s, a time that in every way was an anomaly in human history. We explore the fact that even in the 1950s, most people did not live in SNAFs. Diversity has always been the norm in regard to family structure and a key aspect of this book is its focus on the history and evolution of current family forms. I emphasize that we really cannot understand the health and well-being of a family based solely on its structure. The only way to assess family strengths is by looking inside, moving away from *structure*, and looking at *process*. What are the processes, the dynamics, and the attachment patterns the family members experience? Only with that analysis can we assess whether a family is dysfunctional or has an abundance of strengths that may benefit its members. At its core, this textbook helps students view the world through a strengths-based lens.

Families have evolved and changed continuously since before recorded history and they will continue to evolve with contemporary challenges and trends. If we view these trends with a strengths-based approach, meaning that all family structures are viewed with an eye to meeting healthy relationship potentials, we can each build our strengths through recognition of the many ways healthy families function. I have included a plethora of *Self-Assessment* and *Building Your Strengths* exercises so that students can reflect on their own families' strengths and attempt to reinforce and build on them. When we focus on the positive attributes of families, we see that most of us have a lot in common. These commonalities tie the human family together and unite people from extremely diverse intersectional backgrounds.

Each of us lives an intersectional life, carrying with us our sex, gender, sexual orientation, ethnicity, history, "race," social class, age, religion, language, (dis)ability status, and biochemical make-up. These many intersectional sources of our identity constitute the very fiber of who we are, yet all of us are members of the same global village. It is no longer viable to be socially isolated, insular, or ethnocentric. What happens in one tiny corner of the globe now happens to us all. The 21st-century family is characterized by interactions with diverse others across the lifespan. Each chapter in this text has attempted to show trends within diverse groups in the U.S. and patterns across the world, focusing in particular on intersectional identities. Thus, diversity is the driving force in every chapter, not something that is featured in discrete boxes or sidebars.

Those who learn how to integrate multiple perspectives into their lives can become cognitively flexible, solve problems, and act in more creative, critical, and innovative ways. Multiculturalism leads to cognitive, social, and even spiritual advancement. To enhance this perspective, every chapter features a real family. Families wrote essays about their lives in their own words and provided family photos for students to be able to get a tiny glimpse at the diverse experiences parents, partners, children, and extended kin use to build their strengths.

I hope you enjoy reading this book as much as I enjoyed writing it for you. I welcome your comments and questions. Just send me an email!

Tasha
th28@humboldt.edu

ACKNOWLEDGMENTS

I want to thank everyone who has given their support and encouragement to me as a first-time author: my agent, Neil Salkind; at Wiley-Blackwell, my acquisitions editor, Chris Cardone, now at Sage, for signing me on and supporting my vision throughout the process, Mathew Bennett, senior editor of psychology, for his rational and caring approach to getting the job done, Marilyn R. Freedman, freelance development editor, for making my words fit for public consumption, Deirdre Ilkson, development editor, for her organizational prowess, warm-hearted support for both me and my book, and sense of humor, Nicole Benevenia, editorial assistant, Annie Jackson, copyeditor extraordinaire, and everyone in the marketing and art departments, for making the process and the final product so wonderful. And to the anonymous reviewers: thank you for your eye to detail and suggestions for improvement.

At Humboldt State University, my amazing students collected research, typed references, ran to the library, made spreadsheets, and generally allowed me to stay focused on the writing, especially Rachel Wiseman, Stephanie Bulluss, and Lindsay Weymouth. Thanks are due to my prolific mentor, Ross Parke, for convincing me to spend two years of my life "typing up my lecture notes" to write a textbook and also helping me to make it great and to Melinda Myers, for keeping me in check in innumerable ways.

I am forever grateful to my father, Dr. James Hein, for setting the bar high, and to Mike, Elijah, and Kieran, the steam in my engine: you keep me going with humor, love, and dinner-time conversations; you sacrificed a lot of wife/mommy time to allow me to write this book. Leslie Martin is the most amazing example of an author, woman, and friend, who always listens when I whine.

I want to thank all of my friends, family members, and colleagues whom I can't list individually but who have impacted my life and the writing of this book in myriad ways. Very special thanks to the brave families who shared the intimate details of their lives with my readers, in the personal essays placed throughout the book.

WALK THROUGH TOUR

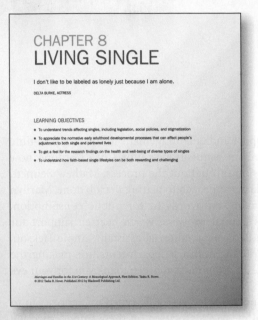

Chapter opening page Each chapter begins with a thought-provoking quotation and learning objectives to help the reader navigate the text.

Key terms and glossary Key terms are given in bold, defined in the adjacent margin, listed at the end of each chapter, and defined in a glossary at the end of the book.

Focus on My Family *Focus on My Family* boxes include essays written by families about their lives along with family photos. These boxes give the reader insight into the diverse experiences of parents, partners, children, and extended kin from many walks of life.

Self-Assessment *Self-Assessment* boxes encourage the reader to reflect upon his or her own family's strengths, focusing on the commonalities that tie the human family together and unite people from extremely diverse intersectional backgrounds.

Building Your Strengths *Building Your Strengths* boxes give the reader tools to examine the ways in which they can strengthen their relationships and families, and highlight the strengths-based approach taken throughout the book.

How Would You Measure That? *How Would You Measure That?* boxes present the details of an innovative research study and encourage students to analyze and critique research designs and conclusions.

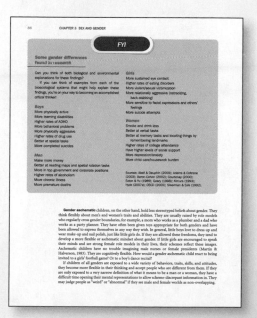

FYI *FYI* boxes highlight specific research findings and information that adds richness and depth to the main text. Critical thinking questions ask the reader to begin to question and apply the knowledge they've gained.

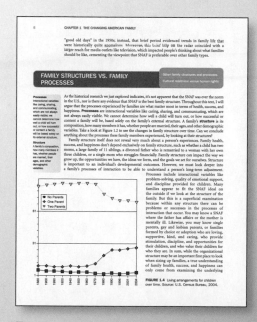

Figures Vibrant photographs and useful tables, charts, and graphs provide information at a glance and support visual learners.

CHAPTER 1
THE CHANGING AMERICAN FAMILY

We are one big family of people, trying to make our way through
the unfolding puzzle of life.

(Sara Childre, President, Heartmath Research Institute)

LEARNING OBJECTIVES

- To learn that there are many different ways to define family

- To understand the impact of the Standard North American Family ideologies on our perceptions of ourselves and others

- To recognize that beliefs about families are in large part social, cultural and historical constructions

- To be able to differentiate between family structures and family processes

- To grasp the general historical and contemporary trends affecting families of the major ethnic groups in the United States

Marriages and Families in the 21st Century: A Bioecological Approach, First Edition. Tasha R. Howe.
© 2012 Tasha R. Howe. Published 2012 by Blackwell Publishing Ltd.

WHAT IS A FAMILY?

The standard North American family

FAMILY STRUCTURES VS. FAMILY PROCESSES

Diverse family structures and processes

Cultural relativism vs. human rights

Regulating family structures and processes around the world

THE EVOLUTION OF AMERICAN FAMILIES

A look at the history of the first Americans

A look at the history of European American families

A look at the history of African American families

A look at the history of Latino and Hispanic American families' experiences

A look at Asian American experiences

Native Americans in modern times

European American families in modern times

African American families in modern times

Mexican American experiences

Puerto-Rican American experiences

Cuban American experiences

Latinos in modern times

Chinese American experiences

Japanese American experiences

Asian Americans in modern times

THE APPROACH AND ORGANIZATIONAL STRUCTURE OF THIS BOOK

WHAT IS A FAMILY?

What is a family? You might think that a formal definition is unnecessary for such a familiar concept. But you will see throughout this book that the way we define a concept is not just a matter of semantics but can have real consequences for the people involved. How we define what a family is or is not can influence what research questions scientists choose to investigate. Our definitions can also affect social policies enacted by governments and can even shape the moral values of a given population. By reading this book you will come to realize that there are many, quite diverse ways to envision family, and that the entity we call family is by nature a cultural and historical construction. In fact, it may be impossible to come up with one agreed-upon definition of what a family is, which makes studying families both difficult and endlessly fascinating.

Take a moment to think about your own definition of family. List your family members and reflect on whom you include on the list and whom you decide to leave out. Who makes up your family? I often have my students do this exercise on the first day of class and I'm always impressed by the great variety of definitions of family they offer, as well as the diverse family structures they describe. For example, last semester Miguel shared his list with our class. It included his mother, father, four siblings, seven aunties, four uncles, 32 cousins, and his grandparents on both sides.

"It seems like Miguel's definition includes only blood relatives," Jasmine commented. She continued, "My list includes my play cousins, my dad's girlfriend, my best friend who lived with us while we were growing up, and my stepbrother on my mom's side." Several members of the class nodded and then Tiffany spoke up, saying "I agree with Jasmine. Your family can include people who aren't blood relations. Like my uncle and his long-term partner, Joshua. They can't be married or have biological kids but Joshua is a big part of our family. Not to mention, that without my dog, I wouldn't have made it through college this far. He's my baby!"

After a few giggles, the class discussed whether those we consider family must be related by blood, involved in heterosexual unions, live in the same household as us, or even be human. Several students felt their college roommates were their primary family members since they were far away from home and they had built a little family at college.

Like my students, even governments and countries define the term "family" in a variety of ways. Why does it matter that we have such different ideas about the definition of family? If you think

FIGURE 1.1 Is Fido family?
Photo reproduced with permission.

about the laws of the United States or your home country, you might see some that apply only to people who are blood relations, legally married, or live together. For example, in some states and many countries around the world, same-sex couples are not allowed to marry, adopt children or visit their partners in intensive care units of hospitals since they are technically not "spouses" (visiting hours are reserved for "immediate family" only).

The definition of family doesn't stop with a country's laws, however. For example, the U.S. Census Bureau defines family as two or more people living together where the members are related by birth, marriage, or adoption. The lead householder (the person whose name is on the mortgage or rental agreement) and all people in the household who are related to him or her are considered to be the family members. If we take the census definition seriously, Jasmine, Tiffany, and Miguel would not technically be "family" with anyone on their lists as they each live with college roommates, away from most of those they consider to be family members.

Compare the Census Bureau's definition with *Webster's Dictionary* definitions, which include "a group of persons of common ancestry," or "a people or group of peoples regarded as deriving from common stock," or "a group of people united by certain convictions or a common affiliation." Would any of these definitions include Jasmine's play cousins or stepbrother? Many people consider a "family" to be characterized solely by a husband, a wife, and a couple of kids. In fact, one of *Webster's* other definitions of family states that family is "the basic unit in society traditionally consisting of two parents rearing their children." To confuse you even further, a group of family researchers defines family thus: "two or more people who are in a relationship created by birth, marriage, or choice. Some families have legal protection and privileges, while others do not" (Silverstein & Auerbach, 2005, p. 33). As you can see, understanding a "simple" concept like family may not be simple after all.

In agreement with Silverstein and Auerbach's definition, some of my students report that they have distanced themselves from their biological families because of abuse, neglect, alcoholism, or being "disowned" due to their lifestyles or belief systems. They went on to create families of their own choosing, consisting of members such as romantic partners and their children, close friends with whom they spend the holidays, and people with whom they work or for whom they are caretakers. These students consider their "family" members to be just as important and as emotionally rewarding for them as Miguel does his biological aunties and grandparents.

We can also belong to different types of families, sometimes at the same time. There's our **family of origin**, the family in which we grew up, and our **family of procreation**, which includes our mate and children. These two families we belong to may have similar structures or we may form a family structure that is completely different from the one in which we grew up. In fact, with today's varied reproductive technologies, divorce rates, and open adoptions, a single child could have a biological mother who contributed an egg for conception, a surrogate mother who carried the child for nine months, an "other mother" who raises the child along with the biological mother, and future stepmothers who enter the picture when a parent divorces and remarries. The same variations in biological and environmental relatedness can occur with fathers, aunts, uncles, and grandparents as well. Today it is not unheard of for a child whose parents divorced and remarried to have up to 16 different grandparents and great-grandparents!

In an attempt to be inclusive of all family forms, family will be defined in broad terms in this textbook. **Family** is defined as a group of two or more people connected by blood, adoption, marriage, or choice, who may rely on each other for social, emotional, and financial support. Tiffany might not like this definition since it requires all family members to be "people" and excludes her prized pooch. Consider whether you like this definition or not and think about which parts of it ring true or don't feel right from your perspective.

The Standard North American Family

Sociologist Dorothy Smith (1993) coined the term **Standard North American Family (SNAF)**, which refers to the image of a homemaker wife, a husband who works outside the home, and their two

Family of origin
The family you grew up in

Family of procreation
The family you form as an adult and often have children in

Family
A group of two or more people connected by blood, adoption, marriage, or choice, who may rely on each other for social, emotional, and/or financial support.

Standard North American Family (SNAF)
The concept articulated by sociologist Dorothy Smith, which consists of a homemaker mother, a breadwinning father, and their children; usually envisioned as white and middle class.

biological children. This is not just a way to describe the family. Smith argues that the image of SNAF carries with it an ideological code by which we judge all families who don't fit into this structure. We may be unconscious of how these ideologies affect our judgments of and interactions with other people. Imagine you meet people with the following family structures:

- a single mother with her three children
- a single father with his three children
- a gay or lesbian couple who have adopted children from another country
- a blended family of six children, three from the husband's previous marriage, and three from the wife's.

What thoughts go through your mind as you imagine each type of family? Do you feel sorry for any of them or think they may not be able to provide a stable or safe environment for their children? If you've ever thought that children would be better off in a married heterosexual household with a mother who stayed home, or if you've ever been surprised when someone who was not raised with a SNAF grew up to be successful and happy, you may be walking around with SNAF ideologies influencing the way you think about your own family and the families of people you meet.

Beyond our ideas about what family structure is best for people, implicit in the SNAF image is that a "family" is both white and middle class. Smith (1993) discusses how school personnel may often view non-SNAFs (e.g., families of color, immigrant families, or same-sex families) as deficient. If a child gets into trouble at school, the first conclusion might be that the problem stems from growing up with a "dysfunctional" family form. Some consider families especially deviant if they are not headed by a married adult male. Interestingly, it was not until the 1920s that even a slight majority of children in the U.S. lived within a male breadwinner SNAF structure (Coontz, 1997). I urge you to continuously assess the messages about families you were taught as you grew up, and try to understand how those ideas impact your perceptions of people and your interactions with them today. To start this process, check out my family in the *Focus on My Family* box.

Because today most families are not SNAFs, contemporary Americans often feel that the traditional institution of family is "disintegrating" or falling apart in modern times. They point to trends like the increase in cross-ethnic and cross-religious marriages, more people choosing not to marry at all, women working outside the home, science-fiction-like reproductive technologies, and the increase in openly gay and lesbian households as destructive to the traditional family. People tend to think that "in the old days" families were happier, more moral, and more stable, and experienced fewer problems like divorce, premarital sex, and abuse. The truth is that violent crime, teen births, and divorce rates have all been *decreasing* over the past decade (www.childstats.gov). Outcomes for children have also improved. More kids of all ethnic groups go to high school and college today than ever before, and they are also less likely to smoke

FIGURE 1.2 Do the Cleavers seem like an ideal family? Still from *Leave it to Beaver*, c. 1957; actors Barbara Billingsley, Hugh Beaumont, Tony Dow and Jerry Mather. © CBS Photo Archive/Getty Images.

FOCUS ON MY FAMILY

The Howe family

This picture shows me with my *family of procreation*. I had the privilege of being able to legally marry Mike. Our marriage is recognized by our home state, California. However, I was not allowed to marry Mike in his church, the Catholic Church. Because of the church's rules on *exogamy*, prohibitions about marrying someone outside of your group, we had to marry elsewhere. After five years of marriage we had a son and then another son five years after that. What ideas pop into your mind as you look at this picture? Do you think we look happy? Like good parents?

You may already know that I'm a college professor with a PhD. Would your perception change if you knew I was raised by divorced parents? That my mother married an African American man and I had a mixed half-brother? What about the fact that my biological father had a child as a teenager, giving me an older half-sister? Does it change your opinion to learn that I lived in poverty and went to ten different schools? What if I told you my mother and brother both died of drug overdoses? Do these facts change your perceptions as you gaze at the four smiling faces looking back at you?

In contrast to my background, Mike grew up in what appeared to be a SNAF. His father worked for Ford in Detroit and his mother stayed home with four children. They went to mass every Sunday and Mike played baseball and football, and was in the Boy Scouts. He lived in the same house his entire life. Sounds idyllic, doesn't it? Does anything change if you know that his father served on the front lines in the Korean War? That he came back with post-traumatic stress symptoms that led him to drink heavily? That he has trouble connecting with people and traveling without feeling anxiety? How might these processes have affected his parenting?

My family *structure*, or observable composition, consists of two legally married European American heterosexual middle-class people with two children. Our family *processes*, or interactional qualities, include us not fighting in front of our children, eating dinner together every night, and using consistent and predictable disciplinary methods. Does it matter that our kids have a male and female parent, or is it more important to know that Mike is naturally laid-back and I am more emotional and expressive? Think about the structures and processes in your own family and analyze which held more importance for the way you turned out. The difference between these two concepts will be explored in depth in this chapter.

The Howe family.
Reproduced by permission.

than they were in the 1950s. In fact, in 2006, 92% of whites, 85% of blacks, and 71% of Hispanic kids in the U.S. graduated from high school. This is a radical improvement over previous decades. Kids today are also less likely to be involved in alcohol-related accidents and to die from drugs than they were in the 1970s (Coles, 2006).

Older generations often think back to TV shows from the 1950s, like *Father Knows Best* or *Leave it to Beaver*, which depicted white American middle-class families who fit the SNAF ideal perfectly. In *Leave it to Beaver*, for example, the mother, June Cleaver, was always dressed immaculately with hair done and make-up on. She cooked and cleaned with a smile on her face. Her husband Ward would come home from work, kiss her, and sit down with the newspaper while she waited on him, bringing him a drink or his slippers. She would then call their two sons, Wally and Beaver, down to enjoy a dinner of meat and potatoes, as they jovially discussed their day. The children in this show were mischievous but never got into any real trouble, and the family solved any problems that arose in about 20 minutes. Media images like these often lead people to wonder whether their own families are as good or as healthy as the Cleavers. We may wonder whether our families are even "normal."

While it's true that the ethnic composition of the United States is becoming more diverse and wider varieties of family structures are being recognized, the reality is that the United States has always been diverse and family forms have changed and shifted continuously since the first colonies began to coalesce into a nation. Today over 46 million people in the U.S. speak a language other than English at home (U.S. Census Bureau, 2007). If the traditional 1950s family ever existed widely at all, it seems to have been a brief blip on the radar because that decade is certainly not representative of most Americans' experiences, either in the past or today. For example, although more people today are delaying marriage to focus on their education and career, the younger marriage ages for men and women in the 1950s were just a historical anomaly. You can see these trends in Figure 1.3.

From sixteenth-century British records (Wrigley & Schofield, 1989), we see that the average age of marriage then was 29.3 years for men and 26.4 years for women. In the United States, similar marriage ages occurred across all decades for the past 100 years, except for a big dip during and directly following World War II (the 1940s and 1950s). Marriage ages were older in earlier generations because men often had to wait until they had learned a trade or had secured land for a home before they married. But after World War II the economy was booming, suburban neighborhoods and affordable uniform tract housing sprang up all over the country, and the GI Bill combined with government subsidies made education and home-buying more widely available. Therefore people had less incentive to delay marriage. Another reason that marriage rates increased during the 1940s is that many young couples wanted to be married quickly before the male partners were shipped off to a very uncertain fate overseas.

It's important to recognize that any historic comparisons we make are relatively arbitrary. Depending on the historical periods we choose and the variables or statistics we use, we can conclude that modern trends in marriage and family life are either worse than, better than, or pretty much the same as previous decades or centuries. Throughout this book, I hope that you will think about what effect SNAF ideologies might have on your thinking. This section has shown that there probably were no "good old days" in the 1950s; instead, that brief period evidenced trends in family life that were historically quite anomalous. Moreover, it coincided with a larger reach for media like

FIGURE 1.3 Median age of first marriage by year.
Source: Wrigley & Schofield, 1989; U.S. Census Bureau, 2007.

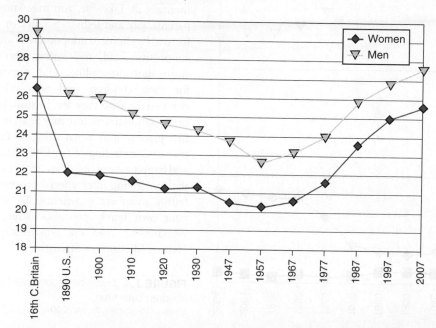

television, which impacted people's thinking about what families should be like, cementing the viewpoint that SNAF is preferable over other family types.

FAMILY STRUCTURES VS. FAMILY PROCESSES

Diverse family structures and processes

Cultural relativism vs. human rights

Processes
Interactional variables like caring, sharing, and communicating, which are not always easily visible; we cannot determine how well a child will turn out, or how successful or content a family will be based solely on its external structure.

Structure
A family's composition, how many members it has, whether people are married, their ages, and other demographic variables.

As the historical research we just explored indicates, it's not apparent that the SNAF was ever the norm in the U.S., nor is there any evidence that SNAF is the best family structure. Throughout this text, I will argue that the processes experienced by families are what matter most in terms of health, success, and happiness. **Processes** are interactional variables like caring, sharing, and communicating, which are not always easily visible. We cannot determine how well a child will turn out, or how successful or content a family will be, based solely on the family's external structure. A family's **structure** is its composition, how many members it has, whether people are married, their ages, and other demographic variables. Take a look at Figure 1.4 to see the changes in family structure over time. Can we conclude anything about the processes these family members experienced, by looking at their structures?

Family structure itself does not reveal very much about a person's experiences. Family health, success, and happiness don't depend exclusively on family structure, such as whether a child has two moms, a large family of 11 siblings, a divorced father who is remarried to a woman with her own three children, or a single mom who struggles financially. Family structure can impact the way we grow up, the opportunities we have, the ideas we form, and the goals we set for ourselves. Structure is important to an individual's developmental outcomes. However, we must look deeper into a family's processes of interaction to be able to understand a person's long-term adjustment. Processes include interactional variables like problem-solving, quality of emotional support, and discipline provided for children. Many families appear to fit the SNAF ideal on the outside if we look at the structure of the family. But this is a superficial examination because within any structure there can be problems or successes in the processes of interaction that occur. You may know a SNAF where the father has affairs or the mother is mentally ill. Likewise, you may know single parents, gay and lesbian parents, or families formed by choice or adoption who are loving, supportive, kind, and caring, who provide stimulation, discipline, and opportunities for their children, and who value their children for who they are. In sum, while the organizational structure may be an important first place to look when sizing up families, a true understanding of family health, success, and happiness can only come from examining the underlying interactional processes those family members experience. To check out your own family processes (strengths and weaknesses), read the *Self-Assessment* box "Rating My Family's Strengths."

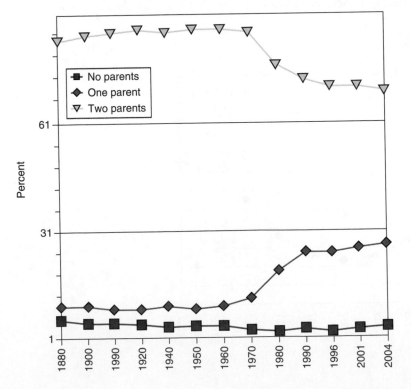

FIGURE 1.4 Living arrangements for children over time.
Source: U.S. Census Bureau, 2004.

Rating my family's strengths

You've learned a bit about the different processes families experience both historically and today. You can also assess your own family processes. Below are ten healthy family processes. Rate your family, a specific dyad or triad in your family (that is, mom and older brother, or husband, wife, and teenage daughter, and so on), or think about your family as a whole. You can do this regarding your *family of origin* as well as your *family of procreation*.

		Never	Sometimes	Always
1	My family members and I respect each others' individuality	1	2	3
2	We try to solve problems without blaming each other	1	2	3
3	We try not to raise our voices or yell	1	2	3
4	We tell other family members we love them	1	2	3
5	We express physical affection to each other (e.g. with hugs and kisses)	1	2	3
6	We try to discuss our problems before they fester too long	1	2	3
7	We don't gang up on specific family members	1	2	3
8	We don't call each other names during disagreements	1	2	3
9	We don't get physical (e.g. slapping or pushing) during disagreements	1	2	3
10	We enjoy just spending time together.	1	2	3

Total score

Scores can range from 10 to 30, with higher scores being best. If you get a 25 or higher, your family has established some pretty healthy processes of interaction. Good for you!

For scores between 16 and 24, you have some key strengths but can definitely do some work to try to improve processes that are lacking.

If your score is 15 or less, you might think seriously about finding some outside help to improve your communication or problem-solving methods. You can usually find free or low-cost counseling services at your university or county mental health office; or search the Internet or look in your local phone book to find other ideas, such as faith-based pastoral counseling at a nearby house of worship. You can also consult the American Association of Marriage and Family Therapists or the American Psychological Association to find a therapist in the U.S. or abroad (www.aamft.org; www. apa.org).

It can be useful to use this assessment as a conversation starter: rate your family yourself first and then have another family member rate the same part of the family without knowing your assessment. Then compare the scores and have a targeted conversation about the strengths and weaknesses you think your family has. Are there weaknesses you think would be easy to improve with a heart-to-heart discussion?

*Please note that all *Self-Assessments* in this text are for informational purposes only. They are not meant to diagnose, cure, or treat any family problems. They are only meant to give you food for thought.

Let's think about a concrete example to be sure you understand the differences between family structures and processes. You may have heard people say that being raised in a single-parent family is not as good as being raised with two parents. It is hard to argue against this idea because the more supports and role models a child has, the better. Do these supportive family members have to be a biological mother and a biological father, though? Can the second parent be a close friend? Or what about a live-in grandmother or an uncle who lives nearby? Researchers have struggled to find ways to examine whether it's true that a single mother is insufficient for raising a child, or whether it's just that one person alone will have a more difficult time, regardless of whether that person is a biological mother. Early research compared family structures and found that children from single-mother family structures are at risk for poor outcomes such as lower education and more problems with the law. But more current research that examined family processes showed that it's not living with a single mother, per se, that is detrimental to a child (looking only at the structure of the family) but that part of the explanation for these children's struggles could be due to the fact that single mothers are more likely to live in poverty than mothers living with partners. Moreover, children who live in poverty are more likely to struggle in school and have problems with antisocial behavior, regardless of the family structure they come from. Why is this?

Let's think about some of the processes that may be at work in this example. First, poor people may have to work so many hours at low-paying jobs that they can't be home when their kids get home from school and can't attend school events or meet with teachers. They may live in more dangerous neighborhoods where, if children can't be supervised while the parents are at work, violent or antisocial role models in the neighborhood may play an important role in socializing the children. So does this mean that if you grew up poor, you're doomed? No. In fact, most children who grow up poor turn out just fine. They are happy, healthy, productive members of society. These good outcomes can probably be attributed to the *processes* each individual experienced, such as a loving family, hard-working parents, caring teachers, and people who believed in them. In fact, most people who overcome adverse childhood experiences cite those very processes as explanations for how they overcame stressful circumstances (Masten & Coatsworth, 1998).

We will return to the ideas of SNAF and "structure versus process" throughout this book. Each chapter includes a *Focus on My Family* box in which families tell their stories in their own words, and describe both the structures and the processes that affect their lives. You will see that while both family structures and processes are important for people's outcomes, families are embedded in larger contextual and cultural systems that impact them. To give you a feel for how a person's culture and context can affect life within the family, let's examine some of the ways people around the world experience diverse structures and processes.

Diverse family structures and processes

Modern family
A family where both adult partners work outside the home but the female partner still completes the majority of the housework and child care.

Before we delve into a deeper examination of the different types of "American" families, let's first look at a few other structures and processes that exist besides the basic SNAF. The **modern family** is a dual earner household where roles and responsibilities in the home are unequal (Silverstein & Auerbach, 2005). Like SNAF, this family structure is composed of a heterosexual married couple and their children. Women in these families still bear the brunt of the child care and housekeeping responsibilities; however, unlike SNAF wives, women in modern families often work full time and earn as much or more than their male partners. You are probably familiar with these families. Most of us know women who work full time but still come home and cook dinner, bathe the kids, and organize birthday parties. Even though men do not share equally in child care, men have tripled the amount of time they spend in child care compared to 40 years ago (Bianchi, Robinson, & Milkie, 2006). And men's housework participation has doubled over the past 40 years, though, they still only do 30% of that work (Fisher, Egerton, Gershuny, & Robinson, 2006). Interestingly, women have also increased the amount of time they spend with their children as compared to 40 years ago, as society now has high expectations for both men and women to participate in parenting, instead of just caretaking. In the 1950s it would be unusual to see a mother sitting down on the floor to play board games or baby dolls with her children, a common sight today (Coltrane & Adams, 2008).

In comparison with the modern family, a **post-modern family** involves a deconstruction or transformation of at least one aspect of traditional SNAF ideas about what a family is (Silverstein & Auerbach, 2005). Post-modern families may have egalitarian gender roles, or consist of a same sex couple or a father who remains single by choice. These families have abandoned the idea that a healthy family must include a European American married heterosexual pairing or traditional gender roles. You can see this kind of deconstruction of SNAF ideas in Figure 1.5, which shows how many children live in single father households, by decade.

In 2008, the United States elected its first multiethnic president, Barack Obama. Look at Figure 1.6 and determine which type of family the Obamas are.

Regulating family structures and processes around the world

In every culture around the world, family structures are regulated—either allowed or endorsed by cultural, religious, or governmental leaders. Most countries, cultures, and religious groups have rules, customs, and policies about the people whom its citizens should definitely *not* marry. This is called **exogamy**, meaning marrying *outside* (*exogenous* to) their own group. For example, many religious groups do not allow their practitioners to marry outside of their religion. Likewise, there are certain people whom groups in power wholeheartedly endorse for their citizens' marriages. This is called **endogamy**, meaning marrying *within* a specific circle of people. For example, many immigrants prefer their children to marry within their own group, and do not approve of their children marrying a person from the new country.

Another practice that is regulated—disallowed or encouraged—by cultural groups is **polygamy**, the practice of one man marrying many women. For example, some Bedouin Arab families practice

Post-modern family
A family where at least one element of the SNAF is deconstructed or transformed.

Exogamy
A set of beliefs, practices, or mandates regarding people who should be excluded as possible marriage partners. People outside of one's own group are often excluded as marriage partners.

Endogamy
A set of beliefs, practices, or mandates regarding people within one's own group who are considered to be one's only viable marriage partners.

Polygamy
The practice of one man taking more than one wife; also known as polygyny.

FIGURE 1.5 Number of children living in single father households by year.
Source: U.S. Census Bureau, 2007.

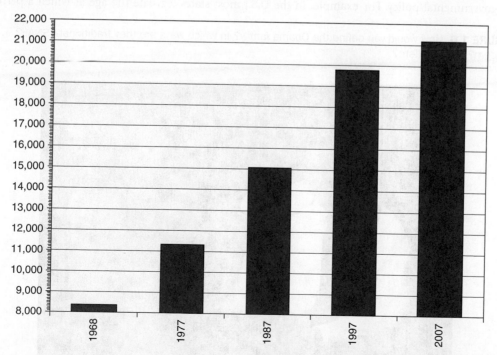

polygamy. The holy book Muslims follow, the Qu'ran, allows men to have multiple wives. For Bedouins, the first marriage is often arranged by family members and then the man himself may choose his subsequent wives. These subsequent wives, chosen due to attraction, liking or loving, sometimes receive more affection, resources or support from the husband than the first wife (Al-Krenawi, Lev-Wiesel, & Sehwail Mahmud, 2007).

Cultural groups also regulate **polyandry**, the practice of one woman marrying more than one man. The Nyinba people from Nepal allow all brothers to marry the wife of the oldest brother, resulting in polyandry. However, this structural arrangement doesn't mean the woman is guaranteed much power in these marriages. The younger brothers can choose whether to engage in sexual relations with the wife and may also choose to leave her for another wife as they become older (Haddix, 2001).

As the above example shows, even when family structures appear to reverse traditional gender role processes, men around the world typically retain more power in family dynamics than women do. In fact, there is no evidence that any human group has ever been **matriarchal**, meaning that women maintain power and control over men. Some societies have been **matrifocal**, however, meaning that a newly married couple moves in with the wife's family. And some groups have been **matrilineal**, where property, privileges, and goods are passed down through the mother's family. In general, however, most societies around the world have been and continue to be **patriarchal** in nature. Men rule and enjoy power, privilege, and control over women and children.

Men are not the only family members to wield power in family dynamics, however. Sometimes elders (including women) and esteemed community members hold even more sway than, say, a person's father. For example, in order to ensure that cultural beliefs and traditions are adhered to, some cultures practice **arranged marriage**, where the wife and husband are chosen by family members, religious leaders, or cultural leaders. While many people in western societies find it very unappealing to think about marrying someone not of their own choosing, research shows the people in arranged marriages often feel happy, learn to love their partner, have lower rates of divorce, and report feeling less pressure to look sexy, attract someone based on superficial characteristics, or date many "frogs" before finding their "prince/princess" (Span, 2003).

In addition to people's marriage patterns being regulated or controlled, the ability to divorce, the right to adopt, and even sexual practices, can be determined by cultural traditions, religion, or governmental policy. For example, in the U.S., most states legislate the age at which a person

Polyandry
The practice of one woman taking more than one husband.

Matriarchal
A social system where women hold power and influence in the clan or family.

Matrifocal
A social system where men marry into their wives' families or clans and often live with them.

Matrilineal
A social system where goods and property are inherited or passed down through the maternal line.

Patriarchal
A social system where men hold power and influence in the clan or family.

Arranged marriage
A marriage wherein partners are chosen by family members, religious leaders, or cultural leaders, and not by the bride and groom.

FIGURE 1.6 How would you define the Obama family? In which ways are they traditional? SNAF? Modern? Post-modern?
© Annie Leibovitz/White House via Getty Images.

can "consent" to having sexual relations. In Arkansas, Indiana, and Iowa, boys are considered old enough to consent at 14 while girls must be 16. Other states, such as California, Virginia, and Wisconsin, require a person to be 18 (*West's Encyclopedia of American Law*, 2004). Why do you think these states chose different ages? And why different ages for boys and girls? It may have something to do with traditional beliefs about personal power or intellectual abilities in older versus young teens, or boys versus girls. Some other exogamy rules that regulate American experiences include laws against marrying within one's own family of origin (e.g., it's illegal to marry one's father, sibling or child). Americans are also not allowed to have sexual relationships with children. In contrast, the Etoro tribe of Papua New Guinea starts initiating boys (around the age of 12) to enter adulthood by having the boys perform fellatio rites on adult men. The thought is that by inseminating the boys with adult semen, they are helping them become men (Wood, 2003). This example illustrates that while one culture excludes certain groups for marriage and sex, other cultures encourage relationships with those groups.

Another example of exogamy in the U.S. includes the fact in most areas, you must marry someone outside of your own gender. In 2010, only five states in the nation (Massachusetts, Vermont, Iowa, Maine, and Connecticut) allowed same-sex couples to marry. Also, 10 countries around the world (Argentina, Iceland, Portugal, Sweden, The Netherlands, Belgium, Norway, Spain, South Africa, and Canada) have also legalized same-sex marriages (marriageequality.org; Vestal, 2008).

Ironically, in the same countries where gay marriage is allowed or civil unions are given many of the same rights as marriages, heterosexual couples are choosing *not* to marry in larger and larger numbers. More than half of couples in Sweden, for example, prefer not to get married but to raise children in cohabiting homes. There are few incentives to get married as these cultures tend to be secular instead of religious, there are few tax incentives for being married, and cohabiting couples receive the same health and insurance benefits as married couples. Is this trend away from heterosexual marriage a good thing? Many people might think trends like these endanger the very fiber of what it means to be a "family." While this is a complex question to answer, you may be interested to know that Western European and Scandinavian countries with low rates of marriage also have some of the lowest rates of teenage pregnancy, violent crime, and child abuse.

In contrast to many western industrialized nations moving away from traditional marriage and the SNAF, other cultures around the world continue to embrace traditional ideas about marriages and families, including separate spheres of existence for males and females. For example, in some Muslim countries such as Afghanistan, women are expected to lead the family in morality and connection to God. Yet women are also expected to serve male family members. They sometimes must marry their husband's family members if their husband dies (Ahmed-Ghosh, 2003). Before the oppressive Taliban regime took over in 1994, however, many women in Afghanistan obtained college educations and performed professional public roles such as being attorneys and physicians.

Similar to current roles for women in Afghanistan, the Masai tribe in Africa practices traditional gender roles where women must take care of the home and husbands have every right to discipline (even physically) their wives (Magoke-Mhoja, 2008). In many countries, women are encouraged, or even required, to be escorted by male relatives in public, and to cover their heads while outside of the home. Do you think these cultures are remiss in endorsing traditional family structures and processes? Or do you believe every society should have the right to regulate relationships and roles as they see fit?

Cultural relativism vs. human rights

With all of these different cultural and legal regulations about who can or should marry whom, it is easy to wonder whether one practice is right and another wrong. Some would argue that we must consider every culture individually and accept their practices as just as valid as ours. **Cultural relativism** refers to the idea that values, practices, and beliefs differ by cultural group and that none are better or worse than any others. From this perspective, we should judge family practices as normal relative to the family's or culture's belief system, even if such practices seem abnormal to us. Do you believe in cultural relativism? Live and let live? The United Nations (UN) has decided that we should allow

Cultural relativism
The idea that each culture's beliefs and practices hold equal value and that one culture should not judge another culture as inferior, wrong, or unhealthy for its members.

cultural and religious freedom to prosper as long as cultural or religious practices do not violate a family member's *human rights*, an individual's freedom to make choices that make him/her happy without the threat of violence, ostracism, or psychological harm. For example, the UN has specific written documents condemning violence against women and children. The UN Convention on the Rights of the Child, for example, argues that all children in every culture have the rights to be loved and valued, to receive education, and to live a life free of violence or abuse of any kind. This means that the international community has decided that individual human rights are more important in some cases than cultural traditions.

Let's look at one example of a cultural practice that may be judged as wrong by people in the West. The Meru people of Theraka in Kenya, Africa, are one of many groups around the world to practice what westerners call "female genital mutilation." However, they call it "circumcision." They "circumcise" young women by removing their clitoris and sometimes sewing their vaginal openings closed. This is meant to ensure a woman is a virgin at marriage, and that she not engage in sexual relations for "pleasure." Her clitoris is thought to cause her to be unfaithful and want sex with men other than her husband. The Meru believe that if a child is born to an uncircumcised mother, that child will be unclean so will not be allowed to participate in cultural rituals. They also believe that if a man marries an uncircumcised woman, he may have a curse put on him by their ancestors. The circumcision ritual is a rite of passage for the women of these communities and marks their development into adulthood (Chege, Askew, & Liku, 2001). So do we have the right to tell these women or their families that what they are doing is wrong? Does female genital mutilation violate UN mandates prohibiting "violence" against women? There has been quite an international social movement against female circumcision around the world and due, in part, to this pressure, many groups are beginning to do "ritual" circumcision where they don't actually cut women's genitals but still perform the other parts of the ceremonies to ensure their cultural rites of passage. I'll leave it up to you to decide for yourself what you think of westerners or the UN intervening in long-held practice and beliefs surrounding family life around the world.

Now let's turn the international lens onto the western family. What do you think about the American practice of leaving infants in cribs in their own rooms to sleep? Many cultures around the world would argue that this is child abuse or, at the least, neglect. Parents around the world feel that infants should be with their parents all the time, especially at night. It is felt that a mother is neglecting her child if she is not there throughout the night to breastfeed on demand and soothe the infant in its sleep (Goldberg & Keller, 2007). Western research has found that when infants sleep alone, they form strong emotional attachments to transitional objects, such as blankets, stuffed animals, or dolls (Hobara, 2003). Do other cultures have a right to tell us what to do with our babies? Is constant contact in the early years better for children, or is encouraging independence through solitary sleeping more helpful for child development? For important questions such as these, researchers have to be creative in designing studies to figure out how to answer the public's demand for knowledge about the best ways to raise children. To get an idea about how we might find answers about co-sleeping versus infants sleeping alone, see the *How Would You Measure That?* box on infant co-sleeping. Each chapter will have such a box, which will help you practice your critical thinking skills by asking you to analyze research methods and conclusions.

I hope that the research evidence reviewed so far has helped you understand that what a "good" family is becomes a complex issue when you consider cultural, religious, legal, and historical factors that impact family relations across many generations. While the picture of the European American post-war middle-class SNAF has been ingrained in many of our minds as the way American families always were and perhaps how they should still be, it's important that students of family relationships understand that diversity has always been the norm. Each ethnic group to live in the U.S. has had unique experiences regarding how they immigrated, what rules and restrictions were placed on their group, and how successful they were in maintaining their traditional family forms while trying to adapt to life in this new land. Stephanie Coontz, a leading expert on the history of the family, writes:

HOW WOULD YOU MEASURE THAT?

Infant co-sleeping
(Taylor, Donovan, & Leavitt, 2008)

Is it better for infants to sleep with their parents, as they do in most non-western nations? Does sending infants to sleep in their own beds in their own rooms harm them? To answer a question like this requires careful research. Many people around the world think independent sleeping amounts to child neglect, yet most Americans engage in this practice. So what's the truth?

In 2008, Taylor et al. attempted to answer this question. Previous research had shown that when mothers co-sleep with their infants, they breastfeed more. Some studies suggested that cases of Sudden Infant Death Syndrome (SIDS) could be prevented by co-sleeping because hormones are produced in the infants to help regulate sleep physiology, more antibodies are produced to fight disease, and parents become more in-tune with their infants' sleeping and breathing patterns. However, other research suggested that more educated and wealthier parents choose both to breastfeed longer *and* co-sleep, so it's not the co-sleeping that matters, but the conscientious parenting the children received. And still other research showed that parents who are forced to co-sleep due to space limitations or child illness do not breastfeed more, so co-sleeping would not necessarily increase breastfeeding. This latter finding may explain why some studies show co-sleeping to be related to sleep disturbances in both adults and children, because they are forced to co-sleep due to other problems.

In research, when one variable is related to another (like co-sleeping and breastfeeding), we say the variables are *correlated*. But we can *never* conclude anything about causality from a simple correlation. Co-sleeping could cause more breastfeeding, or people who choose to breastfeed may then find cause to co-sleep, or it could be that a third variable like higher levels of education cause *both* breastfeeding and co-sleeping. So keep this in mind when you read that two variables are correlated with each other: we don't know what causes that relationship.

Taylor et al. (2008) examined 70 mothers between the ages of 21 and 41 and their 6-month-old infants. They measured the frequency and duration of breastfeeding and looked at outcomes like sensitive responsiveness in mothers and positive affect and play when the infants were 9 months old. They broke the families into three structural groups: nightly co-sleepers, non-co-sleepers, and intermittent co-sleepers (who sometimes co-slept and sometimes didn't). They wanted to see how sleeping *structure* was related to positive family *processes* later on.

What they found was quite interesting. Nightly co-sleepers breastfed their infants more and for a longer duration. The "intermittent" and "non" co-sleeping groups didn't differ on breastfeeding. However, those with consistent sleeping patterns exhibited more positive behavior with their babies, regardless of whether they co-slept; when mothers were consistent in their sleeping patterns, they were also more sensitive to their babies' cues, and they responded more warmly to the infants' behaviors. Thus, the sleep process of consistency had a great impact. It mattered only whether moms did *the same thing* every night. In other words, it was the *consistency* in sleeping patterns that made for the best relationships, regardless of whether they co-slept or the infant slept in his/her own bed. The *structure* of the family didn't have much impact. What mattered most was a *process* of well-regulated, consistent, and predictable sleep every night. It's always best to breastfeed if possible, to give children the richest nutrients, but as far as sleep goes, co-sleep or not, the message from this study is: be consistent!

The "modernization" of the family was the result not of some general evolution of "the" family, as early family sociologists originally posited, but of *diverging* and *contradictory* responses that occurred in different areas and classes at various times, eventually interacting to produce the trends we now associate with industrialization. (Coontz, 2000, p. 25)

THE EVOLUTION OF AMERICAN FAMILIES

> A look at the history of the first Americans
>
> A look at the history of European American families
>
> A look at the history of African American families
>
> A look at the history of Latino and Hispanic American families' experiences
>
> A look at Asian American experiences

As you look around your classroom, you will probably notice that the students may look different from each other. As you get to know other students, you may find that they have distinct cultural or religious backgrounds, speak other languages, or identify with different aspects of the larger culture than you do. One thing most of us have in common, though, is a history of migration or immigration in our families of origin. This section will review some of the key historical and contemporary trends affecting many of our families who originated from the major ethnic groups in the U.S. It's important that we don't just look at people's group or family structures, but that we attempt to understand the processes individuals experience and how those processes affect family health and well-being. We must look beyond static categories like race, gender, or socioeconomic status, and delve deeper into the complex influences on modern family life.

A look at the history of the first Americans

Centuries ago, people from Asia crossed over the land-bridge that once connected what is now Russia to the current U.S. state of Alaska. They migrated all over North, Central, and South America, creating some of the great civilizations of the world, such as the Mayan Empire, which existed from 2000 BCE to 900 CE, and the Aztecs, who reigned in modern-day Mexico from the twelfth to the sixteenth centuries CE. It wasn't until the sixteenth century that Europeans came to these lands and met Native Americans. Spanish conquistadores and explorers enslaved many of the native peoples they encountered. However, the Catholic Church, which funded many expeditions, admonished the Europeans for any treatment that was too severe, such as the violence

FIGURE 1.7 If these Native Americans kept a journal about their family lives, how do you think it might differ from journals of white settlers in the same area at that time? Hunting Horse and daughters, 1908. Photo by J. V. Dedrick/Buyenlarge/Getty Images.

that was routinely experienced by African slaves at the hands of European settlers in the "New World." The Catholic Church also allowed Spaniards to marry indigenous women, which led to openly "mixed race" families. Contrast this practice of open intermarriage with the segregation that occurred decades later in the U.S. when white slave owners had children with black slave women but did not marry them (Coles, 2006).

Native American Indians are a diverse group and comprise over 300 tribes speaking over 150 languages. It is very difficult to make generalizations about their family structures or processes. To paint a clear picture of the history and current status of Native American families, we will focus only on those tribes found in what is now the United States and who have had some level of reliable data published about them.

The first U.S. Census in 1790 showed that 13% of the population was Native American Indian (Schaefer, 2004). Due to contact with Europeans, and through disease, starvation, and genocide, by 1890, there were only 250,000 indigenous people left in the U.S. (Stuart, 1987). The white settlers and the American Indians often engaged in armed conflict with one another, yet many families and small groups got along well, traded, and even intermarried.

Originally, the British colonial regime considered American Indian nations in the colonies to be sovereign; relations with them required public negotiations with written treaties. However, these treaties were difficult to enforce and were often broken. With U.S. independence from Britain came greed for more land. Unlike the British, the U.S. government did not respect American Indian nations as sovereign powers. While some indigenous people stayed on ancestral lands and were not traumatized by their contact with whites, the Indian Removal Act of 1830 forced many Native Americans east of the Mississippi River to move west. Hundreds of thousands died on this journey, now known as the Trail of Tears. The survivors were often put on inferior reservation lands with new climates, strange soil, new plants and animals, and previously unknown diseases. All that these families had ever known was gone.

Imagine being a Native American child who grew up in a forest community, with river fishing as the primary source of sustenance. Your entire family is then relocated to a dry, desert-like climate. The only means you've ever known to survive are gone. Parents no longer know what to do to protect and feed their children. The life skills they once taught their children are irrelevant in this new setting. Government care packages of food and medicine which were promised arrive only sporadically. Your elders' wisdom can no longer be counted on to get you through tough times. Your warriors have new foes to face, whom they don't understand, as you have been resettled on an existing clan's hunting territory. The U.S. government promised to protect these refugees but rarely followed through (McLemore, Romo, & Baker, 2001).

While it is difficult to make generalizations about the original practices of Native American families, we do know that they tended to be fairly permissive parents who didn't use physical punishment. Children were often raised by everyone in the clan and had much freedom to explore the natural consequences of their actions. All caregiving members of a clan could be called "mother" or "father" and people lived in extended family groups with permeable boundaries (Stanton, 1995). Some tribes were *matrilineal* or *matrifocal*, where the mother's side of the family held prominence, men would marry into their wives' clans, and female elders held much power; however, most groups were *patrilineal* and *patriarchal*, with the father's bloodline holding more sway and men keeping the power and decision-making responsibilities. In general, American Indian tribes were collectivist in nature, not having concepts for private property or individual desires.

Native Americans in modern times

In 1887, another blow came to American Indian peoples when the Dawes Act ensured them large parcels of land for agriculture and animal husbandry. Because many tribes had no experience with an agricultural way of life and could not afford farm implements, whites often took over these lands, too. Moreover, in order to "assimilate" American Indian children into American life, they were often removed from their families and sent to boarding schools where they were forbidden to use their own languages, practice any of their cultures' customs, or participate in traditional religious ceremonies. The schools were usually built far away from reservations and native clothing was forbidden, so the children were prevented from feeling connected to their families and old ways of life. Students were often abused and exploited, and made to work long hours under harsh conditions (Lomawaima, 1994). These boarding schools existed well into the 1960s.

With the general social movements of the 1960s and 1970s involving marginalized groups like African Americans and women fighting for greater rights and freedoms, Native Americans also actively sought more power and control over their lives. This was especially true in regard to administering tribal lands on the reservations. They were eventually granted more freedom to control their own school curricula, religious and cultural events, and even child welfare issues like adoption and fostering. Today American Indians are considered dual citizens of their tribal nation and of the United States (John, 1998), yet only 22% still live on reservation land. While many tribes have managed to bring in lucrative industries such as greeting cards, auto parts, and gaming casinos, American Indians living on reservations in general suffer from extreme poverty, unemployment, alcoholism, family violence, and high fertility rates.

Today American Indians make up 0.63% of the American population, with the largest tribe being the Cherokee, with 300,000 members. Many community leaders today are trying to maintain their clans' ties to the past, teaching collectivist ideals and that personal achievements should be seen as a family effort. With a history of trauma, disease, war, and resettlement, it is encouraging that the Native American population has increased to about 2.5 million people today and that families are attempting to rekindle some of their traditional ways of life, while also struggling to help the 22% of their population who live in poverty (U.S. Census Bureau, 2006).

A look at the history of European American families

When most of us learned about American history in school, we were taught the history of *European* Americans. Other groups' experiences were either briefly described or not described at all. In the early colonies of the "New World," there was a shortage of women. For example, in the eighteenth century more men than women made the journey from Europe, and later, in 1830, men crossed the country alone when offered cheap or free land out west. If they did look for a wife, they looked for a hardy, strong woman who could handle the journey as well as the intense work of setting up a homestead. They were not looking for a woman to support financially while she sat at home looking beautiful and cooking gourmet food. These men needed to form a **co-provider family**, what we call today a dual-earner structure, where both partners contribute to the family income. These co-provider families were necessary because everyone had to work equally hard to make an agriculture-based farm life successful. They had to build their own homes, grow their own food, make their own clothes, and often fight off Indians who were struggling to protect their homelands. Pioneer women had to be skilled in many different crafts, from preserving fruit for the winter, to hoeing a field for crops.

Because families were often mobile and their health was marginal, people died early, by about the age of 40 on average. Despite our popular mythology, there were actually very few multigenerational households with warm and loving grandparents welcoming each grandchild's birth. The elderly rarely came west, either across the sea to the colonies or, later, across the western frontier. People typically took in strangers to make extra money. It wasn't unusual to see "families" comprised of eight or nine children, paying boarders, down-and-out community members such as the mentally ill or alcoholic, orphans, and apprentices all living under one roof (Coles, 2006). The term "family" didn't refer to a married couple with their biological children until well into the nineteenth century (Coontz, 1997).

In early colonial and pioneer families, childhood was short to non-existent. As soon as a child could work, he or she was put to the task. All family members worked from sunrise to sunset, and there wasn't much time for socializing, nor was there a verb called "parenting" as we call it today. "Parenting" meant keeping as many children as possible alive to help with the family's work. Fathers were the heads of the households and were responsible for their children's behavior if they got into

Co-provider family
A family where both partners must work to sustain family livelihood.

FYI

Childhood in the Colonies

From: Eugene Aubrey Stratton, FASG (1986). *Plymouth colony: Its history and people 1620–1691*. Salt Lake City, UT: Ancestry Publishing. Available online at: www.mayflowerfamilies.com

Although many families entered the colony in servitude, another important source of servants was the practice of some families of "putting out" one or more children. Samuel Eddy, for example, although the son of an English minister and university graduate, did not seem to prosper in Plymouth, and he and his wife, "by reason of many wants lying on them," were forced to put out several children as servants.

So, too, Samuel Eaton and Benjamin Eaton, after the death of their father, *Mayflower* passenger Francis Eaton, were placed out by their stepmother and were apprenticed respectively to Widow Bridget Fuller and John Cooke, Jr.

On 13 August 1636 Mary Moorecock, by her own voluntary will, and with the consent of her stepfather, was apprenticed to Richard Sparrow for nine years.

Six-year-old Elizabeth Billington, with consent of parents, on 18 April 1642 was apprenticed for fourteen years to John and Mary Barnes.

Sarah Hoskins was apprenticed on 18 January 1643/44 with the consent of her father, to Thomas and Winifred Whitney until she became twenty years old.

Thomas and Anne Savory put their five-year-old son Thomas Jr. out on 2 August 1653 as an apprentice with Thomas Lettice, carpenter, until he reached twenty-one. Young Thomas was to receive meat, drink, apparel, washing, lodging, and all other necessities, and was to be taught the trade of a house carpenter, and be taught to read the English language. In turn he was to give his master faithful and respectful service, not absent himself by day or night without license, not marry or contract marriage during his term, not embezzle, purloin, or steal any of his master's goods, nor give away any of his secrets, and to be obedient. On completing his term, he would be given two suits of clothes and various specified carpenter's tools.

The same Thomas and Anne Savory in November 1653 put out their nine-year-old son Benjamin to John and Alice Shaw until he reached twenty-one, and the father was to receive thirty shillings. Benjamin was to be taught to read and write, and at the end of his term he would get £5 or a cow.

trouble. Fathers were also in charge of any education the children might receive, religious or otherwise (Coontz, 1997). To get a feel for the life of some colonial children, see the *FYI* box, which describes some real children's lives soon after they arrived on the *Mayflower*.

Because life was so difficult for most European Americans, deaths of children and parents were common. Death and desertion in hard times led to the formation of many single parent, stepparent, and remarried families. It was also common for children to grow up with several half- and stepsiblings. Children often lost one or both parents so there were many orphans. These children might be lucky enough to be apprenticed in the trades and perhaps become boarders in a family's home, but many of them roamed the streets and became petty criminals.

To address another stereotype of early American family life, the one that says contemporary generations are declining in morality, you may be surprised to learn that at least one third of marriages in the nineteenth century were *preceded* by a pregnancy (Demos, 1970). Because "courtship" and dating were rare, and traveling long distances was difficult, people who were interested in perhaps marrying each other would often stay for extended periods with their partner's family, which often resulted in a pregnancy and a "shotgun wedding." The joke goes that a man who got a woman pregnant would be forced by her father (at gunpoint) to marry her. This lifestyle sounds like a far cry from *Leave it to Beaver*!

European American families in modern times

Between 1800 and 1850, huge waves of European immigrants came to the United States to find work and build a better life for their families. They settled in ethnic enclaves, and most major cities had Italian, Irish, Jewish, and Russian sections. Most of the European immigrants were poor and had difficulties learning English and finding work. Large factories started springing up, marking the beginning of the Industrial Revolution.

By 1850 more and more farm families had moved to larger cities for a guaranteed wage and shorter work hours than farm life allowed. Women and children also worked in factories, but for lower wages than men received. Children were particularly badly treated, often given the dirtiest or most dangerous jobs, like greasing moving parts in dangerous factory machines or shimmying through small airless caverns in coal mines. Children were often beaten when things went wrong.

After the United States annexed half of the country of Mexico in 1848, Latinos made up 38 million new "immigrants" who came to U.S. cities for work. This new American territory covered modern-day New Mexico, Arizona, Colorado, Utah, Nevada, and California. At that time, the United States also claimed to own most of Texas, but residents and leaders in that region felt that area belonged to the independent "Republic of Texas."

This was a period of great social reorganization as western expansion allowed for innumerable new opportunities. For example, in the 1850s–1920s, many Asian immigrants also sought work in the U.S., particularly in mining and construction. However, those workers, along with newly freed blacks, were felt to pose a threat to European Americans' livelihood. Whites were not only fearful of people they didn't understand, but were also afraid of losing their jobs to groups who would accept lower wages (Mintz & Kellogg, 1988).

As immigrants poured into the country to find work, the emerging European American business owners began to mentally separate themselves from less-educated workers from other ethnic groups. A new concept emerged as "whiteness" became a form of identity for those with European backgrounds. "White" people psychologically and physically separated themselves from non-European immigrants and people of color who experienced the lowest socioeconomic status (Coontz, 1997; Roediger, 1988). People of European backgrounds who looked "white" could change their last names to sound anglicized and could work on losing their accents, strategies that people of color could not use to blend in as "American." Strong anti-immigrant sentiments abounded and whites could now afford to leave city centers and move to suburbs.

Though there was still a large underpaid working class, jobs with guaranteed hours and wages did allow poor people to earn a little bit more money during the Industrial Revolution (circa 1830–1910) compared to earlier periods, so they had more leisure time than their ancestors did. With the better sanitation and medical practices that began to emerge during this period, people began to live longer, and the need for large families decreased. With more leisure time and smaller families, the role of children in the family began to change. By 1880 childhood came to be seen as a special time when skills and character should be molded. Education for white children became mandatory in 1890, and families sought to invest time and energy in their children so that they could become successful and benefit their families substantially over the long term.

When employee unions emerged in the second half of the nineteenth century, wages got even better for European American men, and their wives began to stay home, caring for the home, rearing children, and becoming responsible for the moral and religious education of their children (Mintz & Kellogg, 1988). The middle class began to emerge, with children living easier lives than their parents and grandparents had. Families became increasingly private as the home and workplace became separated. Leisure activities for European American homemakers were often depicted in magazines and fashion catalogs. The early automobiles produced by Ford allowed the rising middle class of the 1920s new freedoms to travel, enjoy vacations, and meet new people outside their own towns. Other groups wanted this lifestyle, too. Unfortunately for most Americans, even most European Americans, the reality was still one of toil, financial struggles, and subsistence living.

By the 1950s, America had recovered from the Great Depression of the 1930s and World War II in the 1940s, and the economy was booming. Single wage-earner SNAFs made up 60% of white American households. Men lived public lives, socializing and holding business meetings. Women occupied the private sphere, rearing children, cooking, and cleaning. With material wealth came appliances to help with housework, but also larger houses and more sets of clothes to clean (Coles, 2006). Women were able to drive their own cars, but this meant they spent the majority of their time doing errands and toting children around town. Longer lives meant grandparents were more likely to be involved in family life. Single-parent families decreased in number as better health brought fewer widows (Coontz, 1992). Families became consumers in a growing economy. Subdivisions of tract homes were being built on a massive scale.

But during these times, women's use of tranquilizers increased. They often felt dissatisfied with their isolated existences as well as the realization that their marriages would be longer lasting than any other previous generation's. They had become financially dependent on men and often felt hopeless (Coltrane & Adams, 2008). An upward trend in divorce rates began and persisted for the next 40 years, until the recent decline over the past decade. Recent declines in divorce rates may be accounted for by fewer marriages occurring in the first place.

White children of the Baby Boom generation (born between 1946 and 1965) often grew up to feel isolated as well. They felt their parents were too materialistic and they wanted to choose a different, more meaningful lifestyle for themselves. They realized their mothers had few rights and that discrimination and racism were still blights other groups faced on a daily basis. Many ethnic and cultural groups recognized that segregation, poverty, and racial hatred were ubiquitous in the U.S. The widespread psychological unrest of this period gave birth to the successful fight for civil rights for African Americans, women, lesbians and gays, and other groups who were no longer willing to be marginalized and denied "The American Dream" (Coles, 2006). While there is not yet equality in terms of income or access to education and health care, most groups today have earned unprecedented human rights guarantees.

The Immigration Law of 1965 lifted quotas and prohibited legal discrimination, so that multicultural issues could rise to the forefront in education and politics. Prohibitions against sexism, racism, gender discrimination, and heterosexism have allowed people to create family forms of their own choosing, such as those many of my students described at the beginning of this chapter, including pets, friends, and domestic partners. Marriage rates have declined in most western nations. For example, as mentioned above, in Sweden over half of couples cohabit but don't marry, and 75% of births are non-marital; the rate is about 33% in the U.S. (Kiernan, 2004).

Today, European Americans, or "Non-Hispanic Whites," make up 57% of the American population. European Americans still enjoy longer lives, better wages, and better health care than most people of color. Yet they also comprise the largest group to receive public assistance (welfare) and white middle-aged males have the highest rates of suicide of any other demographic group. In the 2000 U.S. census, only 23.5% of American homes were SNAF. You can see in Figure 1.8 that Utah is the only state where over 30% of families consist of two married parents with their biological children. Keep in mind that census data consider unmarried couples (gay or straight) with children to be "single-parent" families, so the percentages can be misleading. Again, the ways we define and measure families have important implications for the kinds of conclusions we might be able draw from statistics.

So what do you think of the "good old days"? What might your response be to people who talk about the disintegration of *the* American family? Such a conversation might start with the fact that current families in America closely resemble early American families where both mothers and fathers worked to provide for the household. Also, while divorce rates increased between the 1960s and 1980s, they have since declined. Although non-marital births have increased over the past few decades, teen births have actually declined, especially for African American girls (Martin et al., 2003). Finally, diversity has always been the norm for the U.S. population. Immigration and migration are parts of *everyone's* family history.

FIGURE 1.8 Percentages of households with two parents and children in the Unites States.
Source: U.S. Census Bureau, 2006–2007.

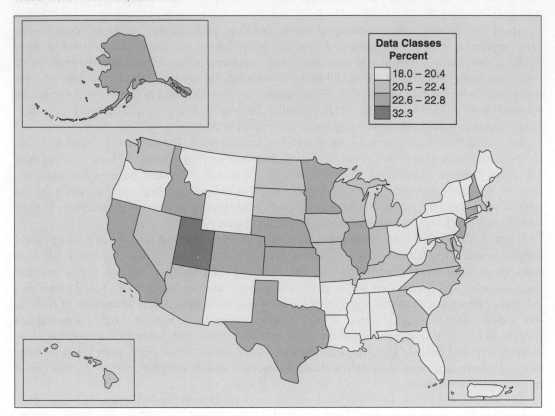

Data Classes
Percent

18.0 – 20.4
20.5 – 22.4
22.6 – 22.8
32.3

A look at the history of African American families

People from the tribes of Africa first arrived in the "New World" in the sixteenth century, to provide indentured servitude for the colonists in Jamestown, Virginia. Slavery had not yet been established so many poor blacks and poor whites could eventually buy their freedom (Coles, 2006). However, by 1700, slavery became entrenched in the British colonies.

The practices of slavery had a widespread and deep impact on how African American families developed. Slave owners feared slave revolts and so did all they could to keep slaves from communicating and forming families of their own. They tried to mix slaves from different tribes and countries, who spoke different languages, so as to prevent slave communion and possible revolt. Plantation owners in the south often used African males as "studs" and African women as "breeders," forcing them to reproduce to increase the available work force (Hamer, 2001). Slave women were forced to give birth frequently and then to quickly return to work, often without their babies (Burgess, 1995). White slave owners raped slave women, often fathering mixed race children, whom they called mulattos, who could be sold at higher prices than purely black children. "Mulatto" children were also treated better than those with darker skin. But mixed children could be a source of scandal for slave owners within their own families and communities, so fathers often tried to get rid of them, sometimes sending them to boarding schools but, more often than not, selling them into slavery on other plantations (Gonzales, 1998; McAdoo, 1998).

While some slave owners, especially on larger plantations that had separate slave cabins, allowed slaves to marry and keep their children, it was common practice for whites to prohibit marriage or to sell a slave's spouse or children to another owner. Stevenson (1995), in an exploration of the lives of former slaves, found that out of the survivors of slavery interviewed, only 43% recalled contact with their fathers while 82% recalled being with their mothers. On the larger plantations that allowed for more freedom and the development of slave communities and churches, the families that did form tended to be **nuclear**, meaning that a married couple lived with their biological children (Kulikoff, 1986).

Nuclear family
A small family consisting of parents and children, without extended kin present.

As early as the Revolutionary War in the latter part of the eighteenth century, many slaves in the north were freed; an estimated 8–12% of blacks there were free. Once the slaves in the south were freed after the Civil War (around 1865), they tried to locate lost family members through the newly developed Freedman's Bureau, which was funded through the 1867 Reconstruction Act (Gutman, 1976). Many children were found living with only one parent or with no parents at all, as they had been orphaned or sold too far away to find their parents. After Reconstruction until the 1940s, 70% of black children lived in two-parent homes (Ruggles, 1994).

Even though the slaves were legally freed, de facto slavery continued through segregation, racism, discrimination, and violent crimes against blacks, such as lynching, in which African Americans would be hanged from a tree, and often dismembered and set on fire. Black families continued to live in poverty and were often forced to work the land of their previous owners or other whites, under a system of sharecropping, where they would work the land and share in the profits of the crops.

African American families in modern times

As former slaves heard of job opportunities in big northern cities during the Industrial Revolution, they migrated north into cities like Chicago and Detroit. However, upon arrival, the former slaves found it was much easier for women to find jobs as domestic servants and nannies. Men had a more difficult time finding jobs and thousands of men were left unemployed or underemployed. Divorce and desertion among black families increased, as did family violence and conflict (Franklin, 1997). With women often bringing home the higher wages, they gained power in the family. However, once the Great Depression of the 1930s hit, African Americans of both sexes became unemployed along with millions of other Americans. Without an extended kin network to rely on, a sense of hopelessness increased in black communities. When the government implemented monetary aid for poor households, African American families received far less than their poor white counterparts. Black families were often forced to move into large, overcrowded housing projects and take on boarders to make ends meet.

During World War II, thousands of black men fought for a country that denied them basic civil rights such as voting and being able to sleep in hotels on public highways. However, black women benefited from new industrial jobs as droves of American women of all ethnic backgrounds entered the workforce to be

FIGURE 1.9 In what ways was African American family life both similar to and different from European American family life after slavery ended? Four generations of an African American family, born on a plantation in South Carolina.
Photo by T. H. O'Sullivan, c. 1890. Photo © Bettmann/CORBIS.

employed in factories to support the war effort. These new jobs enabled black women to leave domestic work behind. One African American woman said, "Hitler … got us out of white folks' kitchens" (cited in Franklin, 1997, pp. 104–105). Unfortunately, African American women earned far less for factory work than European American women did.

After finally being guaranteed civil rights in 1964 and 1968 through their organized efforts, African Americans have slowly gained access to opportunities like higher education and living wages. Along with the right to vote, laws against discrimination have helped them to move ahead in careers, government, and business. In 2008, Americans elected their first president with an African background.

However, even today, African Americans have very high rates of infant mortality compared to whites and high rates of poverty (32% of black children are poor compared to 9% of white children). In fact, 14% of African American babies are born with dangerously low birth weight, in comparison to about 6–7% of infants in all other ethnic groups. African Americans also have higher divorce rates, more non-marital births, and a large gender gap in education, with more college-educated black women and fewer college-educated black men in their communities (Coles, 2006).

Today African Americans make up 15.4% of the U.S. population. Despite the continuing challenges of institutionalized racism, lower wages, and poorer health, African American family resilience is truly remarkable. Through centuries of trauma and turmoil, black people have been able to maintain very strong family ties, valuing family and spending a great deal of time with family members. African Americans often live in intergenerational households where three or four generations help care for children and support the household. The church plays a key role in African American mental and spiritual resilience and there is often a large community support system available for black families (Haight, 2002).

A look at the history of Latino and Hispanic American families' experiences

Familism
A belief common in Hispanic/Latino families (as well as others) wherein the needs and goals of the family, especially elders, take precedence over the needs and goals of any given individual.

Compadrazgo
A belief common in Hispanic/Latino families where many men and women are thought of as co-parents for children (in other words, all "aunties" care for all children in the family).

Personalismo
A practice common in Hispanic/Latino families, where goods and services are exchanged in a face-to-face, or personal manner; people prefer to deal with those in their own community on a personal level.

Like Native Americans, Latinos are an extremely diverse group. They stem from many countries and have a variety of cultural backgrounds. Latino skin color ranges from the black of many Caribbean groups to white, including the blond hair and blue eyes of some Mexicans. With such a diverse group, it is difficult to make many generalizations about Latino families beyond the fact that they mostly speak Spanish or Portuguese (in Brazil) due to their colonial experiences with Spaniards and the Portuguese. Most, but not all, tend to practice Catholicism and to exhibit a sense of communal devotion called **familism**, where respect and reverence for one's family, especially one's elders, are paramount. Similarly, Latinos often live in multigenerational and extended family households where many "god parents" share responsibility for raising children. This spiritual parenting is often called *compadrazgo*, something similar to the idea of "co-parenting." Because of their conservative family values and desire to connect with others in their tight knit communities, Hispanic/Latino peoples tend to prefer to talk about issues face to face and to solve problems from within their close social networks. This preference for *personalismo* allows community and family members to provide favors, help, and assistance for anything from birthing a baby to filling out insurance papers or finding a good deal on a vacation package. As you will see, these values of familism, *compadrazgo*, and *personalismo*, have served Latinos well throughout their varied histories within the U.S. They work together to create family values and communal support networks that are similar to those in the African American community.

Keep in mind that Hispanic and Latino groups vary a lot in their historical, cultural, ethnic, and racial backgrounds. Venezuelans are different from Chileans, who are quite different from Dominicans, who don't resemble Peruvians. To give you a little flavor for this diversity, we will briefly explore the histories of some of the most populous groups in the U.S.: Mexican Americans or Chicanos, Puerto-Rican Americans, and Cuban Americans. These three groups came to the United States in quite different ways and their histories and current states of existence vary quite a bit.

Mexican American experiences

As discussed earlier, indigenous Mexican Indians were colonized by the Spanish starting in the fifteenth century. The Catholic Church allowed the groups to intermarry and Mexican Indians could sometimes buy their freedom (Gonzales, 1998). The indigenous people and the Spaniards were both used to living in patriarchal families but since most of the families were poor and lived in rural areas, they mainly practiced **common law marriage**, a union that is recognized as legitimate even though no formal ceremony or legal documentation has taken place.

After winning the Mexican American War, the United States annexed what are now California, New Mexico, Utah, Arizona, Colorado, and Nevada from the country of Mexico. The U.S. government affirmed that the Mexicans already living in those territories could keep their own land and maintain cultural and familial practices. However, this nineteenth-century land grab usurped the rights of Mexican people, and the land was eventually taken by whites (Gonzales, 1998). No longer able to survive in a traditional agrarian manner, Mexican families moved to work in gold mines, in factories, and on the railroads.

During the Great Depression, when white workers lost jobs and faced poverty, hundreds of thousands of Mexicans were deported so they could not compete for "American" jobs. As the economy recovered by 1940 and more workers were needed, Mexicans were then invited back under a *bracero* agreement, to work seasonally or for certain periods of time to help with infrastructure or war efforts during World War II (Becerra, 1998). After decades of being pushed out of and pulled back into the American workforce, the Chicano rights movement began to take shape during the 1960s when Chicano/Latino groups fought for farm workers' rights, better wages and working conditions, and a voice in government.

Today Mexican Americans make up the largest percentage of Hispanic families in the U.S. (about 67%). Their families tend to live in larger households than non-Hispanic whites. For example, about 31% of Mexican American households have over five members (compared to about 11% of white households) (U.S. Census Bureau, 2003). Mexican American families have higher rates of marriage than non-Hispanic whites, as well as lower rates of divorce.

Puerto-Rican American experiences

While Mexican Americans have lived on the land that is now the U.S. since its beginning, Puerto Ricans began arriving for war-related jobs in the 1940s. The U.S. won the rights to the island of Puerto Rico after the Spanish-American war in 1898. Puerto Ricans were allowed to become U.S. citizens. Today the island is considered a *commonwealth*, neither a state nor an independent nation. Citizens of Puerto Rico don't pay U.S. taxes and cannot vote but are allowed to travel freely to the mainland at will. Puerto Ricans settled mainly on the East Coast and often worked in factories.

> **Common law marriage**
> A marriage recognized in some states and countries where a couple is given all the rights, privileges, and responsibilities of marriage because they've been together a long time, not because they have gone through a formal marriage ritual.

FIGURE 1.10 How did the historic experiences of Mexican, Puerto Rican, and Cuban American families in the U.S. differ? Mexican American women and children, Omaha, Nebraska, 1922.
Photo courtesy of the Nebraska State Historical Society (ref: RG3882–21–163).

Today Puerto-Rican Americans are one of the poorest immigrant groups and have high fertility and low marriage rates. In fact, 60% of Puerto Rican babies are non-marital births. Moreover, 26.5% of Puerto Rican households are headed by women, in comparison to 15.2% and 13.0% for Mexican American and Cuban Americans, respectively (U.S. Census Bureau, 2000a). However, they have higher rates of high school completion (67%) than Mexican Americans (51%) (U.S. Census Bureau, 2003).

Cuban American experiences

If Puerto Ricans have not been able to reap the rewards of a close connection to the American mainland, Cuban Americans have had quite a different experience. When the U.S. obtained Puerto Rico, it also gained control over Cuba (as well as the Philippines and other island nations). The U.S. government allowed Cuba to rule itself in 1902, but American capitalism and influence were entrenched there for the next 57 years (Suarez, 1998). When Fidel Castro overthrew the American-backed Cuban government in 1959, many wealthy and successful Cuban families fled to America. Because the wealthy had the most to lose in a newly communist country, and because they spoke English and had close ties to the U.S., elite Cubans became political refugees and were welcomed. The U.S. government helped them bring their entire families over, provided scholarships for their children, and helped them to become established, mainly in Florida. In a second wave of immigration during the 1960s and 1970s, Cuba's middle class of skilled laborers and small business owners came on flights chartered by the U.S. government (Bean & Tienda, 1987).

With this favored status and much material wealth to begin with, Cuban Americans today are the wealthiest and best educated of the Latino groups in the U.S. Cuban American women have low fertility rates and marry later than women in other Hispanic groups. Only 25% of Cuban American births are non-marital, compared to 40% for Mexican Americans, and 60% for Puerto Ricans (Coles, 2006).

Latinos in modern times

Today, 21% of children in American households are Hispanic/Latino. It is estimated that by the year 2020, one in four children will be Hispanic/Latino (www.childstats.gov). Today large numbers of immigrants from South American countries like El Salvador, Colombia, and Guatemala are arriving in the U.S. and further diversifying the Latino population. Latinos continue to fight for recognition and rights in the U.S., as they often work at the lowest paying jobs and are marginalized due to language and cultural barriers. However, many Latinos have adjusted and fared very well in the U.S. They are reaching the highest ranks of government, business, and education. College campuses are becoming more diverse as people with Hispanic/Latino heritage strive to do better than previous generations. By 2002, 11% of Latinos had college degrees (U.S. Census Bureau, 2003).

A look at Asian American experiences

Just as the group known as "Latinos" or "Hispanics" includes a vast array of histories and cultures, so does the group we tend to call "Asian Americans." People from Asia come from countries as distinct as India, Afghanistan, and Korea. Chinese and Japanese immigrants were the largest Asian groups to arrive in America. But after the internment of over 100,000 Japanese Americans after the bombing of Pearl Harbor, Hawaii, in 1941, fewer Japanese have come to America. Today the largest Asian groups are Chinese, Filipino, East Indian, Vietnamese, and Korean. Two of these Asian American groups will be examined here, to provide a brief glimpse at the diverse histories, experiences, and family challenges of Asian immigrants to the United States.

Chinese American experiences

Similar to the influx and exile of Mexican American workers at the command of U.S. industry, Chinese people came to the San Francisco Bay area of California during the 1840s to find jobs and escape war, poverty, and disease at home. Most of these were men who had to leave their families in China. They were willing to work for lower wages than white workers in the newly discovered gold mines, but they were also required to pay higher taxes on the gold they mined than were white workers (Chan, 1991). As the United States developed its infrastructure, the government recruited Chinese immigrants to build the western half of the transcontinental railroad. However, as Chinese people made money and opened businesses, they were discriminated against and attacked, and unfair policies were implemented to thwart their attempts at success. Their long braids were cut off and new immigration laws forbade them from sending for their families to join them in the United States (Wong, 1998). Thus, most of the Chinese in America were men because their wives were not permitted to join them. In 1924, quotas on the immigration of certain ethnic groups were implemented. This meant that Chinese men had to go back home to have conjugal visits with their wives. Their only hope at forming a family of procreation was to leave their wives pregnant when they came back to the U.S. to work alone. They sacrificed family life for the hope of new financial opportunities that would eventually benefit their children.

Chinese culture was patriarchal and allowed its men to engage in polygamy, as well as take concubines, or legitimized mistresses (Stockard, 2002). The U.S. census of 1870 showed that only 7% of the Chinese population were women, yet American law forbade the intermarriage of Chinese men with white women, which left Chinese men with few options. The Chinese women who were allowed into the U.S. were often oppressed by their husbands, kept inside, their feet tightly bound in the traditional Chinese manner, and they were sometimes attacked and raped if they went out in public. These women often committed suicide (Wong, 1998).

The immigration quotas were lifted in 1965, and we have seen a continuous influx of well-educated and successful Chinese immigrants, usually coming to the U.S. to further their education. Today, 2.7 million people report full Chinese or half-Chinese backgrounds on the 2000 Census (U.S. Census Bureau, 2002). Chinese Americans tend to do well economically and to form traditional families with married, heterosexual parents and their children.

Japanese American experiences

When quotas existed from the 1920s–1960s to disallow Chinese people from coming to the U.S., Japanese people often came in their stead and worked at the same low-paying jobs. White Americans feared that both groups would take away jobs, and in 1905 an organization called the Asiatic Exclusion League took shape to guarantee this didn't occur (Kitano & Kitano, 1998). Since intermarriage between Japanese and Americans was illegal, the U.S. governmental finally allowed Japanese men to send home for wives, whose marriages had usually been arranged for them by family members. Japanese women faced a clash of cultures. Their husbands expected them to maintain very distinct traditional gender roles, while U.S. women had more freedom, owing to the gradually progressing feminist movements of the nineteenth and twentieth centuries (Yanagisako, 1985). Japanese men were strict fathers and emotionally stoic.

The second generation of Japanese children, born in the U.S. between 1915 and 1945, are referred to as *Nisei* and they tended to move away from traditional marriages, wanting to marry for love and romance like their white peers (Gonzales, 1998). Their admiration for and commitment to America was not recognized during World War II. When Japanese Americans were sent to "relocation," or internment camps in 1942, they were stripped of their homes, businesses, and dignity. Most families lost everything they had worked so hard to accomplish in the United States. The camps were closed in 1945 and 1946, and the hatred for Japanese Americans that prevailed during World War II diminished. The *Nisei* generation ended up reaching high levels of educational and occupational success, as well as practicing more liberal gender roles (Kitano & Kitano, 1998). Their children, born between 1940 and 1960, have been almost completely assimilated into mainstream American culture and practice high rates of intermarriage. Today, Chinese and Japanese Americans have higher rates of education than whites, live in more married couple homes, have fewer single-parent families, and have lower rates of divorce (Coles, 2006).

Asian Americans in modern times

Today, Asian Americans make up 4.1% of the U.S. population. Despite racism, poverty, discrimination and unfair immigration policies, many Asian Americans have been able to achieve much of the American Dream. These positive trends can be explained by many factors. First, many Asian immigrants (especially from India and Japan) are not poor or uneducated in their home countries, and they come to the United States specifically to gain access to higher education such as medical school or graduate programs. Also, there were not many Asian *families* at all in the U.S. before World War II, so if men were not successful in America, they might have returned home, leaving the best educated or most successful Asian Americans here.

Their higher socioeconomic status can also partially be explained by the fact that they settled mainly on the East and West Coasts where wages are higher (Coles, 2006). However, keep in mind that the success of Asian Americans is a broad generalization. Many Asian Americans live in poverty and are traumatized, having escaped war and genocide in their home countries. They still face prejudice and discrimination, and even **model minority** stereotypes can be harmful. Model minority refers to the positive stereotypes that paint a group as a "model" to live up to. Model minority ideas can put undue pressure on children from Asian American families to reach high levels of education and economic success. Teachers may have higher academic expectations and lower tolerance for misbehavior from children of Asian backgrounds than they do for other groups of children. We will explore the family life of Asian Americans and many other ethnic groups throughout this textbook.

> **Model minority**
> A belief that a specific ethnic group is characterized by positive traits such as fastidiousness, intelligence, and financial success.

THE APPROACH AND ORGANIZATIONAL STRUCTURE OF THIS BOOK

This book is written from a bioecological perspective, which you will learn more about in the next chapter. In brief, it argues that every system of influence, from a person's biology, to parents, community, and culture affect how we grow up and function in families. Indeed, a comprehensive understanding requires that we look all the way out from our neurons and all the way in from our cultures (Bronfenbrenner & Morris, 1998).

In order to develop educated opinions about families, it's important to understand how research is conducted and be able to analyze the quality of evidence that is gathered. Scientific research examining the very difficult and complex issues of families makes it possible to know if our ideas are true or not. We must also understand the biases of the researchers and the theoretical background behind the research being done. We turn to these topics in Chapter 2.

The rest of the book is organized to unfold the way many family relationships do, in a sequential manner. Before anyone connects with a mate or forms a family, he or she is an established individual with clear personality traits, motivations, drives, emotions, and behavioral patterns. Before diving into an analysis of how families function once all the members are together, I will take you on the journey of individuals' own development. In Chapter 3 we will explore how a person's gender plays a key role in both how he or she approaches family relationships and how others in families respond to him or her. Before someone engages in a sexual relationship, they are first sexual beings who develop sexualities starting in childhood and adolescence. We will also focus on individual sexuality issues in Chapter 3. Relationships tend to unfold in a sequential nature, and our explorations will follow a similar pattern, progressing from sexuality in Chapter 4, to dating and mate selection in Chapter 5, love in Chapter 6, and marriage and committed partnerships in Chapter 7. While the majority of humans pair off into committed relationships, a substantial number of people choose to stay single. We will examine these peoples' lives and experiences as well (Chapter 8), before exploring traditional family topics like parenting (Chapter 9), economic issues (Chapter 10), domestic violence (Chapter 11), divorce (Chapter 12), growing older (Chapter 13), and the future of families (Chapter 14).

CHAPTER SUMMARY

The "good old days" of happy, well-adjusted perfect families from the 1950s is a myth. The 1950s did show higher marriage rates and lower divorce rates, but this was a quick blip on the radar if we examine the historic trends of marriages and families over the past century. Our images of 1950s TV families as the norm never really existed for most Americans.

The concept of the Standard North American Family (SNAF) helps students think about their own beliefs about whether certain family structures are better or worse than others. SNAF was discussed as a lingering ideology that affects how we view ourselves and others when a family is not comprised of a breadwinning father, stay-at-home mother, and their children. To further support the idea that SNAFs have never been the pervasive family structure, historical information was provided about the many ethnic groups that came to the United States as immigrants, and how various contextual factors like economic struggles and discrimination kept them from being able to reach the common SNAF ideal many people thought was best for families.

A key message of the chapter is that family structure (e.g., whether a family is SNAF or not) has less impact on the health and happiness of its members than that family's processes, or the interactional dynamics they experience.

The bioecological model, which is the organizing framework for this textbook, was introduced. It states that families are affected by everything from individual members' neurochemistry and personality, to dyadic relationships, interactions with larger social contexts, and even cultural dynamics. The diverse cultural trends and historic experiences explored in this chapter set the foundation for the rest of book, and serve as examples for broadening our thinking about what a "normal" family looks like or how it performs.

Structure versus process, diversity as the norm throughout history, and the need to examine families through a bioecological lens are the essential points of this chapter.

KEY TERMS

arranged marriage
common law marriage
compadrazgo
co-provider family
cultural relativism
endogamy
exogamy
familism
family

family of origin
family of procreation
matriarchal
matrifocal
matrilineal
model minority
modern family
nuclear family
patriarchal

personalismo
polyandry
polygamy
post-modern family
processes
Standard North American Family
   (SNAF)
structure

WEBSITES FOR FURTHER EXPLORATION

www.ellisisland.org

This website is all about Ellis Island, where many immigrants landed when coming to the U.S. You can place your ancestors' names on the American Immigrant Wall of Honor to maintain your family history, search your ancestors' travel records by their ship's name, read multi-cultural immigrant stories, and see a timeline of immigration history.

www.usa.gov/citizen/topics/history_family.shtml

The U.S. government hosts many resources you can use to study your family's history. You can find ancestors in census records, locate military service records, and find birth certificates, marriage licenses, death certificates, and other vital records.

http://www.time.com/time/photogallery/0,29307,1626519_1373664,00.html

This is a wonderful collection from *Time* magazine of photographs of families from around the world, seated next to the food they eat in one week. You can compare the dietary quality, the amount of food consumed, and the types and costs of food eaten by various cultural groups.

CHAPTER 2
HOW WE STUDY THE FAMILY
Theories and Research Methods

To every complex question there is a simple answer and it is wrong.

(H. L. Mencken, twentieth-century American writer)

LEARNING OBJECTIVES

- To understand key theories that organize thinking and research on families

- To fully grasp the tenets of the bioecological perspective, the key organizing framework of this book

- To recognize the importance of both theory and careful design and implementation strategies in conducting valid research

- To comprehend the basic steps and techniques used in the scientific method

- To recognize the importance of demographic variables and intersectional identities on individual and family development

Marriages and Families in the 21st Century: A Bioecological Approach, First Edition. Tasha R. Howe.
© 2012 Tasha R. Howe. Published 2012 by Blackwell Publishing Ltd.

OVERVIEW: THE NEED FOR GOOD THEORY AND RESEARCH DESIGN

THEORETICAL FRAMEWORKS

- Communism
- Structural-Functionalism
- Family Systems Theory
- Conflict Theory
- Social Exchange Theory
- Social Constructionism
- Feminist Theory
- Attachment Theory
- Bioecological Theory
  - The person
  - Processes and contexts

RESEARCH METHODOLOGY

- Hypothesis testing
- Operational definitions
- Experimental procedures
  - Variables
  - Experimental design
  - Choosing a research time frame
  - Examining results
- Correlational procedures
  - Correlations vs. causal inferences
- Quantitative and qualitative research methods
  - Etic and emic approaches
  - Demand characteristics

DEMOGRAPHIC ISSUES IN RESEARCH

- Race and ethnicity
- Sex, gender, and sexual orientation
- Social class

OVERVIEW: THE NEED FOR GOOD THEORY AND RESEARCH DESIGN

When I was in graduate school and found out my dissertation adviser had grant money to study a group of severely abused children living in a residential treatment center, I was excited about the possibility of learning more about these kids. I read what little research existed at the time, and it noted that many maltreated children had severe social skills deficits. Previous studies had shown that they couldn't make friends, they were unpopular with peer groups, and they were aggressive. I wondered what could explain these patterns. In scouring the literature, I found that one theory really helped me conceptualize why abused children might be socially unskilled: Bioecological Theory (Bronfenbrenner, 1994). This theoretical paradigm helped me understand the complex influences on abused children's lives. I realized that it wasn't just the abuse they suffered that affected their social relationships. Their problems were also the result of the commonly elevated levels of physiological arousal abused children experience, which lead them to lash out at others. Also, their parents often had few role models to teach them parenting skills while they were growing up. Moreover, there was commonly a lack of support by teachers who didn't know how to deal with troubled kids and too few effective interventions were implemented by social service providers. Not to mention that the kids lived in a time period and culture where child abusers faced no real consequences for their actions, leading to the children continuously being returned to their parents' custody.

In sum, I had to consider influences from every ecological system if I really wanted to understand how we could change these kids' lives for the better. In my situation, and in virtually every other researcher's experience, doing good work requires the application of an adequate theory. We use our theories to help us conceptualize and design the appropriate type of study that can best examine our research questions. Strong, coherent theories and sound research designs are invaluable tools in discovering avenues for understanding and improving family relations.

This chapter provides an overview of the theories that guide research on the family and explores the scientific methods most commonly used in research studies. You will see that the theories we endorse can shape the types of questions we ask as well as the methods we use to study a given issue. First, we'll take a look at theoretical perspectives that may direct, guide, or influence the way studies are conducted. When researchers view the world through a specific theoretical lens, this viewpoint helps them to organize their data and generate predictions regarding how families function.

Once researchers have endorsed a theoretical perspective, they are prepared to conduct a study from that perspective. To do this, the researchers must use the **scientific method**, a series of steps they follow to ensure a well-done study, one from which valid conclusions can be drawn. This chapter will explore the scientific method in detail so that you will be armed with the background that will enable you to understand, critique, and apply research findings discussed in the text. A general comprehension of organizing theoretical frameworks and various research methods is essential for forging a true understanding of family health and well-being.

Scientific method
A series of steps taken to conduct accurate research.

THEORETICAL FRAMEWORKS

A **theory** is a set of ideas or principles about how something works. Theories allow us to organize our ideas into a cohesive set of concepts that guide our thinking about issues and allow us to organize our approach to research. Theories should help us to understand a phenomenon and design good studies that accurately investigate a question at hand. They help researchers avoid taking

Communism

Structural-Functionalism

Family Systems Theory

Conflict Theory

Social Exchange Theory

Social Constructionism

Feminist Theory

Attachment Theory

Bioecological Theory

Theory
An organizing set of principles used to guide thinking and predict research outcomes.

Eclectic approach
An approach to research that capitalizes on the strengths of many different theories.

Bioecological Theory
The organizing framework of this book, which assumes that individuals exist within multiple complex systems of influence, from biological to cultural, all of which interact with each other to shape family functioning.

a stab in the dark by providing a foundation for looking at issues systematically. On the negative side, however, the theoretical perspective you choose to use can also be one possible source of bias in research. Once someone endorses a particular theory or set of theoretical propositions, it can cloud his or her vision so that he or she sees the world only through that lens.

Much of the time, researchers use an **eclectic approach**, whereby they incorporate the best parts of several different theories into their work. Every theoretical framework has strong points and can be helpful in aiding our understanding of important phenomena in the social sciences, such as family relationships. However, one theory is rarely sufficient to explain every aspect of a topic of interest.

The theoretical perspective used in this textbook, **Bioecological Theory**, assumes that families are extremely complex and that to understand them we must examine family members' biological make-ups, personal characteristics, interactional styles, culture, religion, and even their neighborhoods. This perspective will be discussed further later on.

Let's begin exploring theoretical perspectives by looking at some classic theories used to explain social phenomena related to the family. Most of these theories have made excellent contributions to our understanding of families, but they may be limited by their simplicity or their failure to take into account the diverse influences on family functioning that the Bioecological Theory provides. You might not consider Marxist or Communist Theory to be relevant to family relationships but several of the theories I present below actually stem from early ideas put forth by Karl Marx and Friedrich Engels in their publication, *The Communist Manifesto* (1848). These theorists specifically focused on social systems like cities and governments, but their ideas also relate to common power struggles many families experience. In fact, sociologists and psychologists gleaned a lot of information from this early theory in their attempts to generate the theories below, which help us understand the experiences of people living in families.

Communism

An early theory of social order is presented in *The Communist Manifesto* by Karl Marx and Friedrich Engels (1848/2004). In this thin pamphlet, Marx and Engels laid out a framework describing how capitalist systems can destroy the underclass of a society, and eventually even destroy themselves, through greed and unfair advantage. Capitalist systems include societies where a free market reigns, and a small wealthy upper class controls most of the resources. Writing about the various cultural revolutions that had taken place in France and Russia, they explained how there is always a class conflict between the rich (the bourgeoisie) and the average worker (the proletariat). The *Manifesto* argued that the rich can only become rich by exploiting and politically oppressing the poor and downtrodden. The poor are often kept illiterate and ineffectual in order to maintain the status quo. In this vein, communists were vehemently opposed to the colonialism and political imperialism exhibited throughout history by countries like Britain and the United States. They argued that these systems oppress the native people who never benefit from their own labor, yet their labor supplies the means for a high standard of living for the already wealthy. Marx and Engels went further by stating that lower classes eventually tire of working to support the luxuries of the rich and often revolt, sometimes causing coups, wars, or government takeovers.

Marx and Engels argued in favor of a society run not by wealthy capitalists but by the community at large, the working masses. They hoped that societies could be restructured to allow the means of economic production to be controlled by the proletariat so that people could rule themselves and ensure a good quality of life, including living wages for all. Everyone would work for the good of the community and everyone would benefit equally from that work, as all goods and services would become communally owned.

Communism
An analysis of capitalist societies that claims the rich will always exploit the labor of the poor and eventually the poor will revolt to reap the fruits of their own labor; it emphasizes the need for a communal way of life where all workers benefit equally from shared work.

Communism tends to have negative connotations today, because we associate it with governments where dictators rule and people have little power, like the People's Republic of China, under Mao Tse-tung, and the island nation of Cuba, under the dictator Fidel Castro. Keep in mind, however, that these countries early on were experiencing a people's revolution meant to topple governments that were seen as being controlled by powerful capitalists who exploited the common person.

The evolution of families in Western societies is not dissimilar to the evolution of cultures described above. For example, it was common historically for women and children to be completely controlled by fathers in families. They were the "underclass" of the family, and had to do as the father dictated. However, over time, women grew tired of not reaping benefits for all of their hard work and women's rights movements fought for them to have equal say in their families and communities. Likewise, there is currently a worldwide movement to provide children with human rights, including the right to speak their minds in their families.

Structural-Functionalism

Building on the ideas of Marx and Engels and using the key idea of conflict between those with more and those with less power, theories were developed to explain the workings of governments, political groups, and even families. The best-known of these theories is **Structural-Functionalism** (Parsons, 1951), which argues that social groups like families have an established structure that allows the group to function as a cohesive whole. Families and larger groups like societies continue to exist cohesively over time because there is an equilibrium, or a normal sort of interdependence, between the parts. Each family member is a piece of the puzzle and must remain in his or her position in order for the social structure of the family to maintain integrity.

> **Structural-Functionalism** Stems from Communist Theory; Emphasizes maintaining the status quo of a society or family, with specific structures remaining in place to ensure the system works as it should, with specific people in power; each person plays a crucial role in keeping the family functioning as it always has.

Any social structure usually includes some members who are wealthy, more privileged, or more powerful (like elders or men) than other members (like children or women), just as Marx and Engels discussed regarding societies. For example, if elders in a community held all the power to make decisions and were revered more than younger people, it is likely that most senior members in that community would like to maintain this social order. They would not want to change the family system so that, say, teenagers, began to make crucial decisions, because that would upset the social order that maintained them at the top of the family's hierarchy. Such a community needs younger people to act in deference to the older people in order to maintain the family system. If adolescents decided to question this hierarchy, a revolution might occur to disrupt the equilibrium. In other words, a family is a system, like the societies Marx discussed are systems, wherein each member is interdependent with every other member. Early Structural-Functionalists often argued that this order should be maintained, that each family member's role is like a spoke in a wheel. If you remove a spoke, the wheel falls apart. Thus they often advocated for the status quo, or leaving the structure of the family (and thereby society) the way it was, to prevent damage to its daily functioning.

This theoretical perspective is helpful in trying to understand why systems continue over time without any changes in their dynamics or power structures. For example, when I ask my students to raise their hands if they like domestic violence, no one budges. In fact, I would guess most people you ask would say they abhor domestic violence. Yet it continues to occur, generation after generation. Structural-Functionalism can help us analyze what function domestic violence might serve in maintaining the current hierarchy and power structure in families. It might argue that when men dominate women, it keeps them at the top of the hierarchy, the way things historically have always been, and some might argue, should continue to be.

However, an important problem with the Structural-Functionalist perspective is that it often assumes the status quo is beneficial simply because it has lasted for so long. In reality, as can be seen in the example above, systems often function in ways that harm their members. Many times, the system requires a shake-up, revolt, or radical change, the kind of change Marx and Engels discussed and that occurred periodically throughout history. Because most cases of severe battering are perpetrated by men, and men have more power and wealth in most families and in society at large, we might argue that we'd have to overturn the status quo and fight for women's rights. And that is exactly what has been happening over the past few decades. One result of the "proletariat" revolt for women's rights is that women are now allowed to divorce battering husbands without having to prove their wrongdoings, which makes it easier for women to leave than it was 30 years ago. Today, we are all used to the idea that if you get caught abusing your power as a spouse and you harm your partner, authorities can step in and take away your power (such as in the case of mandatory arrests of batterers). However, this Structural-Functionalist explanation for domestic violence, one based on maintaining the male power hierarchy, is too simplistic and unidimensional. There are many types of violent families and even though most of us live in a similarly structured family or social system, very few men are violent. Thus, Stuctural-Functionalism helps us understand a piece of the puzzle regarding why a social system or pattern of family interaction is maintained, but it's not the whole story. In order to understand this issue and any other, we must consider the broader, interconnected dynamics of individual families as well.

Family Systems Theory

Family Systems Theory
A theoretical approach stemming from Structural-Functionalism, which examines role and power dynamics present in families, emphasizing that every individual exists within a complex relationship system; the whole is greater than the sum of the parts.

Family Systems Theory (Bowen, 1978; Cox, Paley, & Harter, 2001), an application of Structural-Functionalism, argues that we cannot understand a family without recognizing that the whole is greater than the sum of the parts. Each person's role in the family is crucial for maintaining a balance in functioning between all members. Family systems theorists argue that we cannot understand a family by looking at only one member or even a dyad or triad. We must examine the whole system to understand why one member is having problems or how the family continues to be healthy and happy. For example, if your sister left home, got married, and moved away, this would affect not just you but your parents, both as individuals and a couple, as well as any other siblings in the home. You might feel mature, getting to move into her old bedroom, your mom might feel a sense of loss, your dad might feel excited about the prospect of grandchildren, and your smaller siblings might miss all the games they played with her. Each of you would respond individually, but the move would also change the way each dyad and triad in the system interacts with each other, since a key "spoke in the wheel" is now gone.

An important application of Family Systems Theory is that it influenced the development of family systems therapy, which views entire families as the "patient" during therapy, because every individual in the family exists within a dynamic web of relationships. The power structures, communications styles, and boundaries of each part of the family web (and the whole web itself) provide crucial information for the family therapist. To help a family achieve mental health and happiness, a therapist must treat the whole web of interactions; we cannot "fix" just one person and send him or her back to the same system, expecting any changes to last.

Unlike earlier Structural-Functionalist ideas, Family Systems Theory (and its related approach to therapy) views changing the system as often helpful. With change, the family can gain new skills and achieve a new level of relationship balance. Sometimes when the status quo gets shaken up, a new, stronger family system emerges. With the right systemic intervention involving all members of a family, what began as conflict over power, may lead to new balance and family harmony.

Conflict Theory

Conflict Theory
Argues that conflict is a normal and natural part of family life; people can use conflicts to help relationships mature and grow through renegotiating power relationships.

Another theory stemming from Structural-Functionalism is **Conflict Theory** (Dahrendorf, 1959). From this theoretical perspective, there are always conflicts between individuals and groups in society. These conflicts often involve power struggles. Unlike the communist viewpoint, however, no uniform bourgeoisie is seen as controlling every segment of society. There may be many power holders in different realms of the community (for example, in education, the workplace, and the family). Also, Conflict Theory views conflict in a positive light because it creates movement toward change. Unlike Structural-Functionalism, which focuses on the necessity of maintaining the status quo to keep the system intact, Conflict Theory emphasizes conflict and struggle as an impetus toward necessary change. If people from different political or religious groups have conflicts, theoretically, they can get things out in the open and resolve the conflict or come to some kind of compromise.

The same might be true in families. For example, research on teenagers and their parents shows that conflict tends to rise to its highest level in early adolescence, when teens are about 14 years old.

However, unlike the stereotype of a raging teen and an anguished parent, studies show that these conflicts are actually *positive*. They teach adolescents how to argue for what they want, negotiate their perspectives, and often convince their parents to change rules around the house to allow them more freedom. As long as the conflicts are not violent or habitual, some elevated parent–teen conflict can, just as Conflict Theory would argue, allow the two sides to renegotiate the power in the relationship and come to a new understanding that benefits the adolescent's long term development (Holmbeck, Paikoff, & Brooks-Gunn, 1995). Conflict Theory helps us examine how power relationships influence conflicts and how conflicts can be used for personal and relationship growth. However, like most theories, this theory only explains part of the puzzle of family relationships.

Social Exchange Theory

The "give and take" aspect of the parent–teenager relationship is illuminated by another theoretical framework, **Social Exchange Theory** (Homans, 1958). According to Social Exchange Theory, people are always weighing the costs and benefits of their actions and trying to maximize gains and minimize losses. From this perspective, most of our behaviors are explained through a series of mental calculations in which we weigh the possible outcomes of each choice. An internal monologue from Social Exchange Theory might run something like this: *Should I date John or Frank? Well, Frank is very attentive and sweet, but he reminds me too much of my dad. That would get on my nerves. John is more aloof and doesn't talk about his feelings, but we have so much fun together. For me, right now, I think fun is more important than dating someone like Dad.* According to Social Exchange Theory, if we have an internal monologue like this one, which takes a mental tally of the costs and benefits, we might decide to date John.

For a complex issue like domestic violence discussed earlier, Social Exchange Theory would argue that a husband may unconsciously go through an internal dialogue such as: *If I continue to hit my wife, she may leave me; however, it's very unlikely that she will ever tell anyone, so I can continue to get my way and coerce her into doing what I want through harsh physical treatment.* In this case, the benefits of physical abuse outweigh the less likely costs the spouse might encounter with law enforcement.

Social Exchange Theory is helpful in identifying why people may make the choices they do. There may be hidden benefits to their actions, or the costs of a certain decision-may be too steep. Of course, it's probably rare that people consciously think things over like this, and that's one of the main problems with Social Exchange Theory. People perform a lot of actions and make a lot of choices, both consciously and inadvertently, which have no benefit for themselves and may actually involve steep costs. Can you think of a decision you made or an action you engaged in that had more costs than benefits, yet you did it anyway? Humans are rarely as rational as an accountant's ledger, lining up profits and losses. We often skew things in our minds to fit the way we want the world to be, and often don't view the world the way it really is.

Social Constructionism

One theory that gets at the root of our mental reconstructions of the world is **Social Constructionism** (Berger & Luckmann, 1967). This perspective argues that we cannot know reality, even if there is some objective world out there, because we filter information and then reconstruct everything we encounter through our own viewpoints. In other words, humans socially construct their own realities and live in the reality they've created, not in some objective world "out there."

A good example of Social Constructionism is the concept of race. **Race** is thought to be a biological or genetic characteristic that makes humans different from each other. Its outward signs include skin color, the shape of the face, and the texture of the hair. However, most scholars today agree that there is no such thing as race, nor is there any evidence that there have ever been biologically distinct races of people. Heine (2008) explains that ever since modern humans left Africa to migrate

Social Exchange Theory
A theory arguing that people make a deliberate tally of costs and benefits during decision-making and behaviors they perform in families.

Social Constructionism
The idea that humans construct their own reality, and those constructions affect behaviors in families.

Race
A socially constructed concept referring to different colors of people thought to stem from diverse genetic lines in human history; in reality there are no true races of people.

around 60,000 years ago, every "race" has been mixed. From the beginning of human history, people who came into contact with each other have intermixed. Moreover, even something that is "biological" can be influenced, or constructed, through interactions with the environment.

In an interesting example of this point, Heine (2008) describes how skin color arose from genetic adaptation to the environment. The skin must synthesize vitamin D to help with absorption of calcium and other nutrients. In order for our bodies to synthesize vitamin D, the sun's ultraviolet radiation (UVR) must penetrate our skin. There is a lot of UVR in Africa because it is close to the equator. Perhaps over generations, genetic adaptations occurred, which eventually led to the ability to produce melanin. Melanin darkens the skin and allows UVR to penetrate it without causing damage from severe burns or skin cancer. This adaptation led people with darker skin to live longer and reproduce more, and the tendency for darker skin remained in the human gene pool. As humans migrated to the northernmost climes, their bodies had to work harder to absorb enough UVR to synthesize vitamin D because there was less sun. Over generations, another genetic adaptation occurred that resulted in less production of melanin, and thus whiter skin, making it easier to absorb UVR and synthesize vitamin D. Research shows that dark-skinned people such as Eskimos, who live in low UVR conditions, compensate by eating diets rich in vitamin D (such as can be found in fish and blubber).

Jablonski and Chaplin (2000) found that 70 to 77% of the variations found in skin color can be accounted for by variations in UVR exposure. What we call "race" is determined more by environment than biology. In fact, the American Anthropological Association (1998) issued a statement on "race" which says

> Human populations are not unambiguous, clearly demarcated, biologically distinct groups. Ninety-four percent [of biological variation] lies *within* so-called racial groups. Conventional "racial" groupings differ from one another only in about six percent of their genes. This means that there is greater variation within "racial" groups than between them … All of humankind [is] a single species.

The U.S. Office of the Management of the Budget (OMB), which determines the racial categories for all government documents and surveys, concurs and states that "race" is not a scientifically valid construct, but is a "sociopolitical" construct and should never be thought of in terms of genetically differentiated groups (cited in Walker, Spohn, & DeLone, 2007, p. 10). Therefore, the OMB requires all federal forms to allow for people to identify as belonging to more than one race. The current choices are: American Indian or Alaskan Native, Asian, Black or African American, Hispanic or Latino, Native Hawaiian or Other Pacific Islander, or White.

If there's no biological basis for the term "race," then our ideas about race must be social constructions. But even social constructions can have real and serious consequences. "Race" is such an important demographic variable that virtually every research study done today describes the race of the participants. Access to education, health status, and civil rights all vary by race. And racism is a very real challenge that people of color face. So throughout this book, I will explain how research findings on marriages and families vary by race.

Social constructions are real in their consequences because we create our own reality. The good news is that something that has been socially constructed can also be *deconstructed*, taken apart, or disposed of. Do you think we may get to a point where race is no longer a defining factor in a person's life? Will the ethnic groups become so mixed that there will be very few clear distinctions between them?

Social Constructionism is helpful because it reminds us that our own viewpoints may not be factual or objective. Other people may have valid constructions of their own. Family therapists work hard on illuminating how each member of a family construes the issues at hand because sometimes conflicts can be resolved by a true understanding of another person's construction of the world. We often try to force our viewpoints on others and assume theirs are wrong, which can lead to power struggles and conflict. Try to imagine some beliefs or behaviors you have, which you think are "natural" but may actually be social constructions. Social Constructionism may help you understand these ideas or actions better.

One problem that stems from Social Constructionism, however, is that some things are real. There are objective facts out there, and we can't just assume everything is relative to our experience. Some events like divorce or infidelity are real. They aren't in the eye of the beholder. Moreover, when viewpoints on various issues have been constructed by people who hold an unfair advantage over others, "facts" about those issues can be skewed enough to harm others. For example, my grandmother told me about how when she was pregnant with my mother (in the 1950s), prevailing wisdom by the predominately male medical profession was that women should not breastfeed. Because she was a woman who was less educated and had less power than these medical doctors, she did what they instructed her to do, and fed my mother a mixture of powdered milk and sugar, which today we know has very little nutritional value. During the feminist movement of the 1960s and 1970s, mothers decided to take to the streets and protect their rights to breastfeed, to have natural, unmedicated births, and to construct their own ideologies and birth plans based on the information they gathered themselves. This new, feminist, construction of motherhood empowered women to have faith in their own abilities to regulate their birthing experiences. Out of this movement came a new wave of female theorists and researchers, to whom we now turn.

Feminist Theory

In an attempt to reconcile the historic marginalization of women, **Feminist Theory** was developed to counteract the idea that the male perspective should be seen as an ideal framework for analysis (de Beauvoir, 1952). Instead of using male traits, behaviors, or health trends as "the norm" and comparing women to them (a practice known as **androcentrism**), feminist scholars choose to make their discourse "womanist," or from the perspective of women's experience. In regard to life in families, feminist viewpoints do not privilege the Standard North American Family (SNAF) because they view all family forms as legitimate and normative (Peterson, Bodman, Bush, & Madden, 2000). Thus, a feminist approach can include legitimizing same-sex and single-father families, because feminists argue for complete gender equality for all. They see gender discrimination not only as impeding career and social success, but also as detrimental to mental and physical health.

Up until 1990, researchers conducting clinical trials were not even required to include female participants. Medical trials on heart disease and even such things as breast cancer, commonly associated with women, were researched with male participants (Hyde, 2007b). Researchers in both medical and social science fields typically worked from a **female deficit perspective**, using theories, methods, and interpretations of findings that assumed women were inferior, deficient, or in some way pathological (Chrisler & McCreary, 2010). However, feminists argue that there are very few substantive differences between males and females beyond those that have been socially constructed. Through centuries of oppression, domination, marginalization and sexism, they argue that women's experiences have historically been ignored or pathologized.

Feminists seek to normalize the female experience, document that experience, and study women's biological, social, emotional, and cognitive development as valuable in its own right, not just in comparison to the development of men. This often involves a reimagining of research methods and interpretations. For example, when studying how mothers' speaking styles may relate to children's emotional adjustment, a feminist researcher might argue that it's important to include fathers' speaking styles as well. Similarly, if a study finds gender differences, say in self-esteem, with girls having lower self-esteem than boys, Feminist Theory would argue that it's important for researchers to interpret the findings from the perspective of both genders. Do girls have a *deficit* in self-esteem? Or is it equally likely that boys have *inflated* self-esteem? Without data examining the girls and boys in depth, it would be difficult to answer this question.

Feminist Theory has allowed social scientists to re-examine the questions they ask, the samples they study, and the interpretations they make of their data. It helps us organize our thoughts in new,

Feminist Theory
A broad umbrella term for the many theoretical perspectives espousing the equality of men and women; feminist scholars examine women from their own perspective, often using qualitative research methods, without comparing women to men. This perspective often engenders social activism.

Androcentrism
A world view that holds men and male perspectives as the norm by which women are measured and compared.

Female deficit perspective
The traditional research approach that interpreted gender differences as due to female inferiority, instead of appreciating findings about women as normal in their own right.

inclusive, ways, as well as utilizing more in-depth research methods, such as interviews and focus groups, where the research participants' viewpoints can really be heard. Critics of the feminist approach argue that it puts too much weight on patriarchy and oppression as causes of behavior, to the exclusion of other explanations. Feminists of color and lesbian feminists also argue that traditional feminist theory and research privilege the experiences of the white, middle-class, educated woman, and ignore the needs of other types of women. Feminist Theory also fails to integrate biological processes, psychodynamic ideas, and issues regarding fathers and other men in families. Attachment Theory integrates many of these latter ideas, perhaps providing a more practical perspective, when attempting to help us understand the relationships between parents and their children in diverse families around the world.

Attachment Theory

Attachment Theory
John Bowlby's theory stressing the importance of early caregiving relationships for shaping the way people process information and their social and emotional adjustment in adulthood.

Internal working model
An unconscious cognitive template shaped through interactions with early caregivers, which guides people's thinking and behavior in relationships.

Another important theory for understanding family relationships is **Attachment Theory** (Bowlby, 1980), which emphasizes the important influence that the child–caregiver bond has on a person's mental and physical health both in childhood and later on. One of the main influences on this theory was Freudian psychodynamic theory. Attachment Theory's founder, John Bowlby, was a psychoanalyst trained in the Freudian tradition of emphasizing the important impact of early childhood experiences on adult personalities and mental health. In the Freudian tradition, he also acknowledged the workings of the unconscious mind. Attachment Theory emphasizes that we carry with us a mental template, or **internal working model**, of both ourselves and others, which guides our interactions. Based on the quality of our early experiences with caregivers, this unconscious internal working model is shaped in a more or less positive and healthy or negative and unhappy manner.

Bowlby was a great integrator of many different ideas, in addition to traditional psychoanalytic thinking. From the ethological tradition (studying animals to find out something about humans), he learned that all primate babies cling to their mothers. He also saw that when the famous ethologist, Konrad Lorenz, hatched goslings, they would immediately attach to him and see him as their "mother," following him everywhere he went (Lorenz, 1935). Bowlby also studied juvenile delinquents and noticed that none of the young men he studied had a secure, warm, and loving attachment figure at home to care for them.

At the same time Bowlby was developing his theory, other research was coming out of orphanages, which showed that even when orphans' physical health was taken care of—even when they were fed, clothed, and provided with medical care—they often still developed emotional and cognitive problems or even died when they were not held or did not receive love (Dennis, 1973; Skeels, 1966; Spitz, 1955). Harry Harlow (1963) studied young monkeys and found that they would attach to a soft cloth surrogate mother even if it provided no food. They did not run to a wire surrogate mother when afraid, even if she had a bottle to feed them. These monkeys not only ran to the cloth mother, which provided them with contact comfort, but after they were calmed by it, they were able to confront a feared stimulus or attack a scary object like a toy robot.

Integrating all of these strands of research and theory, along with the theory of evolution, Bowlby developed one of the most important theories of our time to explain family relationships. In brief, Attachment Theory posits that humans are evolutionarily imbued with the tendency to emotionally attach to babies. And babies are naturally inclined to make physical and emotional bonds with their caregivers. This tendency protects children from harm and allows them to develop into mentally and emotionally healthy adults, provided that the family responds to the infant's needs in a warm and responsive manner (Grossman, Grossman, & Waters, 2005). While there are wide variations in qualities of attachment and many ways to parent infants around the world, most societies agree that parents and children form deep bonds that are crucial for the child's optimal development. Most of the societies examined agree that parents have a responsibility to provide tender loving care and respond to their children's needs (Morelli & Rothbaum, 2007). The manner in which parents around the world do this can vary greatly. But key emotional attachments between caregivers and children are critical elements for making a healthy family.

Support for Attachment Theory comes from many sources. Consistent with Harlow's monkey studies, current research suggests that physical touch plays an important part in a human infant's physical, cognitive, and emotional health. When premature infants in hospital neonatal care units are massaged daily, they not only gain more weight than non-massaged babies, but they get out of the hospital sooner, have fewer learning disabilities later in life and experience fewer health problems (Dieter, Field, Hernandez-Reif, Emory, & Redzepi, 2003). In sum, touch, responsiveness, love, and warmth are crucial not only for our happiness, but for our survival as a species.

Attachment Theory is sophisticated and intricate, acknowledging the true complexity of the origins of human relationships. For example, when a father caresses and rocks his newborn infant, the infant's brain releases pleasure chemicals similar to opiates. With thousands of positive tactile interactions over many months, the father and his child build a synchronized "dance" wherein they gaze into each others' eyes, smile, and take turns cooing and eventually talking to each other. During this process of co-regulation, the infant is soothed and comforted by the father's voice and touch and the father's behavior is reinforced by the child's calm and happy demeanor. Over time, the child begins to feel secure enough to look out into the larger world and explore toys, animals, plants, and other people, knowing that there is a secure base to return to if trouble arises. This co-regulation of the child's physiological and emotional states is the foundation for the development of later social skills, academic success, and emotional regulation abilities (e.g., Perry, 2005; Rygaard, 2006; Shore, 2001).

Attachment Theory has generated thousands of studies on topics as diverse as infant speech development and caring for the elderly. Its great strength is its integration of biological and environmental influences. However, it is often criticized for trying to explain too much about people by "blaming" their childhoods and that often people turn out to have very happy families even when they have terrible attachment histories. In spite of these criticisms, we will revisit this perspective throughout this textbook because attachment research incorporates everything from genes and neurons to families and cultures, which you will learn is an essential viewpoint if we want an in-depth appreciation for what makes families tick.

Any given attachment relationship can only explain part of family health and well-being, however, because we all exist within multiple systems of influence. Like Structural-Functionalism, Family Systems Theory, Conflict Theory, Social Exchange Theory, and Social-Constructionism, Attachment Theory tells us only part of the story.

Bioecological Theory

To truly understand the puzzle of marriages and families, we need to consider individuals in the family, their interactions within the family system, and the family's and individuals' contexts in the larger social world. Bronfenbrenner's Bioecological Theory (Bronfenbrenner, 2004; Bronfenbrenner & Ceci, 1993, 1994; Bronfenbrenner & Morris, 2006) does just that. It argues that in order to truly understand a person or a family, we must look at several levels of analysis. We must look across diverse systems of influence for a comprehensive view of family development in context. Bioecological Theory is often described as a *person, process, context* model, as shown in Figure 2.1. Using it, we look at how a person's roles, his or her developmental processes, and his or her life contexts intertwine to create outcomes, such as becoming a tightrope walker or a professional baseball player. True understanding requires complex analyses. It is not as easy as saying "her parents made her a daredevil" or "his baseball skills are in his genes." To understand either the tightrope walker or the athlete, we must frame the question in complex terms, and examine biology, personal characteristics, and the contexts of a person's life. To understand the Bioecological Theory, let's look at each part of the model.

FIGURE 2.1 The bioecological model.

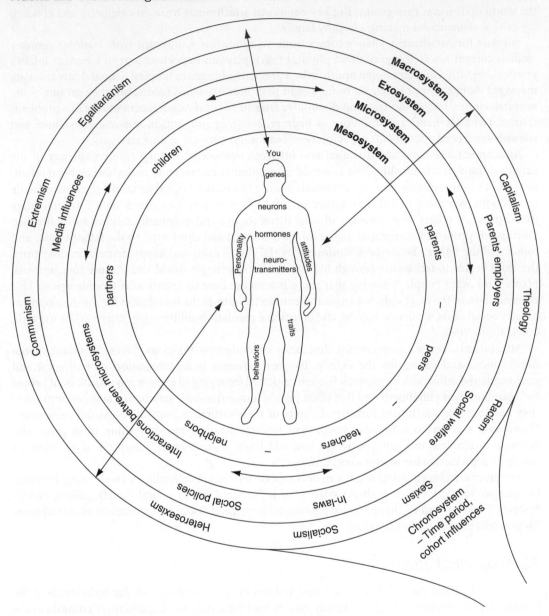

The person

The first level of analysis in Bioecological Theory is the person, you. Think about yourself. You are made up of biological matter. DNA, genes, hormones, neurotransmitters—all of the biochemical processes within you affect your development, behavior, traits, and characteristics.

Students of social science often neglect to consider the importance of biology when trying to understand families. For example, many neuroscience studies have revealed that the brain is an open, dynamic system that can be changed through interactions with the environment. Therefore, you're not born with a brain that you carry with you throughout life. It's constantly under construction, a work in progress. The ways your parents, siblings, and grandparents respond to your overtures, care for your needs, and structure your environment change the structure and functioning of your brain. A study conducted by Paulesu et al. (2000) illustrates this plasticity, or malleability, of the brain. He found that while reading, Italians used the left superior temporal regions that process sound bits called *phonemes*. In contrast, English readers' brains used completely different areas while reading, the left posterior inferior temporal gyrus and the anterior frontal gyrus. These brain areas are used to look for *meaning networks* and for *whole word retrieval* and *naming*. The author believes this cultural difference occurs because the English language is very inconsistent in its use of rules, whereas Italian is much more straightforward. In English, there is a complex letter to sound correspondence. But you can sound out words or sound bits and read Italian easily. I can imagine that having a heated argument with your boyfriend or girlfriend, or writing love songs for your children, might be very different if your brain grew up in Italy versus Iowa. This study shows that the simple act of growing up reading one language versus another significantly changes the way the brain operates, and suggests that our interactions with others in any given language may have divergent qualities. Bialystock, Craik, Klein, and Viswanathan (2004) found that people who use two languages (bilinguals) are better at memory tasks and other information processing skills since they regularly think in a more complex way, using more brain power, than monolinguals do. So it seems it would be hard to win an argument with a bilingual spouse!

In another fascinating study examining the effects of experience on neural plasticity, Maguire et al. (2000) studied the posterior hippocampus, an area that stores spatial representations of the environment, in British taxi-drivers. They found that taxi-drivers had a significantly larger hippocampus than non taxi-drivers. In fact, hippocampal volume was directly correlated with the number of years the people had been working as taxi-drivers. More experienced drivers had a much bigger spatial representation area in their brains than newer drivers.

Together, these studies show that biology plays a key role in how we function, and that how we function changes our biology. Because contemporary research illuminates how crucial biochemical and neuropsychological processes are for every area of individual functioning, it is important to examine such influences when discussing marriages and families.

Each of us brings our brain and body to our relationships and they play key roles in how we behave and process social information. However, it's also important not to over-emphasize the importance of biology when trying to understand families. Keep in mind that, in addition to biology, there is you, the individual, and your personality. You have certain personality and temperamental traits that make you unique. You exist within many systems of influence and your individuality both affects and is affected by the family processes that take place at each level.

Processes and contexts

Moving out from the individual in our bioecological model, we see the first and most immediate system of influence where the *process* level of analysis begins. This system of influence is called the **microsystem** and includes the processes of interactions with others in our immediate environment. This microsystem includes forces and people that regularly and immediately have an impact on you. It can include your parents, peers, teachers, siblings, friends, and partners. Attachment Theory is useful for understanding processes in the microsystem. People in your microsystem—people you are intimately and emotionally tied to—are often your attachment figures. Often, when people seek to understand families, they stop at this level of analysis. They don't go beyond thinking about people's parents in order to understand their behavior at a certain point in time. You often hear people saying things like "No wonder she's crazy! Look at her parents!"

But beyond the microsystem lies the **mesosystem**. In this system, members of your microsystem interact with each other to affect your development in a way that is different from how any individual member of the microsystem could affect you. For example, think about how your parent and your boyfriend or girlfriend interact. How does it affect you if your parent loves this person? How might things be different if your parent were to hate this person? You may have a good relationship and positive attachments with both your parent and your partner; these are microsystem processes. However, if they hate each other or have conflicts, their interactions affect you differently than your interactions with either individual. You may have a great time hanging out with your parent and

Microsystem
Immediate, direct influences on development (e.g., parents and peers).

Mesosystem
Interactions between microsystems which provide a new level of influence on development, separate from the influence of individual microsystem effects.

more great times hanging out with your partner, but if they're vying for your attention, disparaging each other, or bringing negativity to family events, it can completely change the microsystem. The mesosystem, or interaction between microsystems, helps us understand what makes families tick by allowing us to analyze and factor in a new layer of complexity we wouldn't grasp if we only examined your separate relationships with each person.

A third system of influence related to the *processes* in relationships is called the **exosystem**. The exosystem is a system of influences that you do not directly come into contact with. These influences affect you indirectly through members of your microsystem. For example, your parent's boss can have an indirect effect on you. If this boss doesn't allow much schedule flexibility, your parent may be forced to miss your school activities or sporting events. As a result, you may feel disappointed and your parent may feel guilty, which puts a strain on your relationship. Or your parent may come home tired and cranky, which will affect your family interactions. Even though we don't have direct contact with *exosystem* influences, they can have a profound impact on us. Can you think of an *exosystem* influence that affects your own family relationships?

Exosystem
Indirect influences on development, affecting people through their microsystems.

TABLE 2.1 Theories in brief.

Theory	Main tenets
Communism	An analysis of capitalist societies that claims the rich will always exploit the labor of the poor and eventually the poor will revolt to reap the fruits of their own labor; emphasizes the need for a communal way of life where all workers benefit equally from shared work.
Structural-Functionalism	Stems from Communist Theory; Emphasizes maintaining the status quo of a society or family, with specific structures remaining in place to ensure the system works as it should with specific people in power; each person plays a crucial role in keeping the family functioning as it always has.
Family Systems Theory	Stems from Structural-Functionalism; examines roles and power dynamics present in families; emphasizes that every individual exists within a complex relationship system; the whole is greater than the sum of the parts.
Conflict Theory	Argues that conflict is a normal and natural part of family life; people can use conflicts to help relationships mature and grow through renegotiating power relationships.
Social Exchange Theory	Argues that people make a deliberate tally of costs and benefits during decision-making and behaviors they perform in families.
Social Constructionism	Humans construct their own reality, and those constructions affect behaviors in families.
Feminist Theory	Argues that women can be the focus of theory and research in their own right, and not only in comparison to men; urges the use of qualitative research approaches and in-depth analysis of women's perspectives.
Attachment Theory	Stresses the importance of early caregiving relationships for shaping the way people process information and adjust socially and emotionally in adulthood.
Bioecological Theory	The organizing framework of the current text, which assumes that individuals exist within multiple complex systems of influence, from biology to culture, all of which interact with each other to shape family functioning.

Going out to an even more distant set of influences, there is the **macrosystem**. The macrosystem is comprised of larger cultural factors that influence us. These influences may include economic structures like capitalism or socialism. They can include religious views like Christianity or Islam. And they can even include technological advances, such as the use of techno-lingo like "I'll Facebook you" or the recent addition of the verb "to Google" to the dictionary. The macrosystem may also encompass societal and cultural issues such as freedom, racism, classism, ageism, or sexism, which have a great impact on us as individuals, as well as on our families (Spencer, 2006).

Macrosystem
Large cultural and societal influences on development.

Each of these systems in the bioecological model impacts and is impacted by the other systems (shown by the bidirectional arrows in Figure 2.1). For example, if a study finds cultural effects, are these effects part of individual psychological traits, part of something in the macrosystem, or a combination of both (Cohen, 2007)? Cohen suggests that differences we find between cultures may not be due to cultural (macrosystem) practices or beliefs alone. Instead, they may be due to individual traits or the effects of interactions in smaller groups like families (microsystems). Think about what could explain cultural differences we find in, for example, attitudes towards premarital sex. Why does one culture accept its members having sex before marriage, while another culture does not? Do these attitudes stem from the macrosystem, mesosystem, exosystem, or microsystem? The answer to this question is that it's probably a combination of all these systems interacting continuously over time. And that's the exact point of a bioecological approach: all systems matter.

Bioecological Theory also emphasizes a **chronosystem**, or the time period in which we are interacting. The content of a course on family relationships would vary quite a bit if the course were offered in different time periods. A textbook from 1880 may not even mention sex at all, and a textbook from 1950 might discuss sex only within the context of marriage. A twenty-first-century textbook, like this one, has an entire chapter on sexuality because we've amassed decades of research on this topic and have come to understand that sexuality is a key influence in individual development, and thus in families. The time period we live in affects family health and happiness, as we saw in our historical exploration of American families in Chapter 1.

Chronosystem
Time period effects on development.

It might be helpful for you to see all of these theories in one place so you can grasp their main tenets in summary form. See Table 2.1.

To see how the bioecological model works, read *Focus on My Family*, which profiles Jan, a mother of 10. See how Jan describes the various bioecological systems of influence on her life and her children's lives.

Although the bioecological approach is the overarching framework through which we will examine families, you will notice that I often refer back to the other theories discussed here as well. Each theory can help us explain parts of problems or skills that families experience.

Theories help us generate ideas for research and help us understand the results of our studies. It's important to conduct research that stems from a theoretical base so we're not diving in to questions head first without a plan. Like a professional diver, a professional researcher doesn't jump in haphazardly. The theory we use guides our vision, just as most good athletes envision what might happen before they

FIGURE 2.2 What specific examples from each of the bioecological systems of influence can you think of that will affect this baby's development within his family?
© Sajjad Hussain/AFP/Getty Images.

FOCUS ON MY FAMILY

Jan's story

Take a look at Jan's story and see which elements of the bioecological approach you can identify. Which people are in her microsystem? How do you see meso-, exo-, macro-, and chronosystem influences affecting her? Check your answers at the end of Jan's story.

In my forties, I had empty nest syndrome after my children left home. I took in two foster children and from there, my life evolved into what it is today, a single mom of 10 children. I have adopted seven special needs children. Most days are happy, but more hectic than I'd prefer. My kids are healthy today, but the demons from their abusive histories creep up to remind me that our family is unique. It wasn't planned, but as I look back on the last 10 years, I wouldn't trade my life for anything.

We practice open adoption so our birth families come and go from addiction, incarceration, and mental illness. Some we see frequently, others stray for months or years. I believe these bonds are crucial to maintain, though.

On paper, my children's combined diagnoses look frightening. They range from reactive attachment disorder to traumatic brain injury, paralysis, seizure disorder, attention deficit disorder, and depression. I forget that most children can use all their limbs and are rarely aggressive or agitated. It's always odd to see other children focus in school for long periods or eat without spilling.

Early on, the most difficult part was handling the deep anguish I carried, unable to let go of the horrific thoughts of my children being hurt by their birth families; the daily beatings, hunger, being locked in closets, and sexual abuse. Many nights, I would lie beside my sleeping children and sob for hours, unable to put the pain they endured out of my mind. I irrationally blamed myself for not being there to protect them when they needed me. I'm not superhuman. I'm still haunted by the memory of the first time I saw my 3-year-old attached to a web of hospital tubes, after being beaten by his birth parents.

Today, it's not easy to protect them from outside forces. For example, during a community festival, an intoxicated man approached me and screamed "Nigger lover!" He had my car blocked in and was becoming very belligerent. This was the only time I felt hatred could endanger us. I was able to put my children in the car and call the police. The thought of them hearing such unacceptable words makes me crazy! I wish I could protect them forever, but sadly, they will continue to experience shallow, uneducated humans throughout their lives. My job is to give them the knowledge and self-confidence to rise above and shake it off.

Today I still have tears, but they come from a different place. When I watch my son play baseball, batting with one arm and limping around the bases with a huge grin on his face, I thank a higher power that I was selected to be his mom and that we've come so far together as a family. I can tell you, the lesson of forgiveness which comes so naturally to young children, comes to adults, a bit more slowly, perhaps, but it comes and heals the deepest wounds.

Bioecological factors: Jan's children are in her *microsystem*; her children's interactions with each other are in her *mesosystem*; her children's biological parents are in her *exosystem* (indirectly influencing her through her children's problems in the microsystem); *macrosystem* influences include a racist and intolerant culture; *chronosystem* influences include modern approaches to adoption that allow children with multiple challenges to be adopted instead of institutionalized. Many other answers could be correct as well.

Jan and her family.
Photo reproduced by permission.

actually perform a daring feat. However, good research and good performance in sports require more than a theory or vision. They must also include fine-tuned technical skills. For researchers, research methodology helps us perfect our technique and execute our vision.

RESEARCH METHODOLOGY

- Hypothesis testing
- Operational definitions
- Experimental procedures
- Correlational procedures
- Quantitative and qualitative research methods

Chapter 1 of this textbook presented a lot of facts about families, both past and present. How do we know they are facts and not opinions? One way is that scholars who study the family adhere to the scientific method to gather and analyze data. This method consists of a series of steps researchers must complete in order to ensure their study was done ethically and using proper techniques, and that it allows for valid conclusions to be drawn. Following these concrete steps allows all researchers to speak the same language and understand exactly what other scholars are doing so that, if they wish, they may **replicate**, or repeat, the methodology in a study of their own to see if they find the same results. This replication method (repeating someone else's study) allows researchers to evaluate the quality and conclusions of research using a common vocabulary and scientific standards. If researchers all find the same results through many replications, we start to develop a set of facts about the phenomenon under study. Facts, then, are generated over time by many different researchers using different samples and adding to each other's work. It would be bad science to base any firm conclusions on a study that had been conducted only once.

Replication
Doing a research study again to confirm that results are valid.

For example, how did we determine the fact that smoking is bad for us? Sixty years ago many mothers smoked while pregnant and many more Americans smoked than do today. Cigarette packs carried no Surgeon General's warnings informing the public of the dangers of smoking. It was only through decades of research replicated in different laboratories in the U.S. and abroad that researchers discovered how harmful tobacco, nicotine, and even second-hand smoke can be to people's respiratory systems and other organs. Tobacco companies fought the release of these research findings and tried to find flaws in the research designs and conclusions because they are in the business of selling cigarettes. However, eventually, the facts were so well established as to be indisputable, thanks in large part to carefully controlled and replicated scientific studies.

Without scientific research, we might not be able to put the pieces together to realize that cigarettes cause health problems. Suppose your parent, who smokes, develops lung cancer. You may form various opinions about the disease, maybe thinking your parent had a genetic flaw, fell upon bad luck, or was under stress that caused the illness; you may even conclude that the disease was "God's will." Any of these opinions have the potential to be correct, but without conducting scientific research, it's difficult, if not impossible, to determine the causes of diseases. Likewise, without conducting scientific research, it is impossible to determine what specific factors affect family health, happiness, and success.

Hypothesis testing

Researchers cannot examine things that cannot be measured, like supernatural acts or God's will. However, they can measure aspects of each **hypothesis**, or testable statement, proposed regarding how your parent got lung cancer. Researchers can measure genetic markers your parent might have for specific diseases. They can precisely measure stress levels in your parent's life. They can even examine the "luck factor," or randomness, of disease by looking at distributions of disease among various populations.

Hypothesis
A concrete, testable statement employed in research studies.

Without carefully measuring our ideas, we would have to rely on common sense or intuition to understand the world around us, including issues related to families. But, as decades of research have revealed, our common sense is often wrong. For example, people might believe the old adage "opposites attract," but dozens of studies on mate selection have shown us that it is actually *similarity* between partners that both attracts and keeps people together. Instead of relying on common sense, intuition, or opinions, we can use a controlled and thoughtful approach to investigating questions of interest. This controlled and thoughtful approach is the scientific method.

As discussed at the beginning of the chapter, when researchers use the scientific method they begin with a theory, just as I used Bioecological Theory to organize my thoughts on abused children's peer relationships. Using an established theoretical framework helps the scientist develop specific, testable hypotheses to examine. It's important that research begins with a theory so that we can understand what specific perspective spawned the line of inquiry. For example, if I wanted to study the effects of divorce on children, a Conflict Theory perspective might lead me to try to measure the positive aspects of family conflict during divorce. For example, dealing with parental conflict may allow children to develop coping skills. In contrast, an Attachment Theory perspective might lead me to ask how attachment bonds are challenged during a divorce. Thus, the theory we use guides our questions and predictions.

Unbiased
The attempt to keep personal beliefs out of the research process.

A crucial part of the scientific process is being **unbiased**, or not allowing preconceived ideas or beliefs to have an impact on research. However, most research begins with a theoretical perspective, which can affect the types of questions asked, the research designs undertaken, and the conclusions drawn. So we have to be especially vigilant in weighing possible explanations for research findings other than the one the author of a study proposes. Scientists attempt to be objective in their work, but it's difficult to separate the scientist from the person, especially on topics we all care about, like family relationships. Hammersley (2000) argues that researchers cannot possibly remain completely objective because they go into a research project with particular goals to either support or change the status quo. Research conclusions are often used to make political statements and research findings often lead to social activism. He suggests that instead of denying partisanship, researchers should just acknowledge their positions up front.

In the scientific method, we begin with a theoretical orientation, which helps us generate specific hypotheses that we can test in a study. To illustrate how this works, we will explore an example in depth. From an Attachment Theory perspective, we can hypothesize that disruptions in attachment security, such as we find during family conflict, might have negative effects on children's stress levels. The hypothesis must be a very specific statement that can be tested in our study and in future research. How do we come up with a specific, testable hypothesis?

Operational definitions

Operational definition
A concrete, extremely clear definition of research variables which allows others scientists to easily replicate the work.

An important step at the beginning stages of the scientific process is being able to generate **operational definitions** of the variables stated in the hypothesis, the variables of interest. An operational definition is one that is concrete and clear enough that any researcher wanting to study the same phenomenon could *replicate* the study easily by using the same definitions. Operational definitions of variables help us clearly test a specific hypothesis, For example, to study the effects of family conflict on children's development of stress, we would need an operational definition of "family conflict." One operational definition of family conflict is "the number of verbal arguments between parents per week." To make this measurable and testable, we would also need an operational definition of "argument." Is it yelling? Is it a disagreement? How should we measure conflict—by using family members' self-reports? How would the mom's and dad's reports differ from the child's reports? An alternate method would be to place a video camera in the home to capture what the researcher would define as "conflict." But the family might consider the same behaviors as simply teasing. As you can see, creating operational definitions is no easy task. However, creating measurable operational definitions is crucial for good research.

Experimental procedures

After we construct operational definitions for our variables of interest, we must decide on the research design we want to use. The research design depends on whether we want to determine causality or simply an association between two variables. **Causality** is the certainty that one variable causes a specific outcome or change in the other variable. The only way to determine causality is by conducting an **experiment**. Experiments are carefully controlled studies in which the researcher manipulates the participants' experiences. Any results found can be explained solely by the manipulation performed. For example, to study the effects of family conflict on children's stress levels, we could create a situation that imitates the real-world arguments that happen in families. For this study, we couldn't do a perfect experiment because we can't ethically manipulate, ask, or demand that a family argue or fight. So we would have to figure out a way to simulate what families experience at home. When we imitate or simulate real world conditions, we conduct an **analog** experiment. An analog is a simulation of real life. Let's see how an analog experiment might be done on the effect of family conflict on children's stress levels.

Variables

First, we have to decide what our **independent variable** is. The independent variable is the variable that is operationally defined and then manipulated in the experiment. For our example, we want to study the effect of family conflict on children's stress levels. We are manipulating "family conflict," which is our independent variable. We want to see this variable's effect on children's stress. How would we operationalize family conflict? For our analog experiment, let's say we record two adults arguing. We could write a script for them to follow, which could be provided to other researchers wanting to replicate our study later on. One male and one female adult (maybe we'd choose trained actors to make the argument more believable) would argue about, say, one person not pulling his or her weight in household chores; this is a common argument in real families. For our hypothetical study, let's say we make the recorded argument last three minutes.

Our **dependent variable**, the variable we measure at the end of the study, is "children's stress." How would we operationalize that? We might monitor children's heart rate, pulse, and amount of sweating; all of these are signs of physiological stress. We might also interview the children using a questionnaire we have devised that asks them how stressed they feel. Questions might include items like "How happy do you feel right now, on a scale of 1 to 5?" For the operational definition of the dependent variable "children's stress," we are using both physiological and psychological measurements. Once we've determined how to measure our variables of interest, we can move on to placing our participants in groups.

Experimental design

We will set up two groups and randomly assign children to each group. **Random assignment** is a technique that is invaluable for making sure our experiment is highly controlled. It means that every participant has an equal chance of ending up in group one or group two. We can randomize in many ways. We can randomly call every 10th number in the phone book to ask people to participate, and then assign those who agree to be in our study to each group using a random method like drawing names out of a hat. Researchers even use computerized random number generators to assign people to groups. We want to perform random assignment to groups because we want our experimental manipulation to work. We will not be able to determine if the experimental manipulation worked if the groups differ systematically before we begin the study.

One of our two groups will be the **experimental group**, the group that receives the experimental manipulation; in this case, exposure to a recorded conflict. The other group will be the **control group**, the group that doesn't receive the experimental manipulation. To make sure that assignment to the two groups is random, we wouldn't want to put all the kids from conflictual families in the

Causality
A definitive statement about one variable causing changes in another variable.

Experiment
A research method employing strict controls and random assignment of subjects; the only method that allows one to make causal statements.

Analog
A research method that resembles real-life situations but is artificially manipulated in the lab.

Independent variable
The variable that is manipulated in a research study.

Dependent variable
The variable that is measured at the end of a research study.

Random assignment
A technique used in experiments whereby participants are assigned to groups in a random, versus systematic, manner; increases validity of conclusions made from results.

Experimental group
The group of participants that receives the independent variable manipulation.

Control group
The group of participants that does not receive the independent variable manipulation; can receive another similar manipulation if a no-treatment control group is also employed.

experimental group. Likewise, we wouldn't want to put kids with higher heart rates into the control group. Instead, we want a mixture of all different kinds of children in each group. That way, we can see that if we manipulate the kids' exposure to conflict and find an effect of higher stress in those exposed to conflict, we know that it was the recorded argument that *caused* the stress because there are no other systematic differences between the groups. Random assignment should control for any pre-existing biases or systematic differences the participants bring to the experiment.

To make sure our random assignment is successful, we may want to perform a manipulation check, called a **baseline assessment**. To perform a baseline assessment, we measure the dependent variable *before* we do the experiment. That way, we assess whether kids' heart rates and stress interview answers vary in any systematic way before they even go into the experiment. Researchers hope that the experimental group and control group do not significantly differ in any way from each other at baseline. We hope that, on average, both groups of kids have about equal baseline heart rates and self-reported levels of stress. This will ensure that if we find differences between the groups at the end of the study, we can attribute those results to the manipulation of our independent variable, exposure to conflict, and not to some pre-existing difference that biased our results.

In an ideal world, studies would not only use random assignment, but would end up having samples of participants that represent the larger population we hope to make conclusions about (in this case, "families"). **Representative samples** are groups of people that are similar to the larger population we want to make conclusions about. Our samples should look similar to the larger population of families racially, ethnically, and socioeconomically, and should be comprised of gender and age ratios that reflect the larger population. We hope that our sample of kids in this study looks very similar in composition to the population of families at large, so that we can rest assured that our results do not apply to only one type of family (for example, white families, girl-only families, and so on).

The next step in an experimental procedure is exposing the participants to the manipulation. For our hypothetical study they will be exposed to three minutes of a recorded conflict. We have to control for how the manipulation is carried out so that all participants receive it in exactly the same way. We might put each child in a room full of toys and tell them we'll be back in a few minutes to administer a questionnaire. During those three minutes, we could play the recorded conflict so that it sounds like the adults are right outside the playroom door arguing. During these three minutes, we would record the child's heart rate, pulse, and sweat level. The control group children would be treated in exactly the same way, but would not be exposed to the recorded argument, the independent variable. Instead, we could expose them to a recorded adult conversation that didn't involve arguing. If we did that, we might want to add a third group, a **no-treatment control group**, for a manipulation check. The no-treatment control group would hear no recording. This *manipulation check* would allow us to see whether hearing *any* recorded conversation raises stress levels. That way, we could be sure that it was the *arguing*, and not just hearing people talk outside the door, that influenced our results.

Choosing a research time frame

In the study we have been describing, participation in the study is a one-time event. But other studies require that people participate over a longer time span. If we want a picture of how people change over time, or if we want to see long-term effects of a variable like family conflict, we also need to figure out for how long we want to follow families. We could conduct a **longitudinal** study in which we follow the same people over a long period of time. This type of study can be expensive to carry out and time-consuming for the researchers. Longitudinal studies can suffer from a number of problems. One problem is **attrition**, which means that people drop out of the study over time, move away, or die. Scientific measures can change over time, so another problem may be wasting money on a study that is soon outdated. The benefits of a longitudinal study include a real developmental picture of change over time and the ability to assess the same people in a lot of depth.

If we don't have the time or budget to follow a group of families for a long period of time, we may have to settle for measuring children's reactions to conflict at one point in time. When we measure

Baseline assessment
A manipulation check to assess the participants on key variables before the experiment has taken place.

Representative sample
A sample of participants that closely resembles the larger group to whom research results are meant to generalize.

No-treatment control group
A group of participants that receives no level of the independent variable manipulation.

Longitudinal
A study design that follows the same people over long periods of time.

Attrition
The rate at which participants leave a study through drop-out, death, relocation, or refusal to participate.

people at one measurement point, the study design is called **cross-sectional**. Cross-sectional studies measure groups of people all at one point in time, instead of following them for longer periods. They are less expensive and we get results more quickly than with longitudinal designs. However, with a cross-sectional study we can't measure changes over time or long-term effects.

With the time and resources we have, we've chosen to do a cross-sectional design to assess children's stress responses to a recorded argument. Even though it is virtually impossible to design a perfect study, we try to control for as many outside influences on our results as we can. Can you think of any problems with our experimental design so far?

Examining results

Once the study is completed, we would conduct statistical analyses on the data to determine whether the groups differed significantly from each other on stress measures, our dependent variables. If the groups differed significantly and in the direction we hypothesized (that is, children exposed to arguing have higher stress levels than children not exposed to arguing), we would be able to conclude that exposure to adult conflict *caused* children's stress levels to increase. However, before we alert the media, we should probably *replicate* these findings on another sample of children.

Better yet, other researchers in other labs should replicate the findings to be sure that there is sufficient generalizability to make a solid conclusion. **Generalizability** means that our experimental results can be applied to a wider population of people. Generalizability increases when we have a diverse and, especially, a *representative* sample. We don't want to know if only those children in our experiment are affected by adult conflict. We want to be able to generalize our results to all children or to a large majority of children. When our results apply to the majority of children, we can make policies or procedures to address the problem. If our results are generalizable, we would be able to justify spending money on parenting programs that teach parents how to solve disagreements without arguing. Or we would be able to work with families on conflict-resolution skills.

Although the laboratory experiment's great strength is determining causality, it is sometimes not very generalizable to the real world because the experimental manipulation occurs in such a controlled and often artificial manner. We cannot conclude, for example, that children in the real world exposed to *parental* conflict react in the same way as children in the lab experiment who listened to a recorded argument. For one thing, the people on the recording were not the children's parents. Secondly, they were only arguing about one issue, household chores. Third, we could not make the recording too terrifying because it would be unethical to expose children to that kind of conflict.

However, we know that children in the real world *are* exposed to high levels of conflict, and even violence, in their homes. We cannot recreate those real-world experiences in an *analog* lab setting due to ethical protections for human research participants. Therefore, what we gain in laboratory control, we often lose in generalizability. There is always a trade-off between control and the generalizability of our findings. Unfortunately, it's virtually impossible for researchers to have high levels of both experimental control and real-world generalizability. To see how the effects of adult conflict on children were actually studied in a real research study, see *How Would You Measure That?*

Correlational procedures

While experimental procedures can tell us about many important variables related to family health and success, most research studies related to families are non-experimental in nature. Many topics of interest cannot be experimentally manipulated in a lab. We often have two groups to compare, but these groups often occur naturally—we don't randomly assign them. For example, much research is done on gender differences. We can't randomly assign one group to be female and another group to be male. But we are interested in studying gender differences in various topics like communication styles or academic skills. In this case, we might do a **natural** or **quasi-experiment**, an experiment in which almost everything is controlled, except for the assignment to groups. For

Cross-sectional
A study design where one or more groups of people are measured at one point in time.

Generalizability
The degree to which research results can be applied to larger populations based on the sample results found in a study.

Natural/quasi-experiment
A group comparison research design where groups are not randomly assigned but are naturally occurring.

HOW WOULD YOU MEASURE THAT?

Children's adjustment in relation to their exposure to family conflict (Sturge-Apple, Davies, & Cummings, 2006)

These researchers studied 210 mothers and fathers of 6-year old children over a three-year period, so this is a *longitudinal study*. They were interested in the relationships between interparental conflict, the quality of parent–child interactions, and children's adjustment over time. The sample was ethnically and socioeconomically diverse. The parents came into the laboratory for two three-hour visits, one year apart. At the first visit, the parents were asked to engage in a discussion about common issues they disagreed on at home. The content and style of these discussions were used to *operationalize* "family conflict." To measure verbal aggression and hostility, the discussions were coded for insults, expressions of disgust, spite, and cruelty; to measure withdrawal, the discussions were coded for repeated or prolonged tense periods of detachment or avoidance. At the second visit, a year later, parents were asked to engage separately in two tasks with their child, a play session and a session in which the parent directed the child in cleaning up toys. This was done to assess a potential mediating factor: parenting style. Parenting style was measured by their level of "emotional unavailability" during the play and clean-up periods, operationalized by a neglecting or distancing style (in comparison to a warm and supportive style). To assess the *dependent variable*, "children's adjustment," the researchers used parent and teacher ratings, two years later, of children's externalizing (aggression, conflict, negative behavior), internalizing (withdrawal, isolation, depression), and academic adjustment (grades and conduct).

The results were surprising. Interparental conflict at time 1 predicted parent emotional unavailability at time 2 (a year later), which in turn predicted children's poor adjustment at time 3 (two years later). Interestingly, parental withdrawal during problem discussions predicted all three child outcomes (externalizing, internalizing, and academic problems). Moreover, this effect was much stronger than any effects exerted by hostility in parent problem discussions. Of note, fathers' emotional unavailability accounted more strongly for all three child adjustment problems than did mothers' unavailability.

Most family research focuses only on mothers' effects on their children's adjustment. If only mothers were included in this study, as is usually done, the authors would have concluded that maternal hostility, mediated by her emotional unavailability, affects children's adjustment, but for only one of the three child outcomes, academic problems. Mothers' variables had very little impact on the other two child outcomes, externalizing and internalizing. In addition, the effect of hostility in general was much weaker than the effect of withdrawal. This work suggests that *paternal* withdrawal and subsequent emotional unavailability are key variables explaining the negative effect of interparental conflict on children's adjustment.

This study gives us a very specific focus for tailoring interventions or family therapies to key influential family dispute styles: withdrawn and silent avoidance during problem discussions. The authors suggest that withdrawal may be an indicator of very long-standing and chronic problems with no apparent solution. This type of stalemate leaves parents frustrated and disengaged during further discussions. The emotional and cognitive strain may then leave little energy for being emotionally available to their children, which then influences children's emotional and academic adjustment.

What parts of this experiment were well done and which aspects could have been improved, based on what you've learned about ideal experimental designs?

example, we might do the same study about the effect of conflict on children's stress, but instead of randomly assigning children, we might expose a group of women to the recorded argument, a group of men to the recorded argument, and have a control group of men and women who were not exposed to the argument, but whose physiological and questionnaire stress data were still collected as dependent variables.

Another type of natural experiment is done when naturally occurring events happen, such as winning the lottery, getting a divorce, or experiencing Hurricane Katrina. We obviously could not randomly assign people to experience these events. But groups of people naturally experienced them in various ways. Researchers take advantage of those natural experiments and collect data on groups of people involved in those situations. In fact, researchers investigated the effects of the September 11, 2001 terrorist attacks on different naturally occurring groups and found that those who were closer to the World Trade Center experienced more symptoms of post-traumatic stress disorder than those who lived several miles away or only watched the event on TV.

Most social science research is of this correlational nature (rather than controlled laboratory experiments). In this type of design, researchers choose to do a **correlational study**, whereby they look for links, associations, or "co-relations" between variables, but this means they cannot conclude anything about what caused the association. Many scholars studying the family prefer to increase generalizability, even if it means a decrease in control over the influence of other unmeasured variables.

Correlational study
A study that examines links, associations, or relationships between variables but cannot assess causal influences due to a lack of experimental controls.

Correlations vs. causal inferences

With *correlational* results, we can never conclude that *causality* is at play. We can only determine causality by using a highly controlled experimental procedure that is replicated several times. For example, in my work studying abused children's popularity with their peers, I compared a group of abused children to a matched control group of non-abused children; the children were matched on age, gender, ethnicity, school attended, and socioeconomic status. By matching, I tried to control for the influence of as many extraneous variables as I could, not wanting a difference in poverty status, for example, to account for any differences I found between the groups. Indeed, in support of my hypothesis, I found that abused children were disliked by classmates at a much higher rate than non-abused children at their public elementary school. Even though it makes sense that child maltreatment might *cause* these results (maybe abusive parents can't teach their children social skills, or maybe abused children learn to be aggressive with peers through parental modeling), I could not infer causality because this was only a correlational study.

Even though it's tempting to assume causal relations are at play between two variables (and indeed, the media often report correlations as if causality is occurring), it's important for students reading about research to understand that causality can *never* be determined from a simple correlational study. A correlation between two variables (in this case, child abuse and poor peer relations) means just that: a co-relation, a link, or an association has been found. These two variables are correlated, and that's it. As one variable's levels change, so do the levels of another variable. In this case, as abuse rates rise, so do peer troubles, so we say the two variables are correlated with each other.

In a correlation, the causal arrow could potentially run in the direction opposite of what we expect. It could be that children with poor interpersonal skills, genetic defects, or annoying traits—children who would have peer troubles—are more likely to be abused at home. While child maltreatment scholars never want to put blame for abuse on the child victim, in research, we cannot rule out the possibility that child behavior influenced the abuse. Thus, an equally valid conclusion from correlational findings could be that children with poor interpersonal skills are more likely to be abused.

In addition to the causal direction being the reverse of what we might expect, correlations can also be explained by a third, unmeasured variable. While I tried to control for third variable explanations, to be sure variables like poverty couldn't explain the results (both abused and control children were poor), unmeasured variables could be at work. For example, prenatal exposure to alcohol could explain both the abuse the children experienced and their poor peer relations. It could be that alcoholism caused both the parents' maltreatment of their children and the children's poor interpersonal skills. The point is that we really don't know.

This is perhaps the most important lesson any student can learn about research: **we can never determine causation from a correlation (even if the relationship makes sense)**. For some examples

Spurious correlations

The following variables are significantly correlated with each other. You cannot assume one variable causes the other. What explanations can you think of for these correlations between variables?

1 The number of body lice and good health.

2 The consumption of cigarettes and the profits of Nevada gambling establishments.

3 Wearing bras and the incidence of breast cancer.

4 Smoking and decrease in grades.

5 Production of false teeth and number of inmates in mental institutions.

Source: Retrieved from www.junkfoodscience.blogspot.com.

of variables that are highly correlated yet pretty obviously are not causally related, see the *FYI* box. This sidebar lists a number of nonsensical examples. Remember some of these examples when you read about research that appears to be causal in nature (or media reports that imply causality is at play), yet the research design only allows for correlational conclusions.

If we can't determine the causes of most of the behaviors and traits we study in research, you may wonder what the point of doing research is. Even if most social science research is correlational, as mentioned above, after a finding has been replicated enough times across enough different groups and types of populations, we can start to conclude that we have generated a "fact." For example, there is ample evidence from hundreds of studies conducted over the past 40 years on many different populations to conclude that child abuse harms children's social development. Based on these many findings, researchers feel confident in arguing that child abuse is bad for kids' socioemotional skill development. There is enough evidence out there for us to advocate for children, to try to help parents refrain from abusing their children, and to develop social policies and programs that attempt to prevent abuse before it happens.

Quantitative and qualitative research methods

Quantitative
Data that occur in numerical form, as is found in questionnaires or surveys.

The research I have described is largely **quantitative**, meaning that the phenomena under study have been turned into numbers. We measured stress by children's self-reported stress on a scale from 1 to 5, as well as the number of heartbeats per minute. These are good examples of quantitative data. These data can be entered into a computer and statistically analyzed. Our results, then, are also presented in numerical form, for example in frequencies, percentages, averages, or ratios.

Most quantitative results are reported as group averages. For example, a lot of what we know about families comes from large national databases. You've probably heard of the Gallup Poll and the Census. There are numerous national and international surveys of people that give us statistical averages and percentages. We can learn what percentage of Americans are divorced, use drugs, are incarcerated, have children under the age of 5, live in extended families, and so on. While we can usually gain valuable insights about families from quantitative results and large national surveys, some researchers feel this approach is limiting because human traits, behaviors, and relationships are more complex than simple numbers may suggest.

Qualitative
Data that occur in narrative form, as is found in open-ended interviews.

If we want to understand variables from a more nuanced perspective, we might try to collect **qualitative** data. These data are usually gathered by open-ended questions or interviews which allow people to talk freely about the topic of interest. Or they could be gathered by carefully observing people in their natural environments and taking detailed notes on what we see. We might type up transcripts describing verbatim what occurred and then review the transcripts for a *quality* of interest, such as anger, social isolation, connection to one's ancestors, or religious fervor. For example, if our *quantitative* results showed that men react with more physiological signs of stress and report more negative emotions than women after being exposed to a recorded argument, we might then interview the participants to gather some *qualitative* data. We could ask the men how they felt about the recording they heard. We might want to know if they perceived physiological changes in themselves or what types of thoughts were going through their minds during the recorded argument. Our interviews might find something surprising that the quantitative numbers could not reveal. For example, what if men said they felt angry at the man on the recording and wanted to fight him? This could mean that they felt not stress but anger. What if they said they started remembering times when they had fought with their own partners? This could mean that arguments they heard primed their own memories of personal arguments. What if they said they didn't even notice the argument going on? This could mean they are not self-aware enough to recognize their own internal stress. Their answers to qualitative open-ended interview questions would give us a richer flavor for the *quality* of what we found statistically and what the experience actually meant to the participants.

Etic and emic approaches

Many researchers in the social sciences use a *qualitative* approach called **ethnography**. An ethnography involves documenting the lives and experiences of a population or group of people in much depth. This work may consist of a researcher living amongst the group members being studied. For example, a researcher may want to study the arranged marriage practices of families in India. In order to do this from an ethnographic perspective, a researcher would not just show up and interview families about their arranged marriages. He or she might live in a specific village for several months or years, getting to know the families, in order to understand at a qualitative level how children who grow up in that community view marriage. Talking to families after gaining their trust and building rapport is much different from an outsider coming in to "assess" the situation. An ethnographer might live amongst the population and, though an outsider can never become a true insider, try as much as possible to view marriage through the lens of local religious leaders, children, and parents in that community.

Ethnography requires using an **emic** perspective. An emic perspective is when a researcher is able to study his or her research question from an "inside" perspective, through the eyes of the inhabitants, their history, beliefs, and world view.

In contrast, many researchers, especially in the past, have used an **etic** perspective, or an outsider's viewpoint. When studying small clans or tribes of people, for example, a researcher might have described them as "primitive" or "savage." While outright derogatory statements about groups being studied are relatively rare today, research has yet to progress to the point where scholars eschew viewing the groups they study through a Western lens. Researchers may have a difficult time stepping outside of their Western, formally educated, financially stable, often white and male, viewpoint. This etic bias can influence not only the conclusions that are made when we study people from diverse groups, but the actual questions that are formulated in the first place. Compare the following hypothetical headlines and see which one points to research from an *emic* versus an *etic* perspective:

"Waiting a Lifetime to Meet the Partner My Parents Chose for Me"
"Why India Has Yet to Abandon Arranged Marriage Practices"

The first headline speaks from the perspective of a child growing up in a village, waiting to meet his or her spouse. The second headline suggests that arranged marriages may not be "normal" or "progressive" or "appropriate." It also puts an entire country with millions of inhabitants into one category, *Indian*. In reality, not all people in India practice arranged marriage and there are a variety of populations in India, each with different religions, histories, languages, cultural beliefs, and practices.

Ethnography
A research study conducted on a group of people from their own perspective, often after the researcher lives within the society for a length of time; usually qualitative.

Emic
An "insider's" approach to research, looking at a topic from the perspective of the research participants.

Etic
An "outsider's" approach to research, looking at a topic from the perspective of the researcher.

To reduce the problem of etic bias, it helps to read research conducted by scholars who come from the group being studied and to include community members in the research group as either consultants or collaborators. Having a community liaison who is already respected in the community being studied can help reduce mistrust and enhance the rapport between the research participants and the researcher.

We must also be extremely careful in generalizing beyond the actual scope of our findings. Because problems like this are fairly common in social science research, you, as an informed consumer of that research, must take care in interpreting the results of what may be biased or incomplete studies. Every research participant is a complicated person who possesses many qualities that may not be measured or even considered or understood when we make conclusions about our findings. Qualitative approaches are effective ways to help us understand the perspectives of the research participants in more depth than most quantitative approaches can provide.

Unfortunately, qualitative data involve little control over extraneous variables. In gathering qualitative data, we are relying on people's subjective opinions, faulty memories, individual perceptions of what the research questions mean and what answers the researcher might be looking for, as well as their abilities to reflect on or analyze their own lives. Each person may interpret interview questions differently. They may not have a "shared meaning" with the researchers. These issues, of course, may also arise with quantitative data collection. Thus it's important to be cognizant of the limitations of any research design. For example, if an interviewer asked a mother if her child was "laid back," one mother might respond in the affirmative, thinking her child was lazy, while another mother might answer in the affirmative because her child was timid. If our researchers scored a "yes" answer as a "2" using quantitative methods, both mothers would receive the same score yet these two mothers might not share the same meaning of the construct "laid back personality," which limits the conclusions we can draw. Researchers have to be sure their constructs are *operationally defined* and explained clearly, and that their own behavior doesn't change the way participants respond.

Demand characteristics

Demand
characteristics
Characteristics of the researchers or research setting that influence the behavior or thoughts of participants.

Demand characteristics can be a serious problem in any study. A demand characteristic is some trait the setting contains or the researcher possesses which may influence the study participant's responses. For example, in the interview regarding reactions to a recorded argument, could it make a difference to the participants hearing the argument if the lab were decorated with posters of tropical beaches and palm trees versus having undecorated walls that were painted blood red? What if the interviewer asking men about their thoughts while hearing an argument were another man versus an attractive female? Perhaps the interviewer looked like the participant's father and that affected his answers. If the participant was European American and the interviewer was African American, this could affect their interactions and the answers provided. All of these factors, and even less obvious ones, like a researcher's lisp, a personality style, or bad body odor, could affect the way a participant responds in a study.

Because research can become skewed or biased in so many ways, it's important that you critically examine any studies you encounter. Ask yourself who the research participants were. Maybe even more importantly, ask who was *not* studied. Historically, social science research has been conducted on white, middle-class participants and then the results have been unjustifiably generalized to the population at large. Similarly, psychological and medical research on men has historically been generalized to women without women ever having been studied.

Critical thinking
The ability to use reason to find accurate information, to think logically and skeptically, and not be gullible to ideas that have no supporting evidence.

An informed consumer of research must use **critical thinking** whenever possible. Critical thinking means looking beyond the obvious explanation, investigating media and other claims fully, and not putting too much stock in findings that have not been replicated on diverse samples. For more on developing your critical thinking skills, see *Building Your Strengths*.

BUILDING YOUR STRENGTHS

Improving critical thinking

Critical thinking is *purposeful reflective judgment* about what to believe or what to do. When an individual or a group of people is engaged in critical thinking, they are applying their reasoning skills—interpretation, analysis, inference, evaluation, and explanation—to a question or problem. Their purpose is to make a decision—for example, whether or not to believe something they have been told—or to solve a problem—for example, deciding what to do in a given situation. They are being reflective and deliberative, which means that they are trying to be sure that their interpretations, analyses, inferences, evaluations, and explanations are sensible, well-founded, systematic, and carefully considered. If not, then the individual or the group makes the necessary corrections.

Critical thinking is courageous in its open-minded search for knowledge. This means that critical thinking objectively follows reasoning and evidence wherever they lead, even if the answers should diverge from or contradict cherished beliefs or preconceptions. Critical thinking is respectful of those who hold other perspectives, but firm in its demand that those perspectives, no matter how firmly held or personally important, must be evaluated against evidence. For example, just because a person may know someone who is overweight or smokes yet does not appear to have any illnesses, it does not mean that obesity and smoking are not proven health risks. The scientific evidence establishing that obesity and smoking are health risks is solid, good fortune notwithstanding.

Good scientific research methodology is really just critical thinking, refined and applied to scientific questions. Thought of more broadly, *critical thinking is our self-defense against hasty, gullible, uninformed, and unreflective decision-making*. Critical thinking tells us, for example, that if a financial deal is "too good to be true" then it probably isn't true. We might not have experienced the worldwide economic meltdown of 2008 and 2009 had people done some critical thinking before taking on more mortgage debt than they could possibly handle, or before investing in get-rich-quick schemes that turned out to be frauds.

Here are some ways to strengthen your own critical thinking skills and habits of mind:

● Exhibit a bold and adventurous intellectual curiosity about a wide variety of topics.

● Endeavor to become objective as well as informed about issues about which you already hold strong opinions.

● Don't be gullible; evaluate the credibility of the opinions and judgments others offer.

● Trust in reflective, thoughtful, and well-reasoned decision-making.

● Be respectful and open-minded regarding others' views and opposing arguments.

● Be creative and flexible in coming up with alternatives, options, and ways to check the facts before making a decision.

● Be open, honest, and self-critical when you identify your own assumptions, preconceptions, and previously unquestioned beliefs.

● Be willing to reconsider and revise your judgments when the evidence warrants.

(Adapted from P. A. Facione (2009). *Critical thinking: What it is and why it counts*. Millbrae, CA: Measured Reasons and The California Academic Press. Used with permission).

DEMOGRAPHIC ISSUES IN RESEARCH

Race and ethnicity

Sex, gender, and sexual orientation

Social class

Some very important demographic variables affect virtually every research finding about marriage and families. To think critically and clearly about theories and research methods, we must know what these demographic variables are and understand the impact they can have on research results. Important demographic variables include race, ethnicity, sex, sexual orientation, gender, and social class.

Race and ethnicity

One variable we must specify when we publish research is the racial or ethnic backgrounds of the research participants. Although race technically doesn't exist (Walker et al., 2007), the term is used in many research reports and governmental statistics. Therefore, race and ethnic background need to be considered in every discussion of marriage and families.

Keep in mind, however, that race is a thorny issue. For example, in the 2000 census, the U.S. Census Bureau changed its approach to documenting the race of Hispanic people in the U.S. Now if a person states that he or she is Hispanic, a follow-up question is asked regarding which "race" the person is. Because the labels "Hispanic" and "Latino" relate to a large and diverse group of people with varied histories, cultures, and experiences, these are really *ethnic* labels. Hispanic people can be black, white, or brown; they can identify with virtually any "racial" category. Regardless of race, their ethnicity may be considered Hispanic or Latino. **Ethnicity** refers to a shared cultural history, language, and customs. For example, Hispanics may have similar experiences with colonization by Spaniards, speaking the Spanish language, and practicing the Catholic religion. People who belong to the same *ethnic* group typically identify as sharing cultural traditions involving foods, religion, rituals, holidays, and beliefs (Walker et al., 2007).

Because ethnicity and race can be confusing terms, this book uses the term *race* to refer to a person's outside appearance, usually black, white, Asian American, Hispanic/Latino, Native American, or Arab American. Even though these groups are all racially mixed, they are often judged or categorized by their external features. For example, my *race* is considered to be white. In reality, we know there is no such thing as the "white race;" white people, like all racial groups, are mixed. However, people see me as white, and on surveys I always have to check the box next to the "white" or "European American" racial category. *Ethnically*, however, my four biological grandparents came from Wales, Sweden, Germany, and England, four distinctly different white cultures. In their attempts to become assimilated into American culture as quickly as possible, as was common in the early days of U.S. immigration, my relatives did not maintain many of their cultural traditions. Therefore, I have no real ethnic identification, beyond some vague affinity for the Celtic people of Western Europe for their strength in resisting persecution by the Romans for hundreds of years. Other white people I know, however, clearly identify with their homeland cultures. I know a white woman who identifies as ethnically British. And I know a white man who identifies as ethnically Jewish. Look at the images of the "White Race," from a 1932 anthropology text called the *Races of Man*. Would you consider all of these people "white?" Why or why not?

The word *minority* can also be confusing. This book will not use the term "ethnic minority," as it implies that some groups are not as important, or "major," as other groups. In fact, in at least four U.S. states, ethnic "minorities" are actually the *majority*. For example, ethnic "minorities" make up the following population percentages: 50.2% of Texas, 75% of Hawaii, 57% of New Mexico, and 56% of California; African Americans comprise 70% of Washington DC. Ethnic groups will be referred to using either their specific identity (for example, Japanese American) or by the term *people of color*, which puts the person first. As you can see, issues of race and ethnicity are hard to strictly define. We have to be careful when speaking about such groups, and we have to avoid generalizing too broadly, since each ethnic group is comprised of very diverse types of people.

Sex, gender, and sexual orientation

At first glance gender seems more cut and dry than race and ethnicity. It's easier to tell whether someone is male or female than whether someone is Native American or Hispanic. Some scholars talk about *sex* when referring to the biological sex of people and *gender* when referring to social constructions regarding gender roles or gender differences in behavior. However, it's often difficult to tell what causes

Ethnicity
A categorical grouping of people based on their cultural group membership, shared historical experiences, language, rituals, and food.

FIGURE 2.3 Photographs of the "White Race."
Reproduced from: Robert Bennett Bean (1932). The races of man: Differentiation and dispersal of man.
New York: The University Society.

Fig. 61a—REPRESENTATIVE TYPES OF THE WHITE RACE

Gender
The socially constructed aspects of what makes a person male or female.

Intersex
Characteristics that make a person less clearly distinctly male or female; often includes ambiguous genitalia.

Sexual orientation
The sexual attraction one has toward people of a specific gender or genders.

an observed difference between males and females, biology or culture. To address this issue, the term **gender** will be used to speak about topics related to men and women (Hyde, 2007a). *Gender* refers to socially constructed categories of male or female. Throughout this book, we will see that social constructions of gender roles have profound implications for women's and men's lives all over the world. To complicate things further, keep in mind that gender might accurately be conceptualized as a continuum instead of a dichotomy. Many people are not clearly male or female. They may look male but identify as female or vice versa. Or they may have ambiguous genitalia. **Intersex** people do not clearly biologically fit into either the male or female category. But that doesn't mean that gender roles do not affect their lives as much as they affect the lives of other men and women.

Another complication is that your sex and gender often have nothing to do with your **sexual orientation**, or your choice of intimate partners. Like gender, sexual orientation is better conceptualized as being on a continuum than as two discrete categories like "gay" or "straight." In future chapters, you will discover that most people are somewhere between 100% heterosexual and 100% homosexual. If we consider our fantasies, behaviors, and desires, few of us would fit strictly into one sexual orientation or the other (American Psychological Association, 2005).

It's very important that you are aware of the impact of sexual orientation and gender on individuals, which in turn has profound effects on family relationships. A person's sexual orientation has very real consequences. People may be judged, discriminated against, denied access to services, denied the ability to adopt children, and even physically attacked because of their sexual orientation. For example, when the film *Milk* (about the first openly gay politician, Harvey Milk) was nominated for several Oscars at the 2009 Academy Awards, anti-gay protesters picketed during the ceremony. One sign, referring to deceased Oscar-winning actor Heath Ledger's role as a gay cowboy in the film *Brokeback Mountain*, said "Heath is in Hell." As the screenwriter for the film *Milk*, Dustin Lance Black, accepted the Oscar, he stated that his dream as a little boy was to grow up, fall in love, and get married. He stated that he hoped that some day he would be allowed to do so but at the current point in time, same-sex couples were not allowed to marry in California where he lives.

Ethnocentrism
Viewing one's own ethnicity as normative and others' as deficient or foreign; privileging one ethnic group's perspective over that of others.

Heterosexism
Viewing heterosexual orientation as normative and others' orientation as deficient or foreign; privileging heterosexuality over other orientations.

Issues like these reveal the importance of considering demographic variables as real, tangible influences on families, even if the categories themselves are socially constructed. Researchers on family issues need to be especially cautious about both **ethnocentrism** and **heterosexism** in their theoretical frameworks and their research designs and conclusions. Ethnocentrism means using a lens from one's own ethnicity (usually a white or European American lens) through which to view others. We may use our own ethnicity as the yardstick against which we compare others. Other viewpoints or practices may be seen as deficient or deviant if they are different from the researcher's ethnic experience. Heterosexism relates to the fact that many theories and lines of research assume the participants are heterosexual or they may make sweeping generalizations about research on relationships when only heterosexual couples have been studied. It privileges the heterosexual experience as "normal" and other sexual orientations as different or deviant.

Social class

Social class
One's level of income or socioeconomic status.

Like racism, sexism, ethnocentrism, and heterosexism, we also need to be aware of demographic variables related to **social class**, or level of income (also referred to as *socioeconomic status*, or *SES*). While social class is in large part a measure of income, it is often confounded by other variables, such as education level, access to goods and services, health status, and race. For example, in 2004, the median household income was $30,134 for African Americans, $34,241 for Hispanics, and $46,697 for whites. If you consider total assets like homes, cars, savings, and stocks, white Americans have a median net worth of $79,400 compared to $7,500 for African Americans and $9,750 for Hispanics. What do you make of these numbers? How are social class and race related and why?

Sometimes in research we may find racial differences because we fail to consider the effects of SES or social class. Poor people of all ethnic backgrounds tend to differ more widely from rich people of all ethnic backgrounds than they differ from each other. In other words, social class often affects family relationships and processes more keenly than does ethnicity.

To get a glimpse of how these influences might work, consider research that shows that middle-class parents (both black and white) see their job as one of "concerted cultivation," meaning they desire to cultivate a wide variety of academic, social, and emotional skills in their children (Lareau, 2002). This means they regularly create specific opportunities for their children to participate in structured activities like sports and class trips. They regularly debate issues with their children and encourage them to question information in their environment. As a consequence, these children feel confident looking authority figures, such as doctors, in the eye and asking specific questions. In contrast, lower-income parents often do not see their role as one of cultivation, but one of aiding in the "accomplishment of natural growth." They see their job as supporting their children in developing their own skills and interests without a lot of control and structure over their daily activities. They tend to demand respect and obedience from their children so these children do not see themselves as equal to authority figures like middle-class children often do. Thus, they are less likely to look doctors in the eye or ask questions of authority figures.

Researchers have discussed how social class influences the amount of conformity and obedience people exhibit. For example, Kohn (1969) discussed that lower-paying jobs require repetition and manual labor without leaving much room for critical thinking or problem-solving. Workers in lower-paying jobs do not challenge authority and so may raise their children to conform to authority as well, knowing that their children will have to survive in a similar work environment. How do you think living in poverty affects family relationships? How do you think being wealthy changes things? To take a look at this issue, see Figure 2.4, which shows what percentage of different ethnic groups in the United States has a college degree and what percentage of that group lives in poverty.

FIGURE 2.4 Percentage living below the poverty line and percentage with a college degree.
Source: U.S. Census Bureau, 2007.

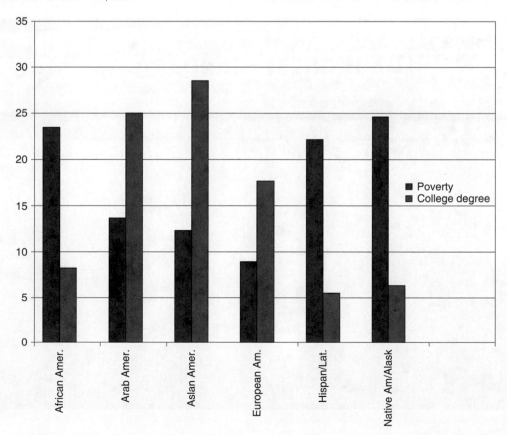

Interestingly, Rank (2003) found that while only a small minority of people at any given time is technically living below the poverty line, poverty is a normative experience for most of us. He found that 60% of people spend at least one year in poverty and that at any given time, 68% of the population lives near the poverty line, just not below it, where most statistics focus. Rank also points out that 65% of Americans will get Medicaid, Social Security Insurance (SSI), or food stamps as adults. These are all forms of "welfare."

Moreover, Rank emphasized that, contrary to the general public's belief that the U.S. spends *too much* money on social welfare programs for the poor compared to other industrialized nations, the U.S. spends very little on protecting its citizens from living below the poverty line. For example, most European nations have universal health care, have free high-quality child care with trained and well-paid teachers, give a comfortable amount of money to families for their daily needs, and have long-term (often six months or more) paid maternity and paternity leaves. In contrast, the U.S. has the highest poverty rate in the industrialized world. For example, in Finland, about 33% of people are poor, similar to the U.S., but the social welfare benefits provided to prevent poverty wipe out all but 4% of poverty experienced by Finns (Rank, 2003).

Hays (2003) conducted a three-year longitudinal ethnography with welfare workers and welfare recipients in the U.S. She found that 90% of people on welfare were mothers and half of those were escaping domestic violence. With the latest waves of welfare reform (Temporary Assistance to Needy Families, or TANF, begun in 1996), which reduced benefits and incorporated sanctions against people who don't find work, we have seen a large reduction in the number of people on the welfare rolls. However, those forced off welfare are often working only part time for minimum wage and

FIGURE 2.5 How do you think race, class, and gender intersect to impact the people in this image, photographed as they wait in a breadline?
Photo by Margaret Bourke-White/Time Life Pictures/Getty Images.

have no health or retirement benefits. Moreover, Rainwater and Smeeding (2003) found that low-income single mothers in the U.S. work more hours for less pay than single mothers in any other industrialized nation. They estimate that at a cost of $90 billion (about $1,900 per family), abject poverty could be virtually eradicated in the United States. Hays (2003) found that the working poor in the U.S. are actually worse off than welfare recipients. They don't make a living wage, have no provisions for high-quality child care, and have no benefits.

By now, it should be clear that all people have a complex **intersectional identity**. Intersectional identity refers to the idea that individuals in families are affected by the interactions between our gender, ethnicity, race, sexual orientation, and social class. When studying marriage and families, we must always keep in mind that these demographic variables interact with each other to influence us as individuals and the families with whom we share our lives. The bioecological approach acknowledges this complexity and steers us away from a simplistic analysis of why families function the way they do. Only when we consider all elements of a person's intersectional identities as well as all the systems of the bioecological model can we truly understand life in families.

> **Intersectional identities**
> The idea that every person is affected by multiple identities stemming from his or her sex, gender, sexual orientation, race, religion, ethnicity, and social class.

The bioecological approach considers how the individual interacts with various social contexts. But before we can understand those complex relationships and interactions in the family, it's important to have a clear idea of what influences individuals' behaviors and beliefs regarding relationships. Thus, let's examine what makes individuals tick before examining complicated family systems like marriages and parent–child relationships. We begin this examination in Chapter 3, which explores the development of sex, gender, and gender roles, and how they affect individuals in families.

CHAPTER SUMMARY

There are different ways to interpret the world around us and theories play an important role in helping us organize our experiences and conduct meaningful research on marriages and families. Many contemporary theories stem from the early ideas of Karl Marx and Friedrich Engels in their groundbreaking publication, *The Communist Manifesto*. This document's exploration of power, privilege, and wealthy peoples' exploitation of the workers of the underclass are key elements in Communist Theory. Communist Theory lent itself to the development of various Structural-Functionalist theories of family relationships. Structural-Functionalists focus on each member of the family as playing a crucial function in maintaining balance and continuity of functioning. Roles and responsibilities are maintained over time by family members continuing their interdependent functions, in order to keep the family, and the larger social structure, in place as usual. However, sometimes these roles and responsibilities fail to benefit all members of the family. In this case, Conflict Theory helps us understand that those with less power often rise up and start conflict with those wielding more power. In this theory, conflict is seen as a positive family process, where new levels of family balance can be attained after the conflict is resolved and new rights and roles are won.

In understanding such complex family functions, roles, and responsibilities, Family Systems Theory emphasizes the need to examine all individuals, dyads, and triads as they interact with each other. The perspective that a family is a system applies to family systems therapy, which incorporates all family members together, in order to address any problems in communication or power differentials, instead of treating one member individually.

Social Exchange Theory focuses on family members' systematic, logical consideration of various options for our interactions with others, with more beneficial choices usually taking precedence over choices that would "cost" them.

Feminist Theory was presented as a contrast to the historical focus on male perspectives in research. This theory places women's perspectives and ideas in the forefront, and does not consider it necessary to compare women to men.

Attachment Theory emphasizes the evolutionarily adaptive behaviors of infants and their caretakers, to stay near each other, care for each other, and seek each other out in times of distress. The internal working model is a cognitive template solidified during early interactions with caregivers. This model provides a framework from which children view the world of relationships, families, and themselves.

Finally, this book's organizing theoretical perspective, Bioecological Theory, was introduced. It posits that the biological, personal, and temperamental characteristics of individuals interact with people and social forces in immediate environments and larger social contexts. Microsystems, mesosystems, exosystems, macrosystems, and chronosystems are graduated systems of influence, ranging from immediate daily interactions to larger cultural and time-based processes that affect families. Each concentric circle of influence adds a layer of complexity that helps us truly understand the way families work and succeed.

The other major topic discussed was research methodology. Using the scientific method allows us to test specific hypotheses about how families work, live, and love. The experimental method was discussed in detail, with special focus on reducing the impact of confounding factors that can skew research findings. These factors include demand characteristics, taking an etic versus emic approach, practicing heterosexism or ethnocentrism, and not having diverse or representative samples. The distinction between correlational findings and causal inferences was illuminated and students were encouraged to practice critical thinking in order to not allow correlational research results to fool them into inferring causality.

Quantitative and qualitative approaches were discussed, as were cross-sectional and longitudinal designs. Demographic variables that comprise our intersectional identities were defined and explored, including race, ethnicity, social class, gender, sex, and sexual orientation. Each of these factors can influence our research findings and we should always consider how these variables interact with each other.

KEY TERMS

analog	ethnography	microsystem
Attachment Theory	etic	natural/quasi experiment
attrition	exosystem	no-treatment control group
baseline assessment	experiment	operational definition
causality	experimental group	qualitative
chronosystem	Family Systems Theory	quantitative
Communism	Feminist Theory	race
Conflict Theory	gender	random assignment
control group	generalizability	replication
correlational study	heterosexism	representative sample
critical thinking	hypothesis	sexual orientation
cross-sectional	independent variable	social class
demand characteristics	internal working model	Social Constructionism
dependent variable	intersectional identities	Social Exchange Theory
eclectic approach	intersex	Structural-Functionalism
emic	longitudinal	theory
ethnicity	macrosystem	unbiased
ethnocentrism	mesosystem	

WEBSITES FOR FURTHER EXPLORATION

www.cornell.edu/stories/sept05/bronf.ssl.htm
   This is a great article examining the life and scientific contributions of Urie Bronfenbrenner, the theorist whose Bioecological Theory forms the backbone of the current text. Interestingly, he was one of the creators of Head Start.

www.csicop.org
   The headquarters of the Community for Skeptical Inquiry. This organization publishes a popular journal called *Skeptical Inquirer*. They fund and support science that tests common myths, especially as they relate to paranormal

activity and pseudo-scientific thinking (such as astrology and psychic predictions). They examine controversial and supernatural claims scientifically.

www.criticalthinking.org

Website for the Foundation for Critical Thinking; they offer webinars, online courses, articles, and other activities to help you assess and improve your critical thinking, a skill they think is vital in a free society.

CHAPTER 3
SEX AND GENDER

The one thing that unites all human beings, regardless of age, gender, religion or ethnic background, is that we all believe we are above-average drivers.

(Dave Barry, humor writer)

LEARNING OBJECTIVES

- To understand the differences between sex and gender

- To realize that gender impacts all people in their family relationships

- To understand the differences between gender identity, gender roles, and sexual orientation

- To appreciate the feminist perspective's idea that both men and women are harmed by sexism and heteronormativity in their families and in society

- To assimilate the theories of gender role development into your knowledge of gender

- To get a feel for the many biological and environmental factors that affect sex and gender development from the prenatal stage to adulthood

Marriages and Families in the 21st Century: A Bioecological Approach, First Edition. Tasha R. Howe.
© 2012 Tasha R. Howe. Published 2012 by Blackwell Publishing Ltd.

OVERVIEW: A BIOECOLOGICAL APPROACH TO SEX AND GENDER

WHAT'S THE DIFFERENCE BETWEEN SEX AND GENDER?

Two genders or more?

Intersexuality

The complexity of gender identity and gender roles

THE IMPORTANCE OF GENDER FOR LIVING IN FAMILIES

Gender stereotypes

Stereotype threat

GENDER AND SEXUAL ORIENTATION

Can sexual orientation change?

Complex family issues related to sexual orientation

Heteronormativity

GENDER DISCRIMINATION AND SEXISM

Sexism

Men and masculinity

Intersectional identities

Gender similarity hypothesis

THEORIES OF GENDER ROLE DEVELOPMENT

Social Cognitive Theory

Gender Schema Theory

OUR DEVELOPMENT INTO BOYS AND GIRLS AND MEN AND WOMEN

Prenatal sexual differentiation	Genes vs. brains
Contextual influences on prenatal and infant development	
Puberty and gender	
Evolution and adult gendered behavior	
The diverse lives of adult men	Men of color
	Contemporary trends for modern men
The diverse lives of adult women	Women of color
	Macrosystem influences on women and their families

OVERVIEW: A BIOECOLOGICAL APPROACH TO SEX AND GENDER

What gender are you and how do you know that's your gender? What biological and social factors led you to believe that? This chapter will examine the complexities involved with gender, particularly the fact that gender may not be a simple dichotomy, with everyone being either male or female. Chapters 1 and 2 of this book gave you a flavor for how complex the study of family relationships can be. We explored a bit of the history of various types of families in the U.S. and around the world and discussed theoretical perspectives and research methods for studying families. We identified the bioecological approach as the theoretical approach that comes closest to capturing the complexity of families and family relationships. Throughout those two chapters, the issues of sex and gender were discussed as central considerations when attempting to understand families.

Remember that at the center of the bioecological model is a person, you. You are comprised of complex chromosomal, hormonal, and behavioral components that help create your gender. As a person of a particular gender, your characteristics affect the family members you live with in your microsystem. Your culture, or macrosystem, also influences how you experience your gender while living in your family. This chapter will take a closer look at these biological, individual, social, and cultural influences on how gender affects our relationships.

WHAT'S THE DIFFERENCE BETWEEN SEX AND GENDER?

Two genders or more?

Intersexuality

The complexity of gender identity and gender roles

Sex
A person's biological characteristics that make him or her male or female.

Gender
The socially constructed aspects of what makes a person male or female.

Because gender is such a basic part of who we are, it's important to be sure we know what we're talking about when we say "gender." Gender is not the same thing as sex. **Sex** refers to the *biological* aspects of what make us male or female. In contrast, **gender** is the *socially constructed* or non-biological characteristics that make us male or female. It relates to people's sense of being male or female based on their socially constructed ideas about what each gender is like. However, it's often very difficult to determine whether traits, characteristics, skills, or abilities are unilaterally biological or social in nature (Hyde, 2007a). In common usage, the term *gender* has come to encompass something with influences from all systems in our bioecological model, from biology to culture. Thus throughout this textbook, unless a topic has a clear biological cause, the umbrella term *gender* will include both biological and social influences.

Two genders or more?

We commonly think of gender as dichotomous: people are either male or female. But it's important to recognize that gender includes more than these two distinctions. Many cultures have conceived of a third and even fourth gender. For example, some North American Indians identify a third gender which is neither male nor female. Anthropologists call a person with this type of gender a "berdache" (Roscoe, 2000). Some cultures consider berdaches to be more important than typical males and females. They may live in a spiritual realm, live an exalted life, are usually revered, and often marry people of their same biological sex. While each tribe has its own name for gender variant people, and many dislike the term "berdache" (they may prefer "two-spirit"), anthropologists use the term as an umbrella to include the hundreds of types of gender variations that exist. Native American cultures are not the only ones with human members and spiritual deities that rise above the traditional male/female dichotomy. For example, in India, a person of a third gender is referred to as a *hijra*, and several Hindu, as well as ancient Chinese, deities can transform from male to female or vice versa (Herdt, 1993).

Intersexuality

While most humans are either biologically male or female, a substantial number—at least 65,000 babies born each year in the U.S. alone—do not fit neatly into either category (Farkas, Chertin, & Hadas-Halpren, 2001). These 65,000 U.S. babies are born with ambiguous genitalia, meaning that at birth it's not clear whether they have ovaries and a vagina, testicles and a penis, or some combination of both. People with ambiguous, or a combination of male and female, genitalia are referred to as being **intersexed**; they used to be called hermaphrodites. Fausto-Sterling and Balaban (1993) argue for the need of an increased understanding of "sexual multiplicity," noting that there may actually be *five* biological sexes. "True" hermaphrodites (people who have one ovary and one testicle) would be one sex; "ferms" (females with ovaries and some male genital characteristics), "merms" (males with testes and some female genital characteristics), traditional males, and traditional females would be the other four. If we add up the people who exist today from just the first three groups, they make up at least 4% of the U.S. population.

> **Intersexed**
> A person who is not clearly male or female and may have ambiguous genitalia.

Researchers have found several different avenues that lead to intersexuality. For example, an enzyme deficiency called congenital adrenal hyperplasia (CAH) causes a fetus to produce insufficient amounts of a hormone called cortisol, which results in the adrenal glands producing excessive levels of male hormones called androgens (Berenbaum & Bailey, 2003). The brain cannot block the high levels of androgen exposure, so androgens circulate in the body in excess, and these genetic females may then be born with ambiguous genitalia, such as a very large clitoris that resembles a penis, or a penis with a vaginal opening.

Any parent would be confused about what to do with an infant who is not clearly a boy or a girl. Many parents have decided to give their children hormone supplements or surgically have a vagina constructed, or they raise their children as females; some parents do both hormones and surgery. Most girls with CAH identify as female and grow up feeling comfortable in their feminine gender role. However, some girls with CAH are "tomboys," play with the kinds of toys that boys prefer, have little interest in dolls or human and animal babies, and appear rather masculine. They grow up to identify as male, yet some have had their genitals altered in infancy, without having had a voice in the process (Berenbaum & Bailey, 2003).

In one of the few studies to examine sexual reassignment surgery's effects in detail over the long term, Reiner and Gearheart (2004) examined 16 genetic males who had cloacal exstrophy (CE), a condition in which genetic boys have no penis or a very small one. However, they exhibit the typical male XY chromosomal pattern, have testes, and experience normal levels of male hormones. In this sample of boys with CE, 14 sets of parents decided to have their infants sexually reassigned with surgically constructed female genitalia, and they raised the children as girls. In measurements years later, six of these "girls" identified as male, three had an unclear gender identity, and five identified as female. The two boys who didn't experience surgery and were raised as boys both identified as male. All 16 children had mostly male friends and participated in typical male rough and tumble play as children, even if they were being raised as female. These findings point to the complex interplay between biology and experience for creating gender. Current medical and clinical recommendations include allowing the child to develop his or her own gender identity because it's impossible to know what the effects of either early surgery or hormonal treatments might be in combination with that child's unique chromosomal and brain patterns (McHugh, 2004).

The sex and gender variations discussed in the sections above point to some issues that can complicate romantic relationships, as well as our relationships with mothers and fathers, brothers and sisters. For example, if your romantic partner is intersexed you may have to adjust your expectations for how intimacy might take place. Or if your brother feels that he is neither male nor female, but perhaps a two-spirit or berdache, this can affect the way family members and friends view him, as well as how willing he might be to marry, have children, or communicate with extended kin. For all of us, gender can impact the types of partners we seek out, the nature of the families we form and how we interact with diverse family members.

The complexity of gender identity and gender roles

Transgendered
A person whose gender identity does not match his or her biological sex.

Gender identity
A person's sense of being either male or female.

Gender roles
Socially prescribed actions, behaviors and traits expected of men and women.

Purging
The attempt to rid oneself of a transgendered identity by acting as stereotypically male or female as one can; these acts are an attempt to confirm that one's gender identity is the same as his or her biological sex.

Many of us experience our gender in a straightforward manner. We look biologically like women or men and feel mentally like women or men. However, some people are born with clearly male or female genitals, yet as they develop they have a nagging sense that they were born with the wrong type of body. People who feel their gender is the opposite of their biological sex are referred to as being **transgendered**. Thus, a woman may feel that she is truly a man, and a man may feel that he is truly a woman. Transgendered people may suffer great psychological stress trying to live in a body that doesn't feel comfortable or accurate for their **gender identity**, or their sense of being male or female. Sometimes they live for decades trying to fit into expected **gender roles**, societal expectations of what are appropriate traits, characteristics, and behaviors of boys versus girls, men versus women. Because society places so much importance on people conforming to expected gender roles, many transgendered people struggle with the realization that they do not fit psychologically with the way their body appears physically.

To deal with their suffering, some transgendered individuals practice **purging**, which is the attempt to be as masculine or feminine as possible, to suppress their feelings and avoid admitting to their true gender identity, which doesn't fit their body's appearance. For example, a male-to-female transgendered person (a genetic male who *feels* like a woman) might join the military or professional sports teams in order to purge the feeling of being a female, so that a masculine appearance is upheld. It is estimated that one out of every 10,000 people is male-to-female transgendered and one out of every 30,000 people is female-to-male transgendered (Swaab, 2007).

Gender role expectations are beneficial in many ways because they help children understand what is expected of their gender within their macrosystem. These expectations help shape family roles and relationships. For example, I always knew as I was growing up that I was expected to marry a man because that's what most women in my community did. However, gender role expectations can also cause a lot of problems, not just for transgendered people, but for all of us.

THE IMPORTANCE OF GENDER FOR LIVING IN FAMILIES

Gender stereotypes

Stereotype threat

While the Dave Barry quote which opens this chapter is funny, it points to a crucial issue for all humans: we tend to organize ourselves into "in-groups" and "out-groups." Being able to categorize people into groups of "us" and "not us" has advantages because we often need to make quick judgments regarding our safety and survival when encountering strangers (Koomen & Dijker, 1997). Most groups that have been studied have some negative views about people not from their own tribe, culture, class, religion, family, or, in the case of this chapter, gender. Besides thinking we're all better drivers than the general population (because they are "not us"), we also may have stereotyped ideas about those other drivers. For example, we've all heard that men don't like to ask for directions and that women drive erratically and unsafely. Whether we're talking about driving, intellectual ability, emotional tendencies in romantic relationships, or the way people parent their children, gender plays a role both in our real behavior and in the ideas we have about what our behavior can or should be like. Gender stereotypes play a role in virtually every realm of family life.

Gender stereotypes

A **stereotype** is a standardized belief that a certain group of people are a specific way or all behave similarly to each other. This belief usually includes an oversimplification of the other group's characteristics and can include prejudices or biases (Rothbart, 2002). To stereotype others is human. We all do it. The key, then, is to understand research evidence in enough detail to think critically about the stereotypes we hold and perhaps begin to see the wide variability within each group, so that we don't lump everyone in a group together in our minds.

Whether you are a male or a female reading this chapter, you probably think there is a lot more variability within your own gender than in the other gender. That's normal for "in-group" and "out-group" thinking. For example, when I have to tell my husband the same thing several times, I often think "why don't men listen?" I'm assuming that most men are bad listeners, while I would probably judge each woman individually. At the same time, my husband is probably thinking "why do women analyze every detail of conversations so much?" He may be thinking all women are like me, but he might judge each man as an individual, not a member of the "man" group. The truth is that men and women are more similar to each other than different. And there is wide variability in all measured traits *within* each gender. So it's probably true that many men listen and many men don't; likewise, many women probably over-analyze conversations but many other women don't. There's a lot of variation *within* each group, but if that group is different from our group, we tend to stereotype its members and lump them all together.

Most of us grew up with a sense of what society expected of us regarding how masculine or feminine we should be. Girls are "sugar and spice and everything nice," while boys are "snakes and snails and puppy dog tails." Girls are sweet, meek, vulnerable, and fragile. They nurture. They help others. Boys are assertive, strong, independent, and invincible. They dominate. They achieve. These are all images we are familiar with, but are these the true characteristics of men and women, boys and girls? Not necessarily. In fact, many scholars consider these to be gender stereotypes, those standardized beliefs that tell us what is expected of men and women. Gender stereotypes are not inherent, but are actively constructed through interactions with others. Therefore, gender is not inside of us, but is constructed "out there" (Bohan, 1993). And when we conform to gender stereotypes, those social constructions become reinforced by others in our group and are eventually perpetuated in society (Courtenay, 2000). Thus, gendered beliefs and behaviors mutually reinforce each other and perpetuate the stereotypes across time.

Remarkable similarities in gender stereotypes have been found across 25 different countries (Williams & Best, 1990). In all of the countries Williams and Best studied, people viewed traditionally male traits (such as being physically active and strong) as more desirable, and they denigrated female traits (such as being dependent and emotional). However, beliefs did vary slightly between different groups. Protestant Christians had more egalitarian gender beliefs than Muslims. In other words, Christians were more likely to endorse the importance of equality between men and women. Also, people living in northern hemisphere countries had more egalitarian beliefs about gender than those in southern countries. More people in Finland, for instance, believed in egalitarian gender roles, while people in Nigeria believed that men have more rights and that the rights, obligations, and roles of men and women are quite different. Moreover, people in industrialized nations viewed the genders as more equal than those in developing countries did. These results suggest that culture, religion, and socioeconomic status impact our ideas about gender. The results are important to understand because egalitarian gender beliefs have clear implications for the structure of any society. For example, 45% of people in the Swedish Parliament are women, whereas only 3% of elected officials in Arab nations (where Islam predominates) are women. Thus, macrosystem ideas about gender roles can affect the types of opportunities available to each gender.

But even within northern, Christian, Western industrialized nations, people tend to view female roles as more malleable or "constructed" and male roles as **essentialized**, meaning inherent or reflecting the natural order of things. They believe men are naturally more powerful and are the natural leaders of societies and families. People think that those who already occupy powerful roles are

Stereotype
A standardized belief about a group of people where all members are thought to be similar to each other in specific ways; these beliefs are often oversimplifications and can include prejudiced attitudes.

Essentialized
When traits or behaviors of a specific gender are believed to be "essential," or natural/biologically determined.

meant to be in such positions, that dominance is part of that group's true "essence." When gender beliefs are reversed, however, such as occurs with some Hindu goddesses, *male* roles are seen as changeable and *female* roles (in this case, females are seen as strong and powerful) are thought to be essential, or innate and unchangeable (Mahalingam, 2003). Such findings point to the social construction of gender since there are systematic variations in beliefs across different types of societies.

As children are born, they are taught to believe that essentialized traits exist in men or women, and they are raised to act in ways that fit those gender role expectations. Thus, the social construction of gendered beliefs continues for another generation. For example, in western countries there is a pervasive belief that women are more talkative than men, that they are "chatterboxes." However, Leaper and Ayres (2007) found that men are actually more talkative than women. Hyde and Linn (1988) found that gender differences in language were very small across scores of studies and that these differences have actually decreased over time. Gender stereotypes like this one can pigeonhole people into narrowing their expectations for themselves or believing that people cannot change because these traits make up their essential nature. This is just one example of how preconceived notions of gender may affect our marriages and families. If we believe women are chatterboxes but we end up with a son who is a chatterbox and talks about his feelings all the time, we may view him as in some way "unmasculine." Likewise, if a man meets a woman who does not talk a lot, cry, or express her feelings as his previous partners did, he may not understand how to communicate with her.

Because gender stereotypes and gender role expectations affect all people, gender is a demographic variable that we must always think of as a key influence on how people experience life in families. Our own experiences related to our gender permeate our relationships. Therefore, it's important to understand the research on how gender affects us as individuals living in families. Kimmel (1986) reminds us, however, that people can play many gender roles in their real lives. There can be many masculinities and femininities so we must try to move beyond the idea that there are only two gender categories that are mutually exclusive (Connell, 1993; Gerson & Peiss, 1985). For example, women and men can be strong, outspoken, driven, and emotional. Likewise, they can be police officers, professional wrestlers, and poets. We can construct masculinity and femininity in innumerable ways. In fact, Butler (1990), referring to the feminine garb called "drag" worn by female-impersonators,

FIGURES 3.1 AND 3.2 Do these images reflect essential gender differences between men and women or are they social constructions?
Rambo: © Michael Ochs Archives/Getty Images; child model Phyllis Leibowitz /Stone+/Getty Images.

famously stated that *all* gender is drag! To examine some of this "drag," look at the nearby pictures of the child model and of Rambo, and think about whether attending cultural events like fashion shows and violent movies might perpetuate traditional gender role stereotypes.

Stereotype threat

Gender stereotypes can have extremely negative effects on people. A theory called **stereotype threat** was developed to illuminate this issue (Steele & Aronson, 1995). According to this theory, women, people of color, and other marginalized groups perform more poorly on psychological or academic assessments because, in addition to the general test anxiety most of us feel, they have the added burden of understanding the stereotypes that other people (including the test administrators) have against their group's performance. For example, if African American students are told that, as a group, black students perform worse on a certain type of IQ test than white students, and they are then given that type of test, the stress they feel may influence their test performance, leading them to perform more poorly than they might otherwise have done. Steele has shown that when stereotypes are not primed, or brought to light in the testing situation, or students are told that people from their group usually perform well, they will perform better. Stereotype threat is one of the many negative influences that stereotypes have on people's lives. This threat can limit what people see as possibilities for themselves, including behaviors, careers, or even intellectual abilities.

> **Stereotype threat**
> The process of a person performing poorly on tasks because of the pressure felt by knowing the negative stereotypes that abound about his or her own group.

If parents feel that children of one gender cannot or should not attempt to do certain things, this can cause conflict in families and can affect a child's sense of self. What do you think some fathers might tell a daughter who wanted to be a football player? If they make statements about her getting hurt, not being strong enough, or messing up her beautiful face, but they never make these statements to her brother, her confidence and effort can be affected. I can recall many times talking to my friends' husbands about politics or philosophy as if we were equals, and then halfway through the conversation, they turned away, and I realized they thought I didn't know anything or I wasn't worth listening to. My husband believes women should speak their minds to men, but some of my friends' husbands leave the intellectual talk for their male companions. These stereotypes can affect the quality of family relationships on many levels.

Huguet and Regner (2007) examined whether Steele's theory of stereotype threat holds true for the impact of gender stereotypes, particularly regarding common differences found in math performance. Read the *How Would You Measure That?* box, which describes this study, to learn how the researchers manipulated gender stereotypes and measured their effect on young girls' and boys' math test performance.

GENDER AND SEXUAL ORIENTATION

Can sexual orientation change?

Complex family issues related to sexual orientation

Heteronormativity

The relationships between sex, gender, gender identity, and gender role behavior are complex. Equally important, these factors don't necessarily relate directly to a person's **sexual orientation**. Sexual orientation is the sexual attraction, arousal and desire a person feels toward people of a certain gender or genders. Like gender itself, sexual orientation exists on a continuum. Just as a person can range from extremely masculine to extremely feminine and from clearly female or clearly male to somewhere in between, people can be strictly heterosexual, strictly homosexual, or somewhere in between (Masters, Johnson, & Kolodny, 1988). If we consider the fantasies we have, our erotic dreams, the images we're attracted to, as well as our sexual beliefs and practices, our sexual orientation might be a little less clearly demarcated than we once thought.

> **Sexual orientation**
> The sexual attraction one has toward people of a specific gender or genders.

The effects of stereotype threat on girls' math performance (Huguet & Regner, 2007)

French researchers were interested in investigating possible explanations for the under-representation of women in math and science fields. Even when women dominate a field, like they do in psychology (75% female) and biology (54% female), they are less likely to get funding for their research and to advance to the highest ranks of their professions. Math skills are crucial for most science careers and scholars believe that math is the main roadblock that stops girls from advancing in these fields. Huguet and Regner hypothesized that math skill differences develop as children hear messages from adults about girls' inferior math abilities. Girls internalize these gender stereotypes and then, through *stereotype threat*, perform worse than they ordinarily might.

The researchers did two experiments to examine this idea. First, they had teachers nominate a highly select group of math students (20 girls and 20 boys, the best in their classes, who also self-reported that they were "better than most students" and placed great importance on math skills). There were no gender differences in these reports. The children were randomly assigned to view a picture made up of 44 geometric shapes. They were then asked to recreate as much of the figure as they could from memory. The *independent variable* in this study was whether the children were told this was a "geometry test," or a "memory test." The *dependent variable* was how many geometric shapes children reproduced.

In support of their hypothesis, girls who were told it was a "geometry" test performed significantly worse than girls who thought it was a "memory" task. Also, girls performed worse than boys only in the "geometry" condition. They performed *better* than boys in the "memory" condition. Remember that all groups received the exact same task. The only thing that differed was whether stereotypes were primed by the name of the task they were given.

In their second experiment, Huguet and Regner used a representative sample of middle schoolers who were not particularly good at math. In this group, before the experiment began, the girls rated themselves as having lower math ability than the boys rated themselves as having. Children were randomly assigned to groups being given different instructions. One group was told it was a "geometry" test and one group was told it was a "drawing" test, since French children show no gender differences in drawing ability. The twist for this study was that the children were also placed in two additional conditions. They were tested in either same gender or mixed gender groups.

In mixed groups, boys performed better than girls when told it was a "geometry test." But girls performed better than boys when told it was a "drawing" test! In the same-gender groupings, girls performed at the same level whether they thought it was a drawing or a geometry test. Importantly, both genders performed best when in same-gender groupings.

The authors argue for the crucial role teachers and parents play in breaking down gender stereotypes so that all children can perform at their best. However, instead of recommending that we create single-gender schools, they argue for teaching students about these types of results and the dangers of stereotyping, while also providing successful same-gender models that break gender stereotypes.

Can sexual orientation change?

In addition to discovering that sexual orientation exists on a continuum, contemporary research also shows that it is not likely to be modifiable. Despite many attempts, both past and present, to change people's sexual orientation, there is no evidence that environmental experiences or interventions can change one's sexual attraction (LeVay, 1996). Just as most gay men and lesbians were raised by heterosexual parents and their parents' sexual orientation didn't make them grow up straight, most children of gay and lesbian parents grow up to be predominantly heterosexual like the rest of the population (Fitzgerald, 1999; Patterson, 2006). Therefore, parenting styles or exposure to one sexual orientation over another do not appear to affect the development of children's sexual orientation.

These facts have not stopped people, though, from trying to modify sexual orientation, usually from homosexual to heterosexual. Throughout history, people have tried brain surgery, hormonal castration, shock treatment, torture, imprisonment, exile, and, currently, "conversion therapy" to change people's sexual orientation. Some argue that through proper treatment, sexual orientation can be reversed. For example, the website for an organization called Exodus states the following:

> For thirty years, Exodus has served men and women who are suffering from homosexuality … freedom is possible through Jesus Christ … we believe that God wants to heal the homosexual through his church … our member ministries support … those leaving homosexuality. (www.exodus-international.org)

On the other hand, in a brochure titled *Just the Facts about Sexual Orientation and Youth*, it is argued that people who try to change others' sexual orientation through the use of conversion therapy are "misguided" and may even harm gay men, lesbians, and bisexual people through psychological stress and pressure to be someone they are not (Just the Facts Coalition, 2008). This brochure's statement has been endorsed by many professional groups across the U.S., including the American Academy of Pediatrics, American Counseling Association, American Psychological Association, National Association of School Psychologists, National Association of Social Workers, and the National Education Association. These organizations argue that any psychological turmoil some gays and lesbians might feel about their sexual orientation may stem from judgments and the discrimination they face in society, not from their sexuality, per se.

Complex family issues related to sexual orientation

Sex, gender, gender identity, and sexual orientation can each contribute to a person's sense of self and impact how he or she is treated in families. If we combine the idea of *gender identity* with the concept of *sexual orientation*, we can come up with quite a few possible combinations (Bockting & Coleman, 1992). Take the example of Jerome, who is a biological transgendered man who is attracted to women. Suppose he decides to have sex reassignment surgery, creating a vagina from his penile tissue. He also takes feminizing hormones, and dresses, lives and identifies as a female. We might say he's a *genetic* male, but now a *biological* female, whose *gender identity* is female and whose *sexual orientation* is lesbian. On the other hand, many women are genetic and biological females who identify as female and whose sexual orientation is predominantly heterosexual. Placing people into clearly defined sex, gender, and sexual orientation categories is not always straightforward, and many people would prefer we not put them "in a box" at all, because then families expect us to fulfill certain stereotypes and it may be disappointing when we don't.

For example, each one of us has experienced the impact of our sexual orientation on our family relationships. If our families expect us to have one orientation and we do, there may be much happiness and harmony as we bring home acceptable partners. If we experience a coming out process, realizing we are gay, lesbian, or bisexual, we risk rejection from our families of origin, our children, or our current romantic partners. Sexual orientation brings with it social acceptance in some families and ostracism in others. It affects our connections with our siblings, grandparents, and children. Because heterosexuality is considered normal, it often takes families aback when they realize a family member is not heterosexual.

Heteronormativity

In scientific and social science communities, the idea of homosexuality being abnormal or being a psychological problem or disorder has been uniformly rejected. Nevertheless, many people still believe that those who do not fit strictly into a single category of the gender or sexual orientation

Heteronormativity
A belief that heterosexuality is normal and right and other sexual orientations are abnormal or inferior to heterosexuality.

dichotomy are abnormal. This **heteronormativity**, or the belief that heterosexuality is normal and other sexualities are not, marginalizes sexual minorities and places heterosexuality in a privileged position against which all others are seen as inferior. Although fitting people into discrete categories is easier to think about, it does not represent the way many people see themselves.

Many scholars would prefer that, instead of placing people into discrete boxes that are judged, we develop dynamic conceptualizations so that we will not see sex, gender, and sexual orientation as hallmarks of what makes us who we are. Bem (1995) suggests that we might one day think of gender and sexual orientation as nothing more remarkable than eye color or shoe size and that gender will not form the core of our identities. Then every child in every family could grow freely, developing skills, talents, and characteristics that are both masculine and feminine. Preconceived notions about men and women would not affect romantic relationship dynamics and families of all kinds could find acceptance in the many ecological contexts in which they live. Currently, many people who do not fit into socially expected norms experience discrimination and poor treatment from others.

GENDER DISCRIMINATION AND SEXISM

> Sexism
>
> Men and masculinity
>
> Intersectional identities

Feminists see gender discrimination as impeding career and social success, but also as detrimental to mental health. For example, out of the 21 most common diagnoses made from the *Diagnostic and Statistical Manual of Mental Disorders*, 17 are more commonly diagnosed in women (Hartung & Widiger, 1998). Are women mentally unstable compared to men? Modern research suggests that they may have higher rates of psychological disorders like depression because they experience **role strain**, the stress on women's mental and physical health that results from balancing the many roles of family, housework, and paid work with the pressure to look good and be nurturing and supportive of their family members and friends (Bianchi, Milkie, Sayer, & Robinson, 2000). Many women today, whether they work outside the home, inside only, or both, feel isolated, perceive a lack of respect, and feel their work at home and with children is undervalued. They have heavy childrearing burdens which make promotions and higher income achievement at work more difficult. Even though men have increased their participation in housework and child care, which lessens the burden on women—especially if both partners work full time—they do not do half of the work at home. Today many women feel like the woman in Figure 3.3, that they are balancing their multiple roles beyond what is healthy.

Role strain
A feeling of stress or pressure experienced by being torn between work, relationships, and parenting roles.

The social construction of gender inequality has profound consequences. In western nations, the prescribed gender roles have evolved and changed toward a more egalitarian place for women in society, but women still experience sexism and discrimination in their families and in their workplaces.

Sexism

Hostile sexism
Negative gender bias which often involves anger and combativeness directed at women.

Benevolent sexism
Covert words or behaviors that express a denigration of women and ensure their continued inferiority; these acts or words may appear kind and positive but they represent a sense that women are helpless or weak.

In western industrialized nations, overt sexism (prejudice or discrimination against women) may be less common today than it was in the past. However, sexism still occurs in often covert or subtle ways (Swim, Aikin, Hall, & Hunter, 1995). Glick and Fiske (2001) distinguish between **hostile sexism** and **benevolent sexism**. Hostile sexism is an overt negative or unkind act that reveals an attitude of bias against women. Someone might make sexist jokes, sexually harass a woman at work, oppress a female partner's goals or desires, or tell a female partner to "shut up" during a discussion. Benevolent sexism, on the other hand, is characterized by positive or kind acts which nevertheless reveal views of women as in some way inferior. Examples include men trying to protect women from pain, anger, the truth, or danger, putting them on a pedestal, thinking they must "take care" of a woman financially

FIGURE 3.3 Women today experience a severe case of role strain.
Source: CartoonStock.

or emotionally, or speaking for a woman in social situations, while they would never do such things with male companions.

The definition of sexism includes discriminatory actions and thoughts regarding women and not women's acts or thoughts about men because sexism stems from a difference in power. Because men hold most of the power in families, jobs, politics, and social situations, women are more likely to be the target of both hostile and benevolent sexism.

Whether men and women truly differ in significant and noteworthy ways, or only our *perceptions* of them differ, the reality is that women and men have very different experiences, and these differences affect life in families. Mothers and fathers are expected to inhabit different spheres (e.g., fathers discipline, mothers kiss boo boos) which affect parent–child relationships. Husbands' and wives' expectations or devaluing of each others' roles can cause conflict in marriages. Extended family members may have opinions about how boys and girls, husbands or wives, should be raised or treated. Different generations may have divergent beliefs about gender, which can affect family balance and harmony. Gender is a key variable influencing life in families, but it is also only one component of family members' lives. As the bioecological approach illustrates, we each exist in multiple contexts and interact in myriad ways based on complex individual characteristics.

Before we end our discussion of the negative effects of gender discrimination and sexism, we can't forget that men are also gendered beings. Men have not only received a privileged role in most societies but, just as women find themselves having to live with gender discrimination and sexism, men are under extreme pressure to live up to masculine expectations.

Men and masculinity

Throughout history men have been expected to fight in bloody battles, remain stoic in the face of death, hunger, or trauma, take care of everyone in their families, and never be vulnerable. Women often take advantage of these male expectations. For example, whenever one of our household pets dies, I cry. My husband doesn't. I tell him I don't want to see the animal dead but want to remember it alive, so that I won't have to do the unpleasant task of burying it. My husband buries the animals stoically and without complaint, regardless of how he feels.

There is also pressure on men to earn enough money to give their wives luxuries and comforts, which means that men often make work their sole outlet for personal pride and achievement

(Levant, 1997). We pressure little boys to grow up measured by their accomplishments and their ability to be tough, to achieve, and not let their parents down. Because of these pressures, men are often more emotionally distant from their partners and children than women are.

When first forming families of their own, men often report feeling helpless in the delivery room because they don't know how to end their partner's pain during childbirth. And at home, they feel their partners know more about children and are "naturally" good at things they have little practice in, like snuggling, singing, and being sensitive and gentle. If women are expected to be natural caregivers for children, men are expected to be naturally sexually skilled in romantic relationships. But little boys are not taught relationships skills. Contemporary feminist men who believe in women's equality are often confused because in their intimate relationships, women want them to be kind, sensitive, and empathic, but not wimpy or too "feminine."

In addition to these relationship and family pressures, men are also expected to financially support their families. Thus, men also feel intense role strain and a pull between their partners, children, and their attempts to advance at work. With many men choosing to focus mostly on work and investing their self-worth in financial achievements, if a man cannot achieve financially, he may feel useless, worthless, and not like a "real man" (Biddulph, 2008). This can be a real blow to the confidence of lower-class men who make little money and often struggle to provide for their families.

Research shows that men are more likely to suffer heart attacks and strokes, and to commit suicide than women are. Boys are more likely to be diagnosed with learning disabilities and behavioral problems, to end up in the juvenile justice system, and to be convicted of violent crimes than girls are (Biddulph, 2008). All signs point to the fact that gender role stereotypes and expectations negatively affect all of us and limit what we think we can or should be able to do (Biddulph, 2008).

Intersectional identities

Recall that intersectional identities refer to our complex senses of self, stemming from demographic variables like our race, social class, sexual orientation, and gender. For example, although it is true that European American women are oppressed due to their gender, they are also privileged and protected by a patriarchal system that values white women over other women (Mullings, 1986). After World War II, when more white women began to stay home and form SNAFs, women of color had to keep working, often doing the housework for white women. White middle-class heterosexual women may not recognize their *own* power and privilege (Baca Zinn & Thornton Dill, 1994; Garcia, 1989; James & Busia, 1993). They are at the same time subordinate (to white men) and privileged (over lower-class women, lesbians, transgendered women, and women of color). Our gender interacts with our socioeconomic status, sexual orientation, and the power, discrimination, and privilege that exist in our macrosystems. The best we can do as human beings is to try to learn about people from different demographic groups and attempt to view our own intersectional identities as different from, but not better than, others.

For example, it's difficult for people who belong to one gender to truly understand the experiences of the other gender. However, transgendered individuals can help us see the world from both sides, and can speak firsthand about their experiences of **male entitlement**. In her groundbreaking book *Gender Outlaw: On Men, Women and the Rest of Us*, Kate Bornstein (1994) discusses her transition from male to female (pp. 108–109):

Male entitlement
The belief that men have certain inherent rights, roles, and responsibilities that are greater and more valuable than those of women.

People ask me what it was like to have had that kind of privilege, what it was like to lose it, why in the world did I give it up. To have it was like taking drugs, to get rid of it was like kicking a habit. I gave it up because it was destroying the people I loved. "Male privilege" is assuming one has the right to occupy any space or person by whatever means, with or without permission. It's a sense of entitlement that's unique to those who have been raised male in most cultures—it's notably absent in most girls and women … Male privilege is woven into all levels of the culture, from unearned higher wages to more opportunities in the workplace, from higher quality, less expensive clothing, to better bathroom facilities. Male privilege extends into sexual harassment, rape, and war … Whatever the idea might be which hopes to end the suffering of women on this planet, it's going to require men giving up privilege, and then all of us giving up this rigid bi-polar gender system. Un-privileging is a necessary prior condition for the deconstruction of the gender system.

Bornstein's profound statement about the privileged position of men is also illustrated clearly by a colleague of mine. Loren described his experience as he transitioned from female to male:

> Just before and during transition I taught at a campus that had a much larger than usual percentage of students who were affiliated with the military. It seemed that the more male I appeared the more respect I received from the students. They called me "Professor" and "Sir" and were quite attentive listeners. Even though I'm a small man, being read as male (and white) brings with it a great deal of white male privilege. Whenever I am in places that tend to be male-dominated, whether it is a mechanic shop or a computer store (my wife knows much more about computers than myself …) there is an assumption of competence. I am usually given the check when I go to lunch or dinner with my wife or women colleagues. In dealing with those that I am unfamiliar with (say in a store or the like), it seems that I am generally more listened to and less interrupted. (Personal communication, 2009)

These two quotes illuminate the complex intersectional identities most women and men experience. Our gender, class, and ethnic backgrounds all influence how society views us and how we experience life in society. They show how large parts of our gendered lives are socially constructed. However, even if we acknowledge the important role of stereotypes and social constructions, because we are using a bioecological lens to understand all topics in this book, we can't ignore the influence of biology. Historically, feminists have tended to under-emphasize the importance of biology in their analyses of gender issues because they did not want to support an essentialist perspective which views gendered behavior as natural and therefore unchangeable (Condit, 2008). However, many modern feminists are using the research from evolutionary psychology, psychobiology, neuroscience, and other fields to help us paint a clearer and more balanced picture of gender from a bioecological lens. The combined efforts of diverse strands of feminists, both male and female, are designed to enable women of all backgrounds to gain access to the opportunities given outright to men for the sole reason that they were born male. Men and women face similar obstacles in overcoming the straitjackets of gender role expectations in their marriages and families. And in the end, we are finding that the genders are actually more similar than different.

Gender similarity hypothesis

Janet Shibley Hyde, one of the premier researchers in the area of gender, proposes a **gender similarity hypothesis**, the argument that men and women resemble each other much more than is popularly believed. She believes that because we grow up with gender stereotypes in our minds and that we feel awkward if we violate gender role expectations, we tend to pay attention to research that *supports* our ideologies, research that confirms gender differences. Hyde has found that when researchers find no gender differences in a study, that study is less likely to be published; and, if it is published, it is less likely to make headlines in the media. But a study that finds significant gender differences, for example, in children's SAT scores for college entrance, makes big news.

To determine whether there is support for the gender similarity hypothesis, Hyde uses **meta-analysis**, a study that compiles the findings of many diverse studies on a topic and statistically analyzes the overall magnitude of the findings. In her two large meta-analyses (Hyde & Grabe, 2008; Hyde, 2006), she found that while many studies find gender differences in various traits, skills, and behaviors, there is actually remarkable similarity between men and women in most cases. The aggregated results across hundreds of studies showed that any gender differences found were extremely small in magnitude, even if the media causes quite a buzz about them.

Hyde emphasizes that the variation *within* groups is much greater than any mean, or average, differences *between* groups. This tells us that two women are likely to be more different from each other on a given skill, behavior, or trait, than a specific man would be when compared to a specific woman. Most studies' results are reported on mean, or average, differences between groups of males

Gender similarity hypothesis
The idea that men and women are actually more similar than they are different and that gender differences are largely overstated.

Meta-analysis
A research technique where the results of multiple studies can be analyzed together to assess the overall magnitude of effects for a given topic.

FIGURE 3.4 Hypothetical distributions of the trait "bossiness" for males and females.

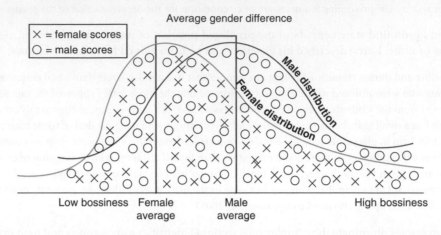

and females, and these differences are published without mention of the overall magnitude of those differences or discussion of the large overlap in the distributions between male's and female's scores. Figure 3.4 uses hypothetical distributions of the trait "bossiness" to demonstrate what Hyde means when she refers to the greater variation within genders than between them.

Look carefully at the distributions for "bossiness" in Figure 3.4. Men appear on average to be bossier than women. However, if you compare any random X representing a given woman's score with a random O representing a given man's score, you can see that many women are bossier than many men. Also, the Xs and Os are more likely to differ between people *within* their gender than between those in the other gender because the distributions of scores for men and women overlap quite a bit.

The gender similarity hypothesis (and much supporting research evidence) posits that men and women are similar in their needs, desires, and yearning for intimate connections with others in their families. However, we are socialized to conform to gender role expectations that limit those possibilities. The good news is that we can also be socialized out of them. Let's look at some of the theories researchers use to explain how boys and girls come to conform to gender role expectations, and consequently, how we can socialize future generations to be less constrained by gender role pressures.

THEORIES OF GENDER ROLE DEVELOPMENT

Social Cognitive Theory

Gender Schema Theory

Gender schemas
Mental representations or cognitive templates that comprise a person's ideas about gender roles.

Boys and girls can accurately label their gender as "boy" or "girl" by about 2 years of age. At a very young age, they start to develop **gender schemas**, mental templates about what is appropriate for both genders (Bem, 1983). The dichotomous messages children receive about males and females affect almost every domain of human experience. Our mental schemas influence our behavior, our desires, and our family relationships. We may believe that boys should be allowed to be aggressive because "boys will be boys." Or girls might desire that new Barbie Corvette for their birthdays. As children, we may think that mommy should not be mowing the lawn or daddy should not be growing his hair long. These mental templates help us organize our world along gender lines.

By the time children reach 2 and 3 years of age, they are developing mental representations or cognitive templates about everything in their worlds (Berthier, DeBlois, Poirier, Novak, & Clifton, 2000). Children store these mental schemas in their memories and compare new information to them. If they receive gendered gifts, toys, and clothing early in their lives, they start to form mental templates of what it means to be a boy or a girl (Denny & Pittman, 2007). For example, a child might think: *I got a pink dress and my brother got a blue set of overalls; that must mean pink is for girls and blue is for boys.*

However, children are not simply molded into fitting a certain gender role. They actively socialize their parents at the same time their parents socialize them. For example, a father may be unable to resist his daughter hugging him around the neck and batting her eyes. She has learned that this behavior gets him to give her a piggyback ride, no matter how tired he is. In addition, children actively construct meaning about the world around them (Peterson, Bodman, Bush, & Madden, 2000) through constantly putting new information into their mental representations. And they store complex information as they interact with every context in their bioecological world.

When a little boy is told "Stop crying!" or "Don't throw like a girl," what do you think he is storing in his mental representations? Boys are often raised to be opposed to anything feminine. This prevents them from emotionally connecting with family as they grow into men, and hampers their ability to develop sensitivity, empathy, and nurturing of others (Adams & Coltrane, 2003). Ironically, these are the exact traits adults usually desire in a male partner. However, socializing forces impair boys' ability to identify and express their emotions, creating young men who are more distant from their families. Boys are taught to suppress and deny their feelings. In some ways, socializing boys to fit into male gender role expectations is a challenging job because they have to deny so much of who they truly are, and then must develop alternative mental representations of what it means to be a man (Adams & Coltrane, 2003).

Similarly, when a little girl is told "Stay inside, it's dangerous in the back yard" while her brother is allowed to hang from the trees, what information do you think she processes about herself and girls in general? Girls are taught that the outside world is unsafe for them, and that it's acceptable to be vulnerable, to cry, and express their natural feelings (Beale, 1994).

Children also receive positive reinforcement for conforming to gender role expectations and punishment for crossing gender lines. They may be praised or receive encouragement for adhering to gender expectations, or receive ridicule or even physical punishment like a spanking for violating gender expectations. Girls may be praised for looking pretty but not for an A grade in math. Boys may be slapped on the hand for picking up their sisters' baby dolls and kissing them. Two theories can help us sort out our understanding of gender role development. These include Social Cognitive Theory and Gender Schema Theory.

Social Cognitive Theory

Social Cognitive Theory (Bandura, 1989) states that behaviors that are reinforced are more likely to be repeated. In addition, the way a child processes social information in her or his environment impacts how he or she might behave in the future. Children learn through imitation of role models in their environments (including those depicted in the media). If a girl sees a woman on TV winning a gold medal for Olympic soccer, that reinforcement might spur her to work hard in soccer. If a boy sees a feminine boy being called "sissy!" or "faggot!" he may try to act more masculine. Because we have been reinforced for gender-appropriate behavior, which has then shaped the way we process information and choose to behave, it's not surprising that by the age of 5, children seek out same-sex playmates and actively avoid the other sex (Fagot, 1985; Feiring & Lewis, 1987). Boys, more than girls, strive to be *unlike* the other gender and will ostracize and tease others who act "like girls."

In an interesting set of studies, Grace, David, and Ryan (2008) showed that when children saw adults as an out-group, they identified with and imitated children, even those of the other gender. In laboratory tasks designed to elicit imitation, children observed role models who were adults and children of both genders performing various tasks. To create an adult out-group and a child

Social Cognitive Theory
A theory of gender role development that emphasizes children's modeling of adult role models and imitating the gender behaviors they see; gender roles are socialized through reinforcing gender appropriate and punishing gender inappropriate behaviors and traits.

in-group, the child participants were told about key differences between how "adults and children" perform on a given task. When given the opportunity to imitate the models they had seen, they chose to imitate what the other *children* did, even if the other child was a girl and the research participant was a boy. So boys preferred to be like child girls over being like adults of *either* sex. This result occurred because the boys were socialized in the experiment to see adults as the out-group and all children as part of their own in-group.

When the situation was manipulated to stress the differences between boys and girls, the child participants identified with and imitated the behavior of their own gender because they were socialized to believe the other gender was their out-group. This study provides evidence that children actively construct, or choose, whom to imitate or identify with. There don't seem to be innate tendencies to identify with members of one's own gender to the exclusion of the other gender. Grace et al. (2008) suggest that "learning about gender involves an integration of social categorical information into one's personal self-definition" (p. 1939).

Maccoby (1995) argues that the distinctive differences we see in gender-segregated play and behavior come from a biological predisposition combined with differential social pressure from adults, cultural socialization, and one's own gendered cognitions (attitudes, knowledge and self-perceptions). For example, a boy may grow up to be a Marine because he has relatively high levels of testosterone compared to girls, his father was a Marine and socialized him to value the military, his culture respects military men, and he perceives himself to be strong-willed, tough, and mentally sharp. This reflects a bioecological explanation for how children develop into more masculine or feminine adults.

Gender Schema Theory

It's important to note that both social pressure and individual social cognitions regarding gender can change. For example, today girls are allowed a little more latitude in crossing gender boundaries than boys are. The feminist movements of the last 30 years and resulting social changes have made it acceptable in western nations for a little girl to wear pants, want to be an astronaut, play sports, and be assertive. The gender roles for little boys are still quite scripted, though. It's less acceptable for little boys to try on mom's lipstick, take ballet lessons, or become preschool teachers. Many people still get nervous if they see men working around very young children and babies because their mental templates, or schemas, do not include "male" and "sensitive" and "caregiver" all together.

Gender Schema Theory
A theory of gender role development that focuses on children's changing gender schemas and the desire to perform socially accepted roles for their gender.

Gender schematic
A way of thinking wherein children's gender schemas are comprised of stereotypical ideas about gender; thinking is inflexible regarding what is appropriate for boys and girls or men and women.

Gender Schema Theory states that boys and girls learn very quickly what is expected of them in terms of gendered behavior, traits, and abilities. Because all children strive to fit in with their families' and communities' expectations, they are highly motivated to please others by behaving in gender appropriate ways (Bem, 1981). As mentioned above, their schemas become solidified over many years of experiencing the separate worlds of boys versus girls, men versus women. Building on Social Cognitive Theory, Gender Schema Theory expands the focus to specific cognitive processes that occur as we build our gender schemas. Bem (1981) emphasizes that our schemas actually affect our attentional capacities, our memories and our abilities to process gender-typical or gender-atypical information. A boy who thinks all nurses are women and all doctors are men may not even notice a male nurse standing next to him, or may remember that the female doctor was the nurse. In other words, our schemas direct our attention to images, people, and activities that confirm our existing schemas, which means we may ignore a vast world of other experiences and images that run contrary to our cognitive templates.

According to Gender Schema Theory, some children are more **gender schematic** than others. Gender schematic children follow traditional gender expectations and hold traditional gender beliefs. They see the world through rigid gender schemas. They may think there are two worlds, one for men and one for women. Women stay home, men work. Men are the bosses, women are the secretaries. Men make the rules, women obey. These types of gender schemas affect not only the child's own behavior and beliefs but the way children grow up to judge and interact with other people. How might a gender schematic child treat a boy who didn't like sports but instead wanted to have a tea party?

SELF-ASSESSMENT

Bem's (1974, 1977) psychosexual androgyny scale

Rate yourself on how often each of the following items is true of you, using the scale below.
(1) Never true, (2) Usually not true, (3) Sometimes/infrequently true, (4) Occasionally true, (5) Often true, (6) Usually true, or (7) Always true.

1 self-reliant ____	22 analytical ____	41 warm ____
2 yielding ____	23 sympathetic ____	42 solemn ____
3 helpful ____	24 jealous ____	43 willing to take a stand ____
4 defends own beliefs ____	25 has leadership abilities ____	44 tender ____
5 cheerful ____	26 sensitive to others' needs ____	45 friendly ____
6 moody ____	27 truthful ____	46 aggressive ____
7 independent ____	28 willing to take risks ____	47 gullible ____
8 shy ____	29 understanding ____	48 inefficient ____
9 conscientious ____	30 secretive ____	49 acts like a leader ____
10 athletic ____	31 makes decisions easily ____	50 childlike ____
11 affectionate ____	32 compassionate ____	51 adaptable ____
12 theatrical ____	33 sincere ____	52 individualistic ____
13 assertive ____	34 self-sufficient ____	53 doesn't use harsh language ____
14 flatterable ____	35 eager to soothe hurt feelings ____	54 unsympathetic ____
15 happy ____	36 conceited ____	55 competitive ____
16 strong personality ____	37 dominant ____	56 loves children ____
17 loyal ____	38 soft spoken ____	57 tactful ____
18 unpredictable ____	39 likeable ____	58 ambitious ____
19 forceful ____	40 masculine ____	59 gentle ____
20 feminine ____		60 conventional ____
21 reliable ____		

Scoring

1 To calculate your score, add up your ratings for items 1, 4, 7, 10, 13, 16, 19, 22, 25, 28, 31, 34, 37, 40, 43, 46, 49, 52, 55, and 58. Divide that total by 20. This is your *masculinity* score.

2 Now add up your ratings for items 2, 5, 8, 11, 14, 17, 20, 23, 26, 29, 32, 35, 38, 41, 44, 47, 50, 53, 56, and 59. Divide that total by 20. This is your *femininity* score.

3 If your masculinity score is above 4.9 (the average score for this scale) and your femininity score is also above 4.9 (the average score for this scale), then you are *androgynous*.

4 Now ask yourself, *why* are those specific items considered to be more masculine than feminine or vice versa? Do you agree with the way the items are scaled? Why or why not?

FYI

Some gender differences found in research

Can you think of both biological and environmental explanations for these findings?

If you can think of examples from each of the bioecological systems that might help explain these findings, you're on your way to becoming an accomplished critical thinker!

Boys

More physically active
More learning disabilities
Higher rates of ADHD
More behavioral problems
More physically aggressive
Higher rates of drug use
Better at spatial tasks
More completed suicides

Men

Make more money
Better at reading maps and spatial rotation tasks
More in top government and corporate positions
Higher rates of alcoholism
More chronic illness
More premature deaths

Girls

More sustained eye contact
Higher rates of eating disorders
More violent/sexual victimization
More relationally aggressive (ostracizing, back-stabbing)
More sensitive to facial expressions and others' feelings
More suicide attempts

Women

Smoke and drink less
Better at verbal tasks
Better at memory tasks and locating things by remembering landmarks
Higher rates of college attendance
Have higher levels of social support
More depression/anxiety
More child care/housework burden

Sources: Abell & Dauphin (2009); Adams & Coltrane (2003); Baron-Cohen (2002); Courtenay (2000); Eaton & Yu (1989); Geary (1998); Kimura (1993); Hyde (2007a); OECD (2005); Silverman & Eals (1992).

Gender aschematic
A way of thinking wherein children's gender schemas are comprised of diverse ideas about gender; thinking is very flexible and children find it easy to imagine and accept people who cross traditional gender lines.

Gender aschematic children, on the other hand, hold less stereotyped beliefs about gender. They think flexibly about men's and women's traits and abilities. They are usually raised by role models who regularly cross gender boundaries, for example, a mom who works as a plumber and a dad who works as a party planner. They have often been given toys appropriate for both genders and have been allowed to express themselves in any way they wish. In general, little boys love to dress up and wear make-up and nail polish, just like little girls do. If they are allowed these freedoms, they tend to develop a more flexible or aschematic mindset about gender. If little girls are encouraged to speak their minds and see strong female role models in their lives, their schemas reflect these images. Aschematic children have no trouble imagining male nurses or female presidents (Martin & Halverson, 1983). They are cognitively flexible. How would a gender aschematic child react to being invited to a girls' football game? Or to a boy's dance recital?

If children of all genders are exposed to a wide variety of behaviors, traits, skills, and attitudes, they become more flexible in their thinking and accept people who are different from them. If they are only exposed to a very narrow definition of what it means to be a man or a woman, they have a difficult time opening their mental representations to allow schema-discrepant information in. They may judge people as "weird" or "abnormal" if they see male and female worlds as non-overlapping.

Today many parents try to raise their children in an *androgynous* way. **Androgyny** means that a person possesses traditionally masculine traits like assertiveness, confidence, and strength, and also traditionally feminine traits like nurturing, sensitivity, and empathy (Boldizar, 1991). If we buy children toys and play games with them that encourage both masculine traits like strength, hand–eye coordination, and confidence and feminine traits like caring for a baby and listening to friends, we help socialize well-rounded children who approach the world with androgynous mental schemas. These children may be better equipped to live in a world with diverse people and complex social and gender dynamics. Check out how androgynous you might be by taking the *Self-Assessment* questionnaire on p. 85.

Much research over the past 50 years has concentrated on gender differences in traits as diverse as intellectual ability, verbal skills, and mental illness. There is much less research on androgyny than there is on gender differences. If we combine the whole body of research, we can see some interesting patterns. Read the *FYI* box for more information on some gender differences that are fairly consistently found in research. Many of the differences related to male death, disability, and illness are hypothesized to be related to the intense demands of achieving proper "masculine" gender roles. Likewise, gender discrimination and sexism are thought to contribute to female mental health and social problems (Kimmel, 2000).

Keep in mind, however, that both genders are more similar than they are different. Geary (1998) argues that the minds and brains of men and women have evolved to help us adapt to very complex and diverse human societies. He posits that since we all have to survive similarly under intense pressure, our brains have evolved to be more similar than different.

You've learned some of the theories scholars use to explain how gender roles and stereotypes develop. Now it's time to learn what we know about the biological and environmental influences on sex and gender.

> **Androgynous**
> People who are characteristically both highly feminine and highly masculine; they do not conform rigidly to traditional gender roles.

OUR DEVELOPMENT INTO BOYS AND GIRLS AND MEN AND WOMEN

- Prenatal sexual differentiation
- Contextual influences on prenatal and infant development
- Puberty and gender
- Evolution and adult gendered behavior
- The diverse lives of adult men
- The diverse lives of adult women

Tune up those critical thinking skills as we embark upon a discussion of the biological, individual, social, and cultural research on sex and gender. The key point to remember here is that there's no longer a nature–nurture controversy in the social sciences. Today there is general agreement among social scientists that most human traits and behaviors are caused by a complex interaction between biology and experience. Gender is no exception.

Prenatal sexual differentiation

Genes direct the process of our brain cells migrating to the proper regions in order to form structures that differ between men and women (Swaab, 2007). These genes, however, just *predispose* the brain to develop in a certain way. This means everyone's brain will be a little bit different depending on experience. There is a large amount of individual and gender-related variation in how our brains develop. There is also substantial overlap in the structure and function of the male and female brain, meaning many aspects of brain development occur similarly for everyone (Craig, Harper, & Loat, 2004). The interaction between genes and environments is complex. For example, Caspi et al. (2002) followed a group of New Zealanders for over 30 years. This longitudinal study examined a specific gene called MAOA, which controls enzymes that affect levels of neurotransmitters like dopamine. Some children were born with low MAOA gene activity and some with normal levels. Those who had low MAOA gene activity and were also abused as children grew up to be violent and antisocial adults. However, children who had the normal level of MAOA gene activity and were abused did not have behavioral problems as adults. Moreover, children with low MAOA gene activity who did not experience abuse were not violent later on either. This study shows that some people are more or less vulnerable to genetic variations as well as being affected differentially by traumatic experiences. Researchers are discovering that genes affect people's behavior through their control over hormones and brain functioning and the environment can determine how genes are expressed. The connection between genes, hormones, and brain development is fascinating.

You may have heard a rumor that all babies start out as girls. The rumor is true. After conception, when sperm meets egg, a baby receives genetic and chromosomal information from each parent. The baby always receives an X chromosome, the female chromosome, from its mother. Sperm can carry either X or Y (male) chromosomes. If the sperm delivers a Y chromosome to the egg, the embryo gets a genetic message to develop into a boy, with the typical male XY chromosomal pattern. If the sperm delivers an X, we get an XX pattern typical of genetic females. So we begin with a female chromosomal pattern and then, as our parents' genetic material combines, we develop into embryos, with both Wolffian (female) and Mullerian (male) gonadal ducts, which will develop into reproductive organs (Holloway, Anderson, Defendini, & Harper, 1993). As the embryo's sexually undifferentiated gonadal tissue begins to develop, sexually relevant genes on the Y chromosome send messages to the gonads (reproductive organs) to start circulating testosterone to make testicles and a penis. If the embryo has two X chromosomes (and so no Y chromosome), anti-Mullerian hormones cause the male Mullerian ducts to atrophy and stimulate new cells to secrete estrogens. The embryo continues on its original journey as a female, with estrogens circulating to create ovaries, a uterus, and a vagina.

Genes vs. brains

Many complex gene interactions are involved in sexual differentiation of the male and female brain, mostly related to selective cell death (Holloway et al., 1993). One interesting aspect of this process is that the gonads are developing at an earlier developmental period than the brain (Swaab, 2007). At the outset, the embryonic brain is not receiving hormonal messages. In genetic males, relatively higher levels of male hormones (androgens like testosterone) circulate during the gonadal development process and masculinize the brain, making it function the way most male brains function, including developing a psychological sense of being a male. In genetic females, relatively higher levels of estrogens and other feminizing hormones create a female brain and, usually, a female gender identity. Some *intersexed* girls experience prenatal androgen exposures equal to that of boys yet still develop female genitalia (Wallen & Hassett, 2009), pointing again to the importance of both genes and hormones in sexual differentiation.

Researchers think a transgendered person's prenatal development may differ from the typical journey (Hutchison, 1997). Since the reproductive organs develop separately from and before sexual differentiation of the brain, it is possible that a person can be genetically male or female yet have a brain that resembles that of the other sex. A woman could be genetically female and born with female genitalia. However, during brain development, feminizing forces could have been halted or altered so that more androgens were circulating (since both males and females circulate both androgens and estrogens, just to different degrees). Thus, a more male brain may develop in a female body, leading a child who seems female at birth to have a feeling as she grows up that she is really a male who was born with the wrong body. The opposite process could occur for a male.

Although researchers haven't figured out the entire process of sexual differentiation in humans yet, they have identified one important biochemical process involving an enzyme called P540 aromatase. This enzyme converts androgen to estrogen in the neurons located in the hypothalamus of the brain. When these brain cells in the hypothalamus receive the enzyme, the estrogen created starts to feminize the brain (Hutchison, 1997). Studies have also shown that if pregnant mothers experience extreme levels of stress (such as that related to domestic violence or homelessness), there is an elevation of stress hormones in their fetus's brain. This leads to a *decrease* in P540 aromatase in male brains, but an alteration of other chemicals in the female brain. Thus, stress hormone effects vary by individual and by gender, depending on the timing of exposure, the intensity of the stress, and the genetic sensitivity of the individual child (Weinstock, 2007).

Remember that female hormones circulate in boys, too. For example, levels of the female hormone progesterone do not differ at all in adult men and women; however, they have different functions. For example, progesterone is used in men to create sperm and regulate sleep quality and cardiovascular health, while in women it is used to help regulate the menstrual cycle, among other functions (Oettel & Mukhopadhyay, 2004).

Many of these biochemical mysteries are only beginning to be solved; much research has to be done on animals because it is unethical to manipulate the hormones or chromosomes of a human embryo. In spite of the difficulties, the fields of developmental psychobiology and neuroscience are ripe for further discoveries. It's amazing to think about all the little enzymes, proteins, and neurotransmitters circulating in our brains and bodies, which help create each individual family member as a unique being. Each of us has a brain that functions slightly differently from everyone else's, which means living in a family is always exciting and challenging.

Contextual influences on prenatal and infant development

In addition to the biological processes that make us male, female, or somewhere in between, social forces are at work long before we take our first breath. Gender expectations and preferences are common in all cultures. For example, with current reproductive technology, wealthy parents can choose the sex of the embryos they implant during in vitro fertilization, and around the world, male babies are preferred so there is often selective abortion of female fetuses (Chunkath & Athreya, 1997; Weiss, 1995). In China and India, male children are preferred so much that if a woman does not provide a male heir, she may be ostracized or divorced. There is also rampant abandonment, neglect, and infanticide of female babies (Hesketh, Lu, & Xing, 2005). Boys may receive more food, attention, and medical care. Historically, this was true in western countries as well. In 1979 the Chinese government implemented a "one child" policy to curb over-population, and many Chinese baby girls were abandoned or adopted away to westerners. Consequently, there is a growing gender imbalance in the population, with not nearly enough women of marrying age available for the larger population of men. This has led to rural women being kidnapped or sold to become urban businessmen's wives (Hesketh et al., 2005). These findings illustrate that we are born into a world that already has gender role expectations and stereotypes about how desirable and valuable we are. What is the first question people ask a woman when she announces she is pregnant? "Is everything OK?" "Do you feel all right?" No, they ask, "Is it a boy or girl?" The question of gender is so important that it's the first thing people want to know.

Parents can look at an ultrasound reading and find out the sex of their baby before it's born. Why do you think they want to do that? You might argue that it's so they only have to read half of the baby names book. However, you could also argue that it stems from the desire to categorize the unborn baby into our existing gender dichotomy. We want to be able to decorate the nursery with the gender-appropriate colors (no pink ruffles for little Freddie). We want to be sure shower guests bring the right kinds of baby clothes, toys, and equipment (no toy fire truck for little Margie). Is it any wonder, then, that research finds children exhibit stereotypical gender-based play before they can even say the words "boy" or "girl"?

Infants as young as 1 year of age show a preference for "gender appropriate" toys: rolling toys, vehicles, and super heroes for boys; and dolls, plush toys, and dress-up sets for girls (Serbin, Poulin-Dubois, Colburne, Sen, & Eichstedt, 2001). Parents swear that they raise their children in a gender-neutral fashion so they often believe these choices must reflect innate biological gender differences. *Boys and girls are just different from day one*, they may say. What response might you have to this statement? What critical thinking skills can you employ to understand why very young children act in gender stereotypical ways?

As children grow into adolescents, they have already assimilated their culture's expectations about their gender, sexuality, and prescribed roles. Now they face new issues related to sex and gender. Their changing bodies and new mental capabilities can affect their romantic relationships, life in their families, and their mental health.

Puberty and gender

The constant interplay between biology, personality, family, and culture helps children develop into gendered adolescents. After a history of genetic, neurobiological, hormonal, socializing, religious, and cultural influences, we reach sexual maturity with quite a bit of gender development already behind us. These influences have created us, become part of us, and molded us. Yet we also have a highly evolved brain with a frontal cortex larger than any other species on earth. With this sophisticated brain, which is capable of self-reflection and knowledge of its own future death, we can *choose* to re-enact and perpetuate the gender roles we grew up with, or to forge our way in a new direction. Even for something so seemingly biologically driven as puberty, the effects of experience, environmental intervention, and personal agency are clear.

Menarche
The beginning of a woman's menstrual cycle; a woman's first menstrual period.

For example, girls who enter **menarche**, the start of menstruation, earlier than their peers are more likely to suffer from anxiety, depression, and eating disorders (Hayward & Sanborn, 2002). Experiencing pubertal development that is out of step with that of peers can be a source of conflict and psychological stress. Interestingly, girls who live in the same household as non-genetically related adult males (for example, a mom's boyfriend or a stepfather) begin their periods about a year earlier than girls who live with biologically related males (Surbey, 1990). Similarly, girls who live in extremely stressful environments and who are sexually abused hit puberty sooner (Wierson, Long, & Forehand, 1993; Zabin, Emerson, & Rowland, 2005). However, when girls have other social support in the form of teachers, peers, or extended family, the effects of stress can be mitigated.

The above findings can be understood better by taking a look at how puberty occurs. Puberty is triggered by a shift in the balance between excitatory neurotransmitters, such as glutamate, and inhibitory neurotransmitters, such as GABA (Hayward & Sanborn, 2002). Gonadal hormones then begin to affect neurotransmitters in the brain (such as serotonin, which regulates mood among other things). Gonadal hormones also interact with other hormones in the hypothalamic pituitary adrenal axis (HPA axis), which is the stress regulation center of the body and brain. Dysregulation of the HPA axis through excessive stress, abuse, or drug use can lead to depression, which is more common in early adolescence when biological pubertal changes are at their height. GABA and glutamate are also related to anxiety and depression, which tend to increase as adolescents experience pubertal changes.

With these types of connections between hormones and neurological function, you might assume that teenage girls are more likely to be depressed than other people. This can be true for some girls, but it does not seem to be the case for African American teen girls, though, who on average begin puberty earlier than white girls, yet tend to suffer from depression less than white girls. African American teenage girls also experience adolescent eating disorders less often than their white peers (Bagley, Character, & Shelton, 2003; Molloy & Herzberger, 1998; Turnage, 2004). This suggests that cultural attitudes about mood disorders or body image concerns may affect psychological adjustment in adolescence more than hormonal changes do. For example, African Americans more readily accept voluptuous body types that European American teens might consider "fat," and African American girls tend to have a larger social support network than white teens, which mitigates depression (Hayward & Sanborn, 2002). Therefore, it is important to remember that biology, personal agency, and social support interact to create physical and mental health.

When we leave adolescence and enter into adulthood, we face decisions about selecting mates and long-term partners, as well as deciding whether to follow traditional or non-traditional gender roles in those relationships. Some theorists, especially those with an evolutionary focus, argue that adult gendered behaviors are biologically driven. Let's examine some of these evolutionary arguments so you can decide for yourself what you think about the impact of species-wide biological change for contemporary adult relationships.

Evolution and adult gendered behavior

Evolutionary arguments try to explain the biological elements of gendered behavior. We often hear about how cave men needed to fight, defend, hunt, and be aggressive, while women had to stay by the hearth and care for babies. These evolutionary arguments have merit in their attempts to understand the function of behaviors we currently see. However, it's important to note that just because we see a behavior or trait today does not mean that it evolved over time to help us adapt to our environments. Even if a trait or behavior did evolve out of our prehistoric past, that does not mean that it's necessary today (charred wooly mammoth meat anyone?). Evolutionary Theory holds that any behavior or trait can be maintained in a species as long as it doesn't interfere with reproduction; a trait or behavior is not necessarily *adaptive* or beneficial just because it continues in a species. Reproduction is really the only trait that truly matters in evolutionary terms. So as long as a species continues to reproduce and can adapt to its environment, other traits that don't impact continuation of the species might be maintained. Let's look more closely at how these ideas relate to the gendered lives of men and women.

People have long believed in evolutionary arguments for gender differences. For example, we often hear the evolutionary argument that men are naturally inclined to spread sperm around as much as possible because sperm is cheap and plentiful, while females need to choose a mate to take care of them and their offspring because women's eggs are all created before birth and only one is released per month. "Bateman's Principle," named for a British mid-twentieth-century biologist who studied the mating lives of fruit flies, supports this argument for gender differences. Bateman found that male flies had a wild need to mate with as many females as possible, at any time. Females, on the other hand, were discriminating in choosing partners (Bateman, 1948). Bateman thought female fruit flies were discriminating so they could ensure the viability of their pregnancies. But what does other research show?

More contemporary work found that complex variables affect mating behavior beyond a simple dichotomy of strategies based on biological sex. For example, Trivers (1972) found that across many species, it didn't matter which biological sex was the caretaker of the offspring, the one that took care of the young was less aggressive, less flamboyant in its colors and behaviors, and more passive. This was true for both males and females. This study shows that parental investment may be more important than biological sex for many traits we associate with natural "male" or "female" behavior.

Nearly 30 years ago, Hrdy (1981) suggested that *female* promiscuity may actually be the best bet for continuity of the species. She argued that it makes just as much sense for females to have multiple partners as males. According to Hrdy, when a woman is with more males, the question of paternity becomes unclear, so females are more likely to have a larger number of males stick around, males who won't kill "other men's" babies. Also, the more mates a female has, the more gifts she will receive, such as food, protection, and shelter. In fact, Hrdy found that across many species, more mates for a female were associated with delivering larger litters and having healthier babies. This suggests that promiscuity helps females' chances of gaining access to the healthiest sperm. In fact, Birkhead and Moller (1998) found that across species, female promiscuity in animals is the rule, not the exception.

Current evolutionary theorists argue that because Bateman was working in a sexist culture, his interpretation of his fruit fly results were colored by his own experience. Hrdy's work, on the other hand, is often referred to as "feminist" evolutionary scholarship. We must always use our critical thinking skills to figure out what the true meanings of research findings are, even for behaviors that seem evolutionarily or genetically endowed and perhaps immutable. Researchers, like all humans, are influenced by gender role expectations.

Some scholars may argue that it is beneficial to animals to be promiscuous, but humans have developed cultures that often frown upon such behavior. Our huge, complicated frontal cortexes allow us to inhibit our impulses, plan our actions, and think about the consequences of what we do.

We know that promiscuity may lead to diseases, or even death, as in the case of AIDS. If we take wedding vows, we often agree to lifelong fidelity with one spouse. It's important to understand the difference between cultural and religious ideologies and the "essential nature" of human beings, because once we consider something biologically innate, we also believe that change is hopeless. But if anyone looks at the diverse beliefs about monogamy, marriage, and sexual behavior across cultures, he or she soon recognizes the importance of the social constructions of sex and gender for both women's and men's lives in families. And we know that if a belief or practice is not working, it can be changed. For example, China is now realizing their one-child policy had some negative consequences for marriages and families and the government is now providing incentives for families to have and keep girl babies (Hvistendahl, 2009). Even though gendered behavior is affected by hormones, and perhaps even evolutionary forces, adolescents and adults make choices that affect their romantic relationships and their lives in families, and these choices differ widely for each individual and across diverse cultures.

The diverse lives of adult men

As boys develop into men, their histories and exposure to the gendered world around them affect everything they do and believe. Beginning in adolescence, boys and men begin to exhibit elevated levels of violence against other men, against women, and against themselves (Kaufman, 1998). They attempt to form families of procreation without having been allowed to develop the nurturing and emotional connection needed to do so successfully. Adolescent male gang members often refer to their gang as their "real family," implying that they feel a sense of connection and belonging, even though this new family is often based on a sense of entitlement and internalization of hypermasculine ideals (Krugman, 1995). Likewise, most school shootings have been perpetrated by adolescent males who had previously been teased, ostracized, or bullied by other boys. Exhibiting fearlessness helps such boys and young men reclaim their masculinity. They lash out in violence to seek revenge for their emasculation. Or they may commit suicide, unable to use the emotional language, social skills, or conflict-resolution abilities that females have practiced their whole lives (Kaufman, 1998). In an attempt to maintain their power and privilege, it's not uncommon for men to harm themselves, as is evidenced by their higher illness, injury, violence, and death rates (Clatterbaugh, 1997).

Men have more chronic health problems and die on average seven years earlier than women. Because males have faster metabolic rates, they require more food to survive, so in situations with poor nutrition or health care, boys may be more susceptible to the negative effects of poverty and deprivation (Geary, 1998). Men tend to smoke and drink more than women, and attend fewer preventive health care visits. In fact, higher proportions of men participate in the top 30 risky behaviors that increase one's risk for injury, illness, and death (Courtenay, 2000).

Because boys are more likely to be socialized to expect power and wealth accumulation as they grow into adulthood, embarking on a journey to maintain power, privilege, and control often means they cannot take the time to invest in self-care or ask for help from others, and a boy certainly cannot admit to suffering physically or emotionally (Bohan, 1993). Men end up working too much, not sleeping enough, engaging in risky behaviors, and refusing to take sick leave. For example, men usually avoid health-promoting behaviors as simple as applying sunscreen. They don't feel they need it. However, they have twice the skin cancer death rate of women (Bohan, 1993). Thus, while men are privileged in most societies, the male role brings with it many challenges. Modern masculinist movements have been fighting to release men from the pressures of traditional manhood, and these negative health trends have been decreasing in recent years.

Men of color

It is important to understand that power and privilege are relative terms. Within the group called "men" there is great diversity. Not all men benefit equally from male privilege and entitlement. Men of color, gay men, those living in rural areas, seniors, poor, uneducated or unskilled men, disabled men, and transgendered men all experience various levels of prejudice, discrimination, and lack of opportunity in comparison to educated European American heterosexual middle-class men. There have always been and still are many "masculinities" (Connell, 1993), even if most of us are only aware of the familiar roles we see.

Majors and Billson (1992) point out that when men are deprived of their ability to achieve the masculine ideal because of oppression in society, they may attempt to overcome their subordinate status through oppressing or attacking others, being tough and aggressive, committing crimes, or taking risks with sexual behavior. The effort of many men on the margins of society does not result in achievement or success like it does in the majority culture. They often cannot conceive of a bright successful future, so they attempt to reach the top of another hierarchy, for example dominating women, children, the elderly, weaker men, gay men, or disabled people. This is yet another example of how traditional gender role expectations for power and wealth can inflict harm upon diverse members of a society.

Men of color are more often unemployed and make lower wages than white men. It's not surprising, then, that 18% of African American men join the military, compared to only 8% of white men. While these men gain income and education from military service, they are also putting their lives at risk while working in a field that gives them the opportunity to develop a sense of achieved masculinity (Blee & Tickamyer, 1995; Diemer, 2002; Hofferth, 2003).

Interestingly, in terms of the variability within the male population, it is often the *more* oppressed group that has the most traditional gender beliefs. Marginalized groups may endorse culturally learned beliefs about masculinity to compensate for their lower position in the social hierarchy (Levant, Majors, & Kelly, 1998). For example, many Latinos follow sharply defined gender roles. Men provide for the family and ensure the honor of their women. They have authority over other family members and can exhibit sexual prowess openly (Gowan & Trevino, 1998). Gay Latino men endorse traditional ideals of masculinity even more so than heterosexual Latino men, who hold a position of privilege in Latino cultures (Diaz, 1998). Similarly, younger, non-professional African American men endorse the traditional masculine ideal more than do older professional African American males (Levant et al., 1998).

Diversity within groups is the norm and many men today do not fit into neat cultural stereotypes. For example, much is made in the media and general social circles about the absence of African American men from family life. Remember that African males were brought to the U.S. against their will and were treated like chattels. Although their status has improved greatly over the past 150 years, being black and male in the United States today is still often a great disadvantage. Today, young African American males and other men of color are more likely to be incarcerated and receive the harshest criminal sentences in American courts. Unemployed men also receive longer sentences than employed men (Walker et al., 2007).

The importance of the powerful effects stemming from the intersections between race, class, sexual orientation, and gender cannot be understated. Some researchers have attempted to examine the issues brought forth in media stereotypes regarding absent African American fathers by looking at both ethnicity and social class. They find that middle-class African American men take as much pride in providing for their families as middle-class white men do. Also, black men from all social classes treat their daughters and sons more similarly with less gender bias than white men in general, and black men are more encouraging of their female partners' employment than white men are (Blee & Tickamyer, 1995; Diemer, 2002; Hofferth, 2003).

Contemporary trends for modern men

African American men are not the only ones living in less gender-traditional families these days. Men, in general, are becoming less gender biased and are looking for something more than traditional gender expectations can provide for them. Thus the contemporary worlds of men are both constrained and expanding. The feminist movement has not only benefited the lives of women, but has changed many men's lives as well. For example, most men no longer think that it is acceptable to beat or rape their wives, actions which were accepted as men's rights in previous generations. Unfortunately, men are still growing up in a world that expects them to be aggressive, assertive, and accomplished. Today, in addition, they are also expected to be tender, emotional, and open with their partners. We expect men to be physically strong yet not dominate in the workplace. They must play well with others in work teams and listen to their partners at home, yet in general, we don't socialize boys to practice these skills as they are growing up (Hyde, 2007a).

At the beginning of the masculinist movement, Pleck (1981) referred to men's family struggles as a matter of contradictory and inconsistent expectations that lead men to feel role strain just like women do. We expect **hegemonic masculinity**, where the male body is privileged, men dominate over women and children, there is a gendered division of labor, and aggression is acceptable (Gmelch & San Antonio, 2001). Yet we also desire for men to truly listen to women, respect their rights to work and make decisions, share their feelings, and be sensitive to the needs of others. Women may want men to treat them as equals yet they expect men to practice old-fashioned chivalry, opening doors and paying for meals. Most women don't want to date short or "feminine" men, but don't want men to be macho or dominant either. When men experience conflict in the roles that are expected of them, they can often suffer from psychological distress and suffer a blow to their self-esteem (Shepard, 2002). Men suffer more ridicule and negative judgments if they violate gender role expectations than women do.

> **Hegemonic masculinity**
> A definition of masculinity that centers on power, control, dominance, and achievement.

To deal with some of these issues, an interesting movement has developed in the conservative Christian community of men. An organization called Promise Keepers brings thousands of men together in large stadiums to discuss how they have let their important role in their families disintegrate. The goal of Promise Keepers is to help men "reclaim their spiritual responsibility as *servant leaders* in the home" (Faludi, 1999). Even though this is a conservative Christian movement, it stemmed from the New Age, leftist liberal men's movement of the 1970s and 1980s when scores of men would go into the woods, beat drums, and openly share about the pain and isolation they felt as boys and men trying to conform to rigid gender role expectations. The liberal men's movement sought to free men from narrowly defined gender stereotypes and stilted emotional lives. They built a brotherhood of open, caring, sensitive men who wanted to connect emotionally with their families. In a similar vein, the Promise Keepers group attempts to create a brotherhood of men working toward restoring wives' and children's love and faith in men as the religious and moral leaders of the home.

Promise Keepers seeks to tear down the commercialization of masculinity, through denigrating macho exploits that objectify sex and violence. They want their members to reject the need for power and money, stop striving for a capitalist dream, and start striving for family harmony and strong marriages. They encourage men to turn off the TV and talk to their families. In this brotherhood, men feel safe sharing their fears and deepest feelings, their sense of failure over not achieving high powered careers, and their sense of disconnection from their wives. They aspire to lead but also to serve their wives. So at the same time they are striving to maintain traditional conservative gender roles (with men as the leaders of the family) they are also seeking to redefine masculinity and create a sensitive, open, and emotionally connected modern patriarch. To learn about a family that chooses to follow similar traditional gender roles in the modern world, read this chapter's *Focus on My Family*, where Dave and Janet follow their own Christian family ideals.

Women often have the responsibility for the spiritual and moral upbringing of the next generation (Gilder, 1986). Some conservative scholars feel that we cannot put these important goals off on the government by increasing our use of day care centers for children. They argue that women have high levels of role strain due partly to the media and the public disparaging traditional women's work and the roles of the stay-at-home wife and mother (Gallagher, 1996). Skolnick (1991) emphasizes that women are more likely to be unhappy and feel role strain if they are forced to work when they don't want to, or forced to stay home when they want to work. These facts and the issues raised in the *Focus on My Family* box illustrate that contemporary women experience life in families in myriad ways.

FOCUS ON MY FAMILY

Dave and Janet's story

Dave says: We have been married for 23 years and have four children ages 6 through 13. We got married too young (at 18 and 19), but our belief and faith in God has seen us through the rough times. At age 21, I began my career as a police officer while Janet worked at various jobs. After nine years, we wanted to have children, and decided she would work inside the home, caring for them. Myriad reasons influenced our decision for Janet to quit work and focus her occupational efforts on childrearing. Some of it was for convenience, such as avoiding having to juggle parental responsibilities between two parents who work outside of the home. Other reasons had to do with our desire to invest more time in our family and children than two working parents could provide. Rather than making a second income a priority, we wanted to invest that extra effort into our children. With a lot of belt tightening, we have been able to succeed financially.

As our children grew, we began to consider their schooling. We were disenchanted with the public schools in our area, due to problems such as gangs, drugs, and plummeting student literacy. Private schools are expensive, and they also have some of these same problems. So, after much soul-searching, we decided to homeschool. We became part of a Christian homeschool network of about 100 families in our town. Initially, some friends and family members were skeptical of our decision to homeschool. They were afraid our kids wouldn't have a chance to socialize with other children, or that we wouldn't be able to provide a quality education for them. Once they saw the many good friends our children have made through extracurricular activities, our children's literacy levels (we can't keep our daughter stocked with enough books to satiate her reading appetite), as well as their happy dispositions, their doubts subsided. In order to make this arrangement work, Janet must use her excellent organizational skills and practice great patience with the constant juggling of so many responsibilities.

Janet says: Homeschooling absorbs much of my time preparing curriculum and presenting the material to the children. In addition to making sure the children receive the basics of instruction, I also try to cultivate each of our children's unique talents, abilities, strengths, and interests, and incorporate their learning styles. I am grateful that Dave helps a lot with the cooking. It's difficult, though, as he sometimes works long hours of over-time to make ends meet. We make it a point to go out on weekly dates to keep our marriage a priority. Regardless of the challenges, we have reaped profound benefits from our family's structure, such as the ability to plan our children's school schedule around Dave's varied work schedule, to include studies in the Bible and our Christian beliefs, and to express to our children their incredible value to us. I feel deeply blessed that I can be a housewife/homeschool mom.

Which aspects of Dave and Janet's family life and gender roles are traditional and which ones are modern?

Dave and Janet's family.
Photo reproduced by permission.

The diverse lives of adult women

It should be clear by now that men's experiences in families vary based on their intersectional identities as well as the influences of their diverse bioecological systems. The same is true of women. The feminist movement has benefited many contemporary women, but women have yet to reach full equality with men, even in western countries.

Men make more money and receive more promotions than women do. In 2008, women in the U.S. made 80 cents for every dollar earned by men of the same age and experience (U.S. Bureau of Labor Statistics, 2009). Only 15 of the Fortune 500 CEOs of the world's largest corporations are women (http://www.fortune.com, Women CEOs, 2009). In the U.S. Congress for the 2008–2010, 34% of senators were women, with only 73 out of 235 representatives in the House being female (http://www.senate.gov; http://www.womenincongress.gov). These statistics show that women's talents continue to be under-utilized and their aspirations thwarted, as they have been historically (Garcia, 1989; James & Busia, 1993). However, it may do our female predecessors a disservice to fail to acknowledge the active roles they played in their own lives in order to overcome tough barriers to success. Remember that, in a bioecological approach, all humans are considered active participants in their own development so it's important to recognize that amidst oppression, there is also personal agency.

Kinship work
The work done in families (usually by women) that maintains strong blood ties; activities include writing letters and sending cards, buying gifts, and organizing parties and gatherings.

Most women today are involved in at least three different kinds of meaningful work: house and child care work, labor market work, and **kinship work**, in which they strive to maintain ties with supportive family members, from grandparents to aunts, uncles, cousins, and their partners' families (di Leonardo, 1987). Women organize visits, gatherings, holiday events, gifts, cards, and so on. Without the intensive efforts women spend keeping close bonds with family members, many families would disintegrate because kinship work takes an enormous amount of time and effort. Women's networking abilities, the effort taken to invite key people over for gatherings, and so on, also can improve a family's socioeconomic status, especially if match-making is involved. For example, in upper-class families in Mexico there is often a "centralizing woman" who brings all strands of a family together to enhance unity. In Japan, women's kinship work encompasses overseeing many financial transactions (di Leonardo, 1987).

Women of color

Even one of the most victimized groups in our history, slave women of the colonies, actively strategized about how to survive and thrive within the confines of their circumstances (Hill, 2005). Many women were so talented in the healing arts, midwifery, or spiritualism that their labor was taxed, an indication of their value (most slave labor was free, or untaxed, as slaves did not earn wages). Many slave women created women's subcultures where their activities were matrifocal, creating goods and services, raising children, and gaining the favor of their mistresses. Some of these women were so favored they would inherit land and privileges for themselves and their children. In this way, they became accustomed to succeeding without having slave men around. This began a system of African American women being strong and independent (Hill, 2005). These historical trends, combined with the current difficulty African American men often have finding good paying jobs and avoiding incarceration, make it less beneficial for many black women, especially in lower income brackets, to marry. Black women are employed at twice the rate of black men (McKinnon, 2003). In addition to these facts, there are only 84 black men of marrying age available for every 100 black women (U.S. Census Bureau, 2000a). Therefore, black girls today often grow up expecting to work, to lead families, and to be involved in large, socially connected communities with or without a husband.

Because feminist movements often exclude working-class women and women of color (Pardo, 1990), we may forget that religious women and women with traditional values can also be political activists, using their personal agency for the betterment of life in families.

For example, the Mothers of East Los Angeles (MELA) is a group of Mexican American stay-at-home mothers who are mostly devout Catholics, most of whom didn't complete high school (Pardo, 1990). This group of 400 women saw government officials exploiting their community and started to fight back. When plans to build both a prison and a toxic waste processing plant in their neighborhood came to light, these mothers built strong political alliances with other groups such as environmental activist organizations, organized protests, and fought the politicians head on. They developed public awareness campaigns showing citizens that 3 out 5 African American and Latino citizens live near a source of toxic waste (this recognition has since spurred a nationwide political movement against "environmental racism"). MELA was successful in that neither the prison nor the toxic waste plant was built in their neighborhood (Freudenberg, 2004).

All women, both historically and currently, have experienced oppression and marginalization, but they also have exhibited extraordinary strength in actively constructing lives of meaning within the most difficult circumstances. They have always had some form of power, whether recognized or not. Interestingly, many cultures, like some Native American Indian clans, practice menstruation segregation, such as having bleeding women go to menstruation huts or "red tents" because they are considered too powerful during that time. They believe that their power might weaken that of men if they roam around in the world during their bleeding time (Hyde, 2007a). Women are often considered extensions of the spirit world and are respected for their unique ability to continue the chain of life (LaFramboise, Choney, James, & Running Wolf, 1995).

Native Americans and other people of color also ascribe more power and wisdom to women as they age. Elderly women are sought for their healing powers, their advice, and their ties to the spiritual world. The Iroquois nation had a "council of matrons" where elderly wise women would consult with each other on pressing issues for their people (Allen, 1986). It is clear that women have always worked many jobs and played many roles in their family and community lives.

Macrosystem influences on women and their families

Governments around the world often implement social welfare programs to help women raise their children with a good quality of life. In fact, since the implementation of Aid to Families with Dependent Children (AFDC, or "welfare") after the Great Depression of the 1930s, American women have received government benefits to help them raise their children with enough food and medical care to enjoy a minimum quality standard of living. Today the Women, Infants and Children's program (WIC) ensures that American children can receive food benefits of staples like milk, bread, and cheese.

Similarly, the women's movement of the 1950s spurred European nations to develop more social welfare programs to enhance the care of its women and children (Cousins, 2005). Since 1979, when many key social welfare directives began, the European Union has provided twice as many benefits for women than men (this includes pay supplements, unemployment benefits, old age care, maternity leave, illness and disability coverage, and so on.). Women's employment in social realms like nursing, social work, and child care spurred discussions about what could be done to ensure that women were retained in a declining labor force while not punishing them by making family life more difficult. Policies were developed to help women and children maintain quality of life while women worked in the labor force. This led to the implementation of high-quality, low-cost child care programs, free access to high-quality health care, and long-term paid maternity and paternity leaves.

Interestingly, the U.S., with one of the strongest feminist movements, has the least extensive social welfare benefits for women and children in the industrialized world. Figure 3.5 compares these policies.

Social democratic welfare states like those of most of the countries in Western Europe have the most family-friendly policies that enhance the quality of living for all men, women, and children. Countries with a Christian Democratic ideology (like the United States and to a lesser extent,

FIGURE 3.5 Comparison of maternity leave benefits in 19 countries.
Source: Table PF2.1.A, Calculating full-time equivalent of paid maternity, paternity and parental leave, 2006/2007, from OECD Family database www.oecd.org/els/social/family/database.

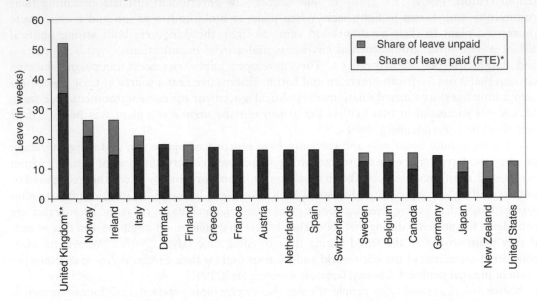

*Full-time equivalent of leave in weeks, as if the claimant were to receive 100% of average earnings.
**Calculates a 90% wage replacement for those who make below the flat rate threshold (£108.85/week).

FIGURE 3.6 More women today are gaining access to the careers that previously put only men's lives at risk. Soldiers of the Indian Rapid Action Force, Chennai, 2009.
© Raveendran/AFP/Getty Images.

Germany) have continued to emphasize SNAF as the ideal family form and so create welfare policies that trap women in low socioeconomic conditions and do not benefit working mothers. In the United States, for example, there's little to no support for high-quality child care centers or elder care (Cousins, 2005). For example, in 2006, 16% of the American population had no health care insurance (over 46 million people), while in France, only 0.005% of the population was uninsured.

Paradoxically, the U.S. spends 15% of its gross national product on health care, compared to only 10.5% spent by France. Moreover, in the U.S., *private* funds account for 55% of health care spending, but only 21.6% of such spending in France. In 2000 the World Health Organization ranked the U.S. 37th in the world in terms of its health care system, with developing nations like Malta, Cyprus, and Greece all ranked higher (http://www.photius.com/rankings/who_world_health_ranks.html). In addition, the U.S. has the highest teen pregnancy rates and abortion rates of any industrialized nation.

This is attributed in part to Americans' opposition to the use of birth control by young people and the moral imperative in favor of abstinence-only education in the U.S. In comparison, Western European countries are more open about sexuality in general, and adolescents grow up using contraception regularly to avoid having babies before they are mature enough to be parents (Moore, 2006). The quality of life of women and children in the U.S. pales in comparison to that of our counterparts in other industrialized nations around the world.

Despite some of the disadvantages American women and families face compared to people in other industrialized nations, we must not forget how very far American women have come in the past century. These changes bring many positive opportunities for women. For example, women have fought for and gained access to once male-dominated professions such as police work and the military. With these increased opportunities, do you think women's rates of illness, injury, and violent death will increase to become similar to that of men? Consider Figure 3.6 as you ponder this question.

CHAPTER SUMMARY

This chapter explores the biological, social, and cultural influences on the development of sex and gender. Sex refers to the biological construct of being male or female. Gender refers to the socially constructed aspects of what makes people male or female. The term gender is used throughout the chapter since it is difficult to determine whether a given characteristic is more biologically or socially influenced. Gender was discussed as a key influence on every person's life as it impacts their sense of self, their behaviors, and their preferences. Gendered individuals interact with romantic partners, parents, children, and extended kin in families. These interactions can be positive or conflicted, depending on how the individual's gendered behavior fits with the family's expectations.

Gender identity was discussed as a person's view of him- or herself as male, female, or another gender variant. Sex and gender variations were discussed in sections on intersexed people, transgendered people, and those who do not fit clearly into any category (e.g., third genders, "two-spirits," or "berdaches" in Native American cultures).

Gender roles refer to social expectations for how boys and girls, men and women should behave or live their lives. Gender roles are culturally constructed with often quite separate spheres for men versus women in families. Gender role expectations can help people understand what roles and responsibilities they have in their families but they can also constrict people's expectations for themselves and the possibilities that exist outside those roles. Social Cognitive Theory explains that boys and girls are reinforced for gender appropriate behavior and they imitate the gendered behavior of those around them.

Gender Schema Theory further explores the role of cognition in gender development. Children's attentional capacities, memories, and information-processing systems are shaped through gendered interactions and they become more or less "schematic" in the way they view the world. Schematic children view gender as strictly delineated between men and women, with prescribed roles for each. Gender aschematic children are more flexible in their thinking and can perceive and remember gender non-traditional roles they see. The benefits of androgyny (exhibiting both masculine and feminine characteristics) were explored in terms of gender aschematic views and cognitive flexibility regarding what it means to be a man or woman.

The chapter focuses much attention on the negative impact of sexist beliefs, gender discrimination, and heteronormativity (privileging heterosexuality over other sexualities).

Sexual orientation refers to one's attraction to romantic partners of specific genders. Sexual orientation is considered to be biologically driven and not a choice people make for themselves. Families have specific beliefs about the acceptability of different sexual orientations and "coming out" as gay or bisexual can cause strife in families with heteronormative belief systems.

Biological and social research was reviewed, which explains how people develop both their biological sex and their conceptions of their own gender. The roles of hormones, neurotransmitters, enzymes, and prenatal environments were examined. Also, intrauterine environments were shown to affect both sex and gender differentiation. Gender development from the prenatal period through childhood, adolescence, and adulthood was examined with both biological (e.g., hormones, evolutionary influences) and sociocultural (e.g., parents and ethnicity) impacts interacting with each other.

Finally, the diverse lives of men and women were examined from a historical and contemporary perspective. Their intersectional identities were highlighted, with particular focus on ethnicity, social class, gender, and macrosystem influences.

KEY TERMS

androgyny
benevolent sexism
essentialized
gender
gender aschematic
gender identity
gender roles
Gender Schema Theory
gender schemas

gender schematic
gender similarity hypothesis
hegemonic masculinity
heteronormativity
hostile sexism
intersexed
kinship work
male entitlement
menarche

meta-analysis
purging
role strain
sex
sexual orientation
Social Cognitive Theory
stereotype
stereotype threat
transgendered

WEBSITES FOR FURTHER EXPLORATION

http://www.now.org

The National Organization for Women. This site is sponsored by the largest feminist activist organization in the U.S. With over 500,000 members, NOW has collected important information on sexism, economic justice, violence against women, reproductive rights, and other key issues. They have ongoing campaigns to help women learn about social policy, legislation, and cultural trends that affect them.

http://www.nomas.org

The National Organization for Men Against Sexism. This group is comprised of male activists who support positive changes in men and the definition of masculinity. They have information and resources, and they monitor social policy related to: custody rights, violence, men in prison, men and spirituality, and other topics.

http://www.ifge.org

The International Foundation for Gender Education. This group advocates for those who cross traditional gender boundaries, including intersex and transgender people. They publish a transgender issues magazine, *Transgender Tapestry*, have a gender FAQ page, monitor social policy and legal cases, and hold conferences devoted to gender issues.

CHAPTER 4
SEXUALITIES

My mom always told me that sex was a dirty, ugly, horrible thing that I was only to do with someone I loved.

(Anonymous)

LEARNING OBJECTIVES

- To be aware of the historical trends influencing sexualities

- To learn some basic research findings on sexuality

- To understand female and male sexual anatomy and typical and atypical functioning

- To understand the bioecological influences on sexuality and sexual orientation

- To be able to master the myths and truths about controversial topics like female genital mutilation, AIDS, abstinence education, and sexualized violence

OVERVIEW OF INFLUENCES ON SEXUALITY

MACROSYSTEM AND HISTORICAL INFLUENCES ON SEX AND SEXUALITIES

- The Industrial Revolution
  - Social Darwinism
- The twentieth century
- The sexual double standard

TRENDS IN SEXUAL BEHAVIOR AND ATTITUDES ABOUT SEX

- Cultural regulation of sexuality
- Recent U.S. trends in sexual behavior
- Cultural variations in sexual behavior
- The bioecological perspective

SEX ORGANS: THE WAY THEY WORK AND HOW THINGS GO AWRY

- Women's sexual organs
  - Hormones
  - Women's sexual response
  - Female orgasms
  - Women's sexual problems
- Men's sex organs
  - Men's sexual response
  - Men's sexual problems
- Men's and women's sexualities in more depth
- Sexual diversity vs. disorders
- Sex therapy
  - Physiological aspects of sex therapy

SEXUAL ORIENTATION

- Biological research on homosexuality
  - Genes
  - Chromosomes
- Social and contextual issues and homosexuality

A CLOSER LOOK AT CURRENT ISSUES IN SEXUALITY

- Female genital mutilation
- AIDS and trends in youth sexualities
  - More on young people and sexuality
- Abstinence education, virginity pledges, and family relationships
- Sexual abuse and sexualized violence

OVERVIEW OF INFLUENCES ON SEXUALITY

As the opening quote illustrates, most of us were raised with some pretty specific ideas about sexuality. Can you remember some of the messages about sex you received, either explicit or implicit, from your parents, religion, media, or culture? Sex has the potential to be one of life's great pleasures. It is more than just a physical act because it can forge emotional connections in a relationship, or it can alternatively tear them apart. At the same time that it evokes desire, it can set a person up for serious illnesses or diseases. Although it seems to occur naturally for all humans, sex is an incredibly complex phenomenon. The micro-, meso-, exo-, and macrosystems of the bioecological approach all play a role in how we experience our diverse sexualities. We have varying hormonal patterns that affect desire levels. Our parents and other members of our microsystem socialize us from specific viewpoints they have about sex. The religions we practice usually deliver messages about sexuality and intimate relationships. Finally, our macrosystems are organized around the formation of intimate relationships and the development of families of procreation. There are cultural norms and traditions that drive how we seek union with others, and this includes sexual norms. Before examining contemporary trends and norms found in research on diverse sexualities, let's take a step back in time and see how micro- and macrosystem influences have shaped sexual attitudes and practices over time.

MACROSYSTEM AND HISTORICAL INFLUENCES ON SEX AND SEXUALITIES

The Industrial Revolution

The twentieth century

The sexual double standard

Historically in most cultures, women's bodies were used for the pleasure of men. Women were seen as property, good only for birthing children. In Greek, the word *gyne* means "bearer of children." Plato said that infertile women were "hysterical," or nervous. Sigmund Freud, one of the first modern theorists to tackle gender and sexuality issues in his nineteenth-century writings, articulated similar ideas: he thought women who did not have children were in anguish and "neurotic," and must have sex in order to cure their hysteria. Early Christians thought that women's sexuality threatened to devour men, to endanger their souls. A famous and very influential early Christian, St. Augustine, ashamed of his own sex drive, announced that sex was only for procreation (Berman, Berman, & Bumiller, 2001). However, other early histories seem more modern by comparison. For example, in the Indian Kama Sutra, a sex manual dating from about the third to the fifth century CE, explicit images taught both men and women many sexual positions.

In medieval Europe, Christian disavowal of sex reached new heights when chastity belts were instituted. A woman was belted into an iron contraption that had small openings for urine and menstrual blood. A woman's husband had control of the key so that no one else could access her genitals. With the Protestant reformation against Catholicism in the sixteenth century, sex was encouraged not only for procreation, but as an experience to bind husbands and wives together emotionally and to relieve stress (Berman et al., 2001). However, the pendulum had swung back by the eighteenth century. In the early colonies of the New World, Puritans felt women were too irrational to control their carnal passions. They were characterized as evil temptresses who would entrap men. Women were prosecuted for alleged sex crimes more often than men were.

The Industrial Revolution

As the massive changes surrounding industrialization and the rising middle class took hold during Victorian times (approximately 1840–1910), women were suddenly viewed as the moral leaders of the family, beholden to God and in charge of the purity of their children. Women were placed on pedestals and were thought to be too chaste and pure to have sexual desires. They had sex with their husbands as a duty, and men did not expect to have their true desires met by their wholesome wives. Victorian women, however, did have sexual desires. Because their husbands were not taught to be aware of their wives' sexual lives, many women developed somatic complaints like fainting spells, pelvic pain, "nervousness," and emotional instability (Berman et al., 2001). Middle- and upper-class women had these "emotional problems" treated by the family doctor. Physicians would massage the women's genitals until they reached "hysterical paroxysm," a condition characterized by such "symptoms" as moaning, muscle tightening, and sharp pelvic thrusts (Maines, 2001).

Relieving housewives' "hysterical" symptoms became a lucrative business as the treatment was reported to return the uterus to its proper state after it wandered upward inside the body during "hysterical" fits of sexual frustration (Maines, 2001). All manner of contraptions were invented to induce hysterical paroxysm, such as giant water hoses (which worked surprisingly well, but left the doctor's office a soggy mess). The first manual pump vibrator (operated by a doctor's foot compressions on an accordion-like pump) was invented in the 1880s, long before other domestic necessities like the electric vacuum cleaner or toaster. The famous naturalist John Muir even patented a vibrator.

In Maines's (2001) groundbreaking book *The Technology of Orgasm*, the author presents Victorian and early twentieth-century magazine ads replete with sex aids marketed for women. These devices were often referred to as "health" aids or anti-aging gadgets. For example, Maines discusses a 1913 White Cross Corporation vibrator ad which read "All the pleasures of youth will throb within you." Most of the early sexual aids were large and cumbersome until 1902 when Hamilton Beach produced a handheld vibrator that women could buy and use at home (about the size of a large hairdryer). In fact, Maines (2001) reports that the race for technologically advanced female sexual aids was the driving force behind the invention of the small electric motor. Between 1900 and 1940 scores of designs were patented under the category of health and beauty aids. In the 1950s to 1970s, as technology advanced, vibrators were made to look like other household appliances, like vacuum attachments or personal massagers.

While these acts of sexual relief were occurring behind closed doors, in public women were expected to deny they had any sexual urges at all. In Victorian times, it wasn't uncommon for wives to publicly endorse prostitution for their husbands in order to let men relieve their natural sexual tension. Travel guides of the 1860s regularly listed the best brothels in towns where people might visit for their holidays (Berman et al., 2001). The spread of syphilis and the realization that many prostitutes were women of color who made fairly good money and so had some power in towns, led to a movement among middle-class white women to advocate for the prohibition of prostitution.

Social Darwinism

Many of these trends regarding women in the 1800s reflect the experiences of the educated white middle class. At the same time that wealthy white housewives

FIGURE 4.1 Victorian advertisement for pelvic massage.

were having medically induced orgasms, a detestable movement was taking shape in the United States and Europe to control the sex lives and stop the reproductive abilities of thousands of poor women. After Charles Darwin published *On the Origin of Species* in 1859, the theory of evolution by natural selection was known throughout the developed world. Around 1870, Charles Darwin's cousin influenced the entrenchment of ideas about white racial superiority. Applying the ideas of evolution to humans, Francis Galton argued that if only the elite or intelligent people (that is, educated white people) were allowed to breed, we could create a superior race of Aryan humans.

Another theorist of the time, Herbert Spencer, called this idea **Social Darwinism**, and felt that humans would naturally evolve into a master race if we didn't implement social programs to help the disadvantaged (like the poor and mentally ill). Without social programs, the "genetically inferior" would die off and we would experience what he called, "survival of the fittest" (Spencer, 1857). The **eugenics movement** grew out of these ideas. This was a movement driven by the desire to reach racial purity and rid society of genetically "unfit" people, especially those considered feebleminded (that is, unintelligent). People were rounded up and put into sanitariums where they were to be sterilized to prevent them from breeding and giving birth to more social undesirables. The eugenics movement was not underground or fringe. It was practiced out in the open, with newspapers touting the benefits of creating a genetically superior race of humans through sterilization of the unfit. It's unclear how many people were sterilized in the eugenics movement, but in the U.S. estimates range from 60,000 to 200,000. California alone sterilized more people by the end of the 1920s than most other *countries* around the world had (Coontz, 2005).

Many in the U.S. and Europe argued that the feebleminded were the causes of social problems like violent crime and alcoholism. People were sterilized without being told what the operation was for. Many people died on the operating table and many women reported being sexually abused by the medical staff. Survivors of eugenics reported genital injuries, sexual dysfunction, and high rates of divorce; as women were expected to bear children in their marriages, so they were blamed for childlessness.

Beyond controlling marginalized populations' sexual and reproductive lives through sterilization, female genital mutilation (usually in the form of removal of the clitoris) was practiced well into the 1950s in the U.S. and Western Europe, as a treatment for "female ailments" like epilepsy, nymphomania, and even lesbianism (United Nations Population Fund, 2009). Social histories usually fail to reveal how life was for many people who never got to know what a healthy relationship or sex life were like.

Social Darwinism
The idea that evolution will take its natural course over time, weeding out genetically "unfit" people so that eventually a master human race will emerge through "survival of the fittest"; this theory was used to justify political attitudes against social welfare programs and in favor of the eugenics movement.

Eugenics movement
A movement stemming from Social Darwinist ideas, which advocated for sterilization of any people considered genetically "unfit." This movement influenced Nazi genocide methods.

The twentieth century

Surveys of women at the turn of the twentieth century show that women felt sex was unimportant for marriage and they had little knowledge about physiology or sexuality. Interestingly, about 30% of those surveyed did report enjoying sex with their husbands, and 75% reported using some form of contraception (usually diaphragms or the withdrawal method) (Berman et al., 2001).

FIGURE 4.2 Historic hand-held vibrator.
Photo © Kurt Rogers/San Francisco Chronicle/Corbis.

At the turn of the century, a doctor named Havelock Ellis widely circulated the idea that women should acknowledge and fulfill their sexual urges. Ahead of his time, he argued that the focus on sex solely for reproduction oppressed women's humanity. Also, in 1916, Margaret Sanger opened the first birth control clinic that advocated the use of contraceptives like the diaphragm. She encouraged middle-class women to be open about their desire for sex outside of procreation (Berman et al., 2001). Between 1900 and 1920 people learned more about birth control and sexuality and so were often relieved from the oppressive sexual tensions characterizing the Victorian marriage. By the early 1920s, the International Women's Suffrage Alliance had spread throughout Latin America, South Africa, China, India, and Palestine (Coontz, 2005).

The 1920s in the western world found women cutting their hair to shorter "boy" lengths (called a bob haircut), wearing short dresses, freeing themselves from corsets and girdles, smoking cigarettes, and dancing and drinking all night without chaperones. Many women decided to remain unmarried and lesbianism increased in visibility. Popular culture from this time was replete with sexuality. Freud's writings had made sex an acceptable pastime and topic of discussion. Soon scantily clad women adorned the pages of advertisements in magazines, catalogs and newspapers. To counteract the "loosening morals" of the time, a film censorship board came into existence in 1910 due to the rampant sexual content and innuendo in silent films (Coontz, 2005). In the 1920s, almost half of women had premarital sex and even gay bars and parades were openly recognized and tolerated. Female impersonators became superstars and made large amounts of money. At this time, it became a more common belief that men and women had to experiment sexually before they settled on a marriage partner. Marriages characterized by all three variables: love, sex, and emotional intimacy, became the norm, and women were expected to enjoy sex to keep the marriage going strong.

It is noteworthy that macrosystem forces played a role in both the more open sexual behaviors of people in the 1920s and the return to conventionality in the 1930s. By the 1930s, the country was in a deep economic depression and the emphasis on frivolous sex and tolerance for homosexual behavior declined rapidly. The pressure on women to be hypersexual led to problems in marriage since the passion of newlyweds normally declines over time. After a couple of decades of free sexuality, women were now expected to submit to sex whenever their husbands demanded it. The good news was that marriage counseling also developed at this time and became a new avenue for strengthening marriages, increasing communication, and allowing couples to talk about sexual conflicts (Coontz, 2005).

Even though women's sexuality has come far since the Middle Ages, many adult women are still afraid to be open about their sexual needs. Women also assume that men know all about sex and should intuitively know what to do to please them. However, men are given very little information about female sexuality and even less instruction on the mechanics of female sexual arousal. Likewise, most women understand little about male sexuality and often fail to ask partners what would please them (Coontz, 2005). As a consequence, many adult heterosexual couples end up with a man doing what he thinks is right and a woman faking orgasms in order to protect her partner from performance anxiety. People still view women as "nice" girls who don't talk openly about their sexuality while men are expected to be hypersexual and figure it all out on their own (Coontz, 2005). The interactions between macrosystem beliefs about sexuality and microsystem communication difficulties make sexuality a complex and challenging part of many relationships.

The sexual double standard

Even though western cultures have become more open about sexuality in general and female sexuality in particular, there is still a **sexual double standard** (Reiss, 1960). Men are viewed in a more approving light than women for the same sexual behaviors. Much research has shown that the sexual double standard has decreased in recent decades, but Jonason and Marks (2009) argue that the old surveys many researchers still use ask questions about behaviors that have become accepted as normal (like premarital sex and oral sex), so their results reveal that not many people today judge men or women negatively for those behaviors.

Sexual double standard (SDS)
The idea that sex is normal and expected for men and disapproved of for women.

Jonason (2007) tried to test this hypothesis by using a new question regarding how people viewed women and men who had had more than 50 sexual partners. You might not be surprised to learn that people viewed men much more positively than women if they had 50 partners. They also rated men with over 50 partners in a lifetime more positively than men who had only one partner. These findings spurred Jonason and Marks (2009) to ask people about another less common sexual behavior, that of having a "threesome." Initial surveys showed that only 8% of heterosexual people surveyed had had a threesome, so this event was rare enough to not be seen as normative. In scenarios in which women were depicted as having a threesome with two men, the respondents rated her *extremely* negatively (which differed significantly from their ratings of a woman having a threesome with one woman and one man). For men, there was no difference in ratings whether the man was with two other men or one man and one woman. In addition, men were rated *extremely* positively for having a threesome with two women, and these ratings were much more positive than him having a threesome with one man and one woman. Interestingly, there was no difference in the ratings of *women* having a threesome with two women versus one man and one woman.

These authors argue that their findings illustrate the "eroticization of lesbianism," in which men from western cultures find any sexual situation involving two women highly erotic, even if those women are lesbians. These findings also reveal the still extant sexual double standard and the privileging of male sexuality even in contemporary western cultures. Male sex is related to power and status, but men are viewed more negatively if they have sex with another man and a woman, revealing the maintenance of homophobia and bisexualphobia in our culture. It's important to examine our beliefs about what is normal or acceptable sexual behavior because those viewpoints can impact perceptions and interactions in our marriages and families. Contemporary trends in sexual behavior help illuminate how this process occurs.

TRENDS IN SEXUAL BEHAVIOR AND ATTITUDES ABOUT SEX

Cultural regulation of sexuality

Recent U.S. trends in sexual behavior

Cultural variations in sexual behavior

The bioecological perspective

Although the mechanics of sex involve biological processes, those processes are largely influenced by psychological, emotional, social, and cultural variables. Sexual arousal stems from a complex combination of cognitive, experiential, emotional, contextual, and physiological factors (Rupp & Wallen, 2008).

Cultural regulation of sexuality

All cultures regulate their members' sexuality in one way or another (Lombardo, 1983). Whether you live in Tibet or Tulsa, Johannesburg or Germany, there are cultural expectations for what you should and should not do with your genitals. Each society has restrictions and controls that define its members' sexual lives. In the United States, the moment we're born, we are bombarded with images and implicit or explicit messages about what is "normal" or "deviant" sexual desire and behavior. We learn that nice girls keep their virginity for longer periods than naughty girls. We hear terms like "oversexed" or "perverted," and many of us learn that sex is a privilege reserved for married people and is wrong if it occurs in non-married people's lives. Parents and religious and cultural leaders give us both overt lessons and covert messages about whether having sex or even discussing sex is appropriate. Schwartz and Rutter (1998) say that "there is no such thing as a truly free sexuality" (p. 137).

However, some cultures allow people more freedom to pursue their sexual desires than others. For example, Sweden is a "sex positive" culture where people expect to engage in sex as a regular part of their growth and development. They expect that sex is to be had for pleasure, that all people are sexual beings, and that sex before marriage is perfectly acceptable (Schwartz & Rutter, 1998).

In contrast, the Catholic Church in Ireland, which remains extremely influential, teaches that sex is shameful and taboo for anyone except married heterosexual couples. Thus, non-marital sex is usually engaged in secretly and often with shame. In addition, the Church prohibits birth control, which can affect attitudes and behaviors related to sex.

Recent U.S. trends in sexual behavior

Recent research has tried to determine what people actually do in addition to what they think. For example, in a study of 813 American college students, 66% of men and 50% of women said they approved of pornography. Of the men questioned, 86% actually used pornography regularly, 48% once a week; 31% of the women reported using pornography, with 3% using it weekly. Pornography use was correlated with a higher number of sexual partners, permissive sexual attitudes, and higher levels of substance use (Carroll et al., 2008). As you can see, gender played a role in both attitudes and behaviors regarding sexually explicit material. In addition, these attitudes can impact people's actual sexual practices.

Other recent findings examining sexual behavior show that the frequency of sex decreases with age for most people (from an average of six times per month in a person's twenties to about six times per year in a person's seventies). This trend holds true for most ethnic groups, social classes, and religions. Women tend to lose interest in sex more than men do as they age (Christopher & Sprecher, 2000).

Research has also begun to examine the types of sexual practices people engage in. Within married heterosexual partnerships, 7–10% of couples engage in anal sex and the majority practice oral sex. Oral and anal sex practices occur most often in white educated couples (Christopher & Sprecher, 2000). Interestingly, the myth of marriage keeping us tied down and miserable doesn't seem to hold true regarding sexuality, as married couples are actually more sexually satisfied than are cohabiting couples or singles (Christopher & Sprecher, 2000).

Statistics and trends like those cited can vary quite a bit based on specific characteristics within each study's sample. Wide variations occur in sexual behavior and quality, based on relationship processes and demographic variables. For example, men tend to prefer a wider variety of sexual behaviors than women do. Important relationship processes include power struggles, conflicts, and communication patterns, which affect sexuality and sexual satisfaction. Also, the higher the social class, the less satisfied people are with their sex lives. This may be due to higher expectations for perfection, a tendency toward workaholism, and the stress of "keeping up with the Joneses," which hamper life satisfaction in the wealthy (Luthar, 2003).

Sexual satisfaction is highly correlated with general marital satisfaction while sexual dissatisfaction is associated with divorce, suggesting that sexual satisfaction plays a key role in the longevity of a relationship (White & Keith, 1990). Sexual satisfaction decreases the odds of relationship break-up for men, while overall relationship satisfaction is a better predictor of relationship stability for women. There are no differences found in the levels of sexual satisfaction between gay, lesbian, and heterosexual couples. For all couples, sexual satisfaction is related to overall relationship satisfaction. However, lesbian couples tend to have sex less frequently than other types of couples. Gay male couples have sex more frequently than others, and approve of non-monogamy at higher rates, although even for gay men, the frequency of sexual activity declines with age (Christopher & Sprecher, 2000).

General attitudes about sex and infidelity have also been studied. In the U.S., 70–80% of adults disapprove of extramarital sex. Men, the highly educated, and those with low levels of religiosity approve of extramarital sex the most. Twenty-five percent of men and 15% of women report having extramarital sexual relations (Christopher & Sprecher, 2000). Males, those with high levels of education, African Americans, people who cohabit, and people who live in urban areas have the highest rates of infidelity. While men get most angry if their female partners have sex with someone else, women are more deeply hurt by emotional infidelity. A male partner sharing feelings or meeting female friends for lunch can hurt deeply as many women want to be emotionally and physically close to their male partners.

Because of macrosystem factors, these trends might be quite different across cultures. For example, many cultures do not consider personal satisfaction to be of any importance in a marriage, and many other cultures consider extramarital sex perfectly acceptable.

Cultural variations in sexual behavior

Sexual attitudes and practices vary widely from culture to culture. For example, in Albania there is a tradition of "sworn virgins," women who, in an attempt to escape radical patriarchy and oppression of women, decide to dress, act, and live their lives as men. In order to receive this privilege, however, the woman must take a vow of celibacy and can never go back to being a woman (Becatoros, 2008).

In another cultural example, Sambia people from New Guinea believe that while "femaleness" is innate, "maleness" must be trained. Young boys live in a female-dominated world with their mothers and they must be rid of their feminine habits as they get older. Male power and strength is referred to as *jerungdu*, and contact with women is thought to diminish a man's *jerungdu*. Thus, young boys obtain their *jerungdu* through ritualized same-sex experiences. Starting at age 7, young boys ingest the semen of older men through oral sex performed on a daily basis. When they are 15, they switch roles with younger children, and by 17, they marry women. As soon as their wives have children, they stop participating in the same-sex rituals and focus on marital sex. Sambians have no word for "sexual orientation." It appears that they start out as homosexual, go through a bisexual stage, and then become heterosexual. But their society does not recognize or have words for these types of categories. They don't conceptualize ideas like "same-sex" relationships or "marital sex." However, it is true that gender role stereotypes play a role in the Sambia culture as they do in all cultures. These same-sex rituals remain in place in order to keep the social structure of male and female spheres segregated (Heine, 2008).

Recall that the Structural-Functionalist perspective legitimizes the status quo and argues that certain familiar roles and behaviors keep society functioning as it "should." Culturally defined gender roles maintain these restrictions on people's sexual lives. If we live in a culture where sexual pleasure is considered "normal" and is healthy and expected for all people, we see very different roles evolve. For instance, in many societies today, people see sex as acceptable for men but shameful for women. Women are scorned or ostracized for the same behaviors that are regularly accepted from men, for example, having sex with multiple partners. These behavior standards maintain a system of male privilege and a society where people view sexuality and gender roles as reflecting the "essential nature" of men and women. Thus, some people are **essentialists** and maintain that male/female sexual behavioral differences are innate. Other people are **constructionists**, maintaining that sexual behavior is malleable and emphasizing how social expectations shape sexual behavior (Schwartz & Rutter, 1998). Table 4.1 summarizes the differences between essentialists and constructionists.

The bioecological perspective

Sexuality stems from a dynamic series of personal and contextual forces interacting with each other. The bioecological model gives us a way to understand how the biological acts occurring during sexual intimacy are influenced not only by physiological health and functioning but by interpersonal relationship dynamics and larger social forces. It will help you understand the multifaceted aspects of sexuality and how those impact life in couples and families. A bioecological analysis begins by looking at the individual at the center of the model. Each person enters into a sexual relationship with years of biological and environmental interactions behind them, which influence how subsequent intimate encounters may take place. To address these individual differences, Bancroft (2005) describes sexuality as a process involving a motivational state in which people strive to experience sexual pleasure and orgasm. This motivated striving must incorporate four key elements:

Essentialist
People who think sex and gender differences are biological, essential, or natural.

Constructionists
People who think sex and gender differences are socially constructed.

TABLE 4.1 Explanations of male and female differences in sexual desire.
Source: Schwartz & Rutter, 1998, p. 139.

Explanations	Causes of desire	Consequences
Essentialist: Desire is biological and evolutionary	Genetically preprogrammed reproductive functions specific to males and females	Male independence in reproduction and female-centered childrearing practices and passivity are the cause, rather than the result, of gendered social institutions
Social constructionist: Desire is sociological and contextual	Social institutions and social interaction signal and sanction "male" and "female" gendered norms of behavior	Support for or opposition to sex/ gender-segregated reproductive and social practices depends on social definitions of men, women, and sexuality
Bioecological: Desire is contextual, process-oriented, and physical	Bodies, environments, relationships, families, governments shape sexualities	Policies address some biological differences (such as pregnancy and work); emphasize the impact of social forces, interactions, societal progams

Information processing
How people judge incoming information regarding possible sexual opportunities.

Generalized physiological arousal
Excitement, nervousness, or tingling in body parts outside of the genital region.

Incentive motivation
A mental process whereby one considers possible incentives or rewards for their actions.

Genital response
Excitement, arousal, or tingling in the genital region.

1 *information processing* (how we understand the information and contexts surrounding us)

2 *generalized physiological arousal* (whether our bodies are relaxed, tense, or excited)

3 *incentive motivation* (our perception that engaging in certain acts will provide us with a reward)

4 *genital response* (how our sexual organs react).

Bancroft's model proposes that the functioning of our genitals and our drive for sexual gratification involves many cognitive, emotional, and social processes acting at the same time. To see how Bancroft's ideas work, let's imagine that you are in the grocery checkout line and an attractive person the next lane over catches your eye. You quickly realize that you've seen this person before in one of your classes and that you've actually spoken to them once or twice during group discussions. You admire how attractively this person is dressed and groomed (not in sweat pants with bed-head, having just stumbled out of bed). You also notice this person is buying juicy, cut-up fresh strawberries in a transparent container. They look really good. This person also looks really good, and has a smile that looks really, really nice, especially because it's directed at you.

According to Bancroft's (2005) model, all four key elements of sexual motivation have to be engaged for you to make a move. You definitely feel a general sense of *physiological arousal*, which might include a sort of tingly feeling, heart beating fast, and butterflies in your stomach. You also experience an *information processing* blitz. Your brain is processing all kinds of enticing cues that you see in this person's eyes and body language. These informational cues can spark a *genital response*, and you may feel sexually aroused. However, before you blurt out the witty comment that just popped into your mind about those "nice looking strawberries," you think about whether it will provide you with a reward (like the person asking you to come over for a meal), or whether this person will think you're a jerk. The *incentive motivation* element has kicked in. Bancroft would argue that without the incentive motivation element—without the expectation that you will get a reward— you will likely just pick up your grocery bag and walk out of the store. Bancroft's ideas illuminate a little bit about how the individuals in the center of the bioecological model might process information and decide to engage in intimate relations with others. If the grocery store meeting ended up leading to a romantic encounter and sexual intimacy, each person's biochemistry would be triggered into action. Let's learn a little bit more about how that physiology works, and then we can put it together with the other systems of the bioecological model.

SEX ORGANS: THE WAY THEY WORK AND HOW THINGS GO AWRY

Many people take physical sexual function for granted. They think we're born with the equipment and when we reach puberty, we develop the urges that successfully lead us to sexual relationships with other people. Even though we know that sexual function is very complex and is more than just a physical event, physiology does play a crucial role in the process. Let's examine women and men's sexual functioning because sexuality is a large part of marriages and intimate partnerships. Sexual satisfaction is an important correlate to relationship satisfaction. It's also necessary that individuals understand how their bodies work so that they can strive to enhance their own and their partners' sexual satisfaction and health.

Women's sexual organs

Women's sex organs are comprised of the entire **vulva**, the external pelvic structures, and several internal areas. The vulva contains tissues that can all play a role in sexual responses, including the external **labia majora**, internal **labia minora**, **urethra**, **vagina**, and **clitoris**, which can be seen in Figures 4.3 and 4.4. Other areas that may be stimulated to give a woman sexual pleasure are the mouth, breasts, perineum, and anus.

There is much variation regarding the organs women prefer to be sexually stimulated. In fact, virtually any part of the body can be an **erogenous zone**, a place on the body that generates sexual arousal when it is kissed, rubbed, or otherwise stimulated. But because every partner is different and has diverse sexual desires, it can be challenging in the initial stages of relationships to learn about and honor these differences.

Internal female organs include the ovaries, fallopian tubes, uterus, and cervix, which can be seen in Figure 4.3. A woman is born with all the eggs in her ovaries that she will ever have in her life.

FIGURE 4.3 Female internal sex organs.

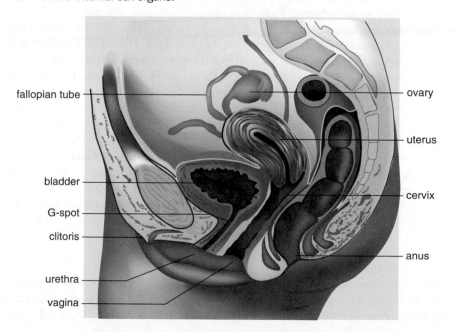

- fallopian tube
- bladder
- G-spot
- clitoris
- urethra
- vagina
- ovary
- uterus
- cervix
- anus

Vulva
The entire external female genital area.

Labia majora
The external folds of skin, or "lips" of the vagina.

Labia minora
The internal folds of skin, or "lips" of the vagina.

Urethra
The opening through which urine passes. In women it is situated above the vagina and may be stimulated during sexual activity.

Vagina
A canal leading from the uterus to the external genitalia; a female sexual organ.

Clitoris
A hard bulb of nerve tissue that responds sensitively to sexual stimulation and assists in the female orgasmic response; located above the vagina and protected by a hood of tissue; includes a base with a shaft that continues into the body.

Erogenous zones
Areas of the body that are sensitive to stimulation and increase sexual arousal.

FIGURE 4.4 Female external genitalia.

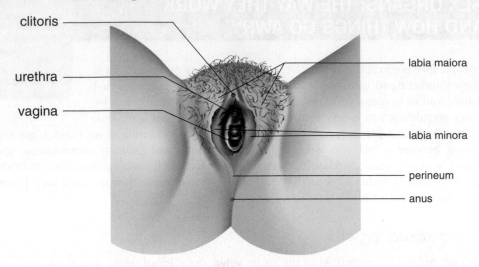

clitoris

urethra

vagina

labia maiora

labia minora

perineum

anus

Ovum
A female germ cell
("egg").

Sperm
A male germ cell.

After she reaches sexual maturity, one ovary each month (they take turns) releases an **ovum**, or egg, into the fallopian tube, during a period called ovulation. The egg usually has about 24 hours during which it is receptive to becoming fertilized by a man's **sperm**. Women's sexual desire often increases around ovulation time to increase the egg's chance of being fertilized through sexual intercourse. If the egg is not fertilized, it will continue to travel down the fallopian tubes, to be washed out of the uterus, cervix, and vagina, along with the uterine lining which is shed each month during a woman's menstrual period. If the egg is fertilized, it will implant in the uterus, and the menstrual period will usually cease during pregnancy and the first couple of months after childbirth. For more information on female genitalia, see Figures 4.3 and 4.4.

Hormones

Beyond their use in reproduction, many of these physiological structures are also involved in sexual desire and the female sexual response cycle. In addition, hormones like estrogen play a role in a woman's sexual response. Estrogen levels change throughout the menstrual cycle, peak at the time of ovulation, and cause vaginal lubrication to increase for better sexual function. In addition to female sexual desire, masturbation frequency and sexual initiation often increase during ovulation and can fluctuate regularly throughout the menstrual cycle (Wallen, 2001). Testosterone levels in women also fluctuate regularly each month and double during puberty (Bancroft, 2005).

Medications and changes that affect women's hormonal processes also affect their sexual responses. Oral contraceptive pills prevent ovulation, which then lowers testosterone levels, and sometimes have the undesirable side effect of reducing the female sex drive. During menopause or after a hysterectomy, testosterone levels also decrease, which partially explains the decline some women find in sexual desire after menopause. If sexual desire is low because of low hormone levels, testosterone supplementation in women (available in a cream) can increase sexual desire. However, women's sexual response cycles vary widely and are influenced by mood, energy level, self-esteem, and general health, so using hormonal supplements is not always the answer to low sex drive (Bancroft, 2005).

Women's sexual response

When women (and men) feel sexually aroused, there tends to be a common cycle of physiology. There is very little research on lesbian or gay male sexual relationships so most of this discussion necessarily focuses on heterosexual sex. Early sex researchers Masters and Johnson (1966) proposed a **four-stage sexual response cycle** common in most people: *excitement, plateau, orgasm*, and *resolution*.

While what each woman finds exciting or sexually arousing differs, biology of the *excitement* phase is pretty similar across women. Most women require a relaxed atmosphere and much foreplay before they can become fully aroused. They usually require stimulation of the clitoris to become excited. The glans, or hard little bulb, at the end of clitoris has the greatest density of nerve endings in the human body. This little organ is extremely sensitive, and its only purpose is to provide sexual pleasure for women. It resembles a small penis in that it has a sensitive rounded glans at the tip and a shaft, which continues inside the woman's body and stiffens during arousal and orgasm.

As women become aroused, their pelvic organs become engorged with blood and swollen. When the vagina becomes engorged, droplets of fluid begin to seep out of the vaginal lining during a process called **transudation** (Berman et al., 2001). In transudation, the lining of the vagina (made up of mucosa tissue very similar to that inside your mouth) becomes lubricated to allow for easier insertion of the penis. This lubrication keeps the vagina moist and creates a chemical balance that keeps bacteria out. As she reaches a state of full arousal, a woman then enters the *plateau* phase. As the woman reaches plateau, her breathing becomes quicker, her pupils dilate, her vaginal tissues continue to swell, her vaginal opening tightens, and she may reach *orgasm*. After orgasm, her body begins to relax and return to normal during the *resolution* phase.

Female orgasms

If a woman reaches orgasm, she will experience rhythmic contractions of the uterus and vagina, forcing the engorged blood back out of the pelvic tissues, leading to *resolution*. There are different types of orgasms, although the research is not definitive regarding how they differ or exactly what physiological processes differentiate them. **Clitoral orgasms**, which occur through stimulation of the clitoris, are described by women as quicker and more intense. **Pelvic floor orgasms** are felt deeper and seem to radiate throughout the body. Pelvic floor orgasms occur by stimulation of the vaginal wall in combination with clitoral stimulation.

Recent research has confirmed what Dr. Ernst Grafenberg in 1950 suspected, that women do have an area within the vagina that can aid in orgasm. Named after Dr. Grafenberg, the G-spot is a mound of spongy tissue inside the vagina, just below the urethral opening. When stimulated (most women find that fingers inserted and then stroking the upper front vaginal wall with a "come here" motion aid in arousal), this tissue swells into a hard lump, and further stimulation can lead to intense orgasms, especially when combined with clitoral or other stimulation (Mah & Binik, 2001). However, without some experimentation, this spot can be difficult to find. Scientists were not completely sure of its existence until the 1980s (Berman et al., 2001; Ladas, Whipple, & Perry, 2005). Some women can also have orgasms when they experience deep thrusting by their partner against the cervix. Other women find this extremely painful. Scholars now tend to agree that there is a hierarchy of organs involved in female orgasm, from most to least sensitive to stimulation. The clitoris is the most sensitive, then the G-spot, the urethral area (from where urine is discharged), and finally the vagina. Unlike what some male partners believe, it's actually pretty difficult for most women to reach orgasm through penises simply being thrust into the vagina. Most women require stimulation of the clitoris before they can reach orgasm.

Women's sexuality has been a topic of scholarly interest since Sigmund Freud first wrote about female sexual frustration in the nineteenth century. We can give Freud credit for being one of the first male scholars to legitimize the study of female gender and sex issues, but his early ideas have not been supported by contemporary research. For example, as regards the female orgasm, Freud argued that "vaginal orgasms" were more mature or somehow better than clitoral orgasms, but these ideas have been thoroughly discredited. Many women find they cannot reach orgasm without clitoral stimulation. In fact, 38% percent of women have never had an orgasm at all during intercourse (Berman et al., 2001).

Four stage sexual response cycle
Masters and Johnson's (1966) discovery that most people go through consistent stages of sexual response: excitement, plateau, orgasm, and resolution.

Transudation
A physiological process during female sexual arousal in which vaginal tissues swell with blood and fluid droplets seep out of the vaginal lining to aid in lubrication.

Clitoral orgasms
Female orgasms that are thought to originate from clitoral stimulation.

Pelvic floor orgasms
Female orgasms that are thought to originate from the G-spot inside the vagina being stimulated in conjunction with the clitoris.

Many women are not familiar enough with the female sexual response cycle to know how to induce orgasm in themselves, and therefore have trouble reaching orgasm during sex with other people. Women often report that it is easier to reach orgasm through oral or digital stimulation. Moreover, some women "fake" orgasms when having sex with men because they fear disappointing their partner or making him feel bad about his performance. Do you think that this means lesbian women might have more orgasms than heterosexual women?

While men are more consistently orgasmic than women, still only 75% of men have orgasms with every sexual encounter. In contrast, 29% of women have orgasms with every sexual encounter. There are individual differences in rates of orgasm as well. We see higher rates of orgasm in older adults compared to young adults, more educated people (who presumably understand more about how the body works), African Americans versus whites and Hispanics, and religious liberals versus conservatives (Mah & Binik, 2001). Women tend to be more orgasmic when they initiate sexual encounters, are aware of female anatomy and physiology, masturbate more often, fantasize during sex, and feel less guilt about sexual experiences (Mah & Binik, 2001). Bisexual and lesbian women report that their orgasms are more intense than heterosexual women report theirs are, perhaps relating to their greater attunement to female anatomy.

Biopsychosocial model of orgasm Mah and Binik's (2001) model which states that orgasms include a sensory, evaluative (cognitive), and affective (emotional) component.

Although scientists are not quite sure what exactly is happening during orgasm and the research is ongoing, some commonalities are reported. First, orgasm seems to induce a state of altered consciousness, with an instantaneous lack of sensation followed by an explosion of sexual pleasure radiating throughout the pelvic region. Most people report warmth and tension throughout the body (Mah & Binik, 2001). Whipple, Ogden, and Komisaruk (1992) found no differences in heart rate, pupil dilation, or blood pressure in lab experiments where women reached orgasm through genital stimulation verses mental imagery. Thus, women can achieve orgasm with their thoughts, and many achieve orgasms during erotic dreaming. In fact, 30% of women report having night-time orgasms during sleep without any bodily stimulation (Whipple et al., 1992). Also, patients with spinal cord injuries can achieve the subjective feeling of orgasm despite having no bodily sensations. Based on this cumulative evidence, Mah and Binik (2001) advocate for a **biopsychosocial model of orgasm**, which has three key elements: *sensory* (stimulation of the body), *evaluative* (stimulation of the mind), and *affective* (stimulation of the emotions), a characterization that fits nicely with the complex and multifaceted bioecological perspective. People may think that sexual activity and orgasms come naturally, but like all complex behaviors, sexuality can take many forms, from healthy and happy to painful and problematic.

Women's sexual problems

Sexual problems are not unusual, but because a large proportion of the general population lacks knowledge about the normal sexual response cycle, they may not recognize that their troubles during sexual intimacy have names and can be treated. Some women experience troublesome sexual dysfunctions, which include:

FIGURE 4.5 Based on the information you read about female sexuality, what sexual advantages and disadvantages might lesbian couples have?
Photo © Imageshop/Corbis.

1 *arousal problems* (the lack of lubrication, tissue engorgement, or sensation)

2 *inorgasmia* (the inability to reach orgasm or having smaller, less satisfying orgasms)

3 *dyspareunia* (pain during intercourse)

4 *vaginismus* (involuntary vaginal spasms that prevent insertion)

5 *low sexual desire* (a level of sex drive that is unsatisfactory).

For both men and women, sexual dysfunctions can be characterized by being lifelong or acquired, generalized or situation-specific, organic (biological), psychogenic (stress or relationship-related) or mixed organic/psychogenic (Berman et al., 2001). Sexual dysfunctions in anyone can be related to medical or social conditions.

All of the following can affect the development, maintenance, or worsening of sexual problems: blood circulation deficits, heart disease, high blood pressure, elevated cholesterol (which can diminish blood flow to the pelvic area), hormonal imbalances, stress, and depression. Diabetes, endometriosis, and fibroid tumors can also lead to sexual problems. People with diabetes can develop neuropathy (nerve damage), numbing parts of the body and leading to poor sexual function. Women with endometriosis, a condition in which endometrial tissues from the uterus grow in other pelvic regions and make the tissues swell, often have painful and irregular menstruation, as well as pain during intercourse. The endometrial cells swell and often tear and bleed, leading to scar tissue that may also cause infertility. Many women suffer from fibroid tumors, benign growths of uterine muscle tissue that must be periodically removed. All of these conditions can be related to loss of sexual desire or painful intercourse, as well as body image and self-esteem concerns.

In addition to biological conditions, some behavioral and environmental factors can also affect sexual quality. Some examples include: medications taken for high blood pressure or depression, smoking, relationship struggles, surgery, and trauma. Also, long-term or intensely athletic bicycle riding can lead to clitoral numbness and can damage genital nerves in both men and women. Sometimes women taking oral contraceptive pills can experience a drop in sexual desire and delay in orgasm or complete inorgasmia (Graham, Bancroft, Doll, Greco, & Tanner, 2007). Drug and alcohol abuse or addiction also play a role in sexual dysfunctions, for both men and women. Moreover, survivors of child sexual abuse often experience sexual dysfunctions ranging from sexual withdrawal and avoidance to orgasm problems and excessive promiscuity (Loeb et al., 2002).

Ultimately, much of female lack of desire and sexual dysfunction is stress-related, especially for women who work and care for children and elderly parents. Role strain is a primary complaint of women whose partners feel neglected in the bedroom.

This section has explored many biological, individual, and social factors that affect female sexuality. Women bring these conditions, experiences, and behaviors into their romantic relationships, marriages, and families. Thus, even though sexuality is part of each individual's development, it can play a role in the health and happiness of relationships and family systems. Men's sexualities are just as complex and worth looking at through a bioecological lens.

Men's sex organs

The male genitals are comprised of the penis, scrotum, and testes. The testes are two spongy balls hanging outside the body, inside a protective scrotal sack. The scrotal sack is an extension of the abdomen; the testes must be external to the body in order to prevent them from overheating and killing sperm. The testes manufacture sperm and hormones called androgens, particularly testosterone. They are lined with extremely tiny coiled tubes called **seminiferous tubules** through which new sperm travel each day. The sperm travel to the **epididymis** where they mature. They then move through the **vas deferens** during ejaculation. The **prostate gland**, a walnut-sized gland lying directly between the anus and the base of the penis, manufactures seminal fluid which protects the sperm and delivers it during ejaculation. Sperm are delivered in a bath of seminal fluid, discharged

Arousal problems
Sexual dysfunctions wherein women may have deficient lubrication, and men or women may experience a lack of tissue engorgement or sensation.

Inorgasmia
The inability to have an orgasm, or having unsatisfactory orgasms.

Dyspareunia
Pain during intercourse.

Vaginismus
Involuntary vaginal spasms which prevent intercourse.

Low sexual desire
A sexual dysfunction where men or women have little interest in sex.

Seminiferous tubules
Located in the testes, these tubes aid in creating sperm cells and helping them travel during ejaculation.

Epididymis
A narrow, tightly coiled tube connecting the rear of the testicle to its vas deferens; sperm mature here so they are able to travel during ejaculation.

Vas deferens
Tubes that transport sperm from the epididymis in anticipation of ejaculation; contractions in these organs propel sperm forward.

Prostate gland
A walnut-sized gland at the base of the penis, that manufactures seminal fluid and delivers it during ejaculation.

through the urethra and out the glans of the penis during ejaculation. Like the clitoris, the glans of the penis is rich with dense nerve endings, making it extremely sensitive to stimulation. You can see these features of the male genitals in Figures 4.6 and 4.7.

Men's sexual response

In addition to the genitals, other organs that can be related to sexual pleasure and arousal in men are the mouth, breasts, perineum, anus, and other erogenous zones similar to those of women. As a man is stimulated, his body experiences physiological reactions very similar to those in women. Most men follow the same sexual response cycle discussed above, with *excitement*, *plateau*, *orgasm*, and *resolution* phases. For example, during the excitement phase, his breathing quickens, his pupils dilate, and his penile tissues become engorged with blood. The spongy tissue in the penis fills with blood and the penis becomes erect, allowing insertion into his partner. When he reaches orgasm, seminal fluid containing sperm cells is expelled through the glans at the end of the penis, in a process called ejaculation.

Prostate orgasm
A male orgasm which originates through stimulation of the prostate gland.

Unique to men is the **prostate orgasm**. This gland can be tricky to locate, similar to the female G-spot, and finding it requires some experimentation. It can only be reached through the anus, which some men are uncomfortable trying. The anal tissues are extremely thin and easily torn. They also don't carry the bacteria-fighting lubricants that vaginas have. The prostate gland can be stimulated most easily during digital penetration with a "come here" motion with the fingers, similar to that described for stimulating the female G-spot. Many men report that the prostate orgasm is much deeper and radiates throughout the body more than a typical penile orgasm.

Similar to women, men may experience a host of sexual problems that cause distress during sexual intimacy with their partners.

FIGURE 4.6 Male internal sex organs.

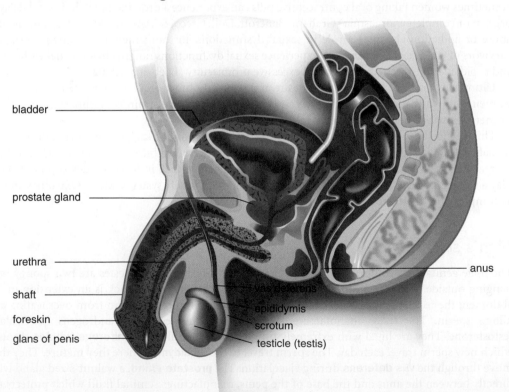

bladder

prostate gland

urethra

shaft

foreskin

glans of penis

anus

vas deferens

epididymis

scrotum

testicle (testis)

Men's sexual problems

Men experience many of the same sexual dysfunctions as women, including low sexual desire and inorgasmia. Testosterone decreases with age, which can affect sex drive, as can anti-depressants, stress, relationship problems, and medical conditions.

Men can also suffer from **erectile dysfunction** (ED), in which the penis does not become or remain erect. Men who suffer from ED can still produce sperm, have orgasms, and ejaculate. Their ED can be treated with sildenafil (trade name Viagra). Ninety percent of ED has physiological, rather than psychological, roots. Periodically throughout their lives, most men have trouble getting or keeping an erection. This is a normal variation in sexual function and does not indicate a disorder. In fact, by age 65, 25% of men have ED. Alcohol and drugs can worsen the problem. ED can be an important influence on the quality of marriages later in life. Couples often have to find new ways to find sexual fulfillment instead of intercourse. They may have to deal with feelings of failure, lack of intimacy, or self or partner-blame (Berman et al., 2001).

Men who have had surgery for prostate cancer often lose their nerve function and suffer from ED. Sixty percent of men having traditional prostate surgery become impotent. However, newer, nerve-sparing surgeries have reduced the incidence of this side effect. Men who go through prostate surgery can still ejaculate, although no fluid comes out; it often backs up into the bladder. After prostrate surgery, it is often recommended that men have sex standing up to prevent veins from leaking (Berman et al., 2001).

Some medications can cause sexual problems for men. For example, medications like beta blockers that lower blood pressure often have unwanted side effects like dizziness, depression, and loss of sexual arousal. Antidepressants can also delay or prohibit orgasm in men.

In contrast to delayed orgasm, many men suffer from **premature ejaculation**, ejaculating immediately upon arousal or sooner than desired. It's not uncommon to find female inorgasmia paired with male premature ejaculation. The male partner may become frustrated and hopeless at the poor quality of the sexual relationship, leading him to give up trying to satisfy his partner in order to satisfy his own need to orgasm sooner (Berman et al., 2001).

The bioecological model can help us understand this cycle. A person's biology, perceptions, microsystem relationships, and cultural views of sexuality can impact sexual function or dysfunction. Sex is one of the most common topics of argument in relationships, and people often have very different sex drives, sexual preferences, and attitudes and beliefs about sex. Macrosystem variables such as discrimination can make sexual fulfillment even more difficult for some groups.

Sexual minorities face even more potential sources of sexual dysfunction than the heterosexual majority. While the sexual problems experienced in gay, bisexual, and transgendered men's relationships are very similar to those described for heterosexual men (ED, premature ejaculation, and delayed orgasm), they can face additional challenges to their sexual health. For example, gay men of color experience racism as well as homophobia, and sometimes are even victims of gay bashing or hate crimes because of what the public thinks about their sexuality, their race, or both. For example, in a study of African American gay and bisexual men, Zamboni & Crawford (2007) found that low self-esteem, male gender role stress, low HIV prevention practices, racial discrimination, and experience of gay bashing all predicted sexual problems in the men's relationships. This held true even when

Erectile dysfunction
The inability of a penis to become erect or maintain erections.

Premature ejaculation
Male ejaculation which occurs directly upon arousal, or earlier than preferred.

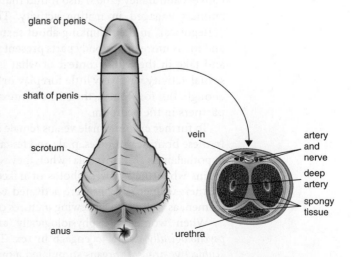

FIGURE 4.7 Male external genitalia. Cross-section shows the spongy tissue which fills with blood during the excitement phase of the sexual response cycle.

controlling for psychiatric symptoms, general life satisfaction, and low social support. Individual variables such as their race, sexual orientation, and HIV status played no direct role in the development of their sexual problems. The variables that predicted sexual problems were all related to sociocultural contexts and their reactions to oppression and judgment in the environment.

Whether gay or straight, black or white, male or female, sexuality can be a source of great pleasure, as well as one of disappointment and confusion. Researchers have been trying to figure out what variables affect male and female sexuality and how men and women's sex drives and attractions might differ.

Men's and women's sexualities in more depth

While male and female sexual arousal works in biologically similar ways, men tend to respond more to visual stimuli than women do. In fact, 72% of pornography consumers are men (Rupp & Wallen, 2008). Women tend to be aroused more by the context or environment surrounding them. Pornography enjoyed by women is usually produced by other women and includes prolonged foreplay episodes set in romantic locales. When women view pornography, they imagine themselves in the scenes. When men view pornography, they focus primarily on the attractiveness of the actors and tend to objectify their body parts, thinking about the specific organs of interest, without considering faces, personalities, or the environment of the acts taking place. When men and women view photos of people masturbating, heterosexual men rate only the female pictures as arousing, while heterosexual women rate both male and female masturbators as equally arousing. Interestingly, homosexual men also rate both genders as equally arousing (Rupp & Wallen, 2008). These are important trends to keep in mind because patterns in sexual arousal play a role in intimate relationships. Marriages and committed partnerships can be more fulfilling when partners understand the way the other thinks and how partners perceive sexual material or situations.

In a study examining how gender and sexual orientation were related to arousal patterns, researchers showed films depicting homosexual or heterosexual sex scenes to heterosexual men, homosexual men, male-to-female transsexuals, and women. Participants' genitals were measured for engorgement and arousal. They were also asked to self-report on their excitement levels (Chivers, Rieger, Latty, & Bailey, 2004). For both measured genital arousal and subjective reports of arousal, all men responded to the films depicting the gender they were attracted to only. They were only aroused by scenes involving the "correct" body parts for their sexual orientation. The women in the same study showed no differences in arousal. They were aroused by *all* films equally. Chivers and Bailey (2005) also found that women become more aroused than men when watching animals engaged in mating activity. These combined findings suggest that men are more "categorical" in their thinking about sexuality. They are selective in the targets of their attraction and focus more on the body parts present in the films. However, women are more *generally* aroused and take in the whole context of what is happening. Men often report being able to engage in sexual activity with very little foreplay or thought about the act. Genital or visual stimulation are enough. But for women, the entire context of her life, her job, family, friends, and self-image are all partners in the bedroom.

To further examine male versus female arousability, researchers conducted PET scans and fMRIs. In these brain scan studies, male and female brains showed activity in the same regions (mainly the hypothalamus and amygdala) when they were sexually aroused. Men only showed activation in their brains when they viewed photos of naked people who were the gender of their preferred sexual partner; women's brains were activated when they viewed photos of both naked men and naked women, as well as when viewing pictures of genitalia alone (Fisher, 2007).

When women are physiologically aroused, however, it does not necessarily mean they *psychologically* desire to engage in sex. They often need to have their cognitive and emotional (*subjective arousal*) organs stimulated along with their genitals. In contrast, men are more ready to engage in sex when simply physiologically aroused (Fisher, 2007). When men and women were interviewed about their sexual arousal, women's reports did not match their brain or genital signs of arousal. Their brain and body are aroused, yet they report lower subjective levels of excitement. Men's reports of arousal match the level of excitement that their genitals and brains show. What do you think can explain these findings? Why are women's physiological and psychological reports of arousal discrepant while men's are consistent?

The female sex drive appears more malleable and flexible than that of males. Sexual desire and functioning can vary widely over a given woman's lifetime, and females respond more to cultural contexts, and even to the temperature of the room, than men do (Baumeister, 2000). Moreover, women's attitudes about sexuality are often not consistent with their behaviors (for example, they may want more sex than they have). On the other hand, men's behaviors and attitudes tend to mesh and their sexual desire and functioning tends to remain fairly constant through the years, though they, too, can experience sexual dysfunction.

Most of the studies described in this section examine regular people in typical relationships. Ordinary folks can have lots of sexual challenges, from lack of desire, to various health and emotional problems that impact the quality of their sex lives and take a toll on their marriages and partnerships. Sometimes, though, sexual variations in desire or arousability can become so extreme that they are classified as disorders. However, we cannot assume that because someone engages in unusual sexual practices, he or she has a disorder.

Sexual diversity vs. disorders

Many people have sexual practices that might be considered different or deviant, such as bondage and discipline practices, a foot fetish, or the desire to be dressed like a baby during sex. However, something is only a *disorder* if a person cannot be sexually satisfied without the behavior being performed, if the behavior is performed non-consensually (as in the case of child molestation), or if the person is experiencing extreme personal or emotional distress over his or her behaviors (*DSM–IV–TR*; American Psychiatric Association, 2000).

More serious problems that can become diagnosable disorders include **sexual aversion disorder**, which is a pathological or phobic avoidance of sex or sex-related material. Because most people have some sexual desire and a need to be intimate with others, an extreme lack of interest in sexuality of any kind is considered atypical and problematic. If it occurs within the context of a marriage, this can lead to unhappiness, guilt, or anger as one partner no longer wants (and is even disgusted by) intimacy with the other person.

There is also a category of disorders related to "deviant" sexual attractions, called **paraphilias**. People diagnosed with paraphilias usually cannot be sexually satisfied or reach orgasm unless the object of their desire is involved. Objects can range from children in the case of *pedophilia*, to *frotteurism*, in which people get sexual pleasure from rubbing up against unsuspecting strangers, to *fetishes* like attraction to rubber, plastic, or chocolate syrup (*DSM–IV–TR*; American Psychiatric Association, 2000).

There is a difference between sexual diversity and deviance. Research on people who engage in unusual sexual practices helps highlight this difference. Sagarin, Cutler, Lawler-Sagarin, and Matuszewich (2009) observed people at several sadomasochism (S & M) and bondage and discipline (B & D) events, which are parties and conferences where people perform various S & M or B & D acts for spectators. One scenario often enacted in these settings is that of "master" and "slave": one partner plays the master and ties up the slave, whips him or her, barks orders, and also massages, kisses, and otherwise sexually stimulates the person playing the slave. Before and during the performances, the researchers examined the participants' cortisol (stress hormone) and testosterone (sex hormone) levels. Before the S & M session began, the people playing slaves had heightened cortisol and testosterone levels. During the session, female slaves' cortisol levels *decreased* and their testosterone levels *increased*, indicating decreased stress and increased sexual desire. Both men and women

Sexual aversion disorder
A diagnosable mental condition wherein people are afraid of or repulsed by sexual behavior.

Paraphilias
Unusual sexual preferences that include objects, behaviors, or other people; paraphilias become diagnosable mental conditions if a person cannot be sexually satisfied without the object or behavior, he or she feels extreme distress over the object or behavior, or the sexual practices interfere with life functioning.

serving as the dominant partner showed increases in testosterone. Women playing the submissive partner in the skits showed an *increase* in testosterone. Men playing the submissive partner showed a *decrease* in testosterone.

When the participants were interviewed after a diverse array of performances, those who reported that their performances went very well also reported increased levels of relationship closeness on a questionnaire. These findings imply that when unusual sexual practices are engaged in consensually, they reflect relationship health and can serve as a way to increase intimacy. We should not assume that engaging in acts that might be considered deviant is destructive. Until 1987, S & M was considered a disorder (*DSM–III–R*; American Psychiatric Association, 1987). But today the diagnostic criteria require that the fantasies or behaviors cause distress or impairment in social, occupational, or other areas of functioning in order for a person to be diagnosed with an S & M paraphilia or other type of paraphilia (*DSM–IV–TR*; American Psychiatric Association, 2000).

Seen through a bioecological lens, it may be less surprising that sexual intimacy issues are so commonly sources of conflict in all types of relationships. Each person has come to the relationship with individualized biopsychosocial experiences, traits, and preferences. Partners have different socialization histories where parents, religious leaders, and cultural forces have shaped them to endorse specific attitudes about sexuality. They have completely different biochemistries and hormonal profiles. They have had diverse experiences (or no experience) with sexual intimacy in the past. If we consider all levels of the bioecological model, it makes sense that when something goes amiss in one or more of these complex systems, sexual problems may arise in committed partnerships. Luckily, a field of psychological practice has emerged to help couples cope with sexual problems, whether they be biological, psychological, or social in nature.

Sex therapy

Positive sexual adjustment or health includes many aspects such as sexual self-esteem, sexual functioning, and sexual arousability (Loeb et al., 2002). Each of these can be enhanced by good general relationship skills, communication, openness, and maturity. A relationship lacking these elements may also experience sexual problems. A good sex therapist can often help with both sex and relationship problems. Sex therapists work with couples or individuals to improve sexual satisfaction and/or performance, but they usually do so within the context of improving relationship skills in general.

Sexual difficulties of any kind may be signals or symptoms of negative or unfulfilling relationship dynamics (Devita-Raeburn, 2006). When communication is poor, couples are uneducated about sexuality, couples are facing stressors, or one partner dominates the other, sexual problems are likely. People often look to their partners to validate them and to heal what is "broken" in their lives. However, these expectations are often unrealistic and lead to unfair demands placed on a partner.

David Schnarch, a marriage and sex therapist, argues that each partner must take responsibility for his or her own feelings. Each person must be able to tolerate that his or her partner has different ideas and that those ideas are valid. To improve a relationship and resolve sexual problems, he suggests that people get over their emotional dependency and start being grownups. This means not expecting a partner to validate your worth or confirm your value. Adults must work hard to value themselves, to learn who they are as individuals, and to open up to their partners with complete honesty. Adults need to recognize that a partner's job is not to soothe their pain from childhood or fill voids in their emotional lives. Schnarch finds that when he helps couples learn these skills and they start becoming completely honest with each other in a spirit of love rather than revenge or a desire to dominate, conflicts decrease. When communication and power issues are addressed, the relationship can open up to more intimate connections and sexuality often improves.

Many people say they are not honest with their partners because they want to avoid conflict. But when two people act like independent adults who accept their own and their partner's failings as part of life, they begin to take responsibility for themselves not only in life but also in the bedroom. One of the intimacy-building exercises sex therapists use is to have couples practice having sex and

FOCUS ON MY FAMILY

Melinda's story

My Irish grandfather was raised by a Native American family on a reservation near where I currently live, after his parents died of tuberculosis. Descendants of theirs have also been fostered by my mother. I'm aware of these connections every day as I perform diverse roles like mom, auntie, daughter, professor, mentor, business woman, counselor, and partner. Although I am a queer, white, rural, monogamous woman, it is my connection to this place around which my identities center.

I moved out of my parents' house when I was 16, and I have had lovers of both sexes since then. I was later married and divorced and bore two sons. I also started a home-based business selling products to enhance sexual experiences, which allowed me the flexibility to continue my education and be the primary caregiver for my sons.

Currently, I am the owner of a lovers' boutique, a business which grew from part-time to a thriving enterprise. After completing my master's degree, I started teaching courses related to sexuality. As I advised students, my frustration with the lack of referral sources for sexual concerns led me to return to school to obtain my doctorate in clinical psychology. Thirty years later, I am now a psychologist with a specialization in sexuality, gender, and relationships, and a lecturer teaching courses on these same topics. Though I love all of what I do, I recommend that my students find a more expeditious path to embarking on their careers. I feel privileged that my livelihood does not depend on fulfilling others' expectations. Practically, this privilege allows me to be "out" about my sexuality and relationship history without fear of losing my job(s).

I have been in a committed, monogamous relationship for seven years. Patrick and I have four sons between us, Jon (24), Samuel (20), Gus (18), and Kinsey (15). Early on Patrick sometimes wondered whether I'd leave him to be with a woman. As he got to know me, the complexities of my identities were easier to understand, and he realized my choices in partners had a lot more to do with character and compatibility than they did with gender. I've frequently been approached by people who assume that because of what I do, I must also be sexually adventurous. I've had to develop quite a repertoire of firm, polite refusals.

My multiple roles also presented challenges for my kids. A school principal minimized my son's experience of being bullied because I was in a relationship with a woman. My other son was embarrassed about my work during middle school. But this became a source of social capital by the time he was in high school. As his peers' interest and awareness of sexuality increased, the family business went from being a source of teasing to one of pride. At work, parenting, or relating, each of these aspects of my life affects the others. It's all just part of the intersections of multiple identities, complexities and connections. It's something we all experience every day, whether we realize it or not.

Melinda with her partner, and Melinda with her sons.
Photo reproduced by permission.

reaching orgasm with their eyes open. Many people find this extremely difficult to do and prefer eyes-closed-lights-off sex. Schnarch argues that adult sex can be extremely intense and satisfying at any age. He suggests that young people may be more easily aroused and have sex more often, but middle-aged people are the most comfortable with their bodies and the most able to reach true intimacy through lights-on, eye-to-eye sex (cited in Devita-Raeburn, 2006).

Other exercises sex therapists may use include education about the sexual response cycle and instruction about how to perform better sexually. They may also help clients by normalizing their feelings or behaviors. For example, they may teach clients that masturbating is normal, not something to be ashamed of. Sex therapists may also teach couples to express openly what their sexual desires and fantasies are, so that couples can work on building a mutually satisfying experience. To learn about the life of another sex therapist, see the nearby *Focus on My Family* box.

Physiological aspects of sex therapy

Treating most sexual problems begins with a full medical examination of both parties in order to rule out the effects of medications, hormones, surgery, blood pressure issues, obesity, smoking, and so on. People who are obese, who smoke, and who are otherwise unhealthy are much more likely to have sexual problems; and those problems can improve with lifestyle changes.

The key to all sex therapy is education. People are taught about the male and female body, how orgasms work, and what realistic expectations might be for sexual activity for their age, health status, and so on. For example, if one member of a couple is an older man with ED, especially if sildenafil (Viagra) has been ineffective, a sex therapist might teach the couple to forget about erections and use a technique called very erotic non-insertive sex (VENIS) (Berman et al., 2001). This technique involves erotic massage, kissing, foreplay, oral sex, and intimacy skills. Many couples find that taking the focus away from erections and intercourse allows a new level of intimacy and sexual communication, and sometimes even better orgasms. This is a non-goal-oriented sex, however, where orgasm is not necessarily the focus. The first few weeks or months of therapy may even involve an intentional avoidance of orgasm in order to build intimacy. Foreplay in this technique is considered an end in itself.

Female low sexual desire can often be treated with testosterone cream—a medical intervention—to increase sex drive and the probability of orgasm. However, if the woman is a young mother of small children who works full time and feels overwhelmed, testosterone cream isn't going to help. This woman may be understandably uninterested in sex. Behavioral interventions might include providing her with emotional support, a night away from the children, a massage from her partner, and other stress relievers. Many times sexual frustrations are merely indicative of larger stresses.

In other cases, sexual problems may be isolated and sex-focused behavioral treatments might do the trick. For example, if a couple struggles with premature ejaculation, a sex therapist might teach them the "squeeze" technique in which either the man or his partner squeezes the end of the penis, just below the coronal ridge, to slow the urge to ejaculate. Another technique for treating premature ejaculation is the "start–stop" method. In this method, the couple may practice either intercourse or fellatio and stop intermittently as the man feels the urge to ejaculate. When the urge passes, they start again. After practicing this for several weeks or months, most men find they can learn how to delay ejaculation.

A medical intervention might also include the use of an anti-depressant like Zoloft, which usually has the side effect of lowering sex drive. In the case of premature ejaculation, Zoloft does not dull the sensation of orgasm, but prolongs the excitement phase before orgasm. Men with premature ejaculation should not take Viagra because it forces blood into the penis and may make matters worse.

Healthy relationship and sexual skills are important to develop for all people. A sexually satisfying marriage or committed partnership allows people to feel connected to their partners and increases self-esteem in the individuals. What can you do to become sexually healthy? Read the *Building Your Strengths* box for information.

Because most of the research on healthy sexual functioning and sexual problems has been conducted on heterosexual couples, we do not know very much about other types of sexual relationships. However, it's important to examine diversity in sexual orientations and to establish clearly how heterosexual experiences are both similar to and different from the experiences of other types of couples.

BUILDING YOUR STRENGTHS

Improving sexual satisfaction

To work on some improvements in your own sex life, try the following ideas:

- Learn as much as you can about your own body, especially regarding anatomy and physiology. This may involve reading books, watching instructional videos, and taking a good look at your genitals in a mirror.

- Practice masturbating to orgasm so that you know what arouses you, then teach these techniques to your partner.

- Work on loving your body, whatever its shape or size; recognize that your body is beautiful and sacred and that no one has the right to touch it without your permission.

- Work on connecting with partners who value you as an individual; when communication, respect, and caring are high, so is sexual satisfaction.

- Ask your partner what he or she likes and doesn't like; open lines of communication make everyone's body happy.

- Always engage in safer sex practices, using both condoms and other forms of contraceptives (such as, pills or patches) as a backup, to prevent pregnancy, STIs, and AIDS. Use condoms during oral sex on male partners and dental dams during oral sex with female partners.

- Never force sex on someone or even slightly coerce them to have sex, especially if either of you has been drinking or is under the influence of drugs. Hearing "no," means you need to stop immediately.

Note: *Building Your Strengths* boxes are not meant to diagnose, treat, or cure any personal or family problems; they are for informational purposes only, and are meant to spur discussion.

SEXUAL ORIENTATION

Biological research on homosexuality

Social and contextual issues and homosexuality

There are wide variations in the experience of sexuality. What turns one person on is a complete and utter turn-off for the next person. What attracts people sexually varies both between and within cultures all over the world. I use the term *sexualities* in this chapter because scholars no longer endorse binary categorizations of sexuality. People are not just gay or straight. As discussed in Chapter 3 on gender, sexual orientation occurs on a continuum. Other sexualities beyond heterosexuality are no longer considered abnormal or deviant by scientists or by much of the lay public. Homosexuality was once considered a diagnosable disorder until it was removed from the diagnostic classification system in 1973 (*DSM–IV–TR*; American Psychiatric Association, 2000).

Queer Theory provides a critique of *heteronormativity*, the privileging of heterosexual experiences over the experiences of other people. Queer Theory questions the simplistic binary view of one type of sexuality being normal and another type being deviant (Riggs, 2007). Heteronormative beliefs include ideas that other sexual orientations are wrong, abnormal, or "queer." Gay men and lesbians have often been called "queer" as a derogatory term in previous generations, but the term "queer" has been taken back by sexual minority communities to turn the previous insult into a source of pride. Queer Theory asks us to question our assumptions about sexuality and think inclusively about all of the sexualities available to and practiced by the human species. Just as Feminist Theory places women

Queer Theory
A theory that was developed to counterbalance the traditional theories of gender and sexuality which privileged heteronormativity and traditional gender roles. Queer Theory seeks to bring marginalized groups to the forefront of scientific study and to recognize the intersectional identities of all people being studied.

in the center of research questions and the design of studies, Queer Theory shifts the center of attention away from heterosexuals and toward sexual minority viewpoints. Some of the most interesting research examines possible influences on the development of a primarily homosexual versus heterosexual orientation.

Biological research on homosexuality

Homosexuality, characterized by same-sex mounting or copulating behaviors (not necessarily by the cognitive "desire" humans have), has been found to occur in many mammalian species. For example, 8% of rams (male sheep) mount other males (Roselli & Stormshak, 2009). As discussed in Chapter 3, many areas of the brain differ in males and females—they are sexually dimorphic. One sexually dimorphic area in sheep is the preoptic anterior hypothalamus, which is naturally larger in male rams. The preoptic anterior hypothalamus has been found to be smaller in "gay" rams as well as in ewes (female sheep). In experimental studies, prenatal ewes were exposed to testosterone, and when they were born, their brains resembled ram (male) brains, indicating the importance of hormones for brain differentiation (Roselli & Stormshak, 2009).

Studies on rats and ferrets have also shown that the sexually dimorphic nucleus of the preoptic anterior hypothalamus is related to sexual orientation in adult animals. These studies provide strong evidence that what makes people gay, straight, or somewhere in between resides in the brain, the development of which is driven by genes and hormones.

Genes

While researchers have not discovered the precise mechanisms underlying the development of sexual orientation, many correlational findings provide clues for how we may develop our sexual preferences. This research is on the cutting edge of science. There are no indisputable facts at this point, and some of the findings are contradictory. So far, three genetic markers have been discovered that may play a role in sexual orientation, two for the neurotransmitter dopamine and one for the neurotransmitter serotonin (Halpern, Kaesle, Guo, & Hallfors, 2007). These neurotransmitters have also been implicated in sexual risk-taking and early pubertal development. Dopamine is related to attraction to novelty and sensation seeking, including activity level, arousal, and attraction to pleasure. Other research shows that gay men are more sexually active and adventurous than both straight men and lesbian women. For example, gay men average about 44 lifetime partners while lesbians average about 20 lifetime partners (Hyde, 2007b). Of people in long-term committed relationships, 79% of gay men, but only 19% of gay women, had sexual relationships with others outside of their primary relationship. In contrast, 11% of heterosexual men and 9% of heterosexual women have sexual relationships outside of their partnership (Hyde, 2007b). These results suggest that dopamine activity may differ in homosexual males compared to heterosexual males.

Hamer (2002) examined a dopamine gene that varies in form between different people (called a genetic polymorphism) to explore its possible influence on sexual orientation. This gene, which affects dopamanine activation, is called DRD4. DRD4 can come in either a long form or a short form. Hamer found that if heterosexual men had the *long* form of DRD4, they were more likely to have sex with other *men* than heterosexual men with the short form. Compared to men with the short version, gay men with the long form had sex with five times as many *women* and had sex with more men. People with the long form of DRD4 were more sexually active and less inhibited, having sexual relations with both more men and more women, regardless of the sexual orientation they told researchers they identified with. So even though men identified as heterosexual or gay, they still had more sex overall with both men and women if they had the long form of this dopamine gene polymorphism.

If dopamine is related to increases in behaviors related to sexual appetite, serotonin does the opposite: it is an inhibitory neurochemical and helps us control our impulses, so we would expect future research to find lower levels of serotonin activity in people with less sexual activity. Neurotransmitter interactions are extremely complex and their combined effects on human behavior are only beginning to be understood. Keep in mind that genes always work in complex interaction with each other and with environments. Many other genes, neurotransmitters, and environmental factors influence sexual behaviors. The bioecological approach argues that, in order to understand sexual behaviors, we have to think about what influences people from the micro level of genes and neurotransmitters all the way out to the macro influences of culture. What is fascinating about sexual orientation, however, is that the environment seems to have little effect on determining one's *orientation*, despite its effects on one's sexual *behaviors*.

Chromosomes

Several studies have implicated X chromosome inheritance in the development of male homosexuality. Evolutionary Theory provides one possible explanation of how this might work. If organisms are meant to reproduce in order to maintain their species' survival, homosexuality doesn't make much sense since gays and lesbians cannot have biological children with their partners. This is often referred to as the *Darwinian paradox*, meaning that if Darwin's theory of natural selection is correct, the genes selecting for homosexuality should have been wiped out because gay people do not reproduce. The genes related to heterosexuality should continue to appear in the human genome as they help us to create offspring. However, modern researchers have found some interesting patterns in the gene pool that may explain the continuation of homosexuality in the species.

Researchers have discovered what they call **sexual antagonistic selection** (Iemmola & Camperio-Ciani, 2009). Sexual antagonistic selection means that in families with homosexual males, females in the family tree have been found to have elevated fertility levels. These women have 33% more offspring than women in families without gay male family members. Women in the maternal (but not paternal) lines of gay men are more fertile than women in the maternal lines of heterosexual men. Thus, the families of homosexual men are significantly larger than the families of heterosexual men, resulting in more aunts, uncles, and cousins in their mothers' families. The X chromosome must be at work in these findings because if the characteristic is passed to female offspring, they tend to be more fertile, while if it is passed to male offspring, they tend to be homosexual. Camperio-Ciani, Cermelli, and Zanzotto (2008) argue that homosexuality is X chromosome linked and that a specific gene allele increases sexual activity toward men in both women and men, explaining both higher female fertility rates and male homosexuality in families carrying this allele.

This X chromosome link has been replicated in several studies on men with European backgrounds and on Samoans (Vasey & VanderLaan, 2007). However, the link has not been consistently found in African American families (Rahman et al., 2008). Interestingly, homosexuality is also more common in brothers of homosexuals (Bailey & Pillard, 1991), especially in the maternal line (versus in the father's

> **Sexual antagonistic selection**
> A term used by evolutionary theorists to indicate that homosexuality has not been weeded out of the gene pool over the eons of human evolution because females in families of gay males have higher than average fertility rates.

FIGURE 4.8 What do you think made this couple heterosexual?
Photo © Jon Feingersh/Blend Images/Corbis.

family) (Hamer, Hu, Magnuson, Hu, & Pattattucci, 1993). In addition, gay men are more likely to have older brothers than straight men are.

Social and contextual issues and homosexuality

While these biological findings are quite interesting, they have not answered the question "What causes sexual orientation?" While most scholars believe that sexual orientation is caused by biological mechanisms, we also know that social forces affect sexual behavior. For example, 75% of white women masturbate compared to 34% of African American women and 60% of Latinas (Hyde, 2007b). What can explain these differences in sexual behavior? Genes? Neurotransmitters? All of these women have the same chromosomal pattern (XX). Therefore, it's very important to consider societal views of sexuality and how the intersections of race, class, and gender affect people's experience of sexuality. For example, lesbian women of color experience triple oppression, being negatively judged, discriminated against and oppressed for their gender, sexual orientation, and ethnic backgrounds at the same time (Hyde, 2007a). While a white middle-class lesbian woman may experience marginalization due to her gender and her sexual orientation, she also receives privileges in our society for being white and middle class.

Identity categories carry with them political meaning (Clarke & Peel, 2007; Riggs, 2007). We must re-examine our tendencies toward heteronormativity and realize that it occurs within the context of a "racialized, classed, and gendered hierarchy" (Riggs, 2007, p. 44). Even within the queer community, there are tensions between groups with various identities. Typically white middle-class gay men have held the power in the gay rights movement and their experiences have been held up as the "typical" or "normal" gay lifestyle. By ignoring ethnicity and class issues, white middle-class gay men's experiences are privileged.

This race privilege is even found in surprising places. For example, gay male pornographic movies often focus on white men's desire for men of color and they objectify men of color, using them as "props" to satiate the white man's desire (Riggs, 2007). This is very similar to how women have been

FIGURE 4.9 In the twenty-first century, more families are openly discussing sexual orientation issues but we still live in a largely homophobic society.
Source: www.CartoonStock.com.

"*Mum, Dad, I've got something to tell you.*
I'm a homophobic."

historically portrayed in mainstream movies, as sexual objects without identities or desires of their own. It should be fairly obvious now that current research and theorizing on sexual issues is complex and is moving away from traditional and stereotypical behaviors and orientations being privileged over others. Sexual minorities still do not have equal rights and recognition, but western macrosystems are moving more in that direction.

These findings bring up interesting points for us to consider when our family members come out as gay, lesbian, or bisexual. Families often struggle with feelings of shame, fear, or confusion when family members are sexual minorities. Parents may fear never having grandchildren. Grandparents may view certain behaviors as immoral or wrong. Younger siblings may fear that they, too, will become gay. Because lesbian, gay, bisexual, and **transgender** (LGBT) people are still not accepted in many parts of society, families often struggle with how to incorporate a gay family member. Do you think it would make it easier for families if they knew sexual orientation was in large part biologically influenced, or would it be more difficult for them to accept if that were the case?

Transgender
A person whose gender identity does not match his or her biological sex.

In 2010, gay marriage rights, bullying and suicide in gay teens, and the repeal of the military's "Don't Ask, Don't Tell" policy were major news headlines. Families all over the country and the world are talking about issues surrounding diverse sexualities. More and more people are openly discussing the impact of sexual orientation on their families and LGBT people are working for equal rights to marry and raise their children. In addition to these trends regarding sexual orientation, there are other trends regarding sexuality that appear in worldwide news headlines. Let's take a look at a few of them.

A CLOSER LOOK AT CURRENT ISSUES IN SEXUALITY

- Female genital mutilation
- AIDS and trends in youth sexualities
- Abstinence education, virginity pledges, and family relationships
- Sexual abuse and sexualized violence

This section will examine some issues that spur much controversy in the media and in the general population: female genital mutilation, AIDS, abstinence education, and sexualized violence. These are examples of how influences from each of the bioecological systems can affect and be affected by human sexualities.

Female genital mutilation

It's difficult for people from western industrialized nations to imagine women being forced to have their organs of sexual pleasure disabled or removed. As previously discussed, however, even in the U.S. decades ago, women's clitorises were removed to prevent them from being "neurotic" or "hysterical." Their sexuality was ignored or denigrated. In many places around the world, the sexual double standard is even more extreme than in the U.S. A key example is the contemporary practice of female genital mutilation (FGM), which occurs in many countries in the Middle East and Africa. There is evidence that ancient Egyptians and Romans may have practiced FGM (United Nations Population Fund, 2009). In one contemporary example, FGM is virtually universally experienced by the women of Guinea, regardless of social class, religion, or ethnicity. Cultural leaders justify the practice by saying it enhances a woman's chances of marriageability, it prevents premarital sex ("protecting virginity"), and it controls the age of onset of sex (Van Rossem & Gage, 2009). The rationale is that if a woman cannot experience orgasm or sexual pleasure, she will remain a virgin until married. The more extreme versions of FGM are the modern version of the medieval chastity belt, keeping the vagina inaccessible except to a woman's husband.

Clitoridectomy
A method of female genital mutilation where the glans and oftentimes the clitoral shaft are removed to keep a woman from feeling sexual pleasure.

Infibulation
A method of female genital mutilation where the entire external female genitalia are removed and the vaginal opening may be sewn shut, in order to ensure virginity at marriage and no sexual pleasure for the woman.

The World Health Organization (2000) outlined the four main types of FGM:

1 *clitoridectomy* (removal of the glans with or without the clitoris)

2 excision of the clitoris with or without the labia minora

3 *infibulation* (partial or total removal of the external genitalia and stitching the vaginal opening closed leaving only enough room for urination and menstrual blood)

4 mutilating genitalia (burning, making lesions).

Types 3 and 4 are rare. In Guinea, about 7% of women experienced type 3 but the majority of women had type 2 and some had type 1. Younger generations are more likely to have type 1. In most countries, types 1 and 2 are most common (United Nations Population Fund, 2009).

Van Rossem and Gage (2009) found that despite the reasons given for practicing FGM, the type of FGM a woman experienced was not related to her age at first sexual intercourse or to having or not having premarital sex. Thus, it appears that sexual desire and behaviors do not depend on whether a woman has a clitoris or not, rendering the rationale for practicing FGM incorrect. This suggests that women engage in sexual intimacy for other reasons than to reach orgasm so FGM does not prevent sexual behavior in women. Yet the practice continues around the world.

Van Rossem and Gage (2009) warn against a simple "sexism" or "patriarchy" explanation for why FGM continues despite public outrage that is expressed by groups like the United Nations who advocate for women's rights. Their work found that the social position of women in cultures that practice FGM is defined by whether they have been cut or not. Good women are cut, other women ostracize those who are not cut, women are perceived as better mothers and wives if they are cut, and a daughter's acceptance in the community is ensured if you have her cut (Gruenbaum, 2006). FGM elevates a girl's standing and acceptance among family and community members. Therefore, it's very difficult to stop the practice when so much of female identity is intertwined with her genital status. Women and girls want to be cut because of what the practice means for their sense of self and womanhood.

In cultures like Guinea, where the spheres of men and women are sharply delineated in everyday life, being accepted by other women as a pure and moral community member is vitally important (Epstein, 2007). The act defines her identity, her sense of belongingness to her community, her social status, and her ethnic identification. Most women see it as a necessary rite of passage that solidifies their social standing (Van Rossem & Gage, 2009). Therefore, it would be extremely difficult for outsiders to come in and demand that the practice end.

One way that other countries have successfully stopped FGM while retaining important aspects of cultural respect for women is to replace the actual surgery with a ritual that closely resembles the surgery, so that all the cultural practices related to entering womanhood are preserved and the dignity of the society is maintained (Toubia & Sharief, 2003).

These trends show how intertwined sex is with marriage, family life, and cultural acceptance. The bioecological lens allows us to explore this complexity and not make simplistic conclusions about sexuality at home or around the world. Another controversial worldwide issue related to sexuality is the AIDS epidemic.

AIDS and trends in youth sexualities

In the 1980s, the free love and sex culture in the western world was brought to a screeching halt with two simultaneous events: the AIDS epidemic and the resurgence of conservative "family values" politics. AIDS led to a return to the more pervasive condom use of the 1950s (then used mostly to prevent pregnancy), and an end to the free sex days of the 1970s. Today, people have to explore the complete sexual history of their partners, and get tested for AIDS and many other diseases. As the epidemic spread, people with AIDS became pariahs in their communities and were discriminated against and shunned. In 1983, Pat Buchanan, the conservative politician, said "the poor homosexuals, evicted—they have declared war against nature, and now nature is exacting an awful retribution" (cited in Jefferson, 2006, p. 36). However, AIDS is not a homosexual disease. It affects people from all sexual orientations and walks of life. The impact of AIDS is devastating. It has killed more Americans than all the wars from World War II to the first Iraq war combined. It has devastated the entire African continent with 25 million people dead by 2006 (Jefferson, 2006).

A positive consequence of the AIDS epidemic is that it has forced the world to face its latent homophobia and has unified people of all sexual orientations in the fight to save lives. It also spurred innovative scientific research on antiretrovirals and universal prevention programs. The LGBT community kept abreast of the changing science and has been exemplary in its use of safer sex practices, political activism, and raising funds for treatments, to the point that now heterosexual people are much more at risk for becoming new AIDS cases than gay men are (Jefferson, 2006).

The fight against AIDS and the gay rights movement have moved the LGBT community to the forefront of our minds. We now see gay characters on many TV shows (albeit often in stereotyped form) and hear about gay issues in the news. In the beginning, AIDS, the "gay cancer," was kept behind closed doors. No one wanted to discuss it because that meant discussing alternative sexualities deemed deviant or sinful. Even though people were dying, politicians and the medical profession were largely silent on the issue. In fact, gay men continued to have sex in bath houses and other anonymous sex locations for the first few years of the epidemic (Jefferson, 2006). Today most Americans are aware of AIDS and people are aware of the groundbreaking research on this deadly disease. All people, homosexual and heterosexual alike, are much more careful about having safer sex, using condoms, and not sharing needles if they are intravenous drug users. The gay community is thriving with fewer and fewer new cases of AIDS diagnosed.

Forty percent of teens and 60% of high school seniors are sexually active, yet unfortunately 49% of girls and 35% of boys still do not use condoms. Because girls often have negative body images during adolescence and are ill informed about changes in themselves, they tend to give the power of decision-making regarding condoms over to boys (Kelly, Lesser, & Smoots, 2005). Many youth in developing nations believe condoms *contain* HIV and think that having unprotected sex with a virgin can cure AIDS. People also still believe that AIDS is a concern only for gay people (Braithwaite & Taylor, 2001). Many youth today are misinformed about AIDS and 25% of new cases of HIV infection are of people between the ages of 13 and 21. To see some of the myths and truths about AIDS, see the *FYI* box, "Myths and Facts about HIV and AIDS."

In addition to risk for AIDS, adolescents have the highest rates of chlamydia, gonorrhea, and human papilloma virus infection (Kelly et al., 2005).

Research shows that young men are much more likely to use condoms when they live in environments that encourage male responsibility for contraception, when they are educated about and fear AIDS, and when their partner expects them to. Contrary to popular belief, embarrassment over talking about condom use or the feeling that condoms numb sensation do not seem to be related to young men's condom use rates (Pleck, Sonenstein, & Ku, 1991).

More on young people and sexuality

Because of the fears of pregnancy and AIDS, many youth practice alternatives to intercourse, like oral sex. In one study of 10th graders, the teens reported engaging in more oral sex than vaginal intercourse. Unfortunately, the majority of those youth did nothing to protect themselves from STIs (Prinstein, Meade, & Cohen, 2003). Many youth also attend sex parties where alcohol and drug use is common and they often have unprotected sexual intercourse, which they report later regretting (Toscano, 2006). Today, most youth don't "date" but attend group activities with friends where they may "hook up" with various friends at different times. These "friends with benefits" are considered to be clean and safe from disease because they have known each other for several months or years.

Gerressu and Stephenson (2008) found that young people's sexual behavior is greatly impacted by their views of a partner being "clean" or "unclean." Young people also exhibit traditional gender role stereotyped attitudes, seeing girls as pure and coy and boys as hypersexual. They place a large value

Myths and facts about HIV and AIDS

MYTH	FACT
You can become infected with HIV by using the bathroom of an infected person, shaking hands with them, kissing them, if they sneeze on you, and through mosquito bites.	HIV is transmitted through vaginal, anal, or oral sex, through sharing needles or syringes with an infected person, and through childbirth and breastfeeding by an infected mother. The jury is still out regarding French kissing as a means of transmission but regular "dry" kissing is safe.
You should not give or receive blood at hospitals or blood banks due to the risk of HIV.	While a few early cases of AIDS were related to blood transfusions, there is no risk from giving blood and all blood since 1985 has been thoroughly tested so the blood supply is safe.
You can get AIDS at a tattoo or piercing parlor.	HIV can be transmitted through dirty and shared needles. Most reputable establishments follow strict sterilization laws and either sterilize their equipment or use new needles on each client. Be sure to inquire and don't allow friends or untrained people to pierce or tattoo you.
AIDS is mainly a "gay" disease.	Lesbians are actually at the least risk of contracting AIDS as female to female transmission is extremely rare. While gay men were the ones who alerted us to the disease, today heterosexuals, and especially young people of color, are most at risk for becoming new AIDS cases.
Using condoms always prevents the transmission of HIV.	There is no 100% successful way to prevent the transmission of HIV during sexual activity. Using condoms accurately every single time you engage in sexual activity is the safest sex, but there is still a slight risk involved in all sexual activity. Latex condoms used properly are the best prevention.
AIDS is a death sentence.	While AIDS is considered a terminal and incurable illness, the drug cocktails available today make it entirely possible to live a long, happy, healthy life if infected. It's not uncommon to live 20 years or more after infection with the right medical care.

Source: HIV/AIDS Basics, 2010. Retrieved from **www.stophiv.com/page.asp?PID=56**.

on their reputations and sometimes may disavow the use of condoms because they say that if your partner asks you to wear a condom, it assumes you are "unclean."

Social pressures to maintain reputations and fit into traditional gender role expectations inhibit the adolescents' ability to communicate openly about sexuality. Marston and King (2006) examined 268 studies across several cultures and found very similar results. Social norms determined the timing and frequency of sex for young people. Teens had more sex when they were left home alone for long periods without adult supervision. Parents who expressed disapproval of sex decreased their child's sexual behavior. On the other hand, when peers' approval of sex was high, so was the teens' sexual behavior. In regard to the myth of familiarity and "cleanliness" (meaning safety against AIDS) see the myths and facts in the *FYI* box.

Research has shown that teenage girls who have a future orientation (they see a positive future for themselves), think highly of their talents and skills, and envision education or a career are more likely to abstain from sex or take precautions against pregnancy and STIs (Schwartz & Rutter, 1998). Girls tend to receive more messages about the negative outcomes of sexual behavior than boys do. Daughters receive more education about sex and are often prohibited from engaging in it at all. Boys, on the other hand, are expected to be sexually active. However, sex in general is not discussed in most American homes. Children are often expected to practice abstinence and deny their sexual development and desires. Schwartz and Rutter (1998) say that "the vision that teenagers should be nonsexual, especially in a hypersexualized society, is simply unrealistic" (p. 77).

With images of sexuality oozing from every billboard, blaring from every TV, and strutting across most computer screens, how can we then ask teens to "just say no"? Societies like Sweden where comprehensive sexuality education begins early in life and is supported by an entire "sex positive" culture actually have *lower* rates of teen pregnancy and STIs than the United States. The U.S. tends to focus more on abstinence than any other industrialized nation. Does this focus on abstinence help youths' sexual development?

Abstinence education, virginity pledges, and family relationships

There is now plenty of research showing that abstinence-only education is not only unreasonable, because sex is a natural and normal part of every person's developmental process, but can actually harm adolescents. Kirby et al. (1994), in a review of such programs, found that abstinence-only programs were related to *higher* levels of teen sexual activity. Also, Rosenbaum (2009) found that after following teens who had made virginity pledges for five years, those who took the pledge were just as likely to have sex as their non-pledging friends. The even more eye-opening finding was that those taking the pledge were less likely to use condoms and contraceptives than the non-pledgers. Perhaps those who take the pledge feel guilty about having sex and are less likely to talk to their partners about safer sex practices.

Wellings, Collumbien, and Slaymaker (2006) found positive results from school-based sexuality education classes that raised awareness about sexual risk-taking, and imparted knowledge about and strategies to use in order to reduce risk-taking. The programs, which raised students' intentions of being safer, actually delayed onset of sexual activity in teens. Thus, comprehensive sexuality education, including information on abstinence, safer sex practices, and, most importantly, sexual assertiveness and communication, can protect teens against some of the negative consequences of sexual behavior.

When education programs focus on the emotional and cognitive components of sex, how to communicate with partners about sexual issues, and how to respect partners' rights to say "no," research finds that teens actually delay sex, and it empowers them to say "no" to unwanted advances. When adolescents are given the power of knowledge regarding their own bodies and those of their partners, as well as concrete strategies for protecting their sexual dignity, programs result in lower rates of sexual coercion and harassment in adolescent groups. In contrast, in abstinence-only programs, teen girls are more afraid of sex, fearing pregnancy and disease. The dangerous consequence of this trend is a rapid rise in oral sex rates, as teens are not educated about the fact that diseases and infections are spread through oral sex as well as intercourse (Berman et al., 2001).

When mothers openly discuss sex, answer all questions honestly, and discuss their own attitudes about sex and relationships, teens tend to delay sex initiation (Davis & Friel, 2001). When parents are closed off from providing information or threaten their children with punishment for sexual behavior, children are much more likely to sneak around and get into risky situations which they are unprepared to handle.

Youth of color are even more at risk for unsafe sexual behaviors that can lead to violence or disease. For example, Latinos are more likely to have sex before the age of 13 and to have four or more partners during adolescence. These rates are 1.5 to 2 times greater than those for European American youth (Trejos-Castillo & Vazsonyi, 2009). Hispanic/Latino youth also have lower rates of condom use than whites. These behaviors put them at greater risk for AIDS, pregnancy, and sexual violation. Latinos account for three times as many new AIDS cases as European Americans each year (Center for Disease Control and Prevention, 2010). While teen sex rates have decreased in the U.S. in general, rates for Hispanic/Latino youth have increased dramatically, while their use of contraceptives has decreased at the same time (Raffaelli & Ontai, 2001). Take a look at these statistics: 50% of white teenage girls are sexually active and 71% of those use contraceptives; 60% of adolescent African American girls are sexually active and 71% of those use contraceptives; but 55% of adolescent Latinas are sexually active and only 53% of those use contraceptives. The teen birth rate for Latinas is two times the national average, and while they make up only 7% of the population, they make up 19% of new AIDS cases (Center for Disease Control and Prevention, 2010).

Hispanic families tend to focus on devotion to and respect for the family and emphasize female virginity and traditional gender roles. This results in many Hispanic/Latina girls not being taught about sex. They tend to be sheltered and kept at home to avoid sexual interactions (Marin & Gomez, 1997). In a study of 20- to 45-year-old Latinas (mostly Mexican American), all of them reported their parents expressing distrust toward men and boys. They were not allowed to date due to fear they might disgrace their families. While 68% of the parents had discussed menstruation with their girls, only 27% of the families had discussed puberty with them and only 36% had discussed sex and pregnancy. The majority of parents had warned them about the dangers of sex, boys, and dating and placed emphasis on morality, with actions like prohibiting revealing clothes or make-up. Despite these trends, 86% of these women had premarital sex and 32% of them got pregnant very young (Marin & Gomez, 1997).

In a study examining whether acculturation to the dominant American culture or the immigration status of Latino youth predicted sexual behavior, Trejos-Castillo and Vazsonyi (2009) found that neither variable played a role in youth sexual risk-taking behaviors. The variables that mattered most for protecting youth against negative sexual behavior were the same ones found in research on European American families: unity of the family, open communication, respect between family members, parental restrictions on premarital sex, and emotional support of the teen. The same findings held for first- and second-generation immigrants and those who were more or less acculturated.

Steinberg and Silk (2002) have found that, for most adolescents, closeness with parents decreases during the teen years, but the warmth families provide and the cohesive sense of togetherness remain. Moreover, while teens may seem less affectionate to their parents, they are still very receptive to parental support. Hispanic/Latino families tend to have strong family ties and this kind of support can buffer teens from risky sexual behaviors if it is combined with open discussion and education about sexuality.

While heterosexual youth of color face many challenges, the continued negative judgments, discrimination, and lack of acceptance of the LGBT community puts LGBT youth of color at even greater risk for depression, substance use, and suicidal behavior and thoughts. Youth of color face enormous challenges as they often must cope with racism and homophobia, along with the everyday travails of adolescent development, puberty, sex, family, and school pressures. Having to negotiate multiple identities at one time is extremely stressful (Andoh & Bogden, 2009).

Interestingly, LGBT youth of color may be well-prepared in some cases because they grew up dealing with racism and race discrimination so they may already have coping skills in place to help them face anti-gay sentiment or action as they become aware of their sexuality (Savin-Williams, 1996). It's extremely important for LGBT youth of color to forge their way into society with a **bicultural identity**, being able to navigate the spheres of their ethnic background and their sexuality while adjusting well to the dominant culture. This is a difficult task but many youth are doing it admirably despite the challenges (Crawford, Allison, Zamboni, & Soto, 2002).

This chapter has focused on the many influences on sexual attitudes, orientations, and behaviors. Biology, family relationships, peers, religion, culture, and historic period can each deeply impact one's sexuality. Unfortunately, no matter which type of family or culture you live in, there is a good chance that you or someone you know has or will become sexually victimized. I would be remiss if I didn't end this chapter on sex with at least a brief overview of issues related to sexual violence.

Sexual abuse and sexualized violence

Tjaden and Thoennes (1998) found that 18% of American women reported having experienced an attempted or completed rape, and 58% report experiencing some form of forced sexual activity or assault. Zawacki, Abbey, Buck, McAuslan & Clinton-Sherrod (2003) found that 14% of women reported being the survivor of a completed rape. The same rates are found in Germany and the United Kingdom (Bohner, Jarvis, Eyssel, & Siebler, 2005). Rape is considered to be an act of violence, not solely a sexual act.

Malamuth (2003) describes two key pathways to men perpetrating sexualized violence against women: **hostile masculinity**, where a man accepts the legitimacy of violence against women, feels hostile towards women, and has narcissistic personality traits; and sexual promiscuity/impersonal sex, where a man usually experienced abuse in his childhood, had a chaotic household, engaged in delinquent acts during adolescence, had promiscuous sex, and views sex as impersonal.

Even non-rapists often exhibit misogynistic attitudes that can lead to sexual coercion, if not outright sexualized violence. For example, in a study of 492 white middle-class male college students, 44% reported feeling an attraction to forcing sex on women (Voller, Long, & Aosved, 2009). Voller and colleagues attempted to answer the question about whether potential and actual rapists also have other antisocial tendencies (the generalist model) or they simply desire to engage in sexual violence and that is their only crime (the specialist model). They found that the students who most endorsed the idea of forcing sex on women also reported being attracted to having sex with children and to committing other crimes in general. This was most true of those who reported that they had already forced sex on or raped women. Thus, the *generalist model* was supported in that general antisocial desires and criminal behaviors tend to go together. Interestingly, the current diagnostic criteria for mental disorders includes attraction to having sex with children as a disorder (pedophilia) but an attraction to raping women is not a diagnosable condition (*DSM–IV–TR*; American Psychiatric Association, 2000).

People from divorced families, those living in rural areas, and those with low levels of religiosity are at higher risk for being sexually victimized. Also, people who exhibited behavioral disorders in youth, who use substances, were sexually abused, had little parental supervision, experienced harsh discipline in the home, and accept violence as a problem-solving strategy are more likely to be victims of sexually violent crimes (Christopher & Sprecher, 2000).

Unfortunately, somewhere between 2% and 9% of women report being forced to have sex with their own husbands. These rates skyrocket for women whose husbands are also physically violent, again supporting the generalist model (Christopher & Sprecher, 2000). Sexually coercive men tend to see love as a game and they feel much ambivalence toward their partners. They tend to discount their partners' protests and ignore their rejection of sexual advances. Sexually coercive men also tend to have poor communication skills and use a predatory approach to meeting partners. While female

Bicultural identity
The ability of marginalized people (i.e. people of color, sexual minorities) to identify strongly with their own group and at the same time function well in the larger society.

Hostile masculinity
A male ideology comprised of negative attitudes about women and an acceptance of violence against women.

coercion is relatively rare, women who force sex on their partners tend to be angry and harbor much hostility toward men in general (Christopher & Sprecher, 2000).

Sexual abuse in childhood is a risk factor for later sexual victimization as an adult. About 30% of women and 10% of men report sexual abuse in their childhoods (Loeb et al., 2002). Keep in mind that the majority of people who are sexually abused never report it, so the actual numbers are probably much higher.

There don't appear to be any ethnic differences in sexual abuse rates. However, culture plays a role in how abuse is defined, how it is detected, and how the victims are perceived. Sexual abuse ranges from exposing children to sexually explicit materials or actions, to fondling, oral sex, and intercourse. Sexual exploitation can include forcing children into prostitution or selling them into sexual slavery. Child sexual abuse increases one's chances for developing depression and substance use. Survivors can also develop symptoms of post-traumatic stress disorder (PTSD), including flashbacks (especially during sex). Boys who were sexually abused are more likely to use alcohol and drugs, exhibit criminal behavior, have higher levels of suicide attempts and ideation, and feel confused about their sexual identity (Heise, Moore, & Toubia, 1995). Many child victims of sexual abuse display sexual knowledge beyond their developmental level (such as a 3-year-old talking about a "blow job"). Children may also exhibit abuse-reactive sexual victimization of other children, excessive masturbation, or the re-enactment of sex acts in their play behaviors.

Because boys (as well as girls) are more likely to be sexually victimized by men, they are often wracked with guilt and internalize a sense of self-hatred involving strong homophobia. This may lead them to eroticize the abuse and remember it as simply "sex with an adult" instead of victimization. Adult men sexually abused as children often engage in painful self-stimulation and even self-injury. They may damage their own genitals, cut them off, request numerous surgeries (such as urethral dilations and penile implants), or ask for orchiectomies (removal of the testes) when incarcerated for sex crimes (Loeb et al., 2002). Because of sexual identity issues involved in male victimization, most boys never report their sexual abuse (Mills, 1993). This has become patently clear in the recent worldwide scandal involving thousands of boys victimized by Catholic priests.

Not all sex between adult males and boys, however, is necessarily abusive or perceived as harmful by the boy. Adult college students who recall sexual experiences with men when they were boys report that those experiences were often neutral or positive, not necessarily negative experiences. Such experiences are most likely to be perceived as negative and abusive if the adult male threatened the child, coerced him, or was a biological relative (Bauserman & Rind, 1997).

When a child is abused by a trusted caretaker, uncle, grandfather, or father figure, it can be devastating. These kinds of sexual violations profoundly affect the developing child's sense of him or herself. Remember from Chapter 2 that our internal working models develop out of the care (or lack thereof) we receive from adults around us. If we are sexually violated or victimized, it can have a debilitating effect on our sexual health, performance, functioning, and satisfaction. It's also related to risky sexual behaviors such as unprotected sex and prostitution. The effects of abuse vary by child and perpetrator characteristics, such as the child's age, and gender, whether the perpetrator was a biological relative, the severity and frequency of the abuse, and whether force was involved (Maikovich-Fong & Jaffee, 2010).

Sexual abuse can interfere with psychological development, but it may also disrupt biological developmental processes as well. For example, sexually abused girls enter puberty earlier than other girls, and they have higher levels of stress hormones like cortisol circulating in their blood and brains (Loeb et al., 2002). During medical visits, these girls are often found to have unhealthy vaginal discharge, vaginal bleeding, lesions in the pelvic area, recurrent bladder and urinary tract infections, and sexually transmitted problems like herpes or genital warts. Butler and Barton (1990) found that half of the pregnant teenagers they studied were victims of child sexual abuse. Moreover, babies of teen mothers who had been sexually abused were less healthy and smaller in size (Stevens-Simon & McAnarney, 1994), revealing that negative effects of sexual abuse carry forward into the next generation.

HOW WOULD YOU MEASURE THAT?

Preventing sexual violence (Banyard, Moynihan, & Plante, 2007)

Testing a "community of responsibility" model of sexual violence prevention, Banyard et al. (2007) wanted to see how teaching college students to intervene could prevent sexual violence incidents with strangers, acquaintances, or friends. The authors stated that there is a lifetime sexual violence incidence rate for college-age women of 50% and an academic year prevalence rate of 20%. This means that in the current school year, 20% of you may fall victim to sexualized violence. While most programs teach women how to avoid dangerous situations where they might be date-raped or stranger-raped, this program focused on both men and women, teaching them that sexual assault prevention is everyone's responsibility. It used peers to teach the material through hands-on active learning strategies. Teaching young people that they belong to a community of responsibility encourages all community members to take an active role in preventing the sexual violation of women. This includes stopping situations that can lead to violence (such as a girlfriend offering a drunk woman a ride home instead of her walking home alone), speaking out against social norms that support sexual violence (such as criticizing sexist or rape-related jokes), and being a supporter of survivors. Much of the curriculum involved debunking rape myths such as "women just say no so they don't appear 'easy'."

The researchers taught the program to 389 students between the ages of 18 and 23. There were two treatment groups (a one-session program group, a three-session program group, and a no-program control group). The dependent variables measured were knowledge about, attitudes towards, and behaviors taken to prevent sexual assault. After the program, students were asked about things like how likely they would be to investigate a woman's call for help or offer help to an upset stranger. They were also asked whether they had performed various behaviors in real life to help prevent possible assaults (such as stopping a friend from leaving a party with a stranger).

The results showed that those who got the three-session program had greater increases in knowledge and positive bystander attitudes, and lower rape myth acceptance than those who got the one-session program. However, all program participants (including both men and women) improved in their sense of self-efficacy in knowing how to help someone, their knowledge about sexual assault, their willingness to help, their appreciation of the personal benefits stemming from preventing sexual assault, and lower rape myth acceptance in comparison to the control group. In comparison to a pre-test, students increased in their reported actual bystander behavior at a post-test, and at 4- and 12-month follow-up tests. This study suggests that a simple 1- to 3-day training session led by same-age peers and using active learning strategies like role play and discussions can increase knowledge and change attitudes and actual behavior that may prevent sexual violence in their peer group and community.

Adult female sexual abuse survivors often feel they are unworthy of love and engage in dysfunctional or abusive relationships. They may experience hypo- or hyperactive sexual desire and inorgasmia (especially if the abuse was familial, occurred over long periods of time, and involved penetration of the vagina) (Berman et al., 2001). Berman and colleagues used sildenafil (Viagra) to treat sexual dysfunctions in two groups of women. The drug only worked for women who were *not* sexually abused as children. This study indicates that treatment for sexual problems in women with a history of abuse must incorporate psychological counseling, perhaps related to trauma processing and relationship skills. For example, research suggests that women who were abused are less likely to refuse unwanted sexual advances as adults and to have a harder time make decisions regarding contraception (Heise et al., 1995). These behaviors put them at risk for further sexual victimization, and child abuse survivors often find themselves being sexually violated or otherwise abused in their adult relationships as well.

Men who were sexually abused as children have higher rates of erectile dysfunction and premature ejaculation, and low sexual desire. There is a strong impact on sexual identity confusion as well. Homosexual men are more likely to have a history of sexual abuse than heterosexual men are. This doesn't mean sexual abuse causes homosexuality. It probably reflects the fact that gay men have a history of sexual encounters with older men, which increases their chances of being victimized as youth, due to the sheer number of contacts with men.

While treatments for sexual abuse survivors can be effective in ameliorating some of the negative outcomes, best practices would include universal education and *prevention* programs. If all youth are educated about their bodies and healthy sexuality, and families are able to discuss and cope with any sexual victimization that occurs, the negative effects of sexualized violence can be mitigated. Prevention techniques can also be taught to older youth in college. To see an innovative approach to preventing sexual victimization in college students, read the *How Would You Measure That?* box.

This chapter completes our study of the individual at the center of the bioecological model. Having learned about individual gender role development, gendered behavior, and a bit about sex and sexualities, we are now ready to move out to the microsystem part of the model, and on to a focus on relationships. The next chapter focuses on the first step in the development of relationships: dating and mate selection.

CHAPTER SUMMARY

People's sexualities have always been influenced by macrosystem influences such as sexism, lack of education, and the desire to preserve traditional views of marriages and families. Historical pressures on women to remain chaste, while men were allowed free sexuality, led to inventions such as chastity belts, female circumcision, and punishments for women who engaged in sex outside of marriage. The eugenics movement was possibly the most extreme example of societal forces endorsing sexual relations between those deemed genetically superior, and it included forced sterilization of the "inferior" underclass. Reproduction was controlled by government agencies seeking to create a master white race where only desirable citizens were allowed to reproduce.

Modern feminist movements allowed for female sexuality to become more acceptable as women gained control over their own sexual and reproductive lives. Today in many places there is a sexual double standard, where women are still expected to remain pure while men are expected to be hypersexual. Gender role stereotypes negatively affect sexual relations between partners who may lack knowledge about the physiology of sex and how to communicate clearly about sexual preferences and desires.

Women and men experience similar physiological processes during sexual experiences, beginning with the excitement phase, continuing to plateau, orgasm, and finally, resolution. Sexual dysfunctions can occur at any of these phases and relationship problems can exacerbate physiological problems, and vice versa. Lack of communication, lack of intimacy, fear, and shame can lead to problems in sexual relationships between partners. Sexual minorities experience sexual physiology and relationship issues very similarly to those of heterosexual couples but it is important to avoid heteronormativity when differences are found. Moreover, sexual minorities often face heterosexist discrimination, racism, and classism, depending on their intersectional identity status.

Biological and evolutionary research findings were examined which suggest that sexual orientation is biologically determined, and not a choice that people make. However, the specific causal factors that lead to a more strongly homosexual orientation have not been discovered. Even though sexual minorities may have some biological differences compared to heterosexuals, all people strive to find intimate partnerships and engage in satisfying sexual relationships.

Sex therapy was established to increase couple communication and education about sexuality, and to help partners engage in meaningful, pleasurable, and mutually satisfying sex. When people dissect cultural expectations for their sexuality and break down the myths regarding male and female sexual experiences, they are able to overcome barriers to sexual freedom and enjoyment.

Some contemporary issues regarding sexuality around the world include the continued practice of female genital mutilation, the AIDS epidemic, and how youth experience sexuality in contemporary society, a focus on abstinence, and disturbingly high rates of child sexual abuse and sexualized violence against adult women. For all of these issues, education, open communication in families, a focus on prevention, and an application of the bioecological model can both illuminate problems and work to reduce negative behaviors surrounding diverse sexualities.

KEY TERMS

arousal problems
bicultural identity
biopsychosocial model of orgasm
clitoral orgasms
clitoridectomy
clitoris
constructionists
dyspareunia
epididymis
erectile dysfunction
erogenous zones
essentialist
eugenics movement
four-stage sexual response cycle
general physiological arousal

genital responsiveness
hostile masculinity
incentive motivation
infibulation
information processing
inorgasmia
labia majora
labia minora
low sexual desire
paraphilias
pelvic floor orgasms
premature ejaculation
prostate gland
prostate orgasm
Queer Theory

seminiferous tubules
sexual antagonistic selection
sexual aversion disorder
sexual double standard (SDS)
Social Darwinism
sperm
transgender
transudation
urethra
vagina
vaginismus
vas deferens
vulva

WEBSITES FOR FURTHER EXPLORATION

www.bermancenter.com/home
Dr. Laura Berman is one of the world's leading experts on female sexuality. This website is for her sex clinic in Chicago where she teaches seminars for individuals and couples meant to improve their relationships and sex lives. The website also links to her store where you can buy books, participate in retreat weekends, read articles about topics like how to talk to kids about sex, and purchase sex toys (like vibrators) she designed based on her research on thousands of women.

www.historyofsexuality.com/top_list.html
A great little site with many articles on the history of sexuality across cultures, most of which are written by anthropologists; articles cover masturbation, sex between family members, Old Testament sex, sex in ancient India (the Kama Sutra), gods devoted to sex, and so on. Beware: this site lists some links to explicit sexual material.

www.webmd.com/sex-relationships/default.htm
A medical site with a section containing articles on sexual issues like foreplay, low sex drive, orgasm, penis size, birth control, virginity, and STIs.

CHAPTER 5
DATING AND MATE SELECTION

I had a lot of dates but I decided to stay home and dye my eyebrows.

(Andy Warhol, artist and pop icon)

LEARNING OBJECTIVES

- To understand both positive and negative contemporary trends in hooking up, dating, and mate selection

- To understand how cognitive and emotional factors (like attitudes and attachment styles) influence dating and mate selection

- To appreciate how factors in each system of the bioecological model impact dating and mate selection

- To learn some theories that are used to analyze dating and mate selection patterns

- To understand the evolution of dating over time, both in the United States and around the world

Marriages and Families in the 21st Century: A Bioecological Approach, First Edition. Tasha R. Howe.
© 2012 Tasha R. Howe. Published 2012 by Blackwell Publishing Ltd.

OVERVIEW OF DATING, HOOKING UP, AND MATE SELECTION

- General processes leading from dating to mate selection
- Attachment processes

A BIOECOLOGICAL EXAMINATION OF DATING AND MATE SELECTION

- Biological factors
  - Research on evolution
  - Neurobiological research
  - Phases of chemical attraction
  - Attachment and biology
  - Micro- and mesosystem influences on adolescent dating
- Person, process, and context factors
- The macrosystem: cultural factors

THEORIES OF DATING AND MATE SELECTION

- Structural-Functionalism and dating
- Conflict Theory and Filter Theory
  - More on filter and market value approaches to mate selection

HISTORICAL TRENDS IN DATING AND MATE SELECTION

DIVERSITY IN DATING AND MATE SELECTION

- Ethnicity and dating
- LGBT communities and dating
- Seniors and dating

CONTEMPORARY TRENDS AROUND THE WORLD

- Dating with technology
- Dating violence

OVERVIEW OF DATING, HOOKING UP, AND MATE SELECTION

General processes leading from dating to mate selection

Attachment processes

If you've ever felt that dyeing your eyebrows might be more appealing than going out on a date, you're not alone. Although many people are super daters with charming personalities and interpersonal skills beyond compare, for most of us, dating is rough. Yet at the same time, the majority of us eventually end up on dates that lead to marriages or long-term committed relationships. How does this happen? After reading the first four chapters of this book, you probably recognize that dating and mate selection, like every other aspect of family life, are extremely complex. **Dating** refers to early stage romantic excursions that serve as a foundation for building a potentially committed relationship. Dating includes romantic outings like going out to dinner, attending entertainment events, or going on weekend getaways. These preliminary liaisons allow people to get to know each other in order to decide if they'd like to pursue a more serious relationship.

Not all early stage liaisons lead to a committed partnership, however. Many people engage in a practice called **hooking up**, which includes casual sexual experiences with strangers or acquaintances (kissing, oral sex, intercourse) without the expectation of any further contact after the fact (Epstein, Calzo, Smiler, & Ward, 2009). **Friends with benefits** differs from dating in that it refers to engaging in sexual activities with friends or acquaintances without expecting the development of a committed partnership (Epstein et al., 2009). Friends with benefits usually involves friends remaining friends after they've been intimate. However, it is often difficult to maintain the status quo because sexual relationships tend to complicate friendships (Epstein et al., 2009). This chapter will explore the ways we hook up and date, what factors influence our dating patterns and preferences, and how we select our mates for a long-term commitment.

Considering all the complexities laid out in our first four chapters—gender, socioeconomic status, ethnicity, religion, personal factors, process factors, contextual factors, SNAF values, and cultural practices coming into play—it is amazing that anyone ever connects intimately at all. Because all humans live in multiple contexts and experience their lives through the intersections of many identities, meeting just the right person for romance can be quite a challenge (Niehuis, Huston, & Rosenhand, 2006).

What is your "type?" Do you ever take a chance and date someone of a different type? What do your parents and religious leaders expect of you in terms of meeting the "right" person? All of us experience pressure to live up to certain expectations in our dating relationships. In more individualistic cultures, such as the United States and Canada, we can often worry less about what others expect and date people who just make us happy. We prefer to focus on fairytale romantic ideals, including passionate love and intense physical attraction, over pleasing our families (Buss, Shackelford, Kirkpatrick, & Larsen, 2001).

In more collectivist cultures, such as India and China, people may have less control over whom they select as their mates, and they may not have the privilege of "dating" at all. Elders, community members, parents, or religious leaders may arrange for people to meet that special someone who appeals to *them*. Around the world, group values and benefits to social network members are of utmost importance in mate selection decisions (Xie, Dzindolet, & Meredith, 1999). For example, in many East Asian groups, family influence and judgments about a potential mate's moral character play large roles in mate selection (Higgins, Zheng, Liu, & Sun, 2002). Chinese people often adhere to *xiao* (filial piety, or obedience and devotion to ones elders) and *guanxi* (adherence to the wishes of social networks). The social network provides financial and emotional support while also helping the dating couple solve problems. Chinese youth want the approval of people in their *guanxi* and do not typically make individualistic mate selection choices (Zhang & Kline, 2009).

While western youth may think parents should mind their own business in terms of their children's mate selection choices, Chinese college students report that not only is family approval important,

Dating
Early stage romantic excursions that serve as a foundation for building a potentially committed relationship.

Hooking up
Casual sexual experiences with strangers or acquaintances (kissing, oral sex, intercourse) without the expectation of any further contact after the fact.

Friends with benefits
Engaging in sexual activities with friends or acquaintances without expecting the development of a committed partnership.

but it influences the possibility of success in a relationship. Students reported that a potential mate must agree to familial piety demands such as respecting their partner's parents' opinions, taking care of the partner's parents when old, helping their in-laws financially, and striving to always make them happy (Higgins et al., 2002). In this study, Chinese students were much more willing than American students to conform to their social network's opinions and ideas. They felt network disapproval of a potential mate would be a large obstacle and reported that they might consider ending the relationship if their parents disapproved of it. In contrast, American students said they would continue dating their partner regardless of what people in their social networks thought. Moreover, when the study participants were asked what purpose dating served, Chinese students reported that dating was expressly for finding a marriage partner while Americans said they dated mainly "for fun."

Recent research has examined the most casual form of "fun" dating, hooking up, and has found that it may not be as much fun as it appears. First, in research on high school and college students, most students overestimate the amount of hooking up their classmates do, and so feel pressured to engage in such casual sexual liaisons to fit in (Fielder & Carey, 2010). Certain demographic variables predict who is more or less likely to succumb to this pressure. For example, youth whose parents have strongly discouraged them from forming serious relationships in college are more likely to have oral sex hook-ups, perhaps as a compromise between intercourse with strangers and looking for serious commitments (Fielder & Carey, 2010).

Despite gender role expectations regarding hypersexuality in males, men are only slightly more likely to hook up than women are. After hooking up, men tend to have fewer feelings of guilt, shame, and low self-esteem than women do (Fielder & Carey, 2010). Women who have more psychosocial stress in their daily lives are more likely to hook up and also to view the experience negatively. However, men with higher self-images are more likely to hook up. Although there are general gender differences, many men feel a sense of regret and emptiness after a hook-up. College men often reported not wanting to hook up with women at parties and hoping to find a more meaningful relationship (Epstein et al., 2009). For most of the college students surveyed, parties were the most common location for hook-ups and the best predictor of whether they would do so was the availability of alcohol. Intoxication has repeatedly been shown to impact the likelihood of casual sex for both men and women, which puts the partners at great risk for sexually transmitted infections, unwanted pregnancy, and risk-taking behaviors like driving drunk and going home with strangers (Owen, Rhoades, Stanley, & Fincham, 2010). European American students and those with higher incomes are more likely to hook up than are students from other ethnic and socioeconomic groups. By the end of the first year of college, about one third of college students reported having an oral sex hook-up and another third a vaginal sex hook-up (Fielder & Carey, 2010).

Despite these trends in hooking up, western youth in general have a great desire to eventually find that one, true love. Interestingly, matches based on personal fulfillment and "love" have actually been pretty rare throughout history and are still infrequent in many parts of the world today. Those who choose their own mates, like western youth, and want to fall madly in love, experience several common dating and relationship processes when deciding on that special person.

General processes leading from dating to mate selection

Our happiest moments in life are those spent with others (Csikszentmihalyi & Hunter, 2003). Fiske (1991) describes four key relationship dynamics, found in most intimate human relationships that are formed by choice:

communal sharing (being open and intimate with a partner)
authority ranking (deciding on power sharing or control issues)
equality matching (finding similarities)
market pricing (figuring out the costs and benefits of being involved in the relationship).

Communal sharing
One of four elements of intimate relationships, characterized by being open and intimate with a partner.

Authority ranking
One of four elements of intimate relationships, characterized by deciding on power sharing and control issues.

Equality matching
One of four elements of intimate relationships, characterized by finding partners with similarities to oneself.

Market pricing
One of four elements of intimate relationships, characterized by a cost/benefit analysis of the worth of a specific partner.

All four of these dynamics come into play when we start dating someone. First, we have to decide how much personal information to share and how open or closed we want to be. As we interact more with our new partner, power issues begin to emerge in terms of making decisions for activities to engage in, whose family to visit, how to handle ex-partners, and how to handle conflicts. If we have been able to find enough similarities in our beliefs, goals, and interests, the relationship is more likely to last and power will be more balanced than skewed. These first three dynamics then feed into our mental calculations about the relative costs and benefits the relationship holds for us. You may recall from Chapter 2 that Social Exchange Theory posits that people rationally analyze their costs vs. benefits as they engage in romantic partnerships. This relates to Fiske's (1991) *market pricing* dynamic. Think about one of your past or current relationships and how you negotiated these four relationship dynamics. Did you decide to stay with the person or move on? Which of Fiske's dynamics played the most important role in your decision?

After people test the waters and get a feel for some of the relationship dynamics, they may begin a **courtship**, the process whereby people select each other as mates and decide to make a committed partnership with each other, such as marriage. Courtship is not only affected by relationship dynamics at the current time, but it is strongly influenced by the characteristics and personal histories each partner brings to the table (Niehuis et al., 2006). For example, each partner's family of origin plays a role in his or her attitudes and behaviors in a romantic relationship. In Chapter 2, you learned about Attachment Theory. This theory has shaped a lot of thinking and research about adult romantic relationships. Recall that this theory posits that early interactions between caregivers and young children shape children's ideas about themselves and about relationships.

Attachment processes

During the development of attachments to our caregivers in childhood, we expand our internal working model, or a cognitive template representing our ideas of what relationships are or should be like. Our internal working models can range from very secure, formed out of loving, warm, responsive childhood experiences, to extremely confused, insecure, or negative, such as those formed in violent or chaotic homes. Secure internal working models of attachment include viewing relationships as safe and inviting, the world as exciting, and one's self as worthy of love. Adults' internal working models include all the information stored from earlier relationships. **Anxious, preoccupied,** or **ambivalent** internal working models of attachment may include excessive worry about relationships, fears of abandonment stemming from partners not being as close as one might like, or alternating desires to be both near and distant from a partner (Pietromonaco, Barrett, & Powers, 2006). People with **dismissing avoidant** internal working models of attachment may be uncomfortable with intimacy, sharing feelings, or expressions of intense emotion. They are very self-reliant and don't see much benefit in getting close to others. In contrast, **fearful avoidant** people both desire and fear closeness so they tend to avoid getting too involved with others in order to prevent rejection and being hurt (Bartholomew & Horowitz, 1991).

Our internal working models reflect our histories of divorce, sexual attitudes, communication skills, power expectations, and so on (Huston, Caughlin, Houts, Smith, & George, 2001). However, when first meeting someone, we may not reveal our inner thinking or show our true behavioral tendencies. Huston et al. (2001) discuss these tendencies in a **disillusionment model**, which involves partners being on their best behavior in the beginning of a courtship but then becoming disappointed as time goes on. They tend to suppress negative aspects of their internal working models, ignoring problems and even idealizing their new mate. The new partners minimize problems like power struggles or bad habits. Once they begin courtship and make a commitment for a longer-term relationship like marriage, they can become disappointed, thinking their partner has changed, because when their true internal working models and interaction patterns come into play, problems begin to arise. In other words, often with commitment comes disillusionment. It seems, then, that a positive course of action would be for people to try to be as honest as possible and be comfortable

Courtship
The process whereby people select each other as mates and decide to make a committed partnership with each other, such as in the case of marriage.

Anxious, preoccupied, ambivalent attachments
Insecure attachments which lead people to fear abandonment, cling onto partners, or alternatively want closeness and then distance.

Dismissing avoidant attachment
An insecure attachment style where people don't value intimacy with others and keep a cold distance in relationships.

Fearful avoidant attachment
An insecure attachment style where people fear being hurt and so avoid intimacy altogether.

Disillusionment model
A model explaining that people often put on false fronts during dating relationships so that when they commit to a relationship, they become disillusioned to find out the flaws in their partners. They feel unhappy that the person has "changed."

enough with themselves so that they choose partners who complement their authentic personalities, attachment styles, and attitudes. To avoid disillusionment may take some courage and the willingness to take a risk by putting one's true self out there for others to see.

Much of the preceding discussion suggests that people have complete control over their mate selection strategies and that it's a very methodical, rational process determined through social and intellectual forces. However, biology always plays a role in our relationships and many researchers have tried to uncover biological correlates of dating and mate selection behaviors. Moreover, these biological factors are always affected by environmental interactions from the contexts existing in each bioecological system.

A BIOECOLOGICAL EXAMINATION OF DATING AND MATE SELECTION

> Biological factors
>
> Person, process, and context factors
>
> The macrosystem: cultural factors

Factors that affect your dating life can stem from every aspect of your bioecological experiences. For example, your biological maturation, hormones, personality, physical attractiveness, and beliefs can affect your dating life. Also, there are important influences from your microsystem (like your parents not letting you date), mesosystem (like your parents' earlier experiences with your sister's dating, which convinced them not to let you date), exosystem (like your parents' knowledge of AIDS, divorce, or other bad things they see in the media, which influences them to not let you date), and macrosystem (like your culture's views of gender role behaviors during dating) all interacting with each other. Let's start this multifaceted exploration by looking at some of the biological research.

Biological factors

Evolutionary forces may influence how we select our mates. For example, the availability of men versus women seems to shape mating patterns (Baumeister & Vohs, 2004). If there are fewer men in a population, females might become more promiscuous, choosing more short-term couplings to ensure they are impregnated (Schmitt, 2005), while at the same time raising their standards for committed relationships (Stone, Shakelford, & Buss, 2007). If there are too few women in a population, marriages tend to occur at younger ages and divorce rates are lower (Pederson, 1991).

Research on evolution

How do we choose the people we date or engage in sexual relations with? Evolutionary psychologists argue that people find others attractive who have characteristics related to healthy reproduction. In general, those who fit the "average" human profile are considered attractive by most people. We can quickly and easily judge as healthy and fit an average person who fits a "human" prototype (Winkielman & Cacioppo, 2001). In fact, when faces from different ethnic groups were "averaged" by a computer into composite faces, people of different racial backgrounds all judged the "composite" or averaged face as the *most* attractive of all the faces of different races (Rhodes et al., 2005).

Some other commonalities are found across cultures. For example, women around the world are attracted to men who are taller than average, have angular facial features, and possess athletic or muscular builds (but not too muscular), with a precise 0.9 waist to hip ratio being rated as the most attractive (meaning the shoulders are slightly wider than the hips and the body has a "V" shape; Hatfield & Sprecher, 1995; Pierce, 1996). Women are also attracted to large eyes, large smiles, and prominent cheekbones and chins (Barber, 1995). They also prefer ambitious men, those who are intelligent, industrious, and have financial potential (Buss et al., 2001). Likewise, men the world over prefer women who appear young (at least three years younger than they are; Kenrick, Gabrielidis,

Keefe, & Cornelius, 1996) and healthy, with a waist to hip ratio of about 0.7 (Singh & Luis, 1995), large eyes, large smiles, prominent cheekbones, and symmetrical features (especially breasts; Jones, 1995). They like women who appear physically attractive and chaste. Men also prefer women who are friendly, intelligent, have a good personality, and a sense of humor (Kenrick, Groth, Trost, & Sadalla, 1993). Across cultures, both men and women rate intelligence, kindness, and understanding as highly important. Men rate physical attractiveness as more important than women do. In fact, men sometimes even seek out women who are more physically attractive than they are. They are less afraid of rejection than women are, as women usually set their sights on men at about the same level of attractiveness. Also, men tend to date down while women tend to date up in terms of the socioeconomic status and education levels of their partners.

Men and women both prefer blemish-free skin and symmetrical features of average size (Montagu, 1986). Interestingly, Shackelford and Larsen (1997) discovered that people who are more *asymmetrical* are less active, more depressed and anxious, get more headaches, are sick more, have fewer sexual partners, and score lower on intelligence tests. Therefore, evolutionary psychologists believe there are universal human traits that potential mates find attractive in order to ensure they mate with the most physically fit and healthy person who might guarantee the continuation of their gene pool through healthy offspring (Rhodes et al., 2001).

Despite the evolutionary similarities across cultures, there are also large variations in characteristics that are considered attractive in cultures around the world. For example, many groups perform elaborate body modification to appear more attractive. In western cultures, this takes the form of women removing the hair from their legs and armpits, wearing make-up, using self-tanning spray to make their skin appear darker, getting plastic surgery such as breast implants, and so on. Men in these cultures may have hair transplants, calf or pectoral implants, or may work out and diet to build a more muscular physique.

Paduang people in Thailand prefer brass neck rings to breast implants. Women wear brass rings around their necks beginning in childhood and continue adding rings over time. The most attractive women have the longest necks and may sport up to 20 or 25 rings by middle age. In Ethiopia, Mursi women pierce their lower lips and insert increasingly larger ceramic disks over time. Eventually, they can fit a disk the size of a musical compact disc in their lower lip (Heine, 2008). In many African nations, being called "fat" is a compliment and women are considered quite attractive the more girth they carry on their bodies (Cogan, Bhalla, Sefa-Dedeh, & Rothblum, 1996; Neff, Sargent, McKeown, & Jackson, 1997).

Within each culture, there are also many individual differences as each of us has our own idiosyncrasies regarding what "type" attracts us. For example, in the United States, African American women feel less pressure to be thin than white women and think the ideal body is heavier than white women do. Nevertheless, we all share the same type of physiological reaction when aroused by a potential mate.

Neurobiological research

At the individual level, when we see someone we are sexually attracted to, our brains are flooded with the neurotransmitter dopamine. This neurotransmitter makes us feel warm and tingly, blissfully happy, and somewhat intoxicated. It circulates in the reward centers of the brain to give us a sense of pleasure and euphoria, as well as more focused attention and motivational drive (Fisher, Aron, & Brown, 2005). Fisher and colleagues (2005) argue that the drive for romantic love is a primary motivational system in humans. It's based on the tenacious drive for brain chemical rewards, is often difficult to control, and is distinct from the sex drive. Sometimes people can't think straight because they become so infatuated with a new-found partner. At times like those, we tend to look past the person's flaws and idealize their strengths. We can't stop thinking about him or her. We fantasize about being with that person almost continuously. And there is an intense physical desire present when he or she is near us. This kind of "love high" cannot last forever, though. It wouldn't be adaptive. The brain wouldn't tolerate us being disconnected from reality for so long. Eventually, we have to come down. Before long, we usually start to see the person in a more objective light and decide whether to pursue a longer-term relationship or not.

As relationships evolve and we fall in love, being with a person for a long time and becoming true companions, we experience a brain awash with another chemical, oxytocin. This chemical gives us a sense of calm security, of warmth and contentment (Carter, DeVries, & Getz, 1995). That's not to say the passion is completely gone. There are still often episodes of intense passion or sexual excitement, but the couple has moved into a state of true friendship, intimate sharing, and safety.

This neuroscience research is still in its infancy, and these findings represent *correlations* between different neurochemicals, human behaviors, and feelings. In spite of how intriguing these correlations are, they cannot tell us whether these chemicals cause these behaviors or vice versa.

Phases of chemical attraction

Helen Fisher and her colleagues have examined the neurochemistry of attraction and have found three distinct phases with different chemical profiles (Fisher, Aron, Mashek, Haifang, & Brown, 2002). In the first phase, **lust** (libido, or sex drive), sex hormones like estrogens and androgens are peaking. This is thought to reflect the evolutionary desire to reproduce. We often lust after a wide variety of people, and in evolutionary terms, we could reproduce with just about anyone, which would conserve the time we usually take to secure a mate. Lust would quickly create offspring to continue our genetic legacy without any emotional conundrums standing in our way.

Lust in men tends to be much more visually stimulated. For example, men in one study reported being aroused by images of women in films they were shown, but women were stimulated by images of both attractive men and women (Fisher, 1999). This research finding calls into question evolutionary arguments that lust is all about the motivation to reproduce. Why would same-sex attractions evolve if the key motivation is to reproduce? There is no consensus on an answer to this question, evolutionarily speaking or otherwise. However, we do know that same-sex couples have the same physiological reactivity, attachment security, and quality of relationships as heterosexual couples (Roisman, Clausell, Holland, Fortuna, & Elieff, 2008). For example, in their studies of gay and straight couples' responses to relationship quality surveys and their attempts to solve common

Lust
The first phase involved in the neurochemistry of attraction; characterized by high libido or sex drive. Sex hormones like estrogens and androgens are peaking. This is thought to reflect the evolutionary desire to reproduce.

FIGURE 5.1 Do you think this couple is experiencing more dopamine or more oxytocin?
Photo © Chris Clinton/Lifesize/Getty Images.

problems in a laboratory setting, Roisman et. al. (2008) found no differences between the different types of couples, except for the fact that lesbian couples worked together the most effectively as a team on cooperative laboratory tasks when compared to gay male or heterosexual couples. As discussed in the previous chapter, no one truly knows how homosexuality develops but it's clear that the phases of chemical attraction and commitment are the same across the sexual orientation spectrum.

The second phase of chemical attraction, **attraction** proper, is characterized by increases in the neurotransmitter dopamine. It also involves increases in norepinephrine (popularly known as adrenalin) and decreases in serotonin (the mood-stabilizing neurotransmitter). Attraction involves heightened energy with attention focused specifically on one person. There is a sense of romantic or passionate love, feelings of exhilaration, and intrusive thoughts. A couple may stay up all night talking, needing little food or sleep. There's a sense of being "amped" and euphoric (Bartels & Zeki, 2000; Fisher, 1998; Wang et al., 1999). These are the same feelings engendered by taking amphetamines or cocaine. Such drugs increase dopamine levels and give a person a sense of exhilaration, energy, sleeplessness, and a lack of appetite (Wise, 1996). Thus, attraction is, literally, intoxicating.

The difficult part of neuroscience research, though, is knowing that these target neurotransmitters affect numerous processes beyond the ones associated with lust or attraction. These same chemicals have been identified as playing roles in processes as diverse as hunger, sex, sleep, problem-solving, and attention skills. Thus, researchers try to piece together a coherent story about what the elevations in certain neurotransmitters mean, but they could be missing some other important chemical changes that have not been measured or that are related to other kinds of behaviors which have nothing to do with mate selection. So make sure you keep your critical thinking muscles flexed, even when reading about fascinating research that makes a lot of sense to you, like Fisher's work on chemical attraction.

In the third phase of chemical attraction, Fisher and colleagues argue that we form an **attachment**. This is the phase when the partners develop a sense of calm, security, and emotional intimacy. Oxytocin is circulating in higher amounts in the brain, as is vasopressin, which constricts the blood vessels and influences feelings of emotional bonding (Carter et al., 1995; Fisher et al., 2002).

These researchers think that the three phases of *lust*, *attraction*, and *attachment* are characteristic of distinct motivational systems, which may function independently from one another, stimulating different chemical pathways in the brain, and different behavioral profiles in the relationship (Fisher et al., 2002). While we must consider these research findings as preliminary for the time being, they raise interesting questions about the impact our actions have on our brains and vice versa. They help us understand that romantic relationships are more than just social. They are part of our deepest physiological make-up.

Attachment and biology

Once a couple reaches the *attachment* phase of their relationship, internal working models are activated, directing and organizing discussions, problem-solving, disagreements, worries, and communication. Mikulincer (1998) found that people who were insecurely attached (with either *avoidant* or *preoccupied* attachment styles) had higher physiological reactivity than securely attached people. They not only had internal working models characterized by betrayal fears and preoccupation with attachment problems, but their bodies were in a heightened state of arousal, with a higher heart rate and blood pressure, compared to other couples.

To further explore this fact, Pietromonaco, Greenwood, and Feldman (2004) examined 76 dating couples. The couples read scenarios that implied threats to attachment relationships (for example, your partner's job has been relocated to another state; your partner is not sensitive to your emotional needs). The researchers assessed how each person in the couple described how he or she might cope with these issues as well as how distressed they reported feeling. Results showed that *preoccupied/ ambivalent/anxious* people reported high levels of emotional distress in trying to solve these problems and exhibited poor abilities to cope with the attachment challenges. *Avoidantly* attached people

Attraction
The second phase involved in the neurochemistry of attraction; characterized by increases in the neurotransmitter dopamine. It also involves increases in norepinephrine (popularly known as adrenalin) and decreases in serotonin (the mood stabilizing neurotransmitter). Attraction involves heightened energy with attention focused specifically on one person. There is a sense of romantic or passionate love, feelings of exhilaration and intrusive thoughts about the person.

Attachment
The third phase involved in the neurochemistry of attraction; characterized by a sense of calm, security, and emotional intimacy. Oxytocin is circulating in higher amounts in the brain, as is vasopressin, which constricts the blood vessels and influences feelings of bonding. Attachment also refers to the emotional bonds between children and their caregivers or romantic partners.

reported coping without asking others for help or even talking to loved ones about the attachment challenge. They said they would simply suppress their feelings. People who were not themselves avoidantly attached but whose partners were avoidant reported the lowest levels of coping abilities. This study shows that each partner's attachment style affects the other's ability to cope and regulate his or her emotions. *Secure* partners helped their mates modulate their emotional lives and regulate their levels of distress, and were not intrusive, controlling, or judgmental while trying to solve attachment challenges. These findings suggest that love and attachment affect not just ours, but also our partner's, neurobiology.

To examine the emotional regulatory skills of partners in more depth, Powers, Pietromonaco, Gunlicks, and Sayer (2006) examined the functioning of the hypothalamic pituitary adrenal (HPA) axis (our body's stress regulation center) via saliva samples before, during, and after a stressful task. The HPA axis includes the hypothalamus of the brain, the pituitary gland of the brain, and the adrenal glands above the kidneys. This three-part system controls the response to stress and the ability to recover from stress and remain calm. A person's saliva reveals how much cortisol, the stress hormone, is circulating in the person's body through their HPA axis. So studies on cortisol use a cheek swab of saliva which is then analyzed for stress hormone levels. These researchers had dating couples discuss a typical issue they often disagreed about at home and asked them to try to resolve the issue in the lab. Results revealed that *insecurely* attached mates had the highest levels of cortisol during this task. Women who were *avoidantly* attached started the experiment with the highest cortisol levels of any group, and their stress levels remained high throughout the task. The researchers argued that because women typically are expected to initiate problem discussions and resolve issues more openly than men, this task was extraordinarily uncomfortable for these women who were avoidantly attached. Perhaps part of the reason for them avoiding intimacy and a secure attachment is to be able to reduce the overwhelming physiological arousal they feel while in relationships.

Preoccupied/ambivalent/anxious men in this study also started out with extremely high levels of cortisol before the task, and their cortisol levels remained high throughout. Interestingly, men with secure partners, regardless of their own attachment style, had the lowest cortisol levels of any group, while men with insecure partners of any type had high levels of cortisol throughout. These results again support the key regulatory functions romantic partners serve. People's attachment style affects their own neurophysiology, but their partner's attachment style can either exacerbate or modulate their own ability to regulate emotions. Thus, your partner changes your biology. Both partners bring baggage and assets to a dating relationship, which researchers are beginning to reveal in neurochemical analyses. To learn more about the measurement of cortisol as a marker of stress regulation and its relationship to risk-taking behavior, see the *How Would You Measure That?* box.

Beyond our neurophysiology and attachment history having interesting links with our dating experiences, larger social forces also play a role in who, when, and how we date.

FIGURE 5.2 Secure attachments allow couples to regulate each others' emotions.
Photo © Andres Rodriguez/Stocklib.

HOW WOULD YOU MEASURE THAT?

Cortisol and Risk-taking (Halpern, Campbell, Agnew, Thompson, & Udry 2002)

Halpern et al. (2002) examined 150 18- to 25-year-old men to investigate whether a person's "stress reactivity" is related to sexual and non-sexual risk-taking. Some people are more "reactive" than others and this is a fairly enduring trait that persists across contexts. *Stress reactive* people have higher cortisol (stress hormone) levels, are more cautious and fearful, and take fewer risks. Low levels of reactivity are related to more risk-taking behaviors.

The men in this study were first exposed to stressful situations. Based on their reactions to these situations, the men were categorized into either the "stress reactive" or "non-reactive" groups. The two stressors used were public speaking and dating interviews. For the public speaking stressor, the men were told they would have 10 minutes to prepare a persuasive speech that they would deliver under spotlight in a darkened room. Researchers would watch from behind a one-way mirror and score their ability to make logical arguments. For the dating interview stressor, men watched a videotape of an interview about dating to get a feel for what types of questions they would be asked in a similar interview later on. The videotape showed a very attractive woman in tight clothing flirtatiously asking questions such as "What do you think about when you masturbate?" The participants' cortisol levels were collected via saliva samples over a three-day period to gather baseline levels and to monitor how their cortisol changed when faced with these stressors. So in this study, the *independent variable* was stress reactivity (with two groups, high and low), with stress reactive men being those who responded with significant cortisol elevations to the stressful tasks. The *dependent variables* measured were various risk-taking behaviors.

These were measured by the researchers having the men fill out questionnaires about their sexual and non-sexual risk-taking behaviors, such as having sex without a condom, stealing things, and driving drunk.

About 17% of the sample was found to be "stress reactive," meaning their cortisol levels increased at least two-fold during the stressful tasks. About 40% of the sample was "non-reactive," and other men fell in between, usually responding to only one stressor and with less than double the cortisol increase. Results showed that stress reactivity was significantly related to the men having fewer total number of sexual partners in their lifetimes, fewer deviant and illegal activities, and surprisingly, lower rates of condom use. These results suggest that people who have elevated cortisol levels are more fearful and cautious. While having sex without a condom may seem like a risky behavior, the authors argue that physiologically reactive men may fear confrontation or open negotiations about condom use. They may be embarrassed and less assertive so they refrain from the conversation all together. "Non-reactive" men (those who were not stressed by public speaking or embarrassing interviews) had two times the number of sexual partners as the stress reactive men, as well as having the highest rates of deviant behavior, and condom use.

This study suggests that physiological reactivity can be both a protective factor (making fewer risky choices) as well as a risk factor (not using condoms). Thus, the way people go about dating and sexual encounters may have a lot to do with their stress reactivity levels. How has your own level of reactivity affected your dating relationships? Have you been a wild adventurer or a cautious loner? Do you think these findings would generalize to women?

Person, process, and context factors

Besides the more biological factors of lust and attraction, many individual and personal factors, as well as larger social contexts, also influence who we choose as our mates. The most obvious contextual influence is **propinquity**, or nearness (Festinger, Schacter, & Back, 1950). We tend to meet people with whom we frequently interact, or who live near us, work with us, share similar hobbies, or belong to our social networks. It's more difficult to initiate and maintain a relationship from far away. At work

Propinquity
In close proximity; people are more likely to date those who are nearby.

Mere exposure effect
The idea that the more we are exposed to a person, the more likely we are to engage in a relationship with him/her.

Similarity-attraction effect
The idea that instead of opposites attracting, most of us actually choose mates very similar to ourselves in attractiveness, personality, and social standing.

Homophily
A liking for people like ourselves.

Expectancy Value Theory
A theory of mate selection which states that people evaluate potential partners based on perceived attractiveness, compatibility, similarity, and whether the person has the attributes and the potential to play roles we consider to be vital characteristics of an "ideal" mate.

here might be the **mere exposure effect**. This idea states that the more often we are exposed to someone, the more we like him or her (Zajonc, 2005) (sort of like how if you try broccoli enough times, you actually start to like it).

Despite the old adage that opposites attract, the reality is that we tend to choose people who are quite similar to us. We usually end up with people who exist in our proximate vicinity, especially if we see them a lot, and most especially if we think they're just like us. The **similarity-attraction effect** states that we are drawn to those who are about as attractive as we are, share like personality traits, have obtained similar levels of education, share religious or cultural values, and have similar interests (Hassebrauck & Aron, 2001; Lydon, Jamieson, & Zanna, 1988; McPherson, Smith-Lovin, & Cook, 2001; Regan & Joshi, 2003).

The similarity-attraction effect varies by culture. For example, the effect is stronger in Native American people than in Japanese people (Lydon et al., 1988). Lydon et al. found that this effect may also be mediated by self-esteem. The Japanese participants in their study had lower levels of self-esteem than the Native Americans and also showed less preference for people "just like them." This implies that you may be more likely to choose people similar to you if you have many positive feelings about yourself. Most people, however, do experience some level of **homophily**, or attraction to partners who are similar to them. For example, partners' self-ratings of their own attachment styles tend to be positively correlated with each other (Feingold, 1988), suggesting that we're attracted to people with similar internal working models. Moreover, it has been found that after one meets a similar partner, those partners then shape and reinforce the similarities in each other so they become even more similar over time (Simon, Aikins, & Prinstein, 2008).

Beyond similarity and propinquity, we also tend to seek out mates whom we predict share similar values and whom we expect will play a vital role in completing our lives. The **Expectancy Value Theory** of mate selection states that people evaluate potential partners based on perceived attractiveness, compatibility, similarity, and whether the person has the attributes and the potential to play roles we consider to be vital characteristics of an "ideal" mate (Murstein, 1970; Overall, Fletcher & Simpson, 2006). Illustrating this idea, in a study of ethnically diverse 10th grade boys, Smiler (2008) found that the top three reasons boys reported for dating were that they liked the person, they were really attracted to the person, and they wanted to get to know the person's values. These results were surprising because the boys did not fit the gender stereotype that boys are just interested in sex. In fact, when asked specifically about reasons for engaging in sex with their partners, these boys reported that they wanted to find out what it was like, that they liked or loved the person, and that *she* wanted to do it as among their top reasons. These relational motives for teen dating and sex are encouraging in that compatibility and connection seem to be just as important for males as for females. Adolescent boys want to get to know their partners' personalities and values. Thus, contemporary western boys appear to be a bit more comfortable sharing their feelings and crossing the rigid gender boundaries of previous generations.

Interestingly, in a study of 7th to 12th grade students, Udry and Chantala (2004) found that the boys and girls who adhered most closely to traditional gender role values were the most likely to have had sex, and they actually had it sooner than less gender stereotyped people. Earlier sexual experience is also more likely if both partners enter puberty early (Phinney, Jensen, Olsen, & Cundrick, 1990). These studies' combined results illustrate how biology, individual factors, and social forces interact to influence sex and dating choices. In addition, they provide evidence to support the Expectancy Value Theory. Adolescents are more likely to become involved with partners who are like them physically and emotionally, and who hold the same values and attitudes.

Micro- and mesosystem influences on adolescent dating

Studies on dating adolescents show that their romantic partners are just as influential as their best friends on their thoughts, feelings, and behaviors (Adams, Laursen, & Wilder, 2001). Therefore, it is important for parents to remember that their children's dating partners are important socializing agents (Collins, 2003). In one study, Simon et al. (2008) assessed students on social and emotional variables before (time 1) and after (time 2) dating couples began dating. At time 1 (6th grade), future non-daters were rated similarly in popularity, body appeal, physical attractiveness, and depressive symptoms as the future daters. Students in the 6th through 9th grades who began dating were seen by peers as more popular, less sad, less physically victimized, and more physically attractive than those who didn't date. Those who were low functioning (sad, depressed, aggressive, and victimized) at time 1 but later dated higher-functioning partners became indistinguishable from popular, well-functioning teens at time 2, post dating. This means dating popular, well-adjusted peers "rubs off" on the less well-adjusted teens, and that the popular, high-functioning students were not dragged down in popularity or other positive ratings by peers if they dated a lower status partner. Similarly, Werner and Smith (2001) found that aggressive, disruptive teens changed their behavior when associating with well-adjusted and supportive partners. These findings are important because teen dating relationships are rarely considered in terms of the important role they play in increasing an adolescent's happiness and social functioning at school. Parents usually worry only about the negative outcomes of dating.

Because over half of teens have special romantic partners and high school students spend more time with their partners than with their family members, it's important that families work hard before the teenage years to prepare teens for dating and mate selection (Collins, Welsh, & Furman, 2009). For example, adolescent girls who have open, secure relationships with their mothers tend to date later than teens with strained parental relationships, and they have higher-quality romantic relationships as well (Scharf & Mayseless, 2008). Mothers who exhibit flexible control (that is, knowing where their daughters are at all times yet allowing them some freedom) and who respect their daughters' privacy, tend to have teens who wait longer to date and have better-quality relationships when they do date.

The same patterns have been found for adolescent boys. When boys are exposed to negative parental interactions like fighting and tension, they begin to view aggression as normative and have more hostile relationships with their girlfriends (Collins et al., 2009). This effect is even stronger if the teen boys also have a negative or hostile peer group, so both microsystem and mesosystem influences take root in teenagers' romantic lives. In fact, Friedlander, Connolly, Pepler, and Craig (2007) found that when parents monitor their boys' whereabouts, the boys' peers are not dating, and the boys experience a relatively late pubertal onset, they are likely to date later and have more intimate and fulfilling relationships with their dating partners.

Looking at this research from a bioecological perspective, we recognize that relationships exist within larger contexts which are each linked to the other. Each relationship influences the development, maintenance, and dissolution of other relationships (Parks, 2007). Even in western and individualistic cultures, we seek approval from those in our microsystems to engage in relationships with new people who will join our microsystem and subsequently become important dynamic players in our mesosystem influences. Parks (2007) argues that without support from members of our microsystem, it's much less likely that a relationship can advance to a more intimate level.

Our social networks can influence the course and security of our intimate relationships. It's not surprising, then, that most of us choose to enter into relationships with people similar to us, as they will most likely be accepted by those in our social networks. As Shanice and Adrian's story reveals, cultural factors can also often play important roles in the maintenance or dissolution of a relationship. While Shanice and Adrian felt very similar to each other in terms of their values, goals, and dreams for their future family, their demographic differences led to many strains on their relationship. They struggled with mesosystem and macrosystem pressures. Check out the *Focus on My Family* box and read about how they persevered despite a lack of support in their social networks.

The macrosystem: cultural factors

As you know from the discussion of gender roles in Chapter 3, women have been oppressed and controlled in most societies. So it may not surprise you that women often have less control over the dating, mate selection, or courtship process than men. In a study of 860 societies, Daly and Wilson

FOCUS ON MY FAMILY

Adrian and Shanice's story

Adrian: I met Shanice one night partying with friends. She drank too much and got sick. I took care of her and since then, we have been inseparable. At the time, it felt like one of those movies where the guy gets the girl and then all these problems start occurring. We had been together for four days straight when I found out she was four months pregnant. I was shocked, but not really surprised because I had had bad luck with women in the past. But I knew that if I didn't stay with this girl, who had such a good heart, life wouldn't be the same. I needed her as much as she needed me. Friends told me to leave her because the pregnancy wasn't my problem. My family was worried about what I was getting myself into because Shanice's father didn't like Mexicans. Even worse, some people in my Mexican family do not like African Americans, so it was hard telling them about Shanice. Even though our family members didn't like it, they knew we made each other happy. Shanice helps me keep my head focused on my goals and I help her as much as I can. I like to go outside and do things but she stays inside a lot. I try to make it so she doesn't have to worry about things. Shanice and I mean the world to each other.

Shanice: When I met Adrian, I was shocked about the pregnancy. I hadn't missed my period and my tests came back negative at first. When I decided to keep the baby, I was glad Adrian stayed with me because I was really scared and I didn't have any emotional support. It wasn't that my father disliked Mexicans, he just didn't think any guy was good enough for me. I felt that Adrian's family was reluctant to let me in because I was black. I often felt left out because I didn't know the language and his aunt, with whom Adrian is really close, only spoke Spanish. Once I expressed how uncomfortable I felt not knowing Spanish, his family started to teach me a few words and now when they do speak Spanish, they let me know what is being said so I don't feel so left out. I believe this was the turning point in our relationship because I started to feel accepted by his family. Having his family finally accept me and my daughter has definitely brought us closer together. I had to make Adrian understand that it's not that I don't like to go out and do things, it's just that I have a busy schedule and I don't have the time to play. I have school, work, and a daughter who needs to be taken care of. It took Adrian a while to understand where I was coming from. We've worked through a lot of our problems and now we both feel we complete each other.

Adrian and Shanice.
Photo reproduced by permission.

(1983) found that women had complete freedom of mate selection choices in only one quarter of the societies. Kin priorities and elder preferences were the norm, rather than the exception to the rule. Women were often considered to be the property of the family and were seen as an economic asset. Their mates were chosen based on what would benefit families, villages, and even whole regions.

Monogamy was the normative marriage system in only 16% of the societies. Other research confirms that the majority of the world practices polygyny (Flinn & Low, 1986). Polyandry is found in less than 1% of those societies and even in those cases, brothers usually marry the same woman and the woman has little choice in the matter (Flinn & Low, 1986; Murdock, 1981). Monogamy is most likely to exist in societies where both parents are needed to raise offspring, especially in poor, harsh conditions (Geary, 1998). Monogamy is also common in large societies that have much political and economic stratification. In societies with socially mandated monogamy, such as in western nations, men and women tend to be more similar than different in the qualities they desire in potential mates (for example, intelligence, kindness, attractiveness) (Geary, 1998). Thus the availability of material resources, cultural traditions, and other macro forces shape our mate selection options and strategies.

Cultural factors are not always static; they are not always unchanging or maintained forever. Instead, cultures change rapidly, so it's not surprising that mate selection and dating also change over time. Several theories can help us analyze these trends.

THEORIES OF DATING AND MATE SELECTION

Structural-Functionalism and dating

Conflict Theory and Filter Theory

Larger social influences work hard to maintain traditional values so the way people date and choose their mates has usually been regulated by forces attempting to maintain the status quo. But the only constant in life is change and such traditions are eventually challenged and practices change sooner or later. The theories that were introduced in Chapter 2 can help us analyze trends in dating, mate selection, and marriage in more depth.

Structural-Functionalism and dating

Gender role expectations play a major role in the dating game. Recall from Chapter 3 that Structural-Functionalist Theory (Parsons & Bales, 1955) focuses on the functional role each person plays in making the larger social system work as it should. Because Structural-Functionalists focus on maintaining social roles as they are, and prefer the status quo over change, they argue that males and females play complementary roles that help form SNAFs in order to maintain the structure of society the way it was meant to be. Men work, women stay home. Men are chivalrous and protective while women are fragile and need protection. Heterosexual dating, then, is a way to fulfill social expectations regarding gender and sexual identities. The traditional western dating pattern is *androcentric* because it centers around girls looking for boys who can take care of them, and when pairs form, the importance of the boyfriend overshadows the girls' previous friendships (Adelman & Kil, 2007). The girl "belongs" to the boy, and with marriage, men hold the most power.

As discussed in Chapter 3, however, more modern viewpoints see these traditional gender roles as conflicted and as impeding each person's ability to develop into a complex, multifaceted romantic partner. The conflict that has arisen over contemporary young men and women challenging traditional gender constructions has led to real changes in how people date.

Conflict Theory and Filter Theory

Recall that Conflict Theory focuses on the obvious as well as the subtle power differentials that affect dating and courtship relationships. It argues that over time, people start to question their traditional roles and want more for themselves than those roles provide. According to Conflict Theory, this conflict is not a problem, but is a positive route toward new realities. Thus role conflicts should help mates negotiate change and develop a new level of balance or homeostasis in their functioning. Through the experience of conflict, problems in power imbalances can be changed for the better.

One specific area of power differences in relationships has been the pervasive influence of male entitlement, the belief that men are entitled to court women of higher education, social class, and attractiveness than themselves, and that they hold power over "their" women. Men also traditionally feel entitled to better treatment than their own behavior might warrant. Men tend to expect more from dating partners than the partners think they deserve. For example, traditionally, men might have expected sex if they paid for an expensive meal. Women expected men to be the pursuers, not initiating sex themselves. Consequently, women often viewed their virginity as their most valued asset.

Similar to the way Social Exchange Theory posits that people logically weigh the pros and cons of specific partner characteristics, and Fiske (1991) discussed the "market pricing" dynamic in which people engage when in a new relationship, Goode (1982) described the process of dating as a "market exchange" enterprise. In this case, before we ever choose a potential mate, the entire pool of eligible partners is weighed in terms of supply and demand. You might not approach someone whose "market value" is excessive. For example, would you walk up to a famous movie star at a party and ask him or her out? What about someone from a prominent wealthy family in your town? Interestingly, men are more likely to pursue a *market maximization strategy* and approach women who are of greater market value than they are. Women are more likely to use a *matching market strategy* and approach men who match their own value. This means that men *overvalue* themselves and feel they are entitled to better partners, better treatment, and more benefits than they might objectively be worth. These differences in value illustrate the crucial role of male entitlement in western heterosexual dating patterns (Goode, 1996). This relates to Conflict Theory because, when one person overvalues him or herself, that sense of entitlement can lead to power struggles, conflict, or even shouting matches in public places where the overvalued party does not take the hint that the other person is not interested.

Being faced with disparate views of your market value partially explains why there is often conflict between people who have different gender, power, or market expectations. According to Conflict Theory, however, conflict with existing partners can be an impetus for positive change. For example, when we are confronted with our flaws or people criticize us, we learn about things in us that may need to change. If we respond to this information, we can often build intimacy with the current partner or make changes within ourselves after the relationship dissolves. These positive changes stemming from relationship power struggles and conflict allow us to keep searching for the next partner, one who may be of equal value to ourselves. As we re-evaluate our own market value and gain some experience in the dating marketplace, we may begin to develop a series of filters through which all future potential mates must be sifted.

In cultures where individuals have a choice in the mate selection process, people often analyze the market value of potential mates through a careful analysis of "perfect mate" selection criteria. **Filter Theory** states that we sift through all possible potential mates until smaller and smaller groups of eligible mates are formed (Kerckhoff & Davis, 1962). First, we begin with a large **pool of eligibles**, the population of people who could potentially be our mates. This pool of eligibles initially includes all single people around the world. Keeping the pool unfiltered would substantially increase the chances of our finding a mate. However, especially in western cultures, people have an ideal "soulmate" in mind. They don't consider that every single person on the planet might be a potential mate. They look for a person who will complete them, make their lives whole, and meet their every need like a fairytale come true.

Filter Theory
A theory which states that people have various cognitive filters through which they sift the pool of eligibles in order to create a perfect soulmate in their minds; the filters usually contain preconceived ideas about what a future mate must be like.

Pool of eligibles
The available group of people who could be potential mates for us.

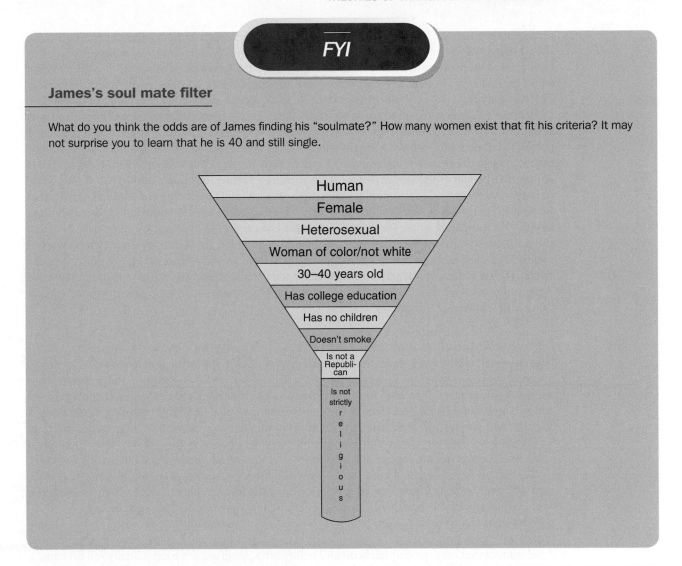

FYI

James's soul mate filter

What do you think the odds are of James finding his "soulmate?" How many women exist that fit his criteria? It may not surprise you to learn that he is 40 and still single.

Human
Female
Heterosexual
Woman of color/not white
30–40 years old
Has college education
Has no children
Doesn't smoke
Is not a Republican
Is not strictly religious

Most youth expect to someday find that "soulmate." In doing so, they use detailed filters to look past many potential mates, trying to find that one person who will fulfill all their needs. The first filter is usually *propinquity*, or being near the person (Murstein, 1976). We have to somehow come into contact with the person before we date them. We often select a person from a pool with which we regularly interact. Next, the pool of eligibles is filtered through the *attractiveness* sifter. We look at which people surrounding us are most attractive and try to get to know them. The next levels include *social background*, *consensus*, and *complementarity* filters. These refer to people wanting someone with similar social status, who shares their attitudes and beliefs, and also balances their lives by complementing traits, lifestyles, and friends they already have. We may use different filters, but for all of us, the more we filter potential mates, the slimmer and slimmer our chances for actually finding a mate. The *FYI* box, "James's Soul Mate Filter," shows how this filtering process can work to a person's disadvantage.

Like my friend James, many of us look past potential mates who might be excellent fits for us because we are looking for an impossible ideal. No one is perfect, including you. Finding a person who shares similar interests and values and is kind, supportive, and attractive, may be enough to make you both happy. Matchmakers often instruct people to find "Mr. or Ms. Good Enough," not "Mr. or Ms. Right." With this new mindset, the market value of people we once thought would never be acceptable for us may increase quite a bit. The more we analyze our filters and sift through those things that are truly "requirements" or "deal breakers," the more likely it is that we may readjust our own market value down to a more reasonable place, and perhaps look at others as of higher market value than they were before. When dating partners stop trying to solve all of their conflicts or differences and stick to just the most important issues, relationships have a better chance of succeeding.

Because we exist in many contexts, we have friends, family members, and people in our spiritual communities who can fulfill some of the needs that our potential partner might not. Expecting a person to be everything we need in all situations is a lot of pressure to put on someone. If we expect our potential mate to be good enough, we may be more likely to stay in our relationships. Shulman (2004) argues that people in the western world want it all in a partner, but that nothing has caused more unhappiness in the world than people looking for a soulmate and not finding one. Shulman argues that we tend to settle for a state of "stable ambiguity," where we are in a relationship half-heartedly, always looking for something better. We expect excitement and passion at all times. We want to be blissfully swept off our feet and when things settle down, we run. Shulman also discusses how many people feel ashamed of their partners if they are not perfect. We want to show off a partner who is physically attractive, has money and a perfectly compatible temperament, and adores us unconditionally. We want to show that our filter system worked beautifully. But we may be overestimating our own market value with that type of thinking.

More on filter and market value approaches to mate selection

In non-western cultures, the perception of equal market value may play an even larger role in the mate selection process than it does in western cultures. The laws of *endogamy* require that someone from within the proper group is chosen for a young person to date (although "dates" are usually chaperoned and occur in family homes). Elders in the community may filter out large portions of the pool of eligibles and choose someone from inside the community who shares the same values, religion, education level, and social standing as the family seeking a mate for their child. Issues of chastity, pride, honor, and a financial agreement between two families often come into play in mating decisions.

It is extremely important in many non-western cultures for women to be virgins when they meet men who will be their future husbands. Virgins carry the highest market value of any woman. If a woman does not bleed on her wedding night, her virginity may be called into question.

What makes a woman a virgin, and why is bleeding on the wedding night so important? Some think a woman is a virgin when she has an intact hymen, a mucous membrane formed during prenatal development that often incompletely divides before birth, leaving a remnant. Usually the first time a woman has sexual intercourse, the hymen tears and bleeds a little. However, because women are very active today and may use tampons, it's not uncommon for a woman who has never had intercourse to have no hymen. In addition, if the tissue divided completely before birth, the hymen never develops. Moreover, many sexually active women still have hymens. Thus, the hymen is an inaccurate method for determining virginity for many reasons (Goodyear-Smith & Laidlaw, 1998).

Nevertheless, some women feel such pressure to prove their virginity that they go to extremes. For example, some Middle Eastern women are now having artificial hymens surgically attached inside their vaginas so that on their wedding nights, the small flap of skin will detach and the desired spattering of blood will occur on the sheets of the wedding bed, proving her chastity and thus her high market value.

So far, this chapter has shown that all levels of the bioecological model come into play during hooking up, dating, and mate selection. Our neurochemistry, personal expectations, attachment histories, microsystem relationships, and cultures each play a role in how we end up building our lifetime partnerships. And even though today in western cultures love and finding a soulmate are of utmost importance, the following section will show that this is a fairly new phenomenon, pointing to the importance of the chronosystem in shaping our beliefs and practices regarding mate selection.

HISTORICAL TRENDS IN DATING AND MATE SELECTION

Historically, most, if not all, mates were chosen based on the financial benefit, political gain, or social standing that person could bring to the entire family, and ultimately, on the ability to reproduce (Ferguson, 2007). Love was not a part of the mate selection game until recently; it didn't factor into the market value of a mate. Romantic love, if it occurred at all, usually took place outside the context of marriage. For example, in medieval times, many of the European elite wrote love poems and songs to their one true love, who was usually someone other than their spouse (Ferguson, 2007).

Love was not a consideration in mate selection for the majority of human cultures until around the 1700s. Changes that occurred during the Enlightenment period of the eighteenth century led people to value personal happiness and fulfillment. In previous generations, most families were so busy trying to survive that personal happiness never even crossed their minds. But during the Enlightenment, people began to base their beliefs on reason instead of tradition. They came to feel they deserved the best mate with the best market value, a person who met all of their filtered criteria for a deep connection.

Beginning in the 1840s, with the Industrial Revolution and a rising middle class, people started working regular hours and so had more leisure time during which they could focus on hobbies and activities of mutual interest. Women began to work in factories and met men from different towns and backgrounds. Large urban centers sprouted up across the United States and Europe, and people's social circles began to expand. Mandatory education brought large numbers of adolescents together in one school building, which led to diverse groups interacting with each other without chaperones (Bailey, 1988).

Then a little invention changed the dating game forever: mass production of automobiles. In 1908 Ford developed the assembly line method of production, which allowed cheaper cars to be produced for the general middle class. Rosen (2004) said that the automobile did more for sexual adventures than any other technology. Middle-class families began to buy automobiles and this opened up a whole new world. Potential suitors no longer had to come calling at the invitation of a woman's parents (Whyte, 1992). Formal courtship with adult chaperones and elaborate rituals began to decline (Rosen, 2004).

Although traditional courting was very formal and young people were chaperoned and monitored by family members, even as far back as 1790 census records show a premarital conception rate accounting for 33% of live births (Smith & Hindus, 1975). So even in the "old days," modern practices like premarital sex still existed, albeit under a blanket of secrecy.

During the days of frontier expansion in the nineteenth century, when people were freed from puritanical and strictly religious families, a first "sexual revolution" occurred (Whyte 1992). As people moved across the Wild West and left the trappings of proper society behind, they gained the freedom to do as they pleased. With a shortage of women, men in the west often visited prostitutes and imported wives through mail order. These matches were certainly ones of convenience and not based on love or mutual attraction. The children's book, *Sarah Plain and Tall*, tells the story of a frontier family, a widowed father left with two children. He desperately wants a mother and wife to care for the children and the homestead, so he answers an ad in the newspaper. When Sarah, the potential mate, writes, she describes herself as plain and tall. She ends up being the perfect match because she can cook and keep a house and they all get along fine (MacLachlin, 1985). This story shows how growing rates of literacy, the availability of newspapers, and a wider set of filters allowed many pioneer men and women to find mates.

But nothing had more impact on mate selection than the advent of the automobile at the turn of the twentieth century. Middle-class men could pick up their dates and go to restaurants, out dancing, or on long country drives. Modell (1989) describes the dance craze of the 1920s when young people could mingle in large crowds of strangers. The new dances were liberated from tradition, exuded sexual energy, and allowed women to fill up their dance cards with the names of multiple partners. Movie theaters began sprouting up. Girls could choose to date several boys at once, some of whom took them to emotional movies in darkened auditoriums where "making out" became all the rage. Young middle-class people had more free time to enjoy leisure activities and women gained more freedom.

These dating trends did not escape the notice of wealthy capitalists. Romantic feelings became linked to consumption as the romance industry began to boom (Illouz, 1997). Romantic books, fashions, fragrances, and "must have" products like flowers, candies, and greeting cards exploded onto the market. With increasing literacy rates, more young people began to read magazines and pine after the clothes and lifestyles of rich, attractive celebrities who appeared to be blissfully in love. Whyte (1992) describes dates as being essentially an opportunity to test out new products.

With new rituals becoming entrenched, gender expectations also evolved. Men exhibited chivalrous behaviors and paid for everything, while women played coy and "hard to get" games. By the 1950s, drive-in theaters, malt shops, school dances, and live rock concerts marked the new life of the American teenager. A burgeoning youth culture evolved where adolescence was seen as a separate stage, and an individual was no longer a child but not yet an adult. Romantic images in the media influenced young men's and women's ideals about their future lives (Illouz, 1997). Middle-class children were expected to marry after high school, buy a house, and have children. Especially for white women, the expectation was that they stay home and make their husbands' lives comfortable.

In the 1960s, middle-class gender role expectations reflected SNAF values as men were expected to earn a living to support their wives. But with the women's liberation movement of the 1960s and 1970s, women started to expect a more equal and free role in relationships, in terms of both power and sexuality. They wanted to make decisions, work outside the home, get an education, and not be told what to do by men or controlled by traditional societal expectations.

The next most important influence on dating came in the 1960s, with the advent of the birth control pill (Rosen, 2004). "Enovid," as the first pill was called, was invented by Polish American chemist Frank Colton in 1960. Before oral contraceptives hit the market, women had lived in fear of becoming pregnant out of wedlock. They would be sent away to boarding schools, forced to have abortions or to give their babies up for adoption. Birth control pills gave women control over both their fertility and their dating lives. Oral contraceptives provided women with the freedom to experiment sexually with as many types of men as they wanted. There was no longer fear of an interracial baby being born or a child being born to unmarried parents.

At the same time, change was seeping into society at large. Dating involved families, religious figures, and cultural elders much less often. Cross-racial dating became more prevalent, especially after legal segregation ended and African Americans won civil and voting rights. From the 1660s to the 1960s the majority of U.S. states had **anti-miscegenation** laws, statutes barring sexual relations and marriage between people of different races (Kennedy, 2002). In many areas such a violation constituted a felony. In 1967 the U.S. Supreme Court halted the ban on interracial relationships in the case of *Loving v. the Commonwealth of Virginia*. In this case, an African American woman and her European American husband fought for the right to love whom they wanted and they won.

Anti-miscegenation laws
Laws that outlaw interracial marriage.

The 1960s and 1970s saw the hippie spirit of "free love" grow, especially on the West and East Coasts. While traditional values were maintained in many regions, some young people (especially in big cities) openly experimented with their sexuality and saw nothing wrong with having many partners across the race and gender spectrum before they married. In many cases, they even eschewed all traditional values related to marriage and family and didn't marry at all. They deconstructed their parents' generation's SNAF ideals, no longer believing in traditional gender roles. Gays, lesbians, and bisexuals started coming out of the closet and fighting for their rights to openly exist on the American landscape.

DIVERSITY IN DATING AND MATE SELECTION

> Ethnicity and dating
>
> LGBT communities and dating
>
> Seniors and dating

Because we all experience intersectional identities based on our gender, social class, ethnic background, religion, and culture, we can't assume that dating is the same for everyone, even if we all live in the same country. Most of the research we have on dating behaviors and attitudes comes from samples of white, middle-class people. Their experiences illuminate much about contemporary trends in hooking up, dating, and mate selection, but in order to gain a comprehensive understanding of these issues, we have to examine studies that utilize people from other demographic groups and give voice to their experiences. Because diverse relationships are becoming more accepted in contemporary society, we can now gain some understanding of dating patterns in mixed race couples, LGBT couples, and older couples.

Ethnicity and dating

Historically, European Americans opposed "race mixing," but today more African Americans than whites frown on cross-ethnic relationships. Part of the reason may be that today, there is only one black man of marrying age available for every three black women, so African American women have a smaller pool of eligibles than European American women do, which makes many black people disapprove of cross-ethnic relationships. This smaller pool of eligibles is probably due to the high rates of poverty among African American men, disproportionate rates of imprisonment, and high rates of death from violent crime. Kennedy (2002) refers to this disequilibrium as a *pigmentocracy*, meaning that the color of one's skin determines how many dating opportunities he or she has.

Many involved in the 1960s Black Power movement opposed cross-ethnic relationships as well, because they wanted to encourage cohesion among African Americans. A famous slogan was "You can't talk black and sleep white." Some activists were disheartened by seeing black leaders in the civil rights movement dating and marrying white women (Kennedy, 2002). Even though black–white marriage has increased substantially in recent decades, it's still relatively rare (less than 1% of marriages). Asian Americans and Native Americans tend to out-marry at a much higher rate than African Americans; an estimated 36–54% of such marriages are cross-ethnic (Kennedy, 2002). For example, 35% of American-born Chinese men and 46% of women marry interracially (Le, 2011). Unfortunately, there is a dearth of research on these populations and their dating patterns. Much more research has been conducted with LGBT youth and adults.

LGBT communities and dating

Historically, sexual minority youth had a very difficult time finding adult role models to teach them about dating, finding partners, sexuality, and creating lasting relationships. They often struggled with identity and intimacy problems because of the social stigma attached to same sex dating (Savin-Williams, 1996). Most lesbian, gay, bisexual and transgender youth begin dating in heteronormative ways, either because they aren't sure how to proceed in other ways or to mask their burgeoning knowledge of being different from their peers. Like all young people, LGBT youth need romantic relationships to help them understand their place in the world of others and understand themselves as co-partners. Like people from all walks of life, finding partners who value who they really are validates LGBT youths' sense of self-worth (Browning, 1987; Isay, 1989).

The general public tends to view same-sex couplings in adolescence as a phase or as simply experimentation. There is no real avenue for these relationships to be viewed as serious or "normal." LGBT youth often see their first same-sex couplings as "deviant" and are shunned, teased, or ostracized for them. Unlike other youth their age, LGBT teens are afraid to hold hands or kiss their partners in the hallways of high schools and colleges. Erik Erikson (1980) described the key psychosocial task of early adulthood as the ability to form intimate relationships. Because this task is partially accomplished after one develops a stable sense of self-identity, this primary need of young people everywhere is often thwarted for LGBT teens by taunts, teasing, and feelings of self-doubt and shame (Savin-Williams, 1996). Moreover, LGBT teens may feel uncomfortable sharing their first loves, kisses, dates, and sexual experiences with their parents and peers, so they are often deprived of essential social support that adolescents need to negotiate the difficult road of early relationships. However, like all young people, LGBT teens desire long-lasting and meaningful committed relationships and finding that "soulmate" (D'Augelli, 1991; Remafedi, 1987; Savin-Williams, 1990).

Sears (1991) interviewed 36 gay southern youth and found that they had all dated heterosexually, but very few had dated same-sex partners. If they had, it was rarely done openly. Those who were publicly "out" and openly dated same-sex partners had the highest levels of self-esteem in the sample. Sears states that "the single most influential barrier to same-sex dating, the threat posed by peers, can have severe repercussions. The penalty for crossing the line of 'normalcy' can result in emotional and physical pain" (p. 167). These youth reported that they were even afraid to stand too close to their platonic same-sex friends, to hug, or even smile at them, for fear that their secret would be "read" or discovered. This led the teens to distance themselves from others, to not date at all, or to date in secret. Others have found that LGBT youth often have a sense that they are not "real" and that they feel utterly isolated from others (Anderson, 1987; Martin & Hetrick, 1988).

Many sexual minority youth report engaging in heterosexual sexual experiences but not enjoying it. They say they did it to fit in with peers, to be accepted, out of curiosity, and even in an attempt to prove to themselves they could be attracted to the other sex (Remafedi, 1990). White same-sex attracted teenage girls suffer the highest levels of depression and the lowest levels of self-esteem, and are more likely to be suicidal (Consolacion, Russell, & Sue, 2004) than other LGBT youth.

Interestingly, Consolacion et al. (2004) did not find these trends in ethnic minority youth of either gender in their sample of gay students. They hypothesize that ethnic minority youth have much experience with racial and ethnic prejudice and discrimination, so they have already developed skills to cope with marginalization by the time they enter adolescence and the dating scene. This points to the importance of looking for heterogeneity, or variance, within groups. Moving beyond the binary gay/straight, male/female categories and examining individual experiences in attraction and romance may illuminate trends more clearly (Russell & Consolacion, 2003).

While dating in LGBT communities may be more difficult, keep in mind that times are changing rapidly and that in many regions, school districts, and families, LGBT youth are valued, accepted, and openly mentored by positive role models in their communities. Many schools now have Gay–Straight Alliance associations and there are gay dances and support groups. Today LGBT youth are "coming out" at younger ages and are living more openly than ever before as society continues to evolve and change in its level of acceptance of diverse dating and mate selection practices (Denizet-Lewis, 2009).

Seniors and dating

There is little research on dating in later life. Issues regarding family relationships in the senior years will be discussed in detail in Chapter 13, but it is worthwhile to explore here what little is known about dating in this population.

People who are psychologically healthy later in life tend to have rich social lives, including remaining sexually active (Nussbaum, Pecchioni, Robinson, & Thompson, 2001). This suggests that dating may have a protective effect on the elderly, allowing them psychological and even physical health. Seniors report that dating relationships are helpful in building intimacy and self-esteem, and maintaining their sexual identity. Early research suggested that seniors who are widowed, divorced, or separated date for the purpose of finding a suitable marriage partner (Bulcroft & O'Connor, 1986). Research also showed that late life dating followed traditional gender roles, with men asking women out and paying for things (McElhany, 1992). Men in later life reported that they enjoyed dating because it gave them an outlet for self-disclosure, intimacy, and sex (Bulcroft & O'Connor, 1986).

More recent research examining older women's views about their dating lives reveals a trend toward changing gender roles and attitudes. For example, Dickson, Hughes, and Walker (2005) found that healthy middle-class senior women enjoyed dating men very much but they did not want to get married. In fact, they were diametrically opposed to living with their partners or ever planning on marriage. They reported that their dating partners often broke up with them because older men seemed to want to date only for marriage. The authors humorously referred to this phenomenon as the women's "nurse and purse" fears. These women enjoyed their independence and financial freedom. They didn't want to be tied down to nurse a man in his old age (many had already done so with their first husbands) and they did not want to share the money they had accumulated over their lifetimes. One 69-year-old woman said, "I raised one husband. I don't want to do it again … I almost prefer to date younger guys because they have more energy and I don't want to hear about how his back hurts" (cited in Dickson et al., 2005, p. 74). The women in this study strongly desired physical affection, companionship, and intimacy but not marriage. They also reported that their friends and family sometimes disapproved of their dating, saying that dating is for young women.

For both men and women, those seniors who are in good health, can still drive, are active in community and religious organizations, and have strong family ties are more likely to date than other seniors (Bulcroft & Bulcroft, 1991).

Let's look at some other dating trends found in contemporary research from cultures around the world.

CONTEMPORARY TRENDS AROUND THE WORLD

Dating with technology

Dating violence

Similar to the trends discussed for senior daters, dating in general is less about finding a marriage partner today than it was in the past. It's often for fun, recreation, practice in understanding and communicating with others, and coming to understand one's self (Laner, 1995). Dating these days is less organized, formalized, and ritualized. People often meet at parties or other group gatherings, and relationships can develop out of close platonic friendships and group activities.

Young people today are more educated about pregnancy, violence, diseases, and divorce. This knowledge can make them cautious. They often refrain from getting serious for fear of failure after seeing many couples around them divorcing (Ferguson, 2007). However, most young people still dream of meeting one true love. Americans, in particular, are very romantic.

Medora, Larson, Hortacsu, and Dave (2002) examined Turkish, Indian, and American college students. In each culture, women were found to be more romantic than men, but Americans in general were the most romantic of all. They reported emphasizing "feelings" as most important over other considerations in dating. They felt that love conquers all, that a person should follow his or her heart; and they believed in "love at first sight." The United States is an individualistic culture where people believe we should freely engage in self-disclosure, openly discuss love, dating, and our desire for a "soulmate" (Sastry, 1999).

In India, by contrast, young people are more often expected to be passive and cooperative, and obey their elders. The group controls dating choices. In many cases, marriages are arranged, and not based on love. Medora et al. (2002) found that Indian students' ideas about relationships were the least romantic of the three groups.

Turkey is a country in transition. It began as more traditional, like India, but is moving toward a western idea of mate selection (Hortacsu, 1997). Young people are usually allowed to date, but dating partners are often still filtered through the family for final approval.

It is interesting to note that globalization has led to many similarities between western and non-western cultures. On a list of 13 possible attributes of a mate, Turkish youth rated intelligence, education level, and a sense of humor as their top three qualities in a good mate. American students ranked having similar interests, being intelligent, and being affectionate as their highest three rankings (Medora et al., 2002).

Western ideals have spread and even in some of the most traditional cultures, we see conflicts now between individualistic and collectivist approaches to mate selection. For example, Zaidi and Shuraydi (2002) found that Pakistani Muslim women living in the U.S. and Canada wanted relationships in which they could express themselves and gain a sense of personal gratification. Yet the Muslim men participating in the same study were less prepared for such individualistic goals in a future wife.

Unfortunately for everyone in modern times, it can be difficult to find *anyone* to date, let alone someone who is a perfect match. Sometimes modern singles have to resort to the use of technology to widen their pool of eligibles.

Dating with technology

Many singles today use the Internet in hopes of snagging that soulmate. Internet chat rooms, dating websites, and social networking sites like Facebook and Myspace have expanded the pool of eligibles to include people from all over the world. Knox, Daniels, Sturdivant, and Zusman (2001) found that college students tend to use the Internet to meet people, to become bolder, and to reduce their social anxiety surrounding relationships. They report that meeting people in bars seems superficial, based on one's physical appearance and the search for sex, and that the Internet is safer than real life. With technology you can meet people from around the world and can also present your best self to them. However, you can also create a false persona through digital photograph manipulation and careful wording so that you may attract a wider array of potential mates (Clark, 1998). Recent research

FIGURE 5.3 How might finding a perfect mate be different for those of upper versus lower socioeconomic status?
Cartoon © Alex Gregory/The New Yorker Collection/www.cartoonbank.com.

"It would never work out between us, Tom—we're from two totally different tiers of the upper middle class."

suggests that, despite people's concerns about meeting manufactured potential partners online, most people tend to tell only "white lies," instead of creating a full blown false persona, because they know they may eventually meet the other person in real life. For example, men tend to lie about their height and women about their weight. This may explain why 85% of people report that they would not contact someone who didn't post a photo (Conkle, 2010). Sometimes when people choose to meet an Internet connection in person, they are actually surprised when the fantasy world they have created does not exist in real life (Waskul & Lust, 2004). "Daters create and invest in a persona while knowing that it may eventually be destroyed" (Waskul & Lust, 2004, p. 200).

Clark (1998) studied the actual posts of teen girls and found that they felt comfortable acting sexy, being bold and assertive, and yet remaining sheltered behind anonymity. Teenagers tend to create personas that are more exaggerated than most adults because adolescents often know they will not meet the partner in person. These personas can prevent a teen from being personally rejected, as correspondence is virtually anonymous. Teens can be brave, saying things they wouldn't say to a person in the real world. They can create a self they wish they were so they are less likely to be judged or get caught in the same relationship dynamics they experience daily with family and friends (Lawson & Leck, 2006). Dating is important for youth development, even if it's "virtual," because research shows that people who date less tend to be shy, lonely, and anxious, have more negative thinking patterns, and are less physically attractive than those who date more often (Lawson & Leck, 2006).

One's real physical appearance, personality, character flaws, race, religion, reputation and even gender can be masked, altered, or completely invented online (Danet, 1998; Lawson & Leck, 2006). Researchers hypothesize that young people may be desensitized to the sex and violence that pervades the media, and this may contribute to them taking online conversations less seriously. They see sexual activity, rapes, murders, and profanity in screen media regularly so they may post things that mirror what they're viewing without considering those posts potentially provocative or dangerous. They feel shielded behind the technology and so can act out fantasies or share secrets more easily than in person.

People communicating through modern technological means also tend to let down their guard more quickly. They charge into full disclosure of their most intimate thoughts and feelings (Rosen, 2004). Subrahmanyam, Smahel, and Greenfield (2006), in a study of almost 600 Internet chatters, found that 55% of posters revealed key identity issues in their posts. They didn't hesitate to post their age, gender, and ethnic backgrounds. Posters with male nicknames often posted sexually explicit comments, while those with female nicknames posted more implicit or coy sexual comments. In a study on moderated versus unmoderated sites, explicit sexual talk increased significantly, as did racial slurs, when sites were unmoderated (Tynes, Reynolds, & Greenfield, 2004).

This rush into intimacy and over-sharing of personal information may impede the natural progression of a relationship. Relationships usually take time to mature, to slowly evolve into one of intimate sharing and vulnerability. When you speed up this process to a matter of days, weeks, or even hours, you may cut potentially good matches off prematurely. Today when people meet someone new, they immediately do secret background checks, violating the person's trust before it's even established (Rosen, 2004). If we Google someone we just met, or friend him or her on Facebook, and find out everything about him or her, our perspective is skewed. We don't come to understand the new partner's own view of him- or herself. We don't get a sense for how he or she might like to reveal career, family, or religious or life experiences or build intimacy.

Today's daters often don't restrain themselves. There is a flood of instantaneous emotions expressed in emails and text messages. When new daters don't get an immediate text reply, they get suspicious. Or they can use texts against the person in arguments. The texted words can be saved indefinitely in their precise form, unlike memories of conversations which can be modified or even forgiven and forgotten over time. When we blog about our first dates and reveal too much information, it deadens the process of discovery. If you rush to a website that posts blogs by your new partner's disgruntled ex-partner, how can the new relationship stand a chance? It's also easier to stalk and harass people with new technologies and it's harder to get rid of people we're not interested in. We have to be good at setting boundaries and keeping relationships as formal or distant as we desire so that the wrong people don't get too close or glean too much information about us.

Intimate relationships evolve from human connections, sometimes involving coincidence, luck, or meeting across a crowded room, and the assessment of body language and non-verbal cues, none of which is available online. An additional problem is that much of the information we may find on the Internet is false. Clark (1998) says that these post-modern relationships are "delivered through the medium of a disembodied 'surface' community, allowing [people] to feel connected to others while allowing them to experience affirmation in an environment that does not risk their current social position" (p. 129). People can be whoever they want to be in the virtual world, and this is different from dating in previous generations because it's harder to be dishonest in person.

Along with all the negatives, there is a positive side to technological dating. There is a much larger pool of eligibles, and we can find and reconnect with previous crushes or partners. We can communicate with people quickly and decide if we want to meet them in person, and we can quickly weed out those whose pictures don't appeal to us or who post things that irritate us. Once we've selected a potential mate, it's easier to connect throughout the day with a quick "xoxo" in a text sent from the office or anywhere. As with all dating trends throughout history, some things are lost but new things are gained.

If you're not in a long-term relationship and are thinking about starting to date someone you've met online or in person, reading the *Building Your Strengths* box can help. It presents some sensible tips from various matchmakers that should enhance the first impression you make on a potential partner. While none of these tips has been scientifically supported, they make good sense. Dating can be dangerous if we connect with the wrong people, and we have to be cognizant of red flags that might indicate that a person could be aggressive or violent.

Dating violence

Whether you meet someone online or in the real world, it's important to recognize that dating relationships can be dangerous. While teen and college-age girls are more likely to be sexually or violently assaulted by dating partners (Molidor & Tolman, 1998), 10% of teen *boys* also report being the victims of dating violence (Howard, Qi Wang, & Yan, 2008). Verbal and physical dating aggression is found in at least 25% of teenage relationships, both heterosexual and homosexual. While boys tend to commit more physical violence that can injure their partners, there are no gender differences in verbal abuse or psychological aggression, such as stalking, belittling, spreading rumors, and bullying (Collins et al., 2009).

There is an important connection between bullying and dating violence. In studies on middle and high school students, bullies and those who are both bullies and victims of bullying have the highest rates of dating violence. Victims of bullying also experience more emotional abuse in their

FIGURE 5.4 What characteristics do you think might make for good "filters" when meeting potential mates on the Internet?
Photo © Photodisc/Getty Images.

BUILDING YOUR STRENGTHS

Improving your first impression on a date

If you follow the tips below, you may make a good impression on your date:

- Arrange for a first date to be brief, about two hours long and in a public place, both to ensure safety, and, if it's not working out, to allow you to leave soon. If it is working out, your date will be anxious to see you again. Be sure to greet the person warmly and with a smile. Use humor to break the ice.

- Pay close attention to your appearance by grooming well, being clean, and wearing clothes that are appealing but never uncomfortable or too tight. Women should not wear clothes that are too revealing (leave something to the imagination). Both genders should dress in a casual enough way that they can be prepared for spontaneous walks or other activities. Try to look put-together but not like you tried too hard.

- Pay attention to your posture. Try not to slump over. Use confident body language and make eye contact.

- Don't appear too desperate. Try to appear optimistic, happy, and positive. This means not talking about previous dating or relationship disasters. In fact, avoid any talk of previous relationships, politics, religion, and gossip until you get to know the person better.

- Be curious about the other person; lean forward and smile; use good manners and try not to appear either too anxious or too cocky/conceited; ask open-ended questions to keep the conversation flowing.

- It's OK to flirt, but save the sex for when you get to know the person better. If the mood strikes you, a brief kiss or a hug are appropriate for a first date.

- It's not a good idea to use alcohol or drugs on a first date, or even on a second date; you don't want to say or do things you later regret (or reveal deep dark secrets that might scare the person away).

- Please, no texting or answering cell phones. This is extremely rude. Your date should feel important and as if he or she is your priority at that time.

dating relationships, as well as high levels of sexual harassment by school peers. Being victimized by bullies, classmates, and dating partners has been linked to high levels of depression, anxiety, and even suicide (Espelage & Holt, 2007).

Risk factors for becoming a perpetrator or a victim of dating violence include early involvement with antisocial peers, lack of school safety, academic problems, and exposure to violence in the family (Schnurr & Lohman, 2008). Children who were maltreated by their parents often fail to develop empathy for others. Parents and peers may reinforce their negative attitudes about relationships. They are more likely to interpret benign acts as hostile in nature, and feel no remorse for aggression toward partners (Wolfe, Crooks, Chiodo, & Jaffe, 2009). Wolfe et al. (2009) found that adolescents fail to take responsibility for dating violence and that boys are especially likely to be perpetrators of dating violence if they were maltreated as children and associate with deviant peer groups. Ryan, Weikel, and Sprechini (2008) discuss that male narcissism and a sense of entitlement are also associated with both young and older men physically assaulting their partners.

Adelman and Kil (2007) point to the fact that most dating today begins in larger platonic friendship groups. These groups, then, can exacerbate, support, or ostracize peers who dominate or violate their dating partners. The mesosystem is critical in preventing or allowing dating violence to occur. Friends can endorse violent acts or protest them. They can kick violent members out of the group or join in attacking the victims.

To avoid becoming a victim, people should keep early dates to public places like restaurants and movie theaters. They should refrain from using alcohol or drugs and should not depend on a partner they don't know well for a ride home. Early in relationships, women, especially, should have a friend or family member available to pick them up if need be, and there should be someone waiting at home for their arrival at a specific time.

If dating violence or sexual assault does occur, survivors should not be ashamed or blame themselves. They should immediately report the incident to authorities and seek out social support from friends, family, and professional mental health workers when necessary. Victims often blame themselves because they like the dating partner, know a lot of the same friends and don't want to break up the group, or feel that they led the person on. The public also tends to blame the victim for putting him or herself in a vulnerable position.

Contrary to what people might think, however, no one deserves to be a victim of date rape or dating violence, no matter how provocatively he or she is dressed, how drunk he or she gets, or how many times the couple has previously dated, kissed, or even had sexual relations. Every dating partner has the right to say "no" at any stage of a relationship and his or her wishes deserve to be respected. "Love" does not mean control, jealousy, power plays, humiliation, secrets, or violence. These behaviors are red flags that should alert you to get out of a relationship as soon as possible. Real love is about support, nurturance, intimacy, and acceptance. It is to this topic that we now turn in Chapter 6.

CHAPTER SUMMARY

Dating consists of early stage romantic excursions that serve as a foundation for building a potentially committed relationship. Hooking up consists of casual sexual experiences with strangers or acquaintances (kissing, oral sex, intercourse) without the expectation of any further contact after the fact. Friends with benefits refers to people engaging in sexual activities with friends or acquaintances without expecting the development of a committed partnership.

Historically, formal courtship rituals took place where families were keenly involved in dating and mate selection choices. Courtship was designed to lead to marriage. However, contemporary trends in western cultures include dating just for fun. Hooking up and being involved with friends with benefits allows young people to be sexually active without the need for commitment or expectations. However, most youth still desire a soulmate, a committed partnership to build a life with. When people evaluate potential mates, they often consider variables such as the level of personal sharing they feel comfortable with, the power dynamics of the relationship, how equitable and fair things seem, and whether their partner is of equal market value.

Filter Theory argues that we have a series of mental filters through which we sift those in the pool of eligibles. These filters include propinquity, attraction, and complementarity. The pool of eligibles becomes quite small after we sift people through increasingly unrealistic filters we have in mind regarding an ideal mate. With modern technology, we can create false personas and often engage in rapid intimacy online, leading to disappointment if we ever meet an online partner in person. The disillusionment model suggests that we put on our best faces for new dating partners and we become disillusioned or disappointed when we get to know them and see them for their true selves.

Dating ideologies and mental filters often begin to develop in childhood as we interact with our caregivers and form internal working models of relationships. Secure versus insecure attachments in childhood can influence the quality of our dating and mate selection experiences later on.

Dating and mate selection are influenced by all levels of the bioecological model. The chapter discussed the neurophysiology of attraction, lust, and attachment, whereby neurochemicals such as dopamine and oxytocin rise and fall in different phases of relationships. Culture also affects how we meet potential mates, what the dating experience is like, and which types of people are acceptable for us to become involved with. People of color, those from LGBT communities, and seniors often have extra challenges in finding dating partners and being accepted by larger society.

Dating violence was discussed as a common experience among college students and young people beginning to date or hook up. No one deserves to be harmed, ever. Controlling, domineering behaviors should be considered red flags that potential violence or sexual assault are possible.

KEY TERMS

anti-miscegenation laws
anxious, preoccupied, ambivalent
    attachments
attachment
attraction
authority ranking
communal sharing
courtship
dating

disillusionment model
dismissing avoidant
    attachment
equality matching
Expectancy Value Theory
fearful avoidant attachment
Filter Theory
friends with benefits
homophily

hooking up
internal working models
lust
mere exposure effect
pool of eligibles
propinquity
similarity-attraction effect

WEBSITES FOR FURTHER EXPLORATION

http://www.boundless.org/2005/articles/a0001451.cfm

This is the site for the webzine *Boundless*, which contains blogs and articles written by the Reform Episcopalian Reverend Skip Burzumato. While there is a Christian undertone to some of the articles, they are all pretty good for general audiences. The one cited in the URL is about the history of courtship and dating in America. There are other historical articles about dating, as well as a great many other dating and relationship related articles and blogs.

http://genealogy.about.com/cs/timelines/a/romance_history.htm

A great little overview of romance through ancient history, medieval times, the Victorian era, and modern Europe.

http://www.about.com has brief answers to most of your questions about dating and romance.

http://www.forbeginners.info.dating/

This is an entire site devoted to dating for beginners (sort of like dating for dummies). It has some interesting articles on dating for teens, seniors, and interracial couples, as well as dating tips for men and women, and information on dating safety.

CHAPTER 6
LOVE

From birth to death, love is not just the focus of human experience but also the life force of the mind, determining our moods, stabilizing our bodily rhythms, and changing the structure of our brains. The body's physiology ensures that relationships determine and fix our identities. Love makes us who we are, and who we can become.

(Lewis, Amini, & Lannon (2000), p. viii)

LEARNING OBJECTIVES

- To realize there are several ways to define love

- To understand the theories that categorize types of love

- To appreciate cultural and historic trends regarding how love has been conceptualized

- To learn the basic biochemistry underlying love relationships over time

- To apply Attachment Theory to adult–child and romantic love relationships

- To understand macrosystem influences on monogamous and polyamorous love

- To recognize the basic ideas and procedures involved in improving love relationships

Marriages and Families in the 21st Century: A Bioecological Approach, First Edition. Tasha R. Howe.
© 2012 Tasha R. Howe. Published 2012 by Blackwell Publishing Ltd.

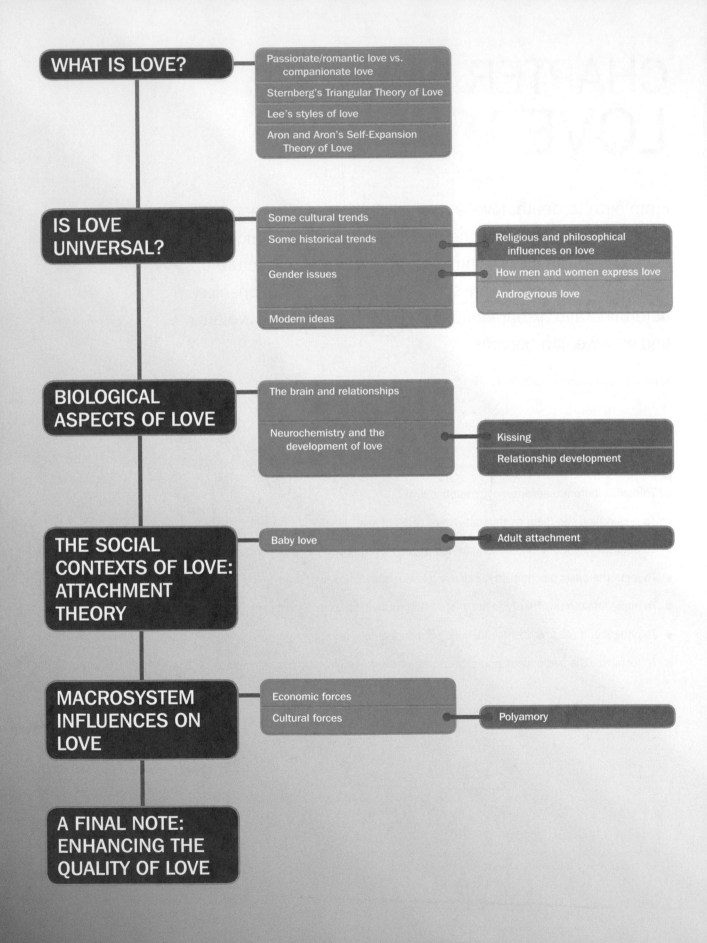

WHAT IS LOVE?
- Passionate/romantic love vs. companionate love
- Sternberg's Triangular Theory of Love
- Lee's styles of love
- Aron and Aron's Self-Expansion Theory of Love

IS LOVE UNIVERSAL?
- Some cultural trends
- Some historical trends
  - Religious and philosophical influences on love
- Gender issues
  - How men and women express love
  - Androgynous love
- Modern ideas

BIOLOGICAL ASPECTS OF LOVE
- The brain and relationships
- Neurochemistry and the development of love
  - Kissing
  - Relationship development

THE SOCIAL CONTEXTS OF LOVE: ATTACHMENT THEORY
- Baby love
  - Adult attachment

MACROSYSTEM INFLUENCES ON LOVE
- Economic forces
- Cultural forces
  - Polyamory

A FINAL NOTE: ENHANCING THE QUALITY OF LOVE

WHAT IS LOVE?

While most of us have felt something we think is "love," it is difficult to put into words exactly what that feeling is. Shaver, Morgan, and Wu (1996) describe love as a physiological reaction that engenders proximity-seeking behavior. Singer (1987) describes love as a search for friendship, beauty, and spiritual connection. Love tends to include a strong sense of attachment to another person and can involve both extremely pleasurable and intensely painful experiences. When we love another person, it's like jumping off the high dive into a pool. Love involves risk-taking. We risk getting hurt for the thrill of something like flying head first through the air. While most of this chapter will focus on romantic or passionate love (usually involving sexual and amorous partners), it will also explore the strong feelings of love we develop for our parents, friends, and children.

Scientists have not yet developed an agreed-upon definition of the concept of love. Baumeister and Leary (1995) discuss that love may be a process that provides evolutionary advantages because seeking communion with others increases one's own chance of survival. For now, let's define **love** as the subjective feeling of emotional connection with another person, often accompanied by intense desire to be near, care for, protect, or share one's life with that person.

Passionate/romantic love vs. companionate love

Long-term romantic relationships often start out pretty differently from where they end up. When we first choose a mate, we are often obsessed with thoughts of that person. We can talk for hours without sleep or food. We can make love for longer and more often than usual. We ignore the bad things about that person and think about our future together as perfect or fairytale-like. This initial stage of a relationship is characterized by passion and romance. We often feel as if we are not living in reality, like we are floating or dreaming when we're with our new love. This experience is referred to as **romantic/passionate love**.

When people have been together for a long period of time, say for many years, however, they tend to experience **companionate love** (Berscheid & Walster, 1978). This type of love is one of affiliation,

Love
The subjective feeling of emotional connection with another person, often accompanied by intense desire to be near, care for, protect, and/or share one's life with that person.

Romantic/passionate love
A type of love that usually exists with newer relationships, where sexual excitement and intrusive thoughts of the person are common.

Companionate love
A type of love that usually exists in long-term relationships where sexual passion may have declined but intimacy, commitment, and a sense of security are high.

FIGURE 6.1 People who have been together a long time enjoy each other's company and are "best friends" as well as lovers; they often experience companionate love.
Photo © Jose Luis Pelaez, Inc./CORBIS.

deep respect, and a "best friendship." The two people enjoy spending time together and feel comfortable being exactly who they really are. While passion and romance may not be completely absent from companionate relationships, they are usually less intense and occur less often than in the beginning of the relationship. However, research suggests that passion is one of the strongest predictors of relationship satisfaction (Contreras, Hendrick, & Hendrick, 1996). Thus, long-term couples may have to work extra hard to rekindle their passion by scheduling intimate dates, going out of town to hotels, or celebrating anniversaries and birthdays away from the mundane happenings of their everyday lives. But don't feel sorry for people in the throes of companionate love. They are usually quite happy. As people get older and build their lives together, passion and sex may become less essential ingredients for maintaining the relationship, although those things still carry some importance for most couples.

Erik Erikson argued that the key developmental task one needs to accomplish in early adulthood is the skill of **intimacy** with others. He defined true intimacy as being vulnerable and open and being able to share yourself with another person without losing your own identity. Those who lack the skills or experiences of intimacy often feel isolated and, according to Erikson, can leave early adulthood feeling a sense of meaninglessness as they enter middle age (Erikson, 1961). Thus, it appears that love, attachment, intimacy, and emotional connection with others are important for both our psychological health and our species' survival.

Although the need for love affects us all, it's extremely difficult to define. Many researchers have developed various typologies to attempt to pinpoint the key elements involved with love. Robert Sternberg's Triangular Theory, Lee's styles of love, and Aron and Aron's Self-Expansion Theory are the best known.

Sternberg's Triangular Theory of Love

Robert Sternberg (1986; Sternberg & Barnes, 1988) laid out a **Triangular Theory of Love**. In this view, love contains three components: *passion*, *intimacy*, and *commitment*, each of which Sternberg considers essential to love. Relationships can be characterized as high or low on each component. *Passion* includes constant thoughts about the person, strong desire to be near him or her, and sexual excitement. *Intimacy* refers to sharing one's thoughts and feelings, as well and being vulnerable enough to reveal one's true self. *Commitment* means that a couple has decided to forego all other liaisons and live in union with one person. They are strongly committed to the welfare of their partner and view life as a shared journey. Whether a relationship has relatively high or low levels of these components determines which type of love they are experiencing. Relationships that are high on passion but low on intimacy and commitment are called *infatuation*. Infatuated couples have a strong physical attraction and are often together a lot of time but they don't open up to share their secrets and they don't decide to stop

Intimacy
The ability to be completely open and honest with another person, merging your lives together without losing your own identity.

Sternberg's Triangular Theory of Love
One typology of love characterized by three parts, passion, intimacy, or commitment.

TABLE 6.1 Which of Sternberg's types of love have you experienced? Which would you like to experience? Source: Sternberg, 1986.

	Intimacy	Passion	Commitment
Nonlove	–	–	–
Liking	+	–	–
Infatuated love	–	+	–
Empty love	–	–	+
Romantic love	+	+	–
Companionate love	+	–	+
Fatuous love	–	+	+
Consummate love	+	+	+

Examples of love stories

Art: partner loved for physical appeal; one person is the admirer and the other is admired.

Business: relationship is a business deal; people are usually in the business together, but sometimes one partner "sells" him or herself to the other.

Democratic government: power shared equally; partners keep score.

Fantasy: one expects to be saved by a knight in shining armor or to marry a princess to live happily ever after.

Game: love is a sport; partners are both players or one may be unknowingly sucked into another's game.

Gardening: relationships take time, nurturing, and care; if properly tended, they will succeed.

Police: one person is in control of keeping the other in line; constant surveillance of the "suspect."

Travel: lovers travel together on a long journey and try to grow along the same path.

Source: Sternberg, 2007.

seeing other people to build a life together. Relationships that are high on commitment and low on intimacy and passion are called empty love. *Empty* couples are monogamous and do not seek to dissolve the relationship but they don't share very much with each other and are not physically intimate. Those who are new to a relationship and have great passion and intimacy but have not yet made a commitment are in the grip of romantic love. *Romantic* couples enjoy spending a lot of time together and may talk all night on the phone when apart, sharing all of their hopes and dreams. They have a fulfilling sexual life but have not progressed to building a committed monogamous life together. A relationship that contains all three components (high intimacy, commitment, and passion) is most likely to be successful, and is considered consummate love. *Consummate* couples enjoy doing things together, feel sexual attraction to each other, share hopes, dreams, and secrets with each other, and they do all they can to stay committed and build a secure life with each other. To see the various combinations of intimacy, commitment, and passion and the resulting types of love, see Table 6.1.

Sternberg emphasized that relationship partners can have compatible triangles or incompatible ones. If one person wants consummate love but another just wants romantic love, this can breed problems. Thus Sternberg urges people to talk about their relationship expectations as soon as they feel comfortable doing so, instead of assuming a partner wants the same thing they do. This is important because Sternberg has found that we create **love stories** in our childhoods. These love stories are ideas we store as templates in our minds, regarding what love should be like, and how we see ourselves ending up in a love relationship. Love stories are based on family of origin patterns, personality characteristics, and exposure to books and media. We may not even be aware of some elements of our loves stories because we store them in our minds unconsciously and they become implicit. See the *FYI* box for some examples of the love stories Sternberg found after interviewing thousands of people.

The most common stories are *travel*, *gardening*, and *democratic government*. Sternberg argues that we should analyze the implicit loves stories that underlie our ideas of what love relationships should be like, in order to be sure that our stories are compatible with our partner's. For example, the *travel* and *gardener* love stories are quite compatible. Completely different love stories can be a source of conflict. For instance, men often endorse *art* stories but women are most likely to endorse *travel* stories. The stories that are related to the lowest level of relationship satisfaction include *business*, *game*, and *democratic government* stories. Disparate stories are not always a source of trouble, however. They can also be used to start a discussion that brings people closer together as they create new stories and try to merge their categories together.

The Triangular Theory of Love is not the only way to think about our love patterns. John Alan Lee has done some interesting research on how people's relationship styles relate to the quality of their matches.

Love stories
Sternberg's idea that we form templates in our childhood based on interactions in our families and exposure to media images of what characteristics should be present in ideal love relationships.

Lee's styles of love

Lee's (1973) research uncovered five different *styles of love*, each with more or less focus on commitment and relationship health. He found that the five different styles that characterize love relationships can be used to predict the health of the match. Eros, the first love style, is like Sternberg's *passionate/romantic love* in that people experiencing it want intense intimacy and commitment from their partner. This style can be healthy, especially in the beginning of a match.

In Ludus, love is taken less seriously. It's seen as an endeavor undertaken for fun or an enjoyable pursuit a person can share with many different partners. In Ludus, love is treated almost like a game. Like Sternberg's *infatuation*, this approach has little intimacy and no commitment. It thrives on passion. Lee's research shows this type of love is related to poor relationship quality and unhappiness.

Like Sternberg's *companionate love*, Lee's idea of Storge (pronounced stor-gee) love involves maintaining a healthy egalitarian relationship with someone who is your best friend. The world *Storge* comes from the Greek idea of "natural affection," or easy love between family members. Couples experiencing Storge are happy and satisfied because they are each concerned with the well-being of the other person and enjoy sharing their lives with each other.

In Lee's fourth love style, people seek out a rational choice, a logical mate, instead of relying on their passions during mate selection. In this case, Pragma love develops, often with the help of matchmakers or through a rational deliberation process. The person chosen must logically fit into one's lifestyle and family configuration. A match must meet several pre-ordained criteria (recall the Filter Theory of mate selection) in order to be chosen. This is the type of love that occurs in arranged marriages. It's a sort of practical contentment that does not necessarily include feelings of personal happiness or sexual passion.

In complete contrast with Pragma, in Mania, the people involved are not logical or rational. They tend to be obsessive and insecure. They fear betrayal and are often involved in emotional drama within volatile relationships. They use only their hearts, never their heads. It can lead to knock-down drag-out fights and then amazing make-up sex. But the partners are not happy, satisfied, or fulfilled. This is similar to the *anxious/preoccupied/enmeshed attachment* style.

Finally, Lee describes Agape love, which is similar to Sternberg's *consummate love*, in that the couple are completely devoted to each other. They care for the very soul of the other person, always wanting to ensure their partner's welfare. They are selfless in their pursuit of making their partner happy. Agape includes true intimacy, passion, and commitment.

Try to categorize your previous or current love relationship, or the relationship of someone you know, using Lee's typologies and Sternberg's Triangular Theory. Table 6.2 summarizes the typologies and relates them to material you have already learned.

To examine the concept of love typology further, assess your love attitude in the *Self-Assessment* box.

TABLE 6.2 Comparing Lee's styles of loving to Sternberg's Triangular Theory and other concepts.

Lee's style of love	Similar concepts
Eros	Sternberg's romantic/passionate love
Ludus	Sternberg's infatuation
Storge	Sternberg's companionate love
Pragma	Filter Theory of mate selection
Mania	Anxious/preoccupied/enmeshed attachment
Agape	Sternberg's consummate love

SELF-ASSESSMENT

Love attitudes – short form
(Hendrick, Hendrick, & Dicke, 1998)

Please rate yourself on each item using the following scale: (1) Strongly disagree (2) Disagree (3) Neutral (4) Agree (5) Strongly agree

Eros Total _____

1 My partner and I have the right physical "chemistry" between us. _____

2 I feel that my partner and I were meant for each other. _____

3 My partner and I really understand each other. _____

4 My partner fits my ideal standards of physical beauty/handsomeness. _____

Ludus Total _____

1 I believe that what my partner doesn't know about me won't hurt him/her. _____

2 I have sometimes had to keep my partner from finding out about other partners. _____

3 My partner would get upset if he/she knew of some of the things I've done with other people. _____

4 I enjoy playing the "game of love" with my partner and a number of other partners. _____

Storge Total _____

1 Our love is the best kind because it grew out of a long friendship. _____

2 Our friendship merged gradually into love over time. _____

3 Our love is really a deep friendship, not a mysterious, mystical emotion. _____

4 Our love relationship is the most satisfying because it developed from a good friendship. _____

Pragma Total _____

1 A main consideration in choosing my partner was how he/she would reflect on my family. _____

2 An important factor in choosing my partner was whether or not he/she would be a good parent. _____

3 One consideration in choosing my partner was how he/she would reflect on my career. _____

4 Before getting very involved with my partner, I tried to figure out how compatible his/her hereditary background would be with mine in case we ever had children. _____

Mania Total _____

1 When my partner doesn't pay attention to me, I feel sick all over. _____

2 Since I've been in love with my partner, I've had trouble concentrating on anything else. _____

3 I cannot relax if I suspect that my partner is with someone else. _____

4 If my partner ignores me for a while, I sometimes do stupid things to try to get his/her attention back. _____

Agape Total _____

1 I would rather suffer myself than let my partner suffer. _____

2 I cannot be happy unless I place my partner's happiness before my own. _____

3 I am usually willing to sacrifice my own wishes to let my partner achieve his/hers. _____

4 I would endure all things for the sake of my partner. _____

Add your scores for each type of love. Those types of love with the highest scores most closely represent your love attitudes. Hendricks and colleagues have found that _Eros_ is related to relationship satisfaction in couples, while _Ludus_ is usually an unsatisfying relationship. Another way you can use this assessment is to assess your _real_ relationship, then assess your _ideal_ relationship, and discuss these differences with your partner in an attempt to build on your relationship strengths and improve weaknesses.

Note: _Self-Assessments_ in this textbook are not meant to diagnose, cure, or treat any relationship problems or struggles; they are for informational purposes only, and are meant to spur discussion.

If you or someone you know have ever experienced Agape or *consummate love*, you can appreciate why the search for love is so important to most people. Experiencing a truly selfless, balanced love where your partner expands your sense of who you are is a pretty great feeling. Aron and Aron (1986) discuss the idea of a true abiding love in more detail.

Aron and Aron's Self-Expansion Theory of Love

Self-Expansion Theory
Aron and Aron's theory that true love stems from one's wish to expand one's self; each partner helps the other become a better version of the self they once were.

In **Self-Expansion Theory**, Aron and Aron (1986) focus on true love and explain that it often stems from a wish to expand one's self, to invite another person to be part of one's self and vice-versa. In *self-expansive love*, partners fill the gaps and balance out their partner's traits. The sheer act of loving that person makes each partner rise to become a better version of the self they once were. This view is similar to Lee's *Agape* love and Sternberg's *consummate* love. Agape, consummate, and self-expansion love are thought to be ideal in many western cultures.

These ideas of selflessness, complete devotion, and a sense of calm security are found in the writings of both eastern philosophical and western religious traditions. For example, in Buddhism, true empathy and pure love are thought to be related to spiritual maturity. True love can only develop through spiritual meditation and practice. Buddhists speak of the exalted states of *mudita* (sympathetic joy) and *karuna* (compassion). Likewise, the Christian Bible, in the passage many couples include in their marriage vows (I Corinthians 13), states:

> Love is patient, love is kind. It does not envy, it does not boast, it is not proud. It is not rude, it is not self-seeking, it is not easily angered, it keeps no record of wrongs … It always protects, always trusts, always hopes, always perseveres.

So these feelings of self-expansive, Agape, and consummate love are valued in many different types of families, cultures, and religions. Do you think the desire for such love is just part of being human?

IS LOVE UNIVERSAL?

- Some cultural trends
- Some historical trends
- Gender issues
- Modern ideas

Feelings of romantic love exist in virtually every culture around the world. For example, Chinese literature over thousands of years discusses passionate love involving personal choice in one's mate selection process (Cho & Cross, 1995). Likewise, ancient Egyptian and Hebrew texts discuss passionate love (Hatfield & Rapson, 1996). Plato thought love helped honorable men remain honorable with their male counterparts and that love for a woman was beneath any honorable man (Coontz, 2005). Some Greeks even thought being in love made people insane. In medieval Europe, this "insanity" was thought to be cured by having meaningless sex with someone else. Royal European families often engaged in adultery as they felt real love could not be found in a spouse. And in China, historically, the word "love" meant a relationship the family did not approve of (Coontz, 2005).

Even if the feelings of love are universal, the importance placed on romantic love varies widely across cultures and has changed throughout history. For example, Russians today don't often consider love to be a necessary precondition to marriage, and Japanese people tend to be less romantic than American people (Sprecher et al., 1994). These results and the following section clearly illustrate that macrosystem forces profoundly impact people's attitudes toward and experiences regarding love.

Some cultural trends

Levine, Sato, Hashimoto, and Verma (1990) examined love in many cultures (India, Pakistan, Thailand, Mexico, Brazil, Japan, Hong Kong, Philippines, Australia, England, and the United States). They found that romantic love was most important to those living in western nations and less important for those in developing and eastern nations. Nyrop (1985) found that in India many people viewed romantic love and emotional attachments as threats to the family. In some Hindu traditions, love is not a valid reason to marry but it is acceptable if it develops after marriage (Coontz, 2005). For many cultures, too much love between a husband and wife is felt to undermine love for family and love of God.

Interestingly, the importance people place on romantic love is inversely related to the availability of large extended kin networks (Goode, 1959). In cultures where people have many extended family members living in close proximity, individuals get their needs met by siblings, cousins, in-laws, and elders, so less pressure is placed on marriages for emotional fulfillment. In many of these extended kin network cultures, marriages are arranged for the benefit of the whole family. The cross-cultural study by Levine et al. (1990) found that people in India, Pakistan, and Thailand were most likely to marry people without love as a deciding factor. In contrast, Brazilians were most likely to say that diminished love should lead to divorce, while people in the Philippines were least likely to believe this.

Some historical trends

Historically, the institution of marriage was created to bind two families together for the mutual political and/or financial benefit of the respective families and even entire communities. Marriage was about political alliance, financial merger, or military strategy maneuvers (Coontz, 2005). While people have always fallen in love, they did not expect it to occur within the context of marriage. The kingdoms of medieval Europe were strengthened by strategic marriages between cousins across France, Spain, Italy, and England, which kept power centralized for centuries. Written or pictorial records from most civilizations reveal evidence of romantic love, whether it is in the form of songs,

FIGURE 6.2 How can extended kin networks affect the emphasis on romantic love in couples?
Photo © Hill Street Studios/Getty Images.

poems, stories, or paintings. But even in classic love stories, like that of Antony and Cleopatra, power and control usually play key roles in the love affair (Coontz, 2005). Both ancient Greek and Roman cultures looked down upon men who loved their wives and valued romantic love only between men who were considered morally superior to women. A man was chastised and considered weak if he exhibited any kind of love toward his wife, and love between strong men was considered the highest love of all. Thus, pre-Christian pagan values led people to envision romantic love very differently from how some of us do today, illustrating the importance of the *chronosystem* for defining love.

Religious and philosophical influences on love

As Christianity spread across the world, a new emphasis on female virginity, piety, and the sanctity of marriage evolved. This led to a system of marriage where romantic love of a partner was considered idolatry, and people were chastised for not putting the love of God first and foremost. While medieval Islam was more tolerant of a husband and wife expressing their love for each other, the love of God was still considered paramount (Coontz, 2005). These types of exosystem influences are very important for most people because what religious leaders teach is filtered through parents and teachers and affects our ideas of love. Even today in many cultures, feelings like love are reserved for parents, kin, and God(s).

These historical trends cautioning against emotional love between men and women do not imply, however, that people did not engage in passionate love affairs. Quite the contrary. As mentioned before, European royalty often had love affairs with people outside of marriage. True love was considered impossible with a spouse so the upper classes often revered the love of concubines and male consorts. Sex with one's spouse was solely for procreation and if the wife did not produce a male heir, mistresses could sometimes legally bear royal sons (Coontz, 2005).

As the philosophies of the Enlightenment period of the eighteenth century began to spread, individual pleasure and happiness became the impetus in many people's quest for a mate. With the founding of the United States and the doctrine of the "pursuit of happiness," people felt their own freedom and individual joy were important. This, combined with the Industrial Revolution of the nineteenth century, led to people socializing with a wide variety of potential mates outside of their village or church circles. City life provided both men and women with many choices. The changes that technological advances brought to courtship and dating rituals (discussed in Chapter 5) also influenced people to take mates for a test drive before they settled down.

People from the American middle class, which emerged from these historical changes, wanted to marry for love. With individual freedom ensconced in society, women were more likely to have the same power as men to choose a mate of their own liking. With freedom and choice often comes a push toward autonomy. Many politicians, philosophers, and religious leaders feared the new focus on individual choice because they felt it would lead to women wanting to be equal to men in power, employment, and family clout. If they gave women the same rights as men to make choices, they would be admitting women had rational decision-making power, which could alter the balance of society. Remember that Structural-Functionalist Theory posits that each part of society plays a key role in maintaining the structure of society as it "should" be. This new trend of marriage for love threatened to undermine traditional power structures (Coontz, 2005).

Gender issues

If women could choose their husbands for love, they could also choose divorce if that love faltered. Thus, the movement toward personal happiness eventually led to the loosening of divorce laws. As the focus on love increased, the rates of divorce increased compared to previous generations (Coontz, 2005). With views of love, sex, and marriage changing, even as early as the late eighteenth century, many more women were getting pregnant without being married. With less responsibility on men to marry their pregnant partners, some women ended up working wherever they could to support their children, even turning to prostitution. This rise in unwed motherhood seemed to confirm the fears of the larger society in that it appeared that our new focus on individual pleasure and love could destroy the traditional family as we knew it (Coontz, 2005).

For the middle and upper classes in the nineteenth century, the Victorian ideal of **feminized love** evolved, where women did most of the loving and men avoided emotional commitment. Women and men were forced to play determined and prescribed roles in the family (Cancian, 1987). Men were expected to be emotionally detached from their wives and children, to be out and about living in the larger society. They had to do all the worrying about finances and deal stoically with business problems or political strife. Men were under intense pressure to bear male heirs so even if they loved their wives, a lack of boys in the family could mean that men took mistresses or divorced their wives. Women were expected to love their children, be naturally good at intimacy, and maintain kin and extended community relationships. They were expected to dress well and be the epitome of manners, grace, and style. While sex was their duty, intimacy with their husbands was not expected.

In many cultures around the world today, women are considered to be the intimacy "experts" (Tavris, 1992). While women used to be considered emotional, irrational, and lovesick, traits that were seen as deficits, today these same traits are often interpreted as the strengths that make women better at love, and more sensitive and caring. What do you think? Are women more able to love and be loved? If so, is this innate or socially constructed? Perhaps some of what you learned about gender in Chapter 3 can help you answer these questions.

Feminized love
The idea that women are naturally skilled at love, are good at empathy and tenderness, and that women's ways of loving are ideal compared to those of men.

How men and women express love

One thing that is commonly found in western cultures is that men show their love differently than women do. This also leads to different expectations for each gender. Men tend to think that love means "action." Doing nice things for their mates, such as washing the car, cleaning the house, or taking care of some unpaid bills, shows their love through action. However, women often want men to express their love through talking about their feelings and processing the relationship in verbally intimate terms (Tavris, 1992). Men often report that they don't know what women want when their partners constantly question their love or commitment. They argue that if they didn't love her, they wouldn't stick around. Statements like "I do so much for her yet she questions my love because I'm not a touchy-feely person" are common. Women, on the other hand, often make statements like "I know he loves me but sometimes I'd like to hear him say it to me and share his feelings about our relationship." These differences in perceptions can be seen even in childhood. Boys tend to talk about their feelings only when they are side by side with a friend, doing something together like playing ball or building something. They also reveal their feelings in a cloaked manner, through joking and teasing.

Teasing is often the main way in which grown men show their affection for their friends as well. Women would be offended if their friends said some of the things men's friends say to them. But for men, being open, accepting, and comfortable with a friend, allows one to poke fun at the other. They don't talk about their flaws and fears directly, however. Girls, on the other hand, prefer to reveal their deep insecurities and vulnerabilities to their girlfriends through intimate sharing, often through sworn confidences.

Grown women like to talk just to be heard by their friends. This act in itself relieves stress. Women talk to solve problems, to have their feelings confirmed, and to share secrets with their friends. Men often feel intimate connections to their partners by just being in the same room doing something together. Women want to engage in both "big talk" and "small talk" about key issues in their lives and the daily events that occurred (Tavris, 1992), but men often don't feel the need to delve deeply into issues.

These gender differences have led to the *feminization of love* mentioned above, wherein women's styles are considered "real love" and men's means of expression are thought to be inferior. Stemming from the Victorian ideals of feminized love, where women were thought to be skilled at love, kinship, and communication and not so interested in sex, contemporary viewpoints now see these feminine styles as most desirable. The way men express love is considered to be inadequate, lacking in intimacy, or superficial. But how can we expect men to express love like women do when their socialization is completely different in most cultures?

Androgynous love

For many people, gender role expectations have been loosening in recent generations. With the evolution of the suffragette movement and changing gender mores of the 1920s, a more **androgynous love** based on intimacy in both partners, where sex, love, and intimacy were combined in one relationship, began to alter people's expectations. The rise in divorce in the 1920s is often attributed to women's new sought-after power, individuality, and rights, their attempts to free themselves from social constraints and seek relationship freedom (Cancian, 1987). Marriage became a form of self-fulfillment, no longer a duty for many. Androgynous gender roles (both partners exhibiting masculine and feminine traits) became more normalized. Keep in mind, though, that these androgynous roles were far from becoming the norm for most families, as most women were still economically dependent on men. Role changes did allow for many men and women to be caring, understanding, and even sexually fulfilled. However, women were still responsible for maintaining the love and keeping husbands interested, attracted to their beauty, well-fed, and comfortable. And men were still expected to wear the rigid mask of masculinity, not allowing people to see their stress, worry, or fears of failure.

For working-class couples and poor families, survival was still more of an issue in their relationships than love was, and most women worked outside the home. Even in the 1970s, when women's liberation was sought by many and women expected others to respect their minds, poor women and more conservative or religious women still believed in SNAF ideals. This trend even exists today, where traditional family values are often pitted against women's freedom to choose, work, and have power over their lives, negotiating their own paths (Coltrane, 2004). Thus, the trend toward true androgyny in love relationships is still growing but not universal.

In general, however, in western cultures, love today *is* considered to be the responsibility of both men and women; each person is expected to sacrifice for his or her partner. Communication between partners is expected; intimacy is desired. For a glimpse of how one American woman integrated love and marriage in her life, throughout the years of changing gender roles, read the *Focus on My Family* feature.

Louise's story of young love following traditional gender roles with her first husband and finding more egalitarian love with her second husband represents a common experience for people marrying in mid-twentieth-century America. Keep in mind, however, that these trends of love, communication, and commitment are not true of all cultures either historically or today. Remember that even today many cultures around the world eschew the value of matches based on love. They feel that personal passions and love are irrational and no reasonable basis for forming a marriage bond. As discussed earlier, romantic love is often seen as interfering with a person's responsibility to their parents, extended kin, God, and community. It's a selfish pursuit, which can bring the downfall of traditional families and values. In support of this idea, it is true that as individualism increases, so does divorce. As socioeconomic status increases in communities, so do the desires for love, personal choice, and the freedom to divorce if desired.

Modern ideas

In modern American culture, we are socialized to believe that we should lock eyes with someone, feel instant passion, fall into bed with each other, and have multiple simultaneous orgasms (Lewis et al., 2000). Surveys from 50 years ago show that people in the U.S. wanted to get married in order to have children. Today people want to get married for love. They want a perfect match, a soulmate to counterbalance their own weaknesses, bring out their strengths, and provide them with unconditional love. We feel we can't possibly stay in a relationship unless we are blissfully happy (Shulman, 2004). This viewpoint discounts the necessity to give of oneself when in a love relationship, to be unselfish and put another's needs ahead of one's own.

However, many western industrialized cultures encourage selfishness and utmost care for individual concerns. With value placed on wealth, power, youth, and sex, modern American culture is based on consumption and materialism. Egocentric self-indulgence is one of the byproducts of

FOCUS ON MY FAMILY

The story of Louise's two loves

My first husband and I were madly in love (as much as teenagers know about love). Back then, one could not have a love affair before marriage (bad policy). I was a virgin as "nice girls" didn't "do it" without a ring on their finger. In the 1940s we got married so we could make love (my mother drummed that into me) and have children. He was going into the Navy and then to World War II. Soon I was pregnant, but he shipped out four weeks before my delivery, in 1944. The baby and I went home to stay with grandparents until the war was over. The war years were horrible. The baby was the shining light in a mad world. But the war did end, "the boys" came home, and soon another baby was on the way, born in 1948. We bought a house in a new development and thought we had reached suburban paradise. But he had not been feeling well so went to the doctor. He was diagnosed with Hodgkin's disease with a grim prognosis, which he fought for several months. Unfortunately, he died in 1954, at the age of 31.

I had to start working for the first time in my life, to support the children. I was a widow with two children and my future husband was divorced with two children. After a lot of persuasion, a mutual friend convinced us to go on a date. I was wary but he was handsome, personable, and well dressed, which diminished my anxiety. We had a wonderful evening, talking for hours, telling each other our life stories. We started seeing each other and fell in love. After two years, he was offered a job in another city. After discussing it with our children, we decided to get married and start a new life. We both worked full time and enjoyed parties, vacations, and participating in work functions with clients and co-workers.

My second husband and I are about to celebrate our 50th wedding anniversary. We have been blessed with grandchildren (one of whom lived with us during her teenage years) and great-grandchildren. I grew up during the Great Depression and we lost everything, so had to move in with my grandparents. That experience affected my life perspective … there is danger out there, don't take chances, security is everything … the struggles and conflicts in our marriage have been primarily due to this feeling of insecurity. Although he lived through the Depression, my husband experienced it differently. The drive for security was not an issue in his life; he is laid back and lets things slide, while I need order and predictability. Other than that, we are both even-tempered, we respect each other and enjoy being together. We both read a lot, love movies and music, and used to enjoy vacations. Health problems have affected us but perhaps have also drawn us closer. We still love each other and make each other laugh, but I think "happily ever after" is a myth. We are very happy at times, content most of the time, and the few times we are angry with one another are offset by good times. What more could one ask from a half-century-long love affair?

Louise and her first husband in the 1940s;
Louise and her current husband in 2006.
Photos reproduced by permission.

this culture. We fail to realize that good, healthy relationships can be simply moderately happy and that even moderate happiness may require lots of work. All relationships have problems, sometimes serious ones. Even the best, most long-lasting relationships include arguments about sex, children, money, and leisure time (Shulman, 2004).

The more collectivist a culture's beliefs are, and the lower the gross national product of a country, the less likely people are to focus on individual needs and desires. They are more concerned with the collective welfare of their groups, kin, and community, and so will often marry based on economic, religious, and familial obligation. This doesn't mean that people from collectivist or poor communities do not feel passionate love towards others. They do, but the objects of their affections may not become their spouses and those feelings may be considered of secondary importance to the welfare of others. Regardless of history, gender and culture, however, we all share common biological functioning when it comes to love.

BIOLOGICAL ASPECTS OF LOVE

The brain and relationships

Neurochemistry and the development of love

Charles Darwin, in his 1872 publication, *The Expression of Emotion in Man and Animals*, argued that emotions have adaptive value and that our emotional expressions serve to communicate our needs to others in order to help us survive.

We now know that hormones like adrenalin raise our alert awareness to our surroundings when we face threats to our survival. For example, when mammal infants are separated from their mothers, they often become extremely alert and conduct a detailed search for their mothers' whereabouts. Experimental studies show that infant animals show an increase in the stress hormone cortisol upon maternal separation. Likewise, humans often stay up all night, wide awake, if they break up with a loved one or a loved one dies. Non-human and human animals alike often go through similar increases in stress chemicals when they experience the loss of a loved one. For examples, prairie voles (small rodents) show increases in blood plasma levels of oxytocin when socially isolated, suggesting this "bonding" chemical urges them to seek out others to bond with (Bales et al., 2007)

In both non-human and human animals, separation from loved ones often leads to initial protest and disbelief reactions. A human may appear dazed and confused, or act as if everything is fine. Eventually, it's not uncommon for both animals and humans to show signs of despair, which is characterized by lethargy, lack of sleep, appetite reduction, and so on. For example, some animal babies, when they eventually stop searching for lost caregivers, show a decrease in blood pressure, an irregular heartbeat, lowered stress hormone levels in their blood, and immune system shut-down (Hofer, 1987). When human children are severely neglected or deprived of caregiving, they often stop growing, their brains develop abnormally, they develop illnesses, and they even die (Nelson, Furtado, Fox, & Zeanah, 2009). Loneliness in adults is related to higher levels of heart disease and lower immune functioning (Kiecolt-Glaser & Newton, 2001). Most of you have probably heard stories of elders who die shortly after their spouse does. This is often attributed to dying of a "broken heart."

Human women engaged in troubled relationships show evidence of an increase in oxytocin levels. In contrast, men in those same troubled relationships show an increase in vasopressin, a hormone that has been linked to male pair-bonding behavior. Thus, it appears with this preliminary research that the bonding hormones oxytocin and vasopressin can be biomarkers of distressed relationships and may influence people to seek closeness or bonds with others (Taylor, Saphire-Bernstein, & Seeman, 2009). Lewis et al. (2000) state that "a relationship is a physiological process" (p. 81). The research results from animal and human studies of separation, loss, and troubled relationships support this observation.

We often take drugs to change our brain chemistry when faced with emotional pain or loss. Drugs like Prozac raise serotonin levels in the brain, reducing depressive feelings and making losses not hurt so badly. However, widespread treatment of loss with medication leads to a situation in which millions of medicated people are not learning how to cope with losses and disappointments. A medicated society may eventually become numb and unable to truly love, or even feel for that matter. Fisher and Thomson (2007) found that serotonin-increasing antidepressants block emotions, including the euphoria of new relationships. They can also inhibit sexual arousal and the ability to have an orgasm. While psychotropic medications are necessary in some cases, to help people struggling with mental illnesses like serious clinical depression, many other people need help learning how to retune their brains and regulate the emotion centers in order to face the world of human relationships in a healthy manner (Fisher & Thomson, 2007).

The brain and relationships

Love can be a powerful connection between two people, leading to intimacy, happiness, and a sense of personal well-being. However, sometimes we don't engage in healthy forms of love and we end up being hurt, depressed, and feeling hopeless that we'll ever find love again. It's important to understand a little bit about how our brain functions so that we can more fully grasp how these social experiences start to influence how we process information in the environment, and how the way we think also affects our social experiences.

Lewis et al. (2000) discuss the facets of the human **triune brain**, the idea that the brain has three key levels or structures. The first level is the **brain stem**, sometimes called the *reptilian brain*, due to its location in the lower or more primitive parts of the brain that control our survival functions (such as heart rate and startle response).

The second, more sophisticated part of the brain is the **limbic brain**, the emotion center, which stimulates touching, playing, caring for babies, bonding to others, distress calls upon separation, and so on. The limbic system tries to integrate internal feelings with experiences of the external world. Most families naturally shape their children's limbic systems into smooth information processors that process friendships and romantic relationships in balanced, constructive ways. Parents teach children to "use their words" to express feelings, instead of hitting others. They hug their crying teenager who just got dumped by a first love and ask them to talk about how they feel. They allow their children's limbic systems to process emotions fully. By talking about feelings and helping them solve problems, limbic systems become balanced in a way that helps children learn how to function in the social worlds of their micro- and mesosystems. If we don't take care of the limbic brains of children or cannot take care of our own as adults, we may create societies of people who cannot regulate their emotions and function well (Perry, 2004).

Some people have not had adequate experiences with limbic regulation in their families of origin. They may not have learned how to reflect on their feelings, process them, and come up with healthy solutions for heartbreak or relational stress. They may try other ways to balance out the strong feelings taking place in their limbic systems, such as taking drugs or drinking alcohol. When we take drugs like opiates (morphine, heroin, and opium), we numb our physical and emotional pain and throw off the fine-tuned chemistry of our natural brains. Introducing artificial chemicals in the form of drugs and alcohol can distort the brain's functioning. For example, rat pups given just enough opium to numb their limbic system no longer cry for their mothers upon separation (Carden & Hofer, 1990).

When children have had severe disruptions in their initial love relationships, such as in the case of parental death, abandonment, abuse, or mental illness, they may develop strategies besides drug or alcohol consumption to numb the pain of loneliness. Cutting, making superficial wounds on the body with razor blades, paper clips, or knives, and other forms of self-mutilation often serve as such coping mechanisms (Sandman, 2009). When a person self-mutilates, **endogenous opiates**, naturally occurring pain-relieving neurochemicals, are released in the brain and dull the greater emotional pain people are experiencing in their lives. Most people who cut are emotionally vulnerable and take losses and disappointments extremely hard, often due to a lifetime history of disrupted attachments to caregivers (van der Kolk, Perry, & Herman, 1991).

Just as people in less healthy family environments learn how to raise endogenous opiates by negative strategies like cutting, many people also figure out how to increase a sense of personal well-being in positive ways that release endogenous opiates, such as by exercising, meditating, and engaging in prayer (Esch & Stefano, 2007; Wachholtz, Pearce, & Koenig, 2007). One of the most common ways we increase these feel-good chemicals in our families is through warm human contact, hugs, kisses, and sharing good times together.

Triune brain
The depiction of the brain as consisting of three parts, from an older more primitive part to a newer, sophisticated part.

Brain stem/ reptilian brain
The most primitive part of the triune brain that controls reflexes and basic behaviors like blood pressure and quick reactions.

Limbic brain
The second level of the triune brain which comprises the emotion regulation centers of the brain involved in emotional reactions and attachment strategies.

Endogenous opiates
Internal chemicals like endorphins that make a person feel less pain and give one a sense of euphoria.

Neocortex
The third level of the triune brain, which controls rational decision-making, executive functions, planning, and analysis.

The third, most sophisticated, and most recently evolved portion of the brain, is the **neocortex**. This bark-like covering over the surface of the brain's two hemispheres helps us to think logically and analytically. Its evolution allowed for the development of one of the most fundamental capacities that separates humans from other animals: language. We use language to communicate about what the limbic brain feels. When we have a supportive, close family, the neocortex allows us to develop a vocabulary that mirrors a calm, balanced limbic brain. A mother whose child did something naughty might feel disappointed but when she sees that her child is also disappointed in himself, might say, "I will always love you, no matter what." Or a husband might look at his wife coaching their child's soccer game and after the game, hug her and express his pride by saying, "You're an amazing coach; our daughter is lucky!" Though powerful in its own right, the neocortex, or reasoning center, cannot necessarily over-ride illogical or passionate feelings. The logical brain cannot easily heal a wounded limbic brain. For example, we often know a relationship is bad for us, yet we can't stop ourselves from seeing the person. Or children who are abused or violated by their attachment figures still cry when separated from them.

The three parts of the triune brain often work in concert, but at certain times, they can be in conflict with each other. For example, teenagers have a well-developed limbic brain but an underdeveloped neocortex. This makes them passionate, emotional, and risk-taking. But they often fail to think about the consequences of their actions or analyze the reasons for why they do things (Giedd, 2004). Even for adults, love is probably not centered in the rational brain. The neocortex can lead us to analyze a loved person to death, rationalize bad or hurtful behavior, or ruminate about conflicts over and over and over again. It certainly doesn't help us many times when we're in a pickle with the object of our affections.

In order to help heal an emotionally bruised limbic brain, one that has had repeated experiences with pain and loss, sometimes it takes a long process of relearning what love is. We need to learn that love does not have to be punishing or intensely painful. If that has been our experience, though, it takes a lot of work to construct a new emotional life. We need to dig deep to truly understand our feelings. We must ask ourselves constantly, "What am I feeling and why? What is the true nature of my emotional life?" When we can calm and regulate our limbic system, then we can stabilize the limbic system and help it to work more effectively in concert with the neocortex (Lewis et al., 2000), creating a finely tuned brain. The passion of a new relationship will get us started on this task, but we must advance beyond romance to bathe the brain with the chemicals of a calm, nurturing love, one that also makes rational sense considering our current life circumstances. Like most behaviors, loving interactions result from a complex interaction between our genes, neurochemistry, and experience.

Neurochemistry and the development of love

Many personality traits, which are largely influenced by our genes, may affect our functioning in love relationships. People who are extroverted, emotionally stable, sociable, and understand both their own and other people's emotions well tend to have better luck with love (Wachs, 2000). They understand their own emotions and the feelings of others. They can solve problems constructively rather than destructively. In contrast, research shows that risk-takers (people who may drive drunk, steal, or have unprotected sex) tend to be more irritable, unable to handle frustration, and highly angry. Some evidence indicates these people have higher than average levels of testosterone (Wachs, 2000). You may not be surprised to learn that these testosterone-linked traits are found more often in men. But even within females there is wide variation in testosterone levels. Research also shows that people with lower than average levels of estrogen (including women) have more emotional ups and downs while higher than average estrogen levels are related to more emotional stability and happiness (Wachs, 2000). These correlations suggest that natural individual differences in the genetic expression of traits as well as hormone levels can affect our experiences in relationships.

To examine changes in chemical reactions over the course of relationship development, let's start with the very beginning. One of the common things we desire in a love relationship is to kiss the person who stimulates our passion.

Kissing

Famous classicist Donald Lateiner (2009) found that kissing was sometimes practiced in ancient Greece and Rome, and studies across cultures show that at least 90% of people kiss (Fisher, 1998). The study of kissing is called **philematology** and more and more researchers are becoming interested in this phenomenon. Wendy Hill and colleagues' (2009) research shows that stress hormones like cortisol dramatically decrease in circulation during kissing sessions, while levels of oxytocin increase, a combination that is linked to a relaxed body and psychological sense of euphoria and bonding. As mentioned earlier, oxytocin has been found in animals to increase pair bonding.

Philematology
The scientific study of kissing.

There are differences between women's and men's responses to kissing. Women's oxytocin levels do not increase like men's do during kissing sessions unless the atmosphere is viewed as romantic (Hill, Wilson, & Lebovitz, 2009). Also, women view kissing as an intimate act in itself while men see it as foreplay to sex. In contrast to women, men prefer wetter, juicier kisses. Scientists have found that testosterone is exchanged with one's partner through saliva, perhaps suggesting a mechanism behind the increase in sex drive after kissing (Fisher, 1998). More research is needed on this phenomenon but these preliminary findings suggest that people who are attracted to each other and kiss will experience an elevation of hormones which increases the chances of emotional bonding, sexual activity, and potentially the development of a romantic relationship.

Relationship development

Once we've built a more committed relationship, we begin to give of ourselves to another person and share a more intimate type of love. We can begin to experience **limbic co-regulation**, which means that our bodily rhythms become synchronized with each other. We can help each other develop our emotional regulation abilities. Lewis et al. (2000) state that we can "remodel the emotional parts of the people we love" (p. 144). When we live with others in an intimate relationship, our hormonal cycles and diurnal rhythms related to sleep, hunger, and sex become more synchronized. As a consequence, we often find it difficult to sleep when the other person is gone, and our eating and regular activities feel "discombobulated."

Limbic co-regulation
The idea that two people who live together or are involved in a romantic bond can affect the functioning of each others' limbic brains.

The ways we talk, share, and experience emotional situations affect our partner's brain functioning. Anthropologist Helen Fisher used MRI scans to record the brain activity of people newly in love while they looked at a picture of their loved one (Fisher et al., 2002). Fisher and her colleagues found that a high level of activity occurred in the ventral tagmental area of the caudate nucleus, which is the reward center of the brain. This means that the reward center of the brain lit up, as if the loved one's photo provided the brain with a chemical reward. This area of the brain is rich with dopamine (the pleasure neurotransmitter) receptors, which help stimulate energy level, exhilaration, attention, and motivation to receive more rewards. The same feeling is engendered when a person attempts a novel and exciting activity like skydiving or riding a rollercoaster.

Remember, however, that these neuroscience studies simply show correlations between a behavior and a brain process. We cannot conclude that the chemical or brain region being studied is *the* cause of a certain behavior or vice versa. In addition, not every participant in brain research shows the same chemical or anatomical profile. Furthermore, each brain region and neurotransmitter is involved in countless human thoughts, feelings, and behaviors, so finding that they are associated with love may not mean what we think it means.

One example of the multiple roles neurotransmitters can play involves serotonin. You may know that serotonin affects mood, as it is altered when one takes antidepressants. People who are depressed tend to have lower levels of serotonin and people who are very happy have higher levels. People who are in love evidence increased serotonin levels while at the same time dopamine is also bathing the brain. This may partially explain why, when we are in love, we can become a euphoric, dreamy, happy mess. Interestingly, people who are extremely jealous exhibit deficits in serotonin (Marazziti et al., 2003). As you might suspect from these brain findings, the brain high on love is certainly not the best one for making rational decisions. Another intriguing finding related to irrational thinking is that while long-term love may be related to increased serotonin levels, brand new love may actually

HOW WOULD YOU MEASURE THAT?

Serotonin in obsessive compulsive disorder and love (Marazziti, Akiskal, Rossi, & Cassano, 1999)

Because both romantic love and mental illness have been linked to the serotonin transporter process in the brain, Marazziti et al. (1999) decided to examine the neurochemistry of people in love in comparison to those diagnosed with a serotonin-related mental illness, obsessive-compulsive disorder (OCD). The authors reasoned that new love and OCD seem to share similar "symptoms," like obsessive thoughts that won't go away. Moreover, OCD is often successfully treated with medications that increase the amount of serotonin available in the synapses of the brain (for example, Prozac, which inhibits the reuptake of serotonin to increase amounts available for use in the brain). The authors examined 20 participants in their early twenties who had "fallen in love" within the past six months. The lovers reported thinking about their new partner at least four hours per day. The researchers also recruited 20 patients of about the same age who had been diagnosed with OCD, but had not taken serotonergic drugs. These two groups were compared to a healthy control group. The independent variable in this study was "group membership," consisting of three levels (love group, OCD group, and control group). The dependent variable measured was the level of serotonin transporter in the blood.

Participants had their blood collected early in the morning after fasting. Researchers assessed platelet-rich plasma for the density of serotonin transporters in a chemical formulation called "H-paroxetine binding parameters" or H-Par. It was hypothesized that those with OCD and those in love would have a lower density of H-Par, which means less serotonin available in the brain. Marazziti et al. (1999) found clear support for their hypothesis. The people who were in love were indistinguishable from those suffering from OCD. Moreover, both the people in the OCD group and the love group had significantly less dense H-Par binding sites than the people in the control group. The difference amounted to people in the control group having double the amount of serotonin circulating in their brains than either people in love or those with OCD.

When those in love were tested again 12–18 months later (presumably when the brain had moved on to *companionate love* chemicals or the couple had broken up), their brains were the same as the brains of people in the control group in the original study. Similarly, people with OCD who had been successfully treated showed an increase in H-Par binding site density (to normal levels) in the same way the individuals in companionate love did at the long-term follow-up. The authors argue that young love induces a state of abnormality in the brain. We obsess over the person, and as we all know, love songs, poems, and irrational behavior follow.

It's important to note that the serotonin system also plays a role in appetite, body heat regulation, sleep patterns, perception of pain, circadian rhythms, impulsivity, and anxiety, all of which can play a role in both love and mental illness. This might suggest that, indeed, love makes you "crazy." If that is the case, is love really something upon which we should base our most serious and enduring life decisions?

decrease the same chemical, leading to emotional instability. The *How Would You Measure That?* box explores how brand new love might change our brain functioning.

Think a little bit more deeply about the idea of people being engaged in a mutually influential physiological partnership. Then take a look at this poem, written in 1921, by the Pulitzer Prize winning poet Edna St. Vincent Millay. What do you think she's trying to tell us about love? How does her message resonate with you, after learning more about the neurochemistry of love?

> I shall forget you presently, my dear,
> So make the most of this, your little day,
> Your little month, your little half a year,

Ere I forget, or die, or move away,
And we are done forever; by and by
I shall forget you, as I said, but now
If you entreat me with your loveliest lie
I will protect you with my favorite vow.
I would indeed that love were longer-lived,
And oaths were not so brittle as they are,
But so it is, and nature has contrived
To struggle on without a break thus far,—
Whether or not we find what we are seeking
Is idle, biologically speaking.

Millay speaks to the complex and often conflicting roles played by our brain stem, our limbic system, and our more sophisticated neocortex understanding of love and long-term relationships. She may not have realized it, but she painted a vivid picture of the triune brain and how the limbic system may not always work synergistically with the neocortex. Our reptilian biological urges lead us in one direction, but our neocortical thoughts can take us elsewhere. Attachments are complicated.

THE SOCIAL CONTEXTS OF LOVE: ATTACHMENT THEORY

Baby love

In her poem, Millay suggests that love is fleeting and that it doesn't matter if we seek or find love because, evolutionarily speaking, all that matters is biological reproduction. In the grand scheme of things, that may be true. But while we are here on earth with a cerebral cortex that allows us to contemplate, ruminate, analyze, hypothesize, and predict outcomes, love can, indeed, be a very real entity that affects our daily lives. And these effects can begin before we're even aware of what relationships are all about.

Baby love

Freudians thought that babies loved their mothers because mothers ensured their survival through feeding. In the 1950s and 1960s, Harry Harlow (1962), a great primatologist, sought to test this idea as well as to try to discover the nature of mother love. In one key study, when baby rhesus monkeys were raised with a wire mesh "mother" who fed them with a bottle placed through the mesh, the babies actually never attached emotionally to her. However, they clung to a terry cloth "mother" (a wooden model wrapped in soft cloth) for the majority of the day; they attached to her emotionally and "loved" her. When scary objects were placed in their cages, they ran to the cloth mother, never to the wire mother; and when they hugged her, they visibly relaxed. The baby monkeys even worked up the nerve to hiss and yell at the feared object (usually a giant plastic insect or a menacing robot) after being "comforted" by their cloth mother. The cloth and wire mothers were heated to the same temperature so these results could not be explained by warmth. These studies showed that babies attach to their mothers to find comfort, touch, and protection, regardless of whether or not she feeds them. Harlow's studies revolutionized our thinking about what "love" is. It's an emotion that allows us to feel safe and secure, and gives us the desire to physically reach out to others who can comfort us in a time of need.

While these results may not be directly comparable to the attachments of humans, human infants do use their caregivers as "secure bases" from which to explore the world around them (Bowlby, 1988). If their caregivers raise them with love, warmth, and caring, infants develop a sense of security about relationships and can venture out into the world with courage. It's a common sight on playgrounds to see small children looking back to their parents as they venture out into the wild world of a jungle gym teeming with loud, strange children. If they fall down or someone takes their pail and shovel, they immediately run back to their secure base, just like the monkeys in Harlow's studies ran back to their comforting cloth mothers. The converse is also true. Research suggests that children who spend their early years in orphanages where their physical needs are met, but they have no consistent attachment figure, experience prolonged periods of social and emotional dysfunction (Wismer-Fries, Shirtcliff, & Pollak, 2008). Thus what happens in our early *microsystems* can have a lasting impact.

Wismer-Fries et al. (2008) found that when orphans who spent their earlier years in stark industrial Romanian orphanages were adopted into loving homes with good parents, they still had trouble functioning. When researchers had the families come into the lab and engage in attachment behaviors (having the child sit in the parent's lap, tickling, playing pat-a-cake, and so on), the children who had been in orphanages experienced sharp spikes in cortisol, the stress hormone. This indicates that they experienced the attachment games as threatening stimuli. This pattern was not found in control group children, and even more interesting, the adopted children did not experience cortisol increases when engaging in the same sorts of games with strangers (research assistants). Thus, the children who experienced early attachment disruption continued to exhibit high alarm-state (fight or flight) hormonal patterns even years after they had been adopted into safe homes. They did not experience close physical contact as comforting. These results suggest that there are early sensitive periods that are difficult to reclaim if our emotional needs are not met in infancy and toddlerhood (Wismer-Fries et al., 2008).

Recall that Attachment Theory (Bowlby, 1980) posits that we develop internal working models that reflect our views of ourselves, our views of other people, and our views of relationships in general. Parents raise children to develop these internal working models, or prototypes, of relationships. These prototypes can then influence what people expect in future relationships. As Sternberg suggested, when we become adults, our ideas about love stem from our childhood love stories. We grow up with images and experiences involving our own parents, grandparents, and extended family. We glean ideas from the media about love and relationships all the time. Our culture and religion teach us about how to connect with other people. And our individual experiences with security, support, care, punishment, shame, fear, and self-esteem shape our ideas about love. Attachment changes our brains and shapes our ability to love (Lewis et al., 2000). Viewing this research through a bioecological lens helps us truly understand love in all its complexity.

Attachment theorists contend that we follow what we know and seek out those who confirm our internal working models, even if it's not emotionally healthy or safe for us. We do what feels familiar, and sometimes this results in our limbic brains being less able to change and grow in order to learn to regulate separation and loss experiences. Our internal working models are like ideologies we develop about love. These ideologies influence the way we seek mates, hook up with people, express or don't express our love for them, fight with them, and ultimately, how successful we can be in love relationships. People who are securely attached see themselves as loveable and so often seek out love partners who value them, treat them with respect, and see their good qualities.

Adult attachment

Like human children and Harlow's monkeys, adults seek out attachment figures to help them regain a sense of security when stressed (Pietromonaco et al., 2006). Securely attached people tend to have constructive conflicts with their mates, where problems are solved without blaming, shaming, screaming, or violent confrontation. People with an *insecure/anxious/preoccupied* attachment style have sometimes experienced inconsistent care from caregivers and often enter adult love relationships with intense fears of betrayal and abandonment. They desire love and intimacy yet they often sabotage relationships through being too clingy and emotionally unstable. In contrast, people with *dismissing/avoidant* styles avoid intimacy at all costs. They may have relationships with others but they do not allow themselves to be vulnerable. They put up walls, do not share emotions, and often appear cold and distant. *Fearful/avoidant* people feel such anxiety over intimacy that they choose to disengage in order to avoid the potential pain of getting too involved with others.

Each of these attachment styles affects the success and health of love relationships. Two securely attached people have the best chances of lifelong health and happiness. But people with any of the other three attachment styles can be involved in healthy relationships, especially if their partner is secure. Any person, but most often those with a secure attachment history, can modulate fear and anxiety in their partners. Romantic partners help their mates to regulate their emotions in order to be able to handle stress better. Even if one has an insecure attachment style, simply loving and connecting with their partner may serve positive functions in helping the person face stress. In the opposite case, and the more likely scenario for people with insecure styles, one partner may influence an escalation of conflict and help their partners to *dysregulate* their feelings and behaviors, leading to emotional turmoil.

Because most of us learned our styles of attachment and emotion regulation in our families of origin, we can also learn a lot about coping with emotional situations by seeing our partners interacting with their own parents. For example, if your partner tends to walk away or clam up during emotional discussions, this may be puzzling at first. But then when you witness your partner's mother doing this at holiday gatherings, it may provide some insight into why your partner may not have developed the skills to discuss issues. This is a perfect opportunity to try to help your partner regulate his or her emotions and learn how to talk without shutting you out. Thus, mesosystem influences such as our parents' interactions with each other when we were children, or witnessing our partner's interactions with their own parents as adults can affect our relationship functioning.

Pietromonaco et al. (2006) posit that **affective reactivity** ("affect" is another word for emotion) underlies the internal working models of the attachment system. Affective reactivity is the frequency with which a person perceives threat, resulting in a need to find security by dealing with feelings in a specific way. This need to cope with perceived threat sets in motion affect regulation strategies, which are patterns of behavior enacted to establish a sense of emotional security. Because internal working models shape our views of others and ourselves, they guide our thoughts, feelings, and behaviors and sculpt our affect regulation strategies. For example, if my internal working model is one of *avoidance*, and I am on the anxious side, I might see my partner looking at another person in a sexual manner and feel threatened. Since I probably have a history of emotional rejection or other forms of insecurity from my parents or previous romantic partners, my affect regulation strategy will include ways to regulate my anxiety as well as my need to avoid intimacy. I will probably not discuss my concerns

Affective reactivity
The extent to which a person reacts with limbic arousal (like the secretion of stress hormones) when potential intimacy threats arise.

FIGURE 6.3 What attachment style do you think this king has?
© Charles Barsotti/The New Yorker Collection/www.cartoonbank.com

"Enemies, yes, but doesn't your moat also keep out love?"

with my partner but will become quiet and distant, and may even move on to forming a relationship with someone else who does not cause me any anxiety. Thus, I have maintained the stability of my internal working model and am likely to continue to be anxious and avoidant in the future. Because insecurely attached people tend to have high levels of affective reactivity, it would take a lot of emotional work for them to change their internal working model and maintain a sense of calm security in relationships. They'd have to retrain their limbic brains to be less threatened by intimacy and remain calm in the face of conflict.

In this same situation, someone who was securely attached might say "Gee, honey, I saw you looking seductively at that person who walked by. Did you think he or she was cute?" Because the secure internal working model views the self as worthy of love and relationships as emotionally stable, no sense of threat is activated by a partner looking at someone else. Secure couples may even allow their partners to have "celebrity crushes" or fantasies about others. Their threat systems are not easily activated and they feel secure in their romantic connections. They have low levels of affective reactivity.

People who have high affective reactivity will frequently perceive a threat to their romantic attachments, their affective threat systems will often be elevated, and they will need to expend a lot more energy on regulating their thoughts, feelings, and behaviors (Pietromonaco et al., 2006). When both partners are securely attached, however, their conflicts are mild, their behaviors are synchronized, one person doesn't dominate the other, they resolve conflicts in a caring manner, and each partner helps to regulate the other's distress. Take a look at Figure 6.4 and see where you think you lie in the attachment classification of adults.

Are you a highly affectively reactive person or are you cool as a cucumber? Do you tend to rely on others or are you pretty self-contained or avoidant? Attachment theorists would argue that if you have a hunch about which type of internal working model you might be walking around with, it could give you some insight into your relationship patterns and perhaps allow you to work toward

FIGURE 6.4 The connection between affective reactivity and regulation.
Source: Pietromonaco et al., 2006.

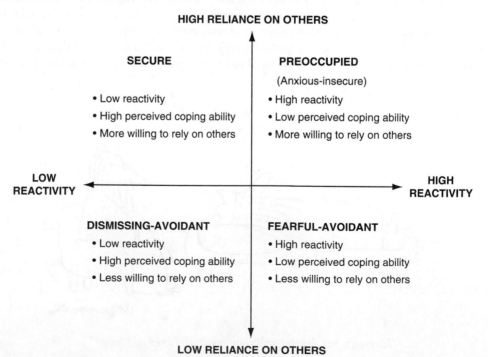

more productive interactions with those you love. Remember, however, that our attachment styles and internal working models (plus their concomitant neurochemistry) are only one part of the big picture of love.

I hope it has become clear that every level of influence, beginning with our biology and personality, and moving out to our microsystem interactions, mesosystem influences, and exosystem, affects, shapes, and molds our love. The bioecological model would not allow us to stop at analyzing our internal working models. It always includes larger social and cultural influences to explain relationship phenomena, and we turn to these next.

MACROSYSTEM INFLUENCES ON LOVE

> Economic forces
>
> Cultural forces

Beyond the microsystem of interpersonal attachments, issues that occur in our larger social and cultural contexts can also affect our experiences of love. Even financial meltdowns like the global crisis that began in 2008 can affect our search for love.

Economic forces

In the current economic climate, we might think that love is the last thing on people's minds. An interesting survey (Opinion Research Corporation, 2009), however, found that people who were the most anxious about the current economic conditions in the U.S. were the *most* hopeful about finding love compared to people who were less concerned about the economy. Also, during economic downturns, the use of personal ads on the Internet and in newspapers increases by around 20%. These two findings imply that people may seek out romantic love as a way to mitigate the stress of economic loss.

Another connection between personal finances and love comes from a recent Pew Research Center report which showed that today wives outearn husbands in over 20% of marriages. Today, we are experiencing the first generation of men (ages 30–44) who can benefit financially from getting married. When the data were first gathered in 1970, unmarried men made more money than married men, who often had to support their stay-at-home wives. Today, more women than men in the 30–44 age group are college educated and women are increasingly making better incomes. Thus, women's incomes offer a socioeconomic boon to many husbands. Women's earnings haven't quite caught up with men's, but women are definitely offering more to men these days than just cooking and cleaning (St. George, 2010). Contemporary trends in socioeconomic status offer new relationship options for both women and men. Of course, these findings apply mainly to western industrialized cultures. Other cultures may experience different economic patterns as well as unique ideas regarding love.

Cultural forces

The cultural climate affects people's views of passionate love. In a study of 166 cultures, Jankowiak and Fisher (1992) found that people in 147 of them (89%) reported experiencing romantic love. But there were large cultural differences in how that love was viewed. The Fulbe people in Cameroon shame and criticize men who appear to be too smitten with their wives or spend too much time with them. In India, 76% of people surveyed would marry a person with good qualities even if they were not in love with him or her, compared with 14% of Americans surveyed.

Each culture also has its own rituals related to the practice of love and romance. Illouz (1997) describes romantic rituals as being of the same nature as religious rituals. She says that romance is like a "staged reality" where rituals are practiced just like in a spiritual ceremony. For example, eating

Illouz's four symbolic assessments
Four ways to examine the rituals cultures engage in to enhance love experiences.

at a nice restaurant is a traditional western love "ritual" and is the most commonly reported romantic event. If we examine this "ritual" more closely, it can be mapped on to **Illouz's (1997) four symbolic assessments of love rituals:**

1 temporal
2 emotional
3 spatial
4 artifactual.

The *temporal assessment* of ritualized love relates to isolated time increments. For example, we tend to view romantic time as different from secular, or ordinary, time. Romantic time seems more special, less ordinary, than our mundane lives. Romantic time often occurs at night rather than in the daytime. We may see specific seasons as more romantic as well ("we cuddled by a winter fire" or "we took a romantic sunset walk during the summer"). Certain times of year are also designated as ritualistic romantic time, such as Valentine's Day or wedding anniversaries. These occur regularly throughout the year, just like religious holidays.

In the *emotional assessment* of romantic rituals, we see romantic feelings as separate from other feelings. Love is special. Our loved one is unique, unlike any other. The feelings we have for him or her are different from the emotions we exhibit toward others. Our romantic love feelings are considered sacred and special, just like our devotion to spiritual or religious paths.

We also set a sacred space for romantic ritual. In the *spatial assessment*, we feel the need to leave ordinary spaces and get away from home. Home is considered an unromantic space so we construct a private space, like a picnic blanket in a park. Or we travel to more romantic spaces like beaches, forests, hotels, or even foreign countries where everyone around us is different and speaks another language. Hearing new sounds and smelling new scents in a foreign land make us feel like we are in a romantic space.

Finally, romance requires an *artifactual assessment*. What artifacts, or objects, do you need to feel romantic? We ritualize the act of eating by using objects that are not of our everyday lives. We may wear special clothing, bring gifts that are more beautiful than ordinary objects, drink wine that's more expensive than what we drink at home, and so on. The restaurant is considered "nice" because its ritual artifacts include crystal, flowers, fancy dishes and silver, candles, and décor.

As you can probably see, the glitzy restaurant experience embodies all four westernized romantic prototypes, *temporal* ("pick you up at eight?"), *emotional* ("you look stunning tonight"), *spatial* ("we'll take that table next to the fireplace") and *artifactual* ("their artwork is so beautiful!"). This kind of love assessment often occurs unconsciously but can engender feelings of wanting to either continue or end the relationship with that one special person. And each culture may have completely different sets of romantic prototypes than the ones I outline above.

Most of this chapter has focused on love between two people, usually referring to the desire for a "soulmate." However, more and more people are questioning this traditional idea, that there can only be one partner with whom we spend our lives. While having more than one special love partner is nothing new historically or culturally speaking, it's becoming more recognized as a legitimate relationship structure in the western world.

Polyamory

Polyamory
Loving more than one person.

In many western cultures, people believe in finding one true love who will meet their every need. That's a lot of pressure to put on one person. Do you think you could fulfill every single need, emotional, mental, physical, and spiritual of another human being? Many people question the idea of monogamy and do not think humans are meant to be monogamous. In fact, the majority of people around the world do not think so. As we learned in Chapter 3, many cultures practice some form of polygamy. But beyond polygamy, **polyamory**, loving more than one person, is gaining in popularity in both heterosexual and gay/lesbian/bisexual relationships (Hernandez, 2006).

Most of us were raised to believe we can only romantically love one person at a time. Sexual relationships are considered exclusive to a committed couple, and "infidelity" is frowned upon by most people in western cultures. We are even opposed to "emotional infidelity" in the form of close, intimate friendships our partners form at work or on the Internet. If we all believe in monogamy, it's interesting to note that the number of women who meet men and have affairs in the workplace is now equal to the number of men (Teich, 2006). Many people today also report falling madly in love with someone on the Internet, dreaming of that person as a potentially perfect mate who would make up for their "real" partner's flaws. In addition, Teich (2006) discusses the Internet as being a new tool for rekindling old romances. Social networking sites like Facebook allow people to find lost loves and create a fantasy space for reminiscing and recreating old desires. Is this wrong? If we flirt, share our deepest secrets and desires, socialize, and talk with people at work or electronically but never have sexual relations with them, is it cheating?

People in polyamorous relationships report that having more than one partner has many benefits. There is always another ear to listen, a person to mediate conflicts, someone to provide a different, unique sexual experience, a third (or fourth) income to support the household and children, more people to share the burdens of housework and bills, and so on. Of course there are also complications. The partners have to be very mature, have good communication styles, lack jealousy, and have a willingness to avoid "keeping score" by trying to make each relationship exactly equal in time spent together, conversations held, or sexual liaisons. To make a polyamorous relationship (or any relationship) succeed, the partners need to talk to each other constructively, be creative in handling problems, make crucial decisions together, have a satisfying sex life, make compromises, and share feelings and ideas even while disagreeing (Olson, Fournier, & Druckman, 1985).

While polyamory may be seen as a relatively new phenomenon in the western world, even in 1950s America "wife swapping" was not an uncommon pastime. Upper-class people would have sexual relations with their friends' spouses yet maintain their marriages. In the 1970s there was "swinging," where committed partners would allow their mates to have sexual relations with relative strangers at swingers' parties (Labriola, 2006). These liaisons were more about sex than love, but they raise the question of whether monogamy should be expected. Interestingly, today in the Netherlands, plural marriage is allowed (Schroeder, 2008). What do you think? Should a committed love relationship mean that we should only have sex with that one person for the rest of our lives? Do you think humans are supposed to be monogamous, or is this practice a social construction? See how you feel about the different types of polyamorous unions that exist.

Schroeder (2008) talks about different polyamorous family configurations:

- **primary/secondary structure**—a couple is committed to each other and any other liaisons are considered secondary, meaning they can never interfere with or join the first relationship

- **multiple primary partners**—there can be polyfidelity in this structure, or group marriage/partnership, where all partners involved are married or committed to each other but no one strays outside of that group

- **open model**—in this structure, the key multiple primary partners are committed to each other but all agree that other sexual or love relationships would be acceptable.

Research is only beginning to recognize polyamorous unions so we do not know a lot about what makes these unions work or dissolve. But more and more newspaper articles and media reports have been emerging in the past couple of years documenting polyamorous families, which suggests they are becoming more comfortable "outing" themselves. With the changes in gender roles, laws regarding same-sex marriages, and declining SNAF expectations, we may eventually see less emphasis placed on monogamy and the potentially unrealistic expectations we often hold for our monogamous partners.

However, not everyone thinks these changes are positive. Kass (1997) wonders whether the move toward more androgynous gender roles and post-modern concepts of love and relationships might inhibit true love from blossoming. He argues that contemporary changes like the "love poisoning doctrines of radical feminism" (p. 111) will destroy all we have always valued about love and marriage.

Primary/secondary structure
A polyamorous family configuration where the initial couple takes precedence over any subsequent partners.

Multiple primary partners structure
A polyamorous family configuration where there can be multiple primary partners; each partner is committed to every other partner to the same degree.

Open model structure
A polyamorous family configuration where the primary partnership is open to other sexual and romantic liaisons.

A FINAL NOTE: ENHANCING THE QUALITY OF LOVE

Do you think polyamory is inherently bad, corrupt, or immoral? Or is this trend just another example of the natural evolution away from strict societal control over our love lives?

Whether we're monogamous or polyamorous, all relationships take work. They involve conflict and the difficult meshing of two or more life histories and sets of relationship expectations. Goldman and Greenberg (2006) posit that conflicts in love relationships stem from a failure to resolve struggles for *identity* (such as power, rank, and status) and *security*. Notice the similarity of this idea to the work on attachment styles. Goldberg and Greenberg (2006) have found in their work that conflicts are often cover-ups for deeper emotional wounds. When people constantly argue over chores not being done or the toothpaste being squeezed from the middle rather than the bottom, the real issues might be related to feeling disrespected, taken advantage of, or not listened to. However, expressing these latter emotions might make a person vulnerable to attack, rejection, or betrayal. Therefore, people tend to cover up such tender feelings and resort to yelling, anger, and hostility. It's much easier to call someone a slob than to say that "the messy house makes me feel like you don't care about me." Family therapists can help couples reveal their true feelings and stop hiding behind the petty conflicts of everyday life.

Emotion-focused couples therapy (EFCT)
An evidence-based practice for improving love relationships which focuses on unraveling the tender emotions underlying harsh emotions like anger.

Some of the most effective couples' therapy is called **emotion-focused couples therapy** (Goldman & Greenberg, 2006; Johnson, 2008). In this therapy, the couple work to identify negative cycles and the threats they feel exist which undermine their emotional security. What makes emotion-focused couples therapy especially impressive is that it has decades of research evidence supporting its effectiveness. It's not a "self-help" movement, but a scientifically based way to improve our relationships and love lives. The therapist's goal is to increase positive interactions on a daily basis, but he or she also coaches the couple through an identification process, helping them to uncover their true and often vulnerable feelings which underlie the conflicts. To reveal their primary or core emotions often requires the couple to risk being vulnerable in front of each other. Softer emotions like sadness, fear, or shame often underlie the overt expressions of anger and exasperation. Our emotions organize our thoughts, feelings, and behaviors (those internal working models of self and others) so it's very important that we come to truly understand our deepest feelings and what is making us tick.

The emotional climate in which we grow up can shape our emotional approach to adult love relationships. We develop expectations for love that are based on what we witnessed as children. These expectations often help determine the negative cycles in romantic partnerships. "Emotions therefore emerge in relationship to the social environment, arising in response to events real or imagined that are appraised as implying possibilities for gratification or obstructing needs, goals, and desires" (Goldman & Greenberg, 2006, p. 233). Too much or too little emotional expression can impede effective responses to environmental challenges or emotional threats. Most romantic partners attempt to understand the emotional needs of their partners and try to fulfill those needs. But often, especially if we come from different types of attachments in our families of origin, our responses to our partners' needs may be inadequate, misunderstood, or even perceived as threatening.

The goals of emotion-focused couples therapy are to increase positive emotions between partners and decrease feelings of shame, fear, and anger. Through uncovering the true, softer emotions underlying anger and contempt, the therapist seeks to bolster self-esteem and solidify identity. Through discussion of our true feelings, we come to discover that dysfunctional patterns with our partners often stem from unresolved wounds from our past love experiences with both parents and past partners. Loneliness, abandonment, shame, worthlessness, inadequacy, anger, and hostility start to control our behaviors and our relationships take on a negative cycle which appears crazy or out of control.

Couples often report that their arguments or fights do not characterize the "real" them. Or they reveal only their "bad side" which comes out because this partner knows how to push their buttons. In other words, they don't see the cycles of dysfunction as representative of their true selves. Their authentic identity is something different. With conflicts, we come to understand the hard outer shell of our partners and ourselves, but we don't get at the underlying emotions when we continue to use defensive or hostile posturing.

Emotion-focused couples therapy focuses on each partner gaining a sense of empathy for where the other person came from emotionally, with both his or her parents and previous partners. It works by bringing the couple together in a sense of empathy and compassion, allowing them to be vulnerable with each other and to feel comfortable sharing their true feelings of loss, pain, and sorrow. Dessaulles, Johnson, and Denton (2003) found that not only did the couples' relationships improve, but women experiencing emotion-focused couples therapy showed greater improvements in depressive symptoms than did women using psychoactive medications like Prozac. This could be explained by the fact that couples learn to control their rage and anger and connect to the softer side of themselves and each other. This can change their limbic functioning. They learn how to regulate negative emotions and proceed in a constructive manner. As Goldman and Greenberg say, "one of the best antidotes to escalation is the ability to soothe the vulnerable in the self and others" (2006, p. 239).

Ideal love is freedom, freedom to share your individuality and be intimate with another. Being exactly who you really are and not being afraid are key elements of a healthy, balanced relationship. Being fearless and vulnerable at the same time can increase exponentially the sense of security and fulfillment that each partner feels (Bellah, Madsen, Sullivan, Swidler, & Tipton, 1985).

It should be fairly clear to you by now that love itself is not going to be enough to keep a relationship together. Love is not enough of a reason to get married. It will not see you through the hard realizations about yourself on its own. Success in relationships takes a lot of emotionally honest communication, mature decision-making, insight into one's own attachment history, knowledge of cultural expectations, financial savvy, and clear communication about what you want out of the relationship, including your goals for careers and childrearing. This means using the entire triune brain. Being able to make it through the tough times means you are able to fight with but not tear down the other, disagree while still exhibiting compassion, and love *yourself* enough to know that loving another person does not necessarily mean you should stay with him or her. Love may get you in the door, but relationship skills keep the roof over your head. For a step in the right direction, check out the nearby *FYI* box for some ideas regarding healthy fighting.

When we work on making ourselves the best partners we can be, long-term committed partnerships become more viable. It is to this topic that we now turn in Chapter 7.

FIGURE 6.5 What do you think emotion-focused couples therapy might recommend for this troubled relationship?
Photo © Jason Stitt / Stocklib.

FYI

**Some tips for constructive conflict
(Adapted from Matta, 2006, p. 71)**

1 When upset about something, don't complain about it; suggest a concrete change you would like to see and clearly ask your partner if he or she would be willing to implement the change.

2 Keep disagreements focused on the present situation. Don't bring up past issues or say "you always…"

3 Remember that your partner's view of the world is just as valid as yours. Start from a place of compassion and compromise; things rarely escalate if you start positively.

4 Don't assume you know what your partner is thinking—directly ask how he or she feels. Don't assume your partner can read your mind or "should just know" how you feel or what you need; assume that if you don't state it, he or she might not know.

5 Do not label your partner or call him or her names. If you really thought your partner was an idiot, lazy, neurotic, or stupid, you probably would not be with him or her in the first place. Do not make sweeping overgeneralizations or judge your partner's feelings. Be very specific about the issue at hand and work on solving that issue, nothing more.

6 Don't attempt to prove how right you are; the goal should be to solve the problem through honest expression of emotion and compromise. Choose solutions over being right.

CHAPTER SUMMARY

Love is defined as the subjective feeling of emotional connection with another person. Love is often accompanied by the desire to be near that person, care for him or her, protect him or her, and share lives together. We can feel love for our children, family, and friends. The majority of the chapter focused on love between romantic partners.

In the typical romantic relationship, people progress from an initial stage of passion and romance to a calmer, companionate form of committed partnerships. Robert Sternberg developed a Triangular Theory of Love, with passion, intimacy, and commitment at each corner of the triangle. There are different types of love based on whether the couple is relatively high or low on these components. Sternberg argues that we come to develop love relationships based on both conscious and unconscious love stories that we learn through exposure to people in our families, media, and books during childhood. People's relationships are more likely to succeed if their love stories are compatible.

Lee also developed a typology of love, with five different types that can predict the health and success of a relationship. Self-Expansion Theory explores how love is often a context for personal growth and emotional fulfillment, helping partners become their best selves.

Historically, love was never the basis for marriage and committed partnerships. It is true that people around the world fall in love, but in many cultures historically and today, love is considered an irrational and unreliable reason for forming a committed partnership. Financial reasons, family obligations, and even military strategies are often reasons for bringing two people together to form a life together.

There are many demographic differences in ideas about love. Gender, culture, socioeconomic status, and sexual orientation each affect how people envision love and experience their love relationships. Western cultures have idealized the feminized version of love, accepting women's "natural" abilities to love, nurture, and communicate as better than the way men typically exhibit their love.

The chapter covered many biological aspects of love, from the bonding neurotransmitter, oxytocin, to the exchange of testosterone in saliva during kissing.

The *triune brain* was presented as way to understand that the emotional limbic system in the brain is often at odds with the more rational neocortical part of the brain. Healthy, happy love relationships are characterized by higher levels of oxytocin and pleasure chemicals like dopamine, whereas conflicted or negative relationships increase stress hormones and even weaken immune functioning. Partners engage in limbic co-regulation of their partners by helping each other modulate and understand their emotional lives, especially if they each have a secure attachment history.

Attachment quality develops during childhood when we learn about relationships from our caregivers. These models of love relationships follow us into adult attachments and can enhance our romantic ties or can cause problems in our ability to connect in a healthy way.

Emotion-focused couples therapy is an effective type of counseling for helping couples understand their attachment histories, how these affect their adult functioning, and how they can improve the quality of their love relationships.

KEY TERMS

affective reactivity	feminized love	neocortex
androgynous love	Illouz's four symbolic assessments	open model structure
brain stem/reptilian brain	intimacy	philematology
companionate love	limbic brain	polyamory
consummate love	limbic co-regulation	primary/secondary structure
emotion-focused couples therapy (EFCT)	limbic system love	Self-Expansion Theory
endogenous opiates	love stories	Sternberg's Triangular Theory of Love
	multiple primary partners structure	triune brain

WEBSITES FOR FURTHER EXPLORATION

http://www.unlimitedloveinstitute.org

The Institute for Research on Unlimited Love, Altruism, Compassion, and Service. This organization studies the benefits of benevolent love for people who both give it and receive it. They focus on enhancing the human race by sponsoring seminars, essay contests, and publications on the religious, humanistic, and artistic expression of pure love.

http://www.links2love.com

This is a frivolous, fun site completely devoted to all things related to love. It has love song lyrics, poems, advice on best practices in kissing and flirting (I can't vouch for these), romantic gift guides, ecards, quizzes, romantic quotes, and even wedding planning ideas.

http://amolife.com/reviews/top-20-most-famous-love-stories-in-history-and-literature.html

This site focuses on "capturing the beauty of life without limits." The specific article linked here covers 20 famous love stories, from Romeo and Juliet to Orpheus and Eurydice and Pocahontas and John Smith.

http://www.iceeft.com/home.htm

This site provides more information on emotion-focused couples therapy. You can also read Dr. Sue Johnson's book, *Hold Me Tight: Seven Conversations for a Lifetime of Love* (Johnson, 2008), which has been published in Spanish and Dutch as well as English. To find an EFCT certified therapist in your area (they are available in 21 countries and most U.S. states and Canadian provinces) check out the website for the International Center for Excellence in Emotion-Focused Therapy (http://eft.ca/findtherapist.php).

CHAPTER 7
MARRIAGES AND COMMITTED PARTNERSHIPS

In every marriage more than a week old, there are grounds
for divorce. The trick is to find, and continue to find, grounds
for marriage.

(Robert Woodruff Anderson, American playwright)

LEARNING OBJECTIVES

- To understand the evolving trends in contemporary marriages and committed partnerships

- To appreciate historical changes that occurred and influenced current ideologies

- To understand the benefits and disadvantages of different types of marriage, including the arguments for and against same-sex marriage

- To recognize the common problems marriages face and how couples can both prevent and solve such problems

OVERVIEW OF CONTEMPORARY MARRIAGE TRENDS

- Sharing roles in committed partnerships
- The deinstitutionalization of marriage
  - Specific forms of deinstitutionalization
  - Examining the modern institution of marriage

HEALTH BENEFITS OF HAPPY MARRIAGES

- Processes underlying the marriage–health link

A HISTORICAL EXAMINATION OF MARRIAGE

- Marriages before industrialization
- Marriage in the nineteenth century
- Kin marriages

TYPES OF MARRIAGE

- Cohabitation and common law marriage
  - A case example of cohabitation in Sweden
- Covenant marriages
- Lavee and Olson's marriage typologies
- Same-sex marriages
  - Key historical turning points in same-sex marriage
  - Domestic partnerships
  - Contemporary views of same-sex marriage
  - Arguments for and against same-sex marriage
- Interracial and intercultural marriages
  - Social dominance beliefs and interracial marriage
  - Demographic variables and interracial marriage
  - Intercultural marriages
  - Immigrant marriages
- Arranged marriages

MARITAL PROBLEMS

- Infidelity
- Unresolved conflict
  - Financial infidelity
  - Problems in relationship perceptions

HEALTHY PROCESSES IN MARRIAGES

- Premarital counseling
- Positive vs. negative interactions
- Peer marriages and feminist marriages
- Lesbian and gay relationships
- Dyadic coping

OVERVIEW OF CONTEMPORARY MARRIAGE TRENDS

Sharing roles in committed partnerships

The deinstitutionalization of marriage

In the previous chapter, we focused on that ubiquitous yet elusive concept called "love." I mentioned that love is a great feeling but may not be the strongest foundation upon which to build an entire relationship. First, the type of love we experience changes over time, from intense passionate love in the beginning, to companionate love later on. Second, basing serious life decisions solely on emotions like love, which may be fleeting, may lead to disappointment about the relationship. Thus, for a relationship to last, we need to have a strong foundation of friendship and the desire to be with the other person for other reasons besides a simple physical attraction or feelings of love.

Because committed partnerships are complex entities, it's important to examine them through a bioecological lens. All couples function similarly, with the impact of brain function, stress-coping, pre-existing beliefs, attitudes, and personality traits showing up in relationship dynamics. Each partner brings a history of attachments, traumas and triumphs, and social and cultural contexts with them into committed partnerships. A person's pre-existing attitudes about sex and gender roles, expectations about the purpose of marriage, and judgments about his or her partner play key roles in the success of a marriage or other committed partnership. Race, class, gender, and family of origin issues all affect the way people interact in their romantic relationships. Both partners' existing traits, including their genes and neurophysiological patterns, combine within specific microsystem and macrosystem contexts to make or break the serious relationship (Niehuis et al., 2006).

This chapter will examine marriages and committed partnerships from a bioecological perspective. It will shed some light on the many ways healthy, committed partnerships benefit the people involved and outline the inevitable struggles that arise along the way. You will find out that the institution we call marriage has changed appreciably over recorded history and that it continues to evolve.

Sharing roles in committed partnerships

Changes in gender roles over the past 40 years provide one easily recognizable example of the evolution of marriages. In 1972, at the height of the women's liberation movement, Jessie Bernard published a groundbreaking book called *The Future of Marriage*, in which she described how very differently men and women experienced marriage. She said that each marriage had two components, "his" marriage and "her" marriage. And "her" marriage was vastly less satisfying and more demeaning than "his" marriage. Women were forced to answer to their husbands, keep the house, raise the children, and not have aspirations of their own. But Bernard envisioned this changing with the women's rights movement, and in her second edition of the book (1982), she saw the trends truly evolving. Men reported wanting to help more around the house and to help with children. Women said their men were more supportive and demonstrative than men in previous generations.

Even though attitudes and desires about sharing roles had become more egalitarian by 1982, not much had really changed in terms of concrete daily behaviors. More and more women were joining the workforce but, as Hochschild (1989) describes, after working their first shift away from home, they then came home to work their **second shift**. The second shift consists of housework, cooking, waiting on husbands, and child care, work that adds up to almost another full-time job for many women. In 1989, only 18% of men shared in second shift duties if their wives worked outside the home. Mattingly and Bianchi (2003) state that marriage decreases "me time" for women, but not for men. Women are constantly on call when married, always expected to care for their husbands, solve problems, and deal with housework and children. But Gilbert (1993) found that where men reported having egalitarian attitudes about gender, 70% of those men did share in second shift work, especially if their wives had higher education, income, or status than they did.

Today, more marriages are characterized by both partners sharing first and second shift duties. Most research on role-sharing in committed partnerships is on heterosexual couples, however, little

Second shift
The work shift that occurs once a person gets home from work, including cooking, cleaning, and child care.

is known about the partnerships of gay men and lesbians. In one early study, published around the same time as Bernard's work on "his" and "her" heterosexual marriages, Blumstein and Schwartz (1983) found that lesbian couples shared domestic tasks much more evenly than heterosexual couples did. Gay men also shared responsibilities equally and divided tasks according to partner interest, not prescribed role expectations. However, some research suggests that LGBT couples over-emphasize their egalitarian roles in research studies in order to appear to exist above the power struggles of heterosexual couples (Carrington, 1999). The controversies about these partnerships will be examined in more detail later in the chapter, as same-sex marriage and other gay rights issues are topics many individuals, families, social groups, and societies are grappling with today.

The deinstitutionalization of marriage

The *institutionalized* form of marriage refers to a union that follows traditional rules and procedures for how people can or should marry (e.g., one man and one woman married legally in front of witnesses). This institution has faced many changes over time. One noticeable trend in marriage today relates to the reasons people get married in the first place. Historically, people around the world married in order to connect kin groups and communities. They married to have children, to share their lives with another person, and to publicly commit to a life of monogamy. In the modern west, people commonly marry for love and to live happily ever after with their "soulmate." People in the contemporary western world (and even increasingly in eastern and developing nations) are looking for this relatively new institution researchers call the **pure relationship** (Giddens, 1991), one entered into strictly for the life satisfaction of the couple. This type of relationship is based on the happiness of each partner. It is entered into not for family, for kin, for children, to be protected by law, or for financial reasons. If personal rewards decline, the pure relationship ends. Interestingly, many people in pure relationships choose not to marry at all. For them, marriage is seen as a choice, not an obligation, and the only reason to marry would be to make the partners happy. Marriage rates have declined significantly in recent decades in western nations as it is no longer seen as something one must do.

    Cherlin (2004) states that contemporary marriage has become **deinstitutionalized**, or changed appreciably from its previous incarnations. The institution of marriage was once a rubric people followed, a set of rules and procedures for how, when, and why people should marry. Most people followed the rules (regarding whom they could marry, especially) and virtually everyone married eventually. But today, the social controls that once influenced people's behaviors are weakening, and in recent decades marriage rates have decreased. Fewer people are choosing to marry and when they do, they do so at later ages than was true 50 years ago. For example, in 1947, the median age of first marriage was 21 years for women and 24 years for men. In 2007, the median age was 26 for women and 27.7 for men (Cherlin, 2004; U.S. Census Bureau, 2008). Deinstitutionalization has allowed people more freedom to negotiate the terms of their relationships as well as define their own roles in marriages.

Specific forms of deinstitutionalization

For heterosexual couples, marriages and weddings have taken on a new meaning compared to previous generations. Virtually 90% of men and women in the U.S. today say they would never marry without love (Allgeier & Weiderman, 1991; Hatfield, Rapson, & Martel, 2007). However, in eastern, collectivist, and poorer countries, marriage for love is still fairly rare (Hatfield et al., 2007). Cherlin (2004) describes contemporary marriage as something people work up to, when their finances, education, and maturity levels are stabilized. Having a wedding is a prestigious event when couples can showcase their mature tastes, lifestyles, and beauty. Many people marry to reveal their personal achievements.

    Another aspect of the deinstitutionalization of marriage is the fact that the legal status of women in western nations today is equal to that of their husbands. For example, women can file for divorce whenever they choose, which they couldn't do in past generations. While previously spouses had to prove some kind of affront to marriage (infidelity, committing felonies, serious harm to children), today people can file for divorce for "irreconcilable differences," a logistically easier process than

Pure relationship
A relationship based on the happiness of each partner; it is entered into for the sole purpose of satisfaction of the couple.

Deinstitutionalized
A radical change in the "institution" of marriage, which was once comprised of a set of rules for how, when, and why people should marry; today, the social controls which influenced people's behaviors are weakening and marriage rates have decreased.

having to prove a partner's wrongdoing. In part due to the loosening of mores, today about one third of marriages end in divorce within the first five years (Cherlin, 1992). Divorce rates increased steadily in a linear fashion from 1910–1990 (except for an anomalous dip in rates in the 1940s and 1950s). After the 1980s, rates started leveling off. The U.S. government stopped gathering divorce statistics in 1999 so it's difficult to know the exact rates today, but a safe estimate using surveys gathered by researchers between 1990 and 2000 suggest that between 43% and 46% of marriages will now end in divorce, compared to about 50% in 1996 (Schoen & Canudas-Romo, 2006; U.S. Census Bureau, 2008).

A third trend in the deinstitutionalization of marriage includes the fact that fewer people believe children must be born within the confines of marriage. For example, in 1980, 18% of births occurred outside of marriage. Today, between 33% and 45% of children are born outside of marriage (Cherlin, 2004; Niehuis et al., 2006).

Cohabitation, or living together, is another increasing trend. The majority of those who eventually marry have cohabited first. One quarter of all stepfamilies in Canada and one half of all American stepfamilies never marry but choose to perpetually cohabit (Cherlin, 2004). These facets of deinstitutionalization are commonly found in many western nations, such as Canada, the U.S., the U.K., and Ireland. People in the U.S. and Canada often see cohabitation as an alternative to marriage, and 36% of Americans feel it is acceptable to cohabit without any plans to marry (Smock & Gupta, 2002). Laws in Sweden and Denmark make cohabiting families legally identical to married families (Kiernan, 2002). However, cohabitation is still rare in some western countries like Spain, Greece, and Italy, where religion still holds more sway over family decisions.

Never before in history have so many people chosen to remain single and have so many single people and cohabitors been given human rights and privileges once reserved for the married (Coontz, 2004). In relation to the rights of unmarried people, in Canada, the Modern Benefits and Obligations Act of 2000 eliminated all existing legal distinctions between married and unmarried people and between same- and opposite-sex couples as long as the couple has been together for over one year. However, non-married and same-sex couples in Canada cannot yet receive any financial protection, such as alimony, if they split up. Similarly, many countries have **domestic partnerships** available for non-married heterosexual couples, policies which give them the same rights and responsibilities as married people.

Domestic partnerships
Policies available for non-married heterosexual or homosexual couples, which give them the same rights and responsibilities as married people.

Examining the modern institution of marriage

What accounts for these marriage and partnership trends in the majority of the western world? The institution of marriage was rarely questioned in previous generations so we always knew what was expected of us. Today, there is such variety in family life, which demands legitimization, that our long-practiced rituals and routines are becoming less common. We're in a state of flux, between traditional and post-modern families. The SNAF is no longer the ideal toward which young people feel obligated to strive. They must now negotiate new rules, which can cause conflicts with people from previous generations. This conflict between generations can result in positive changes, as Conflict Theory would predict. Old roles may be constraining or oppressive, and conflict can be a force that moves society toward positive changes. For example, fewer women are expected to marry a man who will support her financially and control her behavior, and fewer husbands expect that they must bear the pressure of earning wages alone. The new set of social norms is negotiated as the old trends are deinstitutionalized.

While it is true that fewer and fewer people are choosing to formally marry, we still see about 85% of the American population eventually marrying. Why? Cherlin (2004) argues that marriage still has the attraction of being an **enforceable trust**, whereby the formal public commitment of a marriage ceremony makes the couple's vows to each other harder to break. Also, today the wedding itself is seen as a symbol of wealth and prestige. Being able to afford an elaborate "fairytale" wedding elevates couples above others and speaks to their success and power. It sets them apart from the average person, especially in poorer communities. Moreover, many continue to see marriage as a moral choice for legitimizing relationships that will benefit society and children (Flanders, 1996). People feel that marriage is symbolic of their religious, cultural, and personal values, and is a way to show

Enforceable trust
The idea that a formal, legal marriage creates a legal "trust," which reduces the chances of divorce because the public ceremony makes the couple's vows to each other harder to break.

their moral character. When people marry, their legal statuses change and they are imbued with new rights and responsibilities. Many members of society are in favor of marriage because they feel this legal contract helps to preserve the moral fiber of society (Kandoian, 1986).

To fully understand marriages and committed partnerships, we must think about them in a complex and multifaceted manner. The bioecological perspective tells us that a marriage or committed partnership is part of our microsystem. As we've just explored, microsystem committed relationships exist within larger social, political, and religious macrosystem contexts. What impact do all of these interactions have on the people at the center of marriages and committed partnerships? At the most basic level, they have an impact on our health.

HEALTH BENEFITS OF HAPPY MARRIAGES

Processes underlying the marriage–health link

By this point, it is probably no surprise to you that biology has an impact on many facets of marriage. But the converse is also true: marriage has an impact on biology. Biological factors in one partner continuously interact with those of the other partner. Research on the biological effects of marriage gives us some insight into what is going on. There are also some emerging areas of study on people's genetic contributions to marriages.

In general, marriage benefits both men and women. However, the health of people in unhappy marriages is actually worse than the health of single people, and the health benefits decline dramatically in conflictual marriages (Coontz, 2005). For example, happily married partners with high blood pressure showed instant drops in blood pressure when spending even a few minutes with their spouse. However, a few minutes together raised the blood pressure of unhappily married people (Coontz, 2005). Women fare worse health-wise in unhappy marriages compared to single women, while men still get some health benefits from being in distressed marriages compared to single men.

In a 20-year longitudinal study, marriage was found to protect people by lowering their risk of dying, in comparison to those who were never married, divorced, or widowed (Waite & Gallagher, 2000). In this study, widowed women lived longer than divorced or never-married women but not as long as still-married women. Moreover, married men had lower rates of problem drinking and higher levels of income. These results suggest that men may benefit from marriage because their wives make sure they smoke less, eat more healthily, and go to the doctor. Typically, wives serve as the primary social support for their husbands, partially explaining the benefits to men of being married.

Looking at it from the other side, *unhappily* married people are at greater risk for poor health and even mortality. Conflicts within marriage are related to heart rate elevations, increased stress hormone circulation, and poor immune functioning. The risk is comparable to that experienced by smokers, those with high blood pressure, and the morbidly obese (Robles & Kiecolt-Glaser, 2003). In general, people who are in unhappy marriages, are separated, or are divorced have many physical and psychological struggles, from depression to physical illness and violent behavior (Carrere, Buehlman, Gottman, Coan, & Ruckstuhl, 2000). Smith et al. (2009), however, found that wives in unhappy marriages were at risk for heart disease, stroke and diabetes, but their husbands were immune from these negative effects. Both women and men in distressed marriages showed symptoms of depression, but men did not experience any physical or immune system problems, again suggesting that marriage may be more of a buffer for men's health than women's.

To further examine the effect of marital stress on health, Kiecolt-Glaser, Bane, Glaser, & Malarkey (2003) followed 200 people longitudinally and found that stress weakened their immune systems. Their cells showed increased inflammation after stress, which can, over a long period of time, lead the cells to break down. This may result in cardiovascular disease, cancer, and other problems. Marital conflict is a major source of stress. As we know from previous chapters, stress weakens the immune

HOW WOULD YOU MEASURE THAT?

Newlyweds' hormones and marriage quality (Kiecolt-Glaser et al., 2003)

If couples counselors want to prevent couples from breaking up or experiencing severe distress, how would they do that? You have read about some of the psychophysiological effects of distressed marriages. To examine these issues further, Kiecolt-Glaser et al. (2003) examined a sample of recently married people to find out whether neurophysiological reactivity in Year 1 could predict the health of a marriage 10 years later. The authors collected immune system markers, stress hormone, behavioral, and self-report data during a 24-hour stay in a research hospital. The couples averaged 25 years of age for women and 26 years for men, and 61% had lived together before marriage. Participants were fitted with an IV tube that allowed for blood collection by nurses who collected the samples through long tubes from behind a curtain. After the participants adjusted to the IV, they were interviewed about problems they typically discuss at home and were then asked to spend 30 minutes discussing a chosen problem. They also completed a series of questionnaires and had several quiet times to allow their physiological arousal to decrease periodically. The researchers sampled four stress hormones: epinephrine (EPI), norepinephrine (NEPI), cortisol, and adrenocorticotropic hormone (ACTH). During problem discussions, couples were also coded for positive and negative interaction styles.

After 7 to 10 years, 17 of the original 90 couples had divorced. Interestingly, marital satisfaction at Year 1 did not predict those who divorced versus those who stayed together, and neither did hostility during the discussion task or depression measurements. What *did* distinguish the couples who divorced from the couples

who stayed together were their stress hormone levels during the problem discussion task at Year 1. Those who later divorced had higher daytime and nighttime EPI levels. These couples had elevated stress hormone levels throughout the day, and not just during the problem discussion task. In fact, the EPI levels of later divorced couples were 34% higher than those of couples who stayed married, and these couples differed significantly on three of the four hormones assessed. But even among those who stayed together, a substantial proportion reported their marriages to be in distress. Distressed but intact couples showed elevated EPI and NEPI levels in comparison to happy couples at Year 1. Dissatisfied couples' NEPI levels were 34% higher than happy couples'. The only *behavioral* measure that distinguished groups was negative and hostile behavior during the discussion task at Year 1. There were no differences between dissatisfied and happy couples at Year 1 in cardiovascular reactivity, personality trait hostility, or family histories of psychiatric or cardiovascular problems.

These endocrine hormone elevations have serious implications for one's potential to develop long-term illness and they can even affect longevity. Many findings suggest that marital stress harms women's health more than men's. This study adds to the growing literature showing the need to teach individual young people and couples emotion regulation, communication, positive problem-solving, and other conflict de-escalation skills before they enter committed partnerships. Preventing psychophysiological reactivity may prevent relationship distress later on.

system and leads to high levels of circulating stress hormones in the brain and body cells. Marital strain has been linked to stress and the subsequent development of depression, elevated blood pressure, infections and illnesses, and even chronic pain (Robles & Kiecolt-Glaser, 2003).

In another study, Kiecolt-Glaser and colleagues asked married couples to come into the lab and discuss typical problems they fight about at home (Kiecolt-Glaser et al., 1987). They then gave them small blisters on their fingers. The researchers found that the couples who used hostility and anger during their discussion had blisters that healed more slowly. Also, when they took samples of the blister fluid, the couples had lower levels of interleukin-6, a protein that regulates healing at the wound site, which probably slowed their healing. These couples also had interleukin-6 imbalances in general body cells, suggesting a weakened general body immune response. This series of studies suggests that even one argument can spur a negative stress response that can affect partners' health.

Stressful marriages have been related to both self-reported and objectively measured health problems. For example, patients with renal disease and greater marital satisfaction decreased their mortality risk by 29%, while those with hostile relationships increased their mortality risk by 46% (Kimmel et al., 2000). Similarly, women admitted to the hospital with cardiovascular disease and experiencing marital strain were twice as likely to have another cardiovascular event as those in happy marriages. Those with the worst disease levels and the worst marriages (a double whammy) had a survival rate of only 42%, while those with good marriages had a 78% survival rate (Coyne et al., 2001). These results are extremely important as they suggest that the health of your relationship can affect how long you live.

For more on the connection between neurophysiology and relationship health, see *How Would You Measure That?* This box describes a study that examines how newlyweds' stress hormones predict relationship quality 10 years later.

The results of numerous studies using different types of samples in different geographical regions consistently show the benefits of marriage on health to be greater for men than for women; the protection from mortality is 50% higher for married versus non-married women but 250% higher for married versus non-married men (Robles & Kiecolt-Glaser, 2003). Note, though, that these studies are largely correlational. Recall from Chapter 2 that *correlation does not equal causation*. It could be that healthy people are more likely to get married and have satisfying marriages, and not that marriage causes good health outcomes for people. Or perhaps unhappy, negative people have both health problems and strained marriages. It could also be that the same positive results regarding health, happiness, and longevity might be found for other groups, such as *unmarried* LGBT or *cohabiting* heterosexual couples who have certain personality traits like optimism, so the results are not necessarily due to marriage, per se. The health benefits of marriage could be due to social support in general, not necessarily marriage, as social support has been linked to healthy habits and lower mortality rates (Uchino, 2009). And much research suggests that personality traits and cognitive processes can influence the health and happiness of any relationship (Karney, 2010). Let's take a closer look at the underlying processes that might explain these correlational findings between happy marriages and positive health and longevity.

Processes underlying the marriage–health link

McEwan and Seeman (1999) explain four possible ways marital struggles can lead to physical dysfunction: (1) through repeated hits to the immune system (chronic marital conflict leads to proportionally greater physiological stress responses); (2) spouse inability to adapt to continuing stressors (such as criticisms by partner); (3) inability to control physiological responses to marital stressors (e.g., continually elevated heart rate); and (4) inadequate response to stressors (such as drinking alcohol or screaming, which worsen health problems).

Some interesting medical research shows the effectiveness of perceived social support in enhancing longevity. Uchino (2009) emphasizes that simply having access to social support or reporting on the number of people in one's social network are probably poor indicators of the benefits of social support on health and longevity. He distinguishes between two types of support. **Received support** refers to the number of available people or the number of acts of kindness performed. **Perceived support** refers to a real sense that someone cares, listens, and is there for you. Only perceived support is related to positive health outcomes. Received support is situational. People may come to your aid when you're stressed, but if you don't *feel* supported, their attempts to help won't positively impact you. For example, some family members come to help with a problem but then only talk about themselves and don't really listen. Or they may come to help you when you're sick but then give unwanted advice or try to run your life. This is high *received* support but low *perceived* support. If a close friend brings you chicken soup, rubs your back, and listens to you complain about your illness, you may feel a high level of both *perceived* and *received* support. People with high levels of *perceived* support often grew up in securely attached families and have positive perceptions about people in general (Uchino, 2009).

Received support
The objective number of people available to support a given person; does not mean the given person feels supported.

Perceived support
A subjective sense that someone cares, listens, and is there for a given person.

Interestingly, securely attached people have greater levels of perceived support (regardless of whether that support is actually provided). These people tend to have high levels of optimism and low levels of hostility, which are both related to physical health. This finding illustrates the complex interaction between genetically influenced personality traits, microsystem influences in childhood, and cognitive coping abilities in adult relationships (Uchino, 2009). Once again, personal attachment history and family of origin issues emerge as important contributors to adult family functioning.

In the context of marriage, personal health and happiness are relatively new phenomena to examine. They played no important role in marriages in earlier generations. Our ancestors might have chuckled at modern concepts like "marital functioning" and "marital satisfaction." In previous generations, people did not enter into marriage to benefit the individuals involved. No one cared about conflict-resolution skills or a woman's unhappiness. As you will see in the next section, marriage was an arrangement of convenience, not a fairytale where two hearts beat as one.

A HISTORICAL EXAMINATION OF MARRIAGE

Marriages before industrialization

Marriage in the nineteenth century

Kin marriages

As described previously, in earlier generations, marriage was an institution based on the benefits for kin and community, to maintain political alliances, and to secure finances. Hunt (1996) states that marriage was the key avenue by which people amassed possessions, social status, jobs, land, and connections between generations and communities. In most of those marriages, women were considered the property of their husbands and had no real rights of their own.

Marriages before industrialization

In ancient Rome, only the wealthy had the right to formally marry. In the twelfth century CE, Andreas Capellanus stated that love cannot exist between married people (cited in Hatfield et al., 2007, p. 100). He said:

> Everybody knows that love can have no place between husband and wife … for what is love but an inordinate desire to receive passionately a furtive and hidden embrace? But what embrace between husband and wife can be furtive, I ask you, since they may be said to belong to each other's desires without fear that anybody will object?

Since marriage is often considered a sacred bond sanctioned by God, some early thinkers questioned how such a union could involve love and passion. While many people today associate marriage with religious vows, for 1,000 years the Catholic Church merely expected that a man and woman promise themselves to each other in order to be married. No elaborate rituals or ceremonies were required (Coontz, 2004). In fact, early Christians thought marriage was a corrupting institution and didn't think of it as a holy union until around the thirteenth century CE. Instead of being sanctioned by God, many marriages across cultures in the past, and many today, were arranged by parents for the sake of the family. In India, families chose a partner for their child based on social class, educational attainment and the quality of the partner's family (Sprecher & Chandak, 1992). Bumroongsook (1992) discusses that in many cultures, people were forbidden to wed foreigners and even those born under the wrong astrological sign. Horoscopes and supernatural readings by spiritual leaders often influenced marriage arrangements.

In the early colonial years in the New World, it wasn't uncommon for white indentured servants to have sexual and romantic relations with black slaves. Slavery was not fully institutionalized until the 1660s, so before then, there were no formal laws against these relationships (Williamson, 1995). It is estimated that by 1776, about 100,000 persons of mixed race, or 11% of the black population, lived in the colonies. A person of mixed-race was called a mulatto by slave-traders. Slaves were often not allowed to marry each other. By 1865, 67% of the slaves were mulatto, due to liaisons like those described above, as well as the raping of black women by white men. Some slave owners and their slaves did form caring relationships and families, but the mulatto side of the family was always subordinate to the legitimate white marriage and family. And white women often had to look the other way when their husbands had children with black women. Today it is estimated that 75% of African Americans have white ancestry (Coles, 2006).

Because most of the colonists and those eventually moving west were men, many white men also had relations with or married Native American women, or Mexican women in the southwest. Even East Indian and Asian immigrants coming to North America to find work intermarried with Mexican women in the early years of westward expansion. Interracial marriages were eventually forbidden by law as slaves and other people of color were considered property, and not fully human. Moreover, the Mexican and indigenous women in these unions had few, if any, rights to divorce their husbands or have contact with their children if the men left them (Coles, 2006).

Marriage in the nineteenth century

Bouvier's (1856, cited in http://legal-dictionary.thefreedictionary.com) law dictionary states that the wife is the property of her husband and that all of her previous possessions will now belong to him. While wives were allowed to inherit property after their husbands' deaths, husbands were allowed immediate ownership of all of their wives' property and could sell it and retain all the profits. Specifically:

- Marriage gives the husband marital authority over the person of his wife.
- The wife acquires thereby the name of her husband, as they are considered as but one, of which he is the head.
- In general, the wife follows the condition of her husband.

FIGURE 7.1 How do you think this wife's life might have differed from those of wives today? Photo © L. C. Buckley/Hulton Archive/Getty Images.

Martineau (1837), a female writer railing against the oppression of women, and wives in particular, protested the "feudal prejudices" against American women. She despised how they were forced to be party to "mercenary marriages" while eligible men went wildly and freely across the west, land-grabbing, leaving women in the east to marry old widowers. She said "if women and men marry those whom they do not love, they must love those whom they do not marry" (p. 91). In questioning the oppressive system, she asked whether the Declaration of Independence did not also apply to the other half of the human race.

While women may have had few rights within Victorian era marriages, you may be surprised to learn that most women actually married those they knew well, including their cousins. Throughout history, people married those in their villages or kingdoms, most of whom were blood relations. Famous intelligent and successful families, from the Einsteins to the Darwins, from the DuPonts to the Rothschilds, usually kept marriage within the family. It is estimated that 80% of all marriages in human history were between second cousins or closer relations.

Kin marriages

While there is a fear that babies born to married cousins will have birth defects, and 31 states have outlawed the practice, the truth is that the risk of birth defects only increases by about 2% if the parents are biological relatives (Conniff, 2003). However, as with animals and plants, too much inbreeding over too many generations can lead to dangerous recessive genes related to illness or deformity being passed down. If two parents both carry a recessive trait, the trait is more likely to be passed to offspring, so the more genetically related two people are, the greater the chance of passing on recessive traits. We all carry five to seven dangerous recessive traits, but when we marry non-kin, those traits less likely to be expressed.

Marrying kin can also result in strong and healthy traits being reinforced and passed on to offspring, such as immunity to region-specific illnesses. Studies show that kin-breeders have twice as many great-grandchildren as outbreeders, suggesting that inbreeding does not result in low fertility levels (Conniff, 2003). However, today there are many social and legal sanctions against intermarriage with kin. Though marriage between kin is rare in western cultures today, there are some unique types of marriage people experience.

TYPES OF MARRIAGE

- Cohabitation and common law marriage
- Covenant marriages
- Lavee and Olson's marriage typologies
- Same-sex marriages
- Interracial and intercultural marriages
- Arranged marriages

This section will explore the many deviations from the SNAF that are experienced both in western cultures and around the world. As discussed at the opening of this chapter, fewer and fewer people are marrying these days. It's becoming fairly common, especially in western nations, for people to cohabit both before marriage and as an alternative to marriage. In the U.S., each state is allowed to institute its own marriage laws determining who can marry and how marriages can end, although the federal government can always step in. For example, in 1878, the Federal Court ruled that polygamous marriages were illegal, despite religious beliefs that legitimized it in some states (for example, in the case of Mormons in Utah who used to legally practice polygamy). All states now limit marriage to *two* people and will not allow people to marry another person if their spouse is currently living or they are not yet divorced. If people marry a new partner while still married, it is a federal crime called **bigamy**. What do you think? Should people be allowed to marry more than one person if all

Bigamy
The crime of marrying someone while still being married to someone else.

FOCUS ON MY FAMILY

Joel, Todd, and Michael

We are three gay men in a committed co-equal relationship we call a "triad." We started as a couple (Joel and Todd), and after being together 10 years, met Michael, who joined our relationship, and has been with us for eight years. It's important to mention that Joel and Todd had a happy, solid relationship when they met Michael. He was in no way added to the family to fill a void or repair a shaky relationship. As a triad, we face the same situations as most couples, except there is an extra level of complexity because there are three of us with ideas, needs, families, and so on.

As with all relationships, the key to success, as well as the root of conflicts, is open and honest communication. A practical advantage is that one of us is able to mediate when the others are having communication challenges, and things can smooth out more quickly. Each of us also has our own hobbies so we can share them with each other. On the other hand, occasionally someone feels "ganged up on" and resolving conflict is more challenging. But two partners provide more support when each of us needs someone to talk to. It can be great to hear another point of view, but it can be also be tough trying to get three people on the same page. It's easy to forget that you've only shared something with one partner and not the other.

Sleeping arrangements can be tough; there's the issue of fitting all three in one bed (but that has benefits on cold nights). Traveling can be difficult. For example, hotel stays and anniversary dinners can be confusing to arrange for three. Besides being charged for a third person at a hotel, the bed choices can be challenging. Holiday parties at work are also interesting.

Living in a progressive community, we've rarely had to deal with discrimination. Being open about our family seems to alleviate much of the gossip and misconceptions. Of course, it's sometimes challenging explaining our family as our relationship is so far outside of people's experience that they don't comprehend it.

All three of us are completely out of the "closet" with our families. We are fortunate that all our parents accept our relationship, but it was difficult to varying degrees when we first disclosed our triad. The range of family reactions varied from immediate acceptance—Michael's mother bragged about already knowing another triad—to nearly complete rejection from Todd's sister based on religious beliefs and fear. Legal discrimination is also a problem: marriage rights, taxes, medical visitation, inheritance, and so on. We have tried to come close to marriage rights through the use of living trusts and powers of attorney as there is no legal recognition for same-sex families, let alone for triads.

Loving two partners is challenging and joyous. We must constantly work on communicating effectively. We've learned that loving more than one person whole-heartedly is neither impossible nor impractical, making us open to all the possibilities that life may bring.

Todd, Michael, and Joel.
Photo reproduced by permission.

three (or more) people feel truly committed to each other? To see an example of a committed partnership involving three members, see the *Focus on My Family* Box.

Todd, Michael, and Joel from the *Focus on My Family* box seem to have a very strong, committed, caring partnership. They respect each other and communicate well. Based on their description of their relationship, see if you can determine which of the following typologies best describes them.

Cohabitation and common law marriage

Between 1965 and 1972, only 10% of couples cohabited and only 10% of those relationships lasted five or more years. Today, many more couples cohabit and 35% of those relationships have children, although 70% of the children belong to only one partner biologically. Even pregnant women today are less likely to marry and more likely to live with their baby's father (Raley, 1999). In fact, many statistics relating to "single mothers" are actually counting children who are born into a cohabiting relationship (50% for white and Latino/a children, and 25% for African American children) (Smock, 2000). Astone, Constance, Schoen, and Kim, (1999) found that the majority of African American fatherhood occurs in cohabiting relationships, but official census data count their children as living in single-mother homes.

Typically, cohabitors have lower income and education levels than married couples; for example, 33% of cohabitors own homes compared to 80% of married people (Smock, 2000). They also tend to be less religious and more liberal, and have more egalitarian views regarding gender role expectations. Some cohabitors view cohabitation as a temporary step before marriage, some as an alternative to marriage, and some as an alternative to singlehood. These latter folks do not typically have ideas about the permanency of the relationship but just "go with the flow." In this regard, cohabitors typically show lower levels of commitment to the relationship and also feel less satisfaction with their relationships than married people do (Smock, 2000).

Women of color tend to view cohabitation as an alternative to marriage while white women tend to see it as a phase occurring before and leading up to marriage. It is perhaps not surprising that men tend to view cohabitation as an alternative to singlehood while women in general tend to see cohabitation as a step to marriage (Smock, 2000). It's been well documented that people who cohabit before marriage are more likely to divorce than those who don't cohabit prior to getting married, especially if the person cohabits with several partners before marrying one of them (Lichter & Qian, 2008). The reasons why are unclear, but it could be related to the divergent expectations of the members of the couple as well as lower financial resources (leading to higher stress) and lack of acceptance of the couple by their families. Thus, it is important for couples to discuss their specific reasons for cohabiting and to try to reconcile what their future intentions are. Many couples cohabit to save money on rent and to pool resources. But one partner may view this step as a precursor to a future marriage. Cohabitation may be a necessity for some but does not bode well statistically for the future of the relationship.

Married people (both men and women) typically experience greater happiness and joy and are less at risk for mental illnesses like depression, in comparison to unmarried people (Robles & Kiecolt-Glaser, 2003). Married men report higher sexual and relationship satisfaction than cohabiting and single men. Cohabiting adults are likely to be in worse health than married people. In a large recent study on this topic, Wienke (2009) examined over 11,000 people, singles, cohabitors, and marrieds, both heterosexual and homosexual. The results showed that all of the people (across sexual orientation and gender) were happier if they were in a relationship than if they weren't. In support of earlier findings, married people were the happiest, followed by cohabitors (both gay and straight), daters, and lastly, singles. While cohabitation may not seem very beneficial based on these data, it has been fairly normative throughout our history.

Common law marriage
A marriage recognized in some states and countries where a couple is given all the rights, privileges, and responsibilities of marriage because they've been together a long time, not because they have gone through a formal marriage ritual.

Historically, most U.S. states recognized the legitimacy of **common law marriage**, in which there was never a marriage license, legal contract, or formal ceremony. In common law marriage, the partners are viewed as living together exactly as husband and wife except that there was no formal ceremony. By states recognizing common law marriage, children were no longer labeled "illegitimate" and all property rights and other benefits were bestowed upon the family. Unfortunately, inheritance, insurance, and property rights issues became so confusing that most states eventually outlawed common law marriage. Today, only 14 states recognize common law marriage, arguing that they maintain the tradition because it protects religious and social freedoms, as well as allowing marriage for poor people who cannot afford a traditional marriage ceremony, license, blood test, and so on.

FIGURE 7.2 Based on the research in this chapter, what advice would you give this couple regarding cohabitation and marriage, in order to ensure the happiness of their family?
Photo ©Photodisc/Getty Images.

As we recognize now, though, these common law marriages (today known as cohabitation) may have higher rates of divorce than standard marriages.

While decades of research have shown a negative correlation between cohabitation and later marital stability, this trend has been declining in recent years as younger cohorts enter cohabitation without the stigma these couples once experienced and some today choose to never marry at all (Bumpass & Lu, 1999). Cohabitation, for many couples today, is seen as a substitute for the pressures of legal marriage, especially if they would reap no further benefits from being married than just living together, which is the case in many western nations.

In the U.S., though, legally married couples have over 1,000 rights that unmarried couples don't have, including the right to visit each other in hospitals, the right to receive veteran's benefits and pensions of deceased spouses, the right for immigrants to become U.S. citizens if they marry citizens, the right to be housed together in senior care homes, and many others (U.S. General Accounting Office, 1997).

A case example of cohabitation in Sweden

One of the most progressive societies in the world, Sweden, may hold the title for male and female gender equality, and they also have some of the lowest marriage rates in the world (Popenoe, 2006). Only 17.5 per 1,000 Swedish women are currently married (compared to 43.4 per 1,000 American women). This amounts to 60% of Swedish women eventually marrying versus 85% of American women. When Swedes do marry, it tends to be at older ages, 31 and 33 for Swedish women and men respectively, compared to 25 and 27 for American women and men respectively. While Americans are more conservative politically, more religious, and marry more often than Swedish people, the U.S. actually has higher divorce rates and exponentially higher teen and unplanned birth rates. Why the differences?

There are many reasons for these trends. First, the Swedish government provides no incentives for people to get married. It is a largely secular society with leftist politics. All government benefits are given to men and women, gays and straights, equally. There are no joint income tax or spousal insurance benefits. Everyone is entitled to get the same quality health care, education, and retirement benefits just by virtue of being a Swedish citizen.

Women are given maternity leaves that include 80% of their salaries for one year and half salary for another six months in order to stay home with their babies. Men are given two months of paid paternity leave. This means most Swedish children stay home with mom for the first year of life when attachments are forming. High-quality day care and developmentally appropriate preschool after the first year can benefit children's development in many ways. However, research suggests that *full-time* day care, especially if it is low quality, in the first year of life can pose developmental challenges for the burgeoning attachment relationship between mother and child, and can also increase children's behavior problems (Belsky, 2001). Most Swedish women either don't work or work part time when their children are very young; but this means that very few women reach top positions in the corporate world. Nevertheless, this system also ensures that no children live in poverty or live without high-quality care and health insurance.

To pay for this system that reinforces cohabitation, Swedes pay one of the highest tax rates in the world (Popenoe, 2006). In comparison, the U.S. has the lowest tax rate in the industrialized world and the fewest social benefits for its citizens. Swedish people are staunchly egalitarian in their philosophies, and their feminist leanings make them opposed to the patriarchal traditions of marriage, which they feel preserve gendered hierarchies. They feel a sense of "brotherhood" and "sisterhood" for all Swedes and believe it is every citizen's job to care for all other people in the community. They tend to be pacifists with low rates of violent crime and high levels of social conformity.

Theorists argue that the U.S. has such high divorce rates partly due to the large income gaps between rich and poor, leading to a large underclass that struggles just to survive. Minority stress and the constant struggles of living in poverty lead to high levels of relationship dissolution. Also, Americans are highly mobile and ethnically diverse, and marry young compared to couples in Scandinavia, often due to religious or political pressure in their communities.

Scandinavian cultures are also less materialistic than Americans. They tend to have small modest apartments (albeit with all the modern conveniences) and live a more relaxed lifestyle. They spend a lot of time outdoors and have much leisure time. Americans work the most of any western industrial citizenry, leading to high levels of stress and unhealthy habits like eating fast food and getting insufficient sleep. Most European nations grant at least 3–6 weeks paid vacation every year, and small towns virtually shut down in the summer. However, keep in mind that countries like Sweden are very small (Sweden has only nine million people) and the population is homogeneous and less mobile, making a cultural "work ethic" and singular approach to life much easier to institute (Popenoe, 2006).

The sheer diversity of American couples makes their marriages a bit more stressful and difficult to maintain. While Swedes may cohabit out of choice, Americans more often do so as a way to survive financially. Consequently, it's not surprising that cohabitors in the U.S. have higher levels of relationship dissatisfaction than married people and that cohabitation before marriage is related to higher divorce rates.

Despite these cultural trends spurring people in industrialized nations to rethink the necessity for marriage, the vast majority of people in most western countries will still get married. And in the U.S., with its high rates of religious affiliation and a strong conservative political movement, many couples are clinging even more strongly to traditional marriage rituals.

Covenant marriages

Covenant marriage
Marriages that restrict a couple's ability to divorce by having them enroll in premarital counseling, endure a long waiting period for divorce, make every attempt to reconcile during predivorce counseling, and divorce only in extreme circumstances such as domestic violence, abandonment, and adultery.

In reaction to high divorce rates and the perceived disintegration of the traditional family, people in some U.S. states are allowed to engage in **covenant marriage**, which is thought to reduce divorce rates. Covenant marriage restricts a couple's ability to divorce. The couple must enroll in premarital counseling, endure a long waiting period for divorce, make every attempt to reconcile during predivorce counseling, and divorce only in extreme circumstances such as domestic violence, abandonment, and adultery (Baker, Sanchez, Nock, & Wright, 2009).

Baker et al. (2009) found that people who had covenant marriages (versus standard marriages) had more traditional attitudes about religion and gender roles. These couples also described their marriages as public symbols expressing the purity of their relationship and its acceptance in the eyes of God. They denied the argument that these marriages are patriarchal because they said that when you follow a marriage contract that is in service to God, it emphasizes compassion and equality for all. In contrast, the couples in standard marriages felt marriage was just a private commitment between individuals and served no larger purpose. Those who favor covenant marriages advocate teaching young people about the sanctity and commitment involved in marriage, and that divorce should rarely be seen as an option. In one example of this ethic, Florida has enacted the Marriage Preparation and Preservation Act, which mandates that marriage and relationship curricula be taught in public high schools, in order to encourage marriage and prevent divorce. So while the new trends of deinstitutionalization struggle to take hold in society, the forces of tradition push back, positing the need for conventional, religion-based, marriages.

As you can see, there are extremely diverse processes underlying how, when, and why people marry. And there are few universal marriage laws implemented at the federal level which would guide people's behavior across the board in every state.

Lavee and Olson's marriage typologies

In order to discover underlying typologies of modern marriages, Lavee and Olson (1993) examined over 8,000 married couples (mostly white, middle class) who had experienced their therapy program "Enriching Relationship Issues, Communication, and Happiness" (ENRICH). Couples filled out assessments of nine characteristics or dimensions of their relationships (personality issues, communication, conflict resolution, financial management, leisure activities, sexual relationship, children and parenting, family and friends, and religious orientation). Lavee and Olson then used statistical techniques to combine the individual questions into broader categories, or types, of marriage. They found seven main types of marriage, which are defined below. Forty percent of the couples fit in the *devitalized* category, 9% were *vitalized*, 11% were *financially focused*, 14% were *conflicted*, 8% were *balanced*, 8% were *harmonious*, and 10% were *traditional*. Let's look at each type more closely. In addition to thinking about Todd, Michael, and Joel in the *Focus on My Family* box, see if your own, your parents,' your grandparents' or your friends' marriages seem to fit into any of these categories.

Devitalized couples were dissatisfied with all nine dimensions of their relationship assessed on the surveys. Overall, they were the most unhappy and most likely to consider divorce. These couples tended to be younger and had lower incomes than the other types. They tended to have more divorces among their own parents, too.

Vitalized marriages were characterized by high levels of satisfaction with almost all of the nine dimensions. These couples had strong internal and external resources and a solid emotional foundation. They solved problems very effectively and let things slide that couldn't be solved. Recalling the "his" versus "her" marriage from the opening paragraphs of this chapter, even in healthy, stable marriages like the *vitalized* type, 25% of the wives had considered divorce. In fact, for all seven types of marriage, women were less satisfied overall than men were.

The *financially focused* couples tended to be dissatisfied with at least six relationship dimensions, but maintained a strong financial management pattern. Money, or financial stability, tended to keep them together. They were dissatisfied with communication, how conflicts were resolved, and often engaged in negative attacks on their partners, but were comfortable financially.

Conflicted couples showed dissatisfaction with most of the nine dimensions regarding their relationship, but they had many positive outlets outside the relationship. They gained much satisfaction through other relationships, which led them to stay in conflicted marriages.

Balanced couples communicated well and were mostly satisfied with the other relationship dimensions. They agreed on childrearing topics, how to spend their free time, and on sexual issues. They tended to live a fairly balanced life and place high priority on their nuclear family. However, they tended to argue about money management and one quarter of both husbands and wives had considered divorce.

The *harmonious* couples were very satisfied with most relationship dimensions but scored low on the affection and sexuality dimensions. They also saw parenting as problematic but got along well with each other in general.

The *traditional* couples had strong extended kin networks and solid religious faith, but didn't necessarily communicate well with each other or find satisfaction in their sexual relations. They also didn't have very effective conflict resolution skills.

In a study attempting to replicate these seven marriage types in a new sample of over 2,000 couples, Fowers and Olson (1993) found only five of the types during statistical analyses: *devitalized*, *conflicted*, *harmonious*, *traditional*, and *vitalized*. They failed to find couples fitting into the *financially focused* or *balanced* types. A third study also tried to use the ENRICH therapy program to find marital typologies, this time with a sample of 415 African American married couples. Allen and Olson (2001) attempted to generalize the five or seven types found in previous studies to see if black couples experienced similar dynamics that could be categorized along similar dimensions as white couples.

Fifty years ago, the vast majority of black couples were married, while today, only 44% of African Americans report being married. Also, the divorce rate among African Americans has quadrupled over the past two generations. Allen and Olson (2001) hoped to find a marital typology for black married couples that might point to certain dimensions that could be used to enhance their relationships in therapy, just like the results from the European American couples study had done.

Using the same original nine dimensions of marital adjustment and the same assessment procedures, these authors found that at least five of the typologies applied and so posited a five-typology model for African American marriages. They did not find support for the *financially focused* or *balanced types*. Interestingly, 90% of the *vitalized* types of African American married couples were extremely satisfied and, unlike white couples, none had considered divorce. They were very happy with their marriages. Moreover, these couples tended to have high levels of education. The *harmonious* types (12% of the sample) reported extremely high levels of sexual satisfaction and less than 30% had considered divorce. They were also very satisfied with their marriages in general. In the *traditional* couples, men tended to be more satisfied than their wives, and in the *conflicted* couples, both parties were extremely dissatisfied and had considered divorce. Similar to the results among white samples, in this sample of African Americans, the *devitalized* type was the largest group (40% of the sample), and they were dissatisfied in most dimensions. Similar to the white sample, these *devitalized* couples also tended to have lower educational levels, poor employment status, and larger families (three or more children).

In addition to the typologies, Allen and Olson attempted to measure specific Afrocentric influences on African American marriages: extended family and friends, egalitarian

© Mike Baldwin / Cornered

"'Have it all. Be an executive, community volunteer, a devoted wife and mother.' Good article. You should read this."

FIGURE 7.3 Which of Lavee and Olson's marriage types do you think this couple fits into?
Cartoon © www.CartoonStock.com.

TABLE 7.1 Lavee and Olson's (1993) five empirically supported marriage types.

Marriage type	Characteristics
Devitalized	Dissatisfied with all nine dimensions of relationship; most unhappy; most likely to consider divorce; younger; lower incomes; more children; more divorces in family of origin.
Conflicted	Dissatisfied with most of the nine dimensions; many positive outlets outside couple relationship; satisfaction through other relationships leads them to stay in conflictual marriages.
Harmonious	Very satisfied with most relationship dimensions; low on affection and sexuality (African Americans satisfied sexually); parenting problems but get along well in general.
Traditional	Strong extended kin networks; solid religious faith; dissatisfied with several dimensions; poor communication and sexual relations; poor conflict resolution skills. Traditional African American men more satisfied than their wives.
Vitalized	High levels of education; satisfaction with almost all dimensions; strong internal and external resources; solid emotional foundation and good problem-solving skills. Vitalized African Americans more satisfied than whites (fewer consider divorce).

gender role beliefs, and religious affiliation. However, none of these three dimensions differed between the five marriage types. This may imply that these Afrocentric values are equally important to African American couples across all marriage types. The five-category typology has been replicated on numerous samples and is the most valid across a diversity of couples. Table 7.1 provides a summary of the empirically supported five types of marriage.

To learn some strategies for how you might avoid becoming part of a *devitalized* couple, see some tips on how you can solve conflicts with an intimate partner more effectively, in the nearby *Building Your Strengths* box on fair fighting.

While Olson and colleagues' research is exemplary in its attempt to validate its typologies on diverse populations across numerous studies, they failed to examine these typologies in same-sex couples. In fact, same-sex couples have only recently become a focus for family researchers. Although many of these couples cannot get married even if they want to, it is important to consider their marriages and committed partnerships as they are a part of society. Thinking back to the *Focus on My Family* box, some issues Todd has talked to me about include the fact that he cannot visit either of his partners in the hospital and the family cannot receive the tax benefits that heterosexual married couples receive. What do you think about the issue of same-sex marriage? Same-sex marriage is a very controversial topic that is being debated in the public arena daily. Whatever opinion you develop, I hope it will be informed by evidence.

Same-sex marriages

In 1987, the United States Supreme Court delineated four attributes characteristic of a marriage: (a) expression of emotional support and public commitment; (b) spiritual significance, and for some, the exercise of religious faith; (c) the expectation that for most, the marriage will be consummated; and (d) the receipt of tangible benefits, including government benefits and property rights. This ruling, stemming from a discrimination lawsuit, led the federal court to grant incarcerated prisoners the right to marry, a right that had been denied to them in their state, Missouri (Wilkins, 2003). Besides incarcerated prisoners, who now have the right to marry while in prison, what other types of people can you think of who are denied the right to marry? Do you think if people's relationships are

BUILDING YOUR STRENGTHS

Tips for fighting fair

- If you have a problem, think about how to present it and then present it with love sooner rather than later.

- State the problem clearly to your partner using "I" statements, without blaming him or her for the problem. For example, "I have been feeling sad lately when I come home and the house is messy because the clutter makes me anxious."

- The receiver of the information should be prepared to restate the problem so that there are no misunderstandings. For example, "I'm hearing some disappointment from you, because I haven't been keeping the house very tidy."

- The first partner should acknowledge whether the problem was heard correctly or make amendments. Then he or she is responsible for suggesting a solid solution, without blaming or shaming the other person. For example, "Yes, I'm so tired after work that I don't have the energy to clean the house. Would it be possible for you to pick up the living room and put the kids' toys away before I get home? That would be a big help."

- The second partner should then either agree to the request or state other options. Each option should be discussed until there is one that is workable (not necessarily perfect, but one that is not characterized by one partner dominating the other's ideas). For example, "Actually, I think the kids will keep making messes until bedtime, so would it be OK with you if I picked up the living room and put the dishes away but then after the kids went to bed, we could both put the toys away?"

- After the couple has reached an agreement, they must make a concrete plan to implement it and prevent it from being sabotaged.

- Once an agreement is reached, the partners should reaffirm their commitment and acknowledge the compromises that were made on each side.

- Agree to revisit the problem after a while (for example, a week later) to see if the plan needs tweaking. If the plan is not implemented properly, it is not acceptable to yell, whine, or complain. Just start over with the first step.

(Adapted from Matta, 2006, pp. 70–71: Reproduced with permission of ABC-CLIO, LLC.)

Note: These tips are not meant to diagnose, treat, or cure any personal or relationship problems. They are meant for informational purposes, and to spur discussion.

characterized by the first three attributes, that they should be allowed to marry and receive the same benefits as other married people, as described by the Supreme Court's point (d)? While several countries around the western world have legitimized same-sex couplings and have even allowed full marriage equality, the issue in the U.S. came to the forefront in 1993.

Key historical turning points in same-sex marriage

In the 1993 Hawaiian case of *Baehr v. Lewin*, the plaintiffs argued that restricting lesbian and gay couples from marrying violated the *equal protection* clause of the Constitution. While the state court did not legalize same-sex marriage, it argued that the State of Hawaii would have a difficult time proving that *disallowing* same-sex marriage was not a violation of equal protection under the law. The court argued that the state could not deny marriage based on gender or sexual orientation. While the appeals were pending, in response, many other states across the country started to draft legislation that expressly *forbade* same-sex marriage and allowed states to not recognize gay marriages that might be performed in Hawaii at some future date if Hawaii legalized gay marriage.

In 1996, the United States Congress implemented the Defense of Marriage Act (DOMA; Public Law 104–199), which explicitly defines marriages as a union between one man and one woman and allows states to decide whether they want to recognize same-sex marriage performed in other states. Every state maintains the right to determine the rules for marriage within that state and they regularly prohibit certain people from marrying (blood relatives, minors, people with mental retardation). DOMA was enacted out of fear that the Hawaii statute would force all U.S. states to acknowledge and legitimize same-sex marriage. In addition, Congress did not want the U.S. government to provide the same benefits (like tax credits and social security benefits) to LGBT couples as it does for heterosexual couples. Congress needn't have worried, however, as even Hawaii implemented a new law stating that marriage contracts could only take place between a man and a woman. Even liberal members of congress voted for DOMA, which was signed into law by President Bill Clinton, because they favored providing full rights to gay and lesbian couples in a structured *alternative* to marriage, like domestic partnership laws, which will be explored below. After DOMA, by 2002, 36 states had passed laws explicitly banning same-sex marriages or the recognition of such unions performed in other states (Soule, 2004).

Before it legalized same-sex marriage in 2009, the state of Vermont in 2000 passed a civil union bill that allowed same-sex couples every benefit and responsibility of heterosexual marriage (Yep, Lovaas, & Elia, 2003). The lawsuit leading up to this development claimed that denying marriage rights to same-sex couples violated their rights to common benefits and protections of the laws guaranteed by the Vermont Constitution. These benefits include access to a spouse's medical insurance and life insurance, hospital visitations, spousal support, property inheritance and will rights, and hundreds of other social benefits married couples enjoy. Today in over 100 municipalities (such as Seattle and New York City), counties (such as Broward County, Florida), and eight states, registered domestic partners may receive many of the same health insurance and visitation rights benefits as heterosexual couples.

Domestic partnerships

Some areas allow domestic partnerships only for same-sex couples and require that heterosexual couples be married to enjoy the same benefits. Inheritance laws vary widely, with many states forbidding inheritance unless it is specified in a legal will. Also after relationship dissolution, domestic partners typically do not receive help from the courts in dividing property or determining alimony payments. Every region with its own domestic partner policy has different laws, requirements, rights, and responsibilities the couple must follow. Today 267 Fortune 500 companies, 4,000 private companies, and 158 universities provide benefits to registered domestic partners (www.hrc.org; Yep et al., 2003). California alone has 15,000 same-sex couples registered as domestic partners.

The idea of domestic partnership was developed by a gay man, Tom Brougham, in 1982, to bring rights to gays and lesbians, even though many of those same people viewed marriage as an outdated patriarchal institution (http://www.outhistory.org/wiki/Tom_Brougham). In 1984, the city of Berkeley, California, where Tom Brougham worked, was the first city to pass a domestic partner policy for city employees. In 1985, West Hollywood became the first U.S. city to enact a domestic partnership registry open to all its citizens, and soon San Francisco, Berkeley, and Santa Cruz did so as well. In California, heterosexual couples cannot be domestic partners unless one member of the couple is over 62 years of age, due to the ability of the younger partner to then receive a partner's social security benefits, which could be lost if they had married late in life. California's domestic partners are allowed by law to adopt their partner's child and be a stepparent. Unfortunately, people moving to a new area without domestic partner protections will lose all of the benefits enjoyed in their own region. This leads many same-sex marriage advocates to decry that domestic partnerships, like segregated schools for African American children in the 1940s, are "separate and unequal." For more on California's domestic partnership law, see the nearby *FYI* box.

Contemporary views of same-sex marriage

As of 2010, the U.S. Government Code of Laws clearly states that "the word 'marriage' means only a legal union between one man and one woman as husband and wife, and the word 'spouse' refers only to a person of the opposite sex who is a husband or wife"(http://thomas.loc.gov/cgi-bin/query/z?c104:H.R.3396.ENR:). This law means that as long as you are a male and a female of marrying age, you can marry each other.

FYI

California's domestic partnership statute

The California domestic partnership (DP) was the first of its kind in the country and was implemented in 1999. It began with only hospital-visitation rights for same-sex registered domestic partners but the benefits have expanded greatly over time. As of 2007, a California DP gives its members all of the rights and responsibilities of a married couple. In addition to the many rights discussed in this chapter's text, the DP provides for the same sick care and family leave as heterosexual couples, the presumption that both parties are legal parents of children born into the union, the ability to sue for wrongful death of a partner, survivor pension benefits (unless that pension is administered by the federal government; as mandated by DOMA, DPs do not receive federal benefits), assistance in dissolution proceedings, the obligation to file taxes jointly, and the right to take a partner's last name. However, they do not have the other 1,138 rights a married couple enjoys under *federal* law. California's DP code allows for the recognition of DPs or civil unions from other states (such as civil unions from Vermont and New Hampshire). However, same-sex marriages, which are legal in Massachusetts, cannot be recognized in California. A legally married couple in Massachusetts moving to California would need to register as domestic partners. British law recognizes California DPs as equivalent to their civil unions, as have the governments of New Jersey and Switzerland.

Same-sex couples are not allowed to marry in most U.S. states and in most countries around the world. The laws are continuously changing and being challenged globally. For example, although California legalized same-sex marriage in 2008, stating that it was unconstitutional to deny gay couples the right to marry, that same year, the California Supreme Court approved a voter-instituted ban, "Proposition 8," on same-sex marriage in that state. The California Supreme Court allowed the 18,000 legally married gay and lesbian couples to remain legally married. Then the ban on gay marriage was declared unconstitutional by a U.S. District Court in Northern California in 2010. As of 2011, however, the reversal of the ban on gay marriages was being appealed and the case was expected to reach the U.S. Supreme Court. Same-sex couples were not allowed to marry during this court process.

Rostosky, Riggle, Horne, and Miller (2009) surveyed 1,500 LGBT people around the United States and found that amendments that restrict marriage rights for same-sex couples cause psychological harm to LGBT individuals. She found that during the legislative process when these decisions are made, there is often a slew of negative media images. News pundits passionately criticize LGBT individuals' lifestyles and rights to form families by marriage. Rostosky et al. (2009) found that in the 25 states that have recently outlawed same-sex marriage, the LGBT people in her study experienced the highest levels of chronic and psychological stress. The author argues that negative campaigning leads to public stigmatization of sexual minorities and harms their mental health. For example, when Memphis, Tennessee, banned same-sex marriage, research participants reported feeling ostracized from their community and were afraid of violence being perpetrated against them. They feared the negative attention might endanger their jobs or lead people to try to take their children. In general, active attempts to keep lesbians and gay men from committing to their partners through marriage induce feelings of confusion, anxiety, and betrayal.

At the same time, more and more regions are currently drafting legislation to allow gays to marry. In 2010, same-sex marriages were legal in Belgium, Spain, South Africa, Norway, Sweden, Portugal, Mexico City, and the Netherlands (Daley, 2000; Lyall, 2004; www.hrc.org; www.marriageequality. org). In the U.S., in 2010, same-sex marriages were legal in Massachusetts, Connecticut, Iowa, New Hampshire, Vermont, and Washington, DC (www.hrc.org).

At least 57% of Americans believe gay and lesbian people are equal in status to and should have the same rights as heterosexuals (Savin-Williams & Esterberg, 2000). When gay and lesbian couples are compared to heterosexual couples in research studies, their intimate relationships appear very similar in structure and function (Julien, Chartrand, Simard, Bouthillier, & Begin, 2003). For example, they have an equal level of desire to find committed, enduring relationships (Stiers, 1999). Both types of couples value egalitarian relationships and reject power exertion and control. Gay and lesbian couples may share housework loads, financial responsibilities, and family roles more equally than heterosexual couples do; this has most often been found in lesbian couples who may be the most egalitarian. Lesbian and gay couples also exhibit equal levels of relationship satisfaction and experience the same number of conflicts about the same primary problem areas as heterosexuals (such as finances, driving, affection, and sex). They also face some additional struggles, such as coming out as a same-sex couple to their own and their partner's families and dealing with race/ethnicity issues within the context of the LGBT community (Kurdek, 1995; Peplau, Veniegas, & Campbell, 1996).

While people in the LGBT community are not allowed to marry in most places around the world, they often have symbolic rituals like commitment ceremonies or holy unions. These rituals share many of the same elements as a heterosexual wedding, such as fancy clothes, flowers, family members, and vows, but they also differ in many ways (Stiers, 1999). The partners committing to each other may have had to separate from their biological families who rejected them and so the ceremony includes many non-biological "chosen" kin. Secondly, these rituals are often performed in order to validate LGBT relationships and deem them socially acceptable. Many couples also want their commitment ceremony to be a role model for others in marginalized communities, to show that relationships can last a long time and be happy and healthy. Moreover, commitment ceremonies often involve political and personal risk-taking. Not many heterosexuals go through their weddings with an element of fear or daring. But same-sex couples know that publicly "outing" themselves and their partners, for example, with a "wedding" photo on their desk at work, can be a political act. They are publicly refusing to accept their relationship as deviant or inferior and are protesting gendered hierarchies and conservative ideologies. Finally, these ceremonies often happen many years into the relationship for same-sex couples compared to more toward the beginning for other-sex couples (Stiers, 1999).

In a recent news story, a lesbian couple of 13 years, with a registered domestic partnership, and who legally married in California in 2004, are facing the deportation of one partner, Shirley Tan. For heterosexual couples, marriage protects undocumented spouses from deportation. In this case, the "illegal" partner, Shirley, came to the U.S. on a tourist visa, fell in love, and when allowed, married her partner. For heterosexual couples, a green card would be issued, allowing her to stay and work in the U.S. as a permanent resident. Gay and lesbian domestic partners in the U.S. are not allowed to sponsor their partners for citizenship like heterosexual partners are. This couple has been together for 13 years and they are raising two young boys. The boys are devastated that their mother will be taken away from them. The couple lives a very traditional lifestyle. One partner stays home, the other works. They go to church, sing in the choir, and attend school fundraisers. Shirley is the epitome of a U.S. soccer mom, except for the fact that she's being sent back to a country from which she applied for political asylum due to rampant violence. Their only hope may be a currently pending Uniting American Families Act, which would allow the 8,500 documented same-sex couples with an immigrant partner to sponsor their partner for permanent residency, just like heterosexual couples do on a regular basis (Yang, 2009). Many in LGBT communities feel that same-sex marriage is a crucial stepping stone toward equality and full acceptance into contemporary American society (www.hrc.org; Yep et al., 2003).

Keep in mind, however, that even some members of LGBT communities are against same-sex marriage. They feel that it feeds into the traditional patriarchal and religious values of a discriminatory and capitalist society. For example, Baird and Rosenbaum (1997, p. 11) argue:

> Traditional marriage is integral to the corrupt authoritarian structures of society; it is a suspect institution embodying within itself the patriarchy ... the most important issue for gay and lesbian couples is whether or not they should "sell out" to the enemy—the patriarchal culture—that seeks to oppress and eliminate them.

Stacey and Davenport (2002) posit that the pioneering gay rights activists of the 1960s and 1970s never intended to copy heterosexual norms. They could not even fathom that they'd worked so hard to force their way out of the closet only to fall right into traditional domestic bliss. These authors argue that, typically, monogamous relationships are considered normal, natural, and accepted, while polyamory, casual sex, and transient relationships are deemed deviant, bad, and immoral. This allows heterosexual norms to be privileged over those of other individuals who may not share their sexual or relationship beliefs (Yep et al., 2003). Even within the LGBT community, larger social expectations seep in since long-term committed and monogamous relationships are considered more valuable and important, thus privileging heteronormativity even within LGBT communities. They argue that this is why some gay people want to be "married," just like heterosexuals, because even they view heterosexual relationship styles as normative.

Arguments for and against same-sex marriage

Assimilationists
People in favor of the legalization of same-sex marriage who argue that granting this privilege will allow same-sex couples to assimilate their lifestyles into the larger population; gay people who want to be recognized in the eyes of God and the community, and be given the same benefits that heterosexual spouses share through marriage.

Radical argument
A view against same-sex marriages often proffered by feminists and those in LGBT communities, which states that same-sex marriage reinforces heteronormativity and oppression of other lifestyles; they argue that legalizing same-sex marriage will further oppress those who don't or cannot get married.

Yep et al. (2003) outline the **assimilationist** argument in favor of same-sex marriage. This position states that same-sex marriage will lead to LGBT individuals leading more sexually stable and healthier lives within the context of social acceptance. They feel that LGBT people will gain full recognition as citizens of worth, while perhaps reducing dangerous casual-sex lifestyles. The *assimilationists* often argue that LGBT people want to be recognized in the eyes of God and the community, and be given the same benefits that heterosexual spouses share. In fact, many conservative pundits argue *in favor* of same-sex marriage so that the new spouses will feel pressure to conform to society's expectations for "proper" sexual and relationship behavior. They feel that allowing same-sex marriage would strengthen family values for *all* families and protect children by providing a stable, socially sanctioned and economically successful family (Yep et al., 2003).

On the other hand, the **radical argument** places same-sex marriage in the category of perpetuating heteronormativity and oppression of other lifestyles. The *radical* position argues that same-sex marriage will further oppress those who don't fit the mold. People who hold the radical position feel that if same-sex marriage were to be legalized, it would have negative consequences for those not desiring to marry. Many radical feminists feel that marriage is oppressive for women and privileges parenthood, giving "breeders" social clout and approval over those who choose not to marry or have children. They assert that the same oppression and restrictions over human rights, property, taxes, insurance, and other benefits of marriage will continue for anyone who doesn't marry. They feel that legalizing same-sex marriage will never reduce the prejudice and hatred many in society feel for sexual minorities. However, in countries that allow same-sex marriage, the majority of citizens approve of such unions: 82% in the Netherlands, 62% in Belgium, and 56% in Spain. In 2003, polls of Canadian citizens showed that only 46% of people approved of gay marriage. But after a 2005 marriage equality bill passed in Canada, a 2006 poll showed that 59% of citizens approved of gay marriage, which is quite an increase after only three years (Alquist, 2008). Similar trends have been found in polls before and after U.S. states provided more rights in the form of domestic partnerships, civil unions, and marriage for same sex couples. In Massachusetts, approval ratings of marriage equality went from 50% to 59% in a single year; New Jersey showed a change from 43% approval to 56% approval over a three-year period; 47% of New York citizens were in favor of marriage equality in 2004, increasing to 53% in 2006. Thus, legitimizing certain issues can influence public opinion and vice versa. The complex ecological contexts in our lives constantly interact to influence change both within and across populations.

Nevertheless, many LGBT people prefer to fight for the legitimization of *queer* realities and want to steer away from monogamous relationships, toward "chosen" kin structures and a sexual ideology completely removed from reproduction and parenting. Queer activists point to the abject failure of many heterosexual marriages as another reason to avoid heterosexual relationship practices. With an epidemic of divorce and adultery, some people in the queer community wonder why anyone would want to endorse that "normal" lifestyle when it is clearly not working for millions of people.

They argue that rejecting marriage means rising above the powerful grip that churches and governments have over relationships. Moreover, they feel the legalization of same-sex marriage would create a new hierarchy in queer communities that would further marginalize those who will not or cannot get married (such as those in polyamorous relationships like Todd, Michael, and Joel) (Yep et al., 2003).

This is a key question for various factions in the LGBT community: Is same-sex marriage an attempt to be accepted by the mainstream society as "legitimate" or is it a subversive political act to overthrow patriarchal constraints on human rights? Lewin (1998) states that white middle-class gay men are the group most in favor of legalizing same-sex marriage, indicating that white male privilege is a strong force in the movement to legalize it. Some LGBT people of color see the battle over same-sex marriage as shifting attention away from the continual racial injustices experienced in their lives. They argue that while white middle-class gays and lesbians will get married and have children in their accepting suburban liberal communities, people of color will still experience marginalization, poverty, and residential segregation.

Others argue that, with the legalization of same-sex marriage, tradition could be turned on its head and marriage could encompass new ideologies of non-monogamy and equal power in relationships. These theorists argue that marriage is by nature a social construction and by allowing same-sex marriage, we can construct a whole new institution called marriage (Riggs, 2007). For example, today—unlike in past generations—we marry for emotional reasons, and disabled and incarcerated people are allowed to marry, as are people from any race or religion. These changes are reconstructions of the traditional definitions of marriage.

Another argument in favor of the legalization of same-sex marriage is that "domestic partnerships" or "civil unions" are not really "alternatives" to marriage if people don't have a choice. The word *alternative* implies people have a choice between two options. One woman interviewed by Lewin (1998) said she might marry one of her female *friends* for financial and insurance reasons if same-sex marriages were legalized. However, she said that marrying one of her *lovers* would be quite irrational as she'd be building an entire household on changeable passions. The argument is that the entire system needs to change, that all adults and all children should receive the same health, property, and insurance benefits regardless of whom they marry or don't marry. Stacey and Davenport (2002) argue that we should make marriage *and* domestic partnerships available to *all* people, whether they be heterosexual or homosexual, or somewhere in between. As you can see, the legalization of same-sex marriage carries within it complex issues of gender, race, and class privilege, reminding us of both the complexity of the issue and the importance of intersectional identities in our examination of all types of relationships.

Interracial and intercultural marriages

As laws were enacted to prohibit marriage between blood relations in the early part of the twentieth century, they also evolved to outlaw interracial marriage. With the civil rights movement making some headway in the 1940s, the California Supreme Court challenged racial discrimination laws regarding marriage and became the first state to declare that bans on interracial marriage were unconstitutional (Pascoe, 1991). But in the 1940s, interracial marriage was still illegal in 38 states. The key case to come to the courts was *Loving v. Virginia*. In 1958, a white man, Richard Loving, and his African American wife, Mildred, were forcibly taken from their bedroom in the middle of the night by police charging them with violating the interracial marriage ban. They were facing five years in prison but promised to leave the state in exchange for a one-year suspended sentence. They appealed their case and after many years, the United States Supreme Court held that "racial hygiene laws" (recall the eugenics movement described in Chapter 4) unconstitutionally interfered with individual freedoms to marry a partner of one's own choice. But in 1958, a Gallup poll still showed that 94% of Americans disapproved of interracial marriage (http://www.gallup.com/poll/28417/most-Americans-approve-interracial-marriages.aspx).

Finally, in 1967, the U.S. Supreme Court struck down "anti-miscegenation" laws throughout the country, which had prohibited interracial marriage. The Court said that all Americans had the right to marriage and the pursuit of happiness. Interestingly, the 1968 Gallup poll found that in ten years, 20% of Americans had come to approve of interracial marriage (http://www.gallup.com/poll/28417/most-Americans-approve-interracial-marriages.aspx). Furthermore, in 1978, The U.S. Supreme Court said that marriage is "one of the basic civil rights of man" and that "the right to marry is part of the fundamental 'right to privacy'" stated in the U.S. Constitution (Pascoe, 1996). Following this court decision, the 1978 Gallup poll showed a 38% approval rating for interracial marriage. The 1991 Gallup poll showed an increase to 48% approval of people from two different racial/ethnic backgrounds marrying each other and by 1997, the rate was 67% (http://www.gallup.com/poll/28417/most-Americans-approve-interracial-marriages.aspx). These trends show that, as court decisions are made and issues are exposed under the media spotlight, people's opinions may slowly change. In a short *40* years, opinions changed and moved away from the status quo they had consistently held for almost *400* years. If the Supreme Court had waited until the majority of citizens were in favor of interracial marriage being legalized, it would have waited until 1991 to legalize such unions. Most of us today can't imagine living in a world where interracial marriage is against the law.

Social Dominance Theory
A structural-functionalist idea that people naturally form in-group privileging social hierarchies which are validated by policies, laws, and practices in their culture.

Social dominance orientation
A person's viewpoint that groups are not equal and that dominance and hierarchy should be maintained.

Social dominance beliefs and interracial marriage

While the majority of people today approve of interracial marriage, not everyone does. Fang, Sidanius, and Pratto (1998) put forth an intriguing hypothesis about the opposition to interracial marriage. They cite research showing a robust *endogamy* trend in 250 cultures around the world. This means that endogamy is the rule, rather than the exception, and that cultures prefer that people marry "their own kind." Fang et al. (1998) state that these trends are partially explained by a **Social Dominance Theory**, in that people in general naturally form in-groups privileging social hierarchies, which are validated by policies, laws, and practices in their culture. They found that both low- and high-status groups feed into the social dominance hierarchy in order to maintain it. Do you recognize this as a *structural-functionalist* argument? While low-status groups are typically oppressed, they also carry some of the same beliefs about in-marriage versus out-marriage of each group.

Fang et al. (1998) argue that one of the key influences on out-group oppression is a **social dominance orientation** (SDO). This orientation is a person's viewpoint that groups are not equal and that dominance and hierarchy should be maintained. These attitudes and beliefs further entrench the social hierarchy in any given culture and maintain one group's privilege while perpetuating discrimination in the form of racism, sexism, classism, and heterosexism. Fang et al. (1998) have found that, indeed, SDO values exist strongly in many cultures, like Canada, Israel, New Zealand, Taiwan, and China. This perspective is intriguing because it examines the subtle and dynamic interplays between people's histories with dominance and their endorsement of maintaining the status quo.

FIGURE 7.4 How do you think people responded to this interracial family when this photo was taken in 1974?
Photo reproduced by permission.

Demographic variables and interracial marriage

Attitudes about and trends regarding interracial couples vary in relation to demographic variables such as immigration status, ethnicity, age, gender, and education level. Societies differ widely regarding how strongly they disapprove of interracial marriage. Sometimes, however, depending on macrosystem issues like immigration patterns and population dynamics, people may have very little control over the type of microsystem they find themselves in during marriage. For example, when a group makes up a large part of the population, it's much easier to find suitable mates within one's own group. For example, European Americans make up 70% of the U.S. population, so only 4% of them marry someone from another race. On the other hand, Asian Americans make up only 4% of the U.S. population so, not surprisingly, they have high rates of out-marriage, with 59% percent marrying non-Asians.

Interracial couples are more likely to cohabit than marry, perhaps due to lingering attitudes against such unions. For example, only 13% of married black men are married to a non-black wife, but 25% of cohabiting black men are in a mixed relationship (Qian, 2005). Between 1970 and 2000, black–white marriages in the U.S. grew from 65,000 to over 300,000. However, these marriages are still relatively rare, between 1% and 3% of all marriages. The number of whites marrying people of color other than African Americans has increased from 233,000 to over 1.1 million (Qian, 2005). Interfaith marriages are much more common today than interracial marriages and the American public accepts interfaith marriages at much higher levels.

Definite biases still exist in society. For example, 71% of white teenagers with a white boyfriend or girlfriend introduce their partner to their parents, but only 57% of those with non-white partners do (Qian, 2005). Similarly, 63% of black adolescents introduce their black partners to their parents, but only 52% of them introduce their non-black partners. While people "in general" are in favor of mixed ethnicity pairings, they are less favorable when it involves their own children. Parents also report that it's not *they* who are prejudiced, but they are worried about what *other* people might do to discriminate against the young interracial couple. Younger generations, however, are much more accepting of cross-ethnic pairings than older people are (Qian, 2005).

The lighter one's skin is, the more likely he or she is to marry a white person. For example, Hispanics who identify as racially "white," are more likely to marry whites. The darker one's skin, the more likely he or she is to be discriminated against, have a lower education level, have a lower income, and live in a segregated neighborhood (Qian, 2005). Thus, if people with darker skin intermarry, it is often with a white person with less education. If the darker person is college educated, he or she is more likely to marry interracially as people attending college tend both to be more liberal and to meet a wider diversity of people (Qian, 2005). In addition, white women are more likely to marry black men who have a higher level of education than they themselves have; over half of black husbands of white women have college educations, but only 40% of black husbands of black wives do. These findings trouble many African American women who feel that white women are taking all the "good" black men, especially when the pool of eligible educated white men is fairly large. In fact, 74% of black–white marriages include a black man with a white woman, whereas for Asian American cross-ethnic marriages, 58% of the *wives* are Asian American and their husbands are white. For Hispanic/Latino groups and Native American groups, the percentages for wives being white versus husbands being white are about equal. Most of these couples have some experience with marginalization, from people staring at them in public to outright discrimination in housing or other public arenas.

When discrimination occurs, the spouse of color often notices stares, whispering, and negative public reactions more than the white partner does (Coles, 2006). These dynamics can lead to conflicts within the marriage. These marriages may begin with higher stress levels anyway because cultural differences and variations in religion, dress, food, and political beliefs can lead to lower marital satisfaction and higher divorce rates (Bumpass & Sweet, 1989). Fu, Tora, and Kendall (2001) found that in couples with both racial and cultural differences, there were low rates of happiness.

Stark background differences can lead to microsystem, mesosystem, and exosystem challenges for the family members involved. Holidays, rituals, food, visitation, and the beliefs instilled in children can all become sources of discomfort for interactions with the extended family (Chinitz & Brown, 2001).

The healthiest interracial couples will be able to straddle the fences equally between their two ethnic groups, raise their children to identify with both cultures, and feel a sense of pride and connection to both families. This bicultural identity is difficult to accomplish but can lead to an enriched, enlightened, and emotionally fulfilling life for all of those involved.

Intercultural marriages

People of different races who live in the same culture face many challenges, but people from completely different cultures face even more obstacles in their relationships. For example, many cultures privilege **consanguineal relationships** over marital relationships. This means the extended family and blood kin are more important than the married couple. Extended family members' needs are catered to more than those of the married couple. In these cultures, marriage is meant to serve the family and community. Extended family households, non-monogamy, arranged marriage, and lack of co-residency (for example, men and women living in separate huts) may have been the practices in one partner's home country, which can cause many conflicts and power struggles in a marriage (Coles, 2006). Compare the consanguineal emphasis to the traditional western **affinal family** where the marital relationship is given priority and extended family is expected to "butt out." How might a couple with one member stemming from a consanguineal culture and one member stemming from an affinal culture work things out?

Another challenge with which intercultural couples might struggle is that some cultures practice **social marriages**, where there is no legal process, no license, no fees, and simple vows or gifts are exchanged (for example, in the Iroquois Nation) (Coles, 2006). These social marriages are similar to a common law marriage, so if one partner comes from this type of culture and the other person comes from a legal marriage culture, problems can arise. For example, a person from a social marriage background may object to spending $20,000 on a large church wedding and honeymoon.

In successful, happy intercultural marriages, the couples often employ conscious strategies for dealing with their differences, family problems, and societal reactions. They have to figure out how to straddle both worlds, which parts of their own culture to give up, and which parts to maintain. These struggles are the same whether a couple stems from different ethnic groups, cultures, or countries. Gordon's ideas about assimilation might shed some light on these issues.

Gordon (1964) discussed three types of processes people might experience when marrying someone from another culture: **cultural assimilation**, **structural assimilation**, and **marital assimilation**. In cultural assimilation, a person decides to dress, act, speak, and practice daily rituals like those in the new host country. In structural assimilation, the person adopts the educational, employment, and political values of the host country. Finally, in marital assimilation, immigrants intermarry with those from the new culture. Typically, men acculturate faster than women to a new country, except regarding changing their existing gender role ideologies, and divorce rates are higher among immigrant couples than in couples still living in their home countries (Coles, 2006).

While interracial and intercultural marriages are increasing, several social forces will keep the overall percentages low: the strong ethnic identities of people of color, persistent inequality in education and social status, discrimination, residential segregation, and white resistance (Qian, 2005). With Latino groups and Asian groups continuing to immigrate, their in-group pool of eligibles may increase, leading to more in-group marriages for them.

Immigrant marriages

Many people migrate to new places in order to marry. An estimated 200,000 legal marriage migrants enter the U.S. each year to marry someone from their home country or a majority-group American, in order to acquire a green card and work to improve their lives. Although more women than men make this stressful journey, the existence of the stereotypical "mail order bride" is fairly rare. Only

---

Consanguineal relationships
A family where extended family and blood kin are more important and their needs are catered to more than those of the married couple.

Affinal family
A family where the marital relationship is given priority and extended family is expected to be secondary.

Social marriages
A marriage where there is no legal process, no licenses, no fees, but simple vows or gifts are exchanged.

Cultural assimilation
A process whereby a person decides to dress, act, speak, and practice daily rituals like those in the new host country.

Structural assimilation
A process whereby a person adopts the educational, employment, and political values of the host country.

Marital assimilation
A process whereby immigrants intermarry with those from the new culture.

4% of migrant marriages involve some kind of deal through a broker (Thai, 2002). Nevertheless, marriage is the number one reason that people migrate to the United States.

Immigration poses unique problems and opportunities in the search for a marriage partner. The struggles with language, employment, social segregation, acculturation stress, and lack of rights make many immigrants' lives very difficult. One example is the Viet Kieu, Vietnamese people living in the U.S. and other western nations. Immigrant Viet Kieu men often seek wives from their home country, and many of these marriages are arranged. Many Vietnamese people migrated to the U.S. during and after the Vietnam War, in the late 1960s and early to mid-1970s. Goodkind (1997) describes the "double marriage squeeze" in Vietnam: there were very many male deaths during the Vietnam War and a high level of male outmigration. This left many women alone in Vietnam. Today there are approximately 129 men to every 100 women in the Vietnamese diaspora, but only 92 men for every 100 women within the country of Vietnam.

These gender imbalances lead to some creative mate selection strategies. While we typically see women "marry up" in terms of education, income, and social status, the reverse is true for transnational couples from Vietnam. This marriage gradient that most of us expect is turned upside down when the lack of a pool of eligibles gives women and men more freedom to marry "unmarriageables," people whom they would not ordinarily be allowed or encouraged to marry in their home countries. Female "unmarriageables" in Vietnam are highly educated independent women over the age of 25. They typically will not want to marry men in-country who are of a lower social class or education level. However, they are often willing to marry Viet Kieu men who are considered "unmarriageable" by western women in the new country. These men have typically taken low-status and low-pay jobs in the U.S. and Europe in order to stay in their new home country and make money to send home to Vietnam. They are invisible to women in these countries as they are often cooks, dishwashers, and gardeners. They may not speak English fluently and may live in apartments with several other male immigrants. The "double marriage squeeze" leads families to arrange marriages between the educated woman in-country and the lower status man in the western country, in the hopes that her family's money can help him become established in the new country. If he is considered a hardworking man who is honorable and moral and who will not abuse her, he is often considered a good prospect for upward mobility. The couple will then build a successful life together in the western country, building their families' prestige and bank accounts back home.

Problems do arise, however, because many Viet Kieu men still hold traditional values about gender roles and power hierarchies. They may expect their wives to eventually stop working and follow orders. Thus, some women would rather endure the stigma of being childless and unmarried at home than succumb to male domination abroad.

As you can see, the complex intersections between race, class, and gender permeate every type of marriage. Racial, class, and gendered hierarchies are often important factors that influence who parents, grandparents, and religious leaders want young people to marry. And a large proportion of the global population still has their spouses chosen for them.

Arranged marriages

It's not uncommon to see arranged marriages today in couples from Asian, Middle Eastern, and African cultures which make up a much larger percentage of the population than do couples in western cultures. Davis and Davis (1995) discuss how in modern Moroccan tribal marriages, men still wield complete power over their wives and children. They promise their allies that they will give their children to them in marriage to strengthen the alliance. However, in Morocco and in many other cultures, it has been observed that women, cousins, and other family members figure out ways to sway the father's opinion by begging, trying to make the future spouse seem unappealing, and making behind-the-scene deals for other marriage arrangements. People may also use magic or spells to change the father's mind. This points to the diversity that exists within arranged marriages.

Traditional arranged marriages
Parents, elders, and/or religious leaders have complete control over marriage matches.

Modified traditional arranged marriage
Family and community members may choose several potential spouses and the young person is allowed to make the final choice.

Cooperative traditional arranged marriages
The family and the young person have equal abilities to bring in potential spouses, and the final choice is agreed upon jointly.

There are three main types of arranged marriages. **Traditional arranged marriages**, in which parents, elders, or religious leaders have complete control over marriage matches. More common these days, however, is the **modified traditional arranged marriage**, in which family and community members may choose several potential spouses but the young people are allowed to make the final choice. Third, there are now **cooperative traditional arranged marriages**, in which the family and the young person have equal abilities to bring in potential spouses, and the final choice is agreed upon jointly (Stopes-Roe & Cochrane, 1990). Most of the research on arranged marriages is conducted in India, so let's take a look at some of those studies to get a feel for the changing nature of arranged marriages.

East Indians often practice arranged marriage, even if they immigrate to a western nation like the U.S. (Lessinger, 1995). Lessinger describes Indian weddings as elaborate, with large dowries still exchanged by many brides' families. Young people still appreciate the many benefits of a traditional arranged marriage because it protects them from what they see as the rampant heartbreaks of the west, such as being dumped, being rejected by potential mates, the pressure to look attractive or be a certain size, and the pressure to have sex before one is ready. In Indian families, divorce is shameful, so the family and community thoroughly investigate the moral compass and social standing of the families whose children they may choose as marriage partners for their own children. These modern arranged marriages typically occur after both men and women have finished their college degrees, or even graduate degrees, and they occur mostly in middle- and upper-class families. Many young people feel that their parents and elders are wiser than they are and are more capable of finding a suitable mate who would be truly compatible with them over the long-term.

After graduation, all kin and community members join in the search for a mate. There are official marriage brokers, and many Indian families place detailed ads in Hindi-language newspapers. Although India's strict caste system is breaking down, especially when Indians move to other countries, social status and education are still important. Today, it is most important for children of Indian families to marry other people from India, regardless of caste or religious differences (Lessinger, 1995). Thus, parental ads in newspapers will often state "no bars," meaning no restrictions on caste, religion, language, or region. They will also detail their children's personality characteristics and interests, blending traditional with modern approaches to marriage. And often the children are allowed to choose from a set of potential mates selected by parents. These arranged marriages are usually fairly successful in that they have very low divorce rates. Perhaps this is due to Indians' more reasonable expectations for partners; they don't expect the person to be a "soulmate." People assume that the couple will share their lives and have children together, and that love and caring will follow marriage. However, the couple doesn't need to be best friends or have true emotional intimacy because most Indians have large extended kin and community networks to serve that purpose. Thus, many of these *modified traditional* arranged marriages are happy and successful.

If young Indian people cannot find a good match in the U.S. or Europe, often families will send back to India to import a spouse. Instead of a dowry, the promise of a green card brings many young people to the U.S. for marriage and a college education. Second-generation Indian women, though, are fairly liberated and don't want a traditional Indian husband, assuming he will control them.

Today, fully two thirds of young Indians want at least some choice in their marriages. For example, they may hold the right to make the final decision out of a few potential partners their families have chosen for them. They might then court the person for a while (in the company of chaperones) to see if they might like to marry him or her. It's also becoming more and more common for Indian people to out-marry with white Americans or Europeans (Le, 2011; Lessinger, 1995).

In a large study of arranged marriages, Madathil and Benshoff (2008) found that Indians in arranged marriages living in India had higher levels of marital satisfaction if they had at least some choice in their marriage partner. Madathil and Benshoff also examined Indians in arranged marriages living in the U.S. and Americans in choice-based marriages. Their results were quite interesting. Indians in arranged marriages living in the U.S. rated the significance of love in a marriage much higher than arranged-marriage couples living in India did. All Indian couples rated shared values and financial security as more important than American couples did. Moreover, the highest rates of marital satisfaction were in Indian arranged-marriage couples living in the U.S. The authors hypothesized that these couples had the benefits of both worlds. They had the security of an arranged marriage supported by their families back in India, a spouse who shared their cultural and religious values, and the freedom American culture allows for less traditional gender roles. Also, because these couples were separated from their extended kin, they relied on each other more and became emotionally closer to each other than Americans who are used to living apart from extended kin and Indians who have large support networks near their homes in India (Madathil & Benshoff, 2008). This study illustrates the importance of macrosystem influences on marriage values and marital satisfaction within the microsystem.

In addition to benefits, arranged marriages have a number of drawbacks. For example, there is intense pressure for a couple to stay together despite problems. And often husbands in arranged marriages feel they should be the head of the family and can marginalize their wives into a subordinate position. However, this can occur in any type of marriage. Let's take a look at some common problems and suggestions for healthy functioning in all types of marriages and committed partnerships.

MARITAL PROBLEMS

> Infidelity
>
> Unresolved conflict

Two of the most common problems people fear before getting married is infidelity and unresolved conflict. Let's start by looking at a few key findings regarding these unhealthy marital processes. Healthy processes and ways to improve marriages will follow.

Infidelity

According to a survey of marital and couples therapists, an estimated 30% to 40% of women cheat on their spouses, and 50% of men do (Ali & Miller, 2004). These estimates may be high because these professionals work with clinical populations who may face more problems than the general population. In anonymous self-reports of the general population, the numbers are much lower: 15% of women and 22% of men self-reported infidelity.

While infidelity may seem like it would be a microsystem or even exosystem variable, it has also been linked to biological processes within individuals. For example, researchers studying hundreds of twins in Sweden found that men who have two copies of a specific gene (allele 334) are more than twice as likely to have distressed marriages as are men without this genetic marker. Men without the marker are more committed and faithful to their partners. Also, women married to men with either one or two of these alleles were less happy in their marriages than women married to men without the genetic marker. Thus, we must consider that marital happiness is best explained by the bioecological perspective. Part of marital happiness is in the genes, and, as you will see, the other parts stem from personality, context, and culture. One of the contexts that contributes to marital satisfaction is the partners' workplace.

An increasingly common place for developing extra-marital affairs is the workplace, which is part of one spouse's exosystem and the other spouse's microsystem. People tend to dress more nicely, think before they talk, and be on their best manners while at work. They save their holey sweatpants, burping, and silly comments for their spouses at home. Tsapelas, Aron, and Orbuch (2009) found that boredom ("being in a rut, doing the same things all the time") predicted marital dissatisfaction nine years into a marriage. Many people feel that having a fling at work will actually improve life at home because it will make them happy by relieving their boredom, raising their self-esteem, and relieving stress that they would usually express at home when having to deal with the boring and mundane tasks of their "real" lives.

With so many more women entering the workplace and becoming successful—25% of American women now out-earn their husbands—they often feel entitled to a little "action" at work. Women who are more highly educated, earn more, and feel competent may be more willing to risk their marriages by engaging in extramarital affairs, since they are confident they could survive without their spouse. They often have affairs with younger men as well (Ali & Miller, 2004). When husbands find out, women report that their lives do not end up in complete turmoil. They may just peacefully split with their spouse. In fact, 50% of female infidelity ends in divorce, but women are likely to stay with their unfaithful husbands (Ali & Miller, 2004).

Unresolved conflict

Conflict in marriages can range over many issues. The most common issues are financial issues, sex frequency, and communication lapses. The conflict itself is not usually the problem. The problems lie in unhealthy processes that lead to conflicts being unresolved or handled in ineffective ways. This section will examine some financial stressors and some perceptual biases that commonly influence unhealthy processes in marriages and lead to unresolved conflicts.

Financial infidelity

Financial infidelity
Keeping bank accounts, credit cards, or debts outside of the awareness of one's spouse; people may hide income or purchases.

One of the most common things couples argue about is money, and people often choose mates based on their earning potential; this is even true of men. Once they are married, **financial infidelity** causes many problems. This refers to a partner keeping a secret financial life, such as private accounts, undisclosed debt, and personal credit cards. Financial infidelity is increasingly recognized as a source of marital distress and a cause for divorce (Loftus, 2004). Since many people wait longer to marry these days, older couples, especially those with a college education and accompanying debts, are likely to have financial baggage when they enter a marriage. This "negative dowry" is often comprised of student loans, medical bills, auto loans, and unpaid credit card debt. Once they are married, and the financial status of the couple comes to light, women complain that they want their husbands to earn more, while husbands argue they want their wives to spend less. This conflict may end in him hiding money and her hiding purchases. Men may resent their wives wanting to stay home if the wife was an independent earner, especially a high-income independent earner, before the wedding. These conflicts may lead to one or both partners lying about bills, money, or credit cards. They may feel like children hiding from their parents (Loftus, 2004).

The average American couple today has $20,000 in debt, not counting their mortgage. When spouses find out about their partner's financial double life, it can often feel like an intense betrayal. They feel they can't trust their partner anymore, and they often wonder what else he or she is lying about. For it is more than just about money. Our relationships with money tell a lot about our emotional lives, our family history, and our sense of identity. The way we handle money tells people about our priorities and those things we value most. Moreover, money is often used as a tool for power and control in relationships. Partners who earn more may hide their bonuses or dole out an allowance to the other partner. This can feel like an emotional distancing, a lack of trust, and a betrayal of marital vows.

Complete financial independence, when people hold separate accounts and split bills down the middle, is also a bad sign for relationships. Couples who don't want to integrate their financial lives might think twice about integrating their emotional lives because money reflects the type of intimacy a person is willing to engage in (Loftus, 2004). It's extremely important that couples discuss their financial status and their spending and saving philosophies *before* they commit to marriage or domestic partnerships. If one partner earns a lot of money, a prenuptial agreement might be in order to protect assets in the case of divorce or dissolution. Couples are often afraid to broach these topics because they fear their partners will get angry or feel they are untrustworthy.

However, open communication, forethought, and planning are always best in the end. As the old saying goes, "failing to plan is planning to fail." It's crucial that couples take a realistic assessment of their own and their partner's lives ahead of time so that they enter into a commitment with realistic perceptions of what's in store.

Problems in relationship perceptions

One study (Carrere et al., 2000) found that unrealistic perceptual biases in newlyweds were key predictors of marital dissolution five years later. By assessing newlyweds' "perceived marital bond" within the first year of marriage, the authors were able to predict with 80% to 90% accuracy whether a marriage would be intact or dissolved five years later. Carrere and colleagues measured the spouses' relationship perceptions and biases, which are tendencies to selectively attend to only certain types of information over others. Remember that partners enter into a relationship with preexisting internal working models and perceptual tendencies. When problems arise with a significant other, they may judge that partner based on global generalizations or on biased perceptions from the past, and not on the circumstances surrounding the current issue. These global perceptions about partners and the marriage as a whole can be a source of unresolved conflict and can be indicative of future relationship break-up. This results in a sort of mental solidification of negative aspects of the partner and a virtual ignoring of positive traits.

In this study, couples were asked to simply tell the story of their relationship from the time they met to the present day (Carrere et al., 2000). They were also asked about the positive and negative events that had happened to them. If partners expressed disappointment, negativity and perception of chaos in the home at Year 1, these variables predicted marital instability with 87% accuracy four to six years later and with 81% accuracy seven to nine years later. Couples who described their marriages in terms of fondness and "we-ness," and told a very similar marriage story were still together years later. Thus, perceptions and judgments very early on in a relationship can be key indicators of the type of marriage couples might have years down the road.

Benjamin Karney and colleagues have done a series of studies showing that happy couples, when asked to describe their marriages, always report the positive aspects of their relationship. And when they are asked about their partners' flaws, they will usually explain the flaws away as trivial and will redirect the discussion back to the overarching positive elements of the relationship. In contrast, unhappy couples and those who later divorce stay cognitively stuck on negative traits in their partners and focus more on the bad elements of their relationships (Karney, 2010). For example, two women may note that their husband leaves his dirty socks all over the house when researchers ask them about negative aspects of their marriage. A wife in a happy marriage might say "His dirty socks annoy me, but he's such a great dad and works hard, so I let it slide." Meanwhile, an unhappy wife might say "He is so inconsiderate of me; he acts like I'm his mother, having to clean up after him *and* the kids." A happy husband might write off his wife's poor housekeeping skills as of little importance because he focuses on all the things she does so well. An unhappy husband might say that he despises coming home to a messy house and he can't stand her sloppiness. This selective attention is thought to be part of internal working models or cognitive templates that people develop through earlier relationships with their own caregivers and romantic partnerships. And because perceptual biases are so resistant to change, they can be a large contributor to unresolved conflict in a marriage. Karney explains these patterns in a bioecological manner, stating that good problem-solving skills and selective attention are influenced by everything from the spouses' brain functioning, stress management skills, childhood experiences, physical health, stress at work, and financial struggles.

As has been discussed many times in this textbook, people who grow up with secure attachments to caregivers tend to be able to maintain healthier love relationships. They tend to be low in avoidance and anxiety and can tolerate ambiguity and unpredictability (Lopez, 2003). Securely attached couples engage is positive conflict resolution, have reality-based perceptions of the strengths and weaknesses in themselves and their partners, are good at emotion-regulation skills, and have excellent self-insight (Lopez & Snyder, 2003). These are all the skills and characteristics marriage counselors, clinicians, and therapists help couples to develop if they are struggling.

HEALTHY PROCESSES IN MARRIAGES

- Premarital counseling
- Positive vs. negative interactions
- Peer marriages and feminist marriages
- Lesbian and gay relationships
- Dyadic coping

Adults tend to form relationships while they still have emotional needs that were unmet in their childhoods (Matta, 2006). Many couples are not aware of their unconscious internal working models and how they can negatively impact their relationships. In order to embark upon an open, honest partnership with another person that will be successful, people have to get to know their true selves and understand their real feelings. To quickly assess the strengths of your own relationship, read the *Building your Strengths* box.

Because many people have little exposure to or experience with healthy relationship styles, they are rarely taught how to survive and thrive in a marriage. In fact, people tend to spend more time planning a wedding than planning how to succeed in a long-term relationship. Sometimes seeking professional help before committing to marriage or a domestic partnership can help steer people in the right direction.

BUILDING YOUR STRENGTHS

Reducing criticism

Take this quiz and then have your partner take it separately. Compare your scores and discuss areas of relationship strength as well as patterns that may need some attention for change. If you don't have a partner, you can fill this out based on a previous relationship or analyze a friend's or family member's relationship.

Mark each blanks with a T for True or an F for False. There are blanks for each partner.

		You	Your partner
1	I often feel attacked or criticized when we talk about our disagreements.	_____	_____
2	I often have to defend myself because the things my partner says about me are so unfair.	_____	_____
3	When I complain, I think it's important to present many examples of what my partner does wrong.	_____	_____
4	When my partner complains, I often just want to leave the scene.	_____	_____
5	I think it's important to point out when problems are not my fault.	_____	_____
6	I often feel insulted when my partner complains.	_____	_____
7	I think my partner should know what I need without my having to say it.	_____	_____
8	I often feel as though my personality is being assaulted.	_____	_____
9	When I complain, I think it's important to show my partner the moral basis for my position.	_____	_____

	You	Your partner
10 I often think my partner is selfish and self-centered.	_____	_____
11 I am not guilty of many things my partner accuses me of.	_____	_____
12 Small issues often escalate out of proportion.	_____	_____
13 My partner's feelings get hurt too easily.	_____	_____
14 I often feel disgusted by some of my partner's attitudes.	_____	_____
15 My partner uses phrases such as "you always' or "you never" when complaining.	_____	_____
16 I think it's helpful to point out ways my partner can improve his or her personality.	_____	_____
17 When I complain to my partner, I think it's helpful to mention examples of other people who do things the way I'd like them to be done.	_____	_____
18 I often think to myself, "Who needs all this conflict?"	_____	_____
19 If I have to ask my partner for a compliment or a favor, then it really doesn't count.	_____	_____
20 I often feel disrespected by my partner.	_____	_____

Scoring: More than four "true" answers are a sign that your relationship may contain too much criticism. Try the techniques for fair fighting presented in the *Building Your Strengths* box on p. 220, try the communication techniques discussed throughout the chapter, and seek outside help from a clinical psychologist, counselor, or therapist if need be.

(Adapted from Gottman, Schwartz-Gottman, & DeClaire, 2006, pp. 33–34. Copyright © 2006 by John M. Gottman, Ph.D., and Joan DeClaire. Used by permission of Crown Publishers, a division of Random House, Inc.)

Note: *Building Your Strengths* boxes are not intended to diagnose, treat, or cure any personal or relationship problems; they are designed for informational purposes only, and to spur discussion.

Premarital counseling

One way you can develop relationship strengths before you enter into a marriage is to attend brief **premarital counseling**. Premarital counseling is a brief form of therapy that helps couples outline their goals and align their expectations before getting married, in order to prevent divorce. It can be a few short counseling sessions (four to six hours total) provided by a clergy member or mental health professional. The sessions tend to focus on communication skills, conflict resolution, sexual compatibility, finance management styles, childrearing attitudes, and brainstorming potential problems that might arise in the couple or with extended family members. Premarital counseling often includes support, information, and skills development. The goal is to put the relationship on the right footing, nip any problems in the bud, and hopefully prevent unhappiness and divorce.

One such approach to premarital counseling is **solution-focused therapy**, which does not focus on childhood wounds or past conflicts. Therapists using this approach focus on the here-and-now of the relationship and assess each couple's individual strengths, cultural beliefs, and perceptions of reality. Solution-focused therapy stems from a *social constructionist* perspective, in that therapists believe that

Premarital counseling
a brief form of therapy that helps couples outline their goals and align their expectations before getting married, in order to prevent divorce.

reality is less important than the partners' constructed realities and perceptions of the problems they have. The therapist focuses on aligning the partners' perceptions as much as possible and developing concrete strategies for change that will lead to a healthy, open, well-balanced relationship (Murray & Murray, 2004). This process often involves a thorough assessment of the bioecological influences on each partner. For example, the therapist might assess how physiologically reactive a person is to conflict in order to teach new strategies for calming down and listening. He or she might also help the couple analyze how their individual microsystems, like families of origin, friends, and children, might affect their relationship. Exosystem influences such as each partner's workplace might also be explored. Finally, cultural and religious values in their respective macrosystems would be addressed in order to bring their goals and beliefs into alignment before they marry.

Positive vs. negative interactions

Happy marriages and committed partnerships are characterized by partners who see each other as best friends. They respect each other immensely, and show great affection and empathy toward their partner (Gottman et al., 2006). They truly pay attention to the needs and interests of their partner and do what they can to make that person happy. Gottman and his colleagues have studied thousands of couples over dozens of years. They have found that successful, happy couples tend to have a ratio of five positive statements and actions to every negative statement or action. This ratio is necessary in order to keep a relationship healthy, and this research team has been able to predict with astonishing accuracy, by coding verbal and non-verbal positive and negative behaviors, which couples will be divorced within five years. Typically, couples in trouble display 0.8 positive statements and actions to every 1 negative statement and action; that is, the partners have almost equal positive and negative experiences with each other. These authors outline what they call the "Four Horsemen of the Relationship Apocalypse." When the Four Horsemen occur too often, these behaviors may doom a relationship. They are:

- *criticism*, consisting of complaining, blaming, attacking, and saying "you always …"
- *defensiveness*, including using counterattacks to defend oneself and avoid responsibility
- *contempt*, consisting of hostility, disgust, eye-rolling, sarcasm, and name-calling
- *stonewalling*, such as closing down, avoiding eye contact, and acting unaffected.

On the positive side, Gottman et al. (2006) describe potential couple-saving behaviors:

- a *soft start-up*, which involves bringing up a problem gently and with love
- *turning toward*, such as facing one's partner, hugging, and smiling
- *repairing conversations*, consisting of apologizing, smiling through pain, and using humor
- *accepting the influence* of one's partner, such as not dominating or being stubborn, and accepting and appreciating one's partner's ideas and suggestions.

Gottman et al. (2006) argue that if couples improve on even a couple of these behaviors, their relationship will be greatly enhanced. They stress that a marriage counselor can help most marriage partners develop these skills, as long as a couple hasn't waited years into their troubles to seek help because therapy is most effective if sought earlier rather than later. To find a marriage or couples counselor near you, see www.aamft.org or www.apa.org.

The Gottman group provides one final suggestion: when your partner complains, search for the true longing in what they are saying. That longing can reveal their vulnerable emotions, the ones that they are afraid to express or may not even be aware of. For example, a *complaint* might be "Why don't you ever listen when I talk?" But if you search for the *longing*, you might uncover the pain, which really means to say "I wish I had more intimate discussions with you without the distraction of the TV." Another *complaint* might be "There's never any food in this house unless I go buy some!" The hidden *longing* might actually be "I had hoped to share in an equal partnership, to maintain a happy home life with you." By searching for the hidden longing, couples can increase intimacy and build a true partnership.

Peer marriages and feminist marriages

Married couples who are really good at the types of skills Gottman outlines are often living in **peer marriages** (Schwartz, 1994). In peer marriages, the sharing of household labor is at least 60:40 or better, in terms of equal responsibility. These couples see child care, housework, earning money, and power as things to be shared equally. In a study of peer marriages, Schwartz (1994) found that only 40% of women and 20% of men cited feminist beliefs as a reason for their peer marriage. Many couples stated the desire to avoid the oppressive models they had grown up with; others said they had a crisis that led them to reevaluate their marriage; still others said they wanted to be completely present in their children's lives and to truly co-parent. Finally, many couples just said the husband followed his wife's lead, that it wasn't a conscious decision to share equally. These men expected that women were better at relationships and family life and so they would do what their wives suggested. It is interesting to note how traditional gender role ideas led to non-traditional, egalitarian households. In peer marriages, even when men earned most or all of the money, they shared the money equally and said their wives had just as much power over decision-making as they did.

People in peer marriages often disagreed about childrearing strategies but never complained about a lack of affection or intimacy. In fact, in some of these families, the couples shared everything so openly and intimately that they often felt more like best friends or siblings than intimate partners. Again, we see the effect of traditional internal working models of sex and gender roles exerting their influence. These couples had a hard time reconciling how to be completely egalitarian yet have a sexual relationship that might include one partner playing a more passive role than the other. In non-peer marriage couples, sex often helps people bond, feel closer, and forget problems. But in the peer marriage household, the partners already have these other problems worked out, so sex is simply for sexual pleasure and intimacy. For peer marriages to work, the couple must realize that their daily egalitarian roles at home and work do not have to be replayed in the bedroom. It's OK for one person to initiate or for fantasies and sexy garb to be involved.

Beyond these few issues, peer marriages are incredibly strong and stable. The partners' sense of "we-ness" allows them to overcome the stigma and teasing of more traditional family and community members, who might argue that the men are "whipped" or that the women are "butch." These families feel strongly about their equal power sharing and often build a community of other parents raising children in similar egalitarian environments. These couples state, however, that their focus on the family often means a constant psychological struggle to give up potential earning power and material goods, even promotions at work, to maintain equal roles at home. They also must continuously reevaluate whether they are slipping into power plays or whether inequality is sneaking in (Schwartz, 1994). Thus, a peer marriage takes a lot of hard work and constant self-reflection.

Contemporary marriages are often characterized as partnerships with sophisticated communication and problem-solving skills, which help couples to be open and honest, and stay together (Vannoy, 1991). An example of this type of partnership, similar to the peer marriage, is the **feminist marriage**. Feminist marriages are characterized by: (1) open criticism of inequality both inside and outside the home; (2) overt actions to ensure equality between men and women; (3) male support for wives' independent interests; (4) self-reflection; and (5) intimate emotional involvement. Blaisure and Allen (1995) studied a group of self-proclaimed feminist marriages and found that the couples reported constant reassessment of whether they were continuing to maintain equality in their roles.

One aspect of feminist marriages is that women usually keep their own last names. Alternatively, the couple might invent a new last name that combines elements of both (for example, Battelle and Watson might become "Batson" or "Wattelle"). Partners in these marriages often lead independent lives, have accounts and credit in both names, and have friends of the opposite sex (Blaisure & Allen, 1995).

You may be surprised to learn, however, that very few men in feminist marriages actually pull their weight during the "second shift." Men explained this by attributing their lack of second shift work to their wives' temperament or better skills ("She's more organized than I am" or "She's more

Peer marriages
These couples see child care, housework, earning money, and power as things to be shared equally; they are peers without domination or control over their partners.

Feminist marriages
Characterized by open criticism of inequality both inside and outside the home, with constant self-reflection and active strategizing to ensure that women have the same rights, roles, and responsibilities as their husbands.

particular about how things are cleaned"). Women also make excuses for why their husbands don't do more around the house and with the children. This may be because, compared to other husbands, they do exponentially more so the wives are grateful. However, compared to the wives, the husbands' contributions are much less.

While they may not be perfect, both feminist and peer marriages are excellent illustrations of the changing social norms regarding gender roles, marriage, and parenting. Very few women in the western world will partner with someone who doesn't at least believe in equality. One woman in the Blaisure and Allen (1995) study said, "The way to keep the other person powerless is to deny them sufficient finances, sufficient knowledge. So if you're always open and you're always sharing, then you're not denying the other person what they need to establish their power, too" (p. 168).

Lesbian and gay relationships

Research shows that very similar positive dynamics as those described earlier regarding heterosexual relationships increase the relationship satisfaction of gay and lesbian couples as well. Lesbian partners tend to experience closer intimacy, more equality, and more freedom to leave relationships than heterosexuals do (Kurdek, 1998). Gay male partners reported more autonomy and fewer barriers to leaving. But in general, the relationship processes and issues that are important to relationship health are virtually identical in LGBT and straight couples. Gottman et al. (2003) studied gay and lesbian couples who had been living together for at least two years. They were asked to discuss a common conflict in their lives in the lab. Partners' physiological reactivity was measured during the task and later when they watched a video playback of the task. Gay men reported that validation from their partner was most important for relationship satisfaction, while lesbian partners felt affection accounted most for their relationship satisfaction. The authors argue that men are using a more cognitive framework for interpreting support from their partners, while women are using a more emotional framework. This is interesting in light of their physiological findings. Gottman et al. found that high physiological arousal was negatively related to relationship satisfaction for gay men, indicating that they do better in less emotionally arousing relationships. However, physiological arousal was positively related to relationship satisfaction for lesbian couples, indicating that women prefer overtly demonstrative relationships where conflicts are openly discussed and resolved. Thus, the women dealt well with high physiological arousal and saw it as an impetus to have a discussion, while the men found this less comfortable. These findings are consistent with studies on heterosexual men and women and suggest that gender may be a more important factor in understanding relationship success than sexual orientation is. And for all couples, being able to cope effectively without hostility, attacks, or shutting down emotionally is related to better health and longevity.

Dyadic coping

Let's take a quick look at one mechanism that might explain some of the dynamics found by Gottman et al. (2003), and in peer and feminist marriages: dyadic coping (Bodenmann, 2005). Bodenmann puts forth a model of dyadic coping wherein the couple faces stressors (such as loss of a job, one partner's illness, or financial or child issues) together, and a series of attempts to cope together then develop. **Dyadic stress** involves both partners. It is a stressor that causes grief for both partners simultaneously and with which they must cope together within a given time frame. Although both partners experience the same stressor, their individual coping styles may vary, may complement their partner's, or may clash. Stressors can occur from within or outside the relationship (for example, financial struggles in the family versus racial discrimination in the workplace).

Interestingly, Bodenmann (2005) points out that one partner's coping style may actually *be* a stressor for the other person. For example, many women want to bring up a problem and deal with it right away, while many men prefer to just let things go and hope the situation will improve. If the

Dyadic stress
A stressor that causes grief for both partners simultaneously, with which they must cope dyadically (meaning two people together).

woman confronts the man, he may feel anxious and not respond verbally, leading her to then feel unacknowledged and unheard. She may get angry and start raising her voice, causing him to freeze up, turn away, and go for a walk. In this situation, the woman's "in your face" coping method was a stressor for the man. He dealt with his stress by "turning off" and that, in turn, was a stressor for her. This example illustrates a sequence of dyadic coping in which each partner's coping style affects the other's. In dyadic coping, both partners usually make an attempt to restore balance to the relationship, or to their lives, in the case of an external stressor. They will try to work together to cope with the stressor and return to a sense of normalcy and harmony. For example, the couple described in this example may have a calm discussion about the issue after the husband returns from his walk.

Dyadic coping most often occurs after each individual has had a chance to implement his or her own coping style first. For example, if one member of the couple is facing racist remarks from a boss at work, the other partner may use a **protective buffering** strategy. Protective buffering is an attempt to minimize felt stress in a partner. The other partner may try to negate the importance of the comments, ask the offended partner to suppress anger and move on, or just carefully listen and hear his or her pain. Alternatively, the responding partner may use an **active engagement** strategy, in which he or she may initiate constructive ways to handle the problem, such as making a "pro" and "con" list about confronting the boss, or talking about how the partner might get a new job without a reference letter from the old boss. Dyadic coping can often be very positive, as in this example. The partners express unity, face the world as a team, and share their feelings. The responding partner may help the stressed partner cognitively reframe the situation. This means the partner suggests other ways to look at the problem. For example, the responding partner might say, "Your boss always compliments you and gives you raises. Maybe we can just say she's ignorant regarding certain types of language but is really a good person who values your work." Such cognitive reframing helps one's partner think about a situation from a different angle. Another strategy is **delegated dyadic coping**, in which one partner takes over the other's responsibilities. For example, if a wife is under a stressful deadline at work, her husband might feed the kids and keep them quiet while she practices her presentation. Or a wife might mow the lawn for her husband when he throws his back out.

Dyadic coping isn't always positive, however. Couples can be sarcastic, belittling, and humiliating toward their partners. They can minimize the other's feelings ("You always make a mountain out of a molehill!" or "You're such a drama queen!"). **Negative dyadic coping** can also involve emotional withdrawal, in which a partner pretends to care, but rarely listens or responds only superficially (such as "Hmmm, that's too bad" while continuing to watch TV). The type of coping couples use together stems from their individual skills, their upbringing, and their motivations regarding the relationship.

Bodenmann (2005) reviewed 13 studies examining dyadic coping and found that positive dyadic coping was related to marital satisfaction and stability in all studies. Negative dyadic coping was related to clinical-level problems like depression. Moreover, at a five-year follow-up, positive dyadic coping was related to marital stability and negative dyadic coping was related to divorce. Bodenmann (2005, p. 45) states that

> Engaging in positive dyadic coping by jointly discussing the stress experience, reframing the situation, or helping each other to relax increases a sense of solidarity or *we-ness* and is likely to reduce stress, and in so doing, promote marital happiness and cohesion. Individual and dyadic coping are thus seen as protective factors for marital functioning.

For some people, this kind of stuff just takes too much work. A growing number of people decide that they don't want to live their lives always compromising and working things out with someone else. They want to stay single instead of becoming involved in committed partnerships like marriage. Other people end up single due to contextual influences beyond their control, and still others decide to marry their religion and remain romantically single in the service of God. It is to these single people that we now turn.

Protective buffering
An attempt to minimize the stress one's partner feels.

Active engagement
Initiating constructive ways to handle one's partner's problems.

Delegated dyadic coping
One partner takes over the other's responsibilities when the first partner is feeling stressed.

Negative dyadic coping
A partner pretends to care but rarely listens or only responds superficially or sarcastically.

CHAPTER SUMMARY

Historically, marriages were formed due to familial desires, cultural expectations, or other benefits to the larger group. Love and personal fulfillment were not concerns people thought about before getting married. This is still the case in many places around the world. However, in western nations, the traditional marriage of one man and one woman is becoming deinstitutionalized. Fewer people are marrying at all these days, and when they do, they marry at later ages. More and more couples are choosing to have children outside of traditional marriage. Women's rights are now legally protected so they have the ability to divorce for any reason they choose. This means that over the past 100 years, divorce rates have steadily risen in a linear fashion, except for a short period during the 1940s and 1950s when marriages increased and divorces decreased. The 50% divorce rate present in the 1970s leveled out in subsequent decades and now is about 45%.

Another part of the deinstitutionalization of marriage is the increased rates of cohabitation. More couples are choosing to live together than ever before. This can be due to financial needs, lack of social support for the union, couples wanting a "trial run" before marriage, or legal restrictions against them marrying. Those who cohabit before marrying have higher divorce rates, especially if they cohabited with multiple partners. This could be due to increased stress levels and lower incomes in cohabiting couples, or a lower level of commitment from those who choose to cohabit. Individual partners' attachment histories, personality traits, biochemical functioning, and cultural expectations for gender roles and marital functioning all affect the health and happiness of the union, illustrating the need for a bioecological perspective.

Marriage has many benefits for couples, including over 1,000 rights married people have over unmarried people (such as the right to visit a partner in the hospital, pension and health care rights, and real estate and child custody rights). However, in countries like Sweden, all individuals have the same rights whether they are married or not, so marriage rates have plummeted.

Healthy, committed partnerships also impact individuals' health and psychological well-being. Those who have high levels of perceived support (versus only received support) benefit greatly. Relationship support or conflict can affect each partner's heart rate, blood pressure, and immune system functioning.

Many types of marriage were presented, including the most common types, devitalized and conflicted. In *devitalized* marriages partners are generally dissatisfied in all areas. In *conflicted* marriages partners are generally dissatisfied with the marriage but the people have other outlets where they find fulfillment, such as from friends and work. *Vitalized* and happy marriages typically consist of a strong foundation of friendship, love, support, and the enjoyment of similar activities.

Healthy marriages usually have a ratio of five positive interactions to every negative one. They are not defensive, critical, or unwilling to discuss areas of conflict. Premarital counseling, especially that which focuses on all of the bioecological systems influencing partners, can help solve problems before a couple marries, in order to increase the chances of success. The most common problems couples face are financial struggles, differences in sex drive, erroneous perceptions about their partners, and lack of communication.

Besides traditional heterosexual marriages between one man and one woman, other types of marriages were explored, such as peer marriages, covenant marriages, and arranged marriages. Same-sex marriages and committed partnerships were discussed in depth. They tend to be similar in quality and functioning to heterosexual marriages, with perhaps a bit more egalitarian role sharing. The history of gay marriage laws and restrictions was presented, as were arguments for and against the legalization of same-sex marriage. Not all members of LGBT communities are in favor of legalization since they may feel it privileges heterosexual norms over other family forms.

Interracial and intercultural marriages provide particular challenges for couples whose macrosystems do not accept their unions. Various assimilation strategies may work to allow the couple to find common ground and integrate their separate histories and cultures together.

Dyadic coping is a particularly effective strategy for any couple facing obstacles. It involves seeing the world from a sense of "we" instead of "I," and helping each other to think about conflicts differently, talk about their problems, and support one another in achieving adequate solutions.

KEY TERMS

active engagement
affinal family
assimilationists
bigamy
common law marriage
conflicted marriage
consanguineal relationships
cooperative traditional arranged
   marriages
covenant marriage
cultural assimilation
deinstitutionalized
delegated dyadic coping

domestic partnerships
dyadic stress
enforceable trust
feminist marriages
financial infidelity
harmonious marriage
marital assimilation
modified traditional arranged
   marriage
negative dyadic coping
peer marriages
perceived support
premarital counseling

protective buffering
pure relationship
radical argument
received support
second shift
social dominance orientation
Social Dominance
   Theory
social marriages
solution-focused therapy
structural assimilation
traditional arranged
   marriages

WEBSITES FOR FURTHER EXPLORATION

http://www.marriageequality.org

Marriage Equality USA; an organization that seeks marriage rights for all couples, especially those in LGBT communities. It has legislation updates, historical articles, books, FAQs, and a list of the 1,138 federal rights a legal marriage provides.

http://www.focusonthefamily.com

An evangelical Christian site devoted to traditional marriages and families. They have resources they feel will help families thrive, videos on common family problems, a magazine, radio broadcasts and other resources for those who want to raise families with conservative political and Christian values.

http://www.gottman.com

The Gottman Institute is the organization of the world's leading expert on marriages, researcher John Gottman. A great site for research-based advice on communication and other skills needed to strengthen a marriage; they provide workshops, retreats, DVDs, books, clinical training for professionals, and FAQs. An interesting option is for people to buy their books on healthy marriage skills to donate to soldiers serving overseas; research shows soldiers are at high risk for divorce, domestic violence, and suicide stemming from relationship problems after they return from war.

CHAPTER 8
LIVING SINGLE

I don't like to be labeled as lonely just because I am alone.

(Delta Burke, actress)

LEARNING OBJECTIVES

- To understand trends affecting singles, including legislation, social policies, and stigmatization

- To appreciate the normative early adulthood developmental processes that can affect people's adjustment to both single and partnered lives

- To get a feel for the research findings on the health and well-being of diverse types of singles

- To understand how faith-based single lifestyles can be both rewarding and challenging

Marriages and Families in the 21st Century: A Bioecological Approach, First Edition. Tasha R. Howe.
© 2012 Tasha R. Howe. Published 2012 by Blackwell Publishing Ltd.

OVERVIEW OF SINGLEHOOD

UNIQUE CHALLENGES FACING SINGLES

Singlism

Coping with singlism

Singles pride

THE NORMATIVE LIFE CYCLE MODEL

The struggles for identity and intimacy

Emerging adulthood

Types of emerging adults

THE DIVERSE LIVES OF SINGLE PEOPLE

Non-normative singles

Living apart together

Diverse reasons for singlehood

MACROSYSTEM FORCES AGAINST SINGLEHOOD

An example from Mormon culture

Examples from Africa

Examples from the United States

Women's rights in African nations

Fighting for singles' rights in the U.S.

THE PSYCHOLOGICAL AND PHYSICAL HEALTH OF SINGLE PEOPLE

Singles strain

Emotional attachments

SINGLE THROUGH COMMITMENT TO GOD

Priests, monks, and nuns: a historic family necessity

Contemporary faith-based single lifestyles

An example from Thai Buddhist *maechii*

FINAL REFLECTIONS

OVERVIEW OF SINGLEHOOD

With our last three chapters focusing on the developmental stages of forming committed partnerships (dating, falling in love, and finally committing to a partnership, often through marriage), it is pretty clear that romantic relationships are a huge part of most people's lives. Many of us grow up dreaming of a perfect wedding or finding the soulmate who will complete our lives. It's important to realize, though, that many people choose not to pair up. They may decide to just date casually or not date at all. Some people have had messy break-ups or experienced a partner's death, and decide that being single makes them happier than finding another partner. Still others remain single for religious reasons. Keep in mind that being alone does not necessarily mean a person is lonely. Many singles are happy and fulfilled, and have terrific support from friends and family. This chapter will examine the many different types of adults who live their lives without a partner.

In 1950 there were an estimated four million Americans who lived alone. In 2000, there were about 27 million one-person households compared to about 16 million three-person households. In 2004, 26% of U.S. households were single-person, and the numbers continue to increase (Morrow, 2004). Similarly, about 29% of British households have only one member (Coleman, 2007).

While some of these single-person households include young people who simply have not married yet, about three quarters of those homes are made up of middle-aged and older people, for a total of 15 million households (Morrow, 2004). Laumann (2004), in a large study of urban people in Chicago, found that the typical person between 18 to 59 was single for an average of 19 years, cohabited for about four, and was married for about 18 years. This means that the average person can expect half

FIGURE 8.1 One-person households over time.
Source: Morrow, 2004.

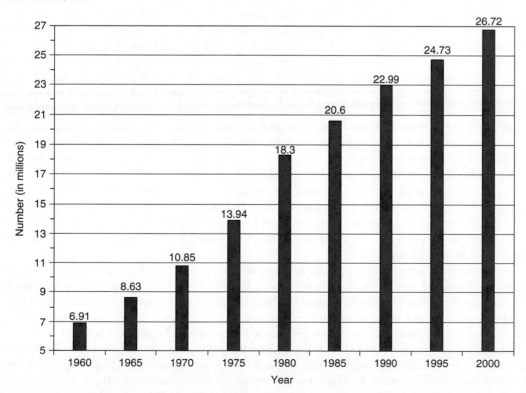

of their life to be spent as a single or dating person. You may be surprised to learn that in 2007 there were 100 million unmarried adults in the United States (Coleman, 2007). This amounts to about 45% of the adult population. These unmarried adults include about 15 million widowed people, 25 million divorced people, and 59 million people who never married.

A study conducted in 2005 found that 55% of single people reported no interest in becoming coupled. You may be surprised to learn that even in the youngest age group of single people (those between 18 and 29), 38% of said they were uninterested in finding a partner (Madden & Lenhart, 2006). Interestingly, the world's oldest woman in 2010 was never married. In fact, in the U.S., there are 51,000 men and 152,000 women over the age of 85 who have been lifelong singles.

Surprisingly little research has been conducted on this large and ever-expanding population of single people. They are virtually ignored in political debates and public policy discussions. Researchers don't spend a lot of time studying them. Nevertheless, it's important that we understand what we can about single people because many of us are adult singles, and if we're not, virtually all of us will have them in our families, so we need to comprehend their lives just as we have tried to grasp issues in the lives of those who partner up. Like partnered people, single people live their lives with intersectional identities and exist within multilayered bioecological contexts. So much of the research we've covered on gender, sexuality, health, and happiness can also be applied to single people. But single people have some unique issues that merit a closer look.

UNIQUE CHALLENGES FACING SINGLES

| Singlism |
| Coping with singlism |
| Singles pride |

For most cultures around the world, marriage is the expected outcome of a life well lived, and the majority of people around the globe eventually marry. Even with more people embracing singlehood these days, it's important to keep in mind that in the United States, even with declining marriage rates, 74% of people eventually marry by age 35 (Fields & Casper, 2001). And only about 10–15% of people will never marry at all (U.S. Census Bureau, 2000b). Long-standing cultural expectations and social norms often make those who remain single feel like cultural pariahs or, at minimum, disappointments to their families. Most cultures legitimize coupling, and do not consider the single lifestyle a legitimate alternative to pair-bonding. Being paired is considered the natural end result of mature human development (Adelman & Bankoff, 1990). Many parents hound their children, especially if they are over the age of 30, to get married and provide them with grandchildren. And virtually all social events are organized around partnered people. Think about the single friend invited to a camping trip with a group of couples, or the unmarried co-worker who shows up to the company holiday party solo. What do people think about your bachelor uncle or the "old maid" living at the end of your block? Historically, people who never married were considered odd, defective, and even scary. They were pitied for their bad luck or judged harshly for their personal failings (Morrow, 2004). Women were "spinsters" or "old schoolmarms," while men might be considered "old codgers" or "ne'er-do-wells." People assumed that these people were inherently flawed or too mean to find a mate.

Fortunately for single people, the use of many of these pejorative labels has declined in recent years. As discussed previously, marriage rates in industrialized nations are decreasing rapidly. Those nations that have the lowest rates of marriage usually provide benefits to cohabiting couples, same-sex couples, and single people at the same rates as benefits given to married couples. Often, however, even in western nations, single people are not given equal rights and benefits.

One benefit that may be denied to single people is the privilege of becoming a parent. In previous generations, for example, unmarried women who got pregnant were expected to give up their babies for adoption. More recently, however, the percentage of never-married mothers who give their babies up for adoption has declined to 1% in the U.S., indicating that more single women are becoming parents (Jones, 2002). Another challenge single people may face is that many states and countries do not allow single people, especially those from LGBT communities, to adopt children. Trends are slowly changing, though. For example, single men are opting to have children by joining their sperm with donated eggs and paying surrogates to carry the babies to term; 80% of these men are heterosexual (Coleman, 2007). With laws around the world relaxing, more gay men and single people of all backgrounds are beginning to foster and adopt children. In fact, about 33% of foster care adoptions are by unmarried adults (U.S. Dept. of Health & Human Services, 1999). The New York Court of Appeals stated that the country should encourage as many people as possible to provide stable homes for children through adoption, regardless of the marital status or sexual orientation of the prospective parents.

Coleman (2007) discusses the Growing Generations surrogacy agency in California, at which 12% of the clientele are single; most are well-educated and financially stable, and about half are gay men. However, there has also been a backlash against these non-traditional single-parent families, with 16% of fertility clinics refusing to serve single people, despite the American Society for Reproductive Medicine stating that it is unethical to discriminate based on marital status (Coleman, 2007).

When single people face discrimination or ostracism, it can lead to stress or loneliness, a topic which has not been widely studied. In one preliminary study by the Yankelovich Monitor (cited in Morrow, 2004), findings revealed that single men who felt stressed and lonely turned to mindless TV watching and alcohol use. In contrast, single women used their time by volunteering to benefit their communities. When they felt stressed, they turned to social support, music, and mediation or prayer. Thus, gender and other demographic variables may impact the experience of being single, and these diverse single lifestyles are only recently being examined by researchers. It's important to keep in mind that the images of single people and the meaning of singlehood are culturally constructed (Darrington, Piercy, & Niehuis, 2005). For example, while single middle-aged women in society may be viewed as "incomplete" or "immature," many people have great respect for nuns who give up their prospects for marriage and children for a pious life devoted to God and performing good works. And not many people have a negative impression of George Clooney, the talented and handsome actor who seems to benefit greatly from the single life, despite being over 50, well beyond the normative age for marriage, even in Hollywood. These trends show a great diversity of singlehood experiences which we don't know a lot about yet. What is clear, however, is that single people tend to be judged negatively compared to coupled people and that this can cause great stress.

Singlism

Continuing the antisingles movement, many U.S. states in the 2008–2010 election years sought to draft legislation to ban unmarried couples and singles from adopting children, along with banning same-sex marriages. DePaulo and Morris (2005) call this **singlism**—prejudice, stereotyping, and discrimination against single people. Singlism includes a set of beliefs stemming from SNAF ideologies, which embrace the idea that committed romantic partnerships are the pinnacle of mature adult development, and encompasses the idea that singles can never be as happy, fulfilled, important, or well-adjusted as married people and those who bear children. DePaulo and Morris (2005) argue that we unconsciously believe that those who are engaged in committed sexual partnerships lead more meaningful, worthier, and happier lives than those who have not developed that kind of relationship. They state that this ideology is never questioned, but simply assumed to be true, and that we negatively evaluate and even discriminate against those who do not toe the line and fulfill society's marital ambitions for its citizens. These authors point out that we constantly negatively compare single people to married people. We even refer to them as "unmarried," yet we would never refer to married people as "unsingle," which would suggest that singlehood is superior to marriage. This ideology socializes people to feel that they can never reach the kind of happiness and fulfillment that marriage provides by forming other types

Singlism
Prejudice, stereotyping, and discrimination against single people.

FYI

Singlehood stigma scale (adapted from Adelman & Bankoff, 1990)

Rate yourself on how much you endorse the following statements. While the scale is geared towards single people, those who are not single can rate how they feel about "people in general" instead of themselves. Use the following scale:

(1) Not true (2) Somewhat true (3) Very true

1 If I (or "people in general") do not marry, my (or "their") life will be unfulfilling. _____

2 If I do not have children, my life will feel empty. _____

3 If I do not marry, I will have no one to blame but myself. _____

4 Being single among friends who are couples is socially awkward for me. _____

5 My married friends regard me as a threat to their marriage. _____

6 It is embarrassing for me to still be single. _____

7 To not marry would make me feel somewhat like a failure, regardless of my accomplishments. _____

Add up your score. Low scores between 7 and 11 indicate little endorsement of the singlism or stigma against singles. Higher scores between 18 and 21 suggest that you have really bought into the idea that singlehood is not a legitimate or acceptable lifestyle.

---

of intimate relationships (for example, with friends, relatives, or co-workers). Are you *singlist*? To assess your singlist ideologies, see the *FYI* box, "Singlehood Stigma Scale."

Most societies are couples-oriented. When people fail to meet societal expectations for partnering behavior, they can be negatively judged and even ostracized or discriminated against. For example, many people think single people, especially those non-normative single people over the age of 35, are immature, self-centered, and emotionally unstable. People think "Why would anyone want to be single? What's wrong with them?" While most western societies publicly disapprove of other "isms" such as racism, sexism, and heterosexism, singlism is accepted and thought to be a legitimate form of judgment (DePaulo & Morris, 2006).

DePaulo & Morris (2006) examined the viewpoints of 1,000 college students and found that they thought singles were unhappy, lonely, ugly, immature, insecure, and self-centered. Only 2% of them viewed singles as caring, kind or giving, compared to 50% who judged married people as such. Judgments became even more negative if the single was over the age of 40.

It's not only college students who have discriminatory beliefs about single people they may come across in their microsystem interactions. Macrosystem laws and social policies can also affect discrimination against singles. For example, Morris, Sinclair, and DePaulo (2007) cite a ruling of a Michigan judge who allowed housing discrimination based on marital status. The judge ruled that landlords could deny housing to unmarried, cohabiting couples if they held strong religious beliefs against cohabitation. This ruling allowed for a direct violation of Michigan's fair housing laws which specifically ban marital status discrimination. Similarly, Virginia's aid to poor families program does not apply to unrelated people. They only assist legally recognized families in buying low-income houses. Thus, low-income cohabitors or roommates in need of housing aid need not apply.

In an interesting study on peoples' perceptions of single people and job discrimination, college students were given various scenarios regarding people who were applying for a job that required relocation. The applicants were either single people or single parents. Single parents were perceived as having a more difficult time relocating, so were less likely to be hired. However, they were more

HOW WOULD YOU MEASURE THAT?

Discrimination against singles (Morris et al., 2007)

Morris and colleagues wanted to examine whether the general public would discriminate against single people in housing decisions. They sampled a group of college students and a group of adults working in real estate agencies and asked them to imagine themselves as landlords evaluating housing applications of several potential tenants. They gave the participants various tenant profiles where they manipulated whether the tenant was: a single man, a single woman, a married couple married for either six months or six years, a cohabiting couple together for six years, or a pair of opposite sex roommates. They then asked the participants how responsible they thought the tenants might be in terms of damaging the house, keeping it clean, being noisy, and paying their rent in a timely manner. Across all conditions, married couples were judged more positively than all of the types of single people (for example, they were judged more likely to pay their rent on time). Single women were seen as almost as responsible as married couples, as were cohabitors if they had been together longer than the married couple (six years versus six months). These results were consistent regardless of the marital status and gender of the participants or whether they were real estate agents or college students.

When asked why they judged the married couple so positively, most people said "because they are married" without any real explanation, suggesting that they believe everyone thinks married people are more responsible and trustworthy. Some participants said "because they have two incomes," even though both the cohabitors and the roommates also had two incomes.

While participants rated single people as least likely to stay in the house for an extended period of time and least likely to pay the rent on time, they never used fears about personal reliability or timely payments as reasons to explain their judgments against single people. They were comfortable explaining that marital status had been the determining factor in their decisions. In fact, when subjects in another experiment by the same authors read about landlords' discrimination against single people, African Americans, women, and the disabled, they rated discrimination against African Americans, women and disabled people as wrong but endorsed discrimination against single people. They felt the landlords were justified in not offering the apartment to single people, despite judging discrimination against all other groups as wrong. Perhaps they judge single people more harshly because single people are actively bucking the traditional system of coupling, whereas people in other marginalized groups cannot choose their status. The authors comment that married couples being judged as so much more reliable and stable than single people is surprising, considering that most people are aware that almost half of marriages end in divorce. The research participants were basing decisions solely on family *structure*, knowing nothing about family *processes*, which could be harmful or dysfunctional, even in married couples. These studies show that single people may face discrimination in the housing market as well as negative judgments from people in each of their bioecological systems.

likely to be offered a job that did not require relocation because the childfree singles were viewed as being too socially immature for the job. The students also viewed childfree single people as less deserving of merit-based pay increases (Eby, Allen, Noble, & Lockwood, 2004). This study suggests that people might not want to hire a single parent because of a perceived inability to meet the requirements of the job, even though the person obviously applied for the job thinking he or she could relocate if necessary. Moreover, if the job applicant was single and not a parent, people would not want to hire them or give them raises due to perceptions about their personal failings. For more on the tendency to discriminate against singles, see the *How Would You Measure That?* box.

Single people themselves report receiving bad service in stores and restaurants as well as experiencing condescending attitudes from various professionals. About 30% of single people and

23% of coupled participants think single people are a group that experiences discrimination regularly. However, single people report that there are many strategies they use to cope with the negative judgments of others.

Coping with singlism

How do singles cope with the stigmatization they face? Many gain social support from friends and co-workers and develop a large set of interests that keep them busy and enhance their life satisfaction. Singles rely on others to help them with tasks, negotiate life's problems, and generally support them (Bellotti, 2008; Malo, 1994).

Zajicek and Koski (2003) found that the pressure to be in a relationship was much stronger for working-class than for middle-class people, who tended to have more education and feel more empowered to buck social norms. These authors found that a group of singles they examined used **resistant thinking** strategies to cope with being single in a couples-oriented world. Resistant thinking refers to the ability to analyze people's comments objectively and not take them personally or internalize negative images of one's self. Single people using this strategy work hard not to buy into the social pressure that tells us that every person should be in a committed relationship to be "normal" or "whole." They also engage in **managed interactions**, where they take control of conversations or other exchanges with people. For example, they may plan very carefully what to say to people ahead of time, thinking of polite ways to decline invitations to non-single-friendly events as well as how to respond appropriately to singlist comments. They reported that people often felt sorry for them or wondered what was wrong with them. Interestingly, they also struggled with coupled individuals feeling threatened by them, thinking that they would potentially steal their mates. Finally, another cognitive strategy single people use is **embracing singlehood**, where they look for all the advantages they have. For example, in a study done on 25- to 35-year-old Italian single people, Bellotti (2008) found that women and men had large social networks of close friends and peer groups that helped them feel happy, secure, and less lonely. Some people (especially women) even had what Bellotti called "surrogate partners" in that they formed extremely close friendships with one other person with whom they did everything and shared all their feelings. Those living in poverty also used their social networks to help them with food, lodging, and other economic support. This 34-year-old man's commentary is a great example of someone embracing his singlehood and relying on close friends for happiness (Bellotti, 2008, p. 322):

> Love for me does not last, while friendship has a higher importance. I cannot compare a few intense months of a [love] relationship ... to twenty years of an intellectual relationship with a friend.

Singles pride

Single people have rarely been given a voice to make a case for the legitimacy of their choices. While you may have learned about civil rights movements for people of color and the women's movement, you may be unaware that there has also been a **singles pride movement**, which advocates for the rights and protections of single people. One of its early proponents, Marie Babare Edwards, wrote in her "Singles Manifesto" of 1974 that:

> I will, by choosing to live a free single life, be helping to raise the status of singlehood. In doing this, I will be strengthening rather than weakening marriage, for only when we truly have the option *not* to marry, will marriage be seen as a free choice rather than one demanded by a pairing society. (Cited in Edwards, 1981)

Luckily for single people, with cultural trends very slowly shifting away from the expectation that everyone must marry, the single person is becoming more widely acknowledged as leading a legitimate and potentially happy lifestyle. In fact, because single people have more money to spend

---

Resistant thinking
A strategy to cope with being single in a couples-oriented world; working hard to not fall prey to the social pressure saying that every person should be in a committed relationship to be "normal" or "whole."

Managed interactions
A strategy to cope with being single in a couples-oriented world; thinking of polite ways to decline invitations to non-single-friendly events as well as how to respond to "singlist" comments.

Embracing singlehood
A strategy to cope with being single in a couples-oriented world; adjusting one's attitude to see all the advantages of such a lifestyle.

Singles pride movement
A civil rights movement which advocates for the rights and protections of singles.

on themselves, not having to buy groceries for multiple family members or save for their children's education, they have become a target for commercial interests and product advertisers who realize that single people buy more alcohol, reading material, and tobacco products, and pay more for rent than households with two or more people (Morrow, 2004). This means they are being courted by the free market interests, which further gives their lifestyle legitimacy.

When single people look to buy a house, they are often interested in places that allow them to walk everywhere so that they can meet local merchants, find nearby hangouts, and build community wherever they go. They also like to buy more quirky homes like artists' lofts or converted cottages, whereas families with two or more members look for large rooms for congregating and eating, and yards for children to play in. Being single allows them to indulge in spending that many couples or people with children might consider self-indulgent. They can take pride in their individual choices and personal style, even though their choices do not follow the age norms of society's expectations for settling down, having children, and so on (Morrow, 2004).

THE NORMATIVE LIFE CYCLE MODEL

| The struggles for identity and intimacy |
| Emerging adulthood |

The **normative life cycle model** suggests that all people will form romantic relationships, settle down into coupledom (usually heterosexual marriage), and have children, in that order. The assumption is that all adults wish to be in committed partnerships and that no one would really want to be single by choice. This model may partially explain why so little research has been done on single people, either heterosexual or those in LGBT communities (Hostetler, 2009). Although the majority of people eventually conform to normative life cycle trends, the life course is partially determined by the opportunities that arise within the context of cultural expectations, which then influence how individuals process information and make life choices for themselves. Not everyone meets the right person or has the kind of finances, job, personality, or lifestyle that would suit being partnered. Just like everything else we've discussed, understanding single lifestyles means taking a bioecological approach and understanding that a person's biochemistry, genes, personality traits, interpersonal style, and many social contexts all play a role in where that person ends up in life.

The struggles for identity and intimacy

In western cultures, it's fairly common to have a prolonged period of singlehood before a person commits to marriage or long-term partnership. Erik Erikson (1969) suggested that at each period of the life cycle, people struggle with certain psychosocial tasks. For example, in adolescence we experience the struggle of **identity versus role confusion**. If a person is to reach middle age in a healthy and positive fashion, Erikson argues that he or she must first gain a keen sense of him- or herself as an individual and not be confused about his or her purpose and goals. If that struggle is resolved in a healthy way and a person is sure of him- or herself, the next task is to face the challenge of **intimacy versus isolation** in early adulthood. He or she must be able form mature intimate relationships, which involve bonding with other people but not losing one's self. These intimate relationships are formed with both lovers and friends. If people fail to accomplish a strong identity or the skills for intimacy, they may enter middle age with a sense of confusion over who they are and may feel isolated and lonely.

James Marcia (1980) expanded on this idea and discussed different ways that people can reach their identity. The most mature way is for a person to experience a long period of searching. This period, called **crisis**, includes meeting diverse people, traveling, trying new things, and experimenting with life. After a period of intense exploration in early adulthood, a person will eventually experience

Normative life cycle model
A SNAF ideology which suggests that all people will form romantic relationships, settle down into coupledom (usually heterosexual marriage) and have children, in that order.

Identity versus role confusion and intimacy versus isolation
Erik Erikson's psychosocial stages for late adolescence and early adulthood. Healthy people search for diverse experiences and then decide upon an integrated identity, which will help them build intimacy skills with others. Negative solutions to these states include a feeling of confusion over identity and a sense of social isolation.

Crisis
A term Marcia used to describe the search for identity, which includes meeting diverse people, traveling, trying new things, and experimenting.

Commitment
A term Marcia (1980) used to describe the process of identity solidification; after a period of intense exploration in early adulthood, one will eventually commit to a set of values, goals, and personal identities.

Identity achievement
The positive outcome of the search for identity, combining a prolonged search with a strong commitment to identity; those who reach identity achievement are considered to be mature and psychologically balanced.

Emerging adulthood
The stage of life from approximately ages 18 to 25 when, in western cultures, young people spend time on improving themselves through education and experimentation (in contrast to getting married right away).

commitment. He or she will commit to a set of values, goals, and personal identities. This positive outcome, combining a prolonged search with a strong commitment to identity is called **identity achievement**. Those who reach identity achievement are considered to be mature and psychologically balanced. They have a clear sense of their vocational, spiritual, social, emotional, and cognitive identities. They know where they're going and who they are in a deep and meaningful way. But before they commit to a solid sense of self, the period of crisis must occur. Imagine having a family member who has not achieved a strong sense of identity or the skills for intimacy. How would this impact his or her interactions with you? With partners or children? Erikson would argue that in order to be happy and well-adjusted in western cultures, we must search for a clear sense of ourselves so that we can truly connect with others.

Emerging adulthood

A person's crisis, or identity search, usually occurs (or at least begins) during a period which is now considered a separate stage of development, referred to as **emerging adulthood** (Arnett, 2000), which spans from approximately ages 18–25. In western cultures, this time is spent improving one's self through education and experimentation in all realms of life. Today, true adulthood is considered to occur much later than in earlier generations, and it's becoming more normative for people to wait to settle down until well into their thirties. Especially for middle-class emerging adults, the focus is on long-term schooling, self-reflection, and experiential learning. Later entry into family and career roles is becoming normative.

For emerging adults in western cultures, with their focus on individual achievements, the mid-twenties are a period for active exploration, trying on different identities, and putting off long-term commitments. Many youth today forgo adult responsibilities and commitments and prolong self-improvement in the form of education, travel, serial monogamy, and activities whereby they are able to solidify their sense of who they really are and what they might want in a committed partnership (Arnett, 2000).

Instead of the old pattern of marrying young, securing a job one might have for life, buying a house, and having children, today's emerging adults focus on self-development first and take small steps through a diversity of relationships and jobs before they settle down. If intimacy is considered a prerequisite for healthy adult development, it might be argued that single people today often lack this skill, which may cause them to be judged as immature by others, as well forcing them to negotiate a more difficult path to adult maturity (Zajicek & Koski, 2003) in a complex, fast-paced and technologically advanced world. However, not all single adults fail to find intimacy with friends and others. There is a wide range of emerging adult experiences.

Types of emerging adults

To examine some of these normative developmental processes at work, Osgood, Ruth, Eccles, Jacobs, and Barber (2005) followed over 1,000 young people longitudinally to see how they negotiated the complex paths to adulthood. They found six main pathways that people took from ages 18 to 24. *Fast starters*, by age 24, had already embarked upon all the adult roles and were on their way to financial stability. They had children, spouses, and jobs. Other emerging adults (mainly women) had children early but did not engage in work roles; these were *parents without careers*. Some young people were *educated partners*, those who went to college and were in committed partnerships or marriages by age 24. And finally, there were three categories of single people at age 24. The worst adjusted group was called the *slow starters*. These folks showed no signs of successfully negotiating the roles of adulthood. They had minimal education and poor job prospects, usually lived at home, and were unsuccessful in relationships. Many of the slow starters were already parents at age 24, yet they engaged in fairly high rates of illegal behavior during their free time (including drunk driving, stealing, taking drugs, and so on). The second group of singles, most of whom were men, was called *working singles*. They usually had some college or technical training, had begun their careers, and were either in good jobs with room for advancement or already involved in jobs to which they expected to make a long-term commitment. They tended to have good success with dating relationships, but most of them still lived with their parents. By far the largest group of single people, 40% of the sample, was comprised of *educated singles*. These young adults were highly educated by age 24 (most had at least a bachelor's degree and many had graduate degrees or were enrolled in doctoral programs), were in steady dating relationships, had no children, and lived either with their parents or in their own rented apartments.

Young adults in the educated singles group tended to come from homes with at least middle-class status, and their parents were usually highly educated. They spent the most time of any of the groups in fun activities, called "me time," especially partying, dating, and even engaging in illegal activities. They spent little time with their families. These educated singles exhibited most clearly the pathway of emerging adulthood that Arnett outlined. Both educated partners and educated singles had strong self-concepts and were highly engaged in school during their senior years in high school, suggesting they had successfully negotiated Erikson's *identity versus role confusion* stage. They all reported having high expectations for their futures, and they participated widely in skill-development activities like sports and community events. While many of these emerging adults appeared to be quite successful and were enjoying a fairly carefree lifestyle, 58% of the single people reported wanting to be in a relationship. In fact, most of them reported being unsatisfied with their dating and romantic lives if they were not married, indicating that they wanted to follow the traditional normative family life cycle model (Osgood et al., 2005).

This research suggests that there are many pathways to both partnering and remaining single. Some of the single emerging adults were happy on a career path with few obligations, while others wanted to settle down and get married. Their personalities, opportunities, education, social status, and parenting experiences all affected their adjustment at age 24. Let's examine in more detail the diverse types of single people that have been identified in the literature.

THE DIVERSE LIVES OF SINGLE PEOPLE

- Non-normative singles
- Living apart together
- Diverse reasons for singlehood

Early on, Peter Stein (1978) posited that there were distinct types of single people, those who are single by choice and those who are single by circumstance. Stein (1978) delineated four types of single people, who might have different life courses and psychological profiles. Stein's typology categorizes single people along two dimensions, choice and time. Those who choose to be single over the long term are called *voluntary stable singles*. Those who choose to be single temporarily (for example, to "figure out what I really want") are called *voluntary temporary singles*. Voluntary singles can include those who choose never to marry or cohabit, those who choose to divorce and not remarry, those who have been widowed and choose to remain single, and those in certain lifestyles that require singlehood (such as Catholic priests). People who wish they were coupled and see that potentially happening in the future are *involuntary temporary singles*. Finally, those who do not want to be single but do not foresee finding a partner are called *involuntary stable singles*.

Shostak (1987) expanded on these categories by suggesting that there are four different types of involuntary singles: people who are ambivalent about their situation (*ambivalents*), seeing some positive and some negative aspects to their lives; those who want desperately to find a partner but have not (*wishfuls*); those who have accepted their single life as meaningful even if lived without a partner (*resolveds*); and those who live a lifetime of regret over having led a single life (*regretfuls*).

Research suggests that people who make a conscious choice to remain single are happier in life than those who are involuntarily single. These distinctions are important because people who are never married versus divorced or widowed may have different psychological characteristics. Some research has suggested that dating after divorce or a spouse's death increases happiness and life satisfaction (Wang & Amato, 2000). However, some widows, especially those who were happily married for many years, might not attempt to date new people (Carr, 2004). They may also not feel the same social pressure from friends and family to date, as never-married people might (Fitzpatrick, Sharp, & Reifman, 2009).

Never-married people tend to be more willing to date than people who have lost spouses, and they tend to be more open to dating diverse partners. For example, in a sample of over 3,000 40- to 69-year-old middle-aged single people, never-married singles, especially men, were more willing to date someone in general, as well as date a person of another race, religion, and socioeconomic status than themselves (Fitzpatrick et al., 2009). Over half of the never-married singles were willing to reach out and date those different from themselves. Fitzpatrick et al. (2009) suggest two reasons for the never-marrieds' open-mindedness. First, they could be unconventional people since they are willing to forego the traditional societal expectation of marriage. Second, they could have been willing to broaden their pool of eligibles because they had not been able to find a spouse within their own social circles. In this nationally representative heterosexual sample, 31% were never-married, 48% divorced, 13% widowed, and 7% separated. With one-third of a national sample like this having never been married, it becomes even clearer that much more research is needed to understand the trends that accompany different types of singlehood. For example, without asking never-marrieds if they were actively searching for a mate or were voluntarily single, it's difficult to understand the results found in such descriptive research.

In a study that examined whether a sample of gay men were single by choice or by circumstance, Hostetler (2009) found that 50% of gay men in the sample described themselves as "single." Although over half of that group said they were single *by choice* on general questionnaires, upon qualitative interviews of the men, Hostetler found that most of them actually wished to find intimate partnerships. They described their single status as temporary. They viewed their singlehood as a time to reflect on what they really wanted in a relationship, a time to recover from previous hurts, to get their priorities straight, and so on. Only 20% of the single sample clearly wanted to remain single. These findings show that "single by choice" may be rare in gay men and heterosexuals alike. In fact, not one participant in the gay male sample spontaneously described his identity as "single by choice" or "lifelong single." Each participant who said he was single by choice, upon closer examination actually talked about a concrete decision he made to be single *temporarily*. And none of the men described shunning heterosexual norms of coupledom as a reason for their being single "by choice." Therefore, Hostetler (2009) describes voluntary singlehood as more of a *process* than an outcome of adult development. Instead of being a source of identity achievement, it might be more of a coping mechanism for these men to deal with the relationship circumstances encountered in their lives. It is likely that some individuals may view their singlehood as a source of identity achievement and as a key part of their sense of self, while others identify more with other aspects of their lived experience (such as race, gender, sexual orientation, or religion).

When does a person actually determine that he or she is *voluntarily single*? When do you think someone actually "becomes" single? Most of us are single at 18. What if someone is unmarried at 25? Do you think of that person as "single" or "never-married?" How would your viewpoint change if the person were 40 or 60? The point is that being single is normative for most adults at some point in their lives. In western cultures, we don't expect people to get married at 18 anymore. Most of us consider it completely "normal" that a 25-year-old is unmarried, especially if that person is in college or graduate school. But once a person starts inching towards 30, we may start feeling like they need to settle down. Especially at 35, and even more so for women, we think, "Hey, isn't it about time you tied the knot and had a couple of kids?"

Because men can have children throughout their lives, there is more pressure on women to get married during their key childbearing years, between 25 and 40 (Shostak, 1987). Kaiser and Kashy (2005) argue that because the average age of marriage in the U.S. is 25.3 for women and 27.1 for men, with a standard deviation of about five years, 95% of people who marry do so between the ages of 16 and 36. Thus, those who are not yet married by age 36 are considered "non-normative" singles.

Non-normative singles

Non-normative singles, people who are still single after the age of 35, face more discrimination and negative judgments than those who are single but are still within the normative age range for committed partnerships and marriage. These younger people are considered to be temporarily single and still "marriageable." Kaiser and Kashy (2005) argue that non-normative singles threaten traditional ideologies about the importance of pair bonding and of marriage in particular. They posit that stigmatizing non-normative single individuals helps people feel secure that their marriage and family ideologies are "right," that the single person is somehow defective, and that being a lifelong single could not happen to them. These authors suggest that seeing non-normative singles being happy and well-adjusted is even more threatening because it questions the long-held belief that people can only be truly happy if they are romantically committed.

But what about the single person him- or herself? When does he or she consider singlehood a source of personal identity? Davies (2003) describes this discovery as a developmental process, like a formal transition period during which people move from viewing themselves as "not yet married" to "single by choice." Davies describes this transition period as a change in personal mental representations, or conceptions of one's self. This change in thought processes takes many years, but eventually, a person realizes that he or she is not going to follow the traditional path of marriage and so begins to identify more and more with being a single person (Davies, 2003). Once this cognitive shift occurs, people may actually make disparaging remarks about married life and disparage that lifestyle in favor of a single life (Shostak, 1987). They may argue that marriage is no longer necessary for a happy or fulfilling lifestyle and that parenting outside of the context of marriage is not only acceptable but may be more desirable. Thus, they embrace non-normative singlehood.

FIGURE 8.2 What type of single do you think this woman is?
Cartoon © J.C. Duffy/The New Yorker Collection/www.cartoonbank.com

"There's a twenty in it for you if you just keep moving."

However, it's important to recognize that even for non-normative singles, singlehood is just one of many identities a person can develop, and for various people, it may not even be a salient source of their self-concept (Kaiser & Kashy, 2005). For example, a single Russian woman may have strong gender and ethnic identities that comprise the core of who she is. If people judge her negatively for not being married, she may not perceive their unfair treatment as stemming from her singlehood, but may think about whether they are perhaps sexist or ethnically prejudiced. Thus, singlehood is something that can only truly be defined by the person living that lifestyle. And some lifestyles are more difficult to put a label on than others. These findings illustrate the significant impact of intersectional identities on our life choices and how we deal with personal circumstances (Major, Quinton, & McCoy, 2002).

Living apart together

Another growing trend in the realm of singlehood is people who are living apart together (LAT). LATs are people who are technically single because they live alone, yet they are in committed relationships (Levin, 2004). People who have gone through messy divorces, are separated, or are dating steadily might be in a LAT situation. People may even be married to each other but move into separate houses due to job relocation or child custody issues, to reduce the intensity of conflicts, to care for elderly parents, and so on. For example, when I was on sabbatical last year, I rented my home out to a man and his wife who had a larger home in a neighboring city. The couple needed some "breathing room," as they had been having marital conflicts and were considering separating. However, they did not want to disrupt their children's lives or schedules. Instead of having the children move from one home to another, each parent spent three days per week at my house while the other parent was at the larger home with the children, where they could continue their routines as usual. Then they would switch. They would be considered LATs until they actually divorced.

LATs define themselves as a couple and others see them as couples, yet they live in separate homes (Levin, 2004). By definition, to be called a LAT, the relationship must be more serious than a simple dating relationship. It is estimated that about 14% of committed couples are LATs, but the Census Bureau and other types of statistical data gathering groups would count them as singles. Many LATs hope to live with their partners someday. Those who don't are usually those who have been divorced and those who are older and enjoy their space and independence. Diversity is the norm within groups labeled as "single" so it's necessary to think about the processes underlying people's lives in families and not just focus on the structure of the household.

Diverse reasons for singlehood

The reasons for being single are as diverse as the people living a single lifestyle. People tend to report three main reasons for remaining single: circumstances never arose which allowed them to marry; they made a personal choice not to marry; or there is something wrong with them that they were unsuitable for marriage (for example, "I'm too selfish," or "I am too high-maintenance") (Frazier, Arikian, Benson, Losoff, & Maurer, 1996; Lewis & Moon, 1997). Similarly, Hostetler (2009) found seven main reasons people may give for being single in adulthood:

- personal past—experiences in childhood or adolescence drove the decision, such as events with parents like divorce, and so on
- collective past—historical events and generational issues, such as that people today are too career-oriented
- learning from experience—not wanting to be hurt or to date "losers" anymore
- particular tastes—sexual or relationship preferences that turn others off, or that most people don't enjoy
- still searching—actively looking but haven't met the right person yet

- loner—beliefs such as "I'm not good at relationships," or "I'm meant to be alone"
- aloner—being single so long that they're stuck in their ways or wouldn't know how to develop a relationship.

How do you think people develop each viewpoint? Some research suggests that attitudes toward being single are adopted through interactions with one's own parents. For example, Cunningham and Thornton (2006) found that young adults adopted the same attitudes as their parents regarding cohabitation and singlehood if their parents were in stable, high-quality marriages. Seeing healthy committed relationships led adult children to identify with and respect parents' attitudes about the acceptability or non-acceptability of singlehood.

Many single people aren't quite certain why they are single or how they feel about it. There may be quite a bit of ambivalence about their relationship status. Lewis and Moon (1997) found that single women in particular often have a sense of ambivalence about their singlehood. They feel a sense of grief and loss for what could have been, while also feeling overall contentment with their lives. They know that people look down on them for not marrying, yet they feel happy most of the time. Most single people, even if they are content with their lives, report that the bias and discrimination they face from society can be unbearable at times.

MACROSYSTEM FORCES AGAINST SINGLEHOOD

> An example from Mormon culture
>
> Examples from Africa
>
> Examples from the United States

So far, we have discussed most of the systems of the bioecological model and how they relate to being single. At the individual level, the stress of experiencing singlism and discrimination can begin to wear on a person's mental health and happiness. In the microsystem, individual family members can be supportive of the single lifestyle and can avoid pressuring the single person to settle down, which can enhance the well-being of the single person. Mesosystem influences can also affect the adjustment of single people. For example, if a single woman's parents treat her sibling who has a husband and children preferentially, those mesosystem interactions between members of the microsystem can make the single person feel like a failure or a second-class citizen. Exosystem forces such as public policies that discriminate against single people, in the form of reduced benefits at work or rejected applications at adoption agencies, can also impact single-person families. Finally, the macrosystem, larger cultural values and practices, can impact a single person's life in profound ways. This section will explore a few examples of how macrosystem cultural expectations can influence a single person's adjustment. It's important to understand how macrosystem forces impact the experiences of single people so that we can empathize with and perhaps help the singles in our own families.

An example from Mormon culture

Even within western cultures, which are more accepting of singlehood in general than are developing nations, there is much diversity regarding the acceptability of singlehood. For example, in a study of single young adults between 25 and 30 in the Mormon community (Latter Day Saint culture, or LDS) in the U.S., marriage is expected of all parishioners. The leaders of the church feel that marriage is sanctioned and expected for all people by God. They feel that God's plan for people's happiness on earth must include heterosexual marriage. In fact, they believe that earthly marriage is required to reach eternal life (Darrington et al., 2005). Most of the young adults in this study saw their singlehood as temporary. They all expected to be married, and felt pressure, especially from church members, to get married. They often felt like something was wrong with them if they were over 25 and still single. Several men said that if they returned from their missions and had no plans to marry, they felt like failures.

Interestingly, many of them reported that church doctrine itself encouraged them to mature first, be patient, and believe that God would provide them with the right partner. However, they heard a different message from church members, one of early marriage and ostracism of those who were in their twenties and not yet married or engaged. Many of the participants also discussed that their parents did not pressure them to marry early, but wanted them to take their time to find the right person to prevent potential divorce later on. Several participants had divorced parents, which was an incentive for them to pray, meditate on their lives, and grow as individuals so that they would find a well-suited mate. This fits well with Erikson's idea of committing to an identity before becoming intimate with others. Many of these young people felt that the church would accept them as real adults if they got married, that they would receive respect and gain in status. Marriage would make them bona fide adults in the eyes of their communities and their God. This study provides further evidence that people exist within dynamic contexts and their families, cultures, and religious contexts shape their sense of themselves and their ideologies about relationships. Issues of gender, race, religion, and socioeconomic status certainly shape the experiences of single people all around the world. Let's look at examples of how this plays out in Africa.

Examples from Africa

Most developing nations adhere to strict gender role expectations and a sexual double standard. Many cultures expect men to be sexually promiscuous and expect women to be virgins at marriage. Men are allowed to participate in polygamous marriages. Unfortunately, these practices can be particularly dangerous in the modern developing world where AIDS has decimated the populations of many countries, especially those in Africa. Marston et al. (2009) report that the longer the time span from first sexual intercourse to marriage (that is, the longer a person is single), the more sexual partners a person is likely to have, and the higher the statistical risk for HIV infection and subsequent AIDS diagnosis. These authors report that later age of marriage in many African nations has been related to the spread of HIV. Thus, single people are at greater risk for AIDS than those who marry early, especially since sexual education is rare and access to safer sex aids such as condoms and hygienic sexual environments are rare. Furthermore, other singles like widows, divorced people, and separated people also have higher HIV rates in African nations (Marston et al., 2009). AIDS is even a risk for older single people. For example, 51% of widows and 61% of widowers in one area of Zimbabwe had HIV in 2003 (Lopman et al., 2003). Heterosexual risk for AIDS increases with marital infidelity and polygamy. In fact, females outnumber males in new cases of AIDS in Africa.

Keep in mind, however, that within any region, there is wide variation in experiences. For example, in two African nations, we see substantial differences. In Umkhanyakude, South Africa, half of the middle-aged men and women are unmarried, while only 15% are unmarried in Kisesa, Tanzania. Also, the percentage of people who are widowed, divorced, or separated varies widely, with 5% in Karonga, Malawi, experiencing these forms of singlehood, but up to 41% in Rakai, Uganda doing so (Marston et al., 2009).

Women's rights in African nations

Another important macrosystem influence that is changing the lives of single people in Africa is the ideology of gender equality. As women's rights issues come to the forefront around the world, we see that even in poor and developing nations, women are beginning to become more independent, pushing back against centuries of oppression. For example, in the African country of Lesotho, many single rural women are beginning to move to the urban capital, Maseru, and open small businesses of their own. They are also being employed in new manufacturing plants where they can earn enough money to rent an apartment or buy a piece of land (Wright, 1999). These new opportunities allow women to become economically independent, not having to rely on men. Their new power to remain single female heads of their own households is pushing the boundaries of gender hierarchies. However, they have a long way to go, as they are still subject to the oppression of their employers and are still at great risk of sexual harassment and even rape as they travel alone.

The right to remain single and in control of your own destiny is increasingly being demanded by women all around the world. They seek education about how to better their lives. For example, in one survey in Nigeria, only 16.9% of unmarried women knew the correct definition of *emergency contraception*, and those who wanted to use it found that it was not available. They said that health workers had negative attitudes toward single women using such methods, often for religious reasons, and did not inform them about their use (Obi & Ozumba, 2008). Women in developing nations need access to safe and effective contraception, especially the use of condoms, as well as proper information about their use, because they are at high risk for unwanted pregnancy, STI/HIV infection, and unsafe abortion practices (Obi & Ozumba, 2008). And single women need empowerment to maintain control over their own health, wealth, and happiness. This is true in both developing and industrialized nations.

Examples from the United States

In industrialized nations there is still quite a bit of legal discrimination against single people. In fact, the Federal Equal Employment Opportunity Act has no prohibitions against discrimination towards the unmarried. Only 21 states have laws on the books prohibiting employers from discriminating against people on the basis of their marital status. You may think this is a non-issue, but discrimination against single people is a very real phenomenon, both legally, and interpersonally. Economic policies in the United States often make marriage a poor choice for people, yet at the same time, other policies penalize them for being single. For example, poor people lose welfare benefits if they marry, even if their combined income is still below the poverty line (Martin, 1996). This means poor people often choose not to marry and stay single instead. In one case study, a young poor single mother eschewed marriage because she didn't want to end up divorced a few years down the road. The men in her neighborhood had little education and poor earning potential. With a limited pool of eligibles and no opportunities for career advancement herself, Jennifer chose to gain a sense of accomplishment through having children and raising them well, all on her own (Edin & Kefalas, 2005). For those living in poverty, there are often few incentives to marry so singlehood becomes normative.

Even for middle-class people, there are some penalties that make marriage unappealing. For instance, tax deductions and earned income tax credits are lower for couples than for two single people. Working-class people with college-aged children may be able to get more financial aid for their children to attend college if they remain unmarried or divorced, for if they remarry, the stepparents' income is factored into financial aid decisions and the child may qualify for less aid. For older people, social security earnings have limits on them, and there are capital gains exclusions on home sales, as well as Medicaid eligibility limitations. In fact, some seniors get divorced just to avoid losing their financial benefits. The wealthy must pay higher income taxes as a couple than as two singles. It's almost never a good idea for rich single people to marry, in terms of financial benefits. American tax laws mainly benefit couples who marry into a SNAF where one person earns the large majority of the income (Martin, 1996).

In other situations, there are biases against single people. For example, unmarried people are often charged more for insurance because they are considered more "risky" or unstable (DePaulo, 2006). Insurance companies may give a policy discount to married people seeking auto and home insurance, but single people, roommates, or cohabiting couples may not be allowed the same discount. Also, the U.S. Federal Government charges 50% in estate taxes when a wealthy single person dies, but if a person leaves a spouse behind, no taxes are imposed. Likewise, if one transfers real estate or vehicle ownership to a spouse, there are no fees, but if a single person transfers a title to a friend, roommate (or domestic partner in many cases), a transfer tax is levied. Inheritance taxes and social security benefits also put single people at a disadvantage. Single men are paid less than married men, even if they have the same work experience (DePaulo, 2006). Travel deals and cruise ships often penalize people traveling alone by incurring "singles supplements" or making packages the same price for singles and doubles.

Furthermore, millions of young adults lack health insurance in the United States because insurers drop them from their parents' policies when they turn 19 unless they are in college. This means that

TABLE 8.1 State laws prohibiting discrimination based on marital status.
Source: www.unmarriedamerica.org/ms-statutes.htm

State	Employment	Housing	Insurance	Credit	Other
Alabama	no	no	no	no	
Alaska	yes	yes	no	yes	
Arizona	no	no	mortgage only	no	violence shelters
Arkansas	no	no	no	yes	
California	yes	yes	some lines	yes	
Colorado	no	yes	no	yes	
Connecticut	yes	yes	no	yes	
Delaware	yes	yes	no	no	
Florida	yes	no	no	yes	club membership
Georgia	no	no	no	no	
Hawaii	yes	yes	no	yes	
Idaho	no	no	no	no	
Illinois	yes	yes	no	yes	
Indiana	teachers only	no	no	no	
Iowa	no	no	no	no	
Kansas	no	no	yes	no	
Kentucky	no	no	no	no	
Louisiana	no	no	no	yes	
Maine	no	no	no	yes	
Maryland	yes	yes	no	yes	
Massachusetts	no	yes	no	no	
Michigan	yes	yes	no	yes	
Minnesota	yes	yes	no	yes	
Mississippi	no	no	no	no	
Missouri	no	no	yes	yes	
Montana	yes	yes	group plans	yes	
Nebraska	yes	yes	no	no	
Nevada	no	no	no	yes	
New Hampshire	yes	yes	some lines	no	
New Jersey	yes	yes	no	yes	
New Mexico	no	no	no	no	
New York	yes	yes	no	yes	

TABLE 8.1 (cont'd)

State	Employment	Housing	Insurance	Credit	Other
North Carolina	no	no	no	yes	
North Dakota	yes	yes	no	yes	
Ohio	no	no	no	yes	
Oklahoma	no	no	no	yes	
Oregon	yes	yes	no	no	
Pennsylvania	no	no	yes	no	
Rhode Island	no	yes	no	yes	
South Carolina	no	no	no	no	
South Dakota	no	no	no	no	
Tennessee	no	no	no	yes	
Texas	no	no	no	no	
Utah	no	no	no	no	
Vermont	no	yes	no	yes	
Virginia	yes	yes	yes	yes	
Washington	yes	yes	some	no	
West Virginia	no	no	no	no	
Wisconsin	yes	yes	no	yes	
Wyoming	no	no	no	no	
Total states with protections	20 yes, 1 teachers only	23 yes	4 yes, 5 some lines	27 yes	2 some areas

if a person is not married and not a college student, health care coverage will likely be elusive. Due to the increasing recognition of the stage of *emerging adulthood*, the health insurance reform passed in 2010 now covers single adult children until age 25 or 26, since people are marrying later and are financially dependent on parents for longer than in previous generations.

Some areas are recognizing the need for rights protection for unmarried people. For example, the Florida Supreme Court expanded the rights of unmarried men who believe their ex-partners have borne their children. These men must now be notified before the child's mother can put the baby up for adoption. Fathers are now given more time to register with the Putative Father Registry so that their parental rights are not terminated prematurely. Most unmarried men are unaware of this registry but 30 states have it (New Hampshire Research Division of the Office of Legislative Services, 2010). These registries allow men to object to their children being put up for adoption without their knowledge or consent, whereas previous policies gave unmarried fathers virtually no rights to their children. To see if your state has laws protecting single people against discrimination, see Table 8.1.

Even zoning laws contain surprisingly discriminatory policies against singles. For example, if a person lives in a "single family" zone in a neighborhood, he or she can have many family members living in a house within that zone, but several unrelated roommates may not be allowed to live in that same house (U.S. Dept. of Justice, Fair Housing Act, 1990). Recall also that the Defense of Marriage

Act of 1996 (DOMA) expressly disallows specific rights for same-sex couples who cannot legally marry. However, in Canada, the Supreme Court ruled that marital status discrimination is unlawful. Canadian federal law recognizes same-sex marriages and there are many legal protections for the unmarried as well (Department of Justice, Canada, 2009).

Fighting for singles' rights in the U.S.

Increasingly, single people are fighting for recognition and society is beginning to take notice. For instance, in many workplaces, the term "family leave" is being replaced with "paid time off" so that all employees, single and coupled, get the same benefits. This helps solve the problem where singles currently cannot use Family and Medical Leave Act benefits to care for unrelated friends, roommates, boyfriends or girlfriends, and so on.

Other issues that arise in the workplace include single people being asked to work more hours if employees with families need time off. Many singles feel that their bosses think they have no life outside of work and can always fill in since they don't have family responsibilities. Also, employers and researchers alike fail to recognize the role strain even single people can feel when trying to balance personal and professional duties (Casper, Weltman, & Kwesiga, 2007). They may have elderly parents to care for, animals who are sick, personal responsibilities such as traffic court or physical therapy, or family events taking place with their family of origin. Single people face many of the same challenges as couples, but couples have another person living with them who can sometimes reduce that burden. It's important, then, for co-workers and employers to recognize those areas of the workplace that may be biased against singles. Casper et al. (2007) delineate several criteria that would ensure singles' rights are respected by creating singles-friendly workplace:

- social inclusion—workplace social events have activities that can involve both families and single people
- equal work opportunities—there is equal opportunity for interesting assignments and promotions for single and coupled people

FIGURE 8.3 What work policies can make a single person happier and more committed to the job? Photo © Robert Daly/Alamy.

- equal access to benefits—all employees receive the same compensation regardless of marital status, such as that described for the Family and Medical Leave Act. For example, if a company provides child care vouchers for employees with children, a single person might be given vouchers of equal value for a gym membership or other perks like contributions to their retirement fund

- equal respect for non-work life—not assuming single people have fewer responsibilities at home

- equal expectations—for hours worked, shifts worked, and holidays and personal days given. For example, just because someone is single does not mean he or she should be assigned all of the graveyard shifts.

Casper et al. (2007) found that if single people perceived their workplace to be singles-friendly, they reported less intention to leave that job and were more committed to the company.

It should be apparent by now that contextual forces can make a single person's life happier or more stressful. Most people assume that single people are less happy, less fulfilled, and less well-adjusted than partnered, especially married, people. What does the research show?

THE PSYCHOLOGICAL AND PHYSICAL HEALTH OF SINGLE PEOPLE

Singles strain

Emotional attachments

As discussed in previous chapters, scores of research studies suggest that married people enjoy both enhanced physical and mental health compared to unmarried people (Umberson, Wortman, & Kessler, 1992). For example, Pedersen and Blekasaune (2003) found that Norwegians were more sexually satisfied the more committed their relationships were, with married couples being most satisfied, followed consecutively by cohabiting people and people in steady dating relationships; single people were the least satisfied. And Warehime and Bass (2008) found that the single men in their sample were the least sexually satisfied compared to married men and both married and single women. Also, in terms of general relationship satisfaction, ever-married individuals (those who were once married but are now single) experienced a noticeable dip in their life satisfaction after they became single. Studies have also shown that partnered gay men and lesbians are more psychologically stable and satisfied with their lives than single gay and lesbian people (Wayment & Peplau, 1995). Moreover, Ward (1981) showed that when never-married people retire, they lose a key source of their identity and social support, the workplace. Thus, they are unhappy and less excited about retirement than married people are.

These studies suggest that marriage is beneficial because it conveys upon its participants well-being, intimacy, and social support. Meanwhile, those without such benefits may struggle with poor mental health and physical decline. For example, in a recent study of an entire birth cohort born in 1946 in England, Scotland, and Wales, physical function was measured at age 53 (Guralnik, Butterworth, Patel, Mishra, & Kuh, 2009). The authors found that never-married men and married childless men had poorer physical health than married men with children. More of the never-married men (28%) reported being forced to take medical retirement from working, compared to only 5% of men who were married, with or without children. No health differences were found in women based on marital status, suggesting that there may be gender differences that need examining in future research on single people. These results are fairly typical of those found across numerous studies, suggesting that marriage protects people from poor health, disability, and even death.

To look at the above findings from a different angle, some theorists suggest that *social selection* is at work: people who are unhealthy, undesirable, or have personality or mental health problems are less likely to marry rather than marriage causing positive health benefits. According to this theory, the causal arrow is assumed to go in the opposite direction than what was implied above, with personal characteristics causing marriage instead of marriage causing poor personal adjustment. However, most of the research is correlational in nature and does not distinguish between the different types of singles so it is difficult to know whether singlehood is a true disadvantage for people or not (Pudrovska, Schieman, & Carr, 2006). While much of the research on single people suggests they are at risk for poor mental health, loneliness, depression, and early death, that research usually fails to distinguish between never-married people, divorced people, widowed people, and those who choose to be single versus involuntary single people. Moreover, even when differences like the ones described above are found for never-married versus married groups, these differences are usually quite small in magnitude and often are over-stated in research (DePaulo & Morris, 2005).

Singlism in society ensures that unmarried women continue to be at a disadvantage both economically and socially compared to married women (Chasteen, 1994). Thus, some of the psychological and physical health findings can be explained by discrimination or stress, and not by the fact that a person is single or not. Some newer research even calls the health benefits of marriage for men into question, and suggests that single men today are just as healthy as married men (Liu, 2009). Liu suggests that in younger cohorts, men are more likely to be emotionally open and to form close intimate relationships with a circle of friends and family, who serve as social support for them, unlike in previous generations when men only had their wives to confide in. She suggests that with the high levels of divorce today, staying single may actually be the less mentally stressful avenue for people to take. Also, if single people have strong emotional ties to their families and friendship networks, they may be just as mentally healthy and satisfied with their lives as coupled people (Adelman & Bankoff, 1990). Indeed, voluntary gay male singles have been shown to have high socioeconomic status, large supportive social networks, and fewer worries about old age, and they feel generally satisfied with their lives (Hostetler, 2009).

In a study on multiethnic seniors, Choi (1999) examined where single people end up living later in life. She stated that previous research had shown Hispanic and African American elders are less likely to live independently of their families than European American elders, regardless of their health or income. However, in her sample of several hundred seniors, she found that 61% of black seniors and 30% of Hispanic seniors lived by themselves. The African American seniors were the most likely to continue to work. One third of both Hispanic and African American single seniors lived as household heads, with their children, grandchildren, or both living with them. Puerto Rican elderly singles were more likely to live alone than Cubans were. For all groups, poor health and older age were related to living in someone else's home. This study indicates that many single seniors of all ethnic backgrounds can and do live long and healthy lives independently and that they even serve as supports for younger family members. They are not incapacitated, dysfunctional, or socially isolated.

Thus, it's difficult to disentangle whether being single, per se, has an effect on mental and physical health or whether forces in the microsystem, exosystem, and macrosystem make single people feel a sense of resilience versus strain in their lives.

Singles strain

Singles strain
A process whereby people may feel stressed over stigmatization, a future old age that may be more difficult, or an isolated daily life.

In an attempt to get a closer look at stress in the lives of single people, Pudrovska et al. (2006) describe a concept called **singles strain**, whereby people may feel stressed over discrimination they face for being single, as well as fearing a less active social life, lack of intimacy with a romantic partner, a future old age that may be more difficult, a lack of caretakers available when one needs help, and an isolated daily life. Some groups may experience more singles strain than others. For example, people who are divorced and people who were never-married usually have some personal choice and agency involved in their single status. Thus, they might be expected to feel less singles strain than those who are widowed, because the death of a spouse is uncontrollable and often unexpected.

Moreover, those who have spent their whole lives as singles have figured out many coping strategies for living alone. They have learned over a lifetime how to be happy and productive and build their social networks. Never-married adults may not find living the single life to be stressful while divorced and widowed people may experience "desolation" (Gubrium, 1974), an increase in social isolation after they lose their partner. People who are divorced or widowed may have experienced most of their social intimacies with their spouse and so when they are separated through divorce or death they may have a radical lifestyle readjustment phase and may feel lonely, depressed, or stressed thereafter. In fact, it may be *more* detrimental to one's mental health to lose what he or she once had than to have never had it at all.

In a study attempting to tease apart some of these issues, Pudrovska et al. (2006) surveyed several hundred older people and found that, indeed, the never-married had higher levels of health, education, and economic security than those people who had been married previously but were now single. The never-married, as a group, experienced less singles strain. However, they did report the lowest levels of social support available to them. Women and men reported similar levels of singles strain as a whole, but never-married women felt more singles strain than never-married men. This may be because these women came of age in a cohort that expected women to marry. The authors suggest never-married women's singles strain may be less prevalent in younger women in today's cohorts. In their study, white widows and widowers felt more singles strain than African Americans who had been widowed. Previous research has shown that African American men and women share household labor more equally and so perhaps when they divorce or their spouse dies, it's easier for both black men and women to adjust to a life alone where they do all the tasks needed. And in general, black women felt less singles strain than white women did. The authors suggest that living non-marital lifestyles is much more common and normative among African American women, who typically have extended social support networks and have always worked to support themselves financially. Interestingly, the singles strain of the divorced and never-married black men did not differ from their white counterparts.

Other research finds that white professional women who have never been married report that they love their independence and their ability to do what they want. While they feel lonely, especially if they have not built a social support network, overall they report feeling very satisfied with their single lifestyles. Interestingly, older white professional women also feel more singles strain than older black professional women (Baumbusch, 2004). In another study on the effects of singles strain, unmarried women aged 40–75 reported being less likely to seek medical attention or make appointments for regular cancer screening than married women, as they felt the medical forms and medical personnel were biased against single women. For example, the forms provide only one space for "spouse's name," and no option to mark that they didn't have a partner, that they cohabited, or that they were in a same-sex relationship. While some single women felt they were not at risk for cancer if they were not sexually active with men, which is erroneous, many others felt marginalized and misunderstood by medical professionals who assumed they were partnered, if not married (Clark, Bonacore, Wright, Armstrong, & Rakowski, 2004). This study suggests that physical health may be in jeopardy as single people get older, especially if they live alone or do not have other social ties to people who encourage them to take care of their health.

Adelman and Bankoff (1990) examined a sample of never-married, highly educated people in their thirties. These people reported fears of growing old alone, coming to regret never having had children, and not being financially secure. Females feared not being financially secure in old age much more than males did. Women also reported being afraid they would have no one to care for them as they aged. Those singles with the highest self-esteem, largest social networks, and best coping abilities evidenced the lowest levels of future concerns. Those who were shy and less open had the most fears about the future. Those who felt the most singles strain and who felt stigmatized for being single had high levels of concern about aging. Thus, social support, a strong sense of identity, an outgoing personality, and good coping skills are protective factors against feelings of single strain for older single people.

FIGURE 8.4 Which personal and contextual factors can help singles resist singles strain and remain mentally and physically healthy as they get older?
Photo © Image Source/Getty Images.

To see an example of one middle-aged woman who feels very satisfied with her single lifestyle, see the *Focus on My Family* box.

Emotional attachments

Single people are most satisfied and less fearful when they have strong social ties. These people have often experienced secure attachments to their families of origin (Granqvist & Hagekull, 2000). Recall that attachment quality in our family of origin sets the template for the development of internal working models about relationships as well as our views of ourselves. When we have a secure base in our original microsystem (like caring parents and involved siblings), we feel more confident living alone and being able to find fulfillment with a single lifestyle (Grandqvist & Hagekull, 2000). We know that we have emotional supports to fall back on when we need them, even if we aren't involved in romantic relationships.

Interestingly, research has suggested that those who are not involved in romantic relationships, as well as those who have lost a relationship through break-up, divorce, or death, tend to turn to religion to fill emotional needs (Byrne & Carr, 2005). Therefore, single people might be expected to have higher levels of religiosity than coupled people do. Faith communities may be considered alternative "families" for those living alone. Grandqvist and Hagekull (2000) argue that God can even serve as an alternative emotional attachment figure for people without committed partnerships. These authors examined a group of Swedish college students (Sweden is a highly secular society in general). They used a measure called the Emotionally Based Religiosity Scale, which examines whether people use God and religion to help them regulate their emotions and enhance a sense of attachment security. The measure assesses whether God can serve as a secure base for people in times of emotional pain or need. These authors found that attachment security was related to better perceived relationships with God. Also, attachment security was related to using God for emotional support. Interestingly, they found that single students had higher levels of religious activity (such as attending church services), increased religiosity, and closer perceived emotional attachments to God than did married students. While these results are preliminary and by no means conclusive, it is interesting to think about the roles that our internal working models play in both the development of our marital status and the connections we make to our spiritual lives.

FOCUS ON MY FAMILY

Leslie and Scirocco

I was barely 20 years old when I got married, and by 29 I was going through a divorce. At first I was certain I would eventually remarry. I relished my newfound freedom but couldn't really imagine being "alone" for the rest of my life. I figured that after a year of autonomy (maybe two or three) I would begin dating, looking for that person who would make my life complete. As time went by, however, I started to entertain the possibility that I might *not* remarry. And now, at age 40, I expect to remain single; I don't know the future, but I can't really imagine having my life intimately melded with someone else's for eternity.

That isn't to say that I don't have deep relationships. Being single allows me to engage in friendships in a way that I believe is sometimes more difficult for married people. Couples frequently approach social situations in tandem—attending events together, consulting one another before accepting invitations, and so on. A single person can spontaneously accept invitations without coordinating schedules with anyone else, can stay late if the conversation is engaging, and can step in to help a friend in need after consulting only one calendar.

I am fortunate to have many good friends, both single and married, who care deeply for me and who invite me to be part of their lives. These same friends, thinking of my happiness, sometimes try to match me up with their single friends and colleagues. Their intentions are good, but these friends struggle to understand that I really *like* being single—I'm not looking for a partner. I've learned to be very direct about my preferences, thus avoiding most awkward situations.

The freedom to live my life as I choose is what I most value about singlehood. But that freedom is sometimes misunderstood to mean that I am less busy or that I have more free time than others do—after all, I don't have a family to take care of. It is sometimes assumed that when there are extra tasks to be done I will be able to make up the difference for those who have family obligations. While I usually can "make it work" more easily than can someone with children and a spouse, I sometimes resent the assumption that I will.

People ask if I get lonely. Occasionally, yes, but doesn't everyone? Sure, there are times when I wish someone were around so I could share a few lines from a book, an interesting thought, a beautiful vista. But there are even more times when I am thankful for the way my life is. My dog, Scirocco, has been my buffer against those lonely moments for nearly eight years. He can't understand most of what I say, but he provides an ongoing emotional connectedness that is fulfilling, without many of the strings that come with human coupling and compromise. Single by choice is not the norm, but I am glad to live in a time and place where it is a real, viable option.

Leslie and her dog, Scirocco.
Photo reproduced by permission.

SINGLE THROUGH COMMITMENT TO GOD

- Priests, monks, and nuns: a historic family necessity
- Contemporary faith-based single lifestyles
- An example from Thai Buddhist *maechii*

One kind of single person that may not immediately pop into your head when you hear the word "single" is a clergy member. Priests, monks, and nuns are people who choose to remain single in the service of their religious or spiritual practices. Some interesting research has been conducted on both the historical and contemporary lives of these singles.

Priests, monks, and nuns: a historic family necessity

In cultures where families live subsistence lives, where mere survival is a challenge, having too many children can be detrimental. Therefore, these cultures often develop mating and reproduction strategies that ensure survival of the most people in their group. Evolutionary Theory usually posits that we want to replicate our genes as much as possible by having many of our own biological children. However, in some cases, a group is more likely to survive in the gene pool if they don't reproduce and leave the childbearing to one family member or a small group of kin.

Crook and Osmaston (1994) describe the harsh life of people living in some high elevation rural villages in the Himalayas. Each family or group may have a small piece of land that must be retained by that family in order for future generations to survive on its agricultural crops. Over-population would decimate these small villages and farms, so they tend to be involved in polyandrous marriages, where several brothers marry one woman, thus, cutting down on the number of potential births. If the family has too many children, surplus sons are often sent to monasteries to become monks.

In their study of these small villages, Crook and Osmaston (1994) found that between 40% and 65% of brothers became monks rather than co-husbands. Similar trends were found in Nepal, Italy, Austria, and Portugal, where virtually every family once had a family member who was a priest, nun, or housekeeper/groundskeeper for monasteries and convents (Deady, Smith, Kent, & Dunbar, 2006). Reproductive strategies in these cultures include the oldest brother being married, the middle brother being a monk, and the younger brothers being married but of lower social status so they typically have fewer children. The goal of these strategies is replacement of the population that dies but not the prolific reproduction as you might find in larger rural areas where food is plentiful. These families also benefit because monk brothers bring their families a level of prestige in the community while also earning money that is sent home to benefit everyone. Female children who become nuns also take care of the elderly and help their brothers' families. Therefore, the celibate lifestyle in these communities allows for the survival of the family's gene pool without each member reproducing.

In sixteenth-century Portugal, only the eldest son inherited land, leaving most men without the resources to marry. Many of these poor men were sent to join the military. The single women remaining—those who did not marry the male heirs—were often sent to convents to become nuns. Their celibate lifestyle ensured their families' livelihood, and if a suitor of equal means became available, they were allowed to leave the convent and marry (Boone, 1988).

Similarly, in nineteenth-century Portuguese families, especially in the northern regions of Minho, land was passed down to only one son, who would marry. Non-heirs would have few prospects to marry and would either emigrate to other countries, thus relieving the burden on their families to support them, or join the Catholic priesthood (Livi-Bacci, 1971).

In a study of the families of Catholic priests in Ireland born at the turn of the twentieth century, Deady et al. (2006) found that the huge increase in the rolls of the priesthood at that time was significantly related to agricultural wealth. Families with large land holdings and one son who could inherit them utilized unmarried daughters to help out on the farm and sent unmarried sons to the priesthood. Unless unmarried sons planned to emigrate, without land holdings they had virtually no chances of securing a bride and so the priesthood offered them many opportunities. Deady et al. (2006, p. 402) conclude that "institutionalized celibacy has provided a safety valve for population pressures … in agricultural societies." Note how bioecological forces all interact with each other in these communities to create an unpartnered lifestyle for many family members.

Contemporary faith-based single lifestyles

While oaths of celibacy may seem undesirable (or impossible to keep) for many of us, as you have seen, they have actually been fairly common throughout history. However, it is true that the number of applications for the priesthood and religious orders has been steadily declining over time in western nations. Today people are not usually placed by their families into the priesthood, but apply of their own accord. With the recent scandals regarding sexual abuse of children in the Catholic Church and other non-marital sexual acts undertaken by conservative Christian ministers, it is easy to wonder if the clergy attracts people with psychological problems who cannot "make it" in regular society.

Research from the 1970s found priests to be more socially uncomfortable, isolated, and anxious than the general public. For the past two decades, however, Thomas Plante and colleagues have been studying successful applicants to the Catholic priesthood. They administered personality tests and tests of mental stability to about 70 of these men. They found that men who made it into the Catholic priesthood were very well-adjusted, with quite low scores on symptoms of mental illness like depression, anxiety, obsessiveness, and antisocial tendencies. They evidenced a strong sense of social responsibility, interpersonal sensitivity, and empathy. They were intelligent, imaginative, emotionally stable, trusting, honest, and self-assured. However, they did tend to be somewhat defensive and to have higher than normal levels of anger and over-controlled hostility. This means they repress hostile tendencies and hide their need to dominate others (Plante, Manuel, & Tandez, 1996; Plante, Aldridge, & Louie, 2005). It appears that successful applicants to the priesthood have many strengths and some weaknesses, just like most of us do. There doesn't appear to be anything unique about them that would make them psychopathological or more likely to harm children. In fact, the majority of Catholic priests do a good job and are well respected by their communities.

All Catholic priests are men but women can serve in the capacity of being Catholic nuns, and other faiths have female clergy. An interesting study examining the mental health of different denominations of women found that single women, mostly nuns, felt the least psychological strain compared to married female clergy. Nuns had the least amount of perceived stress, the lowest rates of depression, and better coping skills than clergywomen in either Protestant Christian or Reform Jewish faiths (Rayburn, 1991). Nuns have also been found to fall asleep more quickly, sleep more soundly, and awake feeling more refreshed than age-matched control group women in the community (Hoch et al., 1987). In Rayburn's (1991) study, female Jewish Reform rabbis had the highest levels of stress, strain, and coping abilities. They also showed the highest levels of approval for reducing gender-biased language in their texts and services. The author hypothesizes that Catholic nuns carry out traditional gender roles and do not "rock the boat" concerning church hierarchy, which clearly favors men. Other religions that allow women to be high-ranking clergy may also still be patriarchal in nature, and so the few women who rise to the top may continue to struggle with acceptance from their congregations and unreasonable expectations from administrators. They may feel alone with only male colleagues at their career level.

Another important variable for explaining the well-being of Catholic nuns may be lifestyle. For example, nuns tend to have very regimented schedules, intense emotional support from their colleagues and congregations, and exceedingly healthy lifestyles devoid of alcohol, tobacco, and poor diets. Protestant and Jewish women clergy who marry and may be balancing home life with a stressful career may not have time to engage in such healthy lifestyles, or may experience more stress in general (Hoch et al., 1987). They must strike a fine balance between being both passive and assertive (Rayburn, 1991). When women face the strain of multiple roles, they can develop symptoms of role overload, depression, and life strain. Rayburn (1991, p. 137) makes a very astute observation:

> A shock wave may go through the religious patriarchy when women become assertive and seek more feminine or androgynous interpretations of scripture. The male religious professionals may then begin to see the women as a threat to the status quo of the religious establishment and to themselves personally. This may lead to the women experiencing depression in the form of unresolved anger, low energy … [and] lower work productivity.

FIGURE 8.5 What characteristics of religious life are related to better mental health for nuns?
Photo © Elvis Barukcic/AFP/Getty Images.

Rayburn's (1991) results show how important the ecological contexts and relational processes are in both single and married women's lives for predicting their psychological adjustment. For example, people might think that nuns have particularly lonely lives, yet Samuels and Lester (1985) found that Catholic nuns and priests most often felt feelings of love, gratitude, hope, happiness, and reverence in their daily lives. In another study, Catholic nuns from war-torn Angola felt much lonelier, felt more dissatisfied with life, and were more emotionally unstable than were Catholic nuns from Portugal (Neto & Barros, 2003). Angola became an independent nation after fighting broke out with Portugal in 1975. Because of constant armed conflict, Angola remains a poor country while Portugal enjoys most of the luxuries of peaceful European statehood. Thus, environmental stressors in the macrosystem can affect the mental health of all people, single or coupled, secular or religious. Oppression and poverty are risk factors for poor psychological functioning no matter who you are.

An example from Thai Buddhist maechii

In a fascinating examination of the lives of the *maechii* (lay nuns) in Thailand, Muecke (2004) found that community perceptions and oppression played a large role in the mental health of these women. *Maechii* are women who shave their heads and eyebrows, wear a white robe signifying their commitment to between eight and ten of the Buddhist Precepts, or ethical guidelines, take vows of celibacy, and live in monasteries with Buddhist monks. Their jobs are to take care of the monks' needs through preparing food, groundskeeping, and cleaning. In the Theravada Buddhist tradition (found in Burma, Cambodia, Laos, Sri Lanka and Thailand), ordained male monks are the highest class of people, followed by women ordained as monks (none of whom exist today). The second class of people includes lay men and women who can gain karmic merit by giving to monks.

While the Buddha established a role for nuns, there has been a lack of commitment to this tradition in Theravada Buddhism, and there have been no ordained nuns for 700 years (Muecke, 2004). Women are seen as inferior and also sexually dangerous to Buddhist monks. Thus, the only females allowed to function in any kind of spiritual capacity are the *maechii*. However, the lay public often views the *maechii* as poor beggars who don't deserve to be in the monasteries. They also view them as sexual temptresses who threaten the monks' celibacy. Muecke (2004) interviewed many monks and *maechii* and found these ideas to be quite prevalent. One monk commented that there are no ordained nuns in Thailand because monks would not be able to control themselves sexually. While *maechii* are not nearly as revered as an ordained nun would be, they are still expected to rise above human sexual desires, show self-discipline, and exhibit selflessness in their support of the monks. However, the *maechii* are not permitted to gain education in the other hundreds of precepts found in the Buddhist tradition. They are limited to a handful of the precepts and remain largely illiterate.

There is a rising movement to protect these single women, educate them about Buddhism, and recruit them to live in new nunneries where they can meditate like monks. Currently, however, many *maechii* are aware of the derogatory images the general public holds about them, as poor, socially unskilled women whom people don't believe can make it in the real world. Because they are thought to sexually tempt monks, if a monk breaks his vow of celibacy, the *maechii* is blamed. However, to become a *maechii*, a woman must give up her family and home, and live alone with minimal possessions. Some in the public recognize their sacrifice and respect them, supporting them with food and money. Most *maechii*, however, live a life unappreciated and often feel sad, lonely, and sorry for themselves, hoping for a change in the system so that they can study Buddhism and rise above their suffering (Muecke, 2004).

FINAL REFLECTIONS

As you can see, simply knowing that a person is single or partnered will not reveal much about their personal adjustment or ability to function in their families. Not all single people are alike and the intersections of race, class, gender, age, religion, culture, socioeconomic status, and sexual orientation play large roles in how people feel about their single lifestyles.

One type of single person we didn't spend a lot of time examining in this chapter is the single parent. Parents are extremely important influences on children as well as on emerging adults' sense of identity, including how those young adults cope with being single. And having children is one of the most significant events in most people's lives. The next chapter will examine many issues related to having and rearing children.

CHAPTER SUMMARY

The majority of people will eventually marry or settle down in a committed partnership. However, more and more people are living single today than in any other historic period. Especially in western nations where women have equal rights to work and become self-sufficient, we see single, well-established women and men living quite happy lives. Even though singlehood is becoming more normative, there is still a problem with singlism, prejudiced views about single people, which may include discriminatory behavior. People often think something is wrong with a single person who doesn't want to marry or settle down with a committed partnership.

The normative life cycle model includes the belief that most "normal" people will marry and have children, and that no one would be single by choice. However, more emerging adults (those between the ages of 18 and 25) are remaining single by choice, in order to explore their own identities, gain an education, and live life as independent persons before they make a serious commitment. This prolonged period of singlehood is becoming more normative in western cultures, and now

it is "non-normative" single people who suffer the brunt of singlism. Those singles who are over 30 are viewed most negatively.

Some single people choose to remain single due to their faith in God or a spirituality-based lifestyle. Priests and nuns are often revered and respected for choosing a single lifestyle.

Not all single people are single by choice, however. Some single people wish to be coupled but have not been able to do so. There are both temporary and permanent involuntary singles, the latter group having given up on the hope of finding a partner.

Some research suggests that single people have higher rates of depression and loneliness but a person's well-being rests largely on factors in the various bioecological systems that affect individuals, from their family of origin dynamics, to financial stability, social supports and friendships, and cultural stigma and discrimination against singles. How happy and satisfied a single person is depends on the complex interactions between many personal and contextual variables.

KEY TERMS

commitment	identity achievement	normative life cycle model
crisis	identity versus role confusion	resistant thinking
embracing	and intimacy versus isolation	singles pride movement
singlehood	managed interactions	singles strain
emerging adulthood	non-normative singles	singlism

WEBSITES FOR FURTHER EXPLORATION

http://www.singlemothersbychoice.com

This website is for established professional women who choose to remain single and then adopt or bear children of their own. It has books, newsletters, articles, a documentary film, and a FAQ regarding things like artificial insemination and surrogacy.

http://www.unmarried.org

This website is for the Alternatives to Marriage Project, a non-profit advocacy group that fights for equality for all singles. It helps people fight discrimination based on their marital status. It has articles and links about "marriage free" lifestyles (including unmarried heterosexual and LGBT people and polyamorous relationships). It is geared toward any person who has made a conscious decision to be unmarried.

http://anunslife.org

This is a fascinating site put together by Catholic Sisters and Nuns in Today's World. It's very contemporary in both its language and the focus of the articles. There's a section for "blogging nuns," some podcasts, discussion boards, FAQs about nuns' lives, and a generally voyeuristic look into lives most of us know nothing about. There is even a campaign for the public to "adopt a sister, friar, priest, hermit, monk, deacon, nun, sanctified virgin, or brother." The public can sponsor novices and support them financially or with letters, support, and donations to help them along their way to living a faith-based single life.

CHAPTER 9
REPRODUCTION AND PARENTING

The test of the morality of a society is what it does for its children.

(Dietrich Bonhoeffer, German theologian and Nazi resistor)

LEARNING OBJECTIVES

- To understand the reasons why people choose to parent or not to parent

- To recognize key ways that parenting and views of parenting have changed throughout history

- To gain a basic understanding of reproductive processes and how people transition to parenting roles

- To understand the causes of infertility and the strategies people use to become parents

- To realize what the basic needs of all children around the world are, and what parenting styles are related to meeting or not meeting those needs

- To understand the many styles of parenting and recognize how diversity affects the parenting experience

Marriages and Families in the 21st Century: A Bioecological Approach, First Edition. Tasha R. Howe.
© 2012 Tasha R. Howe. Published 2012 by Blackwell Publishing Ltd.

OVERVIEW: TO PARENT OR NOT TO PARENT

HISTORICAL TRENDS IN PARENTING

- The work of Leta Hollingworth
- Historical beliefs and practices surrounding childbirth
- Historical views of children and childhood
- Historical views of motherhood
- Historical views of fatherhood
- Diverse families in history
- Modern ideas for insuring child well-being in families

REPRODUCTION AND BIRTH

- Egg and sperm
- Prenatal development
  - The egg and the prenatal environment
  - Sperm and the role of the father
  - The role of genes after fertilization
- Giving birth
  - Natural birth
  - Cesarean section birth
  - Choosing a birth method

THE TRANSITION TO PARENTHOOD

- Mitigating the stress of parenthood
- Post-partum mental health

INFERTILITY AND CREATIVE WAYS TO BECOME PARENTS

- Artificial insemination
- In vitro fertilization
- Reproductive surrogacy
- Adoption
  - Private adoption
  - Public adoption
  - International adoption
  - Unique challenges of adoptive parenting

PARENTING INFANTS AND CHILDREN

Infant brains and the environment
- Stress and the developing brain
- Secure environments and the developing brain
- Over-stimulation of the developing brain

Parenting styles
- Socioeconomic influences on parenting styles
- Baumrind's parenting styles

THE MANY FACES OF PARENTHOOD

Fathering
- Intimate and aloof fathering
- Fathering with fewer resources

Single parents

African-American parents

Transnational and Latino parents

Native American parents

Asian-American parents

LGBT parents

Grandparents as parents

COMMUNITY DEVELOPMENT AND THE MACROSYSTEM

OVERVIEW: TO PARENT OR NOT TO PARENT

While the majority of people wants to and will have children, a growing population of adults chooses to remain childfree. People with children may refer to these folks as "childless," but this implies a deficit or something missing in their lives. Childfree people tend to be just as happy, if not happier, than people with children. Research shows that couples who are childfree by choice and remain childfree have higher levels of marital satisfaction than couples who have children (Shapiro, Gottman, & Carrere, 2000). Compared to the 67% of wives who experienced a steep decline in marital satisfaction after having a baby, wives who remained childfree experienced stability, and for 33% of them, an increase in marital satisfaction over time. Brooks (2008) found that parents were less happy than childfree couples. Also, Gilbert (2006) found that parents felt happier when they were doing any number of other activities than when they were with their kids. Simon (2005), in the National Survey of Families and Households, found that when comparing married, single, step, and empty nest parents to the childfree, all groups of parents felt fewer positive emotions and had lower levels of well-being than childfree people.

How can we explain these findings when most of us grow up believing having a child is the greatest joy a person can experience? The answer to that is extremely complex. Let's look at some processes that may provide some clues.

Even though the above findings suggest that having children lowers life satisfaction, the majority of people across the globe will eventually have children. Upwards of 90% of Americans will procreate. While the numbers of childfree people continue to climb, especially in the western world, for most of us, reproduction and parenting will be key life experiences that will shape us as well as the next generation. As you know from the bioecological model, the influences on development are *bidirectional*. This means that while parents affect and raise their children, children also affect and "raise" their parents. Because human development is a lifelong journey, parents change and grow along with their children and face developmental tasks in physical, cognitive, emotional, social, and spiritual growth along the way. The cultures we live in affect our parenting ideologies while at the same time our own biological, neurochemical, personality, and behavioral tendencies affect the larger contexts in which we exist.

These bidirectional influences make for a complex stew that isn't easy to analyze or examine in research studies. We struggle to figure out how parents decided to parent in a certain way and how children end up so similar to their parents. For example, if your dad is particularly musical, and you are a musical genius, most people will say "It's in the genes!" But how do they know it's not "in the environment"? That possibility may not be as appealing as our intuitive ideas about biological determinism. The truth is that it's virtually impossible to separate out the effects of biology and environment, as they are intricately linked and interact with each other in many complex ways. Our parents provide us with both our genes and our environments, unless we were raised away from our biological parents. Children raised away from their biological parents make for a natural experiment, which helps researchers disentangle the effects of biology and environment, but doesn't give us definitive answers. So whether we resemble or don't resemble our parents on any given trait, we can thank or curse *both* biological and environmental influences.

If we want to understand family development, we must move away from either/or thinking and toward a real understanding of the many bioecological forces that shape all individuals in families. This chapter will attempt to do so, albeit in a necessarily cursory fashion. Space limitations prevent me from covering many important aspects of reproduction and parenting, but you should get a nice flavor for the key issues of the day.

One of the most important contemporary trends is the decision not to have children at all. In most of human history, when the majority of families lived agrarian lives, parenting was about raising children to help out on the farm. Children had a utilitarian purpose. Today we often have children to fulfill our emotional needs. We also have homes where both parents work and we live

FYI

Some methods of contraception

Oral pills (estrogen plus progestogen or progestogen only)	Combined low-dose estrogen and progestogen can prevent ovulation and make cervical mucus hostile toward sperm movement; 99% effective with few side effects for most women
Intra-muscular injection (e.g., Depo Provera); hormone patches worn like a Band-Aid	Progestogen only; lasts about three months for shots and one month for patch; 99% effective
Latex condoms fitted and used as directed.	*If* used properly and kept intact, 95% effective; best to use in combination with oral pills to prevent pregnancy
Periodic abstinence (rhythm method)	Must measure temperature and vaginal mucus carefully to track ovulation; intercourse any time *except* six days before and two days after ovulation should be safe; not effective for women with irregular cycles or those who don't accurately monitor cycles
Coitus interruptus (withdrawal method)	Failure rates are high as sperm are present pre-ejaculation and most males fail to withdraw before ejaculation begins
Diaphragm	As effective as condoms if kept in place at least six hours after intercourse until sperm are dead; must be inserted properly before intercourse and kept in place to block cervix; when used as directed, failure rate of 6–16% versus 2–15% for condoms
Spermicidal jelly	Kills sperm but not very effective on its own; use with barrier methods like condoms
Morning-after pill (e.g., "Plan B")	Levonorgestrel, a synthetic progestogen; prevents ovulation in first half of menstrual cycle and prevents implantation of fertilized zygote later on; extremely high doses of estrogen can have side effects like nausea; does not cause abortion in already implanted embryo (abortion pill is "RU-486").
Intrauterine device (IUD; e.g., "Mirena")	Implanted through cervical canal to prevent implantation of blastocyst; substances in the IUD kill sperm; very effective for up to five years; releases hormones into body.

(Adapted from Brookes & Zietman, 1998; **www.plannedparenthood.org; www.cervicalbarriers.org**)

under the influence of a technologically advanced and competitive macrosystem. We want to ensure our offspring succeed, and we often want to bond emotionally with our children, so we want to invest great amounts of quality time in them. We spend inordinate amounts of money on private lessons, travel, and enriching activities, unlike any other generation in the past. We expend tremendous effort trying to make our children happy, and in doing so, we often feel depleted and disappointed in the results, which can explain some of the findings about the life dissatisfaction of parents mentioned earlier. This doesn't mean that parents don't love their children and don't feel glad that they had children at all. It might mean that their expectations for kids to become successes and for themselves to be wonder-parents are unbearably high.

Thus, many people choose to invest their energy in their own happiness and remain childfree. In order to do this, people must engage in informed **family planning**, a concerted effort to avoid pregnancy. It includes being aware of how the body works, understanding safer versus riskier sexual behaviors, and learning how to use contraceptives effectively to prevent pregnancy. To learn more about how to prevent pregnancy and engage in conscious family planning, see the *FYI* box.

Many people around the world lack access to information about contraception, as well as access to medical services. This means that some populations have more choice in their own reproductive lives and are more able to engage in proactive family planning that would most benefit their economic status and lifestyles. Having little choice in family planning was the plight of most of our ancestors throughout history, who usually had as many children as possible, even if they didn't want them.

Family planning
The act of conscientiously controlling one's own fertility and planning for the timing and number of births.

HISTORICAL TRENDS IN PARENTING

The work of Leta Hollingworth
Historical beliefs and practices surrounding childbirth
Historical views of children and childhood
Historical views of motherhood
Historical views of fatherhood
Diverse families in history
Modern ideas for insuring child well-being in families

Women from all cultures have been expected to bear children. In many cultures, a barren woman's life was seen as worthless. As you have learned throughout this text, patriarchal trends in most societies leave women with little power and few choices over their own reproductive lives. In the past and in some places today, women were little more than baby-making machines, and every man wanted his woman to bear him a son to carry on his legacy. We may wonder, if society did not pressure women to find their life's purpose and fulfillment through childrearing, would they have children at all? Is there a *maternal instinct*? Are women natural nurturers, living to care for children?

The majority of perpetrators of child physical abuse and child neglect are women (Gillis, 1996). And throughout history, women have attempted unsafe and even life-threatening abortion practices to rid themselves of unwanted or unacceptable pregnancies. With historic rates of infanticide and child abandonment quite high, it may make one wonder whether women are "naturally" inclined to want to give birth and raise children. If given the choice, would the majority of women choose to have children or to live their lives childfree?

In western industrialized nations and in middle- and upper-class families, birth rates are quite low. So low, in fact, that without poor people having more children than the average person, wealthier people would not have enough babies to replenish the dying population. Why do you think that when education and wealth increase, birth rates decrease? Perhaps as you read this chapter, you may get some ideas to help you answer this question.

The work of Leta Hollingworth

Leta Stetter Hollingworth was a psychologist who studied with some of the most famous male psychologists in the country in the early years of the twentieth century. However, because she was married, she was not allowed to be a teacher, as that job was reserved for single women. Dr. Hollingworth decided to research the supposed inferiority of women that led men to make such decisions about women's capabilities and potential. She was a pioneer in studying the psychology of women and a staunch suffragette. Dr. Hollingworth's research found no differences between male and female infants that would support women's inferior treatment in society. She also found no alterations in women's cognitive or emotional functioning over their menstrual cycle. A common excuse people gave for women being inferior to men was that they were more excitable and less intelligent than men due to the fact that they had periods (Benjamin, 1975).

In 1916, Leta Hollingworth reflected on the possible existence of "maternal instincts." She argued that if such instincts really existed in most women, we would not need any social pressures to convince or force women to have children. She said:

> Child-bearing … is necessary for tribal or national existence … thus we should ensure the group-interest in respect to the population, just as there is a continuous social effort to insure the defense of the nation in time of war. It is clear, indeed, that the social devices employed to get children born, and to get soldiers slain, are in many respects similar. (Hollingworth, 1916, p. 19)

Hollingworth argues that "social devices" are in place to impel women not only to have children, but to *want* to, just as they are in place to impel people to join the military and fight for their country with pride. Just as soldiers must be willing to die to benefit future generations, she argued that women who, in her time, were at high risk of dying during childbirth, potentially sacrifice their own lives, and like soldiers, experience blood loss and pain, in the endeavor. What are these social devices that impel women to have children? Hollingworth outlined six main ways societies pressure women to have children:

- personal ideals
- public opinion
- law
- education
- art
- illusion.

First are *personal ideals*. These ideals include the mandate that a morally upstanding woman must guard home and hearth. Proper women should want nothing more than to fulfill their duties as wives and mothers. Many people around the world still hold these personal ideals.

Second, *public opinion* about the worth of women impels them to want to conform. Stereotypes of women's roles, capabilities and duties influence women's self-worth and the goals they set for themselves, most of which revolve around the birthing of and caring for children.

Third, often the *law* forces women to have or not have children. Recall that the eugenics movement was entirely legal during Hollingworth's time. Poor women, the mentally ill, and people of color were often forced to be sterilized, while white middle-class women were prevented from divorcing their husbands without proving that they were unfaithful or severely abusive. This ensured that the "proper" types of women had as many children as possible. Similarly, tax laws today may benefit families with children over childfree people. Moreover, laws may prohibit information on birth control or family planning from being disseminated. We see this currently in traditional Catholic beliefs and Leta Hollingworth certainly saw this in the lack of publicly available information on contraception during her time. Thus, laws affect the reproductive lives of women.

Education is another social device used historically and today to prevent women from taking control of their reproductive lives. For example, in nineteenth-century America, women were not allowed to attend most universities. If they were, admission was offered solely to single women as the common belief was that education was for homely or infertile women. People thought it was impossible to be both married with children and also an intellectual. Another belief was that if every woman were educated, the population would decline. We see this belief playing out currently in some fundamentalist Muslim communities, where women are kept out of educational opportunities and their roles are restricted to the home.

The fifth social device is *art*. In Hollingworth's time, this meant paintings and advertisements in which children were depicted as cherubic and precious and mothers were likened to the Virgin Mary, always pious and blissfully happy to be wives and mothers. In our time, art consists of all media, from TV shows where women with a dozen or more children are rewarded lucratively for their fertility, to video games where women are usually depicted as either mothers or sexual vixens. Art reflects and reinforces societal stereotypes and expectations for women's roles.

Finally, *illusion* is Hollingworth's last social device impelling women to have and rear children. Little girls grow up under the illusory belief that motherhood is divine, that having children is the greatest joy in life, and that a woman cannot be truly fulfilled without giving birth. The complications, extraordinary pain of labor, permanent body changes, sleepless nights, and financial and emotional strain are swept under the rug and are not part of the illusion of the mother in the white nightgown cradling her perfect Gerber baby, ready for a lifetime of happiness. In Hollingworth's time, no one talked about what happened in the childbirthing room and high maternal death rates were kept under wraps.

Historical beliefs and practices surrounding childbirth

Before Hollingworth wrote of the pressures that made women feel like failures if they did not have children, most cultures did, at least, provide some support for the pregnant woman while she was giving birth. For example, in most cultures, older women and extended clan members supported birthing women. Many groups had fertility goddesses that could be used in ritual and prayer, for support and comfort during pregnancy and birth. Even early depictions of Jesus Christ included feminine and maternal features (Walker-Bynum, 1983). In fact, the Virgin Mary did not represent holy motherhood until well after the twelfth century CE.

In previous centuries, childbirth was attended by midwives and traditional herbal healers, so there were no rituals involving men in the process of birth. The separate realms of birthing women and their male partners were clearly delineated. **Doulas**, women trained to support laboring women, provided much emotional support for women giving birth, in the form of massages, reassuring talk, rituals, and healing potions (Gottman & Schwartz-Gottman, 2007). Pre-Christian pagan cultures revered the work of wise women healers and midwives, but with the rise of Catholicism, the Crusades, the Inquisition, and witch burnings, these women's crafts were denounced as devil's work and witchcraft (Gottman & Schwartz-Gottman, 2007). However, even with the threat of death looming and Church-sanctioned male doctors made available, many women chose to stick with the support and knowledge of female healers and *doulas* for childbirth.

While traditional practices helped women in birthing their babies, the maternal death rate was high. Without comprehensive knowledge of physiology or biochemistry, and without modern technology available, most women throughout history gave birth at home and got no prenatal care during pregnancy (Gillis, 1996). Beginning in the eighteenth century, in regions that had doctors, they were only called in an emergency. In fact, women often thought that to prepare for birth in any way was to curse the birth. With high rates of infant mortality, people often waited until the baby was born to alter their homes or family routines. Planning for a birth or naming a child ahead of time was believed to lead to certain death of the infant. Furthermore, birth was not the noteworthy event it is today because most women were perpetually pregnant during all of their childbearing years. People also thought that women were meant to suffer for the sins of womanhood, and that the pain and nausea associated with pregnancy were punishments for Eve's original sin. Therefore, women were prayed for and treated with potions.

As industrialization spread in developed nations in the mid-nineteenth century, hospitals eventually became a "cure-all" where women of means thought they could avoid death during childbirth, infections, or the birth defects they so often heard about. If a male doctor in a hospital

Doulas
Professionally trained birthing assistants who support women giving birth.

could deliver their babies, they felt safe (Gottman & Schwartz-Gottman, 2007). Due to lack of knowledge about hygienic practices and the spread of bacteria, however, many women ended up contracting deadly infections in those very same hospitals. As antiseptic was discovered and practices improved, hygienic birth practices became more common in hospitals by the time of the Civil War (1861–1865) (Gottman & Schwartz-Gottman, 2007). Around the same time, chloroform was introduced to sedate women and ease the pain of labor and birth.

However, even in 1900, only 5% of births occurred in hospitals and men were kept outside of the delivery room, wherever the woman gave birth. It was felt that men would be distracting and get in the way. They were encouraged to go socialize with other men and even get drunk while their wives gave birth (Gottman & Schwartz-Gottman, 2007). But more and more men in the 1950s and 1960s started protesting and suing for the right to join their wives in the delivery room during now pervasive hospital births.

A landmark event occurred at Humboldt State University in 1960, when a 23-year-old student chained himself to his wife when the doctor did not allow him in the delivery room. The police were called, but they didn't know what to do. The woman was in labor and her husband was attached to her. The man remained handcuffed to his wife and they ended up delivering a healthy baby. Their story made headlines around the country and other couples started getting involved in fighting for the right to be together during labor and delivery. By 1970, almost all babies were born in hospitals, and more husbands were joining their wives in the delivery room. Men even started to watch films to educate themselves about the processes of labor and birth ahead of time (Gottman & Schwartz-Gottman, 2007). Today in western cultures it is extremely rare to find a partner uninvolved in childbirth education, labor, or delivery.

Historical views of children and childhood

The above discussion of changing views of childbirth shows that men increasingly wanted to be important figures in their children's lives. Today most people tend to view children as worth investing significant time in, and as sweet and innocent. But that hasn't always been the case. Before the sixteenth century, most people were indifferent to children and there was really no such thing as "childhood," referring to a special time of life requiring extra care and consideration (Vinovskis, 2011). Especially harsh in their judgments of both women and children were the Colonial Puritans. These seventeenth-century families felt that children were born evil and that parents must vigorously, through strict discipline and punishment, socialize children, beat the devil out of them, and save their souls (Farrell, 1999). It was necessary to break children's wills to force them into compliance with strict lifestyle mandates. Contrast this with our contemporary images of children as innocents, born pure and good, who must be protected at all costs.

Some groups in the seventeenth century disagreed with the harsh Puritan ethic. For example, Quakers believed that children were innocent and should be protected from the evils of the world (Farrell, 1999). But even in families where children were loved and valued, there was no real sense that each child was an individual. In fact, it wasn't uncommon to give children the same names as previously deceased siblings (Farrell, 1999). Children served mainly an instrumental purpose, to help the family survive. Once children were weaned (usually by age 5 or 6) it was common to send them to live with relatives who needed help around their houses, farms, or businesses. Children were a commodity used to benefit the family's survival. It was quite common for children as young as 8 to be sent as an apprentice, to learn a trade away from home. Poor children were often sent to be servants for wealthier families. In eighteenth-century France, at least 25% of children were sent away permanently, at early ages, many of them to serve the Catholic Church (Gillis, 1996). In fact, only in the 1920s did it even enter children's minds that they should stay at their parents' homes until they were grown up or married.

Children without parents, those whose parents were too poor to care for them, and those who were in trouble often spent years in orphanages, work houses, or reform schools. It wasn't until after

World War II that foster (temporary parental figures) and adoptive (permanent parent replacements) parents took care of these kinds of children in any substantial numbers.

Throughout history, children were commonly raised by strangers, distant relatives, neighbors, and especially stepparents. By the eighteenth century, stepmothers were regularly called "mother" and became the head of the household. Children grew up surrounded by many women who mothered them, including older sisters. In the antebellum south before the Civil War, slave women often nursed white children and were called "mammy" (Gillis, 1996).

With the spread of industrialization in the 1880s, paid wage labor, and the growth of large cities, homes became safe havens from the stress of the outside world. The boundaries between home and community became more insular and closed. With improvements in sanitation, health, technology, education, and medicine, birth rates plummeted and parents for the first time began to invest energy, money, and time into the growth and welfare of individual children (Skolnick, 1994). Intense care for and parental investment in small numbers of children were believed to be the best strategy for benefiting the whole family in the future. After schooling became mandatory in the U.S. in 1890, children's roles slowly changed from that of worker to student, from little adult to child with special needs. Middle-class mothers were now expected to stay home and provide individual attention to each child.

Historical views of motherhood

Interestingly, "maternity" was not equated with "motherhood" until the end of the nineteenth century. Before around 1880, giving birth (maternity) was not necessarily related to our modern idea of "mothering," where a woman brings a baby into a closely bonded family and creates a new identity for herself as "mother." Since historically only about 50% of children lived into adulthood, and at least 7% of women died in childbirth, with more dying before their children reached maturity, women of yesteryear often had many children one right after another. The subsistence living conditions of most families did not allow for a sense of "mothering" children (Gillis, 1996). Even women of moderate means often employed wet nurses to breastfeed their children while they worked. This was especially true in the upper classes, where women had other responsibilities for being the head of their households, which did not involve nursing babies.

Historical views of fatherhood

In previous centuries, the word "fathering" connoted nurturing and caring, but didn't necessarily refer to one's biological father. Giving birth to a child did not mean a man or a woman would be the sole providers for a child. Every adult community member, as well as older teenagers, had the right to discipline children and be mentors to them. Our predecessors would be loath to believe that today we expect one person to be the sole provider for a child's physical, cognitive, social, emotional, and spiritual life for 18 years.

Fathers in colonial America were considered the leaders of the family, in charge of the discipline, education and religious piety of their children. Parenting manuals of the seventeenth and eighteenth centuries were written for *fathers*, who wielded complete power over their wives and children. The pre-industrial home was one sustained by goods and services that could only be produced with the entire family working together. Fathers, mothers, and community members taught children crafts, trades, agricultural skills, and animal husbandry skills from early ages. Moreover, each home in the village or town played an integral role in the community, as a provider of specific goods produced for sale and trade (Vinovskis, 2011). Mothers worked tirelessly in housework, manual labor, and at producing goods and services. They were usually less educated than their husbands and had no knowledge of what we now call "quality time" or time spent specifically for the cognitive and social stimulation of children (Bianchi, 2000). Mothers and fathers worked in the home and outside the home from sun up to sun down, often leaving older children in charge of younger siblings. The boundaries between homestead and community were thin. These trends illustrate that fathers played more parenting roles historically than they are expected to play today.

Diverse families in history

It's important to keep in mind that most historical documents were written by and about European American people. There were no legal, social or economic supports for families of color. For example, because importing slaves was outlawed in the U.S. in 1807, slaves who had already arrived were viewed as "breeding stock" and were encouraged to mate and form large "families" whenever possible (Thornton-Dill, 1988). Rape of black women was common and was used as a tool for power and control over both the women and their husbands. Some slave women killed their own babies to prevent them from facing the hardships of slavery. What little evidence we have, though, suggests that slave marriages were more egalitarian than European American marriages and that the couples often bonded emotionally through their mutual oppression.

Later on, Chinese laborers brought to the United States to build railroads and work in mines in the 1860s were not allowed to bring their wives to join them. However, American-born Chinese men could bring relatives to the States using a limited number of paper "slots"—permission slips that could be used in small numbers to bring relatives to the U.S. This meant the men might go back to China, father children with their wives, bring the children back, or sell their children's slots to relatives or friends in order to earn money. Those who bought the slots were called "paper sons" (Thornton-Dill, 1988). The early Chinese families were patriarchal in nature and women and children had few rights. Discriminatory immigration policies added to the fragmented nature of the early Chinese American family.

When the U.S. colonized the Southwest, they encountered indigenous Mexican populations, people who lived in large, extended families with traditional gender roles and values. While these families were patriarchal in nature, the women were healers (*curanderas*) and midwives (*parteras*). They could also be teachers and often worked to help in their family's agricultural enterprises. They were responsible for the children's moral and religious upbringing as well. In the 1860s, after their land was taken away from them, Mexican men often had to migrate to work on railroads or in mines. This led to the formation of many female-headed households. Sometimes entire families would migrate and follow seasonal work, the stress of which often led to family break-up, instability, and even desertion (Thornton-Dill, 1988).

Modern ideas for insuring child well-being in families

It's important to remember these historical trends because we often think that children have it bad today, that they are abused at increasing rates, and that around the world child labor and exploitation are rampant. The truth is that never in history have children had it so good, especially in western nations. While there are still millions of children living in poverty, diseased, orphaned, exploited, abused, and violated, the world community now at least recognizes their fundamental rights as human beings (Miller-Perrin & Perrin, 2007). The United Nations Convention on the Rights of the Child asserts that all member nations must recognize every child's right to be raised in a loving family, with physical well-being and education, and free from violence of any kind. This is a vast improvement over the earliest discovered written code of laws in human history. Hammurabi's code (from 1790 BCE Babylon) says that children are the property of their father and can be treated as he wishes. In fact, throughout history children were seen as property to be dictated to and controlled. There was an Association for the Prevention of Cruelty to Animals years before similar associations were formed to protect children. Parents had every right to beat and even kill their children, especially if they were unruly. Not until 1879 in the United States did the Society for the Prevention of Cruelty to Children materialize and child abuse and neglect receive national attention. And it wasn't until almost 100 years later that the first federal American legislation was implemented, the Child Abuse Prevention and Treatment Act (CAPTA) of 1974, which allowed for federal funds to be earmarked for research, treatment, and social services to aid abused and neglected children (Miller-Perrin & Perrin, 2007).

While it is still legal for schools to paddle children in many U.S. states, and while girls around the world are still prevented from getting an education or having any rights at all, we must keep in mind that the ideology of the innocence of childhood is slowly spreading to every corner of the globe. People view children as people in need of protection by almost every government in the world. Thus, globalization is affecting the world's community of children in a generally positive way, despite the many obstacles that the world's children still face. Research over the past 40 years has shown that with high parental and social investment in children's welfare, kids are doing great today. Most western children have high self-esteem, strong values for achievement and success, and concrete plans for their futures, and are generally happier today than in previous decades, despite the rise in divorce rates and other structural changes to families (Bengston, Biblarz, & Roberts, 2002). Of course, this is more true for children of middle and upper classes who have their basic needs met.

Every country and every subculture within each country must examine how it treats its children. Each group will be faced with how to ensure children reach their developmental potentials, a task which will be accomplished in many ways. One of the key methods for ensuring child well-being is to consciously plan their births. The more families around the world understand about the physiology of pregnancy and childbirth, the more they can prevent unwanted births and allow children to be born into families who are prepared to parent them.

REPRODUCTION AND BIRTH

Egg and sperm

Prenatal development

Giving birth

We tend to think of reproduction as a purely physiological process and parenting as a purely environmental one. However, using the bioecological perspective, this section will show the incredible interaction between factors in our biochemistry and the complex contexts in which we live.

Egg and sperm

Spermatozoa
Male germ cells, or sperm.

Oocyte
Female germ cells, or eggs.

All of our lives begin from a meeting of two globs of DNA: the sperm, or **spermatozoa**, which is the male germ cell, from our father, and the egg, or **oocyte**, which is the female germ cell, from our mother.

The egg and the prenatal environment

The egg has a fertile life of about 24 hours. If it's not fertilized within that time, it will be washed out of the body through the menstrual flow, the uterine lining shed with it.

A woman is born with all the eggs she is ever going to have, so the health of her eggs, relatively good or relatively poor, depends on her age. After the age of 35, egg cells start to degrade in quality quite rapidly, and we see greater chances of infertility, miscarriage, and babies born with birth defects. One such birth defect is Down syndrome, a chromosomal disorder which leads to physical malformations and mental retardation.

Research shows that, beyond genetic material, the prenatal environment in the womb is related to whether a baby will grow up to have problems as diverse as birth defects, elevated blood pressure, or even diabetes (Nash, 2002; Zambrano et al., 2005). It is important that pregnant women eat well, watch their weight, and exercise regularly. Good health will reduce the stress they place on their own bodies and thereby the prenatal environment they provide for their fetuses. Infants of malnourished mothers can have lifelong metabolic problems. Even atherosclerosis has been shown to be passed to infants, raising their risk for cardiovascular problems later in life (Nash, 2002).

Women who do not get enough folic acid in their diets are more at risk of having babies with spina bifida, an incomplete spine, as the prenatal cells divide improperly. Also, ethyl alcohol—the active ingredient in alcoholic beverages—can cross the placental barrier and reach the infant, increasing its risk for fetal alcohol spectrum disorders which range from mild learning disabilities to severe organ malformations and profound mental retardation (Jacobson et al., 1993). Harmful agents, such as drugs, alcohol, toxic fumes, biohazards, lead, pollution, and radiation, which can cross the placenta and harm the fetus, are called **teratogens**. Teratogens cause the most damage during the first trimester of pregnancy when all of the major organ structures are forming in the embryo (Nash, 2002). However, exposure to teratogens at any time during pregnancy can be harmful. Thus, the advice of most doctors is that women refrain completely from alcohol intake, touching cat feces, which raise the risk for a disease called toxoplasmosis, and other potentially harmful behaviors.

Teratogens
Any substance that can cross the placental barrier and negatively affect a developing embryo or fetus.

Sperm and the role of the father

While you are probably familiar with the idea of a woman's health contributing to the health of her baby, you may be less familiar with the latest research showing that the father can also play a key role in birth defects and the health of the newborn. After the Vietnam war, men who were exposed to the toxic chemical Agent Orange often had children with spina bifida, leading people to wonder about the father's role in the health of the infant. Some studies suggest older men have less robust sperm, which are more likely to contribute to birth defects like dwarfism. Also, men undergoing chemotherapy tend to produce defective sperm (Jensen, Bonde, & Joffe, 2006). While research on the sperm's contribution to prenatal and postnatal health in offspring is limited, there is a growing body of literature suggesting that the father should be just as concerned as the mother about his diet, refraining from drugs and alcohol, and his overall health (Keskes-Ammar

FIGURE 9.1 What advice would you give potential parents about how to provide the safest intrauterine environment for their baby?
Photo © Blend Images/Alamy.

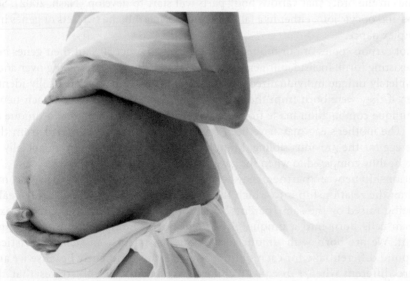

et al., 2003). For example, studies in China show that male smokers have children with higher rates of cancer than children whose fathers don't smoke, even controlling for maternal smoking and second-hand smoke exposure (Reynolds, 1997). Likewise, men who work in toxic environments, where they are exposed to hazards like lead or chemical waste, are more likely to have female partners who miscarry than men who work in safe environments (Savitz, Brett, Dole, & Tse, 1997).

The use of alcohol and other drugs, like marijuana, alters the body's cell composition, often depleting vital nutrients in the cells (Williams, 1998). This means that even though men make new sperm every day, they may be damaging the organs that make the sperm, store the sperm, and transport the sperm. They may even change the genetic or chromosomal environment surrounding sperm production, which can negatively affect the structure and function of those cells. For example, their sperm can be misshapen, with two heads, or can swim in erratic patterns, not reaching the egg. When couples are infertile, the woman is usually the one examined most closely, but researchers are slowly beginning to realize that the role the man plays can be equal to or even greater in terms of the health of the child.

It used to be that sperm count was all that doctors considered as a male contributor to fertility problems. Today, however, there is evidence that men who lack nutrients like vitamin C and folic acid can have malformed sperm, which can affect fertility, pregnancy, miscarriage, and birth defects, like Down syndrome (Eskenazi et al., 2005).

Most of you are familiar with the fact that sperm play an important role in sexual differentiation. An X sperm meeting an egg will create an XX chromosomal pattern, leading to the birth of a girl. A Y sperm meeting an egg will create an XY pattern, leading to a male child. Remember that this process is complicated by hormonal messages, genetic anomalies, and environmental effects, like medications the mother is taking. Thus, as you learned in Chapter 3, gender may not be dichotomous and clear-cut for all babies. Nevertheless, when male genetic material meets female genetic material during fertilization, most babies will develop into either a male or a female and in the majority of cases, that baby will develop completely normally, with ten fingers, ten toes, and two eyes in the middle of its face, which is an unbelievable feat considering the sheer number of processes that must go right.

The role of genes after fertilization

HOX genes
The set of 39 genes that determine the order in which a baby's body structures develop in the womb.

HOX genes have been identified as the genes that determine the order in which prenatal structures unfold. There are about 39 of these genes in humans, and they are arranged along human chromosomes in the order that various body parts will start to develop (Nash, 2002). So when the spermatozoa and oocyte join, either in a fallopian tube or in a lab, the two sets of genes immediately begin a complex dance.

We are not carbon copies of our moms and dads, with an exact 50% of their genes being passed on in their existing form. Instead, our genes combine in amazing ways, crossing over and mixing to form a completely unique individualized genetic make-up. We are not genetically identical to our siblings even if they were born from the same biological mother and father. Each new child in a family is a unique combination made from a unique sperm manufactured at a unique time in the father's life. The mother's egg may have been released from an ovary different from the one that released the egg for the previous sibling. Mom may be older, calmer, more financially stable, and more or less healthy compared to when she gave birth to her first child.

The relationship between partners may be completely different, better or worse, more or less intimate, than the relationship into which the first child was born. Thus, there's really no such thing as "being raised by the same parents." Each of us begins as a unique intermixing of our parents' germ cells born into a unique physiological, psychological, emotional, and cultural environment. We are born with unique temperaments, talents, and characteristics, and our parents respond differentially for each sibling. They treat us differently because *we* are different and *they* are different when subsequent children are born. This illustrates that the various bioecological systems influence us to become unique individuals from the very beginning of our

FIGURE 9.2 The zygote's journey down the fallopian tube.

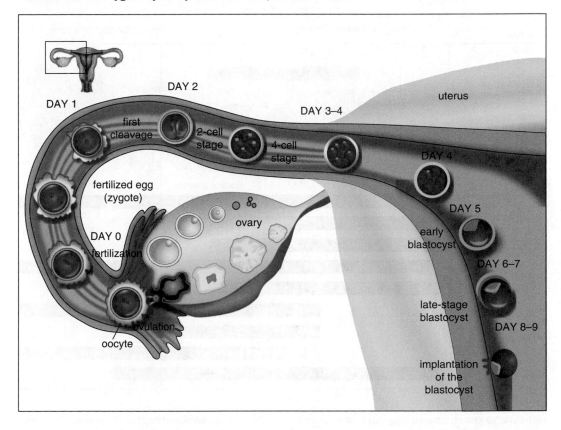

lives. In spite of the different results, when the sperm penetrates the egg, our primitive journeys all look very similar, at least from the outside.

Prenatal development

If an egg is fertilized, the genetic material from the father and mother intermix and combine, leading to a spectacular journey that truly boggles the mind. The new being, the **zygote**, starts replicating its own genetic material after fertilization, and the cells begin to divide. It travels down the fallopian tube as genetic messages as old as the most ancient life forms send messages to proteins that will create a person unlike any of the other six billion on earth. The cells start differentiating into specialized messengers that all have different jobs to perform. By the fourth day after fertilization, it becomes a fluid-filled ball of cells, with two different layers of cells covering it, like respective orange peels. The inner cell mass will become the baby and the outer cell mass becomes the **placenta**. The placenta is a vascularly rich organ that will attach to the uterine lining and serve as the baby's protection and nutrient provider (see Figure 9.2).

This new being, a fluid-filled sphere of layered cells, the **blastocyst**, continues to travel down the fallopian tubes to the uterus, where it will implant into the uterine lining. Once implantation occurs, placental blood vessels attach to the lining of the uterus, sending life-giving and life-protecting organs into the mother's body. These placental vessels will transport nutrients and dispose of waste, and their chemical messengers will trick the mother's body into accepting this foreigner as part of itself.

How is it that most of us are "normal?" It doesn't seem possible that the majority of pregnancies are healthy, all 50 trillion cells in our bodies migrate to where they need to go, and then work the way they should. The genetic surge of life is certainly impressive and awe-inspiring. Just think about how

Zygote
The newly created being that is formed when sperm meets egg.

Placenta
A vascularly rich organ that attaches to the uterus and provides a baby with nutrients while protecting it from waste and toxins.

Blastocyst
A fluid-filled ball of layered cells, which develops by the fourth day after fertilization and travels down the fallopian tubes to implant in the lining of the uterus.

FIGURE 9.3 Stages of prenatal development and key organ development.

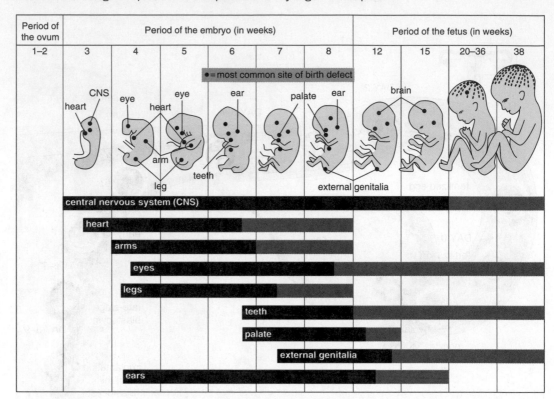

our diverse genetic make-ups interact with innumerable womb environments yet produce so many well-adapted, healthy infants.

Once the embryo has implanted into the uterus (about two weeks after fertilization), we reach the **embryonic stage** of prenatal development when all the major tissue and organ systems begin to form. The first heartbeat occurs a mere 23 days after conception, and the skeleton is fully in place by the ninth week, before many women even know they are pregnant (Brookes & Zietman, 1998). The neural tube is dividing into a brain and spine within the first month after conception. By three months, the embryo will respond to stimulation by recoiling, though it is barely larger than a grain of rice. Women may begin to feel fatigued, nauseous, and emotionally sensitive.

Interestingly, the pregnant woman is not the only one to experience physical changes during pregnancy. Her hormonal changes seem to affect her male partner as well (studies have not yet been done on female partners of pregnant women). Men often show pregnancy symptoms like weight gain, cravings, and backaches, known as sympathy pregnancy, or **couvade syndrome**. Couvade syndrome was once thought to be all in men's heads, but research is showing that men's hormones change right along with their pregnant partner's (Berg & Wynne-Edwards, 2001). To read about some amazing research on male hormonal changes during their partner's pregnancy, check out the *How Would You Measure That?* box.

The **fetal stage** of development begins eight or nine weeks after conception and continues until the birth, usually at about 40 weeks after conception. During the fetal stage, nothing new develops. All of the organs and bodily structures are firmly in place by the start of the third month of pregnancy. What happens after that is a refinement of structures, a continual growth spurt. The fetus grows larger and fatter, and its brain starts a phenomenal proliferation of billions of neurons, more than the baby could ever possibly use in one lifetime (Nelson, 2001). See Figure 9.3.

Another thing we all have in common is the inevitable radical departure from a safe, calm, fluid-filled, dark, and muffled environment into the bright, loud, chaotic reality of our lives.

Embryonic stage
The stage of prenatal development after the embryo is implanted into the uterus (from approximately 14 days and lasting until nine weeks after fertilization); the embryo's organs begin to form.

Couvade syndrome
Male "sympathy pregnancy" symptoms like weight gain and back ache.

Fetal stage
The last stage of prenatal development when no new structures form; growth and refinement of existing structures take place; begins about nine weeks after fertilization.

HOW WOULD YOU MEASURE THAT?

Hormonal changes in men during pregnancy (Storey, Walsh, Quinton, & Wynne-Edwards, 2000)

Men actively parent infants in about 40% of cultures, especially when couple intimacy is seen as important. Men in these cultures also experience *couvade* symptoms more than men in non-fathering cultures do. Only 10% of mammals have much father investment in offspring, but there are examples in primates, rodents, and even some birds. And animal studies show that males in species who exhibit paternal behavior often also exhibit hormonal changes before or shortly after offspring are born.

These findings led Storey et al. (2000) to examine this possibility in human males. They contacted expecting couples attending childbirth education classes. They came to their homes about three weeks before the baby's due date and did experimental manipulations while checking hormone levels in the couples' blood. First, they had the couples put a doll on their shoulders. The doll was wrapped in a blanket that had been used to wrap a newborn within the previous 24 hours. They also played a recording of a newborn crying and had the couples watch videos of a woman breastfeeding a newborn. They then had 30-minute discussions about parenting and childbirth issues. The experimenters took notes regarding which parents put the doll down during the discussion. Men and women were then given questionnaires about their pregnancy symptoms, so men's couvade levels could be assessed. The couples' hormone levels were measured before and after the experimental manipulation, and within two weeks after the birth of their babies. They measured *prolactin*, which is related to caregiver bonding behaviors; *cortisol*, the stress hormone; *testosterone*, a male hormone that has been found to decline in male non-human animals around childbirth, in order to prevent aggression and increase sensitivity; and *estradiol*, a female hormone. All four of these hormones are related to parental responsiveness.

The findings were quite remarkable. Both men and women experienced identical decreasing hormone patterns from three weeks before the birth of their babies to two weeks after. All four hormones decreased significantly after their babies were born. Testosterone levels in new fathers were 33% lower than was found prenatally. This means that new fathers showed steep drops in hormones that may prevent bonding and responsiveness to infant cues. Some of the more subtle hormonal patterns were even more interesting. Men who expressed great concern over the crying baby on the recording showed much greater decreases in testosterone compared to less responsive men. Men who voluntarily held the doll for the full interview also had greater drops in testosterone levels. Men with higher levels of couvade symptoms exhibited higher prolactin levels and lower testosterone levels before the baby's birth. Animal research shows that high prolactin and low testosterone are related to paternal responsiveness to offspring.

This study shows that men living with pregnant partners respond to their hormonal changes in ways that may prime them to be responsive parents. It also shows that men who interact longer with infant-related stimuli show greater hormonal changes than men who do not. In essence, hormone changes in men during their partners' pregnancy and shortly after birth may influence them to be good fathers. Thus, it's important that men attend medical appointments with their pregnant partners, educate themselves about babies, and fully engage in planning for the birth and parenthood, in order to maximize the chances of a hormonal profile that will enhance paternal bonding.

Giving birth

Throughout history babies were, and around most of the world today are, born "naturally." No hospital, no medication, no medical intervention. However, with technological and medical advances, birth in the western world slowly became a controlled clinical experience. In the 1950s in industrialized nations, most women were given general anesthesia and were not even awake for their children's

Episiotomy
A surgical procedure that snips a birthing mother's perineum in a vertical line to allow for easier extraction of the baby.

Cesarean section
A surgical procedure that removes a baby from its mother's womb by cutting directly into the uterus.

births. Because they could not labor to push the baby out, technology was often employed. For example, vacuum extractors were used to pull the baby out by its head. In a procedure called **episiotomy**, doctors snipped the mother's perineum, the flesh at the bottom of the vaginal opening, to allow a quicker delivery of the baby out of the vagina. Medications enabled women to feel less pain. **Cesarean sections**, removing the infant surgically from the womb, allowed the infant to be manually taken from the uterus quickly if labor was not progressing or the baby was in distress. Sometimes forceps were required if the baby was stuck in the birth canal.

While all of these advances saved lives and made some births easier on mothers, for a normal, healthy, low-risk pregnancy, most women can deliver without intensive medical intervention (Stephenson et al., 1993). In fact, many doctors today will not routinely perform an episiotomy because the natural tearing of the perineum during labor can be stitched up and heal much stronger than can a completely straight-line surgical cut that severs fibers in an abnormally vertical line. The naturally torn uneven perineal tissue fibers can "grab" back onto each other and heal with more firm strength than can surgical scars (Hartmann et al., 2005). Also, with better monitoring technology (such as the use of ultrasound) during pregnancy and labor, fewer mothers today need vacuum extractions or the use of forceps. With the feminist movement of the 1960s and 1970s, women desired fewer medical interventions in their births. However, this trend had proponents decades before that.

Natural birth

Natural prepared birth
Dr. Dick-Read's method of educating parents about the physiology of labor as well as working on relaxation and stress management.

The **natural prepared** method of birth was pioneered by Dr. Dick-Read in the 1920s. He advocated educating people about the process of pregnancy, labor, and birth so that they were prepared. He emphasized breathing deeply and using relaxation exercises to help reduce stress. Today women can demand that their births proceed the way they want them to, provided there are no medical circumstances that preclude a natural birth.

In a development stemming from Dr. Dick-Read's (1933) methods and his own work in Russia and France, Dr. Ferdinand Lamaze combined breathing techniques with the psychological method of classical conditioning. He implemented patient education and breathing techniques, but in addition, he had people visualize positive outcomes from the pain of labor. So if a woman is having a contraction during labor, she might focus on deeply breathing and then envision herself breastfeeding her baby. This will eventually lead to a more relaxed mom who can mentally reduce the physical pain by conditioning herself to pair positive images with pain. Lamaze also emphasized the importance of a supportive birth partner, or coach, to help meet the woman's psychological and emotional needs during labor and delivery. Like a *doula*, the partner would help the woman remember to breathe when she started feeling anxious.

Lamaze birth
A natural form of birth where parents use visualization, breathing exercises, supportive partners, and knowledge about the physiology of labor to reduce pain and the length of labor.

Lamaze methods have evolved over time to include more active self-management of labor, with women being encouraged to walk, change positions, sit on a birthing ball, and remain active in order to encourage labor to progress. Partners are no longer considered coaches but are simply support persons to aid the woman in what *she* wants to do during labor. While the Lamaze method has been shown to reduce labor pain, reduce the time to delivery, and reduce the need for medications, it does not make labor painless. It simply helps a woman or a couple take control of her birthing process and work through the pain, focusing on the fact that the pain is essential for the birth of a beautiful baby to occur. It encourages women to feel empowered to handle the pain and control their births (Lamaze International, 2007). With educational services widely available these days, women and men are more informed about their bodies, the physiology of labor, and how to control pain through stress reduction and mental visualization. However, sometimes medical intervention is necessary.

Cesarean section birth

Even with all of the education, preparation, and empowerment in the world, sometimes a cesarean section (C-section) has to be done. The woman's labor may not be progressing or she may have high risk issues such as herpes, a viral STI that can infect babies entering the birth canal and cause blindness; any number of other complications can warrant a non-vaginal birth. C-sections should be used only if medically necessary because they can put extreme strain on mothers' bodies, and the resulting surgical abdominal scars make picking up infants painful and difficult. But the research shows that these procedures are often over-used and used more to prevent medical malpractice lawsuits than to ensure the safety of the mother and infant (Stephenson et al., 1993).

There is some evidence that the anesthesia used during a C-section can dull mothers' responses and interfere with the normal hormonal changes that occur in a vaginal birth. For example, Swain et al. (2008) studied a group of mothers who had vaginal deliveries and a group of mothers who had elective C-sections. They imaged the mothers' brains two to four weeks after delivery and found that when mothers listened to recordings of their own babies crying, the vaginal delivery mothers showed much greater brain reactivity than the C-section mothers did. These results suggest that the baby passing through the cervix, which stimulates the secretion of oxytocin, a hormone related to caregiver–infant bonding, may be a crucial element in developing maternal sensitivity to an infant's needs.

Choosing a birth method

So which method of birth is best? It's really a personal choice. Lamaze birth probably has the best research evidence to support its effectiveness, but women attest to the benefits of other methods as well. Research shows that having a *doula* participate in the birth reduces the chances of episiotomies by 60%, labor time by 25%, the use of medication by 30%, the use of forceps by 40%, the use of labor induction by 50%, and the need for C-sections by 50% (Klaus & Kennel, 1976, 1982, 1997). These findings suggest that social support for the laboring woman is a crucial element in a successful natural birth. Whether she gets that from a formal helper like a doula or from a partner is her choice. As long as the mother and infant are healthy and safe, and childbirth experts or medical personnel (doctors, midwives, doulas) are available to assist, most women can have the kind of birth they desire, medicated or not, hospitalized or not. Although it's important for parents to feel empowered to be in control of their own bodies, pregnancies, and birthing experiences, couples should realize that birthing plans may have to be scrapped if emergencies arise. Labor and delivery often occur in unpredictable ways and the couple's transition to parenthood can become complicated.

THE TRANSITION TO PARENTHOOD

Mitigating the stress of parenthood

Post-partum mental health

Decades of research show that having a baby isn't necessarily the deliriously blissful experience many parents imagine. It can be extremely stressful and can take a real toll on the parents' relationship. In fact, research suggests that marital satisfaction decreases substantially after the birth of a baby and does not increase again to pre-baby levels until the children leave home (Cowan & Cowan, 1992, 1995). Relationship satisfaction declines after childbirth for 65% of couples, while levels of conflict and hostility increase exponentially (Gottman & Schwartz-Gottman, 2007). Emotional intimacy plummets as the parents become exhausted and their physical and mental resources are depleted. They are irritable and argue over the workload, both feeling unappreciated for all they do. Sex is not allowed for the first six weeks after delivery, but even when allowed, the frequency of sexual relations remains low and passion becomes virtually nil. Mothers, especially those who breastfeed, often report having no sex drive whatsoever. They have no energy left for their partner, especially in the first year when breastfeeding every few hours. Each partner reports feeling lonely and overwhelmed. Men report that the mothers have family and friends rallying around them for support but that people fail to recognize the stress new fathers are under. For the most seriously distressed parents, this profile leads to an inability to respond appropriately to the needs of their newborn. They see their baby's cries as irritating or annoying. Furthermore, babies of distressed couples can experience developmental and language delays, fail to establish self-regulation abilities, and be unable to self-soothe (Gottman & Schwartz-Gottman, 2007).

Many working fathers and mothers end up feeling like work has become "home"—a sanctuary from stress—and home has become "work"—a constant to-do list with never-ending duties to perform. For dual-earner middle-class families, especially if they are in the sandwich generation, caring for elderly parents as well as young children, home may come to signify conflicts, tantrums, financial stress, and turmoil. No one pays you or values the work done at home. Contrast this with work, where everyone is dressed well (no spit up or sippy cup stains), uses their best manners, and gets pats on the back, appreciation, and pay raises. Home for many seems unwelcoming (Russell-Hochschild, 1997). Furthermore, women who work in low-paying, unskilled jobs who struggle to find quality child care, especially if they have unsupportive husbands, find even more difficulty in their mothering role (Koniak-Griffin, Logsdon, Hines-Martin, & Turner, 2006).

Mitigating the stress of parenthood

Fortunately, there are parent support groups and parenting classes available in most every community to help couples deal with these problems stemming from the transition to parenthood. The best defense is a good offense, however, so couples can do themselves a favor by working out some of the kinks of life with a newborn ahead of time. Many couples spend so much time preparing for labor and delivery that they rarely think through what daily life will be like with a newborn. They need to plan for juggling parenting and the couple relationship, map out who will do what chores, who will grocery shop and pay bills, and so on, so that they have a workable plan in place and can transition smoothly. For example, detailed discussions about sharing the workload, even with a typed list or signed contract, can help make for a smoother transition. It's important to set a maximum number of hours that will be allowed for each partner to work outside the home. A specific plan for how to balance work and home lives is essential ahead of time (Polomeno, 2000).

Beyond planning for post-delivery workload sharing, another very important preventive step is to learn as much as you can about infant and child development. Knowing what's normal can often reduce stress. If we know that it's normal for a newborn baby to cry often, sometimes for several hours per day, we may feel less frantic when we can't figure out what's wrong. If we know that most couples have reduced sexual intimacy for the first year after birth, we may feel less guilty or abnormal. Paradis, Montes, and Szilagyi (2008) examined over 10,000 parents of 9-month-old babies and found that they had surprisingly little knowledge of child development. They had no idea when babies should be able to reach for things, say their first words, or become potty trained. Parents with the lowest levels of knowledge were less likely to have healthy interactions with their infants and were less likely to cognitively stimulate their babies. Thus, education about couples' communication strategies and normative child developmental stages can be effective stress prevention.

Gottman and Schwartz-Gottman (2007) are two renowned psychologists who run the Gottman Institute, a group dedicated to preventing marital dissolution. They are also a married couple who publish widely on marital relationships. They suggest several avenues toward a healthier post-baby relationship. These include recognizing that all new parents experience the same stress. When we realize others are in the same boat, it helps reduce stress, especially if we seek them out for support groups, informal get-togethers, or babysitting trade-offs. They also suggest being able to soothe your partner but also being able to soothe yourself when your partner is emotionally or physically unavailable. Research shows that new mothers who get daily massages benefit as much in mental health improvement as do mothers who take anti-depressants (Gottman & Schwartz-Gottman, 2007). But when partners are not available, it's important that each parent use self-regulation skills, such as meditation, exercise, reaching out for support from friends, or even listening to music to calm one's self down. It's important also to accept as valid one's partner's viewpoints about conflicts, and try to learn from previous conflicts so those issues can be resolved in the future. This involves compromising and maybe even reading some books or taking some classes on conflict management skills, so that disagreements do not devolve into full blown wars.

While most of the problems described here are fairly typical for all new parents, some parents struggle to a much greater degree with psychological adjustment after having a baby.

Post-partum mental health

While many women have baby blues after the birth of a child, only about 10–15% develop symptoms severe enough to be diagnosed with post-partum depression. **Baby blues** include feelings of sadness, fatigue, exhaustion, being disappointed in parenting or in the baby itself, and general malaise. If the symptoms last for longer than two weeks and occur daily, the woman should contact her doctor or a mental health professional because she may have **post-partum depression**. Symptoms include feeling sad, hopeless, and overwhelmed, eating too little or too much, sleeping too little or too much, feeling worthless and guilty, social withdrawal, unexplained headaches or health problems, problems bonding with the baby, lack of joy about life, and, most seriously, thoughts of harming one's self or one's baby (Hanna, Jarman, & Savage, 2004).

Post-partum depression symptoms can develop from a combination of biological and social influences. For example, hormonal changes during birth can affect thyroid functioning, which can cause fatigue and mood instability. These symptoms worsen if the woman has little social support or other children to care for, which increases her stress levels, thereby leading to further changes in her physiological stress response system. Sleep deprivation also has a huge influence on both mental and physical health, and all new parents are sleep deprived (Hanna et al., 2004).

While many of you may have heard of post-partum depression in new mothers, you may not be aware that new fathers can also succumb to mental health impairment, especially if their partner is depressed. Roberts, Bushnell, Collings, and Purdie (2006) found that postnatal men whose female live-in partners were experiencing post-partum depression had higher levels of depression, anxiety, fatigue, and general malaise than did men whose partners were well. These results point to the importance of viewing the family as a *system* of interdependent parts which all affect each other. As discussed in Chapter 2, each person affects and is affected by every other member (Minuchin, 1985). Thus, it is imperative that *couple* health and well-being are assessed in the post-partum period, not just that of mothers, and not just that of babies. Research suggests that education about post-partum depression shortly before birth, plus short term cognitive behavioral therapy (five to eight sessions conducted by home visitors) can prevent post-partum depression in mothers and can reduce the rates of recurrence in mothers who develop symptoms (Chabrol et al., 2002). It's essential that affected parents receive treatment because much research suggests that infant–parent attachments and quality of interactions are hampered when one or both parents are depressed, which, in turn, is related to poor child developmental outcomes (Murray & Cooper, 2003).

Depressed parents are less positive and child-centered than well parents. Their infants are also more fussy, inactive, and less responsive to the environment (Hipwell, Goossens, Melhuish, & Kumar, 2000). There is little research on effective treatments for post-partum depression, but some work shows that counseling can improve depressed mothers' mood, sensitive responding to their infants, and infants' behavioral problems, at least over the short term (Murray, Cooper, Wilson, & Romaniuk, 2003).

Severe mental health issues after childbirth are rare. In fact, most people feel that the joy and positive emotional health a family experiences far outweigh the negatives. Most parents say they could not imagine life without their children. Most parents report that having children is one of the best things they've experienced in life. And, as discussed earlier, most people will eventually have children. In fact, many people sacrifice a lot, subjecting themselves to numerous medical procedures, being injected with hormones, or spending thousands of dollars and hundreds of hours of time, just to be able to have a child of their own.

Baby blues
A general feeling of malaise or sadness after one has a baby; usually lasts a week or two.

Post-partum depression
A serious clinical disorder arising after childbirth where parents feel sad, anxious, overwhelmed, and may even think of harming themselves or their babies.

INFERTILITY AND CREATIVE WAYS TO BECOME PARENTS

- Artificial insemination
- In vitro fertilization
- Reproductive surrogacy
- Adoption

Many people try to have children and find that they cannot do so. For these families, treatment for infertility is usually the first step taken. Several treatments for infertility will be explored in this section. Creative ways to give birth, like surrogacy, will also be discussed. If the methods used to have a biologically related child don't work, some consider adoption. Other people have always wanted to adopt a child, and they are happy not having their own biological children. This section will explore some options that people who do not have biological children pursue.

About six million Americans suffer from infertility but only about 20% of them seek help from high tech procedures (Weil, 2006). It's awfully disappointing for someone who may have used contraceptives regularly for years to find out she could not conceive a baby anyway. Women who want to but cannot conceive have anxiety and depression levels similar to women who are diagnosed with heart disease and cancer (Domar, 2004). Most women believe infertility is their problem, though today we know the man's health should be scrutinized as much as the woman's.

Causes of male infertility include alcohol and drug use, vascular and prostate malformations or disorders, testicular failure, and sperm transport problems. For example, some evidence suggests that marijuana smoking lowers sperm count (Grotenhermen & Russo, 2002; Martin-DuPan, Bischof, Campana, & Morabia, 1997). How do you think tetrahydrocannabinol (THC), tar, and the many other carcinogens in marijuana smoke affect the environment in which sperm develop and grow inside a man's body?

Endocrine problems, cancer, the STI chlamydia, working in hot environments, and vascular/vein problems (such as enlargement of testicular veins) lower sperm count the most. Obviously, some of these causes can be prevented with lifestyle changes, but hormonal and other treatments are also implemented, with varying degrees of effectiveness (Martin-DuPan et al., 1997; Raman & Schlegel, 2002).

Women who are obese, drink too much caffeine, use drugs or alcohol, are under extreme stress, or exercise excessively can also become infertile (Domar, 2004). Stress is a leading culprit, as the effectiveness of fertility treatments decreases by almost 100% if women are extremely stressed. For example, fertility treatments in general have a 45–50% success rate, but in highly anxious women, that rate decreases to about 20% (Domar, 2004). Turkish researchers found that only 17% of couples using in vitro fertilization alone got pregnant, but 43% of couples who used in vitro fertilization plus cognitive-behavioral counseling, relaxation training, and social support got pregnant (Domar, 2004). These findings point to the importance of *microsystem* influences and individual factors on biological functioning, a key aspect of the bioecological approach.

Much of the time, however, the cause of infertility remains elusive. Couples may try for years, timing ovulation, taking temperatures, and analyzing vaginal secretions in order to increase the chances of fertilization. Having to schedule sex every month at ovulation can kill romance and spontaneity and make a partner feel used. Couples who have been infertile for many years may experience symptoms of depression and anxiety (Tuschen-Caffier, Florin, Krause, & Pook, 1999).

Assisted reproductive technologies
New scientific approaches that help people have babies.

If improving the timing of intercourse doesn't work, more invasive techniques may be implemented. If both partners are healthy and medical professionals cannot determine the cause of infertility as being due to low sperm count, lack of ovulation, endometriosis, the age of the parents, or any of the reasons cited above, numerous **assisted reproductive technologies (ARTs)** are available. ARTs are medical procedures that increase the chances that a couple can have children. These include artificial insemination and in vitro fertilization.

Artificial insemination

Artificial insemination, whereby sperm are medically introduced into the woman's body to increase the potential for fertilization with her partner's sperm, is one of the most commonly used ARTs. Sperm can be placed in the vagina or uterus (Vishwanath, 2003). This method can use either a partner's sperm or, for heterosexual couples where the male partner's sperm isn't suitable, and also for single women and lesbians who desire to have a child, sperm donations from a sperm bank. This procedure can be expensive and it can often take more than a year for success. I have a friend who had to take out a second mortgage on her house to cover her nearly two years' worth of inseminations before she finally had a healthy baby.

> **Artificial insemination**
> The introduction of sperm into the vagina to aid in fertilization.

In vitro fertilization

In 1978 when the first "test tube baby," Louise Brown, was born, the world was in an uproar. People thought this was the beginning of a slippery slope of science interfering with life and playing God, and they were scared of what the future might hold. Horror stories of cloning and making designer babies were rampant. One of the first doctors to perfect in vitro fertilization in the 1970s came out to his car to find a note on it. It read "Test tube babies have no soul" (Kalb, 2004).

Today, more than 30 years later, we hardly blink when we hear that a child was conceived through **in vitro fertilization (IVF)**. In this procedure, a woman's eggs are harvested and mixed with a man's sperm in a lab. Before IVF is attempted, hormonal shots are given to the woman for several weeks to stimulate ovulation. The most common drug used for this purpose is Clomid. While Clomid is effective at stimulating the maturity of several follicles at a time, increasing the chances of healthy eggs being harvested, the drug can also cause emotional changes, weight gain, and other undesirable side effects. For a couple struggling with years of failed attempts to have a baby, the side effects of these hormones add to existing relationship strain in many cases; also, the cost is quite prohibitive for many couples.

> **In vitro fertilization**
> The introduction of a zygote or blastocyst into the uterus to increase the chances of pregnancy.

Weil (2006) estimates that for those who end up having a baby using IVF, which often requires several attempts, the cost averages around $100,000. For those who have good insurance or can afford it, there is about a 40% success rate for this procedure. After the sperm and egg are joined in a laboratory (in a Petri dish, not a test tube), fertilization is closely monitored. The *zygote's* cells begin to divide, and they can be assessed for genetic malformations and disorders before being implanted into the woman. This is called **preimplantation genetic diagnosis (PGD)** and can be performed for many genetic anomalies if the couple knows one or both of them has a genetic atypicality (Kalb, 2004), but this is also expensive.

> **Preimplantation genetic diagnosis**
> An optional procedure occurring during in vitro fertilization where genetic disorders are screened out and only healthy embryos implanted.

Today parents can even choose the gender of their future baby with almost 100% certainty for an additional fee over the price of the IVF procedure. A new technique, **microsort sperm sorting (MSS)** uses dye to mark X or Y chromosomes on sperm. There is a 90% success rate for identifying female sperm and a 76% success rate for identifying male sperm (Kalb, 2004). Sperm sorting is a good alternative if the couple does not want to waste embryos, as only embryos of the desired gender would be implanted. Couples considering this option may already have children of one gender and may only want a baby if it is the other gender. Or they may carry genes for sex-linked disorders so choosing the gender could avoid this problem.

> **Microsort sperm sorting**
> An optional procedure occurring during in vitro fertilization where chromosomes are marked with dye so that gender selection of babies can take place before implantation.

Because multiple births can put the mother's life and the health and development of the babies at risk, Canada, Australia, and New Zealand limit the number of embryos that can be implanted to two; currently there are no limits in the U.S. Thirty-seven percent of IVF births are multiples, compared to only 3% in the general population.

With IVF, if the embryo actually implants, the woman will usually have a successful pregnancy. There is an even higher chance of pregnancy occurring if the embryo has been kept in the lab for about five days. The average success rate of IVF is 37% for women under 34 but only 20% for women aged 38–40. The success rates increase if women use a donor egg and non-frozen, fresh sperm; this procedure leads to about 49% success rates, regardless of maternal age.

Weil (2006) warns that there is virtually no regulation of clinics that provide IVF and no legal restrictions in the U.S. on how many embryos can be implanted, as is evident from news stories about Nadya Suleman, "the Octomom," who had eight embryos implanted although she already had six children. In recent years, 60-year-old women have conceived using in vitro fertilization, and a widow has had sperm extracted from her deceased husband for use in in vitro fertilization. There have also been custody battles over frozen embryos (Weil, 2006).

There is even talk of a new "fertility tourism" movement, whereby people can travel to unregulated countries to get whatever infertility procedures done that they want. For example, Denmark is considering offering a "fertility cruise" whereby people can take ships to international waters and sidestep the regulations of all countries (Weil, 2006). Without regulation, clinics have every right to discriminate. They can choose to deny services to single people, older people, the disabled, or gays and lesbians. These reproductive technologies have advanced quickly and many people are concerned about the ethical issues involved when we engineer the types of children we have and screen out possible differences or atypicalities. Can you think of any ethical arguments against couples using some of the above techniques?

Reproductive surrogacy

Reproductive surrogacy
The use of a "donor" womb to carry one's child.

In **reproductive surrogacy**, a woman gestates a baby for a couple or single person who wants a baby. Couples usually choose surrogates through careful selection and legally binding contracted processes. Embryos created either from both parents' germ cells, or from the male partner's sperm and the surrogate's own egg cell, can be used. When the surrogate's egg cells are used, the baby is genetically related to the surrogate. In the case of complete embryo transfer, the baby is not genetically related to the surrogate but its development is vitally affected by her health, behavior, and intrauterine environment. This is an extremely expensive option as the prospective parent(s) must pay for all medical costs and living expenses for the surrogate, plus labor, delivery, and after-care. Many surrogates are paid a salary or stipend. Parents sometimes fear the surrogate will want to keep the baby so hefty legal fees related to contracts and other documents can be additional costs.

Adoption

Adoption involves a person or couple becoming the legal parents of and raising a child born to another woman. Norway has the highest rates of per capita adoption of any country and about one million children in the United States live in formalized legally adoptive homes (Ward-Gailey, 2004). Millions of other children live in homes with extended family or friends who have not legally adopted them. About 24% of foster children live in **kinship care**, foster care with biological family members who are not the child's parents (U.S. Dept. of Health and Human Services, 2008). Today, kinship care families often receive the same benefits of health insurance, stipends, and other services that other foster parents get. For adoption to occur, a mother must decide to give up a baby, or a baby must become parentless for other reasons. There are three types of adoption: private adoption, public adoption, and international adoption.

Kinship care
Foster care provided to children by their biological relatives.

Private adoption

Private adoptions
Adoptions conducted through private agencies, usually working with birth mothers in order to obtain a newborn or infant; babies are usually European American.

In **private adoption**, a birth mother decides to give up her newborn or infant and work with an agency to help her choose a suitable family to adopt. A suitable family may be of the same ethnic background as the mother, hold the same values, practice the same religion, and so on. The adoptive parents are often responsible for the mother's medical care, education, clothing, lodging, labor, and delivery costs. The majority of private adoptions involve European American infants. Private adoptions are extremely costly, and it can take years for prospective parents to find a birth mother. Unlike in previous generations, most white women now keep their babies, even if they were not planned or the father is absent. Private adoptions can be open, where the adoptive family gets to know the birth mother, provides her with pictures of the child and update letters over the years, or even invites her into their family to be an "auntie" or friend of the family. The level of openness in adoptions is rapidly increasing. Forty years ago every adoption file was sealed forever, but today children may grow up having intimate knowledge of and regular interactions with their birth mothers. Private adoptions can also be anonymous where the agency arranges the placement without the birth mother and adoptive parents getting involved with each other. Much more common, however, is the public adoption.

Public adoption

Another type of adoption is **public adoption**, in which people usually adopt relatively older children out of foster care. These children often have histories of abuse and neglect, in-utero drug or alcohol exposure, and multiple residence changes and foster care placements. Relative to their numbers in the general population, children of color are disproportionately represented in foster care. It takes several months, if not years, for a biological parent's rights to be legally terminated, so children in foster care who are adoptable are usually over a year old, and most of the adoptable children in foster care are older than 5 years of age. Today over 500,000 children in the U.S. live in foster care (U.S. Dept. of Health and Human Services, 2008). Fifty-two percent of foster children are boys who are on average 10 years of age.

A number of regulations govern public adoption in the U.S. Gay and lesbian people often find that public adoptions through the foster care system are easier to accomplish than private agency adoptions, which can discriminate against single or LGBT prospective parents. It is illegal in many U.S. states for single people or those from LGBT communities to adopt, even if they are allowed to foster children who have been removed from their biological homes (Ward-Gailey, 2004). Also, children affiliated with Native American tribes must be adopted by those with Native blood. It is very rare that an Indian child is placed with non-Indian adoptive parents. Tribal governments have their own child welfare and adoption systems that carefully oversee Native American adoptions in an attempt to prevent the dissipation of tribal communities.

Public adoptions Adoptions conducted through the foster care system; more often these children are older or children of color.

International adoption

Besides private and public adoptions, more and more **international adoptions** are taking place these days. Each country has its own adoption laws and procedures, so western prospective parent(s) must study those requirements and work with agencies both within their own country and in the child's country. They must also follow all U.S. immigration laws and work with immigration services in their home and adoption countries. The 1993 Hague Convention outlines formal rules for international adoptions. Countries who signed the convention must abide by these rules, including having only federal level standardized adoption agencies working with foreign adoptive parents and a transparent fee and child-exchange procedure (http://adoption.state.gov/hague_convention/overview.php).

International adoptions Adoptions conducted across country lines; usually western parents adopting children from developing nations.

International adoptions can be extremely expensive, costing between $10,000 and $40,000, but many people feel that the children are more likely to be healthy and less likely to have been abused or exposed to prenatal alcohol or drug use than domestic children in foster care. Moreover, a family can more easily find a newborn or young infant or toddler internationally than in the domestic foster care system (McMillan, 1993). People from LGBT communities find that it's sometimes easier for one of the partners to adopt internationally as a single parent than it is at home. The second parent can then, in some states and countries (but not universally), adopt the child at home, becoming a second legal parent. See Susan and Karen's story in the *Focus on My Family* box to get a feel for what can be involved in international adoption.

The macrosystem implications of adoption trends are telling. Prospective parents can adopt an older child of color very quickly and virtually for free in the United States, with the state even reimbursing many medical and other costs. However, adopting a white newborn infant can cost thousands of dollars. Adopting a newborn baby from China can cost $40,000, with several

FOCUS ON MY FAMILY

Susan and Karen adopt internationally

When I met Karen, she was in medical school and pregnant, but miscarried. We both unsuccessfully tried to get pregnant. I couldn't see children without pangs of jealousy and yearning. We decided against domestic adoption; I couldn't endure the thought of the birth mother changing her mind. Our adoption agency told us that healthy infants could be adopted in Vietnam. My life as a social justice activist began with Vietnam War protests—and now, a baby from Vietnam? It seemed like fate. International adoption is *very* expensive. The home study was invasive and uncomfortable. We scoured the house and filled it with homey smells. Then came endless checks—finances, child abuse check, criminal checks, fingerprinting, references, health exams, interviews about our lives and parenting styles ... the paperwork was overwhelming; hundreds of pages had to be notarized.

I kept thinking of all the people who become parents with no scrutiny at all. Our social worker told us that most people didn't believe lesbians should adopt, but that *she* thought "better with you than 'dying in an orphanage in Vietnam.'" (Quite a compliment; I became practiced at keeping my mouth shut.) Finally came a picture of a 2-month-old baby. We got Immigration and Naturalization Services approval. Then we waited. Endlessly. Painfully. Karen and I had fight after fight. I despaired; I couldn't believe it would ever happen. Imagine giving birth to a baby and then waiting five months to see him.

Finally, the call came. Karen was the experienced baby-sitter and older sister but couldn't leave her medical residency. I had never even diapered a baby. Luckily, three of our dear friends came with me. I'll never forget the day I called Karen to tell her I held our son in my arms. He had adorable feet, the sweetest smile, and his hair stood straight up. I remember walking off the airplane, putting Jesse into Karen's arms, and watching her incandescent smile blossom. Without an outpouring of help from our friends and families, it would never have happened.

Jesse had so much energy that we were run ragged. But soon it was Karen's turn to travel—this time to Cambodia (we didn't want Jesse to be the only non-white person in the family). The only hitch was that we couldn't afford it. But a generous gift from a friend solved that problem! In a week Karen was back. Eleanor was beautiful, with curly hair and chubby cheeks.

When Jesse and I met them at the airport, the first thing I said was "Give me that baby!" I later said that "parenting is like being inside joy." Our children are 11 and 9, healthy, smart, and delightful. They make us very happy. They are polar opposites in temperament, but have the exact same smile. People always ask if they are biological siblings. Karen and I were legally married in California in 2008, after 15 years together. Our children were with us, and sang "Give Yourself to Love." The song title says it all.

Susan and Karen with Jesse and Eleanor.
Photo reproduced by permission.

years of waiting time. International adoptions reflect western geopolitical power as many adoptive children come from countries that are economically dominated by western countries, such as South Korea, Latin American, Vietnam, and Russia (Ward-Gailey, 2004). In addition, people from marginalized communities, such as gay or lesbian parents, are more likely to adopt children from marginalized communities, such as poor children of color. What do you make of these trends? Do you think they reveal that certain children are more valued in our society than others are? Ward-Gailey (2004, p. 380) states that adoptive parents

> seek acceptably colored, healthy infants and toddlers … occasionally, as in the Romanian floodgate of international adoptions following the collapse of the Soviet bloc in the 1990s, color trumps age, and older children may be acceptable because they are categorized as white.

Race, class, gender, sexual orientation, and many other demographic influences affect the adoptive relationship, just as they affect all parent–child relations. Most adoptive parents are concerned about how well their newly adopted children will fare in their care, having experienced numerous transitions and often some traumatic events. They may take classes on parenting adopted children. Adoptive parents, like biological parents, sometimes have a difficult time with the transition to parenthood.

Unique challenges of adoptive parenting

Adoptive parents put tremendous effort into the process of finding their child. Even though adoptive parents usually view their children as their own, surveys show that the general public doesn't view adoptive parents as "real" parents, and people assume they have fewer emotional ties to their children, especially if they are of a different race (Ward-Gailey, 2004). Adoptive mothers are often told by other mothers how lucky they are to have done it the "easy way"—they didn't have to go through labor or breastfeeding. However, people fail to realize how stressful adoption can be. It can consist of many sleepless nights, great expense, international travel, many fears, and insecurity; once the child arrives there can be child behavior problems, especially if the child has a history of trauma (Page, 2003).

Adoptive parents, like biological parents, can experience depression. **Post-adoption depression syndrome (PADS)** can occur in men or women and has the same symptoms as post-partum depression. These parents have often spent years trying to have biological children. They have wanted a child for so long that they may often have unrealistic expectations regarding how happy they will be when their little bundle arrives. They may never tell anyone about their fears or insecurities, especially for fear that social workers may deem them inadequate parents or even take their children away (Page, 2003). Parents with PADS may feel they can't share their parenting difficulties with friends and family, who may be unsympathetic. Adoptive parents have waited so long for a child, and they worry that others will not understand how they can complain now that they have one. Prospective adoptive parents should know that it takes time to build an attachment and that the first few months with an adoptive child may be just as difficult as dealing with their own newborns. Parenting for all of us, whether we are biological parents or adoptive, is a learned skill. Scientific information can help us learn the best ways to help children achieve their developmental potential.

> **Post-adoption depressive syndrome**
> Similar to post-partum depression but occurring in adoptive parents who are disenchanted, sad, or overwhelmed by their new parenting duties.

PARENTING INFANTS AND CHILDREN

> Infant brains and the environment
> Parenting styles

Most parents are concerned about their children's well-being. Fortunately for new parents, science has discovered many key ingredients to positive child development and can provide parents with easy ways to ensure their infant's well-being, as well as healthy outcomes for older children.

The definition of child well-being is fairly similar around the world. We can define well-being in terms of children having caregivers from whom they can seek protection, a safe environment in which to grow and learn, and people who will actively help them deal with stress and solve problems (Lahikainen, Tolonen, & Kraav, 2008). A child's level of well-being is socially influenced within all social contexts, from micro- to macrosystems. Young children are vulnerable in that they have little control over the social contexts influencing them. They gain in autonomy and influence as the years progress but, in general, they are at the mercy of the adults and cultural influences surrounding them and their brains are designed to assimilate all of the information those contexts provide.

Infant brains and the environment

Neural plasticity
The ability for children's brain cells to respond to environmental stimulation; makes the brain malleable and able to adapt to its specific environment.

Earlier you read that more brain cells are generated in the fetus than a person could ever use in a lifetime. The infant brain is like a giant sponge, just waiting to soak up all the information it possibly can. **Neural plasticity** refers to the brain's ability to absorb information from the environment and organize its own functioning to work well in that specific type of environment. This has both advantages and disadvantages for the developing child. If the child has all the requisite aspects of an environment that leads to healthy development—a nurturing caregiver, good nutrition, safety, and stimulation—this neural plasticity allows for a tremendous amount of information to be productively processed and organized by the developing brain, leading to a child who is curious, energetic, and ready to learn (Nelson, 2001).

Any baby in the world is prepared to learn any language, practice any religion, go to any type of school, live in any family, and thrive in any culture on earth. Because the brain is so *plastic*—meaning malleable or responsive to influence—it can lay down neural pathways that perfectly suit its environment. For the average baby, this means becoming emotionally attached to one or more stable caregivers, developing a sense of familiarity and security in his or her home surroundings, learning the skills required to become a productive adult in the community, and so on. Parents who use warm and responsive parenting and form secure attachments with their children have children who are able to regulate their emotions effectively, thereby being successful in both cognitive and social tasks (Valiente & Eisenberg, 2006). However, neural plasticity can also put a child at an extreme disadvantage because the brain will record any and all experiences occurring in the child's life. If a child is abused, neglected, sexually violated, malnourished, ignored, locked away, underfed, or exposed to violence, war, or exploitation, the child's brain will record these experiences while it lays down neural connections that direct how it processes information and behaves in the future.

Stress and the developing brain

The amygdala and hippocampus of the brain process emotional stimulation and signal the release of corticotropin releasing factor (CRF) by the hypothalamus. CRF then in turn stimulates the pituitary gland which activates the adrenal gland to produce cortisol. Recall that cortisol is a stress hormone. When too much cortisol is released too often, parts of the limbic system can be damaged and emotion regulation abilities hampered. At first glance, this may appear to be a biologically driven, innate or hard-wired stress response system. However, much research shows that environmental stress activates this process and can lead to chronic hypervigilance in traumatized children.

Davies, Sturge-Apple, Cicchetti, and Cummings (2008) examined the brain reactivity of children exposed to inter-parental conflict. They found that children with high cortisol levels in their blood after witnessing inter-parental conflict also had high levels of glucose (sugar) in their brains' emotion regions. High cortisol secretion is related to a fast heart rate, quickened pulse, and more oxygen being circulated in the cardiovascular system. It is also related to the processing and storing of emotional events into long-term memory. Thus, children who witness continual inter-parental conflict show elevated levels of distress and hypervigilant physiological responses, and report feeling less secure in their relationships with caregivers. Other research has shown that insecure attachments are related to higher cortisol reactivity and stress. Long-term or chronic hyperactivity of the stress response system can eventually wear down both brain and body, leading to lowered physical health (such as poor immune functioning) and mental health problems (Davies, Winter, & Cicchetti, 2006).

Secure environments and the developing brain

When children are fed well, nourished emotionally, have strong bonds to caregivers, receive training and education, know that they are loved, and feel they are vital members of the family, clan, or community, they will thrive. Our brains are eternally responsive to the environment and we can overcome early deprivation, abuse, or trauma later in life. However, never again will our brain be more plastic, more malleable, than in the first five, and particularly in the first two, years of life (Knudson, 2006). One of the most valuable things a parent can do for brain development during the first year of life is breastfeed. Breastfeeding is the best nutrition a baby can get. It provides crucial immune system builders to prevent infection and illness, and it has been repeatedly linked to higher IQ scores in children. In an interesting twist on this latter finding, Caspi et al. (2007) found that breastfed babies had IQ scores almost seven points higher than their formula-fed counterparts when they reached elementary school. However, this was only true if the breastfed babies had inherited a specific gene allele that helps convert fatty acids in order to enhance brain development. This is a great illustration of how all aspects of the parent–child relationship are influenced by complex gene–environment interactions, and that we always need to consider biological influences as important factors in microsystem relationships.

Over-stimulation of the developing brain

Proper stimulation of the brain is needed for healthy development and eventual adult functioning. However, in western cultures, we often interpret this research to mean we should try to create baby geniuses. We can play Mozart to our bellies with headphones while we're pregnant to create mini-Mozarts. Or we let toddler Sally watch educational videos. We can send little Billy to an academic preschool to ensure he gets into a good college later on. Paying for music lessons, sports, and foreign language classes is the norm for many western middle-class parents. However, for proper brain development, babies and toddlers need only interactions with their families in the real world. They need to be talked to, sung to, read to, held, touched, cuddled, and massaged. They need to see nature, animals, and the world around them. Music does influence both physiological and neurological development, so hearing music is certainly beneficial (Sacks, 2008). But this natural, easy kind of unstructured stimulation is all they need in the first couple of years because *play* is their work. Play helps them learn problem-solving, communication, and creativity skills. They take on roles, imagine, and create. They don't need to adults to teach them academic lessons or involve them in disciplined or competitive activities at early ages.

Caregivers can nurture children's attempts at autonomy just by encouraging their interests, and then watch them blossom and thrive. Parents don't need to try to over-stimulate infant learning through computer games or educational television. In fact, numerous professional organizations such as the American Academy of Pediatrics recommend *no* screen media at all in the first two years of life because proper brain development proceeds from live face-to-face interactions, and TV is passive (American Academy of Pediatrics, 2010). Screen media discourages time spent in active play with humans, animals, and the natural environment. No more than two hours of screen media per day are recommended for children aged 2–18 years of age. Limiting the use of screen

FIGURE 9.4 How do chronic stress, abuse and neglect affect the developing child's brain?
Photo © Lucille Khornak/Taxi/Getty Images.

media will ensure children are physically active and engaged in the world around them. Every day, family stimulation is what the brain needs for optimal functioning.

Parenting styles

Most children are naturally curious and when given a secure base in terms of strong attachments to caregivers, they will feel safe to explore their environments and learn new things (Bowlby, 1978). A lack of secure environments, or even worse, the existence of threatening and scary environments, impedes the child's ability to investigate the world and assimilate new information in a productive manner (Lahikainen et al., 2008). More difficult environments can impair parenting and lead to lower levels of well-being for children. For example, Lahikainen et al. (2008) found that both children and parents in Estonia had lower levels of physical, emotional, and behavioral health than children and parents in Finland. Estonian families had more struggles with money, stress, and health problems like alcoholism, and children had more psychological and behavioral problems. Estonia is a post-Soviet society in transition, winning its independence from the Soviet Union only 20 years ago, and struggling to build a strong economy. In contrast, Finland is a financially strong Nordic state with socialist leanings, where a high standard of living is enjoyed by the majority of its citizens. Even though both countries enjoy the benefits of membership in the European Union, are geographically similar, and have citizens who speak similar languages, these larger macro- and exosystem influences—standard of living, economic struggles, stress, alcoholism— shape the way parents are able to parent their children and thereby influence children's outcomes.

Beyond larger systemic influences on development, there are key *microsystem* influences. The way parents raise their children has much to do with their histories with their own parents. If parents were spanked, they will probably spank their children. If they were raised in the church, temple, or mosque, they will more than likely do the same. Even when we try to undo what our parents did to us, we find that the internal working models laid down in the early years of brain plasticity are awfully hard to change. It takes a strong will and knowledge of how to do so, to radically change the caregiving models we grew up with (Masten & Coatsworth, 1998).

Much of what we do as parents depends on our **socialization goals**, the ideologies that drive parents' plans for their children's future, and influence the parenting tactics they implement.

Socialization goals
The ideologies that drive parents' plans for their children's future, and influence the parenting tactics they implement.

FIGURE 9.5 What specific things should parents do to ensure their babies experience healthy brain development?
Photo © Tomas van Houtryve/VII Network/Corbis.

What goals do we hold as most important for our children's proper development? Do we want to socialize them to be obedient and quiet? Independent and strong? Elements of our intersectional identities, such as ethnicity, social class, and religion, influence how we socialize our children. For example, research shows that people from lower socioeconomic classes tend to follow a more authoritarian parenting style, where they stress the socialization goals of obedience, conformity and deference to authority. They do not encourage children to analyze the world around them but to accept the parents' wishes without question.

Socioeconomic influences on parenting styles

Kohn (1969) argued that many lower-income parents grew up in tough neighborhoods with few job opportunities. The jobs they were able to obtain required repetitive unskilled labor with few opportunities for independent thinking. These lower-income parents may raise their children to survive in this same environment, to stay out of trouble and do what they're told. In contrast, many middle- and upper-class parents work in professions where there is a new challenge every day. They may have flexible schedules that allow them to make choices about their working hours, take time off for family, and have room for advancement in their work within a context of challenging assignments. These parents' *socialization goals* may include critical thinking, questioning authority, and envisioning new and exciting paths for one's self. Middle- and upper-class parents may allow their children to challenge their rules and may even negotiate with them. They strongly encourage independence and autonomy (Kohn, 1969). These ideas suggest that parenting styles and socialization goals stem in part from the very real demands of our individual social environments, as well as from the internal working models and ideologies of our parents and their parents before them.

Lareau (2002) extended these early ideas in her fascinating study of African American and European American families from lower and middle socioeconomic statuses. Instead of *racial* differences in socialization goals, she found more pronounced *class* differences. Middle-class parents tended toward **concerted cultivation**, a parenting style consisting of efforts to cultivate a child's individuality. These parents enrolled their children in numerous extra-curricular activities, from sports to music training. They used language, reasoning, and in-depth conversations to explain things to their children and often solicited ideas from the children themselves. Families with concerted cultivation goals might ask a child what he or she thinks about a current news story or a family crisis. Children are encouraged to ask questions. In interesting observations with these families at doctors' visits, the children often questioned what doctors had to say and felt comfortable asking questions about their medical care. In essence, these parents were socializing an "emerging sense of entitlement." The children felt entitled to respect and fair treatment. They were entitled to success in a world where schools and other social institutions would work for their benefit.

Lareau (2002) found that in both black and white lower socioeconomic status families, parents were more concerned with the socialization goal of **accomplishment of natural growth**. This parenting style consists of the feeling that as long as parents provide love, safety, and security, children will naturally grow and develop well. These children were not involved in extra-curricular activities but instead spent time engaged in rich extended family activities, playing with children in their neighborhoods, and attending church activities. They had much more free time than the middle-class children and deeper ties to family and community. But their parents expected obedience from them. The parents had virtually no extended conversations with their children. They would tell them what to do and expect it to be done. While they often supported their children in "bucking the system," such as defying an unfair teacher, they were not teaching them strategies for how to manipulate larger social systems to work in their favor. During their doctors' visits, these children rarely made eye contact with the doctor and had few questions about their care. In essence, these lower socioeconomic status parents were preparing their children for an "emerging sense of constraint." They felt their children would be constrained within existing authority structures and so they expected the children to conform.

Concerted cultivation
A parenting style used by middle-class parents to cultivate their children's individuality, self-confidence, and independent thinking.

Accomplishment of natural growth
A parenting style used by working class or poor parents to allow their children to develop naturally within strict power hierarchies and expectations for obedience.

Interestingly, Lareau (2002) found that white and black middle-class parents were very similar in their parenting styles, and that white and black lower-class parents also approached parenting in similar ways. The only *racial* differences found were that African American children of both classes were engaged in more religious activity than European American children (such as church-based camp for the middle-class black kids versus a state park based camp for middle-class white kids). They also had more contact with extended family than white children from both classes. This research strongly suggests that parenting styles emerge from historical, structural, and economic pressures.

Baumrind's parenting styles

To examine parenting styles in more depth let's look at Diana Baumrind's (1967) groundbreaking classifications. She examined several hundred families over two decades and found that she could classify most of the families' parenting styles along two dimensions, warmth/responsiveness and control/demandingness. She found that many families were high on both warmth/responsiveness *and* control/demandingness. She called these families **authoritative**. They had high expectations for their children's futures. They expected good grades, good behavior, autonomy, and responsibility. However, they were also extremely nurturing and responsive to their children's needs. They would have democratic discussions about family rules and would change rules if the children persuasively argued for such. They explained their positions and expected children to do the same. In essence, they were raising their children to exist in a world where anything is possible, where, if you work hard, you can have control over your life and you will be supported in all you do by loving parents. Contemporary research shows that children raised in this *authoritative* manner are happy and successful, stay out of trouble, can resist peer pressure, think for themselves, and are very well-adjusted. These kids are confident in themselves and have few behavioral or psychological problems (Lamborn, Mounts, Steinberg, & Dornbusch, 1991).

Baumrind (1967) also found a parenting style called **authoritarian**. Parents using an authoritarian style were low on warmth/responsiveness but high on control/demandingness. Authoritarian parents see obedience as a primary socialization goal and do not allow children to question authority. They do not solicit children's opinions about family business nor do they respond warmly to children's attempts at autonomy. They have high expectations for good behavior and staying out of trouble. Authoritarian parents love their children and want what's best for them, just like authoritative parents do. However, they are raising their children to make it in the world with their heads down, by keeping quiet and doing what they're told.

Contemporary research (e.g., Lamborn et al., 1991) has shown that children from authoritarian homes are more likely to be conformists with few goals for themselves. They tend to be well behaved and often stay out of trouble. They do well in school but lack confidence. However, children raised with an authoritarian parenting style can also be depressed, have trouble-making behaviors, and can sometimes rebel as they get older. Because authoritarian parents are likely to use corporal punishment, children can also be more aggressive as they get older since corporal punishment has long been found to be associated with elevated levels of aggression in children (Gershoff, 2002; Kazdin & Benjet, 2003).

Parents on the complete opposite end of the spectrum from authoritarian parents are **permissive/indulgent** parents, who are high on warmth/responsiveness but low on control/demandingness. Permissive/indulgent parents have few rules or expectations for their children. They love them unconditionally and warmly respond to all of their desires and interests. They cherish their children and think they will make the right decisions if they are given the freedom to explore. These parents are raising children who can do no wrong in their eyes. While most children raised using a permissive/indulgent parenting style "turn out OK," they can be aimless, having no goals for themselves, and narcissistic, thinking the world revolves around them. They tend to have high self-confidence and good social skills, but they often disengage from school

---

Authoritative parenting
A parenting style that is high on warmth/responsiveness and also high on control/demandingness; the style related to the best child outcomes in western cultures.

Authoritarian parenting
A parenting style that is low on warmth/responsiveness but high on control/demandingness; emphasizes conformity and obedience.

Permissive/indulgent parenting
A parenting style that is high on warmth/responsiveness but low on control/demandingness; few rules or expectations are placed on children.

SELF-ASSESSMENT

Parenting quality in family of origin (adapted from Gottman & Schwartz-Gottman, 2007, pp. 187–188)

Take this self-assessment twice, once in relation to your father and once in relation to your mother. If you had same-sex parents or a single parent, adjust accordingly.

1	My father/mother was not there for me.	true	false
2	My father/mother was cold; he/she wasn't warm.	true	false
3	My father/mother could be scary.	true	false
4	My father/mother hit me.	true	false
5	My father/mother had a real temper that scared me.	true	false
6	My father/mother said some mean things to me when I was little.	true	false
7	I really never understood my father/mother.	true	false
8	My father/mother was not affectionate.	true	false
9	My father/mother did not tell me he/she loved me.	true	false
10	My father/mother did not praise me.	true	false
11	My father/mother did not kiss or hug me.	true	false
12	My father/mother did not make me feel safe.	true	false
13	There was no pleasing my father/mother.	true	false
14	My father/mother did not attend my special events (e.g., games).	true	false
15	My father/mother never showed me he/she was proud of me.	true	false
16	Sometimes I was scared of my father/mother.	true	false
17	My father/mother did not treat my mother/father very well.	true	false
18	My father/mother was violent toward me.	true	false
19	My father/mother had a problem with alcohol or drugs.	true	false
20	My father/mother sometimes favored other siblings over me.	true	false
21	My father/mother was unfair.	true	false
22	My father/mother neglected me.	true	false
23	I avoided my father/mother whenever I could.	true	false

24	To this day, I am upset about how my father/mother treated me.	true	false
25	I never really knew my father/mother.	true	false
26	My father/mother never really knew or understood me.	true	false

Scoring: add the number of times you circled "true." If your total is 5 or higher, you may have lacked a good role model for healthy parenting behaviors. You may struggle with how to be a good parent. If this is the case, it's important to be sure you've worked out these issues before you have your own child; or if you already have children, it's important to work on these issues now. Obtaining counseling from a licensed therapist or psychologist, reading parenting books written by legitimate experts, and getting social support from friends, family, and issues-based support groups (e.g., Adult Children of Alcoholics) can help.

Note: Self-assessments are not meant to diagnose, cure, or treat any personal or family problems. They are meant for informational purposes only, and to spur discussion.

TABLE 9.1 Baumrind's parenting styles.

	High warmth/responsiveness	Low warmth/responsiveness
High control/demandingness	Authoritative	Authoritarian
Low control/demandingness	Permissive/indulgent	Neglectful

and engage in deviant behaviors with peers, such as drug use and truancy (Lamborn et al., 1991). They can also be creative, intelligent, and happy.

While all three of these parenting styles can be related to good outcomes in many children, authoritative homes produce the most well-adjusted children of all, especially in middle-class environments.

The worst parenting style is low on warmth/responsiveness *and* low on control/demandingness. In these **neglectful** families, children are virtually ignored. There is a lack of positive interactions between parents and children, in contrast to what we see in all of the other three parenting styles. In neglectful families, children are not stimulated or cared for. They may be malnourished or exposed to drugs and violence. They may miss many days or months of school, and their medical needs may be ignored. Not surprisingly, these children often have learning disabilities and language delays at far greater rates than other children (Teicher, 2002). In addition, they have higher aggressive and antisocial tendencies than children who were physically abused (Lamborn et al., 1991). Neglecting a child's basic needs is about the worst thing you can do to a child who needs to survive and thrive in a complex world. To see more clearly how Baumrind's parenting styles map out, see Table 9.1.

To assess your relationship with your own parents while you were growing up, take the *Self-Assessment* questionnaire on parent–child relationships.

When you complete the assessment, think about how differently your father parented you compared to how your mother parented you. Research shows that fathers employ different parenting styles than mothers. Moreover, people from various cultural, sexual orientation, and age groups also parent uniquely. The next section gives a brief glimpse of how parenting can take a variety of forms.

Neglectful parenting
A completely uninvolved parenting style, low on both warmth/responsiveness and control/demandingness.

THE MANY FACES OF PARENTHOOD

In keeping with our bioecological viewpoint, this section will examine how intersectional identities stemming from gender, marital status, race, ethnicity, social class, religion, and age can be key players in the parenting experience. We start with dads. We'll also look at single parents, African American parents, transnational parents, Native American parents, Asian American parents, LGBT parents, and grandparents as parents. Keep in mind that these are just snapshots to illustrate key influences on parenting. These sections are not meant to be exhaustive in their coverage of each type of parent. Moreover, some groups of parents have very little research on them and their sections are necessarily brief.

Fathering

Contemporary fathers are often confused about the roles they should play in families. Their roles throughout history were clear and sharply delineated from those of mothers. Today, however, men are often torn between traditional patriarchal values and attempts to fit in to new feminist and other non-traditional family forms. Mothers' roles are more clear-cut, and fathers' roles are more ambiguous. Fathers often receive mixed messages that leave them confused (Parke & Brott, 1999). For example, women say they want their male partners to help out more around the house and with the children, yet many women try to control those domains. They often criticize the way men do jobs around the house or care for the children, leading men to feel incompetent and unappreciated. Many new fathers report feeling like errand boys, waiting at the beck and call of their partners, without feeling an intimate connection to the new baby.

Psychologists recommend that women encourage fathers to play intimate, active roles in parenting from prenatal periods on, so that they know their contributions will be appreciated. Note that it's important for partners to work on communication and problem-solving issues *before* they have children so that the baby is born into a healthy and stable relationship environment. It's also necessary for social policies to allow men flex-time and paternal leave at work in order to build those bonds early on. Much research shows that fathers who care for newborns by changing diapers, feeding, and holding babies, often have more secure attachments with their children throughout life (Parke & Brott, 1999). This is not always easy to do, practically speaking. For example, Townsend (2002) found that fathers reported judging their own success as men based on a "package deal" of various roles: marriage, fatherhood, work, and owning a home. These roles may seem complementary but the fathers in the study reported an awful lot of tension in trying to balance the demands and contradictions inherent in their perceived jobs. They felt they had to provide for their families, protect their families, and also be emotionally available. The men reported a sense of not being able to do everything well and feeling much pressure, but they kept trying to spend quality time with children as well as perform well at work and be good emotionally available partners.

Current research shows that fathers engage directly with children about 1.9 hours per day on week days and 6.5 hours per day on weekends; these numbers add up to about 83% as much time as mothers spend engaged with children. Women do about 11 more hours of work per week inside the house than men do, but men do nine more hours of outside house work (like gardening and painting) than women do (Coltrane & Adams, 2008). If commuting time is included, in dual-earner families women work on average a total of 60 hours per week in paid and unpaid labor combined, while men work a total of 59 hours per week. So while it's true that men do less housework and child care, women do less outside house work and less paid work than men do; about 72% of women work, 73% of those full time, while 95% of men work, 97% of those full time (Coltrane & Adams, 2008; Parke & Brott, 1999). So while the work balance is different, for dual-earner families, we see a lot of very hard-working mothers and fathers. Keep in mind that these findings apply mainly to middle-class western families. We know less about how working-class families balance paid and unpaid work at home and on the job.

Research also shows that fathers have a unique way of playing with children compared to mothers (Carson, Burks, & Parke, 1993). Fathers engage in more rough and tumble play, like wrestling and tag, while mothers engage in more verbal interactions. Fathers allow children more independence, boys more so than girls, and exploration (Carson et al., 1993). They *talk* less and *do* more with their kids. Interestingly, by 2 weeks of age, infants respond differentially to fathers and mothers. They greet fathers with wider eyes and playful and bright looks on their faces (Parke & Brott, 1999). Sixty-five percent of 2-year-olds choose fathers over mothers as *play* partners. Dads are fun, and research shows that fathers who play a lot with their children have children who are skilled at interacting with peers later on (Parke & Brott, 1999). Involved fathers influence their children's cognitive and emotional development and have a positive impact on self-esteem. Also, research shows that if fathers spend at least 40% of their time at home, their children develop less gender-stereotyped ideologies (Coltrane, 2004).

Intimate and aloof fathering

Intimate fathers
Calm, peaceful dads who believe in gender equality; they desire intimacy in their families.

Coltrane (2004) describes two main types of fathers, the **intimate** father and the **aloof** father. Intimate fathers are calm and peaceful, and believe in gender equality. They believe that women have equal rights and strive for intimate relationships with their partners. When fathers care for and respond warmly to infants, their adult children become independent, strong women and emotionally sensitive men (Coltrane, 1998; Parke, 1996). Thus, the intimate fathering style can reduce sexism and perhaps even protect women from violence in future generations.

Aloof fathers
Dads who follow traditional gender stereotypes and expect to contribute to their family mainly by providing material goods.

Aloof fathers tend to follow traditional male identities, which leads them to eschew activities considered "feminine." They usually believe in stern male gods, emphasize separate spheres for men and women, and feel wives should obey their husbands. They base their identity on the **good provider role**, meaning that men work outside the home for pay and women care for the home and children. Their sense of masculinity is based on how well they provide for their families. This aloof style is

Good provider role
A traditional male gender ideology where men gain most of their identity from working and providing material goods for their families.

FIGURE 9.6 What are some unique contributions fathers make to children's development?
Photo © John Howard/Getty Images.

losing popularity with most western families, which is good because when men share in housework, women are less depressed and more satisfied with their marriages (Coltrane, 2004). As expectations for fathers continue to change, men will rely less on the good provider role to give them a sense of worth.

Fathering with fewer resources

For the poorest families, different struggles prevent father involvement in many cases. For example, welfare laws, such as Temporary Assistance for Needy Families, or TANF (previously Aid for Families with Dependent Children, or AFDC), prohibit women from receiving benefits if a man lives with them. This rule obviously stems from the old fashioned *good provider role* ideology, where it is expected that men can provide for their families financially and only if they don't should women receive government benefits. Welfare workers have been known to make unannounced night-time raids to discover children's fathers living in the home so that they can cancel the woman's welfare benefits (Parke & Brott, 1999). However, even when two parents work full time at minimum wage, unskilled jobs, they cannot make enough money to pay for both child care and their living expenses. This means that welfare could help lift poor working families out of poverty and keep men connected to their children. Instead, it punishes poor women for staying with their children's fathers or other men who might contribute to the children's welfare.

African American men in the United States have a legacy of slavery, migrant work patterns, incarceration, and early death that leaves many African American children without live-in fathers. These men are often extremely poor, uneducated, and unskilled. They live on the cultural, economic, and educational margins of society (Hamer, 2002). If they do find work, it's often for low pay, with erratic working hours and no benefits. These low-wage jobs are often physically demanding and may be located quite a distance from their homes, requiring long hours of public transportation. The men often have no power or opportunity for advancement. Their low income, long hours, and often distant workplace, lead many fathers to live away from their children's homes and give up attempts at seeing their children. They feel their children's mothers judge them negatively if they don't show up with money or gifts. Shame over not being able to contribute is common. Hamer (2002) interviewed poor African American live-away fathers who said they often didn't come around their children in order to avoid having conflicts with the mothers in front of the children. They felt they were not welcome if they didn't have money or goods to contribute. Just getting to the children's homes could be a half-day event using public transportation or finding rides with friends.

Hamer (2002) found that the poor fathers he studied had big dreams for their own children and hoped they could influence them positively. Many of them who did live near their children's mothers helped out with daily tasks of child care, taking children to doctor's appointments, playing ball with them, and watching them at the mother's home while she worked. These men all felt they were doing a better job with their children than their fathers had done with them. They did not see the good provider role as essential to being a positive influence on their children. However, they often felt powerless because the women controlled their visits, and if they failed to toe the line, visits with children were cut off. These fathers were usually raised by single mothers themselves and so expressed respect for women. They often asked their own mothers to mediate visitation, payments, and other logistics between them and their children's mothers.

Neither these men nor their children's mothers reported wanting to go through formal child support channels because the women feared the men would stop visiting their children if enforcement agencies went after them. They also felt that their own welfare benefits would be reduced (which does, in fact, happen) if the father paid official child support. The men agreed. They preferred to bring cash from their paychecks and let their children's mothers spend it as they needed, instead of having the government involved. Hamer (2002) found it particularly noteworthy that these men expressed deep caring and concern for the welfare of their children. They were not uncaring, callous, selfish men who left fatherless children abandoned around town. However, many of them struggled with basic skills of daily living, having had no role models or social support themselves, very little education, and sometimes substance abuse and incarceration histories. Nevertheless, many of them managed to see their children regularly and maintain positive relationships with the children's mothers.

In another set of studies examining poor, unmarried parents, parents were found to be strongly motivated to provide for their children, but they didn't want to marry their partners unless they created what they perceived to be a perfect life. They only wanted to marry if they had enough money for a nice wedding, their arguments, infidelity, and relationship struggles had ended, and they felt they could work together to raise their children. Because their general lives were so stressful, these parents chose to keep their promises to do right by their children by not entering into a marriage that they felt might end in divorce, like most of the marriages they had grown up around had done (Edin, Kefalas, & Reed, 2004; Gibson-Davis, Edin, & McLanahan, 2005).

As evidenced by these studies, the intersectional identities of race, class, and gender have powerful influences on parent–child relationships. The fathers described above were trying to meet societal expectations for masculine gender role fulfillment while also working to build secure attachments with the children in their microsystems. They leaned on their own mothers, friends, and family, and tried to provide for their children as best they could. Another group of parents that faces many challenges is single parents, who often struggle to be everything their children need in one body.

Single parents

Although single parents have always existed through death, desertion, and divorce, they are becoming more common today. The women's movement allowed women to get more education, enter the workforce for higher wages, and feel confident in caring for themselves. Today we see many women staying single by choice as well as choosing to mother as single parents. These deliberately single mothers are usually highly educated and financially stable, and have family and friends to support their mothering. They have no desire to find a mate but would like to nurture a child (Mannis, 1999).

A growing number of children are also living in single-father families today, more than ever before. Over two million children currently live with single fathers, which amounts to 15% of single parent homes (Sugarman, 2004). Courts are more willing to provide men with custody of their children than they were in previous decades. Men are also stepping up to become single parents as maternal drug use and child abuse are factored into custody decisions (Elrod & Dale, 2008). Single fathers on average tend to have more financial stability than the average single mother. There is very little research on this population, so the processes within these homes await further study.

Most of the research on single parents focuses on single mothers. The majority of single mothers struggle financially, making about half as much as their single male counterparts. Twenty-five percent of single mothers live below the poverty line, but most of them work and only 30% receive welfare benefits (Sugarman, 2004). Today, 70% of African American children live in single-mother homes. Social security in the U.S. provides for survivor benefits to help single mothers after the deaths of their husbands, but there are no such benefits for divorced women whose husbands fail to pay child support, or for never-married women whose ex-partners abandoned the child (Sugarman, 2004).

Early studies on child outcomes in single mother homes were distressing because they showed that such children were socially, emotionally, and cognitively delayed, compared to children in two-parent homes (Biller, 1974). People assumed that the family *structure* (single parent) impacted children's outcomes negatively. However, more recent research began to look at family *processes* and found that it wasn't single parenting, per se, that influenced negative outcomes. For example, McLanahan and Sandefur (1994) found that the best predictor of poorer adjustment in children from single mother families was their income level. It appeared that the decline in family income after divorce is what had the most impact on children, not the fact that they lived in single-mother homes. They had experienced the stress of divorce as well as a sharp decline in quality of life. When research controls for these contextual influences, they find virtually no differences between children in single-parent versus two-parent homes (Crockett, Eggebeen, & Hawkins, 1993). Recent research like this may also be evidence of a cohort effect. When earlier research was conducted, single parents were anomalies and were stigmatized. However, single parenting is more normative today so children may be experiencing less stress than earlier cohorts did.

When negative outcomes for children of single mothers are found in more recent research that considers process and structure together, interesting patterns emerge. For example, Weinraub, Horvath, and Gringlas (2002) found that children of single mothers had more behavior problems, worse school performance, and poorer social skills than children in two-parent homes. However, these outcomes were most strongly affected by measurements of high levels of maternal stress and low levels of maternal support for children's emotional needs. This illustrates that *process* mattered more than *structure* for predicting children's outcomes. It also brings to light that single mothers are a very diverse group. Some are responsive to children's needs and some are not, just like parents in two-parent homes.

In a fascinating study that followed children of single heterosexual mothers, children of single lesbian mothers, and children in two-parent heterosexual families longitudinally for many years, very few differences were found in children's outcomes (MacCallum & Golombok, 2004). These families were all middle- to upper-class professionals with high levels of education. This sample composition allowed the researchers to bypass any confounding factors related to poverty or stress in the single-parent homes. They found that single mothers (both lesbian and heterosexual) spent more time interacting with their children than did mothers in two-parent homes. Also, single mothers reported they had more disputes with their children. Boys raised by both types of single mothers showed more feminine characteristics, like warmth and emotional sensitivity, but did not differ from boys in two-parent homes on masculine characteristics. Beyond these differences, the children in all three groups were virtually identical on mental health, self-esteem, academic performance, peer relations, behavior problem levels, and teacher-rated adjustment to school (MacCallum & Golombok, 2004).

Although there is less research on single-father families, research suggests that single mothers are similarly happy and satisfied with their lives as single fathers are, and that both groups' parenting quality is usually quite good. However, single mothers show more emotional support, praise, and affection to their children than single fathers do (Amato, 2000). They also set more rules and have more consistent consequences for misbehavior. There are no differences in children's behavioral problems in single-mother versus single-father families.

This section has shown how changing gender roles and advances in cultural understanding of children's needs have influenced single-parent families. Such macrosystem influences can impact the unique challenges and struggles that parents face when trying to raise their children. One aspect of our macrosystem that puts unique pressure on families is discrimination and oppression. Research is limited on families of color, LGBT parents, and grandparents as parents, but the following sections will explore some of the parenting styles exhibited and some of the challenges these family forms face.

African American parents

Patricia Hill-Collins (1986, 1994) uses the term "shifting the center" to help people recognize the Eurocentricity that drives most research on families. She argues that if we shift the center away from the white middle class, we might recognize that engaging in both paid work and housework/child care has always been the norm for women of color. Also, we cannot assume that they struggle with male dominance in the family like European American women do. Hill-Collins (1986) emphasizes that people from the majority culture sees modern motherhood as a struggle for personal independence and appreciation, as they mother children who have unlimited possibilities for their lives. Meanwhile, women of color are struggling for their children to survive into adulthood in a racist culture that continually degrades people who look like them. Poor single women of color have struggled historically for the right to keep their children, and currently struggle for their children's survival. They do this through the support of rich kin networks, including "other mothers" like aunties, grandmothers, and friends, who share with biological mothers their financial, spiritual, material and emotional resources. An *Afrocentric feminist* perspective emphasizes that African American women have deep self-respect and strength, and demand respect from others. Hill-Collins (1986) argues that survival, power, and identity shape motherhood for all women of color.

Bell-Kaplan (1996) studied middle-class and lower socioeconomic status African American mothers of pregnant teenage daughters and found that they had constructed identities of strength, power, respect, and moral righteousness for themselves. None of the mothers studied approved of their daughters getting pregnant. The middle-class single black mothers in this study had worked diligently to raise themselves and their children out of poverty. They were terribly afraid of sliding back down in social acceptance. They felt guilty about the teen pregnancies, as if their parenting had failed. The lower socioeconomic status mothers in this study discussed how much they desired to get out of poverty and that teenage pregnancy ruined those chances (many of them were themselves teenage mothers and wanted more for their daughters). This study contradicts the erroneous belief many people have that African Americans approve of teenage pregnancy or consider it a normative event. Instead, many African American parents rely on traditional values and church teachings to create moral lessons for their children. They construct routines of intimate connection with church and community to form a foundation from which children can grow to be successful.

Parke and Buriel (1998, 2006) discuss the importance of tradition and ritual in families of color. African American families often teach their children lessons through stories of people they have known or experiences they have had. Storytelling and other oral traditions are long-held practices in many families of color. They also celebrate traditional rituals, holidays, and routines in order to solidify family intimacy (Wolin, Bennett, & Jacobs, 1998). Children from families who engage in regular rituals and routines have lower levels of alcoholism and higher levels of self-esteem as adults. Parents of successful black children work hard to instill a sense of ethnic pride, the development of self-confidence, a keen awareness of racism, and the ability to negotiate a bicultural identity (McAdoo, 1993).

Transnational and Latino parents

Contextual influences make it impossible for some families of color to spend quality time with their children. The experiences of transnational mothers form a striking illustration of parental drive to ensure a positive future for children while living separately. These mothers immigrate to a country where they can find better work and more pay and must leave their children behind. In the United States, we see this trend particularly in Mexican and Central American women who come to the U.S. for low-paying domestic work. They send money home to support their children and are sometimes separated from their families for years. They often provide housework and child care for white middle-class mothers, which allows those mothers to work outside the home. In this way, transnational motherhood deconstructs SNAF values for both types of women (Hondagneu-Sotelo & Avila, 1997). Both the dominant European American ideology and Latina Catholic ideology value mothering as an important job. Many Mexican and Central American women coming to work in the U.S. value motherhood and wish to do it full time, but their work separates both them and their employers from their own children.

Cultural brokers or gatekeepers
Children who serve as liaisons between their home culture and the larger dominant culture, providing key services for their families and often taking on adult-like responsibilities.

Immigration status and the level of acculturation to the new culture impact parenting. In new immigrants or second generation parents who don't speak the dominant language, children often serve as **cultural brokers** or **gatekeepers** (Parke & Buriel, 1998, 2006). Children translate the new culture for their parents and communicate with the dominant culture for their parents. These children, sometimes very young, take on the worries and responsibilities of adults. They help fill out medical forms, pay taxes, file insurance claims, translate school memos, and talk to employers. When children are from traditional cultures, they must balance the difficult challenges of being cultural brokers with maintaining deference and respect for their parents as heads of the household (Buriel, Perez, DeMent, Chavez, & Moran 1998).

Chicano/Latino parents emphasize a strong sense of identity with *la raza* (the race), and they take pride in their *mestizo* identity (a mixture of Spanish and Native American heritage). Parents place value on interpersonal functioning, good manners, and polite social interactions. They feel social skills are just as important as cognitive skills for children to develop. One of their main goals for children is that they become *bien educado* (socially skilled and respectful). Families tend to be patriarchal, but women actually wield quite a bit of power in family decision-making and childrearing. Hispanic mothers wish for their children to exhibit respect, harmony, cooperation, and self-denial, as well as great social responsibility (Buriel, 1993).

Native American parents

Native American families often experience life as immigrants in a country where they lived long before white settlers arrived. They are a diverse people, with 450 tribes speaking 100 languages (Trimble & Medicine, 1993). While 70% of Native Americans live outside of reservation land, most of the research on Native families is done on reservations. What little research we have shows that Native American grandparents play a significant role in family life. Families value cooperation and harmony with nature. They tend to see time as fluid, focusing on the here and now, not looking at events as linear. They also believe in teaching children through having them listen, watch, and then practice new skills in private (Lum, 1986; Suina & Smolkin, 1994).

Because many Native American grandparents and parents grew up away from their tribes in boarding schools (even until the 1970s), they were not exposed to Native methods of childrearing and so may have little knowledge of how to successfully raise children. Child neglect is five times higher for Native Americans than for the general population (Harjo, 1993). In general, however, these parents desire their children to be proud of their heritage and competent tribe members. In addition, they want them to adapt to the majority culture while maintaining ties to traditional ways.

Asian American parents

Asian Americans also struggle with living bicultural identities, maintaining traditional ties while adapting to the dominant culture. Asian Americans come from about 28 countries or ethnic groups and they often instill Confucian principles in their children. This includes a strict social hierarchy with deference to parents, family loyalty, moral obligations, and denial of individual needs (Parke & Buriel, 1998). Chinese and Vietnamese families tend to be more traditional than Japanese families, due to differences in immigration and acculturation patterns. Chinese mothers tend to be more restrictive and controlling than Chinese American mothers (Chiu, 1987). In American research examining families from many ethnic groups, Asian American families tend to score high on authoritarian parenting styles. However, Chao (1994) reminds us that Chinese families value *chiao shun* and *guan*, which have no equivalent words in English, but mean something close to "training with support and concern." So while Americans may view Chinese families as high in control/demandingness and low in warmth/responsiveness, these parents and children actually see the parenting style as one of governing children while caring deeply for their success. Zhou, Eisenberg, Wang, and Reiser (2004) found that most parents in China used a parenting style closer to authoritative than authoritarian and when they did, their children showed excellent emotion-regulation skills and social functioning.

LGBT parents

When gay, lesbian, bisexual, or transgender people decide to become parents, they often already exist within unique family forms. Many have had to separate from their biological families who did not accept them, so often LGBT people bring children into "chosen family" networks, groups of non-biologically related people who form an emotionally supportive network (Dalton & Bielby, 2000). It is estimated that one out of five lesbians and one out of ten gay men are parents. In a survey of LGBT non-parents, 49% said they would like to become parents some day (Bos, van Balen, & van den Boom, 2005).

Many children of gay and lesbian parents were born into heterosexual marriages or relationships before their parent came out of the closet. Research shows that when divorced lesbian women form new committed lesbian partnerships, their children accept her female partner much more easily than other children accept a new stepfather (Tasker, 2002). This may be because a stepfather is seen as a rival to or replacement of their biological father, whereas a new female adult is seen as a friendly supporter. In fact, lesbian divorced mothers are more likely than heterosexual divorced mothers to allow their children regular contact with their biological fathers.

LGBT parents face many struggles heterosexual couples do not have to deal with. For example, in same-sex households, the non-biological parent must adopt the child formally in order to be ensured any rights should the biological parent die or the relationship end. They are not legally or socially recognized as legitimate parents (Dalton & Bielby, 2000). They cannot sign permission slips for school functions or approve of medical treatments. Biological gay parents are thought to be the child's "real parents," while the non-biological mom or dad is seen by outsiders as more of a friend. In some U.S. states, sperm donors have more rights to children if the custodial parent dies than does a same-sex partner, even one who raised the child from birth (Tasker, 2002).

Gay fathers are doubly marginalized, as heterosexual fathers often confuse homosexuality with pedophilia, leading them to stigmatize and judge gay stepfathers. In addition, parenting in the gay male community is relatively rare, so gay fathers often feel stigmatized as belonging to that marginalized group of "breeders," to which other gay men can't relate (Tasker, 2002).

The women's movement of the 1970s and 1980s helped develop greater approval for lesbian mothers than gay male fathers, as women are widely assumed to be naturally good parents. Parenting for gay men is still stigmatized. Gay fathers feel like better parents and report being more successful at handling challenges with their children if they have a live-in partner, suggesting that two partners, regardless of sexual orientation, makes parenting easier (Tasker, 2002). McPherson (1993) reported that gay fathers shared an even distribution of child care and household chores with their partners, more so than did heterosexual couples. They were also more satisfied with the quality of their relationships.

Gay fathers report that their daughters accepted their coming out as gay much more easily than their sons did, probably because male children face more challenges with traditional views of masculinity and rampant homophobia (Tasker, 2002). Bigner and Jacobson (1989) found that gay and straight non-residential divorced fathers had equal levels of quality relationships with their children, but the gay fathers were less indulgent in their parenting style, perhaps feeling less pressure to compete with the children's mothers.

Planned same-sex families
Gay or lesbian families that planned to have children together in their union.

Divorced same-sex families
Gay or lesbian families that contain children who were born into previous heterosexual unions; these children have experienced divorce and a parent's "coming out."

Over two decades of research examining child outcomes for LGBT parents finds no evidence that the children fare worse than kids from heterosexual homes (Patterson, 1995, 2009). They do well in school, have good social and cognitive skills, are happy, and mentally healthy. They actually benefit from having same-sex parents in some ways. For example, they endorse gender and racial stereotypes less often than children from heterosexual homes, and they are more tolerant of non-traditional relationships and family forms (Patterson, 2009). The girls tend to strive toward gender non-traditional careers like science. Some evidence suggests that children of lesbian parents are less aggressive than children of heterosexual parents (Bos et al., 2005; Steckel, 1987; Tasker, 2002).

There are two types of lesbian and gay families, planned and divorced. **Planned** same-sex families are those who planned to have children together within the context of their current same-sex relationships. This is an important distinction, because children from **divorced** same-sex families have experienced more stressors: a divorce occurred in the parents' previous heterosexual relationship, and one of their parents came out of the closet. Studies show that when parents are open about their sexual orientation at work, with ex-partners, and with their families and children, their children are much less likely to suffer psychological problems than if parents remain closeted (Bos et al., 2005). Interestingly, lesbian parents are much more likely to be open with their children about their conception through sperm donation in comparison to heterosexual couples, who are less likely to tell their children because they want them to feel like they are from a "normal" family (Brewaeys, Devroey, Helmerhorst, van Hall, & Ponjaert, 1995). Also, some literature shows that in *planned* lesbian families, the non-biological mother is more sensitive and responsive to her children than heterosexual fathers are to theirs (Bos et al., 2005).

Many people are concerned that children from LGBT families are more likely to grow up with a homosexual sexual orientation. However, there is no evidence in the literature to support this (Bos et al., 2005). In a study of children born through sperm donation, comparing those from single-parent households vs. two-parent households (of any gender), and those from lesbian vs. heterosexual households, there were *no* family structure or sexual orientation effects, and no differences in children's psychological adjustment (Chan, Raboy, & Patterson, 1998). For *all* families examined in this study, high parenting stress, inter-parental conflict, and low relationship satisfaction were consistently related to higher behavioral and emotional problems in children, regardless of the composition of their family structures.

Grandparents as parents

With the AIDS epidemic and drug and alcohol problems affecting parents from all ethnic, sexual orientation, and socioeconomic status groups, grandparents in greater numbers are raising their grandchildren. Today, six million children in the United States and Canada are being raised by grandparents (Hansard & McLean, 2001). There have been 150,000 children in the U.S. alone orphaned by AIDS, not to mention the millions around the world. Many grandparents, in the fight to gain custody of their grandchildren, must destroy their own children's reputations in court. They must testify to drug use, theft, and child endangerment, often while experiencing extreme guilt over the feeling that they themselves failed as parents to their own children.

FIGURE 9.7 What family processes do you think will most benefit this child? Can they occur within the context of *any* family structure? Iraqi woman with her baby, 2008.
Photo © Robert Nickelsberg/Getty Images.

While grandmothers of color have always been intimately involved in helping to raise their grandchildren, grandparents from all walks of life are now more likely to be the sole parental figures of their grandchildren. Grandparents face the additional challenges of being older and having less energy to care for young children, and they must use their retirement money to care for those children (Hansard & McLean, 2001). They may have no knowledge of child development, especially knowledge of how to cope with traumatized children or children with multiple learning or behavioral problems. The children may express anger towards them and constantly test boundaries, wondering if their grandparents will also leave them. These grandparents have no free time to spend with other grandchildren and often after years of raising them, face losing custody if the biological parents get their lives together. Grandparents raising grandchildren is quite a challenge. They need societal support including respite care, health insurance, counseling, and financial support from foster and kinship care systems (Hansard & McLean, 2001). When it works out, though, children raised by grandparents can do very well developmentally, having similar health, well-being, and school adjustment levels as other children (Solomon & Marx, 1995).

There are many ways to raise children, and most of them result in positive child adjustment. As discussed in Chapter 1, research from all over the world supports the notion that it is not the *structure* of the family that matters. A child can be born to single parents, parents from LGBT communities, interracial, transnational, or any other family structure, but what really matters is how the parents shape intimate connections with their children. Meeting their basic needs and providing for the rights the United Nations endorses for all children, in order to ensure emotional health, are key *processes* that matter. And oftentimes, entire communities are needed to support children's positive development.

COMMUNITY DEVELOPMENT AND THE MACROSYSTEM

Community development
Collective efforts by all public agencies to provide goods and services that support all parents in helping their children meet their developmental potentials.

If we are to ensure that all children receive their basic human rights for positive development, the principles of **community development** must be followed. Social problems cannot be solved at only the individual, microsystem, level. In community development approaches, governmental, non-profit, social welfare, religious, economic, and employment agencies band together to create a safety net supporting families' welfare (Perkins, Crim, Silberman, & Brown, 2004). All stakeholders put forth concerted effort to support families in their desire to raise healthy, happy, emotionally secure, successful children. Community development includes keeping neighborhoods safe from toxins and pollution, teaching parents about positive parenting and discipline strategies, supporting marriages and committed partnerships with basic rights and benefits, and supporting family values through maternity and paternity leave, high-quality child care with trained teachers, and job flexibility. If this sounds expensive, it is: the investment on the front end would be expensive. But the price we are paying right now for *not* supporting families is far greater. The costs of mental health, welfare, incarceration, drug treatment, custody battles, child abuse, and foster care are enormous. And many other after-the-fact interventions cannot possibly help strengthen families like comprehensive preventative community development efforts can.

Strober (2004), an economist, sees children as a "public good." She argues that we must begin to view children as a valuable asset. When we treat them well, all of society reaps the rewards. Strober posits that it will take collective social action to take care of the nation's children and that we can't expect parents to do it alone. It comes down to how much society is willing to pay to support families and prevent social problems like crime and neighborhood destruction. People in other western industrialized nations pay much higher taxes than Americans do in order to ensure the health and well-being of all citizens. These countries also have fewer ultra-rich citizens who acquire massive quantities of material goods. Neither doctors nor rock stars make the kind of money they make in the U.S. But most citizens have free health care and free high-quality child care, and make a living wage at their jobs. Some pundits argue that the economic downturn beginning in 2008 may have helped people begin to reprioritize and move away from an economy of consumption, and into an economy of compassion. Do you think this is possible? Desirable? Your generation will be the one to make the call.

CHAPTER SUMMARY

"Mothering" and "fathering" are relatively new concepts in human history, terms that imply that parents engage in an active and deliberate process of socializing individual children. Throughout history, infant mortality rates were high and most families engaged in subsistence living. They had as many children as possible to help maintain the health and well-being of the family. It wasn't uncommon for children to nurse on hired wet nurses instead of their own mothers. Also, children were often sent away from home at young ages, to apprentice with employers and earn money.

As industrialization spread, better medical care, hygiene, and education ensured that more children would live better and longer. Families began having fewer children and investing much time and energy into each individual child. These trends were mainly true for European American middle-class families. Other families still struggled to make ends meet and to this day, families from lower socioeconomic classes raise children with socialization goals geared toward obedience and conformity, instead of toward shaping one's individuality.

Parents around the world use a variety of parenting styles according to their socialization goals. Styles can range from authoritarian to quite indulgent. Research suggests that the best parenting style for the majority of children in western nations includes high levels of warmth and responsiveness, combined with high expectations and demands (the authoritative type of parenting). Moreover, secure attachments and proper levels of stimulation ensure that a child's extremely plastic brain will develop to its full potential.

The chapter explored the many ways that parents have children, from natural childbirth, to cesarean section, to using artificial insemination, surrogacy, and adoption. Regardless of how a child is conceived or which type of birth he or she experiences, every child has the same needs for a secure environment structured to provide nurturance, proper nutrition, and culturally appropriate socialization. Inordinate amounts of stress can harm children's well-being and lead to improper brain functioning. Stress or exposure to teratogens can be particularly damaging to the baby during the embryonic stage of prenatal development when all of the organs and tissues are forming. Both fathers and mothers should take care of their physical and mental health prior to conceiving children in order to ensure the best chances for survival of the baby and its healthy development.

Many parents focus a lot of energy on pregnancy and planning for the birth and are unprepared for the great challenges they face in the transition to parenthood. Sleepless nights, a crying infant, less time for each other, and post-partum depression can all be problems for new parents. These problems can be mitigated or prevented by planning carefully for the sharing of roles and workloads, open communication, and obtaining counseling.

Both fathers and mothers face many challenges in balancing family, work, and couple roles. And parents of color, LGBT parents, and grandparents face even more obstacles as they raise children under the macrosystem forces of racism and oppression. Each cultural group has a set of values and socialization goals that shapes how they parent their children. Intersectional identities impact the type and quality of parenting that parents are able to provide. Race, ethnicity, social class, gender, age, and sexual orientation all affect socialization processes within families.

If entire communities come together to provide for infants' and families' basic needs, we can ensure that, regardless of their backgrounds or family structure, children will have what they need to thrive and many social ills can be prevented

KEY TERMS

accomplishment of natural growth
aloof fathers
artificial insemination

assisted reproductive technologies
authoritarian parenting
authoritative parenting

baby blues
blastocyst
cesarean section
community development

concerted cultivation

couvade syndrome

cultural brokers or gatekeepers

divorced same-sex
    families

doulas

embryonic stage

episiotomy

family planning

fetal stage

good provider role

HOX genes

in vitro fertilization

international adoptions

intimate fathers

kinship care

Lamaze birth

microsort sperm sorting

natural prepared birth

neglectful parenting

neural plasticity

oocyte

permissive/indulgent parenting

placenta

planned same-sex families

preimplantation genetic diagnosis

private adoptions

post-adoption depressive
    syndrome

post-partum depression

public adoptions

reproductive surrogacy

socialization goals

spermatozoa

teratogens

zygote

WEBSITES FOR FURTHER EXPLORATION

http://www.actagainstviolence.org

This is a site devoted to the Adults and Children Together (ACT) Raising Safe Kids program developed by the American Psychological Association. It's a program designed to encourage non-violent and positive parenting. It provides handouts, articles, information, and training for both professionals and parents. The website includes public service announcements, as well as articles about improving parenting skills.

http://www.nlb.nih.gov/medlineplus/infertility.html

The National Library of Medicine and the National Institutes of Health have collaborated on this site, which covers anything you'd ever want to know about infertility. It has a dictionary of terms, information on anatomy, drugs, the latest research, coping skills, adoption, treatment, and a list of clinical trials for new treatments currently underway.

http://www.gaybboom.com

This is an excellent site about parenting in LGBT families. While much of the information—discussion forums, resources, and community events—requires you to register (it's free), a great table is available for anyone to view. This table explores the many parenting options available, from in vitro fertilization, to home insemination (turkey baster method), to surrogacy, to adoption. The table covers the cost of each option, how long you might wait to complete each option, and the emotional and social issues you might face in each case.

CHAPTER 10
THE ECONOMY OF WORKING FAMILIES
Balancing Mental, Physical, and Financial Health in the Twenty-First Century

No government can love a child, and no policy can substitute for a family's care. But at the same time, government can either support or undermine families as they cope with moral, social and economic stresses of caring for children.

(Hillary Rodham Clinton)

LEARNING OBJECTIVES

- To understand the roles historic and contemporary economic trends play in the lives of families.

- To get a feel for how diverse types of families experience life in the workplace

- To appreciate the economic pressures that impact family relationships

- To recognize how work and family pressures differ for men and women

- To gain insight into how work stress, income levels, and family-friendly policies or the lack thereof can influence people's physical and mental health.

Marriages and Families in the 21st Century: A Bioecological Approach, First Edition. Tasha R. Howe.
© 2012 Tasha R. Howe. Published 2012 by Blackwell Publishing Ltd.

OVERVIEW OF ECONOMIC TRENDS

- Contemporary issues
- Historic patterns in work and income

DIVERSITY IN WORK AND FAMILY LIFE

- Men in families and work
- LGBT issues and work
- African American experiences with work and family
- Diversity in social policies around the world
- Working women in families
  - Women and career advancement
  - Sexism
  - Challenges for working women of color
  - Tokenism
  - Wage penalties for women

BALANCING WORK AND FAMILY

- Family-friendly policies
  - Child care issues
  - The impact of performing multiple roles
  - Policies that benefit families
- Work stress
  - The role of personality in work stress
  - Economic downturns and unemployment

LIVING ON THE EXTREMES OF THE SOCIOECONOMIC CONTINUUM: POVERTY AND WEALTH

- Living in poverty
  - The consequences of poverty
- Living in affluence

OVERVIEW OF ECONOMIC TRENDS

We are in the midst of a global economic crisis of enormous impact. In recent years there has been a keen economic downturn in once prosperous nations. Wealthy countries played high-risk games in the financial market and now we feel the impact, with debt increasing and wealth being leached away from the west (*The Economist*, 2009). Interestingly, developing nations like Brazil and India have generally been more conservative in their financial dealings and many of them are showing a remarkably quick recovery from the crisis. More money is flowing into developing nations and their economies have been growing about 6% per year since 2008, versus about 2% in the west (International Monetary Fund, 2010). Western banks are holding on to money, not lending, and deficits remain high in the developed world.

The average U.S. family experienced a decline in annual income of more than $2,000 between the years 2000 and 2007. Meanwhile, the cost of living has increased dramatically, with energy and health care costs skyrocketing. People, especially men, earn less now, in dollars adjusted for inflation, than they did 10 years ago (www.whitehouse.gov/issues/economy). From 2008 to 2009, the unemployment rates for men jumped from 6.1% to 10.3%, and for women from 5.4% to 8.1%. During that same period, unemployment duration increased from an average about 10 weeks to over 15 weeks (U.S. Bureau of Labor Statistics, 2009). The national unemployment rate in 2010 was over 9%. Moreover, once middle-class families who have lost their homes through the sub-prime mortgage crisis, declining wages, job loss, or exorbitant health care costs are now joining the ranks of the homeless (Hardy, 2009). For example, Hardy describes the situation in Charles County, a wealthy Maryland suburb and the twentieth richest county in the U.S. Since 2007, this county's homeless school pupil population has grown by 50%, and now 2% of all students are homeless. With only 25% of homeless students graduating high school, schools and community agencies are scrambling today to house families and keep children in school (Hardy, 2009).

This chapter, more than any other, will focus on the exosystem portion of the bioecological model. Recall that the exosystem is comprised of elements that affect our family members indirectly, through contact with our microsystems. Thus, whenever work life bleeds over into home life, the exosystem is coming into play. We may never come into direct contact with our spouse's or parents' jobs, but they nevertheless have dramatic effects on the quality of our family's life. Financial and economic trends in the macrosystem also work their way down through the exosystem to the microsystem, and can even change our biological functioning (for example, through malnutrition or physiological stress reactions). The bioecological approach can help us understand the impact of economic issues on family life.

Contemporary issues

The current economic climate has increased the pace at which companies are downsizing and outsourcing work to cheaper workforces in foreign countries. The economic trends of the past few decades—shrinking wages, layoffs, furloughs, deterioration of bonuses, and declining health and retirement benefits—make the previous SNAF career track virtually impossible for most families. People can no longer count on working for one company for a lifetime. The average person now has seven different jobs over a lifetime, and the average job search today takes about five months, leading to long periods of no income and having to spend savings (Kadlec, 2003). Today's college graduates can expect to make less money at their jobs than the previous generation. A look at incomes over a one-year period from 2001 to 2002, prior to the current economic downturn, shows declines in salaries for certain previously steady professions. For example, dentists in 2001 made an average of $86,000, while a year later in 2002 they made an average of $72,000. Similarly, public relations specialists made $53,000 in 2001 and only $47,000 in 2002 (U.S. Bureau of Labor Statistics, 2002).

Because of the Internet, cheap shipping, and competition from international companies, many U.S. companies must slash wages to stay competitive (Kadlec, 2003). For example, a computer programmer in the U.S. might make $80,000 a year, but someone in India can perform the same job for $20,000, which is a high level of income in that country. Likewise, a call center worker in India makes $2,500 per year, but $20,000 per year in the U.S. (Kadlec, 2003).

Today people have to constantly learn new skills, diversify the way they market themselves, and be prepared for layoffs or labor redistribution. Skills in the current workforce must include knowledge of technology beyond that of any previous generation (Orecklin, 2004).

The current economy means employees are just part of the balance sheet, like office supplies or equipment costs. Wages and benefits are not determined in order to make an employee stay with a firm and exhibit years of unwavering loyalty. Today employees are expendable and wages are always negotiable. Annual cost of living allowances and wage increases used to be the norm. Most employees today do not expect them and know that raises are now based on superior performance. Companies are also ceasing their contributions to retirement funds and are cutting out paid vacations. With United States health care costs being the highest in the industrialized world and with today's workers living longer, retirement and health benefits comprise larger percentages of every company's costs. As a consequence, new hires are receiving fairly meager benefits packages. In fact, only 62% of large companies currently provide health benefits for retirees. This number used to be 80% (Kadlec, 2003). The new Health Insurance Reform bill signed by President Obama in 2010 may change some of these trends but the net effect on the average worker remains to be seen. To check out some of the bill's aims, see the *FYI* box on health insurance reform.

FYI

The U.S. Health Insurance Reform Act ("Affordable Health Care for America")

By the time you read this, the health reform bill will be in the early stages of implementation. Judge for yourself whether you think the bill delivers as it was supposed to, and whether you or your loved ones are benefitting from it.

The non-partisan Congressional Budget Office (CBO) states that the U.S. Health Insurance Reform Act will extend insurance coverage to 32 million more people, or more than 94% of Americans, while lowering health care costs over the long term. The deficit may be reduced by $143 billion over the next 10 years. The bill purportedly will:

- bar insurance companies from discriminating based on pre-existing conditions, health status, and gender
- provide better coverage and information to make informed decisions about health insurance

- create health insurance exchanges—competitive marketplaces where individuals and small business can buy affordable health care
- offer premium tax credits and cost-sharing assistance to low- and middle-income families and small businesses
- insure access to immediate relief for uninsured Americans with pre-existing conditions on the brink of medical bankruptcy
- create a reinsurance program in support of employers who offer health coverage to retirees age 55–64
- invest in Community Health Centers to expand access to health care in poor communities
- empower the Department of Health and Human Services and state insurance commissioners to conduct annual reviews of plans demanding unjustified, egregious premium increases.

Currently, health care costs rise at least 20% a year. Compare that to a 4% raise a worker *might* receive for a cost of living increase, and you will begin to see the problem.

With a gargantuan Ponzi scheme resulting in the loss of billions of dollars of retirement and other investments, the downfall of the automotive and banking industries, a plunging stock market, and the mortgage crisis, Americans and most people around the world are feeling the strain of an economic emergency. The Insight Center for Community Economic Development (2010) found that while some statistics show that people of color and women are gaining in income and that the gaps between majority and minority incomes are decreasing, if you look at *wealth* accumulation (homes, retirement funds, and other assets), the gap is actually widening substantially. For example, while married white women average about $160,000 in total wealth, married Latinas average about $18,000 of wealth. Figure 10.1 shows the full results of this study.

Moreover, Harris Interactive Polling, on behalf of the American Psychological Association (APA), conducted a Stress in America survey in 2008 and found that 80% of Americans rated financial issues and the economy as the top stressors, out of a list of 10 possible stressors. Two thirds of Americans reported feeling stressed about work, health care, and housing problems. A majority also reported being worried about job stability. Sixty percent of respondents reported feeling irritable and angry, lying awake at night, and experiencing physical stress symptoms. Unfortunately, almost half of Americans surveyed reported dealing with stress in ways that put their health at risk, like over-eating. Others reported skipping meals, shopping, and using alcohol or smoking to cope with stress, and 58% said they would *not* be willing to seek professional help to deal with stress. Job stress, heavy workloads, and home/work conflicts are related to higher levels of depression, myocardial infarction, diabetes, hypertension, and increases in blood lipid levels. Job stress is also related to lowered immune functioning (Kawakami & Haratani, 1999). Only 28% of the American population of workers report

FIGURE 10.1 Racial differences in median wealth.
Source: Insight Report on Wealth Disparity, 2010; http://www.InsightCCED.org

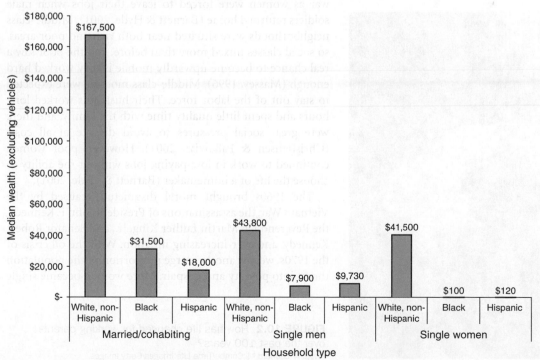

that they are in excellent health. Over one third experience symptoms of clinical depression, and 49% report that they get virtually no exercise (Aumann & Galinski, 2009). The American Psychological Association suggests that distressed people visit its Help Center to find healthy ways to manage stress and prevent physical and mental health decline (http://www.apa.org/helpcenter/index.aspx). With these disconcerting trends, it's remarkable that so many people today actually thrive in the workplace, enjoy their work, and find a way to balance their work and home lives.

Many students reading this book may have experienced some of the effects of the current economic climate first hand, and many others may have seen the effects on their friends and family members. Putting the contemporary situation into historical perspective may enhance your understanding. Then we can examine how contemporary families manage to balance the stress of work and family roles successfully.

Historic patterns in work and income

Since the beginning of time, most humans around the world lived in poverty and eked out a subsistence living. From hunter-gatherers in early Africa to the agricultural civilizations of the Mediterranean, right on through to the industrial advances of Western Europe and the United States, the general population has always been poor. Until recent times, most societies were geographically isolated and populations were less dense. Poor people were the most populous and could survive and have children fairly successfully without feeling deprived, especially if they didn't live near large castles or cities run by a ruling elite. Everyone they knew lived under subsistence circumstances (Massey, 1996).

As industrialization grew in the nineteenth century, huge numbers of poor people flocked to cities to find work and began to see the effects of extreme wealth all around them, with automobiles, large mansions, and fancy dress permeating society. The new high density city living led to many of the effects of poverty we see today: crime, disease, violence, and family disruption.

After World War II, a wave of affluence spread across the western world, with a rising middle class enjoying all the comforts once belonging only to the rich. Women's participation in the workforce peaked during World War II but fell again at the end of the war as women were forced to leave their jobs when male soldiers returned home (Barnett & Hyde, 2001). Middle-class neighborhoods were situated near both rich and poor areas, so social classes mixed more than before, and the poor saw a real chance to become upwardly mobile if they worked hard enough (Massey, 1996). Middle-class mothers were expected to stay out of the labor force. Their husbands worked long hours and spent little quality time with the family, and there were great social pressures to avoid divorce at all costs (Christiansen & Palkovitz, 2001). However, poor women continued to work in low-paying jobs without the ability to choose the life of a homemaker (Barnett & Hyde, 2001).

The 1960s brought moral disquietude caused by the Vietnam War, the assassinations of President John F. Kennedy, the Reverend Dr. Martin Luther King, Jr., and Senator Robert Kennedy, and ever-increasing inflation. With the oil crisis of the 1970s, we saw another large proportion of the population thrust into poverty and despair. More women became single

FIGURE 10.2 How has life changed for working parents over the past 100 years?
Photo © Leonard McCombe/Time Life Images/Getty Images.

mothers. The women's liberation movement began a fight for equal rights in the workplace. And with an ever widening gap between the rich and the poor in the United States, more so than in any other industrialized nation, poor people became keenly aware of their state of relative deprivation. At the same time, rich people clung more tightly to their wealth, endorsing conservative economic policies that further deprived the "have nots" from receiving government-sponsored income, housing, child care, and health care supplements (Massey, 1996).

Since 1973, there has been no relative increase in American family wealth, so families for the first time in history can no longer expect that their children will do better than they did economically (Teachman, 2000). If we examine the employment trends of American workers over the past 40 years, we do not see much change in the average number of hours worked per week—43 for men and 37 for women (Jacobs & Gerson, 2004). Remember that *averages* mean that some people work more and some people work less than the average. If we look at the data more closely, we see that with companies downsizing and outsourcing work to foreign countries, American workers are now working more hours for less pay. This means that people from the lower socioeconomic classes have a harder time finding full-time stable work and so are **underemployed**. Being underemployed means that a person wishes to work full time but cannot find a full-time job. They may be forced to take jobs that fail to utilize their skill sets or challenge them. Unfortunately, unemployment statistics do not differentiate between unemployment and underemployment. The true rates of unemployment might be staggering if we knew the actual numbers of people who are working a little bit but can't make a living wage. Jobs for people with both low and higher levels of education or skill are moving overseas and middle-class people are increasingly willing to take jobs for which they are over-qualified, further worsening the situation for poor workers (Jacobs & Gerson, 2004). Underemployed people experience much psychological distress compared to fully employed people. In fact, people report that when their jobs fail to take advantage of their range of skills, have limited opportunities for advancement, have little challenge, variety, or autonomy, and pay less, they are more depressed and distressed (Barnett & Brennan, 1997; Loscocco, 1990).

Underemployed
The group of people who want to work full time but cannot find full-time work; they are counted as "employed" in government statistics.

While incomes have decreased dramatically for some people, other people's incomes have greatly increased, leading to an ever-widening gap between the rich and the poor. While there used to be many good paying jobs with benefits for people with little education, today very few jobs are available for those without at least a high school, and increasingly, a college degree. But these economic trends vary greatly and have differential impacts on diverse groups of people in the population. Let's examine these differences in more detail.

DIVERSITY IN WORK AND FAMILY LIFE

- Men in families and work
- LGBT issues and work
- African American experiences with work and family
- Diversity in social policies around the world
- Working women in families

Remember that behavior of any kind is the result of a complex interaction between biology and environment. It's true that people are socialized to work in either more masculine or feminine careers, but even before we are born, various hormonal and genetic effects may drive us to be more masculine or feminine in our interests and abilities. For example, women with high levels of androgen exposure while in the womb grow up to prefer more traditionally masculine activities like electronics and sports (Berenbaum, 2005). They also express interest in male-dominated careers like engineering and airline piloting. These findings are more pronounced at higher levels of androgen exposure, with those girls exposed to the highest levels of androgens reporting being less nurturing and less interested in having children. Thus, hormone effects can influence variations in humans' interests and activities, including women being unusually good at traditionally male spatial problem-solving skills and men being good at traditionally female social relationship skills (Berenbaum & Korman-Bryk, 2008).

HOW WOULD YOU MEASURE THAT?

Young women's desires to enter male-dominated professions (Frome, Alfeld, Eccles, & Barber, 2008)

Frome et al. (2008) were interested in following a group of young women who expressed a desire to enter male-dominated careers. Male-dominated careers are defined as those jobs that have less than 30% participation by women. Previous research had shown that girls underestimate their abilities in math and science and may also receive less support from parents and teachers for entering science, technology, engineering, and mathematics (STEM) careers. Having a positive attitude toward one's ability in math and science predicts majoring in those fields in college. However, female college students who greatly value having a family in the future are less likely to choose STEM careers. It may be that girls who want a family see male-dominated careers as untenable. Thus, Frome et al. (2008) wanted to see what happened to girls who in 12th grade expressed great interest in entering male-dominated professions.

As part of the longitudinal Michigan Study of Adolescent Life Transitions, the authors examined 104 12th grade lower- and middle-class women. They were asked what jobs they would most like to have when they were 30. They were provided with a list of male-dominated, gender neutral, and female-dominated jobs. Male-dominated careers included engineer, architect, and pilot. Gender neutral careers included manager and pharmacist. Female-dominated jobs included day care providers and nurses. The girls were then contacted seven years later when they were 25-year-old women. By then 43% had gained a bachelor's degree and 25% had some college education.

By the time they were 25, 87% of the girls who wished to enter a male-dominated career had actually switched over to female-dominated careers like nursing and secretarial work. Even though 20% of the sample had expressed a desire to be a lawyer or judge in 12th grade, only 4% actually entered the law profession. Similarly, 31% wanted to join health professions like medicine or dentistry, but only 1% actually entered these professions. The key variables that predicted the change from male- to female-dominated careers were: desiring a family-friendly job, the job demanding too much time, and a low value placed on science in 12th grade. The authors concluded that the desire to have both a family and a career coupled with a negative attitude toward math and science predicted women abandoning their desires to enter male-dominated jobs. They cite other research showing that young women know early on that they are not willing to work 50–70 hours per week because they greatly value family time, while many male-dominated professions still demand this type of investment. This study suggests that if we want girls to enter STEM professions, we must encourage them to engage in and value math and science education. Teachers and parents must support girls' career aspirations by exposing them to female role models in those professions and affirming their abilities. Moreover, social policy must ensure that family-friendly workplaces become more normative so that girls see the possibility of having a prestigious and well-paying career while also raising a family.

In combination with biological influences, parents' gender role stereotypes affect their children's perceptions of the skills and abilities of men and women in the workplace (Chhin, Bleeker, & Jacobs, 2008). As mentioned in Chapter 3, children receive reinforcement for conforming to traditional gendered behavior. It's unlikely that a boy will receive parental approval for a career in hairdressing, or that that a girl will receive much encouragement for a career in professional football. Parental attitudes and socialization practices affect the careers children can envision for themselves. For example, parents often reinforce the false stereotype that math and science are natural for boys and more difficult for girls (Eccles, Freedman-Doan, Frome, Jacobs, & Yoon, 2000). While girls and boys do not differ in early math performance, girls come to reflect parental stereotypes and doubt their abilities in math and science in later grades, especially by high school. Bleeker and Jacobs (2004) found that when girls' mothers doubted their daughters' abilities to succeed in math-related careers, these girls were less likely to pursue science, technology, engineering and mathematics (STEM), careers.

Chhin et al. (2008) found that mothers' and fathers' predictions of the prestige levels of their children's future careers at age 15 were positively correlated with those students' actual career prestige ratings in adulthood. These children, at age 28, were engaged in careers that confirmed their parents' earlier gendered beliefs during their teen years. For example, girls at age 17 whose parents held traditional gender expectations for their daughters were much more likely to be in gender traditional occupations at age 28. Interestingly, this did not hold true for sons. This could be because the majority of sons grew up to engage in traditionally male occupations regardless of parental influence, as very few men are willing to take traditionally feminine jobs. This again illustrates the point made in Chapter 3, that contemporary girls are allowed more freedom in transgressing gender boundaries than boys are. Boys are shunned and judged more negatively if they engage in female behaviors or careers. To support this point, Chhin et al. (2008) found that almost one third of girls in their study grew up to work in traditionally male careers but only 7% of boys took female jobs. It is clear that parental socialization and exposure to cultural beliefs can shape children's career aspirations. Similarly, O'Connell, Betz, and Kurth (1989) found that college students whose mothers worked planned to work full time themselves when they graduated. Moreover, young women who planned to pursue gender non-traditional careers (for example, in medicine) expected to work full time, regardless of whether they planned to have children or not. In contrast, women who planned to enter traditionally female-oriented fields planned to work only part time at twice the rates of women pursuing non-traditional careers. These findings suggest that family experiences and knowledge of gender stereotyped careers affect women's career planning.

These trends point to the complex bioecological influences on both career and family roles. All levels of influences, from biology to culture, are important to consider. Take a closer look at a longitudinal study following a group of women who desired gender non-traditional careers when they were in high school in the *How Would You Measure That?* box. See where they ended up years later.

Intersectional identities profoundly affect work and home lives. Gender, sexual orientation, ethnicity, and socioeconomic status all affect the way jobs impact our families and vice versa. For example, while poor women can still find work relatively easily in domestic labor, caring for the homes and children of middle-class and wealthy women, the situation for poor men is far worse. Wages have decreased most noticeably for poor men who have experienced the greatest decrease in earning potential of any group over the past few decades (Aumann & Galinski, 2009; Teachman, 2000). Interestingly, 30% of all single parents working today are men (Bond, Galinsky, & Swanberg, 1998). Let's take a closer look at working men in families.

Men in families and work

Although poor men tend to experience the most negative repercussions of economic downturns taking place in their macrosystems, even upper-level male managers can experience negative impacts of the economy. For example, in economically challenging times, male managers tend to make less money and get promoted less often if their wives work because they are viewed as having more family obligations that make them less committed to work than men whose wives stay home. These men also fear taking paternity leave because they might be labeled as being on the **daddy track**, meaning they are less committed to work, and might lose respect and opportunities for advancement. It seems these fears are well founded because research on CEOs shows that they tend to think that men should take *no* days off for paternity leave. As a consequence, many men save up their vacation time to use when their wives give birth. Parke and Brott (1999) tell the story of David Williams, a football player for the Houston Oilers, who, in 1993, missed one game for the birth of his child. He was fined $25,000. Professional sports teams have not improved much since that case. For example, Major League Baseball has nothing in the players' contracts regarding work–family balance. They typically give players a couple of days off after the birth of a child but work individually with players

Daddy track
A negative stereotype of working fathers that believes they are less committed to their jobs if they are committed to their children; results in fewer promotions or raises.

on a plan. For example, in June, 2006, Los Angeles Dodgers infielder Cesar Izturis was allowed an extra three days off when his wife suffered from childbirth complications (Behson, 2008). However, this several days' allowance is a far cry from the 12 weeks of unpaid leave middle-class workers may get in order to spend time with newborns. Therefore, many professional sports players decide to work as free agents in order to maintain more control over their work–family balance (Behson, 2008).

Despite the pressures on men to make work their top priority, a survey conducted by *Time* Magazine along with the men's channel SPIKE TV found that only 13% of men surveyed reported measuring success by their work performance. Instead, 31% reported their faith in God as marking their success, 26% measured their success by being a good person, and 22% by their success with family. The majority of them (72%) said they would sacrifice work to improve family relationships, and 66% would risk upsetting their boss in order to ask for paternity leave. Nevertheless, 68% of them also reported working more than 40 hours per week, and those with children worked even *more* hours (cited in Mainiero & Sullivan, 2006). This could be because the majority of men still view providing for their families as a key indicator of their love and support. In fact, men from all ethnic groups think that if a father loves his family, he should financially support them (Townsend, 2002).

In a study of men in SNAFs, Townsend (2002) found that men were very proud of being able to provide their children with a mother at home who did not work. If she did work, these men said it was to earn her own pocket money or give her a break from the kids, not to provide for the family. They explained that it was natural for a man to work and a woman to stay home and control the home front. They allowed their wives to plan and arrange their interactions with their children and felt participation in housework or child care was optional for them. However, other research shows that even in SNAFs, 56% of fathers feel some conflict over work and family balance (Parke & Brott, 1999). In general, contemporary men feel they are under increasing macro- and exosystem pressure to be more involved with their children (Henwood & Proctor, 2003). Maurer and Pleck (2006) found that men tend to use other fathers they know as role models and when they see fathers being involved with their children, they feel pressure to play similar roles with their own children.

In spite of increasing pressure for men to be involved with their children, caregiving for children is still considered more *optional* for men than for women. Women are still expected to play the major role in the home. Much research shows that men's caregiving responsibilities are more voluntary and discretionary than mothers' roles (Maurer & Pleck, 2006). For example, Singley and Hynes (2005) found that wives fought hard for flex time and other work–home balancing strategies in order to reduce the burden on their husbands to have to do so. Thus, husbands in this study failed to seek out or use available family-friendly policies at their own places of work.

Despite these trends showing a bit of an internal struggle for contemporary fathers, the data show that, increasingly, men are both taking on caregiving duties and desiring to do so more than any other generation in the past. Modern dads want to be involved and feel much of the same tug in their hearts that mothers feel when work calls. They fight the same internal battles that working mothers do, to not let work stress affect their parenting.

Family process model of economic hardship
A model showing that when families experience economic or job stress, it spills over into marital/couple, and parent–child relationships.

Conger and colleagues (2010) put forth a **family process model of economic hardship,** wherein economic problems like unemployment and loss of income affect family interaction processes negatively. For example, they found that when fathers experienced high levels of emotional stress related to their jobs or income, they experienced depressive symptoms and demoralization which led to conflicts with their wives, disrupted parenting of their children, and child behavior problems. This model suggests that the entire family system is affected by exosystem influences in the parent's/ spouse's work environment. Similarly, in a study of male air traffic controllers, Repetti (2006) found that when fathers had stressful days at work, they often emotionally withdrew from their children at home. Moreover, they reported emotional spillover in the form of anger and increased discipline of their children. Chronic stress at work led them to view their children less positively.

Parenting is a very difficult job and when a father experiences economic hardship, unemployment, pay cuts, or extreme job-related stress, the whole family system can suffer. And much research shows that fathers play essential roles in the lives of their children. They physically play with children more than mothers do. They often serve as moral guides and role models, as well as sources of emotional support. And children with absent fathers are much more likely to have behavior problems. For example, children whose fathers left were more likely to engage in early sexual activity and teenage girls were more likely to get pregnant (Ellis et al., 2003), suggesting that fathers play an essential role in helping children negotiate their sexual development. In addition, LGBT youth who have supportive fathers are much less likely to be depressed or have behavior problems (Eisenberg & Resnick, 2006).

LGBT issues and work

Members of the LGBT community often experience discrimination and lower wages in the workplace (Klawitter, 2002). For this reason, gay and lesbian workers often decide not to come out of the closet at work, to reduce the risk of gay bashing, impairing relationships with co-workers, or limiting their chances of advancement. If an LGBT person is already in a top position, coming out could put their job at risk. Research shows that gay men make less money than heterosexual married men, but about the same as single heterosexual men. Also, lesbians actually tend to earn more than heterosexual women (Klawitter, 2002). This may be due to the fact that lesbians are more likely to be single and have fewer children than heterosexual women. It could also be explained by the fact that lesbians work more hours than heterosexual women, since their female partners probably earn less than heterosexual women's male partners. In general, same-sex couples in dual-earner families tend to have higher levels of education than heterosexual couples in dual-earner families. Thus, it's possible for gays and lesbians to earn more money if they stay in the closet or if they can pass as heterosexual.

There is still much bias and prejudice against gay and lesbian workers. Today, only 55% of Americans think LGBT people should be hired as schoolteachers, and only half think a gay man or lesbian could be president of the United States. South Africa was the first country to include sexual orientation as a protected category in its constitution in 1996, and the U.S. is currently considering instituting the Employment Non-Discrimination Act, which would forbid employment discrimination based on sexual orientation. Currently, many LGBT workers face negative attitudes of co-workers, a lack of social support, and under-appreciation of their performance. They also receive domestic partner benefits at far lower levels than heterosexual spouses do for their partners (Klawitter, 2002).

To live as an openly gay person in the workplace greatly depends on a person's economic security. People who accumulate more wealth have more choices and can deliberately structure their lives to avoid gay bashing or discrimination. For example, middle- to upper-class people have more freedom to choose to live in liberal, higher status neighborhoods, and have more freedom to be completely open. Because LGBT people often experience discriminatory and sub-par service at straight-owned businesses, with enough resources they can choose to shop in gay-owned establishments. There are more and more gay-friendly businesses and more neighborhoods where LGBT business owners congregate into enclaves where gay coffee houses, upscale fashion stores, and other shops cater to the LGBT community and also welcome heterosexual customers. Many products are now aimed at niche markets in these "gayborhoods," which confirm a sense of identity for those in LGBT communities and allow them to have a family life that is open and comfortable (Klawitter, 2002).

However, even within LGBT communities, people of color can experience marginalization and discrimination. Let's look at some trends for people of color in the workplace.

African American experiences with work and family

Today women in general make about 77 cents for every dollar men make, controlling for education, numbers of hours worked, and previous experience. For white women, this amounts to 80 cents on the male dollar (Weinberg, 2007). Black women in relation to black men, and Hispanic women in relation to Hispanic men, make about 83 cents on the dollar; but remember that black men make less than white men, so overall earnings for these women may be less than white women make. In terms of earned income, Asian American women fare the best. Asian American women make 76 cents on the male dollar, but earn significantly more in total dollars than women of any other ethnicity. For example, they made $31,000 per year in 2003 versus $27,000 per year for white women (Costello, Wight, & Stone, 2003).

In a study of over 1,600 managers, half African American and half European American, and their supervisors, Greenhaus and Parasuraman (1993) found some interesting trends. When judging the success of their female and African American managers, supervisors attributed their success to the managers getting help from others. In contrast, they judged male and European American managers' success as due to their personal abilities. The longer they knew the manager personally, however, the less this trend held true. These findings show that people's gender and ethnic background, and presumably their sexual orientation, can influence their supervisor's attributions regarding their performance. Supervisors judge employees more superficially if they don't know them, but realize their personal attributes if they get to know them better.

Interestingly, the way we socialize future workers can have a large impact on their expectations for life in the workforce. Bigler, Averhart, and Liben (2003) found that black children rated careers in which they saw African Americans working as less prestigious than careers European Americans held, even if the jobs were identical. However, African American parents tend to socialize their boys and girls to have similar types of goals. In particular, black girls are often raised to aspire to career independence more than white girls are. In one study, only 60% of white parents emphasized the importance of finding an occupation while raising their daughters, but over 90% of black parents did. About 20% of white girls saw marriage as a primary goal in their lives, while only 4–6% of black girls did (Higgenbotham & Weber, 1992). In fact, black girls tend to view marriage as a separate issue from economic security. It's uncommon for them to expect their future husbands to support them. African American girls are not typically raised within the context of the same traditional gender roles that European American girls are. For example, they have little experience with being treated as passive or fragile. They do not grow up with domesticity as a goal, nor do they expect to find a man to make their dreams come true (Higgenbotham & Weber, 1992).

Young African American female college students often join sororities that specialize in community service. The organizations help young women build connections and network to enhance their chances of future success. In an interesting study on African American and European American college sororities, Berkowitz and Padavia (1999) found that the black young women's groups focused on career goals, improving skills, and helping their communities. The young white women belonged to groups that structured their activities to interact with men's fraternities, and they held formal dances and candlelighting ceremonies. The emphasis was on dressing attractively and finding a man. Traditional sorority structures still encourage female subordination and allow functions involving large amounts of alcohol, which disinhibits sexual behavior. The black sororities had *no* alcohol-related events and *no* functions related to looking good or being chosen by men to dance or date. Black women have always been in the workplace and have rarely had the luxury of being cared for by a man. This may be why black sororities focus on self-sufficiency and career competence. In fact, highly educated black women outnumber highly educated black men by 2 to 1 (Strong & DeVault, 1994).

Services that focus on building career competence are vital for young people of color soon entering the workforce because there is still a wage gap between ethnic groups. Statistics show that white families out-earn families of color by a great margin. For example, the median white household family income in 2004 was $46,697, while that for African Americans was $30,134 and for Hispanics was $34,241. An even more disturbing indicator of racial disparities is the median family net worth of each group. While white families in the year 2000 averaged a net worth of $79,400, African Americans averaged a net worth of only $7,500, and Hispanics only $9,750; the lower net worth of African American and Hispanic families is due in large part to their lack of home ownership (U.S. Census Bureau, 2003, 2005).

These sobering facts illuminate the continuing financial inequities in American family life. Families who struggle financially and have fewer options for their children can experience stress, role strain, and higher levels of depression. All people experience life in families and in society through the intersectional identities of gender, race, sexual orientation, and social class. Can you think of any potential policies or system changes that could reduce such inequities for the diverse families in the United States?

Diversity in social policies around the world

What can be done to reduce the inequity between the rich and the poor in the United States? It's a difficult question to answer and political debates often revolve around how much responsibility the government or the wealthy have for closing the wealth gap. This section will illustrate how important macrosystem beliefs, policies, and programs are to the health and welfare of individual families. The bioecological model allows us to understand the complex effects of continuous interaction between macrosystems and microsystems in people's family lives.

The U.S. is the only industrialized nation with such a wide gap between rich and poor and such a large proportion (25%) of children living in poverty. Other wealthy nations have more interdependent views about the diverse members of their populations, seeing it as everyone's responsibility to ensure their fellow citizens' well-being. For example, in the U.S., 60% of Americans believe the poor are "lazy" while only 26% of Europeans do (Alesina & Glaeser, 2004). In terms of total income, many western nations have averages similar to the U.S. For example, the average income per person in the U.S. is $39,700 and in Austria it is $35,800. This is not a large difference but cultural work patterns different greatly because it takes Americans working 1,822 hours per year to make that much money, while it takes Austrians only 1,550 hours per year; the French work only 1,431 hours per year for an average income of $39,000 (OECD, 2005). In cross-cultural examinations of developed nations, only the Japanese work more hours than Americans do. In fact, Japanese people work more hours per week than Belgians, Israelis, Netherlanders, and Americans (Snir & Harpaz, 2006). Despite the fact that Americans work almost 300 more hours per year than Austrians, the percentage of poor people in the U.S. is three times higher than that in Austria (Weidenholzer & Aspalter, 2008). In addition, Austria provides health care, child care, and paid maternity and paternity leave for its citizens. Much of the higher income that Americans make goes to pay for those expenses.

Following an in-depth examination of the cultural belief systems that may contribute to the rich-poor gaps we see in the U.S., Weidenholzer and Aspalter (2008) argued that the U.S. prefers a *penalizing* system instead of a *social welfare* system. Over two million Americans are imprisoned, most of whom grew up in poverty without the benefits of comprehensive social welfare programs. We spend more money building prisons and fighting wars than we spend on schools. These authors emphasize that high spending on punitive measures and warfare reduces the funds available to spend on improving family life for American citizens. Many pundits argue that providing more funding for social welfare programs will reduce individual freedoms and the motivation to work. They also argue that it will weaken U.S. competitiveness in the business world. However, in the Growth Competitiveness Index of the World Economic Forum, the top 10 world performers included the eight countries that spend the *most* on social welfare programs. For example, in 2006/2007, Switzerland, Finland and Sweden ranked at the top for economic competitiveness in the world market, and each of these nations has extensive social welfare spending programs (Weidenholzer & Aspalter, 2008). Weidenholzer and Aspalter (2008, p. 10) state the following:

> a flourishing economy requires public efforts in the field of social protection, and even constitutes a vital precondition for high economic growth. Anyone who puts the case for cuts in social services thus puts economic prosperity at stake, too. Perhaps we (still) find it difficult to propagate this. In a nutshell, we would like to conclude that the social costs of non-social policy are high … and that the consequences of non-social policy are dramatic.

What do you think? Would the U.S. be more prosperous if we spent more on social welfare programs for the poor or is that just wasting money? Would closing the huge gap between rich and poor improve the standard of living for most American families and reduce the necessity for interventions like incarceration? Some scholars argue that the entire community of Americans would benefit if companies made family life easier for people and if social programs allowed people the freedom to be both good parents and productive workers (Hyde, 2007a). They posit that when people earn a good income and don't have to worry about child care and health care costs eating up their salaries, social ills like mental illness, violence, and homelessness will decrease, allowing more and more families the ability to focus on the quality of their relationships instead of mere survival.

One goal that the United Nations has been working toward is bettering the lives of working women. Because women play such a crucial role in maintaining the health and well-being of their families, their financial success is a burgeoning area of focus (United Nations Entity for Gender Equality and the Empowerment of Women, http://www.unwomen.org/focus-areas/?show=Violence_against_Women). Many countries around the world are working tirelessly to get women educated and into the workforce because there is a growing fundamental belief that the prosperity of a nation depends on the welfare of its women.

Working women in families

Today in western nations, there are more women than men in both college and graduate school (Peter & Horn, 2005), and women make up half of the U.S. labor force. Employed women experience a greater sense of personal well-being than do non-employed women, especially those who have both children and high-prestige jobs (Barnett & Hyde, 2001). While women now make up 50% of middle management positions, they still comprise only 2% of Fortune 500 CEOs (Catalyst, 2011). In a study of 31 European countries, women made up 44% of the workforce, 30% of middle management jobs, but only 3% of corporate CEOs (Catalyst, 2007). Women of color are even less likely to be in prestigious positions (England, Garcia-Beaulieu, & Ross, 2004). Less than 5% of managers of Fortune 500 companies are women of color (U.S. Bureau of Labor Statistics, 2006a). Even though women have made large advances in the workplace, they still face a gender pay gap in both the U.S. and Europe (Perfect & Hurrell, 2003), despite laws enacted to prevent discrimination in the workplace (Emslie & Hunt, 2009).

Barnett and Hyde (2001) reviewed decades of research on working families and found that, despite continuing challenges for women in the workplace, women who worked were no more depressed than women who did not work. In fact, balancing rewarding work and family roles can increase a woman's health, self-esteem, and mental health if she *wants* to work, feels she is treated fairly at work, and can rely on high-quality care for her children while she works (Hyde, 2007a).

Statistics show that married mothers work on average four fewer hours per week than married non-mothers do, which translates into lower wages. In addition, both poor and middle-class mothers face societal pressure to conform to gender role and class expectations. For example, white middle-class mothers in the U.S. feel pressure to stay home with their children, while poor single mothers feel pressure to work and leave their children for long periods of time while earning little pay. In a sample of Israeli workers, Snir and Harpaz (2006) found that the more people valued their families, the fewer hours they worked. These findings point to the complex interactions between gender, marital status, and social class. Some women have a choice in how many hours they work, while for others, working full time is a necessity.

The reality for most families today is that both mothers and fathers must work. In married couples, 60% of women work today, over half of them full time. Dual-earner families are now the norm for most children growing up in the twenty-first century (White & Rogers, 2000). Dual-earning families are more able to protect themselves from poverty in comparison to families where only one partner works. They are often able to live in better, safer neighborhoods, live above the poverty line, and receive at least some health care and retirement benefits (Benokraitis, 2000). In fact, two-parent dual-earner families are the only group that has increased (increasing by 25%) their earned income since the 1970s (DeVault, 1991). This increase is most likely due to women's increased wages, as men's wages have remained relatively stable or even decreased over the same timeframe (White & Rogers, 2000).

FOCUS ON MY FAMILY

Leah and Kamara

Kamara and I have been together for 14 years and have three kids (Jerome, 10, and Ziamara and Amaya, 3). Many people hate the idea of scheduling their lives, but with three kids and owning a business, carefully scheduling everything works well for us. Kamara and I decided to start our own business so that one of us could always be home with the kids. We run two group homes serving autistic and developmentally challenged children. I run the program and he does the books. Both of us worked hard to get our degrees so that we could open a business that meant something to us, our family and the community.

We eat dinner together every night and spend a lot of time with our extended family. Kamara and I split the work load, but to say it's 50/50 is not accurate. There are days when it is 90/10 or 60/40, depending on work and family demands. Some days Kamara or I just need a break so the other steps in. We plan weekly menus on Sunday nights as a family to prevent eating out. On a typical day, Kamara gets up with the kids, gets them dressed, fed, and so on. This is my time to shower and get ready without the kids under foot. I take Jerome to school and then start my day working at the group homes. Kamara gets the girls to preschool and then does his work. We split preschool pick-up duties as well as weeknight chores. I do dinner and clean up one night while Kamara does homework and baths, and then we switch. We all read together for 30 minutes and then tuck everyone in by 8pm.

Saturday is Kamara's day to sleep in and Sunday is mine. We deviate from this when Jerome has practice or a game. We schedule dinner around his activities but we all still eat together. Daddy likes to go to practices and he is usually the assistant coach. The girls and I will then prepare dinner, get the house picked up, and make it as easy as possible for daddy and brother when they get home.

Our extended family is amazing and great support; they come to all of the kids' activities and support us when we need a break. Kamara and I feel that it is very important to have our own time to hang out with friends so he plays poker every Friday night and I go out with my friends. We both plan trips with friends once a year as well as a family trip, so that we can have time both together and apart. It makes us appreciate each other more than ever when we return from our trips without the kids. We volunteer at the kids' schools, do field trips and stay involved with extracurricular activities. There isn't any easy answer for balancing marriage, work, and kids. Just make a commitment to work hard together and always stay involved.

Leah and Kamara and their family.
Photo reproduced by permission.

Many people don't want to live in dual-earner families because they feel that children suffer when mothers work. However, there is no evidence to suggest that children whose mothers work suffer emotionally or cognitively in the end (Harvey, 1999). In fact, economic hardship is worse for children than having a working mother. And despite common belief, the children of working mothers do not experience attachment problems with their parents (Chira, 1998), nor do they experience higher levels of delinquency in adolescence (Vander Ven, Cullen, Carrozza, & Wright, 2001), provided that they receive high-quality child care. They benefit economically if their mothers work and endorse less stereotypical gender role ideologies as they develop. As long as children are supervised while their mothers work, feel connected to their schools, and have positive peer groups, their developmental outcomes in adolescence are generally positive. I will discuss the effects of day care quality on young children's development in more detail later on. For now read the *Focus on My Family* box to see how one family handles work and home life challenges.

Women and career advancement

This section is focused on women's careers but it's difficult to discuss women without first framing the issue around traditional male career paths and the challenges both men and women face. Traditional male work patterns after World War II that led to career advancement consisted of almost unilateral commitment to one's company. This included long work hours, travel, no missing work for family obligations, and even geographic relocation. There was never a consideration of employee mental health or stress. The hardest worker got the prize. This pattern fit well in the SNAF environment and usually benefited educated, white males whose wives stayed home. This traditional pattern is becoming less and less tenable and is certainly less desirable for all workers today, especially white men. Today, men in general want a family-friendly workplace where they can participate in a degendered career path (Deutsch, 1999). We can no longer assume that in dual-earner couples, the woman will be the one to either end her career or go on the **mommy track**, losing seniority and benefits as she removes herself from the workplace for several months or years due to pregnancy and child care. Today, modern, equally sharing families include partners who both want to limit their work hours so that they may enjoy quality family time. Both men and women report passing up promotions or career advancement if they involve relocation or working excessive numbers of hours (Deutsch, 1999). Parke and Brott (1999) cite a DuPont Corporation poll of 18,000 employees, which showed that 41% of them refused to relocate because of family responsibilities and 11% refused a promotion for the same reason. Even blue collar workers turned down overtime and extra shifts to spend time with family. These findings suggest that both men and women are finding ways to improve family relationships while they remain active in their work roles.

Women are making great strides in the workplace today. They are constantly challenging the **glass ceiling**, that invisible barrier that prevents them from receiving promotions and equal pay. More and more states and countries around the world are implementing anti-discrimination legislation to prevent workplace inequities between men and women performing the same jobs. This legislation, often referred to as **comparable worth legislation**, requires a standard pay scale for people of similar educational levels with similar job responsibilities and experience (Hyde, 2007a). Interestingly, companies that have larger numbers of women at the top actually make a greater profit than those that are male dominated (Catalyst, 2004), so it makes sense for corporations to take a comparable worth stance in their hiring and promotion practices.

Studies show that employees find no differences in the effectiveness of their female versus male supervisors or leaders. However, women leaders who behave in traditionally male ways are rated as less effective by their employees. For example, if they are seen as pushy, dictatorial, and not nurturing, they are rated as less effective leaders; men with these same styles are *not* rated as less effective leaders. Women supervisors who use an empowerment style of leadership, wherein they are good listeners, give employees positive feedback, have open communication, and compromise, are rated as most effective (Astin & Leland, 1991). It's important to note that there's no evidence that women *are* more effective leaders when they use a more traditionally feminine style. Employees just like them more. This points to sexism in the workplace.

Sexism

Sexism includes any discriminatory or differential treatment based on gender. As discussed previously, men are valued for certain traits, like assertiveness in the workplace, but women might be disparaged for the same traits. Cikara and Fiske (2009) argue that "rare is the successful woman who is seen as both brilliant and kind" (p. 73). This implies that successful women who make it to the top

---

Mommy track
A negative stereotype of working mothers that believes they are less committed to their jobs if they are committed to their children; results in fewer promotions or raises.

Glass ceiling
A hypothetical barrier women face when trying to reach the top of their careers; often due to sexism or discrimination in the workplace.

Comparable worth legislation
Laws that mandate equal pay and benefits for men and women when they have comparable experience, skills, and education.

Sexism
Any discriminatory or differential treatment based on gender.

TABLE 10.1 Percentage of various careers held by women.
Source: Hyde, 2007b.

Career	Percentage of women
Airline pilot	5.3
Auto mechanic	1.3
Dentist	22
Dental assistant	98.8
Physician	29.4
Nurse	92.2
Child care worker	94.5
College teacher	46
Bus driver	48.5
New MD degrees awarded	44.4
New law degrees awarded	48

must not be nice, or conversely, that nice girls finish last. This is an important point for women in powerful positions to remember, as gender role stereotypes and role expectations influence all levels of work status. Sexism also occurs when people judge women with and without children. For example, women with children are viewed as less competent by co-workers than are childless women, and even as less competent than themselves before they had children (Cikara & Fiske, 2009). In general, women are less likely to receive a promotion if they work at the same job, have the same education, and same experience as a man in that job (Costello et al., 2003; Gutek, 2001b). If a woman takes over a job from a male employee, she often receives less pay than her male predecessor (Greenhaus & Parasuraman, 1993). Today women fill less than 24% STEM positions (Cooper & Weaver, 2003). Many careers are still difficult for women to break into. See Table 10.1 for a listing of various careers and the percentage of women in those jobs.

Sexism in the workplace is illegal in most western nations that value equal rights for all. However, it's not always easy to determine whether an act is sexist or not. Many acts are clearly and overtly sexist, such as a secretary's boss calling her "honey" but not calling his male assistant similar names. Some acts that are also considered sexist may not seem quite so obviously demeaning because the intent behind them is benevolent, or done out of kindness. There are two main types of sexism, benevolent, and hostile. **Benevolent sexism** includes gender-biased beliefs and actions that attribute positive qualities to women that ensure their inferior status. It is paternalistic in that it sees women as relatively helpless, passive, and best-suited for inferior positions. For example, male supervisors who consider women employees to be naturally nurturing, patient, and kind, may have extremely negative reactions when women act in gender-atypical ways (Cikara & Fiske, 2009). Or because people think women are naturally inclined to wear make-up, those who don't wear make-up may be harassed for not being "pretty enough" to greet clients. Benevolent sexism negatively affects women's work lives and makes it difficult for them to act in gender neutral or traditionally "masculine" ways, such as speaking up assertively for their rights or dressing similarly to men.

Co-workers and supervisors may see professional women as threatening or intimidating because they have high levels of education and self-confidence. They may not defer to men in decision-making and can argue for what they believe is right. These women may be *respected* but are often *disliked* and are described as competent yet cold (Eckes, 2002). People may react to them

Benevolent sexism
Covert words or behaviors that express a denigration of women and ensure their continued inferiority; these acts or words may appear kind and positive but they represent a sense that women are helpless or weak.

Hostile sexism
Negative gender bias which often involves anger and combativeness directed at women.

negatively and disparage them behind their backs, describing them as "mean" or "cold." **Hostile sexism** is differential or discriminatory treatment of women that is often combative in nature. For example, if strong, assertive women have a disagreement with colleagues, they may be described as a "bitch" while men exhibiting the same behaviors would not be similarly derogated. People who practice hostile sexism may take a position which argues that women try to "castrate" men, try to control men, or use their sexuality to manipulate men. People who exhibit hostile sexism may envision feminism as a man-hating or lesbian-inducing movement (Cikara & Fiske, 2009). For example, male students who receive poor grades in a course taught by a female professor may write on her teaching evaluations that she is "conceited" or "arrogant." Meanwhile, a male student receiving the same grade in a male professor's class might write that the professor is "extremely challenging" or "makes us work hard."

As a consequence of the varieties of sexism, women must be extremely careful as people may doubt their competence or they may be paid less if they exhibit traditionally female characteristics like kindness and empathy. Their "niceness" or warmth may be doubted if they exhibit traditional male qualities like decisiveness and assertiveness. However, women can play an active role in co-constructing this workplace process. They must try to cultivate a sense that they are both warm and competent, while recognizing that men have to fight for neither (Hyde, 2007a).

Because there is sexism and discrimination in the workplace, women must advocate for themselves to receive equal treatment. They must examine the treatment they receive, their pay, and other benefits, in comparison to their male counterparts. For example, women who only compare their wages and benefits to those of other women feel they are doing fine, if not better than their female co-workers. However, women who compare themselves to male workers think they are entitled to more, bargain harder, and end up making more (Glick et al., 2000).

In studies in over 15 countries, examining more than 15,000 people, researchers demonstrated that, while benevolent sexism may seem benign, it works in conjunction with hostile sexism to keep women in their place and allow discrimination and inferior pay to continue at work (Glick et al., 2000). Interestingly, benevolent sexism may benefit women who work in gender traditional careers like secretarial work. People may compliment women on their competence as long as they stay in their expected gender roles. For example, a boss may tell his secretary how neat her handwriting is or how nicely her friendly smile welcomes clients. The problem is that people who score high on benevolent sexism also accept sexist promotion, pay, and treatment practices in the workplace. Hostile sexism, however, may be more prevalent for women in non-traditional careers. For example, women fire fighters may be called "dikes" or may be asked who they slept with to pass the exam. Hostile sexism is related to openly sexist joking in the workplace (Glick et al., 2000). Education is negatively related to both hostile and benevolent sexism so one solution to reducing both forms of sexism would be sensitivity training and educational requirements for being hired on jobs (Cikara & Fiske, 2009).

Challenges for working women of color

Men who endorse gender role stereotypes are more likely to engage in sexual harassment in the workplace as well as act aggressively toward women in general (Bargh & Raymond, 1995). This may be even more pronounced when the target is a woman of color. For example, over half of female lawyers of color, but only 3% of white men, experience belittling comments and harassment in the workplace (Hunt et al., 2009). In addition, Latinas often report that their competence and intelligence are called into question at work. Many women of color feel they cannot be their true selves at work. They must put on a front of "acting white" or downplay their femininity to become "just one of the boys," in order to be accepted as equal in worth and competence (Hunt et al., 2009).

Imagine a woman of color experiencing these sexist and racist biases at work and then coming home to her partner and children. She may feel stressed, drained, and hopeless. These exosystem influences can have a dramatic impact on parent–child and partner–partner relationships, illustrating how microsystems can either suffer or benefit from family members' work lives.

In order to prevent job burnout and problems in personal adjustment, Hunt et al. (2009) recommend that all women, but particularly women of color, find several mentors across color, class, and occupational lines in order to enhance their social support networks in the workplace. Mentors should be diverse, and as often as possible come from upper management levels and majority cultures, because research has shown that when supervisors know employees personally they are more likely to support their attempts at promotion and recognize their positive contributions to the company.

Unfortunately, workers of lower status are often judged more harshly, with their behaviors being scrutinized more often as "deviant" or "weird," than higher-status workers. Lower-status workers, such as women, people of color, and low-status job holders, are expected to conform to workplace rules and strictly adhere to policies much more than are higher-status workers such as men, European Americans, and supervisors. Supervisory evaluations tend to be more biased when the evaluator has a higher social status than the person being evaluated. In contrast, the same behaviors exhibited by fellow high-status workers are judged to be acceptable and normative (Bowles & Gelfand, 2009). In recent years, many low-status employees have sued their employers over such bias and discrimination.

Tokenism

In response to gender discrimination lawsuits and women's movement protests and lobbying, many companies today might promote one woman or one woman of color, in order to prove they are not gender- or race-biased. This practice of hiring or promoting a single woman or person of color, called a token, in order to suggest a lack of bias in the workplace is called **tokenism**. While seeing a few token women in top leadership or management positions may be viewed positively, research shows that tokenism makes people think sexism does not exist at their company (Schmitt, Spoor, Danaher, & Branscombe, 2009). For example, about 16% of Representatives in Congress are women. If we see a group of these women on television, we may feel that the government is reaching gender balance. However, this is obviously not the case as 84% of Representatives are still men. A Catalyst (2006) study calculated that it would take 70 years for women to be equitably represented in the workplace if we continue our *token* improvements at the current rate. Even worse, the few women who are hired or promoted as tokens experience extreme gender discrimination, face more negative personnel evaluations from male subordinates, and lose jobs more quickly. They also become marginalized by existing employees who view them as incompetent (Schmitt et al., 2009). Comments like "She just got the job because she's a minority" are fairly common. While female tokens bang their heads against the glass ceiling, male token hires in traditionally female professions ride a **glass escalator** right to the top. The glass escalator refers to the quick ride to supervisory positions for men in female-dominated professions. They are promoted at greater rates than their female colleagues. So while a female police chief may face sexism, derogatory remarks about her competence, or sexual harassment, a male nurse would more likely be promoted to department supervisor and granted pay raises.

Despite these findings, many women in companies with token hires in leadership positions are more likely to endorse the belief that if a woman only works hard enough, she can also reach high levels of success in the company, ignoring the structural and cultural obstacles in her way (Schmitt et al., 2009). In an interesting set of studies, women who compared the current state of affairs for women in the workplace to women throughout history reported that there is little discrimination against women today, and they did not expect to face sexism themselves. However, those who analyzed the current state of affairs for women versus *men* in modern times viewed discrimination as rampant in the workplace and felt that they, personally, might experience sexism (Spoor & Schmitt, 2011). Tokenism and comparisons with the past perpetuate sexist attitudes and work practices aimed at women (Schmitt et al., 2009). Sexism can make women feel they have to choose between a career and a family if they know that to succeed in business, they have to follow a more "masculine" personality or management style and sacrifice their personal lives to succeed.

Tokenism
The practice of hiring or promoting a single woman or person of color in order to suggest a lack of bias in the workplace.

Glass escalator
A hypothetical pathway to the top of the career ladder, which is often "ridden" by men who engage in traditionally feminine careers.

Wage penalties for women

While there are still many inequities in the work lives of women, some things might be improving a bit for the current generation. For example, Crittenden (2001) found that women *without children* between the ages of 27 and 33 make 98 cents to the dollar of a comparable male worker. Today, many young women are highly educated. They can be financially successful and not depend on men for financial stability.

However, if they choose to have children, they will still face discrimination and reduced earnings. The reduced wage disparity between men and childless women shows that being a mother puts women at a disadvantage in the workplace. Though women with more children may have less experience working, when studies control for level of work experience, there is still a wage penalty of 5% for mothers versus non-mothers (Budig & England, 2001). This is even higher for married women with children, perhaps because companies who knowingly hire married women expect that their husbands can provide for the wages they don't get. Some research suggests that this wage penalty for motherhood is greatest for white women, who make an average of $6,000 per year less than white non-mothers. Latinas show virtually no wage penalty for motherhood, and African American women only experience a penalty if they have more than two children (Glauber, 2007). Budig and England (2001) posit that all members of society benefit from the hard work mothers perform by raising well-adjusted children, but the sole costs of mothering are borne by mothers themselves.

Women also experience a **mommy tax**, wherein they receive reductions in pay if they leave their career tracks to have or care for children. The pay gap between the income of mothers and non-mothers is even greater than the gap between men's and women's income in the U.S. (Crittenden, 2001). These reduced wages can amount to over one million dollars lost over a woman's lifetime, in addition to loss of benefits (Crittenden, 2001). For example, a couple earning $80,000 per year will lose approximately $1.35 million over the lifetime of one child, in days of work missed without pay, health care costs, education costs, unpaid leave, and so on. Having a child can throw low-income couples without health care, child care, paid leave, or living wages into poverty.

Mommy/caring tax
Loss of wages or benefits for employees, usually women, who take time off from work to care for children or elderly parents.

With people living longer than ever today, more and more middle-aged workers will be caring for the elderly as well as children. Without social policies to help them manage, people will increasingly face penalties on their earnings, a **caring tax**, or loss in income due to performing caregiving roles, from which their income may never recover. About 25% of American families care for an elderly family member and many experience a reduction in wages while doing so. These trends make it exceedingly difficult for workers to balance the demands of a job and a family.

BALANCING WORK AND FAMILY

> Family-friendly policies
> Work stress

You have learned that most of the industrialized world provides a variety of supports for families: long paid maternity and paternity leaves, high-quality health care and child care available to all, fewer work hours, and longer paid vacations. In contrast, only three countries *don't* provide paid maternity leave: Swaziland, Papua New Guinea, and the United States (Lawrence & Fitzgerald, 2011).

We know the consequences of macrosystems not providing support for families. In the U.S., paid maternity leave and the provision of high-quality child care for all young children would help reduce the pay gap found between mothers and non-mothers (the mommy tax). Crittenden (2001) followed women for 5 to 15 years after they graduated from high school and found that those mothers who took a total of less than 12 months off work during that time experienced pay reductions when compared to non-mothers of the same age, education, and experience. Thus, the effects of even small career interruptions can be seen 15 years later. Blue collar workers who take time off for family lose seniority and hours, get laid off first, lose promotions, and so on.

However, in recent years, more and more companies are beginning to realize that when workers are able to effectively balance the demands of home and work, they are more loyal to the company, fewer sick days are taken, there is less employee turnover, and there is higher productivity. This growing awareness among companies and also in the government is prompting the implementation of family-friendly policies.

Family-friendly policies

In 1993, the United States implemented the Family and Medical Leave Act (FMLA), which guaranteed 12 weeks off—without pay—for employees having babies or adopting children. Both fathers and mothers have the right to take these 12 weeks while keeping their jobs or getting a similar job upon their return. However, most workers cannot afford to take off 12 weeks of work without pay, so many people do not take advantage of this. Furthermore, FMLA only applies to companies with 50 or more employees. People who work for smaller companies still receive no leave, and only about half of the U.S. workforce is covered under FMLA (Kamerman, 2000). While some larger corporations voluntarily provide more leave or even paid leave, most people will not experience that benefit in their lifetimes (Hyde, 2007a).

The family leave situation is slowly improving, however. In 2004, California was the first state to implement a 12-week paid leave under FMLA. This benefit is paid through an employee payroll tax fund. Washington has a similar program, and Illinois, Massachusetts, New Jersey, and New York are considering such programs as well. Currently, across the U.S., when a child is born men currently take an average of five days off, usually using their vacation pay, and women take about eight weeks off. In contrast, the average leave for parents in European nations is 10 *months* (Brooks-Gunn, Han, & Waldfogel, 2002).

Child care issues

The issues of maternity and paternity leave and high-quality child care are vitally important because over half of women return to work before their children are a year old. Some research suggests that spending over 30 hours per week in child care during the first year of life can impair children's cognitive development (Bachu & O'Connell, 1998). In a study of over 1,300 children at 10 day-care sites, researchers found that those whose mothers worked full time before their children were 9 months of age were less prepared for kindergarten and had lower verbal intelligence scores. Especially detrimental was if mothers began working when their children were between 6 and 9 months of age and worked 30 or more hours per week. Recall that infancy is a crucial time for the formation of secure attachment relationships between children and their caregivers. These findings held true most strongly for white boys who had insensitive mothers. Attachment problems arose more often if a child had an insensitive mother who worked 30 hours per week (Brooks-Gunn et al., 2002). The findings were also strongest for families in which mothers worked over 30 hours per week and had their children in low-quality day care. These trends suggest that working long hours, having poor-quality child care, and being insensitive to a baby's needs can combine to put a baby at risk for negative outcomes. Due to the scarcity of maternity leave policies in most workplaces and the difficulty of finding high-quality child care in the U.S., more babies are probably exposed to these three risk factors than people might realize. Contrast this with findings showing that Swedish children who attended child care in their early months actually had *better* cognitive outcomes. Why the difference? In Sweden, parents are guaranteed paid leave and a job where they can work part time for up to eight years after a child is born. All children receive high-quality child care with trained and well-paid teachers (Weidenholzer & Aspalter, 2008).

So what can we learn from the cross-cultural research on family leave and child care? Most mothers and fathers have to work today in order to make ends meet. At the same time, they need to spend quality time with their children in the early months to enhance attachment and cognitive development. If parents are going to succeed at both critically important tasks, then they need family-friendly policies so that they can care for children. They also need universally available high-quality child care so that when they have to work, their children do not suffer cognitive or social impairments, but reap the benefits of a stimulating, loving child care center. Moreover, parents need to be able to work fewer hours and receive social support for their parenting, so that they can remain sensitive in their caregiving, since insensitive parenting combined with low-quality day care are most detrimental to children under a year old.

The impact of performing multiple roles

It is not necessary for a woman to stop working when she has children. She just needs supports in place to ease the work–family strain, especially in the child's first year. Research shows that both men and women who experience multiple roles in life (worker, parent, spouse, friend, and organization leader) actually have *lower* levels of stress than do people who take on only one or two roles (Barnett & Marshall, 1993; Crosby & Jaskar, 1993). Employed women, even those who are married or are parents, have a higher sense of personal well-being than those who do not work (Barnett & Hyde, 2001). When women add the worker role to their parenting role and men add the parenting role to their worker role, both physical and mental health are enhanced (Barnett & Hyde, 2001). Multiple roles allow people to move in numerous contexts where they can receive social support, encouragement, and a sense of appreciation for their talents and strengths. They gain a more complex and nuanced sense of who they are as people and travel in multiple circles where they meet diverse individuals who expand their world view.

In spite of these benefits for the individual, if too many demands are placed on a person, mental and physical health can decline. If a woman or a man has responsibility for numerous poor-quality, unsatisfying roles, morale and health can decrease. Thus, if someone works for low wages, has no social support, is discriminated against, has low-quality child care, and comes home to a violent or dangerous neighborhood, those multiple roles can be more stressful than helpful for their identity (Barnett & Hyde, 2001). A terrible job working with awful people and then coming home to a strained marriage is associated with high levels of distress. Therefore, it is important that those in control of the workplace culture do all that they can to enrich the lives of their employees and value them as individuals even when they have family responsibilities.

Policies that benefit families

A few companies have taken it upon themselves to support their employees in their family relationships. In 1991, the Los Angeles Department of Water and Power began implementing the Doting Dads program. This includes a four-month paternity leave, a child care referral service, and support groups for new parents. They found that this program led to

FIGURE 10.3 What social policies around the world allow parents to balance their work and home lives? A working mother picks up her daughter from a "Kangaroom'" run by Japanese cosmetics firm Shiseido in Tokyo, 2008.
Photo © Yoshikazu Tsuno/AFP/Getty Images.

lower absenteeism and turnover rates in their employee pool, which improved productivity (Parke & Brott, 1999). Similarly, IBM found that the money it invested in paternity leave was more than made up for by increased employee morale, loyalty, and productivity (Hill, Jackson, & Martinengo, 2006). The Japanese cosmetics company, Shiseido, opened a "Kangaroom," or nursery for working mothers, because the birth rate for middle-class women in Japan is very low. The company wants to make mothering and working as easy as possible in order to encourage career women to have children (http://www.shiseido.co.jp/e/csr/stakes/employee04.htm).

Today employees are fighting for family-friendly policies like **flex time**, which enables them to work the same number of hours but, for example, work fewer days for more hours, or split the day in half to be able to pick up children from school in the afternoon. Other techniques employers are using today to lure new employees, while not sacrificing productivity or profits, is **job sharing**, through which they may hire two people to fill a single job so that each person can spend more time at home. **Telecommuting**, in which the Internet and other technologies allow people to work from home and save commuting time, gas, and the cost of purchasing work apparel, is also becoming more and more popular. Larger corporations are also offering on-site child care so that employees can spend their lunch times with their children, women can take breaks to nurse infants, and there is less stress in finding child care and commuting to off-site child care centers. Surveys show that parents have better attitudes and worry less at work when their children attend on-site child care centers (e.g., Kossek & Nichol, 1992). They report that the commute to work is more relaxed because they can spend time chatting with their children in the car, and so on. In studies of companies who use these techniques, the employees are happier and more committed to the company.

Today, about 43% of companies provide flex time, but many employees are still afraid to use it, for fear of being seen as less serious about their jobs (Blair-Loy & Warton, 2004; Tang & Wadsworth, 2010). They fear they may lose assignments or not be given raises. However, Powers (2004) reports that flex time is effective for both employees and their employers. Employees perform best when they are given choices, provided with challenges and opportunities to grow, and given support for their efforts to make decisions.

Sabattini and Crosby (2009) argue that benefits alone do not make a company family friendly. A family-friendly company is one that engenders a culture of respect for its employees as human beings. It recognizes the need for people to allocate time and effort into maintaining their family relationships. It makes clear that career promotions, raises, or assignments will not be affected by people taking advantage of programs meant to enhance the balance between work and personal life. It also has an extensive support network including mentors, and may include child care, support groups, wellness training programs (such as stress reduction training), and other programs that lead to a positive emotional climate for employees. These things lead employees to work hard for a company, miss less work, and perform at their peak, being loyal to their employers (Sabattini & Crosby, 2009).

Moreover, alternative work arrangements designed to enhance the family–work balance should be available to all employees, regardless of marital status, parental status, or gender. This makes family-friendly work policy no longer a women's issue, but a quality of life issue for all employees, whereby no one is stigmatized or penalized for taking advantage of such programs. To further encourage companies in this direction, take note of the findings of Harter and Schmidt (2000), who found that companies with the highest number of employees experiencing positive mental health and a sense of well-being actually made the highest rates of profit. People who have high levels of job satisfaction are more cooperative and helpful at work, arrive on time, and quit less often (Keyes & Magyar-Moe, 2003; Spector, 1997). In contrast, depression is related to low productivity. In fact, depression is the number one cause of disability and loss of productivity in the American workplace (Keyes & Lopez, 2002).

What happens when people are stretched too thin, work too much, or have a family-unfriendly workplace? Let's take a look at the effects of work stress on employees and families.

Flex time
A family-friendly work policy that allows people to create their own schedules that fit in with their family lives.

Job sharing
A family-friendly work policy that allows more than one employee to share a job so that they have time to spend with family.

Telecommuting
A family-friendly work policy that allows people to work from home and attend meetings by videophone, etc.

Work stress

Most jobs have some level of stress involved. We have rough days, our bosses get disappointed in us, or we have conflicts with co-workers over tasks. However, sometimes job stress becomes so overwhelming that we cannot function well at home, and the exosystem pressures really start to take a toll on the quality of life in the microsystem. Bakker, Demerouti, and Burke (2009) put forth a **role scarcity hypothesis**, wherein they argue that people have only a limited amount of mental and physical energy and resources. With limited amounts of mental and physical energy and limited time to do all we have to do, we must be able to perform each role in moderation, with clear boundaries between required activities.

Some jobs may be so demanding, or people may have such little control over their schedules, that they have no choice but to sacrifice family time for work. For positive mental and physical health outcomes, though, it's important to refrain from devoting an inordinate amount of time or energy to only one thing, such as work. If at all possible, families need to try to minimize work stress and to manage the balancing act between work and family life. Some people are better at managing their commitments than others. For example, people who are generally optimistic and exhibit positive emotions in most contexts of their lives tend to be viewed positively by employers and so may be granted more freedom of choice that helps them balance work and family life (Wright & Cropanzano, 2000). To see how you are doing in managing your various responsibilities, see the *Self-Assessment* box.

The role of personality in work stress

Some personality types are more likely to succumb to the negative pressures of work than others are. For example, people with **Type A personality** characteristics are more likely to succumb to stress at work. They are more likely to have physical problems and depression. Type A personality consists of being extremely competitive, driven, and controlling, and more committed to work than to maintaining personal relationships. The key variable that is related to the decline of mental and physical health in Type A individuals is their level of hostility. Hostility is detrimental to both physical and mental health, and is even a predictor of heart failure at a young age. For example, Jiang, Yan, and Li (2004) found that among 290 Chinese doctors and nurses, those who had a Type A personality had the worst levels of job satisfaction and the highest rates of mental health problems. This was especially true if the Type A personality was combined with an **external locus of control**, a world view wherein a person sees events as out of their hands, as being controlled by external forces. They have a low sense of confidence in their ability to solve problems. Type A characteristics plus external locus of control can be a deadly combination, leading to heart problems and emotional despair.

In the study by Jiang et al. (2004), doctors and nurses with **Type B personalities**, which are laid back, happy, caring, and carefree, had the greatest job satisfaction and the highest levels of mental well-being. This was especially true if they also had an **internal locus of control**, a world view wherein people believe they can control the stressors in their lives and approach work with a positive, relationship-centered style. Workers with Type B personalities plus internal locus of control are more satisfied at work and happier in general. They are able to balance the strains of work and home life and are not over-committed to work success at the expense of their health.

High **over-commitment** to work can be detrimental to a person's health. Over-commitment means that a person commits the vast majority of mental energy and time to work, to the point of isolating family and friends. People who are over-committed to work engage in excessive striving, have a high need for control and for approval, use maladaptive coping strategies, and have an inability to forget work problems while at home. Over-commitment can lead to increased risk of coronary heart disease (Kuper, Singh-Manoux, Siegrist, & Marmot, 2002) and elevated blood pressure (Steptoe, Siegrist, Kirschbaum, & Marmot, 2004). At the neurochemical level, over-commitment has been related to stress responses in the body, including the secretion of *low* levels of norepinephrine (adrenalin) and cortisol, the stress hormone (Wirtz, Siegrist,

---

Role-scarcity hypothesis
The idea that a person only has so much energy for each role in life so that physical and mental resources devoted to one role necessarily mean less available for another role.

Type A personality
A personality style involving extreme hostility, competitiveness, and a drive to succeed.

External locus of control
The belief that one's life is outside of one's own control.

Type B personality
A personality style involving a happy, carefree approach to life.

Internal locus of control
The belief that one's life is within one's own control.

Over-commitment
An extreme form of career striving where people commit too much energy to work at the expense of family relationships.

The energy project audit

HOW WELL ARE YOU MANAGING YOUR ENERGY?

1. Almost never
2. Infrequently
3. Sometimes
4. Most of the time
5. Almost always

SCORING GUIDE:

By Category

20–25	On fire. You have nailed this dimension.
17–21	Good energy management skills, but room for improvement.
13–16	Some energy management skills but this dimension needs attention.
10–12	Serious energy management deficits, needs significant work.
Below 10	Crisis-level deficits. Demands your immediate attention.

Overall Scores

111–125	You are a model of balanced energy management.
95–110	You have many strengths, one or two weaker areas.
75–94	Moderate strengths, significant deficits.
50–74	You are at very high risk for burnout.
Below 50	It's amazing you are functioning. Take action now!

PHYSICAL

I exercise at least three times a week. _____

I eat small nutritious snacks every two to three hours. _____

I get 7 to 8 hours of sleep a night. _____

My level of energy is consistent and high throughout the day. _____

I eat a nutritious breakfast. _____

Physical Score _____

EMOTIONAL

When I experience setbacks at work I am able to recover my positive outlook quickly. _____

I feel relaxed and in control despite the pressures at work. _____

I have a good balance between taking care of myself and caring for others. _____

I feel secure and confident. _____

I am optimistic and forward-looking, rather than negative and blaming. _____

Emotional Score _____

MENTAL

I focus well and shut out distractions at work. _____

I take time to think about long-term issues and strategy at work _____

I set priorities and manage my time well. _____

I can step back and see the big picture even under pressure. _____

I am creative and imaginative. _____

Mental Score _____

SPIRITUAL

I feel that my work makes a significant positive contribution to others. _____

I act in accordance with my most deeply held values, even under stress. _____

I am passionate about my work and highly committed to what I do. _____

I derive a sense of meaning and purpose from my work. _____

I have a mission in life that is bigger than myself. _____

Spiritual Score _____

RENEWAL

I create clear boundaries between work and home. _____

I am able to leave work behind at the end of the day. _____

I take a break every 90 minutes to 2 hours at work. _____

I create time in my life for activities that I find enjoyable and satisfying. _____

I am still energized and able to engage when I get home at night. _____

Renewal Score _____

OVERALL SCORE _____

This questionnaire created by Tony Schwarts. For more information go to www.theenergyproject.com.

Rimmele, & Ehlert, 2007). Why would a person with high over-commitment experience *low* stress activation in the body and brain? Wirtz et al. (2007) argue that after prolonged chronic stress, bodily systems shut down. A chronic condition of elevated stress response leads to complete exhaustion and, thus, reduced responsiveness in the normal stress chemicals. In fact, Wirtz et al. (2007) found that high over-commitment in middle-aged working men was related to *vital exhaustion*, perfectionism, chronic stress, and high levels of depression. This means that when we overtax our vital stress response system, it may slow down completely to resemble the physiological profile of a clinically depressed person who is listless and sad, lacks joy and spontaneity, and cares little about others or one's self. This set of findings illustrates the bioecological processes involved in family life. When a family member works so hard and so much that other family members become lower priorities, family conflict can increase and relationships can become strained. These exosystem processes at work affect the microsystem relationships at home, and eventually, a person's physical health begins to suffer.

Workaholism
A condition where people work too much and cannot enforce proper boundaries between work and home life; they are often disconnected from family and work to avoid intimacy.

Over-commitment is also related to another personality style, **workaholism**, a condition in which people cannot separate the boundaries of work and home. People suffering from workaholism gain most of their self-worth from work-related activities and do not stop thinking about work when they are with family. Due to self-imposed demands, they may bring work on every family vacation or not go on vacations due to work. Workaholics tend to engage in compulsive over-working and tend to use work as a way to avoid intimacy with others. In fact, Robinson, Flowers, and Ng (2006) found that workaholism is related to marital problems, over-controlling behavior at home, and dysfunctional communication patterns. Workaholics show little support for their family members (Bakker et al., 2009). They often work at the expense of all other activities in their lives. They show little attachment to or caring about others, have negative feelings about their partners, and report less physical attraction to their spouses than do non-workaholics (Robinson, Flowers, & Carroll, 2001).

Bakker et al. (2009) examined 168 dual-earner couples in the Netherlands and found that workaholism was related to high levels of reported work–family conflict. Couples where one or both partners were workaholics experienced reduced relationship quality and low levels of partner emotional support. Research suggests that many wives of workaholics simply abandon their personal goals and careers in order to keep the household running in support of their husband's workaholism (L'Abate & L'Abate, 1981). Partners of workaholics report less emotional connection with their spouses and feel helpless, exhibiting external locus of control beliefs about their lives (Robinson et al., 2001). Moreover, children of workaholics also have external locus of control patterns, in combination with high levels of depression and anxiety (Robinson & Kelley, 1998).

Unfortunately, many jobs reinforce workaholism because people receive pay raises, promotions, and positive feedback about their commitment to the company (Piotrowski & Vodanovich, 2006). In a study of over 200 MBA students, Burke (2000) found that those who were workaholics failed to endorse the importance of a work–family balance when they

"It's the Old Man's idea. Reckons his young executives should see more of their families."

FIGURE 10.4 What personal and social factors maintain workaholism and over-commitment to work? www.CartoonStock.com.

graduated. They emphasized the importance of complete commitment to work, indicating that new graduates may be setting themselves up for some of the family conflicts and struggles described above with established career workaholics.

Economic downturns and unemployment

As discussed at the beginning of this chapter, we are currently facing an economic crisis of monumental proportions. People are losing jobs by the millions and families are suffering the effects. Unemployment affects families in profound ways. It has been related to increases in domestic violence and depression (Cunradi, Todd, Duke, & Ames, 2009; Mossakowski, 2009). Mossakowski (2009) found that the longer a man was unemployed, the stronger his potential for developing depression.

In 2008, 43,500 businesses went bankrupt, double the rate in 2006 (Irons, 2009). This means that tens of thousands of families have been affected by economic struggles. This can affect everything from child support to family planning. For example, child support payments are stalled in divorced families when the non-custodial parent loses his or her job (McCarthy, 2009). More and more non-custodial parents are going to court to get their child support obligations reduced, and custodial parents are filing more contempt orders than ever before. There has also been a marked increase in the use of birth control and vasectomies, with Planned Parenthood seeing an increase of about 50% in their patient base. People are reporting that they just could not afford the prospects of a pregnancy right now (McCarthy, 2009).

During times of economic downturn, people often have to move to worse neighborhoods, change their children's schools, reduce their standard of living, and do without health care (Gardner, 2003). Thousands of previously middle-class families may lose their pride and self-confidence if they cannot find work. They may no longer travel as much, attend entertainment events, or shop like they used to. These trends may cause strains on marriages and committed partnerships. If one partner is unemployed, the other may question whether the unemployed person is trying hard enough to get a job. He or she may face daily questioning and feel unsupported by family members. Moreover, poor economic conditions tend to strike people of color most dramatically. With job loss and unemployment come family stress and strain, and research shows that African American men are often the first fired during restructuring or downsizing (Rubin, 1995; Wilson & Roscigno, 2010).

Irons (2009) talks about "economic scarring" that occurs in times of recession. This means that the effects on all types of families are not short term but lasting. For example, if a family member loses a job or must be under-employed, this means that children may receive poorer nutrition. It may also lead to an inability to save for children's education, leading to fewer children in the current generation being able to attend college. Lower levels of education in the population can then impact the levels of technological innovation and business start-ups that become possible in the next generation. This means that economic downturns can have multigenerational effects, illustrating clearly the multiple systems in the bioecological model that are impacted by macrosystem financial pressures.

However, there may be a positive aspect to economic downturns. People may reprioritize their lives, spending more time as a family, at home interacting. They may reconnect with neighbors and friends in their mesosystems, and focus less on acquiring more "things" and more on finding meaning in life (Gardner, 2003).

Regardless of your personality, neurophysiology, and family connections, there is no doubt that being of middle-class socioeconomic status is definitely beneficial. Having all of your basic needs met plus being allowed some luxuries like travel and well-running cars definitely make life easier. Unfortunately, with the current economic climate, we're seeing a decline of the middle class. With job loss, medical costs, and legal costs during divorce, it's often more than two working parents can handle. The old saying goes "the rich get richer while the poor are getting poorer." This may be the case right now, and as the next section reveals, being at either of the extreme ends of the socioeconomic continuum can be detrimental to physical and emotional health in families.

LIVING ON THE EXTREMES OF THE SOCIOECONOMIC CONTINUUM: POVERTY AND WEALTH

Living in poverty

Living in affluence

Most of us wish we had more money than we do. Even when we double our income or get huge raises, we simply adjust to the new lifestyle and continue to feel like we don't make enough. For example, I lived on $11,000 a year while in graduate school and lived a perfectly happy, comfortable life. But that seems preposterous to me now. I can't imagine making that little. This is the plight of most middle-class people. We're always striving for a newer car, house, or electronic equipment, better vacations, and so on. And with the economic downturn, many of us are struggling to keep up with mortgage payments for houses whose values are diminishing, as well as covering health care costs and clothing and supplies for our children. However, it's important to realize that being middle class—making somewhere between $35,000 and $90,000 for a family of four, depending on the cost of living in your area—is beneficial, even in such trying times. Being very poor or very rich can both have a negative impact on families.

Living in poverty

The number of children living in poverty has increased dramatically in the past 40 years. One quarter of American children live below the poverty line. This number is higher for different ethnic groups: 50% for Native American children, 30% for African American and Hispanic children, 15% for Asian American children, and 10% for white children (Rank, 2000). The three developed nations with the highest rates of child poverty are the United States (25% of children), the United Kingdom (18.5% of children), and Australia (15.4% of children), but the U.S. has the highest rates of poverty out of the 17 developed nations of the world (Rank, 2000). Americans also have fewer social programs to help the poor, so American poor people are actually worse off than poor people in other industrialized nations.

The consequences of poverty

What would it take to make you poor? Or what might protect you from sinking deeper if you're already poor? Research suggests that most Americans are only one to three paychecks away from being poor, homeless, or both (Rank, 2000).

I once heard a poor grandmother say "Finding a machine gun in this neighborhood is easier than finding a fresh tomato." This is true as grocery stores and other service merchants are less likely to be located in poor areas, leading to poor nutrition, inferior health, and social disorganization in poor neighborhoods. Wen, Browning, and Cagney (2003) cite research showing that poor neighborhoods have higher mortality rates for all age groups than middle- and upper-income areas. Also, both mental and physical health tend to decline the longer people live in chronic poverty.

In a study of chronic disease in poor residents of various African, Asian, and Central American nations, Russell (2004) found that having tuberculosis (TB) or HIV/AIDS financially devastated poor families even further. They could no longer afford the necessities of life if they had to cope with a serious illness. He estimated that poor families spend between 8% and 20% of their income on transportation, medication, special foods, hospitalization, lost earnings due to missed work, funeral expenses, and so on. Some families were completely decimated if a family member became ill. For example, in Zambia, TB treatment costs 99% of a family's annual income. Likewise, AIDS treatment for families in Thailand costs 50% of their annual income. How would a serious illness impact your family? If you have insurance, how much would your insurance pay until it ran out? For many of us, health care costs, even in developed nations, can be crushing.

In the U.S., poverty exerts negative effects on families and communities. Poor women have less access to quality prenatal care and have more birth complications (McLaughlin et al., 1992). They have babies with lower birth weight, which is related to both health and learning problems later on (McLaughlin et al., 1992). Poor children have more physical illnesses and injuries, and exhibit more behavioral and cognitive problems than middle-class children (Teachman, 2000). Children who experience chronic poverty before the age of 6 are most at risk for negative outcomes, as brain plasticity and crucial times for learning peak in the early years (Duncan & Brooks-Gunn, 1997). They attend inferior schools with high teacher turnover rates and inferior learning materials (Kozol, 1992). Poor teenagers are more likely to drop out of school, become pregnant, and experience violence and drug use (Foster, Brooks-Gunn, & Martin, 2007). Between 1985 and 1992, the rate of violent deaths for poor adolescents rose 10% in European American youth and 78% in African American youth (Lerner, Sparks, & McCubbin, 2000). People living in poverty tend to have higher birth rates and lower access to information and technology related to birth control and medical care, leading to a population with many physical and emotional disadvantages.

As discussed earlier, people with financial struggles can experience mental and physical health problems. Poor people face more parenting stress and role strain as they struggle to find appropriate and affordable child care. You learned earlier that high-quality child care plus sensitive parenting can enhance children's social, cognitive, and emotional development. When poor children are enrolled in high-quality child care centers they experience success in school all the way up to 2nd grade, and this finding holds true above and beyond the influence of parents (Peisner-Feinberg et al., 1999).

High-quality child care centers in poor neighborhoods are those that receive substantial social welfare funding (Hofferth, Phillips, & Cabrera, 2001). Sixty percent of federal monies go to low-income child care centers serving mainly welfare recipients. For example, Head Start was designed to equalize the playing field for all children starting kindergarten, regardless of their background. But Hofferth et al. (2001) found that poor children get the worst early childhood care because only 17% can go to Head Start. Moreover, the waiting lists for subsidized care centers are long, and most families who work do not get any help in finding suitable child care or paying for it. Only 18% of the *working* poor—people who work full time but make little money—receive financial help in covering child care costs, but 37% of the *non-working* poor do. For both groups, the majority get no help. This system is a disincentive for poor or unskilled workers to look for jobs, when they know they may have to leave children at home unsupervised or in low-quality care. Mistry, Vandewater, Huston, and McLoyd (2002) found that when parents are both poor and distressed, they have trouble being responsive to their children and feel less capable of disciplining them. They are also less affectionate toward their children. Similarly, Lempers, Clark-Lempers, and Simons (1989) found that poor parents were more likely to be inconsistent and rejecting in their parenting. These findings suggest that relieving the burden of poverty would enhance parental mental health and facilitate higher-quality parent–child relationships, ensuring positive outcomes for children.

While most of us are familiar with the plight of poor people at home and around the world, we may not realize that families at the other extreme end of the socioeconomic continuum could also be at risk for problematic outcomes. But recent research is discovering that the lives of the affluent are not as carefree as many of us might think.

Living in affluence

We tend to have little pity for the rich because their lives seem so easy. It's important to realize, though, that with more money comes greater responsibility and more pressure to maintain one's wealth, status, and image. It's true that a higher socioeconomic status provides much buffering against some of the hardships impoverished people experience. For example, in the LBGT community, wealthy community members can buy large homes, take vacations, and invest in entertainment. They have the freedom to build a life away from family members who may have rejected them and can construct a "chosen" family that supports them emotionally (Carrington, 1999). Moreover, people who live in affluent regions usually are surrounded by more peaceful settings, trees, parks, and large yards. They have adequate shopping resources for healthy food, many good schools for their children, and strong crime prevention programs. They also face less daily stress like fear of crime, environmental health hazards like toxic waste and pollution, and less social disorganization (Wen et al., 2003).

You may be thinking "If only *I* had such problems!" But the truth is, being rich isn't always easy. It's difficult to know who your real friends are and who may be using you for your money. Constant pressure to be perfect and achieve can lead to a sense of insecurity, helplessness, and depression for those who don't live up to the potential for which they have been groomed their entire lives (Luthar, 2003).

Affluence can cause a variety of problems for family life. Many wealthy parents work extensively to maintain their wealth, so they hire help to care for their children. Their children often grow up with a sense of isolation from emotional support. Luthar and D'Avanzo (1999) compared white suburban youth from white-collar families to youth of color from low socioeconomic neighborhoods. What they found surprised them. The wealthy youth suffered higher levels of anxiety, depression, and substance use than the poor youth. They smoked more and used more alcohol and drugs. In fact, 20% of rich girls exhibited clinical levels of depression, three times higher than the poor girls. The same was found for anxiety and substance use. For the wealthy, but not the poor, substance use was linked to depression and anxiety, suggesting that the youth were using substances to cope with stress. Moreover, substance use was associated with popularity with peers. This was not true for the poor youth.

Similarly, Luthar and Becker (2002) examined children of families making over $125,000 per year. In 6th grade, these students reported good mental health, but by 7th grade, they had elevated levels of depression, anxiety, and substance use compared to the national average. Affluent children face many pressures to excel in all areas. In fact, being "average" or "mediocre" is actively shunned by the wealthy. Children are expected to get the highest grades, be the best in sports, and attend the best colleges. Meanwhile, they are often left home alone or with hired help for many hours each day, leaving them both time to get into trouble and a feeling of being disconnected from family members. Any failures they face are made public so many wealthy children develop anxiety and somatic symptoms like headaches and stomach aches (Luthar, 2003). Csikszentmihalyi and Schneider (2000) found that affluent teens reported the lowest levels of happiness and poor teens the highest. These rich teens often acted out, becoming sexually active early and taking drugs, sometimes to attract attention and even elicit discipline from their absent parents. The U.S. Department of Health and Human Services (1999) found that a feeling of closeness to parents was negatively correlated with income. This means that the closer a child feels to his or her parents, the more likely he or she is to be poor versus rich.

On a larger scale, depression is higher in wealthy countries than in poor countries. People in rich countries have cars, TVs, and cell phones, take luxurious vacations, have leisure time, buy nice clothes, and yet feel a sense of emptiness. They have a lot of "stuff," yet their levels of emotional well-being are low (Buss, 2000).

If an individual has every material good possible, appreciation for small or simple things in life, such as nature, family time, spirituality and friendship, may decline. Affluent people may live in giant houses spread far apart from neighbors, and live behind gated and locked protective walls. Children are unlikely to spontaneously play with neighbors. And people do not get involved with their neighbors' problems, preferring to stay out of personal issues like domestic violence, divorce, or family deaths.

Affluent youth may feel guilty for their sadness and existential angst because they know they should be happy, having been provided with all the material wealth they could ever use. They know people may wonder what right they have to complain when they have everything. This can deepen their sense of depression and can even lead to isolation and suicide (Luthar, 2003). Similarly, eating disorders are much more common in the wealthy, reflecting a desperate sense of trying to be perfect in a stressful household. Children may be suffering because all of the emphasis has been on their performance and not on their intrinsic worth as human beings (Luthar, 2003).

Affluent survivors of domestic violence and clinical depression report that service providers never took them seriously (Csikszentmihalyi & Schneider, 2000). People may question the validity of their suffering, and at some level, the public even enjoys seeing the rich come crashing down. Even school personnel may be reluctant to intervene in a struggling wealthy student's emotional problems for fear of reprisal from the family as a consequence of their "reputation" being ruined.

Csikszentmihalyi (1999) argues that money, to a certain extent, is a protective factor. But too much of it is harmful to the human psyche. The rich are less likely to make true human connections because everyone around them is on their payroll or is as rich as they are. In contrast, people with fewer material comforts have no choice but to reach for community, friends, family, and professional service providers, and they have the luxury of enjoying the simple things in life.

In the grand scheme of things, middle-class socioeconomic status has the greatest chance of increasing mental, financial, physical, and spiritual health in families.

CHAPTER SUMMARY

We are experiencing the effects of a recession that began in 2008 which affected the lives of millions of people. The stress of job loss and under-employment can influence family functioning in many ways. Families can experience increases in conflict, depression, divorce, and physical health problems. Children may suffer from poor nutrition, lack of higher education, and parents who are distracted from providing care and support.

When parents are employed, men and women can face role strain while trying to balance the demands of work and family life. Pressures at work can bleed over from the exosystem into the microsystem and create tension in personal relationships. Especially for mothers, there is a wage penalty for having children. Even brief exits from the workforce can impact lifetime salaries, benefits, and promotions. Women often experience a glass ceiling, the barrier to work promotion and success. Sexism in the workplace negatively affects women's mental health and can affect their ability to care for their children at home. People of color and those in LGBT communities may be particularly marginalized and discriminated against in the workplace, leading to much stress at home. Tokenism can put undue strain on women and especially women of color, who often have no mentors or supports in place at work to help them cope with discrimination or harassment.

Many countries around the world have established social policies that provide high-quality health care, child care, and parental leave benefits that ease the burden of balancing work and family pressures. In the U.S. recent trends show more companies implementing family-friendly policies like telecommuting and flex time, but this is still relatively rare, especially for people in low-paying jobs.

Several personality factors can affect how people adjust to life at work. Type A personality is related to mental and physical health problems, while Type B personality is related to good co-worker relationships and personal satisfaction and health. Over-commitment to work and workaholism are traits that lead people to gain their self-worth from work at the expense of family relationships. Workaholics can be hostile, excessively striving, and competitive. They cannot leave work at work and the boundaries between work and home become blurred.

The chapter concluded with the negative effects of both poverty and affluence on family functioning. Disease, depression, conflict, and strained attachments can result from living at either extreme of the socioeconomic continuum; thus, being middle class provides many benefits for a happy and peaceful family life, even under times of economic downturn.

KEY TERMS

benevolent sexism	glass ceiling	role-scarcity hypothesis
comparable worth legislation	glass escalator	sexism
	hostile sexism	telecommuting
daddy track	internal locus of control	tokenism
external locus of control	job sharing	type A personality
family process model of economic hardship	mommy/caring tax	type B personality
	mommy track	underemployed
flex time	over-commitment	workaholism

WEBSITES FOR FURTHER EXPLORATION

http://www.familiesandwork.org

The Families and Work Institute is a non-profit, non-political research organization which seeks to change workplace policies and practices to benefit family life. They have some great videos on various governmental positions on workplace issues, many publications, and resources for working families.

http://www.workingmother.com

Working Mother magazine's website has a lot of helpful information for working mothers. There are "mom blogs," real working mothers' stories, articles on how to balance work and family, information on preparing quick meals, information on seeking out "green" businesses and family vacations, and some very informative lists of the best companies parents can work for.

http://www.fatherhood.org

The National Fatherhood Initiative seeks to improve the well-being of children by helping fathers stay involved in their lives. It provides public service announcements, education for fathers, mentors to help new fathers, and clubs and email lists for working fathers. There's a great survey dads can take to see whether their jobs are doing all they can to help fathers balance work and home life.

CHAPTER 11
FAMILIES IN CRISIS
Violence, Abuse, and Neglect

No peace in the world without peace in the nations
No peace in the nations without peace in the town
No peace in the town without peace in the home
No peace in the home without peace in the heart.

(Tao Te Ching)

LEARNING OBJECTIVES

- To realize how pervasive violence is, in every system of the bioecological model

- To gain an understanding of the different forms of elder abuse and neglect

- To see the connections between animal abuse and family violence

- To understand both sides of the gender symmetry controversy regarding domestic violence

- To understand the dynamics of intimate partner violence, including issues related to survivors, batterers, and their children

- To gain insight into the many ways children are maltreated and how we can prevent child abuse and neglect

Marriages and Families in the 21st Century: A Bioecological Approach, First Edition. Tasha R. Howe.
© 2012 Tasha R. Howe. Published 2012 by Blackwell Publishing Ltd.

OVERVIEW: THE PERVASIVE NATURE OF VIOLENCE

ELDER ABUSE AND NEGLECT

Forms of elder abuse

- Neglect
- Self-neglect
- Physical abuse
- Psychological/emotional abuse
- Sexual abuse
- Financial/material abuse/exploitation

Diversity in elder abuse

ANIMAL ABUSE

Risk factors for animal abuse

Childhood cruelty to animals

INTIMATE PARTNER VIOLENCE

Historical trends in intimate partner violence

The importance of terminology

Marital rape

The gender symmetry controversy

- The World Health Organization study
- Research on western families

The dynamics of IPV

- Cycle of violence
- Power and control
- Why is it so hard to leave a batterer?
- Supporting battered women

Biological processes resulting from IPV

Risk and protective factors related to victimization

Victims or survivors?

Lesbian IPV victims and survivors

Ethnicity and IPV

Feminism and IPV

BATTERERS

Types of batterers
- Dysphoric/borderline batterers
- Antisocial/violent batterers
- Family only batterers

Attachment issues

Treatment issues
- Duluth Model
- An innovative treatment model for latino immigrants

Children exposed to intimate partner violence

CHILD MALTREATMENT

Cultural issues in maltreatment

Types of child maltreatment
- Physical abuse
- Abusive head trauma
- Neglect
- Sexual abuse
- Psychological/emotional abuse

Intervention and prevention
- Legal issues
- The need for evidence-based practice

FIGURE 11.1 Overview of the material presented in this chapter. Image © Alexander Raths, 2010. Used under license from Shutterstock.com

OVERVIEW: THE PERVASIVE NATURE OF VIOLENCE

You know someone who has been abused or neglected. You may not realize you do, but unfortunately, violence is so pervasive that almost all of us know someone or have ourselves been exposed to violence. This is not a new phenomenon. The opening quote comes from a Chinese philosophical text dating from the sixth century BCE, and it illustrates very well the bioecological nature of violence. The causes and consequences of violence occur within individuals and extend to every context of our lives, all the way out to our macrosystems.

Violence occurs in many settings where families interact. Whether it's child abuse, domestic violence, elder abuse, animal cruelty, or exposure to violence in your neighborhood or community, all of us are affected in some way. The World Bank estimated that if we add up the number of preventable years of life lost around the world, fully one out of every five years is lost, not due to disease or hunger, but due to violence inflicted upon us (Koss, Heise, & Russo, 1994). Indeed, violence against women has a greater overall cost to women's health around the world than HIV/AIDS and cancer combined.

How many wars are going on at any one point in time around the world? At the time of this writing, wars or major armed conflicts are going on in Afghanistan, the Democratic Republic of Congo, Israel and the Palestinian Territory, and Algeria, to name a few. In each of those places where battles rage, where militants and warring tribes reign, families are affected. For example, in studies of Palestinian children living in the Gaza Strip, both adults and children exhibit high levels of post-traumatic stress disorder (PTSD) symptoms. They live in fear, with high levels of anxiety and depression. When parents are traumatized by war or conflict, their ability to sensitively parent their children is impaired. They can't make a living and support their households and their emotional distress affects children's levels of psychopathology (Thabet, Tawahina, Sarraj, & Vostanis, 2008). Palestinian children in Gaza show signs of poor appetite, nightmares, anger, fear, phobic avoidance of areas where they witnessed violence, inability to concentrate in school, and survivor's guilt. Thabet et al. (2008) found that 98.5% of Palestinian children had seen mutilated bodies on television, 89.8% had heard jetfighters flying overhead, 74.5% had seen tanks firing into their neighbors' homes, and 75% had seen people killed by rockets. On the other side of that conflict, Israeli children and adults in the town of Sderot suffer ongoing post-traumatic stress responses as their region is continuously attacked by mortars and rockets. It is estimated that 400 people have been seriously injured in this small town, with dozens killed. In 2008, almost 4,000 rockets and the same number of mortars were fired from Gaza into this area of Israel. Families in Sderot seek mental health services at a rate three times higher than other cities in Israel (Diamond, Lipsitz, Fajerman, & Rozenblat, 2010).

DeJong et al. (2001) found that political strife and warfare resulted in PTSD symptoms experienced by 37% of the population in Algeria, 28% in Cambodia, 16% in Ethiopia, and 18% in Gaza. Pham, Weinstein, and Longman (2004)

FIGURE 11.1 These infants were orphaned through the intense violence in the Democratic Republic of Congo, November 2008.
Photo © Uriel Sinai/Getty Images.

found that 28% of Rwandans exhibited PTSD symptoms. These symptoms are highest in people who are closest to a conflict, have their own safety threatened, struggle to survive, or are displaced from their homes (Thabet et al., 2008). If people can escape the violence or are forced to flee, they often face personal injury, loss of property, hunger, disease, and complete disruption of their lives. Unfortunately, these refugees also experience racism and discrimination when they flee to a new country. For example, Somali refugees moving to the United States experienced PTSD symptoms from the trauma they lived through (68% had symptoms), and almost 80% of them reported discrimination and racial taunts in their new home (Ellis, MacDonald, Lincoln, & Cabral, 2008).

These kinds of experiences are found not only in people living in developing nations or fleeing from developing nations. It is estimated that 25–65% of children living in crime-ridden impoverished inner cities in the United States exhibit post-traumatic stress symptoms (Foster, Kuperminc, & Price, 2004).

The United States has the highest rates of both family and community violence of any industrialized nation (Richters & Martinez, 1993). And even among middle-class people with private insurance, who are assessed by their own doctors in the U.S., it has been found that exposure to family violence is linked to the development of heart disease, tobacco addiction, cancer, lung disease, teen pregnancy, substance abuse, unemployment, and obesity, to name a few outcomes (Felitti et al., 1998).

Researchers estimate that one in three women will experience domestic violence and that one in four children will be abused or neglected over their lifetimes. Look around at the faces in your classroom, church, temple, or mosque, in your grocery store, neighborhood, and the schools where local children play. In each one of those settings are people who have experienced violence, abuse, or neglect in their families, their communities, or both. While this state of affairs is certainly sad and disheartening, it may also help many of you reading this book to realize that you are not alone. Your experiences are shared by millions of people.

Most of you are probably somewhat familiar with the issues of domestic violence and child abuse, but two forms of family violence are lesser known, and very little research examining them is available: elder abuse and animal abuse. While we will study each type of abuse separately, it's important to recognize that many families experience several types of violence at once. In fact, it's common for law enforcement officers investigating cases of animal cruelty to discover that the perpetrators are already known to child welfare or other agencies that investigate domestic violence. When people harm elders and pets, it's a safe bet to assume that children and adult partners may also be experiencing harm. That's why it's important that we have some understanding of all the forms of family violence, because they often co-occur.

ELDER ABUSE AND NEGLECT

Forms of elder abuse

Diversity in elder abuse

With improvements in sanitation, hygiene, quality of life, and health care (at least in the western world), we are seeing a global phenomenon: the graying of the population. Never before have so many people lived for so long. Currently in the United States, 13% of the population is over 65. Longer life spans, increases in the retirement age, and women's changing gender roles have combined to create a dilemma of how to care for the increasing numbers of elderly. In previous generations, care of the elderly was the responsibility of the family, particularly women. But changing gender roles and work outside the home have relieved some women of the expectation that they must care for older or infirm family members. Family mobility and a change in cultural beliefs regarding obligations to our elders has led to the current situation of a large percentage of seniors being left alone, abused, or neglected (Barnett, Miller-Perrin, & Perrin, 2004). Childless seniors and homosexual seniors are even less likely to be cared for in their old age.

It is estimated that one to two million seniors in the U.S. are abused or neglected each year. But only one out of 14 cases actually comes to the attention of authorities like the police or Adult Protective

Services (Pillemer & Finkelhor, 1988). The Senate Special Commission on Aging estimates that true numbers could be as high as five million victims per year (www.ncea.aoa.gov), with 65% of victims being European American and 32% being African American. Prosecutions for these crimes are rare.

Teaster (2003) reports that in 2003 in the United States, 472,813 cases of elder abuse or neglect were reported but only 166,019 could be confirmed by authorities. In surveys using self-report methodology, about 4% of elders report being victims of abuse or neglect. Emergency room reports show about 33,000 confirmed elder abuse injuries. Elderly women are particularly likely to show up in emergency departments for genital injuries due to sexual assault (Teaster, 2003).

In spite of these statistics, seniors do not identify with words regarding victimization and do not envision themselves as victims. Therefore, to prevent or intervene in these cases, Barnett et al. (2004) suggest that outreach efforts to the senior community should not mention words like "abuse" or "rape" but should ask people to call to get help for "concerns of older women" or "issues that face the aging population today." Moreover, those who intervene should do so with respect, by maintaining the senior's dignity and autonomy in as many ways as possible. While seniors may be frail or disabled in some ways, we must not infantilize them or consider them dependent in the same way children are (Penhale, 2003).

The U.S. and Canada report that about 5% of elders are abused each year and that most of these are women abused by spouses, other kin, or institutional caregivers (Lachs & Pillemer, 2004; Podnieks, 1990). Other countries are beginning to assess rates of elder abuse but accurate statistics are difficult to gather, as most cases are not reported and many places do not have systematic data-gathering protocols in place. However, studies show that about 18% of seniors in Israel experience some form of abuse or neglect (Eisikovitz, Winterstein, & Lowenstein, 2004), rates in Hong Kong are estimated at 21.4% (Tang & Yan, 2001), and in the UK, estimates vary from 2.6% to 5% (Ogg & Bennet, 1992; O'Keeffe et al., 2007). Across countries, the World Health Organization estimates that between 1% and 35% of elder experience mistreatment but that the vast majority of cases go unreported (WHO, 2008).

While a few publications attempted to alert people to the problem occurring in the U.S. and elsewhere in the 1970s, it has only been since the 1980s that the United Kingdom and other western nations began taking steps to deal with elder abuse and neglect (Penhale, 2003). The development and enforcement of laws protecting seniors occurred even more recently, primarily in the 1990s. In Ireland, failing to care for an elder is a misdemeanor crime, and in India children are legally bound to care for their aging parents (Barnett et al., 2004).

Forms of elder abuse

Six main forms of elder abuse take place: neglect, self-neglect, physical abuse, psychological/emotional abuse, sexual abuse, and financial/material abuse/exploitation. Let's explore each of these in turn.

Neglect

Neglect
The failure of caregivers to provide for the needs of children or dependent adults; neglect can take many forms, like not providing food, shelter, clothing, health care, or emotional support.

Neglect is the most common type of abuse and is perpetrated mainly by spouses or partners and adult female kin caregivers (that is, daughters). When people face a caregiving burden for their parents, especially if that parent abused or neglected the adult caregiver as a child, abuse or neglect of the senior becomes more likely (Penhale, 2003). Neglect includes not feeding the older person, withholding medicines, failing to transport the senior to scheduled medical appointments, failing to provide clean bed linens, failing to change diapers, or failing to provide the senior with adequate personal hygiene. There may also be emotional or spiritual neglect, where caregivers refuse to talk to the senior, don't allow visitors in the home, or prevent the senior from practicing his or her religion.

Self-neglect

You may be surprised to learn that self-neglect represents the majority of cases of senior neglect. In fact, 21.6% of abuse/neglect reports in 2004 were reports of elders neglecting themselves (Teaster et al., 2007). When seniors are neglecting themselves, it usually means they have become socially isolated and they have no family to care for them. Their families are either neglecting to check in on them or live far away, or their attempts at care are thwarted by an independent-minded senior (Barnett et al., 2004). Elders who are experiencing **self-neglect** have usually become too frail or mentally or physically challenged to care for themselves. They may be dirty, be emaciated, live in a filthy house, suffer from dementia, or have drug or alcohol problems that impair their ability to care for themselves. But they can also be mentally lucid yet have just decided that hygiene and regular eating habits are of no interest to them.

Physical abuse

After neglect, **physical abuse**, wherein usually male caregivers will slap, hit, kick, tie up, or otherwise physically harm elders in their care, is the most common form of elder abuse. About 19% of reported abuse cases are physical in nature. This type of abuse is more commonly found in residential facilities than in situations where the elder is being cared for at home (Lachs & Pillemer, 2004). In the most severe cases, the senior can be killed, and most states now have a fatality review team, which investigates all suspicious deaths of older people in order to determine not only what killed the person, but what can be done to prevent similar cases in the future (www.ncea.aoa.gov).

Psychological/emotional abuse

Psychological/emotional abuse includes verbal or non-verbal acts that torment, humiliate, embarrass, or attack an elder person's character. Emotional abuse inflicts distress and mental anguish on the victim (Parra-Cardona, Meyer, Schiamberg, & Post, 2007). In a sample of Chinese elders, Yan and Tang (2001) found that verbal abuse was the type of harm most strongly related to psychological distress. These victims felt anxious and depressed, and had many somatic complaints. While emotional abuse is difficult to detect or prove, some research suggests that at least one third of all cases of other types of abuse include some element of psychological harm to the elder (Teaster et al., 2007). Emotional abuse is more likely to occur when perpetrators experience high levels of **caregiving stress**. Caregiving stress can include fatigue, feelings of being overwhelmed, and symptoms of depression or anxiety. Caregivers today may be particularly stressed because of the large birth cohort in the Baby Boom generation, which is also referred to as the **Sandwich Generation**. This generation is stuck in the middle of two other generations they must care for: children and elderly parents. This "sandwiching" can lead quickly to a feeling of being overwhelmed. For members of the sandwich generation, retirement is more likely to consist of caring for elders than playing golf or traveling the world.

Sexual abuse

Sexual abuse of elders is most commonly perpetrated by male workers in nursing homes, rather than by kin caregivers, and often involves seniors with deteriorated cognitive capacity, such as dementia or mental illness. In a study of elder sexual abuse, Grossman and Lundy (2003) found that Korean Americans endorsed family privacy more than other groups and so were the least likely to report sexual abuse in comparison to African American, European American, and Hispanic elders. Moreover, four times as many Hispanic women and three times as many white women were sexually abused as African American women were. These differences could be due to certain groups residing in nursing or care homes at higher rates than others. African Americans, in particular, are more likely to care for their elders at home instead of in an institution. It could also reflect differential rates of reporting in various communities of color.

Financial/material abuse/exploitation

Financial/material abuse/exploitation is unique to elders and involves taking advantage of an elder's home, investments, or other accumulated wealth for the personal gain of a caregiver. For example, elders with Alzheimer's disease or other forms of dementia can be asked to sign checks, change their wills, sell their property or real estate, or transfer funds in ways that benefit the caregiver. Some elders give their caregivers *durable powers of attorney*, the legal right to act on the senior's behalf, which

Self-neglect
The most common form of elder abuse, wherein a senior fails to care for his or her own basic needs.

Physical abuse
Physical harm of a family member in the form of hitting, slapping, kicking, choking, or other physical acts.

Psychological/ emotional abuse
Humiliation, put-downs, criticisms, and threats that attack the core character of the person and make him or her feel worthless.

Caregiving stress
The overwhelm, depression, or loneliness felt by adult caregivers who must fulfill the needs of elderly or dependent adults.

Sandwich generation
Adults who are responsible for caring for both elderly parents and young children at the same time.

Sexual abuse
Any act of a sexual nature that is perpetrated against the will or without the knowledge or consent of the victim.

Financial/material abuse/exploitation
A form of elder abuse where the senior is taken advantage of and made to write checks, change wills, or otherwise give money to the perpetrator.

caregivers can abuse. Elders are also commonly the unwitting targets of exploitative telemarketing and email schemes that promise them goods or services for small up-front "investments" (Barnett et al., 2004).

The federal government has recently created **Fiduciary Abuse Specialist Teams (FASTs)**, which are responsible for prosecuting those who financially abuse seniors. These multidisciplinary teams do all they can to catch the perpetrators of financial exploitation and bring them to justice, as well as returning any lost resources to the older person. FASTs consist of accountants, FBI agents, insurance claims detectives, computer experts, and other professionals who can work together to catch perpetrators of financial abuse (www.ncea.aoa.gov).

All forms of elder abuse and neglect are difficult to research because most cases never become public. It is difficult to determine when an elder death is due to abuse or neglect, and even when reports are taken, often little can be done by social service personnel. Elders tend to be invisible as they stay in their homes and crimes against them go unrecognized. They often do not report these crimes due to being incapacitated, not recognizing that they are experiencing abuse or neglect, being afraid of the perpetrator, being afraid of having to leave their homes and lose their independence, and a sense of humiliation or shame, especially if the abuser is their own child. If they are elderly victims of domestic violence committed by a spouse, they are very unlikely to ask for help and potentially be forced to separate from a partner they have lived with for decades.

Abusive partner relationships may be at risk of developing later in life if unexpected changes occur that put undue stress on one partner. For example, if a spouse is forced to bathe, feed, toilet, and otherwise care for every need of his or her partner, the stress of caregiving, mixed with grief or depression over the loss of autonomy and joy, can create a volatile situation (Penhale, 2003). This may be even truer in relationships that were previously stressed, troubled, or financially strapped.

Diversity in elder abuse

Parra-Cardona et al. (2007) discuss how Hispanic/Latino elders may be at particular risk for abuse due to traditional gender role expectations that lead women to be subservient to and financially dependent on others. Foreign-born Latino seniors may be at even greater risk because of their financial and emotional dependence. Language barriers, immigration status, and lack of financial stability make them especially vulnerable. Moreover, divorce is frowned upon in this mostly Catholic population. Thus, married Latinas are at highest risk of elder abuse in this community, compared to single seniors. Also, Latinas experience caregiver stress, including depression and anxiety, at higher levels than white women do. This may be due to the higher levels of poverty in this population, which means caregivers often work one or more jobs for low wages and long hours, and then must come home and care for their elders. Caregivers with personal problems like substance abuse, mental illness, or financial struggles, may be particularly likely to exploit or abuse their elderly parents.

Older generations may affiliate more with their home country than their host country and a particularly insidious type of elder neglect includes social isolation. Caregivers may neglect the senior's social or spiritual needs by keeping them away from others from their home country, or from their churches, and the elder may become depressed and develop a sense of hopelessness. Kin caregivers may refuse to speak their native language, often indicating a sense of internalized racism due to identity stress combined with caregiving burdens. Immigrant caregivers may distance themselves from their native culture when faced with oppression and discrimination in their host country (Parra-Cardona et al., 2007). These factors combine to place immigrant seniors, especially the undocumented, at very high risk for abuse and neglect. However, these seniors are unlikely to report abuse or neglect due to fear of deportation for themselves or their loved ones. Elders may be particularly reluctant to report their children for mistreatment because they love them or don't want to lose their caregiving services. They may be dependent on their children for their survival. Unfortunately, statistics show that sons and daughters kill about 11% of elderly homicide victims (Teaster, 2003). The experience of immigrant elders illustrates the complex influences from each

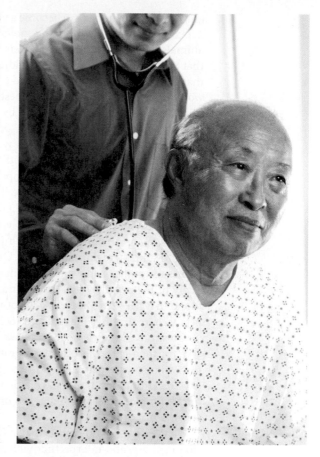

FIGURE 11.2 What can we do to protect our elders from abuse and neglect?
Photo © Supijono Suharjoto/Stocklib.

system of the bioecological model, from individual characteristics (e.g., caregiving stress), to macrosystem forces (e.g., immigration policies).

Yan, Tang, and Yeung (2002) studied elder abuse in Chinese families and found that the younger generation of Chinese families adheres less strictly to Confucian principles of familialism and devotion to elders. With elders living longer, fertility rates dropping, and most Chinese women working today, the caregiving burden placed on the small number of caregivers still available in the home can lead to elder abuse in the same way it does for families in the U.S. Because of China's one-child policy, most adults grow up with exactly four grandparents, two parents, and no siblings; as a consequence, only children are the sole caregivers for the elderly. The 1980 Revised Law in the People's Republic of China requires children to care for and support their parents. Yan et al. (2002) discuss Chinese culture being at a "crossroads between modernism and traditionalism" (p. 168). Young Chinese adults do not see any benefits for themselves if they exhibit extreme devotion to their parents and they feel that modern women should not be forced to care for the elderly at home. These authors found that the majority of abusers were usually married males living with their victims. These men often had financial struggles, drinking problems, and psychological problems. The more physically or mentally impaired the elder was, the more at risk he or she was for abuse by a live-in son. Because Chinese values placed on preserving family harmony are still prevalent, most of these cases are not reported.

While elder abuse and neglect are illegal in most western countries, there are few processes in place that guarantee safety and a place to live for a mistreated senior who is often dependent on his or her abuser. Adult Protective Services are usually financially strapped and over-burdened with cases. There are limited placement options for dependent adults as there is no uniform foster care system like there is for children. Moreover, the majority of cases never even come to their attention. If you see signs of an elderly person or an adult of any age who is mentally or physically disabled being abused or neglected, please call the National Center on Elderly Abuse at 1–800–677–1116, or report the case to your local Adult Protective Services agency.

ANIMAL ABUSE

> Risk factors for animal abuse
>
> Childhood cruelty to animals

If you think about the list of family members you completed in Chapter 1, when we were defining the word "family," chances are there was a pet on the list of many students. My students consider pets part of their family and talk about how their animals provide them with love and support. In the U.S. population, 75% of families with children have a household pet, but the general population usually doesn't think of animal abuse as a form of family violence. Pet owners usually love their animals and do all they can to minimize their suffering. However, just like all other members of a family, an animal family member can become a victim of abuse or neglect. In fact, if family violence of any kind is occurring (such as domestic violence, child abuse, or elder abuse), it's likely that the family's animals are also being abused or their needs are being neglected. For example, Ascione (1997) found that 85% of women and 63% of children surveyed while living in domestic violence shelters reported that their pets had also been abused by their perpetrator. Similarly, Ascione et al. (2007) stated that women staying in shelters for domestic violence reported animal abuse by their partners at a rate 11 times higher than that reported by women in non-violent relationships. These women said they had strong emotional ties to their pets, they were highly upset by their pets' mistreatment, and they reported that not wanting to leave pets in harm's way was a large factor in their decision to stay with the batterer for as long as they did.

Because batterers know that their partners or children love their pets, they may use them as leverage for exploitation and emotional abuse. They want to come between the love and emotional support pets often provide for battered victims. Therefore, pets are used as a means of power and control over victims of abuse (Ascione, 2000). For example, batterers will often tell their partners that if they leave them, the pets will be tortured or murdered. Or pets will be physically harmed in front of women or children in order to scare them into submission. One study of children surveyed after they had been removed from homes where they had witnessed domestic violence found that among their top three concerns was the safety of the pets they had left behind (Mullender et al., 2002). Similarly, other researchers have also found that between 18% and 48% of women delayed entering shelter care due to concern over their pets' welfare (Carlisle-Frank, Frank, & Nielson, 2004; Faver & Strand, 2003; Flynn, 2000).

Currently, there are no federal laws in the United States regarding animal abuse or animal cruelty, save for their care and transportation across state lines. However, all states have laws on the books forbidding the perpetration of undue pain and suffering on companion animals. There are also strict laws regarding dog fighting, cockfighting, puppy mills, the mistreatment of farm animals, undue duress on race horses, undue stress on circus animals, and the use of animals for scientific research (www.aspca.org).

McPhedran (2009) reports that animal abuse has been discovered in conjunction with child abuse, sibling abuse, and interpartner violence in both heterosexual and same-sex couples. However, only 27% of the abuse survivors surveyed by Ascione et al. (2007) reported that they were asked about possible animals at risk during intake procedures by helping professionals or police. This is disturbing in light of the heinous nature of many of the animal abuse crimes they reported their male partners had perpetrated. Incidents reported ranged from threats to hurt or kill a pet, to a batterer starving a pet, preventing the survivor from taking the animal for medical care, and torturing or killing animals. Moreover, violence toward pets was particularly sadistic, ranging from setting kittens on fire to bludgeoning dogs to death. What's even more noteworthy is that when these women leave their batterer, the pets often stay in his custody. Very few shelters for battered women have facilities to care for battered or endangered pets. The Humane Society reports the need for nationwide safe havens for pets living in homes where family violence occurs (www.hsus.org). If you suspect animal abuse or neglect, please contact the humane society or your local animal control agency or police.

Risk factors for animal abuse

Concern for animals in society is widespread, despite the many people who skirt the laws and find ways to treat animals inhumanely, whether it is through restricting the wings of chickens on poultry farms or keeping dogs tied up on short leashes for hours every day. The Humane Society of the United States (www.hsus.org) puts forth some recognizable signs that animals might be victims of abuse or neglect, which include:

- being outside without shelter on very hot or very cold days
- areas of missing fur
- thin, starving appearance

- infected or injured areas; severe flea/tick infestation
- untreated medical conditions
- being chained and unable to walk
- lack of food or water provision
- animals who cower in fear or act aggressively to their owners.

Beyond the obvious forms of abuse or neglect is another abusive practice, **animal hoarding**. People who obtain and rescue large numbers of animals without permits or the space, medical knowledge, or financial means to care for them are committing animal *hoarding*, a form of neglect. These people often have good intentions but their actions may actually endanger the health and well-being of the animals involved because they are not receiving proper medical care and attention.

> **Animal hoarding**
> A form of animal abuse wherein the person attempts to help animals but has neither the money nor skill to do so; excessive numbers of animals are held in deplorable conditions.

Even though survivors of domestic violence love their pets, research shows that even if their pets are not abused by their batterers, the majority (55%) of battered women do not or cannot properly care for their animals through preventative medical care or vaccinations (Ascione et al., 2007). Also, abused women harm animals at higher rates than non-abused women do (11% versus 2.5% for the general population). In addition, 37.5% of children in shelter care compared to 11.8% of children in the general population were found to have hurt or killed pets (Ascione et al., 2007). Because victims of domestic violence and child abuse often begin to experience blunted emotions, a lack of empathy, and other emotion regulation problems that stem from abuse, their symptoms may contribute to their own patterns of animal cruelty.

Carlisle-Frank et al. (2004) found that compared to spousal abusers who did not harm pets, spousal abusers who were cruel to pets talked less to their animals, showed less affection to them, used pets as scapegoats for family problems, and reported that pets' behaviors pushed their buttons or made them angry. Also, Carlisle-Frank et al. (2004) found that batterers did not view pets as sentient beings or members of the family. They were seen instead as objects or property. In addition, those who were cruel to animals were often abused in their own childhoods or witnessed domestic violence between their parents. These risk factors can increase the chances that children will be cruel to animals both in childhood and adulthood. Merz-Perez, Heide, and Silverman (2001) found that violent offenders from a maximum security prison were much more likely to have been cruel to animals as children than non-violent incarcerated offenders were (56% versus 20%). Many perpetrators of domestic violence and child abuse harmed animals when they were children, particularly if they themselves were also victims of abuse.

Childhood cruelty to animals

Childhood cruelty to animals is a red flag for potential serious problems down the line. Animal cruelty is one of the key symptoms of childhood conduct disorder, a disorder whereby children consistently violate the rights of other people and property through violence and antisocial behavior (*DSM–IV–TR*; American Psychiatric Association, 2000). Duncan, Thomas, and Miller (2005) found that antisocial children who were also cruel to animals were much more likely to live in abusive homes than antisocial children who were not cruel to animals. Similarly, Currie (2006) found that children who witnessed domestic violence were more often cruel to animals than matched control group children not exposed to violence. Boys seem to be more affected by exposure to violence than are girls, and they are also more likely to externalize their trauma in aggressive and violent ways (Currie, 2006). Being violent toward animals may give traumatized children a sense of control over chaotic environments. Children may also be identifying with the violent adults in their homes and simply modeling what they see (Ascione, 1993).

However, McPhedran (2009) reminds us that many children exhibit some cruelty to animals, from putting salt on snails, to squashing bugs, to pulling wings off flies. Ascione (2005) found that caregivers in the general population report that 5% of their children are cruel to animals. McPhedran

(2009) emphasizes that the level of sentience of the animals should be taken into account when examining how children treat animals. There is a continuum of normal exploration, for example with invertebrates, with less violence exhibited toward cold-blooded vertebrates than invertebrates, and even less toward warm-blooded vertebrates like dogs and cats. Ascione (2000) argues that it may be fairly normative for very young children such as toddlers and preschoolers to engage in **exploratory/ curiosity animal abuse**, especially with invertebrates or cold-blooded vertebrates. Exploratory/ curiosity animal abuse occurs when a child plays with animals to see what will happen if they alter or dismember them in some way. These children lack knowledge and skills regarding empathy and protection of living things. Simple information, guidance, and modeling kindness to animals may stop this behavior. For example, when a child squishes a small frog, or hits a cat with a toy, it is important that caring adults respond by discussing the need to respect all living things, and that key adults in the child's life model kind and empathic behavior towards animals. However, older children may exhibit **pathological animal abuse**, a more extreme form of abuse, which is often a symptom of emotional disturbance, a reaction to trauma, or both. Pathological animal abuse is severe or frequent harm of animals, and includes injuries to warm-blooded vertebrates.

It's necessary to realize that just because a child hurts animals does not mean the child is a victim of abuse or will grow up to be antisocial. We must consider the severity and frequency of their animal cruelty, as well as other psychological characteristics of the individual before we become alarmed. If a child is exposed to interparental violence, this is an especially significant risk factor for the existence of animal cruelty.

Let's take a closer look at this topic, which has perhaps the largest body of research evidence, domestic violence between partners. This literature has shown that one is more likely to experience violence perpetrated by family members than by any other person or group.

Exploratory/curiosity animal abuse
A child plays with animals (usually invertebrates) to see what will happen if they alter or dismember them in some way.

Pathological animal abuse
Severe or frequent harm of animals in an attempt to cause them pain or gain sadistic pleasure; includes injuries to warm-blooded vertebrates.

FIGURE 11.3 The most common place to experience aggression and violence is in the family.
www.CartoonStock.com

INTIMATE PARTNER VIOLENCE

Intimate partner violence (IPV) occurs in all types of partnerships: rich poor, gay, straight, western, non-western, and so on. People from any gender, sexual orientation, or ethnic group can be both perpetrators and victims. In these terms, domestic violence is an equal opportunity crime, one that has persisted for millennia.

Historical trends in intimate partner violence

Although violence can occur in any intimate relationship, the majority of serious cases involve men battering their female partners. Throughout history in most cultures, men have held the power to make decisions and own property, and could control women and children at will. For example, in the Hindu text the Skandapurana, it states that wives should eat after, sleep after, and sit below their husbands. Women should also never lose their tempers if husbands assault them. The Bible also tells wives to obey and submit to their husbands. English common law stated that the wife should be controlled by the husband, who could use force to control her, especially if she did not fulfill her wifely duties, such as having sex with him and obeying his wishes (Dobash & Dobash, 1979).

As Islam became an established religion by the prophet Mohammed in the seventh century CE, some forms of patriarchy were being challenged. For example, the Muslim sacred text, the Qur'an, allows women to inherit property and divorce their husbands. In fact, Islam allowed women many more rights than were given in most cultures at the time. Thus, feminist Muslim scholars argue that patriarchal oppression of women, including things like female genital mutilation and wife beating, are cultural inventions, not religious dictates of the Muslim faith (Hyde, 2007a).

In 1871, the first U.S. court to ban wife beating, which was then legal in all states, was Alabama (Heise, 1998). But not until the feminist movements in the west in the 1970s did violence against women emerge at the forefront of political and social agendas. Feminist activists fought for the establishment of safe houses or shelters for battered women and lobbied for public and social service agencies to acknowledge the pervasiveness of violence against women in the home. They argued that communities must protect victims and confront perpetrators, arresting them and implementing legal and social consequences for battering women (www.theduluthmodel.org). Feminist activists fought for better training of police and mental health workers to protect, rehabilitate, and care for the perpetrators, victims, and children involved. In particular, they advocated for treatment for the offender; shelter, psychological help, and financial assistance for the survivor; and a coordinated community response stemming from a common definition.

Despite these early social movements toward improving the situation for battered women and their children, it was only in 1994, when Nicole Brown Simpson's brutal murder was widely publicized and her estranged abusive husband, NFL football hero O.J. Simpson was tried, that the Violence Against Women Act became law. O.J. Simpson was acquitted of criminal charges but found guilty of civil responsibility for her death and was fined millions of dollars. The current Vice President of the United States, Joseph Biden, was a strong advocate for that legislation protecting women from domestic violence, as well as providing funds for detection, prevention, and treatment services (Cherlin, 2008).

The importance of terminology

Up to this point in the chapter, I have often used the term *domestic violence* to refer to violence and abuse that occurs between romantic partners. This term refers to committed partnerships, marriages, and both heterosexual and same-sex couples. However, the term preferred by today's researchers is

Intimate partner violence (IPV)
The preferred term used today for "domestic violence," which is more inclusive of all types of couples and does not have the conceptualization of "domestic," or "home-like" associated with it.

Intimate terrorism
A form of intimate partner violence where one partner wields complete control over the other and uses power tactics to isolate him or her from family and friends.

Violent resistance
Violence used by victims of intimate partner violence to fight back against their abusers.

Situational couples violence
The most common form of violence in community samples and young western couples; mutual slapping, pushing, or other forms of less severe violence which rarely result in injury and are often initiated by women.

Marital rape
Any act of psychological coercion, or physical force, used to induce a female partner or wife to engage in sexual activities for which she has no desire.

intimate partner violence (IPV), which encompasses all forms of domestic violence and includes married, non-married, heterosexual, and same-sex couples.

Because the words we use conjure up images and gut reactions in us, it's important to choose our words carefully. For example, when people read or hear the word *domestic* what comes to mind is often images like "homey" or "cozy" or "good food." In the phrase *domestic violence*, the word *domestic* tends to temper the word *violence* and make it seem less severe than it actually is. *Domestic violence* may sound like a lover's spat or a private disagreement in the home. The reality is that if the same types of assaults were committed in *non-domestic* settings, say, on the street or in a bar, the crime would be simply be called "assault," and the consequences would be much more severe for the perpetrator than is often the case with perpetrators of *domestic* violence. Many people advocate for the use of more graphic words, such as *spousal assault* or just plain *assault*.

Michael P. Johnson (2001) suggests we go a step further, and call physical violence in romantic partnerships **intimate terrorism**. He advocates this term because domestic violence includes many of the same elements as terrorism: intimidation, threats on family and friends, social isolation, deprivation of essential needs, and mentally breaking down the victim. In intimate partner violence, coercive control is at the root of the relationship. One partner, usually a man, controls virtually every aspect of the victim's, usually a woman's, life.

Many people criticize the idea that men are usually the controlling and violent partners because they argue that women are just as violent as men. Johnson (2001) finds that when women are violent or aggressive toward men, it is usually in the form of **violent resistance**, or self-defense. In intimate terrorist/violent resistant families, 97% of the *perpetrators* are men and 96% of the *violent resistors* are women. However, some feel that because *terrorism* is for many people now mentally associated with Muslim fundamentalist groups and other political militants around the world, it loses its impact when we are looking at families.

Intimate terrorism and violent resistance are most often found in clinical and shelter samples, while other types of violence are found in general community members' relationships. Johnson makes a clear distinction between intimate terrorism and the kinds of violence experienced in community samples of typical relationships, which experience virtual gender symmetry in their violence. Typical relationships sampled at random from the community or from college campuses experience violence and aggression perpetrated by both male and female partners. This type of violence is found most often in young couples. Johnson calls reports of almost equal levels of male/female violence (56% perpetrated by males and 44% by females) among college students and non-shelter populations **situational couples violence**. He reports that this is the type of violence experienced most commonly in the general population, in about 1 out of every 8 couples, and is usually not very severe. *Situational couples violence* includes slapping, pushing, and pinching, and rarely involves the type of serious injury or even death that is found in families experiencing *intimate terrorism*. Intimate terrorism includes many forms of sadistic control, including sexualized violence.

Marital rape

It is estimated that between 10% and 14% of married women have been raped by their husbands (Martin, Taft, & Resick, 2007). Marital rape is the most common form of rape, occurring more often than stranger, acquaintance, and date rape (Basile, 2002). Moreover, 40–50% of battered women have experienced marital rape. **Marital rape** includes any act of psychological coercion, or physical force, used to induce a woman to engage in sexual activities for which she has no desire. Marital rape is most often associated with other types of intimate partner violence. It is usually the endpoint of long sessions of psychological torment, verbal abuse, and physical abuse (Martin et al., 2007). Although the term includes "marital," this type of sexualized violence can occur between heterosexual intimate partners who cohabit as well as partners who are of the same sex. Most of the research, however, has been conducted on heterosexual married couples.

Early British law from the eighteenth century endorsed the view of "unity," wherein once a woman married a man, the couple was considered united as one. Thus, the woman no longer existed as a separate person. British judges ruled that husbands could not rape their wives because it would be like stealing from one's self, an impossibility (Bennice & Resick, 2003). Women were considered to be their husbands' property, without rights. Legal professionals feared that if these provisions were repealed, the courts would be inundated with vengeful wives seeking to harm their husbands (Green, 1988).

The first case of an American woman prosecuting her husband for marital rape occurred in 1978 (Bennice & Resick, 2003). The first successful conviction occurred the following year in another case. Today, all 50 states have laws against marital rape, but many states do not allow prosecution of marital rape if the couple is cohabiting or homosexual (National Clearing House for Marital and Date Rape, 2005).

About 80% of the U.S. population believes that husbands use force at least sometimes, in order to have sex with their wives (Basile, 1999), but most people do not consider marital rape to be as severe or as devastating as stranger rape (Bennice & Resnick, 2003). For example, Kirkwood and Cecil (2001) provided college students with various scenarios of rape (stranger, date, marital, or ex-partner) and students rated the marital situation as least likely to be "real" rape. Many students feel that there is no such thing as marital rape because sex is an expected activity in a marriage.

Risk factors for the occurrence of marital rape include marital dissatisfaction, poor communication, drug use, low education, a male partner with hypermasculine gender identity, and a history of abuse in either partner's family of origin (Martin et al., 2007). Both men and women in these relationships believe that sex is a woman's wifely duty, so most women never report it. Women who experience marital rape can exhibit symptoms of post-traumatic stress disorder, depression, anxiety and severe health problems, from chronic gynecological troubles to recurrent illnesses and stomach ailments (Martin et al., 2007). Those women who report the crime to police or social service agencies are more likely to escape and recover.

Most of our discussion of IPV, and especially marital rape, has focused on male perpetrators and female victims. The gender balance in IPV perpetration is a source of much controversy in the literature and with the general public so let's examine this issue further.

The gender symmetry controversy

Not all people believe that the victims in serious cases of IPV are most often women. To further examine the hypothesis that men and women are equally violent towards partners, (the **gender symmetry hypothesis**), Phelan et al. (2005) studied a sequence of emergency room admissions. They found that 100% of the women admitted were admitted for injuries stemming from IPV. Only 39% of men admitted had IPV-related injuries. This mirrors research cited by Cook (1997), which found that over one third of female hospital admissions were due to IPV, but very few male hospital admissions were.

Gender symmetry hypothesis
The idea that men and women are equally likely to perpetrate domestic violence.

When Phelan et al. (2005) interviewed the patients, 36% of the women and none of the men reported that they were intimidated by their partners. Moreover, 70% of women, but only one man, reported being intensely afraid of their partners. In fact, 85% of the men interviewed said they experienced no fear when their female partners initiated violence against them. While it may be true that men may be ashamed to admit vulnerability and fear due to society's gender role expectations, the severity of the injuries inflicted upon women versus men, who are often larger and stronger, is undeniable. Rennison and Welchans (2000) cite the Bureau of Justice Statistics' findings that in 1998, 75% of the 1,830 murders committed by intimate partners, were women murdered by men. Also, 900,000 partner assaults were reported by women in that year, while only 160,000 men reported being assaulted by their female partners.

Even if some men are under-reporting, it is unlikely that the numbers of incidents initiated by both genders are equal and that thousands of seriously injured men in need of medical care or shelter go undetected. In addition, many women also fail to report IPV, which would again raise their victimization numbers to higher than those of men. In looking at these numbers, we can see that 160,000 men in the U.S. need help dealing with and, perhaps, protection from their violent partners. The seriousness of these crimes against men should not be dismissed. Keep in mind though that women and children are the ones most likely to be gravely injured or killed (Brown, Williams, & Dutton, 1999). Women are six times more likely to be victims of IPV than men are (Bureau of Justice Statistics, 1995). They use more mental health and medical services for serious IPV injuries than men do (Tjaden & Thoennes, 2000). Women are also more likely to be stalked than men are. Their length of victimhood lasts longer than that of men, and they lose more time from work due to the effects of violence, such as injuries and emotional distress. The National Center for Injury Prevention and Control (2003) found that if we combine the lost productivity of all victims of IPV, we get eight million days of lost work per year (about 32,000 full-time jobs). To read about one woman's incredible survival story, see the *Focus on My Family* box.

FOCUS ON MY FAMILY

Paula's story

I met my husband over ice cream. As he scooped a cone for me, his large hands looked strong and protective. He presented himself as a feminist, appreciative of my independence. After we married and had two children, he suddenly declared himself a "traditional man," expecting me to be a subservient woman. He was reverting back to what his father taught him. His father had physically and emotionally abused him, and his mother abandoned him.

The first time my husband struck me, my infant daughter was next to me. He acknowledged it was wrong and there were no incidents for two years. The next time, he struck my head and ruptured my eardrum. I left with the children and told him I would not come back unless he entered therapy. He did, and I returned home. I also entered therapy to deal with this as well as my own abuse history. From 3 months to 6 years of age, I was abused by my married babysitters and their friends. After moving away, I repressed the horrible memories but my husband's violence awakened them. Nevertheless, after therapy, I shared my trauma with him and he loved and supported me. Sometimes he was so kind and eased my pain. Then he would use something I told him to blame me for his violence, claiming I was damaged or insane. But I wanted to believe we could both heal from our childhood experiences. This hope anchored me to him.

For a time after his therapy, he wasn't violent, but in hindsight, I see how he controlled me. I talked about his violence during couples' counseling, but he contained himself during those sessions. Then at home, I paid the price as he silenced me. My daughter called me "the dancing bear" as I tried to maintain a façade of happiness amidst violence. He would strangle me unconscious and tell me how long I had to live. He twisted my arms and terrorized me, with long stretches between incidents, during which he was kind and loving.

After 20 years, I was able to permanently leave with my teenage children, due mainly to their growing understanding of the situation. They became more confrontational with him so I felt increasingly responsible for their safety. Though he never physically harmed them, they were deeply affected. Both children have serious reservations about relationships, especially marriage, which saddens me.

For years after leaving, my husband continued to harass and threaten me, leading to restraining order violations. Like most batterers, he was ordered into treatment with no jail time. Because we share two children and a grandchild, we still cross paths. I would not feel safe being alone with him but no incidents have occurred for several years. My children and I continue to heal and support each other. They have their own relationships with their dad and believe he's made some positive changes. Sometimes I'm still amazed no one is waiting at home to hurt me. My life is peaceful, filled with family, good friends, fulfilling work, and a safe home. These things may not seem like much, but they are everything to me.

In light of the statistics, why do people still insist that women are just as violent as men? The answer could have to do with their macrosystem experiences. For example, Archer (2006) examined 52 nations and found that in countries with higher relative levels of gender equality and high rates of individualism in the population, situational couple's violence was more common, and more men were victimized by women. In contrast, women were much more likely to be the sole victims of domestic violence in countries where sexist attitudes were more pervasive and the community approved of violence against women.

The World Health Organization study

In a study of 10 countries around the world, no more than 15% of women reported initiating violence against their partner if he was not first abusing her. The more traditional a society is, then, the lower the rate of situational couple's violence and the higher the rate of intimate terrorism. For example, in rural Bangladesh and Ethiopia, less than 1% of physically abused women ever initiated violence against their partners (WHO, 2005).

International bodies are adamant that intimate partner violence is a global crisis against women. The World Health Organization (WHO, 2005) has stated unequivocally that women around the world are at greater risk than men of experiencing violence in their intimate partnerships. WHO and many international human rights groups argue that violence against women violates their basic human rights to exist peacefully and happily without being assaulted or victimized. WHO argues that all countries of the world must take it upon themselves to eliminate such violence. One of the United Nations' Millennium Development Goals for the twenty-first century focuses on educating girls, empowering women, and institutionalizing gender equality around the world. This includes work by the World Health Organization to protect women from violence. In fact this is one of their top priorities (WHO, 2005). In an attempt to convince nations that violence against women is an international epidemic of pervasive human rights violations, as well as an international public health problem, they undertook an ambitious study of over 24,000 women in 10 countries (Bangladesh, Samoa, Thailand, Japan, Serbia and Montenegro, Thailand, the United Republic of Tanzania, Ethiopia, Namibia, and Peru). They found women's self-reported rates of physical violence perpetrated by male partners ranged from 14% in Japan to 61% in rural Peru. Japan also had the lowest rates of sexual assault, at 6%, with 59% of Ethiopian women experiencing sexual assault. Women who reported sexual abuse by a partner ranged from 6% in Japan and Serbia and Montenegro, to 46% in rural Bangladesh. Almost one third of rural and urban Ethiopian women reported marital rape or being forced to have intercourse against their will by a domestic partner. Moreover, across all countries, between 25% and 50% of women had been assaulted by their partners while they were pregnant.

With the alarming rate of AIDS in Africa, these results should be a wake-up call to health professionals everywhere. Family violence is a public health crisis. Women in the WHO study who had been abused had much worse health status than women who were not. They complained of memory loss, problems walking, dizziness, and vaginal problems. More of them also had signs of depression and anxiety, and had both thought about and attempted suicide than non-victimized women.

Across countries, violence was more common in rural than in urban areas. WHO suggests that this may be due to higher education and better resources in urban areas. The study found that education was a protective factor for women, with the most highly educated women being least at risk for violence. Women in urban areas tended to believe that no one deserved to experience partner violence. However, some women, especially those in rural, traditional communities, reported that it was acceptable for a man to beat his wife if she did not do her housework, refused sexual relations with her husband, disobeyed him, or was unfaithful to him. Those who had been abused were most likely to accept these reasons for abuse, especially for a woman "disobeying" her husband or being unfaithful. Women in rural, traditional communities may see violence as normative and expected in relationships. In fact, in rural Bangladesh, Peru and Tanzania, 10–20% of women felt a woman had no right to ever refuse sex with her husband, even if she were sick, he was drunk, or he was mean to her. To see some results across all ten countries, see Figure 11.4.

Research on western families

Western scholars and media outlets are more embroiled in the controversy over whether women are actually equally as violent as men than international groups are. This may be because most research is done in western nations where the rates are more equal. Studies on dating college students in western nations show that college women are just as likely as college men to slap or hit their partners, and even initiate such acts more frequently (Archer, 2000; Johnson, 2001). In more serious cases than this typical *situational couples violence*, women tend to throw things to keep a safe distance from their partners, while men cause serious injuries through punching and kicking their female partners (Cook, 1997). Men therefore suffer a greater percentage of eye injuries from glass and ceramic objects being thrown at their heads. Cook (1997) reports that many serious female batterers have previous histories of violence, and report not being afraid of their partners. He argues that women tend to attack men where they are most vulnerable, in their groin area, and often use psychological tactics that threaten their manhood. For example, they may publicly criticize his sexual performance or attack his masculinity. Cook (1997) argues that men do not trust that police will take them seriously if they report battering, so they keep it to themselves. They feel ashamed and don't want to be ridiculed for letting the "little lady" hurt them. He emphasizes that many couples obtain mutual restraining orders when police are involved, suggesting equal levels of violence.

It is important to remember that when data are collected on less severe IPV (situational couples violence), they are collected on general population groups, often young dating or college couples. When data are gathered by law enforcement, domestic violence shelters, child welfare services, mental health practitioners, fatality review teams, and international organizations, the result is almost uniformly in the direction of women being severely battered by men. There are lesbians and

FIGURE 11.4 Prevalence of lifetime physical violence and sexual violence by an intimate partner, among ever-partnered women, by location.
Source: WHO multi-country study on women's health and domestic violence: summary report.

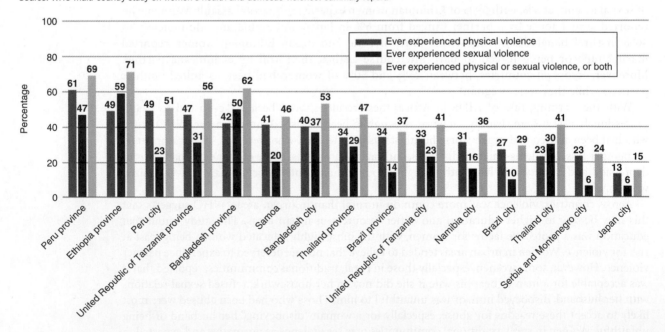

gay men in these samples, as well as some men who seek shelter from battering wives, but in general, the most severe, debilitating, and ultimately fatal forms of violence are perpetrated by men against women. This is true in both western and non-western nations.

In the U.S., a 2009 Department of Justice study found that over 45% of female murder victims were murdered by intimate partners, compared to 5% of men being murdered by intimates (Catalano, Smith, Snyder, & Rand, 2009). Also, women who do kill their partners tend to do so after years of enduring chronic abuse. They feel trapped and desperate when they kill. They often kill in self-defense during a battering episode. And women use weapons to kill their partners, keeping a safe distance, while men tend to use brute force. Men tend to kill their partner after long periods of domestic violence when they feel they can no longer control her, she may be leaving him, or he suspects she has been unfaithful. In these cases, men will often hunt the woman down, stalk her, torment her with barrages of phone calls and emails, and violently murder her while in a rage. Murder-suicides are almost always committed by men (Dobash, Dobash, Wilson, & Daly, 1992). Specifically, the Violence Policy Center (2006) found that 94% of murder-suicides were committed by men.

While most research on IPV focuses on adult heterosexual partners, IPV occurs in all types of relationships, including those of dating teenagers, newlyweds, LGBT couples, and men who are battered by women. Liz Claiborne, Inc. (2006) conducted a survey of dating teens and found some startling results. One quarter of teens reported feeling pressure to date and 33% who dated said sex was expected of them. The most alarming result may have been that 61% of teens said they have had a boyfriend or girlfriend that made them feel bad about or embarrassed about themselves and fully 47% said they compromised their own values to maintain a dating relationship. Fourteen percent said they would do just about anything to keep a boyfriend or girlfriend (www.ndvh.org). These are dangerous warning signs that a relationship could turn abusive. The teens in this study reported that 20% of their boyfriends or girlfriends had hit or slapped them and 30% actually worried about their own physical safety. It's vitally important that all adolescents (and adults) know that when a partner is controlling or makes you feel bad about yourself, it's time to get out of the relationship before it escalates.

We must educate all young people to believe that violence and aggression in families are never acceptable. We must understand the dynamics of violent relationships so that all people will understand the warning signs and get out before it's too late.

The dynamics of IPV

The National Family Violence Survey (Tjaden & Thoennes, 2000) found that over two million men and women were experiencing intimate partner violence in the year 2000. This means a lot of people are *reporting* IPV and thousands more are suffering in silence, not reporting the crimes committed against them and often living for years under extremely stressful circumstances.

The dynamics of family violence and our responses to those dynamics can vary widely. Some people can be exposed to violence and consciously decide to work on stress reduction techniques to help them cope and not aggress against others. They may take meditation classes and enroll in parenting classes to teach them how to use non-violent discipline with their children. Other people may act impulsively, reacting in a rage whenever their safety is threatened. To understand these differences, let's examine some of the interactional processes in families experiencing violence.

Cycle of violence

While there are many variations in how families perpetrate and respond to violence, there is also a typical pattern seen in many abusive relationships called the **cycle of violence**. The cycle of violence consists of a repetitive pattern of violence escalation, cooling off, and re-escalation. The cycle includes

Cycle of violence
A repetitive pattern of domestic violence escalation, cooling off, and re-escalation; violence is often followed by apologies, forgiveness, happiness, and then escalation back into violence.

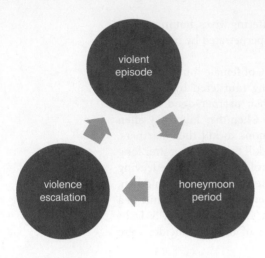

violent
episode

violence
escalation

honeymoon
period

FIGURE 11.5 The cycle of violence.

a violent episode followed by a period of relative calm. In this calm cooling-off period, the batterer often apologizes, swears his love for his partner, and promises never to do it again. During a **honeymoon period** there may be happy or romantic times, fun times with the children, and a sense of normalcy. But soon the tension builds. The violent partner gets more irritable over time, snaps at his partner, yells at the kids, and may even kick the dog. The abused partner begins to walk on eggshells around him and does everything in her power to make him happy. This period of **escalation** is extremely stressful for the victim as she tries to prevent the violence from occurring. However, the violence usually happens again, and then the cycle continues. While not all violent relationships follow the cycle of violence, this pattern is fairly common. Some families have no honeymoon period and experience consistent, chronic violence. Others have sporadic violence every few months or years. What most families share, however, is the use of violence in order to gain power over others, dominate and control them.

Power and control

The general public may view IPV as a lovers' quarrel or jealousy that turns into rage. These views assume the perpetrator is "out of control." However, research shows that violence is often perpetrated against partners in a deliberate manner in order to gain **power and control** over his partner. Power and control are the two key elements in the cycle of violence, and explain many of the interpersonal dynamics found in violent relationships. Such tactics are used to enable the violence to continue without fear that the abused partner will leave. For example, the abuser may control his partner's every move, timing her arrivals and departures, or monitoring the gas tank in her car. He may discourage her from seeing friends or family, and tell her he wants her all to himself.

In the beginning, many women are flattered by controlling men's devotion and desire to be with them all the time. But this is a clear warning sign of which all women (and men) should be aware in the early stages of a relationship. A new partner who keeps you isolated from other people and needs to know where you are at all times is not exhibiting love and devotion. This is controlling behavior and can evolve into violent power struggles. As their control tightens, in order to keep their partners with them, batterers often humiliate their partners by sexually assaulting them, insulting their character or their looks, or embarrassing them in front of others. They may force the victim to clean and reclean the house or they may throw freshly cooked food away, complaining that the partner can't cook. Calling her names, and saying she is fat, ugly, or unlovable, are also common. Women caught in the grips of ultra-controlling partners often begin to believe the insults and their self-esteem plummets.

Long-term victims of IPV may develop a sense of **learned helplessness**, in which they don't even try to leave because they feel their attempts won't succeed, that they couldn't make it on their own, or that they don't deserve better. They may even think they are the cause of the violence, that if they were better wives or partners, he wouldn't be so angry. Women also know the soft side, the good and charming side of their partners, so they hope that with enough love and support, they can bring out that side again. They may stay with him in the hopes that he will change (and he often promises he will). They may stay because they have children in common and the woman doesn't want to deprive them of their father. On the more sinister side, many batterers threaten to kill the children, kidnap them, or kill the woman's family members, if she leaves. Pets may be injured, tortured, or killed in order to keep her from leaving. The woman may be financially (and emotionally) dependent on the man and may have nowhere to go.

Honeymoon period
Part of the cycle of violence, which occurs after violent episodes; the batterer has apologized and things are calm and happy for a while.

Escalation
Part of the cycle of violence, which occurs after the honeymoon period and is characterized by increasing tension and foreshadowing of violence to come.

Power and control
The two key elements in the cycle of violence, which explain many of the interpersonal dynamics found in violent relationships; these tactics are used to continue to perpetrate violence against a partner without fear of him or her leaving.

Learned helplessness
A psychological state where victims of IPV feel so beaten down and unskilled that they could never leave the batterer or succeed on their own.

FIGURE 11.6 What are some of the commonly used tactics batterers use to gain power and control over their victims?
Source: Domestic Abuse Intervention Project, www.duluth-model.project. Reprinted with permission.

Why is it so hard to leave a batterer?

These dynamics point out that a woman cannot just get up and leave after many years in a battering relationship. People tend to think that if she stays, it's not that bad, she may like it, or she deserves it. But if she leaves, she may also be leaving her in-laws, her pets, her home, her community, her church, and everything else she knows in order to move into a temporary shelter, often without the ability to work, support her children, or keep her pets and other family members safe. Cohabiting women who are not legally married, members of same-sex couples, and immigrant women may think they have no legal rights and so do not leave. They may have been told that their batterers will keep the children if they leave. Some women actually do lose custody of their children if they report IPV because the courts feel her staying with her batterer has endangered the children's welfare and that she is an unfit parent for not leaving (Whitney & Davis, 1999).

Women may also be afraid of the police looking down on them. This fear may be warranted. Feder (1997) found that only 41% of police officers surveyed said they would arrest a man for slapping his wife. Many officers feel that IPV is not that serious or that if the woman stays, she must deserve what's coming to her. But even if a woman reports her partner for battering and he is arrested, he may spend only one night in jail, and his first conviction is only a misdemeanor, which leaves her right back where she started.

In addition, businesses and services practice "pink-lining," which occurs once a woman reports IPV or leaves her batterer. Pink-lining means that a woman is considered a risky client, and so various services may be canceled. Health insurance, auto, home, and life insurance companies often cancel women who leave an address due to battering. And most seriously, statistics show that a woman is most likely to be killed by a batterer when she is attempting to leave him. This is one of the key fears that keeps women living with a batterer (Barnett et al., 2004). Sometimes the cost of leaving is greater in many women's minds than the price paid for staying (Cook, Woolard, & McCollum, 2004). Without financial support and assistance in securing housing, work, and psychological treatment for herself and her children, many women do not see a way out. If you suspect someone you know is being abused, please see the helpful hints and contact information in the *FYI* box.

Supporting battered women

If you or a friend is experiencing intimate partner violence, try to devise an escape plan. Start storing money, documents, and clothes somewhere. Think of code words, safe places to live, and secret locations for people to pick you up, so that with a moment's notice, you can leave the house safely. Many women are in the most danger as they attempt to leave a batterer, so escape plans need to be

FYI

What to do if you think someone is being battered

- Stress to the person how concerned you are and that battering is not normal or deserved.

- Tell them that there is help available and that they are not alone.

- Emphasize that you believe them and can listen without judgment. Realize how hard it is for them to share scary or embarrassing information with you and listen empathically.

- Never try to guilt or shame a person into leaving his or her batterer. He or she needs support. The more isolated he or she gets, the closer he or she may get to the batterer.

- Make proactive attempts to involve the person in gatherings and events with family and friends.

- Help your friend create a safety plan such as a code word to say if he or she calls you, which will

tell you to come pick him or her up; store money and clothing in a safe place if needed; arrange a relocation plan that ensures his or her safety. Do not confront the batterer.

- If the person leaves, allow him or her to openly grieve the loss of a relationship and realize he or she may still love the batterer.

- If your friend leaves his or her batterer, help him or her to find support services such as counseling, a lawyer, or a new job. Go along for moral support.

- Realize that you cannot save a person in a battering relationship or force someone to leave a batterer. All you can do is provide information and support.

- Call the National Domestic Violence Hotline to report abuse, get help, or ask questions at 1–800–787–3224.

carefully planned and implemented with much social support. Law enforcement should also be notified. Never force a woman to leave or disown her if she can't leave.

Because law enforcement has become more aware of the dynamics of IPV, most communities today have **mandatory arrest** policies whereby women no longer have to voluntarily decide to press charges against their batterer. Police called to a domestic violence situation automatically arrest the person who initiated violence, especially if there is an injury visible on his or her partner. Also, pink-lining has been outlawed in 33 states. Moreover, restraining orders and protection orders are now given full faith and credit in all states. This means that victims of IPV who file a restraining order can expect that order to be enforced if they move to another state. However, there is no centralized database yet, so a woman must register her protective order every time she moves. While these are all steps in the right direction, many communities still suffer with traditional police officers who believe women should obey men and who don't refer battered women to mental health or substance abuse treatment in order to help them leave for good (Cook et al., 2004). And in poor communities, services are limited and shelters are virtually non-existent.

For a woman without transportation or a job, leaving a batterer may be all but impossible. Furthermore, batterers routinely violate protection orders, which makes many victims feel helpless and leads them to develop physical illnesses, and symptoms of anxiety and depression. Let's take a closer look at some of the biological effects of couple distress.

Biological processes resulting from IPV

Gottman, Driver, Yashimoto, and Rushe (2002) compared the relationships of happy couples, distressed/unhappy but non-violent couples, and violent couples during problem discussions in a laboratory setting. They found that happy couples exhibited laughter and support during problem discussions in a laboratory setting. However, violent couples compared to both other groups exhibited criticism, sarcasm, and attempts to coerce the woman into obedience. Wives in these marriages showed increased heart rates compared to their husbands, but wives in happy couples had lower heart rates than their husbands. These results suggest that coercive and domineering tactics during problem discussions increase arousal levels in victims. Thus, again, we see the biological effects of microsystem relationship dynamics.

Beyond victims of violence exhibiting high levels of physiological arousal, trauma may also induce PTSD symptoms such as cognitive and memory impairment or even amnesia. Stress alters people's ability to pay attention, learn new things, and use memory and visual-spatial skills (Hage, Griebel, & Belzung, 2006). In animal laboratory studies, when mice are exposed to a predator-stress condition, in which they see a cat from which they cannot escape, they show a reduced ability to learn new maze configurations. They make more errors in judgment and take longer to learn tasks than mice in a control group who experienced no stress. A single exposure to a cat impaired these mice's memories and learning skills for up to a month post-exposure. In repeated trials of a challenging maze task, control mice got better and better and made fewer errors, while the stressed mice continued to make numerous errors and took longer to navigate the maze. In addition, they showed signs of anxiety and fear when put into the maze. While studies on animals cannot directly be generalized to humans, they do give us an indication about some of the physiological process that might be at play in the human traumatic stress response during periods of *learned helplessness* where one cannot escape a stressful situation.

Sterling and Eyer (1988) discuss a process called **allostasis**, in which the body and brain work together to reach equilibrium of internal processes while trying to meet the demands of the external environment. When the external stressors are too great for people's stress systems to handle, we face a large **allostatic load**, and it is much more difficult to maintain homeostasis, or balance, within the system. Allostatic load refers to increasing pressure on the nervous system, which prevents internal balance or equilibrium. When faced with a stressor, our stress systems correctly activate and throw the brain and body into a state of hypervigilance, or hyperarousal. Then our stress centers return to normal as our nervous system responds to the allostatic load placed on it.

Mandatory arrest
Laws whereby police officers must arrest perpetrators of domestic violence, regardless of whether the partner wants them to.

Allostasis
A homeostatic balance between the demands of the environment and one's neurophysiological systems.

Allostatic load
Increasing pressure on the nervous system, which prevents internal balance or equilibrium; leads to stress reactions.

However, if we live in an environment where there is constant threat, the system may short-circuit and abnormalities may occur. Allostatic loads may increase so that the nervous system is burdened by too much stress and cannot adequately reach a state of equilibrium (Charney, 2004). For example, the neurotransmitter dopamine allows us to process both reward and fear stimuli. When a person's brain is exposed to too much stress, the prefrontal cortex of the brain, the nucleus accumbens, and the amygdala, become involved in dopamine imbalance. If there is too much dopamine in the prefrontal cortex and too little in the nucleus accumbens, the person will start to feel depressed and helpless. Too little dopamine in the prefrontal cortex can lead to a strong sense of anxiety and fear (Charney, 2004). Likewise, a perfect balance is required between testosterone and estrogen so that the person can regulate emotions and not feel elevated levels of stress, anxiety, or depression. People with PTSD often have low testosterone levels, and people with high estrogen levels may be more depressed. Thus, neurotransmitters and hormones that are naturally in balance (in allostasis) in most humans play a large role in how some people can become psychologically vulnerable to stress, or how another person can be resilient in the face of that same stress (Charney, 2004).

We are all born with individual differences in the reactivity and responsiveness of our hypothalamic pituitary adrenal axis (HPA axis), the stress regulation center of the body and brain. As a consequence, our reactions to trauma are the result of an infinitely complex interaction between our genes, brains, neuroendocrine functioning, social support systems, social risk factors, the types of coping strategies we learn, and the experiences we have in specific cultural milieu. This multifaceted picture is the crux of the bioecological approach to understanding family violence and its effects.

To see if you tend to use positive or negative coping strategies to deal with stress, see the *Building Your Strengths* box "Positive Coping Skills Assessment."

Beyond biological stress reactions and illnesses, we need to examine the victims of IPV in more depth. It's important to understand which factors in our bioecological systems put us at greater risk for being victims of violence. Research has uncovered some factors that many survivors of violence tend to have in common.

Risk and protective factors related to victimization

Heise (1998) points out that some key risk factors for being both victims and perpetrators of violence are exposure to IPV as a child and being abused or neglected as a child. This pattern is found throughout western countries, as well as in Nicaragua, Cambodia, and Chile (Ellsberg, Peña, Herrera, Liljestrand, & Winkvist, 1996; Johnson, 1996; Larrain, 1993). Also, people who are emotionally needy, dependent, and jealous, have low frustration tolerance, cannot regulate their emotions, and have mental health or substance abuse problems tend to be more at risk for becoming both perpetrators and victims of violence (Heise, 1998). Poverty is a major risk factor for violence of all kinds.

Heterosexual female victims of IPV tend to come from troubled backgrounds where they experienced multiple stressors like poverty, violence, low education, and victimization in childhood. Women who exhibited conduct disorder symptoms in childhood, such as stealing, lying, and fighting, tended to form friendships with deviant peers who are often truant from school and use drugs and alcohol. As they spend more time away from home, these young women often end up in dangerous relationships and contexts where women's rights are often violated (Heise, 1998).

Although young, poor mothers with little education are most at risk for IPV, violence occurs in homes of all kinds. Wealthy and middle-class women experience IPV as well. They are just more likely to have the resources to cope with it in terms of large social support networks to help them leave their batterer, private therapists and physicians to help deal with the resulting symptoms and injuries, and higher levels of education to help them understand the dynamics and leave sooner. Nevertheless, there are thousands of examples of highly educated, well-functioning women from good families

BUILDING YOUR STRENGTHS

Positive coping skills assessment

Each item below represents a way people might react to situations in life. Using the scale below, enter a number from 1 to 4 next to each statement to indicate how true each statement is.

Scale: (1) Not at all true (2) Barely true (3) Somewhat true (4) Completely true

1   I am a "take charge" person.   _____

2   I try to let things work out on their own.*   _____

3   After attaining a goal, I look for another, more challenging one.   _____

4   I like challenges and beating the odds.   _____

5   I visualize my dreams and try to achieve them.   _____

6   Despite numerous setbacks, I usually succeed in getting what I want.   _____

7   I try to pinpoint what I need to succeed.   _____

8   I always try to find a way to work around obstacles; nothing really stops me.   _____

9   I often see myself failing so I don't get my hopes up too high.*   _____

10   When I apply for a position, I imagine myself filling it.   _____

11   I turn obstacles into positive experiences.   _____

12   If someone tells me I can't do something, you can be sure I'll do it.   _____

13   When I experience a problem, I take the initiative in resolving it.   _____

14   When I have a problem, I usually see myself in a no-win situation.*   _____

Scoring: Before you add up your points, the three items marked with an asterisk (*) must be reverse-scored. This means you cross out a "1" and make it a "4," cross out a "2" and make it a "3," cross out a "4" and make it a "1," and cross out a "3" and make it a "2." Do your reverse-scoring only for the items with an asterisk. After reverse scoring these three items, add up your final numbers to calculate your total score.

Scores between 42 and 56 suggest that you are a person who can overcome stress, make sense of bad events, learn a lesson, and move on with a positive attitude.

Scores between 28 and 42 indicate that you sometimes cope positively but could use some help (such as cognitive-behavioral therapy) in maintaining more motivation and the confidence to take control of your life.

Scores below 28 may indicate a sense of *learned helplessness*, meaning you feel things just happen to you and there's not much you can do to cope. Counseling or therapy may be quite helpful in empowering you to cope more positively with the stressors in your life.

Source: Greenglass, Schwarzer, & Taubert (1999)

Note: *Building Your Strengths* assessments are not meant to diagnose, treat, or cure any psychological or family problem; they are for informational purposes, and to spur discussion.

who experience horrendous violence from their intimate partners, many of whom are killed. Most of you have heard stories in the media about wealthy men who engage in murder-suicides, killing their wives who tried to leave them, and then killing themselves. Many wealthy actors, athletes, and musicians have been convicted of battering their wives and partners. Thus, no one is immune from the risk of violence in the home. Statistics can only point out who is *most* at risk, even though every person could be a potential victim.

There are also a number of protective factors that reduce the risk of victimization through IPV. Any variable that is the opposite of a risk factor can be a protective factor. For example, since low education is a risk factor, education about relationships, communication, and warning signs of violence can protect partners from becoming victims. Protective factors can come from individuals, microsystems, exosystems, and so on. In terms of the macrosystem, countries with the lowest rates of violence tend to be those where citizens' welfare is considered the responsibility of all people. They tend to have high standards of living, with good wages, health care, child care, and low levels of poverty. Societies where people view the family not as private, but as amenable to public help and intervention, tend to have lower rates of violence (Heise, 1998). Countries with high standards of living and low crime of all kinds also have social policies against the death penalty and against government involvement in military offensives; and they maintain strict gun control policies. This ethic of non-violence in the macrosystem filters down to individuals and families in the microsystem and reduces the incidence of IPV. Also protecting people from IPV are excellent tools for coping that millions of people use to overcome risk factors that they may face, such as intelligence, social support, and professional intervention (Masten & Coatsworth, 1998).

Victims or survivors?

Reports of crime statistics focus on victims. However, many family violence scholars recognize the active strategizing that women use both to cope with abuse and leave their abusers. Because scholars and professionals in the mental health fields choose to focus on women's strengths and build on those for a positive future, they tend to refer to women as **survivors** and not victims (Cook et al., 2004). *Survivors* are people who use their protective factors and coping skills to get themselves out of a dangerous situation. This term implies active attempts to help one's self and reach out for support. Those who make it out of a battering situation are really incredible, and their hard work, use of social support, and personal resilience should be recognized. While the general public often questions why battered women stay with their partners, the truth is that many women make active, concerted efforts to leave, and often do so successfully. For a woman to leave an IPV relationship is a long process. It's not something that can be done hastily because of the danger to themselves, their children, and their pets, as well as the complex negotiations that must occur first.

> **Survivors**
> The preferred term for "victims" of IPV; refers to people who use their protective factors and coping skills to get themselves out of a dangerous situation. This term implies active attempts to help one's self and reach out for support.

Even if they get out, survivors of IPV can have many psychological and physical symptoms both during the abuse and after they leave. Not surprisingly, survivors can suffer PTSD symptoms such as flashbacks, reliving the trauma, irritability, inability to concentrate, and panic attacks. IPV is related to chronic health problems and illnesses, from stomach pains to back problems, pelvic pain, chronic headaches, nightmares, depression, anxiety, poor self-image, poor coping skills, drug and alcohol dependence, and violent tendencies (Krishnan, Baig-Amin, Gilbert, El-Bassel, & Waters, 1998). Survivors of IPV are about five times more likely than non-survivors to suffer from severe depression and to make suicide attempts (Stets & Straus, 1990). Thus, it is important to remember the extreme mental, and often physical, health challenges many survivors face. They need intensive support, both logistically in setting up a new life, and emotionally, in learning to cope with their symptoms of depression or anxiety. All of these factors must come into play in order to turn a victim into a survivor. And while scholars are beginning to really understand the plight of heterosexual battered women, researchers are only beginning to understand the complex dynamics of lesbian battering relationships.

Lesbian IPV victims and survivors

As mentioned earlier, survivors of abuse can be male, female, gay, or straight. Lesbian couples experience rates of violence similar to those of heterosexual couples. Lesbians are most likely to experience violence when one partner is overly dependent on the other (Renzetti, 1992). In Renzetti's study of lesbians experiencing IPV, batterers tended to be very emotionally dependent on their victims, and violence occurred when their partners tried to break up with them or distance themselves. The batterers tended to be extremely controlling and tried to isolate the victim from her friends and family. Violence tended to co-occur with intoxication, and this led many of the victims and perpetrators to write off the battering as due to the alcohol. Many of the batterers had been abused as children, and they and their partners used this as a reason to excuse the battering. Interestingly, the survivors tended to make more money in this sample. Renzetti (1992) suggests that having less financial power, a history of childhood abuse, plus high levels of emotional dependence and jealousy, make for a toxic combination for lesbian relationships.

Lesbian victims and survivors of IPV relationships face a number of problems that heterosexual women do not face. The women in Renzetti's study who sought help felt that shelters would not welcome them and that police would not consider lesbian-battering to be a serious crime. Lesbians may even face scorn from their own community because lesbian communities usually have a strong feminist and equality-based ethic. Their egalitarian image may be shattered if lesbian-battering were fully acknowledged. Because most women in lesbian communities know where the battered women's shelters are located, lesbian victims may have a harder time escaping dangerous partners. To deal with this issue, Renzetti (1992) suggests that an underground network of lesbian safe houses for battered partners may be necessary. Lesbian victims, who have often been rejected by their biological families, may become completely socially isolated without the support of their community and thus may have little incentive to leave their batterers, who might be their only source of social support.

Service providers and law enforcement must overcome entrenched homophobia and gender-bias in order to serve all victims of violence equally. Police officers must realize that same-sex battering and the battering of men are serious crimes and real violence. Shelters must explicitly state that they accept victims of all genders, sexual orientations, and ethnicities.

Ethnicity and IPV

Statistics show that white women are more likely to be victims of IPV from spouses than are other races, while African Americans are more likely to be victimized by boyfriends. African Americans make up about 15% of the population but 46% of homicide victims. Arrests for crimes against family members are 67% white, 30% African American, 1.3% Native American, and 1.2% Asian American. White women are victims of sexual assault at a rate of 21 out of every 1,000 women. Twenty-six out of every 1,000 African American women, 19 out of every 1,000 Latinas, and 51 out of every 1,000 mixed race women are sexually assaulted (Walker et al., 2007). White women are more likely to be victimized than black women in rural areas, but in urban areas, black women are more likely to be victims than white women. What factors from the bioecological model do you think can explain some of these differences?

A study of South Asian women from Bangladesh, India, Pakistan, Nepal, and Sri Lanka living in the United States found that between 20% and 25% of these women had experienced IPV. Women from South Asian cultures tend to believe that IPV is their "fate." Thus they feel they must tolerate it and do not attribute any blame to their batterers (Krishnan et al., 1998). They say that their religious faith protects them from harm. These women are raised to be faithful and obedient wives, righteous women, and must be selfless and subservient. Because they spend most of their time in their homes, they have little knowledge of IPV laws in their host countries and are not aware of services available for battered women. Being married makes them respectable women and their social status depends entirely on their husbands, on whom they are financially dependent. Thus, they are very unlikely to seek help or leave. Helping these women leave their batterers would involve providing culturally and linguistically appropriate services that incorporate their religious and social beliefs in a respectful manner. They need comprehensive services related to transportation, child care, legal help, immigration services, job training, and so on (Krishnan et al., 1998).

Due to under-reporting and differences in research methodology, it is very difficult to gather accurate information on violence rates and victim characteristics. For example, Rennison and Welchans (2000) found that black women in the U.S. are battered at higher rates than other women; this holds true for black men as well. However, other statistics show that Native Americans and Alaskan Natives have higher rates of violence than blacks or whites (Tjaden & Thoennes, 2000). Some other studies suggest that if we control for socioeconomic status, there are no major differences in violence against women for various ethnic groups (Walker et al., 2007).

Asian Americans usually exhibit the lowest rates of IPV of all groups in the United States. However, Kim, Park, and Emery (2009) found that 30% of a sample of South Korean women in their native country reported being abused by their husbands. They also reported high rates of verbal abuse from their own parents, which impaired their psychological well-being. Keep in mind that statistics only reflect *reported* crimes. Most IPV goes unreported, so the rates in South Korea and other countries may be even higher.

Though most IPV goes unreported in all groups of women, African American women are the most likely to report IPV (Coles, 2006). Black women enter into marriage with high expectations for gender equality, which may explain their higher reporting rates when they are battered. Most black women work outside the home and most black men do more housework than white men do. However, black men still tend to hold traditional beliefs regarding gender relations. With many black men experiencing relatively low educational levels and high rates of incarceration and death, black women feel they have less to gain from marriage than white and Latina women feel they do (Coles, 2006), which explains them being battered by boyfriends more than husbands.

Latinas are expected to obey their husbands, to be pure of heart, and to have many children. But the reality is that many Latinas must work outside the home and tend to expect more independence and power in the family than their partners want for them, which can lead to conflict and violence meant to control them. Likewise, many Asian American women are expected to obey both their husbands and their fathers (as well as older sons), but modern demands of work and independence often clash with these traditional ideas (Coles, 2006).

Due to common experiences of racism and discrimination in the workplace and society at large, women of color are often unlikely to trust law enforcement or social service professionals, so in general do not report IPV. Cultural beliefs about family privacy, obedience to male will, and allowing family elders to solve problems, rather than law enforcement, may lead to higher rates of both IPV and lack of reporting. Women of color may want to prevent their partners from facing further oppression from social systems. They may also have less access to social services and shelters in their communities. Moreover, undocumented immigrant women may fear they or their partners will be deported. They may not understand the legal system of their host country and may experience language barriers (Coles, 2006). Language minority women often report that police use their English-speaking intimate partners who allegedly battered them as translators during IPV investigations (Yllo, 2005). These trends illustrate the importance of including intersectional identities such as race/ethnicity, class issues, and the pervasive patriarchal and gender-biased norms in cultures as variables when researching IPV (Yllo, 2005). We must always remember the intersectionality of race, class, gender, age, disability status, and sexual orientation when attempting to understand complex issues like family violence (Crenshaw, 1994).

Feminism and IPV

Yllo (2005) emphasizes that IPV is so pervasive because gender and power pervade every relationship in some way. Institutionalized gender-bias and sexist norms and institutions allow violence against women to continue unmitigated. Feminist scholars such as Yllo (2005) maintain that violence against women, including female genital mutilation, sexual harassment in the workplace, rape, date rape, sexual assault, and IPV, serve a purpose: to maintain male supremacy, power, and control over women. Even *men* who are physically or sexually assaulted are usually victimized by other men (Tjaden & Thoennes, 1998, 2000). For example, gay men are more likely to be assaulted by their male partners than are straight men who live with women. About 23% of men who live with men, but only 7% of men who live with women, report being raped, stalked, or assaulted by their partners (Tjaden & Thoennes, 1998, 2000). Hurtado (1996) posits that these trends are maintained over time because women, especially white women, live in male-dominated power structures that need them to give birth to the next generation of patriarchs (recall Structural-Functionalist Theory).

Women of color are not part of this system of institutionalized power, so we must recognize that even when white women are victimized by partners, they still hold a position of privilege in society that gives them more rights and respect, and willingness to intervene, than many women of color ever experience. Browne and Bassuk (1997) found that 83% of very poor women of color experienced physical and sexual violence. This is quite a high percentage compared to the estimated 30% for white women.

In an eye-opening study examining the issue of race disparity in responses to violence, Abel (1999) examined women in batterers' groups and in victims' groups. She found that 42% of the female *batterers'* groups were made up of women of color, but only 25% of the *victims'* groups were comprised of women of color. What was most interesting was that when Abel looked into the case histories of these women, the batterers and the victims had exhibited similar symptoms, had similar experiences, and had shown similar levels of violent resistance against their battering partners. However, women of color were referred to *batterers'* groups for defending themselves while white women were referred to *victims'* groups. So even though white women experience high rates of violence and sexual assault, they also experience a level of protection and privilege by virtue of being white, middle class, or both. Thus, contemporary feminists argue that we must consider the plight of all women, and look beyond the statistics and research findings that relate mostly to white women's experiences.

Issues of patriarchy, gender-bias, sexism, and oppression of women are key indicators of a society where IPV is likely to run high. However, we must remember that *all* of us live in the same society, yet very few men are actually violent toward their partners. If we go with the rate of about 25–35% of women being battered, with a few more percentage points given for those who fail to report their experiences, we still end up with the majority of men *not* battering their partners. While it is true that women are *more* likely to be battered in communities where men dominate women, make all the decisions, bring in all the money, and there are strict admonishments against divorce (Levinson, 1989), *all* men live in patriarchal societies where they have more power than women. Yet most men choose not to abuse that power and oppress, violate, or otherwise harm their partners. This is even true in developing nations and places where women have very few rights. Not all of the husbands in traditional societies mistreat their wives.

If IPV were caused solely by patriarchy, as many feminists argue, then we would probably see much higher rates. In fact, quite a few men are involved in the struggle *against* IPV and other forms of violence. For example, the California Department of Health and Human Services and the California Coalition Against Sexual Assault have joined forces to include men in the prevention and cessation of sexual assault and violence. This program, called "My Strength," works with young men to teach them that they can use their strength not to perpetrate violence, but to stop it. Recruiting young men as advocates for non-violence is an effective strategy for changing gender norms and interpersonal dynamics (see www.mystrength.org for more information on how you can become involved).

No one variable, including patriarchy, can explain something as complex as family violence. As the bioecological approach suggests, there must be a combination of factors, from individual biology and temperament to personality characteristics, family factors, community factors, and lastly, societal factors like sexism and oppression of women. Indeed, a bioecological approach is the most effective method for helping us understand what leads some people to become victims of violence (Heise, 1998).

Pets and children, harm to the victims' family, financial and emotional dependence, and love for the batterer all play into a woman's decision to stay in an IPV relationship. Cook (1997) reports that battered men stay with their partners for the same sorts of reasons. The most important question we must try to answer, however, is not "why do victims stay?" but "why do people batter?"

BATTERERS

Batterers, like all groups of people, are quite diverse. There isn't a specific unique species of people called "the batterers." They are similar to other people in many ways. They struggle with the same issues we find in all families: balancing work and family responsibilities, living up to cultural expectations for proper gender role behavior, raising children, and coping with issues they experienced in their own childhoods. This section will explore some of the things we know, but this research is in its infancy, and there's probably more that we don't know than we do know about batterers.

Types of batterers

Batterers tend to distance themselves from the partners they batter. They either dissociate from their violent actions or minimize their actions. They discount others' (for example, therapists') negative statements about their actions (Goodrum, Umberson, & Anderson, 2001). In contrast, non-battering male partners tend to listen empathically to their partners' and others' views of them and try to assimilate those views into their ideas about themselves. Goodrum et al. (2001) posit that batterers choose to batter their partners after they consider the costs and benefits along with ideas regarding their own personal characteristics (recall Social Exchange Theory). They batter after a lifetime of experience has accumulated into their current sense of self in relation to others. Because they often endorse traditional gender roles, view women as property to be controlled, and wield the power in relationships, batterers really have very little reason to empathize with their partners' pain and suffering.

These are general characteristics of batterers, but there are also three specific categories that most batterers fall into: dysphoric/borderline batterers, antisocial/violent batterers, and family only batterers.

Dysphoric/borderline batterers

**Dysphoric/
borderline batterers**
A type of batterer who feels he is not responsible for his actions, blames his partner, and often suffers from mental illnesses like depression and personality disorders.

When confronted with negative judgments or consequences for their actions, **dysphoric/borderline batterers** tend to distance themselves from responsibility, stating that their partner brings out the worst in them, or that they don't act like themselves around her. They feel that the violent acts are "not me" and feel detached from their partners. They have low levels of empathy for their partners and experience high levels of psychological distress, often in the form of mental illness or personality disorders. This profile is fairly typical of batterers but we don't yet know which systems of the bioecological model influence a person to become this type of batterer over another type (Jacobson & Gottman, 1998).

Antisocial/violent batterers

**Antisocial/violent
(cobra) batterers**
A type of batterer who is cold, callous, and calculating; they see their victims as objects and feel no love for them or remorse for their battering.

A second type of batterer, who often say their violent actions were their partner's fault, are the **antisocial/violent** type. They exhibit the lowest levels of empathy for their partners and exhibit strong psychopathic propensities. They tend to be cold, callous, and calculating in their violence. Other research on this type of batterer has found them to be like **cobras**. Cobra batterers are cold and uncaring and strike out violently without remorse. They are very self-centered and narcissistic. They have a sense of entitlement in relationships, and feel their partner should be available to fulfill their whims on command. There are low levels of true intimacy in these relationships and they feel absolutely no sadness when their partner suffers or when she leaves. They are not threatened or jealous and often inflict intense emotional turmoil on their partners (Jacobson & Gottman, 1998).

The antisocial/violent or cobra batterer is often a substance abuser who was maltreated in childhood. He tends to be highly intelligent and charismatic so women are drawn to yet fear him. These antisocial men, previously referred to as sociopaths, can easily con therapists, law enforcement officials, and judges. They often easily complete mandated therapy and continue immediately in cobra-like relationships, being calm, cool, and collected, and then striking rapidly. Punishment often has no effect on these men. While they should be offered therapy, their completion of therapy should be voluntary and not tied to any reductions in sentencing or early release from prison because they can easily con treatment professionals (Jacobson & Gottman, 1998).

Family only batterers

Holtzworth-Monroe and Stuart (1994) discovered that many men are **family only** batterers. They aren't generally violent and their violence toward partners is typically moderate in severity. They tend to feel badly after battering incidents, apologize, and empathize with the pain they caused. This is the most common type of batterer to engage in the cycle of violence pattern. They recognize that their partners often have had abusive or neglectful childhoods, which can impact adult romantic relationships. They feel bad for their partners' low sense of self-worth and want to work out a healthier relationship. Jacobson and Gottman (1998) labeled them the **pit bull**. Pit bulls can be loving and usually feel tender feelings toward their partners. They are less likely to have a criminal past but usually have witnessed IPV in their families of origin. They tend to be extremely emotionally needy. They cling to their partners and depend on them for their psychological well-being. Pit bulls are extremely jealous and often batter out of fear of abandonment or betrayal. It's very difficult for women to leave these men because they hold on to their tender side, and their violence can be severe if they feel threatened. Both the survivor and the batterer are strongly emotionally attached to each other. Because not much research has been done on the neuroendocrinology of batterers or influences from their meso- or exosystems, it's hard to pinpoint variables we might address to prevent someone from becoming a batterer. But one mechanism that has been found to affect the quality of adult relationships is one upon which we have focused throughout this book, attachment security.

> **Family only (pit bull) batterers**
> A type of batterer who reacts to conflict with violence but usually feels guilty and apologizes; can respond well to treatment and often loves their partners greatly.

Attachment issues

In an attempt to examine how batterers vary in their attachment styles, Babcock, Jacobson, Gottman, and Yerington (2000) examined both violent and maritally dissatisfied, stressed, but non-violent husbands. They found that violent husbands were twice as likely to be insecurely attached as non-violent, distressed husbands. In particular, when the researchers watched these couples in laboratory problem-discussion tasks, they found that *dismissing/avoidant* husbands were extremely controlling and distanced themselves from their wives. They would clam up, ignore her, or give her the silent treatment. These men tended to act violently at home when their wives tried to defend their own opinions or state their positions about issues. The authors found, therefore, that dismissing attachment styles are risk factors for men using violence as an instrument to dominate and control their wives. These men exhibited high levels of contempt for their partners but did not display much anger at all. These findings indicate that some dismissing/avoidantly attached men may be similar to the *dysphoric/ borderline* or the *cobra* type of batterer. In support of this, Babcock et al. (2000) found that the dismissing/ avoidant husbands had high scores on both antisocial and borderline personality disorder assessments. Keep in mind that most people with dismissing/avoidant attachments do not batter their partners, so this is a correlational finding of people who are at *increased risk* for being perpetrators of violence.

The other insecure attachment style is *preoccupied/enmeshed*. The preoccupied/enmeshed men evidenced the least amount of distancing during problem-discussions in the lab. They tended to keep a disagreement going on for too long, never letting an issue drop or be resolved. At home, they were most likely to batter when their wives withdrew from a conflict. These findings suggest that for preoccupied/enmeshed batterers, the fear of abandonment leads them to react harshly with violence. They tended to emotionally abuse their partners and could not tolerate anger or any negative emotions from her. They are more akin to the *pit bulls* and the *family only* type of batterer. Thus, preoccupied/enmeshed attachment puts men at risk for becoming batterers, even though most men with this attachment style are non-violent.

Babcock et al.'s (2000) results are very interesting in that they point to the key role attachment history and emotion-regulation skills play in healthy relationships. Securely attached people respond to negative emotion as a wake-up call, indicating that they need to proactively discuss and work through a problem. In contrast, insecurely attached individuals may respond to negative emotions by either *deactivating* their emotional reactions, like the dismissing/cobra batterer, or *hyperactivating* their emotional reactions, like the preoccupied/pit bull batterer, (Babcock et al., 2000).

The insecurely attached husbands in this study reported high levels of witnessing IPV between their own parents, as well as being harmed themselves as children. Because violent husbands are more likely to be insecurely attached than non-violent husbands, this research suggests that incorporating an element into treatment which involves the acceptance of negative emotions as normal, and enhancing skills that lead to the ability to productively regulate those negative emotions may prove promising. Gottman et al. (2002) have cited preliminary data suggesting that when both gay male partners and heterosexual married couples can down-regulate their own emotional responses, calming themselves down and rationally thinking about their actions, their relationships may last longer. Also, the ability to repair a negative emotional interaction during a disagreement bodes well for both the individual's emotion-regulation skills and the health and success of the relationship.

Treatment issues

It is important to note that marriage or couples counseling is *not* recommended for couples experiencing IPV. Couples counseling is based on the idea that each partner can share his or her feelings openly and have those feelings accepted, and the couple can work together to improve the relationship. This approach places equal responsibility on the survivor of IPV to repair a violent relationship. When one person is completely dominated and controlled by another partner, not only can she not be open and honest in counseling with him, but if she is, he may retaliate violently when they return home, as you saw in Paula's story in the *Focus on My Family* box. Any counseling or treatment should involve each partner separately coping with his or her own issues while living apart. For example, he might work on changing his belief that women are property or that she provokes him to batter. She might focus on changing her sense that she can't live without him and she might actively try to use counseling to reduce her depressive symptoms. This method ensures that if he *chooses* to stop his violent behavior, he is given the tools to help him do so, but if he doesn't change, she is empowered to stay away and stand on her own two feet. Couples experiencing more mild situational couples violence may benefit more from couples counseling than those involved in intimate terrorism, for whom couples counseling is almost always contraindicated.

Batterer intervention programs have notoriously low rates of success, most likely because men rarely take full responsibility for their actions and continue to desire power and control over their partners. Also, in terms of LGBT relationships, since batterer intervention programs are usually designed for heterosexual men, and those men tend to hold gender-biased and homophobic beliefs, where does a lesbian or gay male batterer go for treatment? Most batterers who are caught are sentenced to short jail sentences, have restraining orders filed against them, and are required to attend counseling. Unfortunately, most of the counseling programs they attend are not developed from a scientific evidence base, so it's difficult for the programs to help batterers, even if they want to change. The most widely implemented model will be discussed next.

Duluth Model

Duluth Model
The most commonly used model of batterer treatments; the focus is on rehabilitation of the batterer and support for the survivor, without a focus on maintaining their relationship; includes all community agencies working together to prevent further violence.

In the most widely used treatment model, the **Duluth Model**, the focus is on rehabilitation of the batterer and support for the survivor, *without* a focus on maintaining their relationship; this model includes all community agencies working together to prevent further violence in the couple. About

35% of men stop battering without treatment but only about 40% do with Duluth Model treatment (www.theduluthmodel.org). While this 5% increase in those who refrain from battering after treatment seems small, it could amount to tens of thousands of women being spared future battering. Nevertheless, these statistics also show that the majority of men continue their violent ways after incarceration, treatment, or both.

The Duluth Model's developers state that this model is based on a belief that a survivor's safety should be our topmost concern. We should hold perpetrators responsible for their actions, and they should receive the appropriate punishments for their crimes, as well as ample opportunities to rehabilitate themselves. Duluth emphasizes that the goal is to stop the violence, not maintain the relationship between the couple. Professionals must tailor interventions to the needs of the specific relationship. While most battering relationships are characterized by long-standing attempts to dominate a partner and include various control tactics, each couple is also unique in terms of life circumstances, ethnic background, cultural beliefs, economic privilege, and immigration status. Thus, treatment should focus on culturally responsive and supportive techniques. To this end, Duluth includes a special program called "Mending the Sacred Hoop," which works within Native American cultural and religious frameworks to reduce violence in Indian communities.

To fully implement the Duluth Model, communities must provide a united front against IPV. Law enforcement, the courts, social services, shelter and mental health professionals must come together to form a concerted community effort to conceptualize, intervene, and treat IPV from a similar ideological framework. All institutions must work together to minimize retraumatization of survivors and their children. Duluth emphasizes mandatory arrests for batterers, plus emergency housing, transportation, and economic support for survivors. They advocate for increasingly harsh penalties for repeat offenders and do not advocate for couples' counseling or anger management classes in most cases. Offenders must be confronted with their sexist ideas and must choose to overcome their long histories of power and control (www.theduluthmodel.org).

An innovative treatment model for Latino immigrants

Not all IPV professionals agree with the Duluth Model. For example, Lohr, Hamberger, and Parker (2006) found that several different treatment models worked just as well, or had just as low success rates, as the Duluth Model. Some also feel that it is not always appropriate for men to be forced to view women as their equals, and that as long as they are respectful and non-violent toward their partners, inequalities may be culturally acceptable. For example, the Duluth model was attempted with a group of Latino immigrant men and was found to be ineffective. The practitioners realized that gender-equality was not a realistic goal for these men who came from very traditional, patriarchal, Catholic communities. Their female partners also held similar cultural and religious beliefs. However, their beliefs did not include violence towards women. These women were often denigrated, being called less than human, they were forced into sexual intercourse, were accused of being terrible mothers, and were threatened with being reported to immigration officials. The poverty, substance abuse, and loss of cultural supports they had in their home countries were often cited as stressors for these families. Therefore, Hancock and Siu (2009) implemented a treatment program for Latino immigrants wherein they had the men work through the stress they faced as immigrants. They discussed the racism, oppression, discrimination, and economic hardships they faced. They talked about how they came to the U.S. and how their life stresses affected their relationships with their partners. There was a concerted effort to make the men realize that their own trauma had influenced the trauma they inflicted on their partners. The men talked about working for long hours of manual labor for little pay. They often worked in hot, dirty conditions or were unemployed.

The therapists did not try to convince these men that patriarchy was wrong. Because of their strong cultural beliefs in masculinity and as men being the leaders of the family, the therapy instead focused on positive aspects of *machismo*, such as being a strong, powerful man who does all he can to protect his family. The focus was on relating respectfully to women, valuing their roles as wives and mothers, and cherishing their contributions to family life. By healing their own traumas, these men were able to emerge with a stronger sense of self, pride in their identity as leader of the family, and a lower likelihood of abusing women to gain power and control. By being able to recognize the source of their negative emotions and work on successfully regulating those emotions, they increased their empathy for their partners and could interact in non-violent ways with their children. This study is another example of how attachment experiences and emotion regulation can perhaps be key aspects of batterer intervention in the future.

Children exposed to intimate partner violence

Much of the research on children's exposure to IPV has been discussed in earlier chapters, but a few key issues are important to touch on in the context of IPV. Children may be present for up to 70–85% of violent incidences between adult partners (Jaffe, Wolfe, & Wilson, 1990). Because somewhere between 40% and 70% of families experiencing IPV also experience child abuse, neglect, or both, it is important to understand that children may experience multiple traumas (Cherlin, Burton, Hurt, & Purvin, 2004; Higgins & McCabe, 2003). They may be exposed to animal abuse, watch their parents become involved in IPV, and experience maltreatment themselves. Some children might also witness elder abuse and violence in their communities. About ten million children witness IPV in the United States every year (Cherlin et al., 2004). Thus, there are children we all know in our local schools and neighborhoods who are suffering from the effects of multiple forms of violence.

Children witnessing IPV are at risk for negative outcomes, including substance abuse problems, aggression, depression, eating disorders, intense fear, and suicide (Adams, 2006; Mignon, Larson, & Holmes, 2002). When men abuse their female partners, it increases the chances that the women will harm their children (Slep & O'Leary, 2005). These stressed mothers may be unable to cope with the challenges of parenting or may displace their anger at their partners onto targets who won't fight back. Hilton's (1992) work suggests that IPV often occurs when male partners are upset that mothers cannot keep the children quiet or make them obey. So women may lash out in an attempt to prove they are good mothers who can control their children, thereby reducing their own chances of being victimized. Slep and O'Leary (2005) found that 59% of children in their sample were harmed by *both* parents. They found a rate of 45% for the occurrence of both partner and parent violence. When categorizing the various patterns of physical aggression in their study, the most common pattern they found was the existence of *both* partner and parent aggression.

In addition to behavioral and emotional outcomes, children exposed to IPV can have many negative physiological symptoms as well. For example, Saltzman, Holden, and Holahan (2002) found that 6-year-olds exposed to IPV had elevated heart rates compared to a matched control group. An elevated heart rate can lead to children becoming hypervigilant, and they can develop a **hostile attribution bias**. This means they scan the environment for warning signs and trouble and are on hyperalert for attacks from others. They may view benign social situations, such as a classmate spilling milk on them, as hostile in nature, and they may retaliate with aggression (Crick & Dodge, 1994). Children with elevated heart rates may also be at risk for anxiety disorders, as research shows they tend to secrete abnormally high levels of cortisol (Saltzman et al., 2002).

It is necessary to intervene early and provide services for children because after the stress system is exhausted, children may become abnormally unresponsive to their environments. Consistent with this idea, people with extremely violent tendencies and callous or unemotional dispositions show *low* heart rates and *low* nervous system arousal. They also experience no guilt for violent behavior, no empathy for others, and are quite unresponsive to treatment or intervention. Punishment has no effect on them (Frick, Cornell, Barry, Bodin, & Dane, 2003). These findings point to the importance of emotion regulation skills in the development of both mental and physical health for children and adults experiencing violence. Let's look more closely at the children who are themselves direct victims of child abuse and neglect.

Hostile attribution bias
A cognitive style of interpreting ambiguous social stimuli as negative or hostile in nature; often leads to aggressive or violent reactions.

CHILD MALTREATMENT

In 2007 there were 3.2 million reports of child maltreatment involving 5.8 million children in the U.S. (www.acf.hhs.gov). However, only about 25% of these could be substantiated through investigation and documentation of evidence. This amounted to 794,000 children being confirmed victims of child abuse or neglect. The U.S. Department of Health and Human Services Administration for Children and Families publishes an annual summary of child maltreatment, which can be found on their website. The following information is from the 2007 *Child Maltreatment Report*. The Federal Child Abuse Prevention and Treatment Act (CAPTA) and the Keeping Children and Families Safe Act (2003) define child abuse and neglect as:

> Any recent act or failure to act on the part of a parent or caretaker which results in death, serious physical or emotional harm, sexual abuse or exploitation; or an act or failure to act which presents an imminent risk of serious harm.

Interestingly, out of the three million reports of child maltreatment, virtually no reports were ruled intentionally false, meaning that we should always err on the side of believing the victim of or witness to abuse. Most of the reports are made by professionals like teachers or police officers and the majority of cases are of neglect (60%). The highest rate of victimization is for infants under a year of age (21.9 out of every 1,000 children). Boys and girls are equally represented in these cases and about 50% of the victims were white, with 21.7% African American and 20.8% Hispanic. About 10% experienced physical abuse and 8% sexual abuse, with 4% documented to experience psychological maltreatment.

In 2007, 1,760 children were confirmed to have died from abuse or neglect (2.35 deaths per 100,000 children). Most of the deaths were due to neglect, and the children who died were usually under the age of four. Perpetrators were largely the children's parents or parent figures (80%), usually the mother (56.5%). This can be attributed to the large numbers of poor, single mothers who neglect their children. Most of these cases involve young mothers under the age of 20, pointing to the great need for social support and services provided to young, distressed women who are pregnant. If they get resources like child development education, resource referrals for health care, food, and child care, plus job training and substance abuse treatment, they may be less likely to neglect their children.

Cultural issues in maltreatment

It's important to recognize that while child abuse and neglect occur in every society around the world (Krugman, 1996), some cultural practices which are not abuse may be deemed abuse. For example, immigrants may use traditional healing practices that are unfamiliar to western social service agencies. Mexican immigrants may heat glass cups and place them on a sick child's back to draw an illness out. These children may then go to school with several circular burns on their backs, which do not hurt them, yet may appear frightening to school personnel. Similarly, Vietnamese people may engage in coining, where they rub hot coins along their children's backs for the same reason. The coins may leave reddish track marks on the skin, but the children are not harmed and understand this is a traditional healing practice. Also, children of Native American or Asian descent may have dark purplish birth marks across their buttocks which may look like bruising to babysitters or day care providers changing their diapers. It's important that we consider the macrosystem and cultural context of any actions parents use with their children and not jump to conclusions.

While taking culture, religion, and family beliefs into account is vitally important, we must always protect children whose rights are being violated, especially when practices would be considered abusive by state and federal definitions. It is not acceptable to use culture as an excuse to sexually or physically abuse children or neglect their basic needs. It's important that we all understand the legal definitions of abuse so we know what would and would not be reportable crimes.

Types of child maltreatment

Children can be maltreated in many ways. They can be physically harmed by caregivers hitting, kicking, punching, burning, or choking them. Emergency rooms regularly treat child victims of physical abuse who have characteristic marks left by belts, electrical cords, and cigarettes. Children can also be neglected, sexually abused, or emotionally abused. Each of these types of maltreatment will be discussed below.

Physical abuse

Children are most likely to be physically abused before the age of 5. Most maltreatment fatalities are infants and toddlers. These very young children are not verbal and are very active and curious. Parents can easily become exasperated and physical punishment can escalate into abuse (Straus & Stewart, 1999). Young children cannot fight back and are easily injured.

The majority of child physical abuse occurs during difficult interactions revolving around feeding and toileting. Parents with unrealistic expectations for when children should be potty-trained can become very frustrated over accidents and messes (Krugman, 1996). It's not uncommon for children to be punished by being placed in scalding water, leading to characteristic burn patterns often seen in emergency rooms. "Sock and mitten burns" typically occur when children are punished for touching things or going where they are not supposed to go. Their hands or feet are placed in hot water, and they are admitted to the hospital with second- or third-degree burns in the shapes of socks or mittens. Genital and buttock burns also occur when they are placed in hot bath water after toileting accidents.

Many parents do not realize that all young children are curious, and that it's perfectly normal for them to get into all the cabinets and closets. Putting away breakables, child-proofing the home, and allowing very young children free rein of much of the house can prevent frustration on the part of both the child and the parent. Education regarding the normal ages and stages of development can help parents recognize that, for example, most children are not potty-trained until well over 3 years of age, and accidents even in kindergarten are quite common.

Children also receive injuries when spoons are jammed into their mouths when they refuse to eat. Parents must be taught that children do not need to eat very much. They should never be forced to eat. Parents only need to provide them with healthy snacks and meals throughout the day so they can "graze" when hungry. Most children will eat what they need to be healthy and will not starve themselves, so parents should not use meal time as a time for power and control. This can only lead to eating problems, anxiety in the children and frustration on the part of the parent. Dental professionals are trained to recognize mouth, teeth, and throat injuries that may be signs of abuse or neglect revolving around eating issues. Very young pre-verbal children can be frustrating to raise for any parent, and oftentimes multiply stressed parents act out their frustration by shaking infants and young children to the point of injury.

Abusive head trauma

You have probably heard of "shaken baby syndrome." This syndrome (formally called abusive head trauma) includes concussions, brain bruises, and diffuse neurological injuries leading to breaking and stretching of the axons at the ends of brain cells (Ashton, 2010). These types of abusive head traumas occur when a young child is shaken, slapped, punched, thrown, or dropped violently. Medical research shows that infants under 2 years of age are the most likely age group to experience all forms of traumatic brain injury (Rivara, 1994). When the entire population of traumatic brain injuries in infants is examined, between 20% and 50% of them are confirmed to have resulted from shaking or abuse (Eisele, Kegler, Trent, & Coronado, 2006). Part of the reason infants experience more head trauma is because their skulls have an open fleshy part at the top, called a fontanelle, which means their skulls cannot reduce the impact of blunt force on the brain. Older childrens' and adults' skull fissures have closed so the same force used against them would result in less severe injuries (Ashton, 2010). Abusive head trauma results in death for between 6% and 50% of children, depending on the age of the child and type of injury (Richardson, 2000).

The effects of abusive head trauma include convulsions, induced epilepsy, sensory deficits, language delays, cognitive processing and memory problems, and social/behavioral problems (Ashton, 2010). Many of these effects can be mitigated by the proper occupational, educational, and psychological therapies. While physical abuse is usually what comes to mind when we hear the term "child abuse," the most common form of maltreatment is actually child neglect.

Neglect

Child neglect can take many forms. **Physical neglect** can occur when parents do not have enough food, shelter, or clothing for their children. Neglected children are often malnourished, dirty, hungry, and tired. They are most often referred to child protective services agencies by concerned teachers and neighbors.

Parents neglect children for many reasons. When parents suffer from mental illnesses like depression or schizophrenia, they may be incapacitated and cannot care for their children, leaving them unsupervised or abandoning them. Parents who abuse substances often live in filthy apartments with animal feces and garbage throughout the residence. Children in these situations can also be exposed to drug paraphernalia like hypodermic needles used to inject drugs and toxic chemicals like those used to make methamphetamine. Exposing a fetus to alcohol or drugs in utero can also be considered a form of neglect. Some states mandate that substance-exposed newborn infants be immediately placed in foster care after birth. Other states prefer to place the mother in drug treatment and work on building her parenting skills with her newborn.

Mothers with low levels of education and abuse histories in their own pasts often do not know how to bond with their babies and need to be taught how to love and stimulate their children to prevent **emotional neglect**, which can lead to attachment and emotion regulation problems later on. Emotional neglect can also influence atypical brain development and cognitive and language delays. Children can also experience **medical or educational neglect** when their parents fail to provide them with proper medical attention or do not ensure they attend school.

Child neglect is one of the most insidious forms of child maltreatment because it greatly impacts children's normal brain development (DeBellis, 2005). Chronic neglect can permanently alter a child's ability to perform normal social, emotional, cognitive, and behavioral tasks required for competent development. Animal studies have shown that neglect impairs the ability to learn, hampers memory development, stunts the ability to plan and problem solve, inhibits sensory-motor skills, dysregulates the stress-response system, and leads to the inability to form social bonds or rear healthy offspring (DeBellis, 2005).

Human studies show that even when children's physical needs are met, if they are raised in institutions with little human contact or emotional attachments, they still suffer in all areas of development and often die unexpectedly. DeBellis and Putnam (1994) found that chronically neglected human infants have high rates of illness, infection, and early death. Infants can even die from the stress of hours and hours of prolonged, unanswered crying. Moreover, neglected infants and toddlers develop high levels of anxiety and will engage in self-stimulatory behaviors like head-banging and rocking motions. Neglected children exhibit extreme dysregulation of the stress-response systems and many brain functions, including the metabolism and transfer of neurotransmitters like dopamine and serotonin (DeBellis, 2005; Perry, 2004). Girls may be particularly vulnerable to HPA axis chemical dysregulation (DeBellis et al., 1994).

When children experience chronic stress, lack of stimulation from their caregiving environments, or both, they can exhibit neurobehavioral problems such as attentional deficits, hypervigilance, inability to remember information, psychosis, dissociation, and paranoia (DeBellis, 2005). Abused and neglected children have also been found to have smaller brains in general, larger ventricular spaces within their brains, and smaller corpus callosum bands of connective fibers between the two hemispheres of the brain (Teicher, 2002). Boys may be more vulnerable to brain structural changes than girls and exhibit more externalizing symptoms, such as aggression, hostility, and hyperactivity.

Physical neglect
Not meeting a child or dependent adult's need for food, shelter, clothing, or hygiene.

Emotional neglect
Not meeting a child or dependent adult's need for love, affection, and validation of who they are.

Medical/educational neglect
Not providing adequate preventive medical or dental care; denying access to education.

Given what you have learned about brain development in earlier chapters, you may not be surprised to find out that maltreatment occurring in the earliest years is more detrimental to the smoothly orchestrated processes of brain development than is maltreatment occurring in later years when key brain areas are already established to a large degree (Perry, 2004). To learn more about how the effects of neglect have been discovered, see a fascinating study on the orphans of Romania in the *How Would You Measure That?* box.

HOW WOULD YOU MEASURE THAT?

The Romanian orphans study (Nelson, Furtado, Fox, & Zeanah, 2009)

When Romania experienced a political revolution after the execution of the dictator Ceausescu, over 170,000 children were found suffering horribly in state-run institutions. These children had been abused, neglected, or orphaned. Babies languished in cribs all day, with white walls and mattresses all around them. No toys, color, music, or attention was provided to them. Untrained staff who knew nothing about child development cared for hundreds of children who were herded like cattle to meals, showers, toileting, and so on. They got no cognitive or emotional stimulation as their mechanical routines were performed in silence. They had little to eat and many children were physically and sexually abused by staff and older children. When their plight was publicized, thousands of parents rushed to adopt these Romanian orphans. However, they never suspected that love was not enough to rehabilitate them. Severe and chronic neglect, and often abuse, had led to malnutrition, developmental delays, disturbing behavior, and emotional problems. The children could not form attachments to their new parents and had poor emotion regulation skills.

In response, Nelson et al. (2009) recruited children from all Bucharest orphanages and randomly assigned some of them to live with trained foster parents who could stimulate them and cope with their many special needs. They selected healthy children who had no major handicapping conditions. They put half in high-quality foster care and continued to monitor the rest who remained institutionalized. They also used a control group of children in the community who lived with their parents. At four years of age, 65% of the control children were securely attached to their parents, 49% of the therapeutic foster children were, but only 18% of the institutionalized children had formed secure

attachments to their favorite staff. The institutionalized children had IQ scores of 73 (mildly retarded), the therapeutic foster care group scored 81 (approaching low-average), while the community group scored 109 (approaching high-average). Institutionalized children also showed deficits in brain functioning for tasks like reaction time and recognition of human faces. They had a hard time paying attention and displayed more negative emotions. At 4 years of age, 55% of those who had ever lived in institutions had high levels of diagnosable psychopathology like anxiety or depression, but only 22% of the control group did. The foster care intervention did not reduce levels of attention deficit hyperactivity disorder (ADHD) or internalizing or externalizing problems.

This study shows that therapeutic foster or adoptive care with trained parents prepared to deal with special-needs children can improve their cognitive and emotional development. Mental disorders may be more difficult to change and may require intensive therapeutic and social services. The children who were placed into foster care before 2 years of age showed the greatest improvements in language, cognitive, and emotional development, especially the ability to attach to caregivers. Language gains were most noteworthy for children who entered care before the age of 15 months, again indicating the importance of very early intervention whenever possible. Because of this research, Romania outlawed the institutionalization of children under 2 years of age. Today there are only 30,000 Romanian children still living in institutions and their quality of care has improved greatly. These results also show that children around the world need loving, stimulating, safe environments to grow and develop, in order to prevent serious emotional, cognitive, language, and behavioral problems.

Other effects of child abuse and neglect include eating disorders, high levels of aggression toward self and others, post-traumatic stress reactions, dissociation and emotional numbing, and sexual promiscuity (Cicchetti & Lynch, 1993; Trickett, Kurtz, & Noll, 2005). Maladaptive social information processing and cognitive and emotional biases place victims of abuse at high risk for perpetuating the cycle of violence as they grow up (Egeland, Jacobvitz, & Sroufe, 1988; Pettit, Lansford, Malone, Dodge, & Bates, 2010). In fact, many people who sexually abuse children were themselves abused.

Sexual abuse

Sexual abuse can be any sexual act committed on a child, from fondling, to digital penetration, to oral, anal, and vaginal intercourse. Other sexual exploitation of children includes exposing them to pornography, using them in pornographic materials, forcing them to watch or participate in adult sexual behavior, and forcing them into prostitution. Most children are sexually abused by someone they know, either a family member, friend, or community member like a coach or youth worker.

When children are sexually violated by other children, the age of the perpetrator must be taken into consideration. Two 7-year-olds fondling each other is not considered sexual abuse. However, a 13-year-old fondling the genitals of a 7-year-old would be considered sexual abuse. Most laws specify a "five year rule," wherein sexual behavior between anyone five years older than a child is considered exploitative or abusive. Many children who perpetrate sexual crimes against other children were themselves sexually abused, and they are often re-enacting what was done to them. Children may also re-enact their sexual abuse in their play episodes. Many mental health professionals prefer to call these children *abuse-reactive*, instead of referring to them as sexual abuse perpetrators, since they are victims themselves and need treatment, not incarceration.

Sexually abused children with PTSD exhibit elevated cortisol, norepinephrine, and dopamine levels, leading to mental health and cognitive and emotional problems (DeBellis, 2005). For example, depression, anxiety, and low self-esteem are common in sexually abused children. They may experience sexual acting out and excessive masturbation. In addition, they may be diagnosed with sexually transmitted infections like genital warts, herpes, and HIV/AIDS; and girls may become pregnant. Boys may experience gender identity confusion because their sexual abuse perpetrators, like those of girls, are almost always men. They may have fears of being gay or may neglect to tell a trusted adult about the abuse due to their fear of being labeled homosexual. Boys may also feel confused because they may have been sexually aroused during the abuse and may think they are at fault or that they led the person on. They may even internalize a sense of it being consensual sex in order to avoid admitting being victimized, since male gender role expectations include boys being tough, confident, and never being taken advantage of.

Sexual abuse most adversely affects children if the perpetrator was a biological relative and if force was involved. Much sexual abuse is non-coercive and non-violent. Instead it consists of a process of psychological manipulation referred to as **grooming**, tactics sexual abusers use to gain the trust of a victim and proceed slowly to sexual interactions without fear or violence. Perpetrators often seek out children who are lonely or come from broken or troubled families. They befriend the child and often give gifts and compliments to the child, who is usually emotionally needy and responsive to these attentions. They may begin by kissing the child on the cheek during a session of video game playing. They may ask for a back rub in return for a gift of jewelry or money. They tell the child how beautiful, smart, and special he or she is. This friendship then leads to a gradual advancement of the sexual relationship. The child is then trapped, feeling loyalty to this friend, who has often told them that what they share is special and secret. In more violent cases, the perpetrator will threaten the child not to tell anyone or he or she will be killed. Or perhaps pets and family members will be targets of threats if the child tells anyone what happened. Thus, most adult sexual abuse survivors report that they never told anyone.

Educational programs must make it clear to children that they should always tell a trusted adult if they are touched or otherwise violated in a sexual manner. Parents should assure children that they

Grooming
The process sexual abusers use to gain the trust of a victim and proceed slowly to sexual interactions without fear of violence.

would believe them and they would be loved no matter what they share. Sexually abused children often internalize great guilt over what happened to them and feel responsible for the sexual acts they believe they engaged in and feel they should have prevented. It's important that sexually abused children receive treatment to process what happened to them and help them make some sense out of it and realize that it was not their fault. Children who can come to a sense of closure and not let abuse control their lives have a great prognosis for living a normal life after sexual abuse. Beyond the sexual acts, however, the emotional trauma that occurred often takes longer to overcome.

Psychological/emotional abuse

It's fairly uncommon for a child to experience only one type of abuse or neglect. Multiple forms of victimization are common, including witnessing IPV in conjunction with being abused one's self. And each type of maltreatment carries with it psychological consequences. Physical abuse, neglect, and sexual abuse are not just physical acts with physical consequences. Wrapped up in all forms of abuse is psychological harm. Children experience psychological exploitation whenever they are abused or neglected. They cannot care for themselves and are often dependent for their very survival on those who victimize them. **Psychological/emotional abuse** includes verbal attacks, insults, and humiliation. The child is told that he or she is fat, ugly, stupid, and that the perpetrator wishes he or she were never born. Parents or other perpetrators make children feel useless, worthless, and insignificant. Their physical appearance and personal characteristics are disparaged.

> **Psychological/emotional abuse**
> Humiliation, put-downs, criticisms, and threats that attack the core character of the person and make him or her feel worthless.

Compared to physical abuse, neglect, and sexual abuse, the effects of psychological/emotional abuse are less well researched. Because this form of maltreatment is rarely reported, we do not know much about it except for what adults report in retrospective studies. And they report that psychological abuse is more harmful in the long run than physical or sexual abuse. This kind of attack can result in destruction of the child's self-worth and can inculcate a sense of hopelessness, despair, and often suicidal thoughts or attempts. Adults emotionally abused as children carry lingering feelings of self doubt and insecurity which they bring to their own romantic relationships. While this type of harm is a crime, it is difficult to prosecute because the evidence is all internal. There are no bruises, sexual infections, or dirty clothes to see. But the scars can last a lifetime, especially without intervention.

Intervention and prevention

What do we do when we discover that a child is abused or neglected? First, to report child abuse or neglect, please call the Childhelp national hotline at 1–800–4A-CHILD or report the incident to your local child welfare agency.

In the past, when people reported abuse, officials used to try with all their might to keep biological families together. The child welfare system implemented every effort to send the parents into counseling or parenting classes and then reunite them with their children. However, years of research have taught us that family reunification is rarely successful. In fact, it may actually violate the child's need for safety, stimulation, love, and support as many families continue to struggle with drug addiction, crime, violence, and residential instability. Professionals realized that, sometimes, family reunification could harm children. Therefore, today, the focus may be on parental reunification for the first offense, but the ultimate goal is to ensure what would be best for the child's well-being, which may be concurrent planning for adoption (Lederman & Osofsky, 2004).

Legal issues

Today, courts focus on caring for the child's physical and mental welfare while working with the family to provide services. However, once a family has reached a court situation, great harm has already been inflicted on the child, and today the larger focus is on permanency, getting the child a stable and loving home as soon as possible.

The Adoption and Safe Families Act (ASFA, 1997) was an attempt to minimize the amount of time a child spent bouncing between foster homes and back into the biological home after the parent had completed yet another drug treatment or parenting class. ASFA mandates a one-year deadline for the courts to decide on a permanent placement for a child who has been abused or neglected. It favors adoption whenever possible. The goal is to prevent retraumatization of already distressed children. If a child has been in foster care for 15 of the previous 22 months, there must begin a procedure to terminate the biological parents' rights and the court may then seek adoptive homes.

Children who have been abused have already missed most of their preventative medical and dental appointments, have sporadic school attendance, and have moved a lot, often into one substandard living situation after another. They need intensive intervention within the context of a stable, consistent, loving environment with parents who understand the many challenges faced by abused and neglected children (Lederman & Osofsky, 2004). At least half of the children in foster care show severe developmental delays in several areas of functioning (Dicker & Gordon, 2001). Many of them were born small for gestational age or were premature, suffering from infections and illnesses at high rates (Dicker, Gordon, & Knitzer, 2001). As infants, they tend to display little to no curiosity about their environments, show no or dysfunctional attachment patterns, do not engage in pretend play, are fearful, withdrawn, and often aggressive (Lederman, Osofsky, & Katz, 2001).

Lederman and Osofsky (2004, p. 163) provide some insight into the daily struggles of abused children and the courts that serve them:

> Each judge is responsible for approximately 1700 cases annually. Each week, more than 100 families appear before each dependency judge, creating an apparent sea of chaos, despair, and uncontrolled emotions, ranging from anger, confusion, desperation, and hope. It is not unknown for tears to be shed from the bench, from the lawyers' lecterns, and from the courtroom gallery. Despite the thousands of adults and children who pass through the courts, it is rare to witness an expression of caring, love, or contrition from a parent to a child. Unlike the positive and hoped for "good enough" parent–child relationship … the courtroom is rarely the scene of a parental caress, a gesture of concern, or an expression of maternal or paternal pride. The juvenile courts in this country are teeming with dysfunctional families, emotional impoverishment, and every conceivable form of deprivation a child can endure. It is a difficult, if not impossible, context from which to promote healthy child development that, by necessity, requires both sensitivity and the difficult task of modifying maladaptive behavior that may have become the norm in these families, passed on from generation to generation.

In the U.S., there are currently 500,000 children in foster care. This means 2% of the U.S. population of children is without a permanent placement (Lederman & Osofsky, 2004). With the shortage of available foster parents these days, more and more children are being officially placed in family **kinship care** homes, where biological relatives can receive the same governmental and health care supports that non-kin foster parents receive. While in the U.S. there are more children than foster parents available, the situation is even worse in developing nations where there may be no foster care system or one is just emerging (Carbarino, 2006). Other countries are beginning to make progress. For example, Japan, Argentina and Hungary are working to construct alternative care systems that reflect their cultural values. Likewise, many countries work from a **community care model** where an abused or neglected child is cared for within larger family kin networks and their biological families are still included in their lives. If the child must be removed from the kin network, the advice and counsel of elders and community members are sought (Cameron & Freymond, 2006). This model has been used in Native American, Canadian First Nations, and Australian Aboriginal cultures, as well as in Korea.

Unfortunately, many abused and neglected children around the world are simply abandoned or given over to institutions. In Brazil, for example, homeless children (many of whom are AIDS orphans) continue to live on the streets (Pasztor & McFadden, 2006). Science is only recently discovering what the best standards of care are for children.

Kinship care
Foster care provided to children by their biological relatives.

Community of care model
A model of caring for families and children in order to prevent or intervene in family violence; includes multi-agency culturally sensitive practices.

The need for evidence-based practice

The situation for many families is dire. Family violence tends to be intergenerational, with abused children growing up to be violent in their own families. While not every abused or neglected child will grow up to harm his or her own children, it is estimated that at least 30% do (Panel on Research on Child Abuse and Neglect, National Research Council, 1993). In order to break this cycle, it is vitally important to get the youngest victims out of the courts and into families where they can receive occupational and speech therapy, counseling for emotional issues, and tutoring or other interventions to raise their cognitive skills to age-appropriate levels (Lederman & Osofsky, 2004). All social service personnel (including teachers, social workers, doctors, police officers, judges, and counselors) need to be educated about the research findings regarding the importance of brain development for very young children. Professionals must make colleagues and new graduates aware of scientifically sound interventions and encourage them not to follow trends or fads.

It is widely known to psychologists that cognitive behavioral therapy (CBT) is highly effective in helping people cope with trauma. In a review of 31 treatment studies, CBT was more effective than any other form of treatment for abused children, including play therapy, art therapy, psychodynamic therapy, group therapy, and the use of medications (Wethington et al., 2008). CBT utilizes relaxation techniques and helps children change maladaptive stress responses, thinking patterns, and aggressive behavior through role playing, homework assignments, and other "here and now" activities that keep the focus on the present in terms of aiding in communication, problem-solving, and social skills. CBT improves children's anxiety, depression, and PTSD symptoms. However, other therapies that have no evidentiary support are still being performed in clinics and centers around the world.

The most effective way to address child abuse is to prevent it. There are many examples of evidence-based practices that are very effective in reducing the incidence of child maltreatment (e.g., Bekemeier, 1995; Olds et al., 1998), which should be used in lieu of practices that might just sound like good ideas. Many of these programs include home visitations to stressed or young parents, child development information for parents, health information, service referrals, and transportation and nutrition assistance. There is ample evidence that *early* intervention works to help children meet their developmental potentials (Ramey & Ramey, 1998). All infants "in the system" should receive developmental evaluations and services should be provided so that they do not suffer the negative consequences of a lifetime of abuse or neglect (Dore & Mullin, 2006). Once attachment patterns, emotion regulation strategies, and behavioral tendencies are in place, it is very difficult to modify them later on when the brain is less plastic and years of trauma have accumulated in the nervous systems and behavioral repertoires of children (Perry, 2004; Shonkoff & Phillips, 2000). People who recover from abuse and trauma and break the cycle of abuse have typically found alternative attachment figures to provide them with emotional support, have experienced some form of intervention or counseling, and have worked to modify the way they process social information (Masten & Coatsworth, 1998).

Almost all researchers agree that prevention is more effective than intervention. It is easier and costs less to prevent violence and neglect than to spend billions of dollars and innumerable hours on law enforcement, mental health, welfare, substance abuse counseling, and

FIGURE 11.7 ACT campaign poster.
This image has been reproduced with the permission of the American Psychological Association and the Advertising Council. Copyright © 2002 by the American Psychological Association. For information about the ACT Program please go to http://actagainstviolence. apa.org.

incarceration later on. If we can reach young people before they have children, or when their children are very young, we can teach them the skills they need to be good parents (Masten & Coatsworth, 1998). Many programs exist that inform people about the normal ages and stages of development and provide people with the resources they need to seek help for nutrition, education, and substance abuse treatment before they harm their children (Conduct Problems Prevention Research Group, 2002). For example, the American Psychological Association (APA) and the National Association for the Education of Young Children (NAEYC) have teamed up to create a violence prevention program called Adults and Children Together (ACT) Against Violence, Raising Safe Kids Program. This program includes a national media campaign with the slogan "What a child learns about violence, a child learns for life. Teach carefully." This message is portrayed on billboards and in public service announcements on television and radio. It reminds parents that children learn from what they see around them, and that parents are always teaching. The program also includes an eight-week parenting curriculum that teaches parents about early childhood development, how to discipline positively without hitting, how to manage anger, how to solve social problems non-violently, and how to prevent children from being exposed to violence in the media (Guttman & Mowder, 2005; Miguel & Howe, 2006; Porter & Howe, 2008; Silva & Randall, 2005). We must make universal prevention efforts a national and international priority so that we can circumvent harm to children before it ever happens and keep families from breaking up.

CHAPTER SUMMARY

Violence is pervasive in families around the world and different types of violence tend to co-occur. If someone is abusing animals, it is likely that children, intimate partners, or elders might also be at risk. Family violence occurs in all ethnic groups, all social classes, and in heterosexual and same-sex couples.

Elder abuse is one of the least researched types of family violence. Seniors can be physically, sexually, or financially abused. They can also be victims of neglect, either from family members, or through self-neglect. Adult child caregivers who experience caregiving stress, or who were abused by a senior in childhood, are at risk of perpetrating elder abuse. Ethnic and language minorities are especially likely to suffer elder abuse in silence, having few resources to turn to. Most seniors do not report abuse because they do not recognize they are being abused, or they are reluctant to report abuse out of shame or fear of losing their independence, or fear of the abuser.

Animal abuse often occurs in homes where family violence exists. Batterers use animals as weapons to manipulate their partners, threatening to harm or kill animals if their partner doesn't toe the line. Abusers often torture animals, seeing them as property not worthy of humane treatment. Many battered women and children living in shelters report that among their top concerns is the safety of pets they left behind with their batterers. Some battered women stay with batterers out of fear for their pets' safety.

Intimate partner violence can occur in any type of relationship, gay, straight, married, or cohabiting. It often involves attempts at power and control by one partner over the other, a form of violence called intimate terrorism. While there are many types of batterers, most of them view partners as property, and many of them were abused themselves as children. There is much controversy over whether women can be batterers as commonly as men. Depending on the types of research samples studied, findings differ regarding gender symmetry in IPV perpetration. For example, in college samples, partners are often both aggressive, hitting or slapping each other, in a form of family violence called situational couples violence. In shelter and hospital samples, the most severe cases of abuse are almost always female victims and male perpetrators. Survivors of IPV can experience psychological problems like depression, anxiety, and suicidal thoughts.

Marital rape often co-occurs with IPV, as the final escalation after long-term sessions of battering and abuse. Marital rape is illegal in all 50 U.S. states but the general public still views it as a less severe event than stranger rape. Many people don't believe a husband can rape a wife since sexual activity is a normal part of marriage. Nevertheless, marital rape can result in PTSD, depression, anxiety, and health problems for the victims.

Over three million children are reported abused each year. Most of these cases are of neglect, but children can also be physically abused, sexually abused, and emotionally abused. Many children experience more than one type of maltreatment and the negative consequences of each type can be similar. Abused children often develop feelings of depression, anxiety, and sadness. They can become aggressive and victimize other people. They tend to have cognitive distortions and can experience dissociative states. Infants and toddlers are most likely to die from abuse, especially if they experience abusive head trauma in the first year of life.

For all forms of family violence, there are treatments for victims' symptoms that can improve their functioning and mental health over time. Treatment for perpetrators is less successful. However, the best antidote to family violence is universal prevention strategies. These would consist of good health care, child care, and living wages for all families. Educating parents on normal child developmental milestones can prevent much frustration during childrearing, which contributes to abuse. Adults who were abused as children can be trained in new problem-solving, communication, and emotion-regulation skills, so that the cycle of violence can be broken in their families of procreation.

KEY TERMS

allostasis
allostatic load
animal hoarding
antisocial/violent (cobra) batterers
caregiving stress
community of care model
cycle of violence
Duluth Model
dysphoric/borderline batterers
emotional neglect
escalation
exploratory/curiosity animal abuse
family only (pit bull) batterers

fiduciary abuse specialist team
financial/material abuse/exploitation
gender symmetry hypothesis
grooming
honeymoon period
hostile attribution bias
intimate partner violence
intimate terrorism
kinship care
learned helplessness
mandatory arrest
marital rape
medical/educational neglect

neglect
pathological animal abuse
physical abuse
physical neglect
power and control
psychological/emotional abuse
sandwich generation
self-neglect
sexual abuse
situational couples violence
survivors
violent resistance

WEBSITES FOR FURTHER EXPLORATION

http://www.americanhumane.org

The American Humane Association is the only protective organization to work for the welfare of both animals and children, which it has done since 1877. Their work has led to policies like the "no animals were harmed in the making of this film" disclaimer that is required in movie credits. Their website has great articles on the links between animal abuse and family violence, excellent fact sheets on topics like neglect and abuse fatalities and the human–animal bond, links to events, and a description of their PAWS (Pets and Women's Shelters) program, where they are fighting for battered women's shelters to be able to care for pets.

http://www.nrcdv.org

The National Research Center on Domestic Violence aims to improve responses to domestic violence, as well as work on prevention programs. They provide technical training, information packets, electronic materials and publications, statistics and charts, and information on LGBT battering and teen dating violence. They list the national domestic violence hotline where you can call to report abuse or get help (1–800–799–7233).

http://www.childwelfare.gov

The Child Welfare Information Gateway is a one-stop shop for all topics related to child abuse and neglect. It promotes safety programs for children, disseminates research information and statistics, and has resources on foster caring and adoption. It contains lots of great information sheets and articles about topics like maltreatment's effects on the brain and children witnessing domestic violence. They also have a video to walk you through the site. They list the national Childhelp USA hotline where you can call to report abuse or get help (1–800–822–4453).

CHAPTER 12
DIVORCE AND REMARRIAGE

When two divorced people marry, four people get into bed.

(Jewish Proverb)

LEARNING OBJECTIVES

- To understand the evolution of and contemporary trends in divorce practices over time

- To grasp the complex processes involved in divorce and remarriage

- To gain a better understanding of the effects of divorce on diverse men, women, and children

- To learn some strategies that can help minimize the negative impact of divorce on families

- To understand the unique challenges and rewards stepfamilies experience

- To learn techniques for ensuring the health and well-being of stepfamilies

Marriages and Families in the 21st Century: A Bioecological Approach, First Edition. Tasha R. Howe.
© 2012 Tasha R. Howe. Published 2012 by Blackwell Publishing Ltd.

OVERVIEW: TRENDS IN DIVORCE AND REMARRIAGE

- Historical trends in divorce
  - Historic trends in the U.S.
  - Contemporary legal trends
- Contemporary trends
  - Comparing legal trends in other countries and the U.S.

THE COMPLEXITIES OF DIVORCE

- The process of divorce
  - Some psychological processes related to divorce
- The stations of divorce

THE EFFECTS OF DIVORCE

- Effects of divorce on women
  - Psychological issues for women and children
  - Biological aspects of women's response to divorce
  - The effects of abuse on divorce outcomes
- Effects of divorce on men
  - Financial issues
  - Psychological processes fathers can experience
- Effects of divorce on children
  - Should parents stay together for the kids?
  - Positive outcomes of divorce

REDUCING THE NEGATIVE IMPACT OF DIVORCE

- Co-parenting
- Couples coping enhancement training

REMARRIAGE

- Variables influencing remarriage rates
- Special challenges in stepfamilies
  - Legal and financial issues
  - Challenges for stepmothers vs. stepfathers
- Different viewpoints on stepfamilies
- Healthy ways to remarry and stepparent

OVERVIEW: TRENDS IN DIVORCE AND REMARRIAGE

Historical trends in divorce

Contemporary trends

Most people who marry think it will last forever. They say their vows sincerely, feel immense hope for the future, and feel love for their new spouse. Despite their best intentions, however, almost half of couples fail to stay together. Fully 40% of children in the United States will live in a divorced home (Cherlin, 1992; Phillips & Sweeney, 2006) and 50% of Americans will be part of a stepfamily at some point in their lives (Neuman, 1998; Sweeney, 2010). If we include couples who separate but don't legally divorce, rates are estimated at about 66% for the break-up of first marriages (Castro-Martin & Bumpass, 1989).

Some variables that are related to higher chances of divorce include low education, divorce or separation in the partners' families of origin, having a partner from a different ethnicity, cohabiting before marriage, early age of marriage, and having children before marriage (Phillips & Sweeney, 2005). Instead of these factors causing divorce, however, it's important to think about macrosystem factors that may differentially place groups of people into these risk categories. For example, people of color are more likely to experience poverty, family break-up, and lower education levels. They are also at greater risk for divorce than European Americans. It could be that racism, discrimination, and living with the constant stress of trying to scrape by are the real influences on divorce rates (Phillips & Sweeney, 2005). See Figure 12.1 for marriage, divorce, and remarriage rates by ethnicity and see if you can think of some influences stemming from different systems in the bioecological model that might explain these trends.

Despite the poor odds of success, people still firmly believe in the institution of marriage. Two thirds of divorced women and 75% of divorced men remarry (Sweeney, 2010). However, divorce rates are even higher for second marriages (Cherlin & Furstenberg, 1994). In light of these trends, it's important to find out why people divorce, how they divorce, and how we can prevent divorce or minimize its negative impact on parents and children when it does happen. A bioecological lens can help us develop a true understanding of such a complex phenomenon. This chapter will focus on

FIGURE 12.1 Marriage, divorce, and remarriage lifetime prevalence for adults of all ages, by ethnicity, 2004.
Source: U.S. Census Bureau 2007.

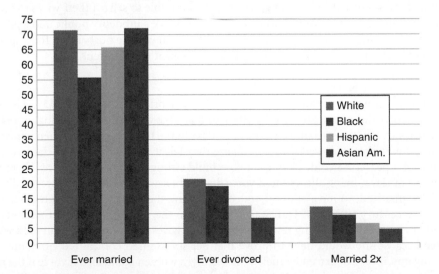

contributing factors from all systems of the bioecological model. For example, it will explore biological factors such as stress reactivity, microsystem factors, such as family communication styles, exosystem factors, like job loss and economic downturn, and macrosystem factors, which include cultural beliefs and social policies related to divorce.

To set the stage and better understand where we are with divorce today, let's explore divorce from a historic perspective. Recall that paying attention to historical influences means we are using a chronosystem analysis.

Historical trends in divorce

Men in ancient China (tenth century to fifth century BCE) were allowed to divorce wives who failed to serve them adequately, and who talked too much, were jealous, or who could not bear children (Day & Hook, 1987). The ancient Chinese word for divorce is *ch'u-ch'i*, which means "oust wife" (Day & Hook, 1987). Early Jewish cultures allowed men to divorce their wives and send them away for displeasing their husbands (Amram, 2009).

Ancient Romans divorced quite readily, and women were allowed to remarry numerous times without scorn. In early pre-Christian cultures, marriage was formalized by simple rituals such as "jumping the broom." A bride and groom would lay a broomstick at the threshold to their home and jump over it to symbolize their formal union. Likewise, divorce could proceed easily by jumping over the broom backwards out of the house (Day & Hook, 1987). Some Anglo-Saxon groups allowed divorce if a woman stopped wearing her wedding ring, or by the couple exiting a building through separate doors. Some early Christian churches even held rituals where those wanting to divorce would meet at the church and run around in circles while blindfolded, reaching out for another spouse. They would then marry that spouse and vow to try to live together for one year.

However, under the Roman emperor Constantine, divorce laws became very strict and divorce could only be granted for adultery, prostitution, or other crimes committed by wives. Women could only divorce their husbands if the husband never returned from war. By 1200 CE, divorce was outlawed in most Christian communities (Day & Hook, 1987). The Bible clearly disapproves of divorce, yet Deuteronomy does say that a man can divorce a woman if she displeases him. Women and children were considered the property of men. The Christian father was considered lord and king over the family and women were expected to obey their husbands.

After its split with the Roman Catholic Church in the sixteenth century, Scotland allowed divorce, and many English couples fled to Scotland to break ties with their spouses (Day & Hook, 1987). Before that, the only other way British Christians could divorce under strict laws was to attend the cattle market for a session of "wife selling," where men were able to sell off their wives to the highest bidder. It is thought that this process was meant to make a wife's infidelity public and legitimize her moving to live with another man (Day & Hook, 1987). It allowed the husband to free himself from all financial obligations to care for his wife and he usually kept the children.

Historic trends in the U.S.

The first recorded divorce among settlers of the "New World" occurred in 1639. The Puritans granted this divorce due to an egregious violation of marriage vows, bigamy (having more than one wife). The perpetrator (the husband) was put in stocks in the town square and then banished back to England. The Puritans allowed divorce because they felt it would increase social harmony and their vision for a peaceful world. They wanted to build strong and happy families. There are even sparse records of slaves being allowed to divorce due to their wives' adultery. However, divorce was still largely stigmatized, so most spouses ended up leaving their partners through desertion until the nineteenth century (Riley, 1991). It wasn't unusual in the 1800s to see advertisements in train stations and in newspapers offering rewards for runaway wives. It was very difficult for a wife to file for divorce because she would have to prove that her spouse had committed egregious acts like infidelity, bigamy, incest, or extreme cruelty. Interestingly, women could also divorce if the male was impotent. And if a husband was lost at sea or had not been heard from in several years, a woman was usually allowed a divorce so that she could remarry.

Divorce was legally allowed in Deseret (modern day Utah) in 1850, a century before it was legalized in most U.S. states. In fact, in South Carolina, divorce was illegal until 1949. Mormon leader Brigham Young granted church divorces in Utah in the 1850s to those who had previously practiced polygamy. Lenient divorce laws in Utah led couples from other states to flock there. Attorneys got wealthy off of administering over the proceedings and Utah became known as a **divorce mill**. Divorce mills were states or regions to which people flocked to get easy divorces.

Divorce mills allowed a new industry to take root, focusing on divorce and its aftermath. For example, South Dakota businesses, hotels, and stores advertised in neighboring states, welcoming couples to stay with them and shop while they waited for their divorces to be processed. Pennsylvania was also an early hotbed of divorce. Couples moved there for the required year and then could legally divorce (Day & Hook, 1987). These are examples of **migratory divorce**, the practice of leaving one's hometown and traveling long distances to obtain a divorce. Migratory divorce became common as the individualistic ideal of personal happiness collided with the gradual loosening of divorce laws in northern states. Southern states continued to be conservative and followed the teachings of the Bible.

As people began to move to burgeoning cities during industrialization, greater numbers of women were working and people developed more progressive attitudes. They felt that in a true democracy, women should have the right to end an unhappy marriage. Both men and women had started thinking about the need for personal fulfillment in their marriages. Recall that people married in previous centuries to benefit a family, clan, or larger group, not because of love or personal feelings. After the turn of the twentieth century, however, more people were getting divorced and there were fewer stigmas attached to it. Divorce rates reached a peak in the 1880s (Riley, 1991), with 1 in 14 marriages ending, which is still quite low compared to the modern average of between 40% and 50%.

Historically, most divorces were initiated by men. When courts granted a divorce, it was usually in response to petitions by men. Men's cases were more often heard and approved, while women were forced to stay in difficult marriages. Men just had to argue that they were suspicious that their wives had committed adultery and the woman could be socially ostracized, whipped, jailed, or made to wear a red letter "A" on her bodice. Those convicted of infidelity were not allowed to remarry, in order to prevent the formation of another "unstable" union. Women usually lost custody of their children if they *were* granted a divorce. They were then socially shunned and expected to live with their parents and become "old maids."

In the 1920s silent film *Children of Divorce*, starring Clara Bow, Esther Ralston, and Gary Cooper, divorce was depicted as a "fate worse than death" because the main character kills herself over putting her daughter through a divorce. The film takes place in France, at an American "divorce colony," where couples marry too soon and divorce quickly. Divorcees in the colony party all night, drinking and living it up, while they send their kids to live in a convent.

The mere existence of this film illustrates the negative connotations divorce had in our culture in previous generations. Today divorce is much more accepted, if not a normative transition that most of us will experience in some way in our lives (Bray & Hetherington, 1993).

While divorces became more common at the turn of the twentieth century, when thousands of men returned from World War II in 1945 there was a marked dip in divorce rates, accompanied by an increase in marriage and birth rates. Divorce was at an all-time low from 1945 to 1955, a decade uncharacteristic of the general decline in marriage and increase in divorce taking place over the past 100 years.

In the past 50 years, divorce rates have doubled from about 25% to 50% of marriages, and even though the increase in divorce rates has slowed down a bit, probably due to fewer people getting married in the first place, divorce still occurs in about 45% of first marriages (Teachman, Tedrow, & Crowder, 2000). In 1959, almost 80% of marriages lasted at least 15 years, but today only 57% last that long (U.S. Census Bureau, 2008).

Divorce mills
States or regions in the nineteenth century where people came to get easy divorces.

Migratory divorce
The trend where couples move to other cities, states, or even countries to obtain divorces that are illegal in their area.

FIGURE 12.2 How was divorce viewed in 1920s America? Esther Ralston as Jean Waddington and Gary Cooper as Ted Larrabee in *Children of Divorce* (1927).
Photo © John Springer Collection/Corbis.

Contemporary trends

Americans have always been individualistic, willing to pick up and leave, or forge new frontiers, and our personal relationships are no different. People in the United States have always moved with the spirit of taking risks and changing their lives dramatically. That's why people originally came to the colonies, to escape the strict rules and religious control of British law. They had lived oppressed for centuries and wanted personal freedom in their new lives. Allowing people to divorce aligns well with American values of social democracy and personal happiness. Reflecting these values, divorce laws changed substantially in the 1970s.

By the 1970s, most divorces were initiated by women, and, for the first time in history, divorce petitions listed issues like incompatibility and falling out of love (Riley, 1991). Gender role ideologies had shifted by the twentieth century, so that men were no longer considered the primary parent, as they had been. Women were now considered naturally good at caretaking and their rights to keep custody of their children were more steadily enforced in courts of law. By 1970, as the feminist revolution took hold, women became even less willing to stay in oppressive, unhappy, or violent marriages. The legal victories of the twentieth century (the right to vote, anti-gender discrimination laws) gave them more rights than women in previous generations had. Many courts began awarding joint custody of children to both parents in the 1980s. Joint custody refers to a legal ruling allowing both divorced parents to have equal access to and responsibility for their children. Practically, however, women almost always retained physical custody of children after divorce in the late twentieth century. These trends show how gender ideologies can affect divorce practices. Check out how gender roles and divorce rates of various cultures are related in the *How Would You Measure That?* box.

No-fault divorce
A contemporary trend where no one has to prove fault or wrong-doing for a divorce; divorce can occur unilaterally, or without the consent of a second party, and possessions one owned before the marriage remain his/hers.

Contemporary legal trends

The 1970s brought implementation of **no-fault divorce**, which means a divorce can occur unilaterally, or without the consent of a second party (Allen & Gallagher, 2007). Each party goes his or her separate way and they don't have to prove wrongdoing on either side; one person can simply cite "irreconcilable

HOW WOULD YOU MEASURE THAT?

Divorce rates and gender equality (Yodanis, 2005)

Many people think the increase in divorce rates is certainly a bad thing. What do you think? Can higher divorce rates be indicative of positive changes in society? In order to assess this question, Carrie Yodanis (2005) studied the divorce policies and gender role beliefs and behaviors in 22 countries. Yodanis noticed that countries with high divorce rates have lower rates of domestic violence. For example, in the U.S., no-fault divorce led to a decrease in domestic violence, as women were allowed to leave marriages at any time. Also, when women work in the labor force, divorce rates are higher, suggesting financial independence. Thus, Yodanis expected to find that in the countries with a high divorce culture, women would be more equal to men. She assessed "marriage culture" (beliefs that all people should marry; marriage is forever) and "divorce culture" (beliefs that marriage is just one of many lifestyle options; divorce is always possible if marriage doesn't work). She used questionnaires of over 9,000 married women gathered by the General Social Survey, which is conducted around the world each year. Women were asked about the division of labor in their homes, their beliefs about the equality of men and women on various topics, and whether the husband or the wife made more money. She also examined national marriage and divorce rates.

Divorce rates were lowest in Ireland, where it was illegal until 1997, and the Philippines, where it is still illegal. Surprisingly, most women in all countries had fairly liberal attitudes toward divorce. They felt that if a woman was being treated badly or if the marriage was very unhappy, divorce was acceptable. Nevertheless, divorce rates were highest in the United States, which also had the greatest "divorce culture." Those countries where Catholicism was widely practiced (for example, Italy), which had collectivist value systems (like Poland), and were very familialistic (like Ireland) scored lowest on the "culture of divorce" variable. In other words, they were "cultures of marriage."

In all countries, women performed the preponderance of the household tasks, and in no country was housework distributed equally between husbands and wives. However, in countries with low scores on "divorce culture," women did exponentially more housework than men. In contrast, high "divorce culture" countries had a gendered division of labor that more closely approached equivalence and women earned more money than women in "marriage cultures" did. There were no countries that scored high on divorce culture *and* high on inequality between the sexes. There were also no countries that scored low on divorce culture *and* low on equality. Thus, when the "divorce culture" ethic is stronger, there is more gender equality. And when the "marriage culture" ethic prevails, there is less equality between men and women.

In sum, in cultures where divorce is common and less stigmatized, women's standing in terms of earnings, equal treatment, and division of labor is greater. Yodanis (2005) emphasizes that divorce is not just something that happens between individuals at the *microsystem* level, but is also affected by *macrosystem* influences. Moreover, divorce may not be a completely negative event, as can be seen by the positive quality of life for women living in divorce cultures.

differences" as the reason for the divorce (Allen & Gallagher, 2007). This legal arrangement allows people to leave a marriage with the property they had when they entered the marriage. Each state's no-fault divorce law may vary in terms of how property, alimony, and child support are decided, but the commonality is that with no-fault divorce, women can leave their marriages without having to justify their desire to divorce or prove their husband was a bad person (the same holds true for men). This has helped countless battered women leave toxic marriages without having to involve law enforcement or prove they were battered. In fact, female suicide, domestic violence exposure, and murder rates all decrease in areas that implement no-fault divorces (Wolfers & Stevenson, 2006).

There is some debate about whether no-fault divorce laws have led to the increases in divorce rates we saw in the 1970s and 1980s. Some statistical analyses suggest they have influenced these rates

(Wolfers, 2006), while others suggest they have not (Day & Hook, 1987; Droes & vanLamoen, 2010). What is clear, however, is that divorce rates have pretty much leveled out since the 1980s (Schoen & Canudas-Romo, 2006).

While the idea of a no-fault divorce sounds equitable, the results have not always been. Women work significantly more hours after a no-fault divorce (Allen & Gallagher, 2007) and a woman's income typically declines after divorce, while a man's actually increases (Riley, 1991). Since the inception of no-fault divorce, the socioeconomic status of divorced women has declined substantially, and divorce has meant a descent into poverty for millions of women and children. In the previous fault system, if a woman proved her husband cruel or adulterous, she could be awarded large monetary compensation in the form of alimony and child support, as well as usually keeping the family home. In the no-fault system, monetary issues are decided by each judge individually based on state laws, and this has often led to custodial mothers experiencing extreme economic hardship (Wolfers & Stevenson, 2006).

Because divorced mothers have to work more hours, their income declines, and they also spend more time with their children than divorced fathers do, this can be a challenging experience for women. For example, while women and men often have **joint legal custody** of their children, meaning the courts have awarded them equal parental rights, women actually spend much more time caring for children. Thus the couple usually does not share **joint physical custody**, which means each parent caring for the children for equal amounts of time. It is usually women who arrange children's activities, buy school clothes, take children to medical appointments, etc. They also bear most of the financial burden of raising their children.

It's important for mothers to encourage a more equitable balance approaching true joint physical custody. Sometimes both ex-spouses accept the new unequal physical custody balance as natural, and men become reluctant to pay child support for children they rarely see. It's important for mothers to encourage visits with fathers, for their children's well-being, and because research shows that only about 2% of men willfully avoid paying child support if they are allowed to visit their children regularly, while 36% of men denied visits do so (Parke & Brott, 1999).

Poor men who are allowed visitation may still not be able to financially support their children, however. Even with welfare benefits, pay from minimum wage employment, or both, these families struggle to keep their heads above water, often without health care, child care, transportation, or proper nutrition (Phillips & Sweeney, 2006). Thus, it's important to remember that social class and gender both play key roles in the experience of divorce.

In the current economic climate, there are reports that divorce is starting to occur less often because neither spouse can afford to pay for attorneys, court fees, or a new home for themselves (Elkin, 2009). They can't sell their current homes due to the economic crisis and subsequent declines in home values. One attorney reported that people are opting for legal separations, which cost a mere $2,000, over divorces, which can cost much more. Under legal separation, people may not have sexual relationships with others or remarry, and they are still jointly responsible for children and financial responsibilities. They may file a formal **Separation Agreement**, a document that outlines custody, visitation, and bill-paying schedules, among other things. This separation agreement makes boundaries and responsibilities clearer for couples living separately while still being legally married. Some couples feel that legal separation is enough, and that divorce should only occur if one of the partners wants to remarry (Elkin, 2009). Many other couples who cannot afford to legally separate are moving into separate bedrooms and living solitary lives in the same house, since they can't afford alimony, child support, or the maintenance of two separate homes and cars. Despite these trends, the United States still has the highest divorce rate in the industrialized world.

Comparing legal trends in other countries and the U.S.

Divorce is harder to obtain in Europe than in the U.S. European countries typically impose long waiting times—an average of three years—and require mandatory counseling for the couple (Crouch 2007). Not surprisingly, European countries have lower divorce rates than the U.S. Bulgaria, Italy,

---

Joint legal custody
A legal ruling allowing both divorced parents to have equal access to and responsibility for their children.

Joint physical custody
The actual practice of both divorced parents spending equal amounts of time and taking equal responsibility for their children.

Separation agreement
A document that outlines custody, visitation, and bill-paying schedules, among other things.

and Spain have the lowest divorce rates in Europe and they each require mandatory counseling before a divorce is granted (www.divorcereform.org). However, couples usually enter this counseling far too late, rendering such therapy ineffective in most cases (Widmer, Cina, Charvoz, Shantinath, & Bodenmann, 2005). And when therapy seems to strengthen the relationship, the results are often short-lived and divorce ensues anyway (Widmer et al., 2005). Thus, in many ways it seems that if a couple is determined to divorce, nothing can stop them. Interestingly, research in several countries has shown that religion has an impressive effect on whether a couple will reconcile after such pre-divorce counseling. When the two partners share the same religious beliefs, they are more likely to get back together after a separation followed by counseling (Wineberg, 1994). Also, partners of the same age and those who cohabited before their marriage are more likely to reconcile instead of divorce (Wineberg, 1994).

Why do you think that the U.S. has the highest rates of divorce of any country? Some scholars point to the fact that divorce is relatively easy to get in the U.S. so people don't try hard enough to keep their marriages together. In support of this idea, the 10 U.S. states with the lowest divorce rates have the longest waiting periods (averaging 18 to 24 months). These states have about 3.1/1,000 divorces per capita versus 4.0/1,000 in other states (Riley, 1991; Sweezy & Tiefenthaler, 1996). In an opposing argument, Riley (1991) posits that when divorce is harder to obtain, people will sabotage their marriages (such as engaging in infidelity) in order to meet more stringent divorce criteria, or they end up just abandoning the marriage. Also, it isn't clear how cases of domestic violence, cruelty, infidelity, or abandonment would be treated under a stricter set of divorce laws. Would prohibiting divorce or making it harder to obtain lead to stronger, happier, and more stable families? Before we can answer this, we must explore in more depth some of the complex issues surrounding contemporary divorce, including factors from our *micro-* and *macrosystems*.

THE COMPLEXITIES OF DIVORCE

The process of divorce

The stations of divorce

Divorce is not an isolated event, where someone is married one day and divorced the next. Instead, divorce is a long process, sometimes evolving over years or even decades. It usually follows months or years of marital dissatisfaction. And both partners are rarely at the same level of desire for uncoupling. There is usually a "leaver" and a "leav-ee." Because one person leaves the marriage and the other is left, divorce resembles death, the death of a relationship that began with two people in love but ended in conflict, silent resentment, or both (Everett & Everett, 1994).

Today, women initiate most divorces. Recall from earlier chapters that there is often "his" marriage and "her" marriage, with women reporting lower levels of marital satisfaction than men throughout their lives together. Women are more in tune with emotional disconnects in marriages and report being unhappy in their marriages for a much longer time than men do (Gottman, 1994). Many men say they are caught off guard when their wives ask for a divorce and report that they were not aware there were serious problems in the marriage. Women often report that they stayed in their marriages for years while feeling unhappy because of their inability to financially support themselves. They also report extreme dissatisfaction with the quality of their marriages because many husbands do not want to spend time with them but have their own hobbies or prefer to go out with the "boys." Women are also unhappy about the *quality* of their sex lives, while men report dissatisfaction with the *quantity* of sex (Hetherington, 2003).

Men cite reasons for divorce that include their wives' nagging, criticizing, alcohol use, or infidelity. Upper-class women are more likely to cite personal dissatisfaction with communication, intimacy, or emotional connection as the main reason for divorce than poor women are. However, Matta (2006) argues that many couples confuse "intimacy" with "infatuation," and states that what they are really missing is the original infatuation they had with a new relationship. They may still share emotional and lifestyle intimacy, but they interpret the normal reduction in passion that occurs over time as a loss of intimacy and thus grounds for divorce.

Matta (2006) reports that most couples divorce within the first two years of a marriage, when the passion (their view of intimacy) decreases. However, he also found that another peak period for divorce occurs at the empty nest stage when children leave home, as couples find they have nothing to talk about if their old conversations always revolved around the children. They interpret this new lifestyle with their partners as lacking in intimacy as well. Interestingly, women from lower socioeconomic status are less likely to complain about a loss of connection with their partners. Instead, they report violence and hard living as reasons for divorce. Their partners are often absent from home, drink too much, have unstable employment histories, and are unfaithful (20% report infidelity) (Kurz, 1995). These trends illustrate how very different processes can be in families experiencing divorce. This means that knowing someone comes from a "broken home," or a divorced family, is not very informative. We can't understand a lot about them based only on their family structure. What helps is a more in-depth analysis of the processes each family member went through before, during, and after the divorce.

The process of divorce

The *process* of divorce isn't cut and dried, either. One person doesn't just walk out the door as they did in previous centuries, where desertion was more common than divorce. Instead, today they negotiate (or battle) over child custody, visitation, religion, discipline, holidays and birthdays, education, medical care, negotiating life transitions like children's graduations, and so on. They must work out relocation, remarriage, taxes, insurance, debts, property, assets, retirement plans, and numerous other issues that become entwined when two people are married for a long time (Everett & Everett, 1994). It's clear that divorce can be a stressful transition for many families. To see the story of how one contemporary woman experienced divorce in the United States, see the *Focus on My Family* box.

Uncoupling is even more complicated for LGBT people in long-term committed relationships or marriages. With same-sex marriage only recently becoming legal in a few countries and U.S. states, we have virtually no research on the divorce process in same-sex couples (Brown & Groscup, 2008). However, we do know that if they live under domestic partnership agreements or are in committed cohabiting relationships, there are no laws protecting them or helping them negotiate their break-ups. They cannot use family courts to help them end their relationships equitably. There are no resources for helping them negotiate property or custody arrangements. Civil courts require couples to hire an attorney, which many people cannot afford to do, and most attorneys are unfamiliar with the needs of LGBT clients. Legal professionals may not consider same-sex relationships real or valid and their problems may not be taken seriously. Their partnerships are often of "ambiguous status" under the law and their partner and child losses in court cases are thought to be in some way dissimilar to the losses of other families (Allen, 2007; Sweeney, 2010). Moreover, federal law denies LGBT couples rights that their own states might grant them, leading to different treatment under the law than heterosexual couples receive when their relationships end. Also, LGBT partners may be particularly vulnerable to feelings of depression and guilt after a break-up because social sentiment was already against their unions in the first place. They may receive less family support if their family members have distanced themselves from them because of their sexual orientation or gender status (Brown & Groscup, 2008). People judge their relationship dissolutions and custody battles more negatively because they are already marginalized by society.

Some psychological processes related to divorce

The media is replete with stories of contentious or even vicious divorce and custody battles among heterosexual couples, with couples who once loved each other becoming enemies who can barely be in the same room with each other. However, there are many couples that divorce well, with both

FOCUS ON MY FAMILY

Loretta's story

Much to the disappointment of my Christian parents, I married and converted to Islam at 19. On my wedding day, I remember never having felt surer about anything in my life. My husband was so different, charismatic and much older than me. I was enchanted by him, his culture, his family values, and his strong religious beliefs. We quickly started a family and I was truly happy to be a stay-at-home mom of five children. My mother asked me what happened to my ambition for becoming an actress and graduating from college. But I was happy—until my husband started working sporadically and neglecting his responsibility to support our family. His views of our religious beliefs became extreme and twisted. He became controlling, violently angry, and unreasonable. He alienated friends and stayed in the house for days at a time. He attempted to keep me from my parents and friends, refused to allow me to leave the house, and his daily verbal assaults were excruciating.

This type of behavior was not an example of the beliefs of equality, justice and fairness that I knew Islam to be. His behavior also affected his parenting. He was particularly harsh with our two eldest children. I don't understand how I tolerated this misery. I was trying to be happy and thankful, complaining to no one but God. My faith increased and I believed one day my circumstances would improve. I attempted to tell him his behavior was contrary to Islam, but his abuse worsened. He humiliated me in front of my children, friends and family. I realized I was the only person who could take a stand.

I felt his behavior was morally wrong and against everything Muslim. The Qur'an states, "He has created spouses for you … so that you may console yourselves through them. He has planted love and mercy between you" (Qur'an, 30:21). Surely, God would understand my frustration. Islam validates marriage with a written agreement that specifies rights and responsibilities for both parties. It allows women to initiate divorce (known as *khul*). Although Islam allows divorce, it is also known as "the most hated of all permissible things by God." The Qur'an increased women's rights at the time it was written, but sometimes more recent *cultures* decide to restrict these rights.

I finally confided in an Arabic male colleague from my community. He couldn't believe what I had gone through. The emotional support I received from him and his wife gave me encouragement to finally end the madness. Within two weeks I found a house, enrolled the children in school, and filed for divorce. My community wholeheartedly supported me because my ex-husband blatantly violated his responsibilities as a husband and father. It was ironic that the female American convert received the support of fellow Muslims over the Arab male. The Islamic community here is very educated, especially in terms of their religious traditions, which led them to support the person who was following Islam's teachings, not the person who was violating them.

These first two years have had many ups and downs. However, my faith in God remains strong and I look forward to living my life in a quest for happiness and solace for myself and my children.

Loretta and family.
Photo reproduced by permission.

parents, their own four parents, and all eight grandparents working together to make the transition cordial and less traumatic, especially if children are involved. We rarely hear about these successful divorces, but many of us know people who have managed them. Some of us have been to weddings where stepsiblings and half-siblings, grandparents, aunts and uncles all get along, sometimes very well. This is especially true if people manage their own anger and feelings of being hurt or betrayed and can think about what would be most psychologically healthy for the children and other family members. This psychological distancing from personal hostility and the ability to think rationally about the future make positive divorces much more likely. People don't like to think of divorce as an event that can reduce tension and lead to happiness for the people involved. Nevertheless, divorce doesn't have to traumatize people (Ahrons, 2004). If we fail to research or even pay attention to these positive divorces, we perpetuate the idea that all divorce is bad and that we can all expect our families to be torn apart by it.

The truth is that there is wide variability in how couples divorce, and this is often related to their microsystem dynamics early on. For example, Gottman and Levenson (2002) found that there are two main types of emotional climates related to divorce. First, there is an **emotionally distant or neutral affective style**, where partners avoid discussing topics that may provoke emotions and they disengage from each other. Secondly, there is an **emotionally volatile** affect regulation style wherein the couple is continuously engaged in an attack–defend pattern and emotions (both positive and negative) run high. For those divorces that occur early, in the first seven years of a marriage, couples are more likely to be characterized as emotionally volatile. They are engaged in conflictual interactions characterized by emotional attacks and contempt (recall the "Four Horsemen of the Apocalypse" from Chapter 7). However, when divorce occurs in the later period, around the "empty nest" time, couples are more likely to drift apart or be characterized by a neutral affective style. Couples may be more likely to stay together longer if they are not overly hostile and angry, but eventually, that alienation, avoidance, and dissatisfaction may lead to the desire to divorce in mid-life (Gottman & Levenson, 2002). This illustrates that divorce can occur years after marital dissatisfaction has taken root.

Emotionally distant or neutral affective style Emotional disengagement from one's romantic partner.

Emotionally volatile affective style Continuous engagement in an attack–defend pattern and emotions (both positive and negative) run high.

The stations of divorce

Divorce is much more complex than just changing residences and ending a romantic relationship. As the research above suggests, we often emotionally disengage from our spouses long before a divorce occurs. People don't just rush into such a decision. They usually think about their options, lament over their feelings of failure in the relationship, and weigh the pros and cons of their decision. People realize that when they divorce, they don't just divorce a spouse, but all of the spouse's family members, and any mutual friends or community members, who may feel torn, like they have to form alliances with one partner over the other. Partners think about how they might successfully parent their children from two different homes, as well as envisioning how life will be after they start dating or having sexual relations with a new person after being intimate with only one person for so long. These processes illustrate that all bioecological systems play a role in both the decision to divorce and the way we adjust after a divorce. Bohannon (1970) argued for six *stations of divorce*:

- *emotional*—which involves falling out of love, losing intimacy, drifting apart, feeling sad, angry, and lonely; this is the only station that typically occurs *before* a couple is legally divorced
- *legal*—which involves filing official court papers that legally dissolve the union
- *economic*—which involves creating a new life with more or less money, selling property, alimony arrangements, child support issues, insurance, debts, assets, and so on
- *parental*—which involves ceasing to be co-parents in one home and beginning a new relationship of co-parenting with children moving in and out of one's home with visitation and custody arrangements; re-establishing rules and discipline
- *community*—which involves being accepted or ostracized by previous neighbors, co-workers, merchants, church members, and so on; perhaps moving to a new community and forming new friendships and connections

- *psychic*—which involves finally feeling that one's life is truly separate from the old life, the person is psychologically independent, and has a stable new life.

With so many changes occurring simultaneously and in quick succession, it's no wonder that most people think of divorce as a highly stressful event. As discussed earlier, divorce can be extremely traumatic for some people, but it can improve the lives of others. Therefore, once again we must emphasize family *process* over family *structure* in our analysis of family members' well-being and happiness. Let's look at the research on the effects of divorce and what factors make it more or less painful for the people involved.

THE EFFECTS OF DIVORCE

> Effects of divorce on women
>
> Effects of divorce on men
>
> Effects of divorce on children

Because each divorce occurs under varying circumstances, it's not surprising that there are diverse effects on different types of people. However, research has been able to reveal a few general trends in how divorce affects the people involved, as well as establish some guidelines for minimizing negative effects on families. This section will focus on the effects of divorce and tips for how to minimize the traumatic impact of divorce on men, women, and children.

In the first year after divorce, both men and women experience anger, loneliness, ambivalence about the divorce, continued attachment to their ex-spouse, and especially for women, fantasies about reconciling (Hetherington, 2003). Within six years after a divorce, however, most men and women are remarried or have built satisfying new lives for themselves. They have recovered from conflictual post-divorce relationships with their ex-spouses and have overcome the pain and anger they once felt. Emotional problems, use of alcohol, impairments in parenting, and other problems decline dramatically after the first two years post-divorce (Hetherington & Kelly, 2002).

Fisher and Alberti (2006) outline several issues with which both women and men struggle in the aftermath of divorce. These issues are normal and the majority of people begin to overcome these psychological struggles after about two years following the divorce:

- self-acceptance, including questioning whether they are good people, failures, and so on
- feeling rejected and unworthy or guilty over rejecting their spouse
- loneliness and grieving the loss of their previous lives
- finding a new concept of self, which involves asking and answering the question "Who am I now, without this other person?"
- being willing to find love again; letting go of the previous relationship
- overcoming the dysfunctional relationship dynamics of the previous relationship and learning new, healthy ways to interact
- coming to terms with anger and sadness; expressing true feelings in open, honest, and constructive ways versus suppression or lashing out
- understanding one's self as a sexual person; assessing sexual needs and how to open up sexually with a new person
- overcoming lack of trust and fear of betrayal or emotional pain
- eventually feeling energized, excited, alive, vibrant, free, and ready to move on.

There are wide variations in the way in which both men and women cope with and adjust to life after divorce. In a longitudinal examination of life post-divorce, Hetherington (2003) identified six *patterns of adjustment* people exhibit after a divorce. People who exhibit the first pattern of adjustment are called **enhancers**. This group of divorced people adjusts very well after divorce. Their lives are actually better

Enhancers
Post-divorce, these people are successful in employment, relationships with their children, and physical and mental well-being.

a few years after divorce than they were before. Enhancers are more likely to be women than men. Ten years after divorce, 25% of women are living enhanced lives, but only 12% of men are. Enhancers are successful in employment, relationships with their children, and physical and mental well-being. Many enhancers went to college or embarked on new careers after their divorce, giving them a renewed sense of self-confidence. As their economic prospects improved, enhancers often made new friends and joined new social groups, leading to satisfying dating and even marital relationships a few years after divorce.

The second group consists of the **goodenoughs**. Forty percent of women and 45% of men fit into this category 10 years after divorce. They tended to do fairly well after the divorce without major traumas, but also without noteworthy successes. They tended to marry second spouses who were similar to their first spouses. They are good parents and are relatively happy. They just do not exhibit the kind of drive to achieve a higher quality of life that the enhancers do. Thus, their new lives resemble their old lives; they are good enough.

At one year post-divorce, fully 35% of men and 20% of women fit into the **seeker** category, but at 10 years after divorce they make up only 10% of the female and 18% of the male divorced population. Seekers anxiously seek a new partner to marry right away. They tend to have low self-concepts and are highly emotional. Men in this category need a woman to take care of them. Both men and women in this category gain their self-worth by being in a relationship. They have little sense of autonomy and can experience high rates of depression and anxiety. They tend to commit to a relationship too quickly and often repeat the same patterns they had in their first marriages.

At one year post-divorce, about 20% of men are **swingers**, about double the rate of women. At 10 years post-divorce, swingers make up less than 10% of the male population and less than 5% of the female population. Swingers tend to spend a lot of time in bars and clubs, take more drugs, have more sex, and engage in more antisocial behavior than most divorced adults. They also experience high rates of depression. Although swingers appear to live a fun-filled party lifestyle, they feel guilty about their divorces, miss their children, and several years after divorce end up in the *goodenough* category.

Some people end up as **competent loners** after a divorce. Ten years after divorce, 15% of women and 5% of men decided to stay single. These people are independent, happy, and self-confident. They have successful careers and many friends.

Finally, the **defeated** group is pretty large at one year post-divorce. About 38% of men and 27% of women were in this category. They had low self-concepts and high rates of depression and antisocial behavior. They tended to drink and use drugs, get into trouble with the law, and had many health problems. They had few skills to know how to move on after divorce. Fortunately, however, most people in this group did overcome their sense of loss and despair, so that by 10 years post-divorce, only about 10% of men and women are still defeated. They feel helpless, desperate, unhappy, and confused.

These findings illustrate that the majority of people experience early distress, confusion, and loneliness after divorce but most of them pull themselves out of despair and end up with relatively successful and happy lives. Interventions, counseling, and social support are crucial in those first two years, not only to prevent people from remaining in the *defeated* category, but for enhancing the positive role models their children see, role models who are able to cope with stress and still live positively.

Most children spend the majority of their post-divorce time with mothers, so let's see how women fare after divorce.

Effects of divorce on women

The most consistently reported effect of divorce on women is the sharp decline they experience in their income. Because many women must begin working for the first time or must work more hours than usual, as well as maintain primary physical custody of their children, their lives become more hectic and stressful. Custodial mothers face burnout, distress, social isolation, residential moves, and job instability, especially in the first two years after a divorce (Bray & Hetherington, 1993).

Over half of single mothers in the United States live in poverty (McLanahan, 2002). Compare this to only 24% of single mothers in the Netherlands and a mere 7% of single mothers in Sweden.

Goodenoughs
Post-divorce, these people do fairly well but do not exhibit the kind of drive to achieve a higher quality of life that the enhancers do; their new lives resemble their old lives.

Seekers
Post-divorce, these people anxiously seek a new partner to marry right away; tend to have low self-concepts and are highly emotional.

Swingers
Post-divorce, these people spend a lot of time in bars and clubs, take more drugs, have more sex, and engage in more antisocial behavior than most divorced adults; also rate high on depression.

Competent loners
Post-divorce, these people are single, independent, happy, and self-confident; have successful careers and many friends.

Defeated
Post-divorce, these people have low self-concepts and high rates of depression and antisocial behavior; tend to drink and use drugs, get into trouble with the law, and have health problems.

The very poor are in an even worse situation as their welfare benefits are docked one dollar for every dollar their ex-husbands pay in child support. Thus, if a poor man makes minimum wage and sends his ex-wife $100 per month in child support, she will lose $100 in her monthly welfare benefits. This means that laws meant to enforce child support payments will not necessarily improve the lives of poor women and their children after divorce. Regardless of child support laws, 60% of mothers who don't receive sufficient child support payments report that their ex-husbands simply cannot afford to make the payments (Parke & Brott, 1999). About 80% of fully employed men make their complete child support payments, while only 45% of men with unreliable or low-paying jobs do. Thus, *exosystem* influences can really affect the quality of mother–child relationships post-divorce.

Psychological issues for women and children

Regardless of who has custody or who is more financially viable, both mothers and fathers are at risk of psychological disorders and health problems after a divorce (Bray, 1990; Kiecolt-Glaser et al., 1987). Mothers are particularly at risk for psychological challenges because they spend the most time with their children after divorce and experience a marked decrease in parenting quality. For example, they monitor their children's behavior and whereabouts less consistently, and engage in more conflictual interactions, especially with sons (Bray & Hetherington, 1993). Mothers also find parenting adolescent daughters particularly difficult and their relationships often experience much conflict as their daughters start to break away from home and become more independent and mature, many times engaging in early sexual intercourse (Hetherington, 1992). Adolescent boys may emotionally and physically disengage from their mothers. However, most research suggests that these problems tend to even out after the first two years following a divorce, and that many teenage children, especially girls, form extremely close, mutually satisfying relationships with their mothers (Bray & Hetherington, 1993; Hetherington, 2003).

If children remain close to extended family and have peer and community support, both they and their mothers can bounce back from the initial stress of a divorce and can do extremely well both physically and emotionally. In fact, all parties may function more competently in a peaceful single-parent family than in a hostile and conflicted married family. Divorced parents experience more life satisfaction than parents who stay in unhappy or high-conflict marriages, especially in collectivist cultures or communities where the divorced parents have much social support and are not isolated from others (Gohm, Oishi, Darlington, & Diener, 1998). Reaching out to extended family and religious and community groups is especially important because it is difficult for most divorced parents to maintain a harmonious, cordial relationship with each other after divorce. Most families, even with joint custody, rarely discuss discipline or other co-parenting issues with each other. They live parallel lives that often do not intersect (Maccoby, Depner, & Mnookin, 1990). Unfortunately, it's fairly common for children to be dropped off and move from home to home delivering messages to and from each parent. This leads women and their children to experience high levels of stress.

Biological aspects of women's response to divorce

While challenges described above are fairly common in most people after divorce, there are individual differences depending on the mental health, financial stability, and social support the individuals have both before and after the divorce. There may even be biological differences. For example, in one study, women's brain firing rates (event related potentials or ERPs) were measured in waves called N400 amplitudes (Zayas, Shuda, Mischel, Osterhout, & Takahashi, 2009). The researchers exposed women to rejection-related words and acceptance-related words. Women whose N400s were extremely high in response to partner rejection-related words (their brains reacted by firing a lot) were also high on anxiety and low on avoidance. They paid more attention to threatening stimuli and could not avoid looking at rejecting words. Thus, their brains were highly vigilant, searching for threatening stimuli more than other women's brains were. This leads to a more intense experience of personal rejection than the ordinary person perceives, and a resultant level of high physiological arousal such as anxiety (high heart rate, sweating, and nervousness). These are all signs of insecure adult attachments, which can predict a much worse response to divorce than other, more physiologically and neurologically calm individuals might have. Thus, individual neurophysiology affects microsystem relationships and vice versa.

E. Mavis Hetherington (2003) conducted decades of research on divorced families, and found that securely attached women came to find a new sense of self-confidence, pursued their dreams, accomplished professional goals, and could live alone or with a new partner in a happy, harmonious life. Hetherington (2003) found that women's mental and physical health, as well as life satisfaction and sense of well-being, were lowest if they were involved in **pursuer-distancer** or **disengaged** types of marriage. *Pursuer-distancer* marriages involve nagging, hostility, and back-biting by wives. Their husbands then retreat and withdraw. These couples have intense angry conflicts. The *disengaged* couples live independent lives in the same house. They have few interests in common and different sets of friends. They don't fight but don't engage emotionally in positive ways either, including having very infrequent sexual relations. Women from either of these types of marriages exhibited high levels of anxiety, depression, alcohol problems, and physical ailments (such as stomach problems and infections) while still married, but all of these problems decreased within two years after their divorces, even though they were financially less well-off. Kiecolt-Glaser and Newton (2001) also found that women in high-conflict marriages showed immune system suppression responses during marital conflict and break-up. These results suggest that some women are more biologically vulnerable to the effects of stressors such as divorce, and that the relationship processes and attachment styles they experience can make divorce more or less stressful for them.

The effects of abuse on divorce outcomes

Other issues complicate divorces for wives who have experienced physical, sexual, or emotional abuse while married. Divorce becomes quite complicated for them because the mechanisms in place to help couples navigate through the court system, as well as the typical procedures of divorce, can further traumatize abused women (Bryan, 2006). Battered women have become accustomed to never asking for what they want, and always bowing down to their husbands' desires. They are often convinced they cannot live without their partner, that they are ugly, unlovable, and incompetent. It is very difficult for these women to navigate **divorce mediation** or other legal proceedings. In divorce mediation, each spouse sits in the same room with a mediator—often an attorney, psychologist, or other professional trained in divorce proceedings—who helps them come up with an amicable agreement on custody arrangements, dividing up property, child visitation, child support and alimony, dealing with scheduling activities, and so on. If the mediator is unaware of domestic violence issues, the woman may acquiesce to all the man wants and may end up with nothing after the divorce. Also, she may be stalked, attacked, harassed or otherwise tormented for anything she tells judges or attorneys involved in the divorce case. These women are often socially and financially isolated. They have no independent means to pay for their own attorney or learn about their legal rights. They also have little self-confidence and live in fear of voicing their desires or concerns (Bryan, 2006). Even when women disclose abuse, many attorneys and judges dismiss this information, consider it to be in the past, or fail to recognize its effects on the wives and children involved. They may further traumatize the victims by awarding the man the lion's share of joint property or minimizing his payments for child support because the woman was unable to express her needs adequately. Her husband may have also threatened her, telling her that she would lose custody of her children if she spoke out against him in court.

Just as divorce for women can range widely, from a life-enhancing experience to one of extreme fear and danger, likewise, men's reactions can run the gamut.

Effects of divorce on men

Men often fare better financially but worse psychologically after a divorce. This could be because they are more often the "leave-ee," and must deal with rejection and losing their main source of social support. Because men tend to discuss their feelings only with their wives, when a wife files

Pursuer–distancer marriages Marriages involve nagging, hostility, and back-biting by wives; husbands then retreat and withdraw; couples have intense angry conflicts.

Disengaged marriages Couples live independent lives in the same house; have few interests in common and different sets of friends; don't fight but don't engage in positive ways.

Divorce mediation A trained professional (attorney, psychologist) helps a couple devise an amicable agreement on custody, dividing up property, child visitation, child support and alimony, scheduling activities, etc.

for divorce, a man loses the person who has cared for him, has done the majority of the housework, cooking, child care, and other work that made his life easier. Men, like women, can suffer from depression, anxiety, loneliness, a sense of failure and grief, and insecurities about their self-worth after divorce (Hetherington, 2003). Divorced fathers often feel confused about their new roles. Are they their children's friend? Should they discipline the children or will this add to the children's distress? Many men have never spent substantial time alone with their children, responsible for all of their needs for long periods of time. Their wives facilitated and arranged their time with their children so they are now are unsure about what to do in terms of giving baths, choosing healthy menus, transporting children to activities, and so on (Lawson & Thompson, 1999).

Men in interracial marriages may have an especially difficult time because they may fear their ex-wife will marry someone of her own race, leaving their mixed-race children confused about their identities and perhaps feeling bad about their father's race. Lawson and Thompson (1999) found that black middle-class fathers kept consistent contact with their children after divorce and that black stepfathers encouraged the children's interactions with their natural fathers as well. All parents involved in this study of African American family divorce were extremely concerned about the adjustment of black children of divorce living in a racist society. African American mothers considered their stepchildren to be their own and wanted to ensure their well-being. African American fathers from lower socioeconomic classes reported needing support from other black men, helping them to get on their feet financially, and preventing their children from suffering the negative effects of divorce.

After a divorce, many men lose their sense of masculinity. They feel their worthiness as a father and provider has been shattered. They often feel the courts have unfairly ruled on the side of their ex-wives and that their needs have been ignored. Men may try to maintain a sense of independence and control over their lives, and not paying child support is one way they may reaffirm their identity as powerful and maintain control (Arendell, 1992).

Financial issues

While men in general benefit financially from divorce more than women do, financial struggles affect many divorced men who desire to provide adequately for their children after divorce. Laws have become more stringent in recent years in terms of requirements for hunting down "deadbeat dads," yet these laws may not actually be protecting women and children. For example, the federal child support enforcement law (Deadbeat Parents Punishment Act of 1998) allows the courts to garnish the wages of men who fail to pay their child support. This sometimes leads to men quitting their jobs or working under the table for cash. The government will then confiscate the man's tax refunds, and even put him in jail for failure to pay. They will revoke the men's business licenses, restrict their travel, and cancel their drivers' licenses. While these actions may ensure that some men pay their child support, they guarantee that many men will not be able to drive to work, conduct their business, and so on. In fact, poor men are unduly affected as research shows that the most common child support evaders are painters, roofers, truck drivers, mechanics, and those working construction (Parke & Brott, 1999). Most of these men are in unstable and low-paying jobs. Very poor men are penalized even more. Their welfare checks can be stopped if they fail to pay child support.

Interestingly, one study (U.S. General Accounting Office, 1992) even found that 14% of deadbeat dads on record were actually dead. Thus, statistics reflecting the number of men who do not pay adequate support may be inflated. Because research shows that the best predictor of whether a man will pay child support is the amount of visitation he is awarded, courts and ex-wives should ensure that divorced men spend ample time with their children (Parke & Brott, 1999). However, 20–50% of custodial mothers try to prevent such visitation or sabotage visits by saying a child is ill or unavailable when the father shows up for visits, unwittingly making both parents' and the children's lives more unmanageable.

Psychological processes fathers can experience

In an in-depth examination of divorced men's viewpoints, Arendell (1992) found that men characterized themselves as rational, logical family leaders who strove for an egalitarian marriage with their ex-wives. However, most of them were socialized under traditional gender ideologies and saw themselves and women as fundamentally different types of people. Many reported that their "rights as men" had been violated during marriage and divorce. This included a sense that they were seen as "sperm donors" or "bank accounts." Their "rights" were often referred to in a manner suggesting their masculinity was threatened. They no longer held complete control over their lives and their identity had suffered a blow. They felt they had been emasculated and were going to fight for their "rights" and even "snatch" their children if their ex-wives interfered in any way. Confused by societal pressure to be "real men," these fathers used anger and power struggles to mask their sense of loss, grief, sadness, and confusion over the divorce.

Interestingly, about 10% of the men in Arendell's (1992) sample were called "androgynous" in that they eschewed traditional male gender roles after their divorces and actually became more loving and better fathers. They felt personal responsibility for some of the divorce issues and knew that it was completely up to them to forge a positive relationship with their children. They wanted to co-parent positively with their ex-wives. Very few of the fathers in this study had ever had role models for being a good father. The best parents they knew were their mothers, sisters, or ex-wives, and so they had no understanding of how to merge the roles of masculinity with those of fatherhood in a positive, loving way, especially since most of their children lived with custodial mothers. However, this trend is becoming increasingly less common since the study was published. Today fathers are being awarded sole physical custody of children much more than they were back in 1992 when the Arendell study was conducted.

When fathers are given sole physical custody of their children, they report role strain and stress like custodial mothers do. To balance their many roles, they will often assign more responsibility to their children for chores and household upkeep than custodial mothers do. Also, they have more financial resources to pay for child care providers or housekeepers. Moreover, single fathers often elicit sympathy from female friends and relatives who come over to offer their services for cooking, cleaning, helping the children shop for clothes, and so on (Bray & Hetherington, 1993). Research shows that when men are involved in their children's lives post-divorce, children fare much better in the long run (Kelly, 2007). Let's look more closely at the effects of divorce on children.

Effects of divorce on children

Children of divorce are at increased risk for poor outcomes, so anything parents can do to improve their own functioning can benefit their children. Decades of research on the effects of divorce on children have led to some fairly mixed results. Some researchers suggest that divorce has long-lasting negative impacts on the majority of children (Wallerstein, 2005), while others find that negative effects may vary by age, gender, and personal characteristics of the children (Hetherington & Elmore, 2003). The largest effects seem to be for declines in father–child relationships after divorce and the smallest effects appear to be for self-concept changes in children (Lansford, 2009). Also, children examined in these more recent studies look more similar to children from non-divorced families, as compared to children from older research, who had more clear problems in adjustment after divorce (Amato & Keith, 1991b). This suggests that with divorce becoming more common in our *macrosystem* and the stigma of divorce declining, the negative effects of divorce in our *microsystems* also decline. This could explain the more positive adjustment of children from divorced families in recent cohorts. Moreover, those negative effects that do occur happen mostly in the year or two directly following the divorce and are mitigated over time.

Even when researchers discover negative child outcomes, they are rarely found in the majority of children examined in any given research sample. For example, poor adjustment indicators such as depression, anxiety, aggression, and relationship problems may be found in about 10% of the population of children who haven't experienced divorce, but in 20% of the children who have (McLanahan, 1999). A research result like this could be reported as "divorce doubles the risk for depression and anxiety in children" or it can be reported as "80% of children suffer no long-term effects from divorce." Both can be true at the same time and different researchers emphasize varied aspects of similar findings.

In general, it is true that children from divorced families have higher levels of internalizing symptoms like depression and anxiety and externalizing symptoms like aggression. They also suffer from higher rates of academic and social difficulties (Amato & Keith, 1991a). Very young children struggle with feelings of abandonment and often feel the divorce was their fault. They fear rejection by their non-custodial parent as well (Wallerstein, 1983). Children who experience divorce between the ages of 5 and 10 exhibit more internalizing and externalizing symptoms (Lansford et al., 2006). Older children may exhibit anger toward their parents and have problems in peer relationships and school work. Divorce occurring when children are between 11 and 15 years of age may result in a decline in academic performance (Lansford et al., 2006). Adolescents may take drugs, get pregnant, or drop out of school (Furstenberg & Teitler, 1994). As adults, children of divorce are more likely to be divorced themselves or suffer from unhappy marriages. They also tend to have lower levels of education and income, poorer health, and dissatisfaction with life (Cherlin, Kiernan, & Chase-Lansdale, 1995). Young adults whose parents were divorced often feel great anxiety and fear over failing in a future marriage (Wallerstein, 2005). They also feel less confidence in their ability to succeed in committed relationships (Whitton, Rhoades, Stanley, & Markman, 2008).

In one study, college students whose parents had been divorced exhibited decreased salivary cortisol levels, indicating their hypothalamic pituitary adrenal (HPA) axis (the brain's stress response system) had been altered. HPA axis abnormalities characterized by abnormally low levels of circulating stress hormones are related to immune functioning problems and frequent illnesses (Meinlschmidt & Heim, 2005). These students from divorced parents had salivary cortisol levels as low as students who had experienced the death of a close relative. These findings suggest that without good coping skills, social support, or counseling, adult children of divorce can be both physiologically and psychologically unprepared to enter into committed adult relationships. In fact, parental divorce has been repeatedly shown to increase an adult child's risk of poor marital relationships and future divorce (Amato & DeBoer, 2001). When both partners come from divorced families, their risks increase even further.

However, finding a patient, committed, mentally healthy, and emotionally supportive romantic partner can give the person confidence and can perform as a corrective attachment experience, helping the adult child of divorce break the cycle of dysfunction (Hetherington, 2003). As you know from previous chapters, we tend to search for adult romantic partners who confirm our internal working models regarding relationship quality and our views of ourselves as partners. Thus, we may attract people who have struggled with divorce themselves and it may take a conscious effort to look beyond the troubled folks and find a securely attached partner who can help us overcome the problems we experienced with our parents' divorce.

Despite the negative outcomes children of divorce often experience, it's difficult to separate the effects of divorce from the effects of problems that existed before the divorce. For example, many adjustment problems such as substance abuse, hostility, aggression, depression, poor communication and problem-solving skills, and financial struggles have been found in families who later divorced (Amato, 2001; Davies, Avison, & McAlpine, 1997). In fact, declines in children's academic achievement *after* divorce are almost completely accounted for by children's achievement and their family's conflict *before* the divorce (Sun & Li, 2001). Some scholars even argue for an **assortative mating** process, wherein people with similar challenges in personality, antisocial behavior, impulsivity, and poor relationship skills find each other and marry, increasing the risk for both divorce and poor outcomes in their children (Hetherington & Elmore, 2003).

Assortative mating
A theory that says people with similar challenges in personality, antisocial behavior, impulsivity, and poor relationship skills find each other and marry, increasing the risk for both divorce and poor outcomes in their children.

Therefore, we need to understand what factors, specifically, lead to poor outcomes in children of divorce. Most scholars would agree that family *processes* are much better predictors of child outcomes than is a simple *structural* evaluation of whether the family is married or divorced (Dunn, Deater-Deckard, Pickering, & O'Connor, 1998; Hetherington & Elmore, 2003; Lansford, Ceballo, Abbey, & Stewart, 2001). Unfortunately, many parents get caught up in SNAF ideals and stay together for the appearance of an acceptable family structure.

Should parents stay together for the kids?

In light of the poor outcomes that children of divorced families often experience, people wonder if parents should stay together for the sake of the children. Hetherington and Stanley-Hagen (1999) suggest that children in low-conflict families are *not* better off if their parents divorce, even if their parents are dissatisfied with their marriage. Similarly, Amato, Loomis, and Booth (1995) found that children's adjustment problems *declined* when *high*-conflict parents divorced, but that children's adjustment issues *increased* when *low*-conflict parents divorced. This increase in adjustment issues may be due to children in low-conflict families having no idea that their parents are unhappy so the divorce is a complete surprise. However, even children in high-conflict families only do better if the divorce actually *reduces* conflict. For example, if parents use the child as a pawn in their conflicts, question the child about the ex-spouse's dating life, make the child side with one parent over the other, or involve the child in hostile interactions between ex-spouses, those children will show more psychological problems after the divorce than they had when their conflicted parents were together (Amato & Afifi, 2006; Buehler et al., 1998). On the other hand, if an unhappy couple fights daily in front of the children and then they divorce and the conflicts end, the children will likely benefit from the divorce. Thus, it appears that the processes involved in family *conflict* are more detrimental to children's well-being than divorce, per se (Cui, Fincham, & Pasley, 2008).

If a divorce will reduce stress, conflict, and hostility in the home, it *is* better for parents to divorce than to maintain a negative home environment. If parents can live relatively happy lives in a lukewarm marriage, having two parents in the same home may be better for children than their parents divorcing. Keep in mind that, beyond the stress of the divorce itself, children also experience multiple transitions, such as changing schools, changing residences, the absence of previous friends and family, and parents' remarriage (Lansford, 2009). Therefore, many of the negative effects of divorce can be attributed to the cumulative nature of the changes children experience.

Divorce transition guides

Trained professionals (social workers, psychologists) who consult with families in order to minimize conflict and counsel parents on the best way to talk to their children about divorce, as well as co-parent after divorce.

Divorce transition guides, trained professionals such as social workers, psychologists, and lay relationship experts can consult with families in order to minimize conflict and counsel parents on the best way to talk to their children about divorce, as well as the best way to co-parent after divorce. Ahrons (2004) urges parents to consider the personality, coping skills, and maturity level of their children, in addition to the following points before deciding to divorce or stay together for the benefit of the children:

- Is your marriage so unhappy that you cannot parent your children effectively?
- Is the energy between spouses so negative that the children feel uncomfortable being at home?
- Do you and your spouse set a poor example for your children in terms of respectful, caring interactions, so they cannot learn how to be in a healthy relationship?
- Would divorcing mean extreme financial hardship, or a change in schools or home towns for your children?

If it's likely that the parents' and their children's lives will be better after a divorce, then divorce is usually better than staying together for the kids and being martyrs who may resent each other and the children later on. Adult children who leave home and find out their parents are divorcing often feel guilty and confused because they feel they made their parents stay together in an unhappy marriage. They can also feel angry that their lives may have been a sham or a lie. My students often tell me that they wish their parents had divorced early on so that they could have been happy, instead of staying together for the students' benefit and being miserable, or divorcing as soon as the student left for college.

Research results reveal that divorce can be extremely traumatic for children, but it can also be positive if it occurs in the right way.

Positive outcomes of divorce

Many children gain important strengths after recovering from the effects of divorce. They can become mature and responsible, exhibiting high levels of self-confidence and empathy, and good perspective-taking skills (Hetherington, 1998). Some children of divorce experience no ill-effects whatsoever, especially if their parents were able to keep their conflicts behind closed doors, support the mental and emotional health of their children, and engage in positive co-parenting with the child's best interests as their primary concern. Children with good coping skills who have positive relationships with both parents and are exposed to minimal levels of parental conflict tend to do well after divorce (Braver, Hipke, Ellman, & Sandler, 2004).

It's fairly common for parenting skills to be disrupted shortly after divorce. Parents are overwhelmed by the financial and daily life changes and they feel guilty, lonely, and confused. Contact with non-custodial fathers is greatly reduced (Braver et al., 2004). However, children who are able to maintain high-quality relationships with non-custodial fathers are better adjusted, even if the total amount of time spent together is less than it was previously (Amato & Gilbreth, 1999).

Research suggests that custodial mothers have a difficult time maintaining authority over children after divorce. They tend to become more like friends to their children and even engage in role reversals, where they tell their problems to their children and ask them for advice (Arditti, 1999). While adults may find this disturbing, the children themselves often report that their new relationship with their mothers is fulfilling and that their mothers sharing things with them is not a burden. They report that their mothers are still good mothers, guiding and even disciplining them. They like being treated like mature, responsible people, and girls especially rise to the challenge and really enjoy their newfound egalitarian relationships with their mothers (Arditti, 1999).

Children are not passive recipients of their parents' problems. They actively react to and construct the divorce experience for themselves. They decide to recreate their own ideas about family and accept or resist what is happening to them. Two children in the same family may respond to divorce in vastly different ways. They may enjoy their new lives or feel devastated over the changes they've experienced. Some may love seeing their non-custodial parent less, particularly if that person instigated a lot of conflict or was unfaithful, or they may feel a gaping wound left by that person's absence. This all depends on the child's maturity level, personality, temperament, coping abilities, and the social support provided (Smart, Neale, & Wade, 2001). For example, Smart et al. (2001) found that many children benefited from divorce in that it made them really appreciate their parents' strengths and how hard they (especially their mothers) work to ensure the child's happiness. They appreciated all the efforts parents made to minimize the negative impacts of divorce on them. They enjoyed being support systems for their parents and did not find their new confidante role to be a burden. Many of these children reported being like detectives, checking in on the well-being of their parents, and monitoring their behaviors for nuanced changes in personality or action. They paid close attention to their parents' friendships and work activities, to ensure their parents were doing as well as they said they were. They were worried about their parents' well-being and actively voiced their opinions about new partners.

Children actively cope with their parents' divorce and the majority of children grow up being well-adjusted adults, especially if they do not have to face other major life stressors or traumas after the divorce (Amato, 2001; Lansford, 2009; McLanahan, 1999). Dr. Robert Emery has constructed a wonderful website outlining many resources for divorcing families, including custody and visitation guidelines delineated by children's ages and stages (www.emeryondivorce.org). He has also devised a Bill of Rights for Children of Divorce. To see this list of rights, see the *FYI* box.

FYI

The children's bill of rights in divorce

Divorced parents still must fulfill their responsibilities to their kids, and in Dr. Emery's view, children should have rights in divorced families. Here is a Children's Bill of Rights in Divorce. If you can give your children these rights, you will have gone a long way toward fulfilling your responsibilities as a parent.

Every child whose parents divorce has:

1 The right to love and be loved by both of your parents without feeling guilt or disapproval.

2 The right to be protected from your parents' anger with each other.

3 The right to be kept out of the middle of your parents' conflict, including the right not to pick sides, carry messages, or hear complaints about the other parent.

4 The right not to have to choose one of your parents over the other.

5 The right not to have to be responsible for the burden of either of your parents' emotional problems.

6 The right to know well in advance about important changes that will affect your life; for example, when one of your parents is going to move or get remarried.

7 The right to reasonable financial support during your childhood and through your college years.

8 The right to have feelings, to express your feelings, and to have both parents listen to how you feel.

9 The right to have a life that is as close as possible to what it would have been if your parents stayed together.

10 The right to be a kid.

REDUCING THE NEGATIVE IMPACT OF DIVORCE

Co-parenting

Couples coping enhancement training

Best interests of the child
The contemporary legal standard whereby all decisions made in divorces and custody rulings include individualized decisions regarding what would benefit the children most.

Some early research suggested that joint custody was best for all children but today it's more difficult to make such blanket statements. There is some indication that no-fault divorces are better for children because fault-based divorces drag out personal problems and expose children to more conflict (Lansford, 2009). Courts are aware that each family is different and children have different skills and difficulties they face in their families. For example, joint custody would work for some children while others don't want to visit their non-custodial parent as often, especially adolescents who are involved in many school and community activities. Strict visitation schedules and forced custodial arrangements can actually harm children depending on their age, gender, relationships with their parents, and coping skills (Kline, Tschann, Johnston, & Wallerstein, 1989; Wallerstein, 2005). Today the focus is on the **best interests of the child**, the contemporary legal standard whereby all decisions made in divorces and custody rulings include individual judgments about what would benefit the children most. Therefore, judges will examine the individual family's situation in deciding divorce decrees and custody, visitation, and alimony/child support arrangements (Bryan, 2006). Today, long-term alimony payments to custodial mothers are rare. In fact, only 57% of custodial parents even receive a formal child-support award (Grall, 2007; Katz, 1994). The best interest of the child is usually established through the use of mediation (versus litigation). Parents who can come to an amicable compromise in their divorce and custody arrangements engender better relationships between family members and garner more involvement from non-custodial parents (Emery, Sbarra, & Grover, 2005). However, even with mediation, the mental health of parents and children can still be compromised and require counseling or therapy (Hetherington & Stanley-Hagen, 1999).

Most previous divorce interventions focused on the children and were implemented in schools, usually in the form of support groups where children whose parents were divorced could share their feelings with each other and form a supportive network of friends (Hetherington & Stanley-Hagen, 1999). Facilitators would help children reduce the stigmatizing feelings surrounding their parents' divorce and aid them in developing skills to cope with it. These interventions, while well-meaning, have not been found to be as effective as psychotherapy with individual families. Interventions with parents, teaching them coping, communication, and co-parenting skills, tend to be quite effective in easing the parents' transition into a new lifestyle. Interventions for both parents and children (involving psychoeducation about divorce and how to handle conflicts) have also been found to make the immediate transition period easier for children, but they have not yet been shown to improve children's long-term functioning (Gilman, Schneider, & Shulak, 2005; Hetherington & Stanley-Hagen, 1999; Pruett, Insabella, & Gustafson, 2005).With a dearth of promising results stemming from divorce intervention studies, parents are best off taking a preventative approach and proceeding with their divorce in a way that might mitigate any negative effects on family members.

Ford (2001) argues that instead of seeing divorce solely as a negative experience, people can choose to view it as an avenue for self-improvement. They can learn from the experience and live a better life than they lived before. In order to do this, first people must accept that the divorce happened and surrender to that fact, instead of fighting it or ruminating over "what ifs." They must take responsibility for their part in the failure of the relationship, forgive both themselves and their ex-spouse, consider all the choices now available to them to empower their lives in a positive direction, and then take concrete steps to create a new future. Part of this is letting go of the past is to develop new social circles, hobbies, and skills, and redefine one's view of family and parenting roles (Everett & Everett, 1994).

In order to minimize a divorce's impact on children, parents must make a concerted effort not to demean their ex-spouse. They must work together to make a consistent routine, enforce consistent rules and discipline, and encourage children to express all the feelings they have. Each parent must encourage the children to maintain a positive relationship with the other parent and give age-appropriate honest answers to any questions they ask about the parents' relationship and the divorce. Parents should be honest about their own feelings but not act out in anger, rage, jealousy, or resentment. They should also recognize that their ex-spouse and their children may not share their feelings and be able to accept that as legitimate. Parents need to communicate directly and not use children as go-betweens, spies, or messengers. If the ex-spouse forms a new romantic partnership, the divorced person should not ask the children questions about this new partner or make any negative judgments (Matta, 2006).

Co-parenting

Many parents are embroiled in anger, resentment, feelings of betrayal, loss, confusion, and loneliness. It's often difficult for them to see their ex-spouse, communicate about the children, or be present psychologically for their children's needs.

In this regard, **co-parenting classes** can help parents negotiate these tasks. These courses help parents understand the effects of divorce on children, develop co-parenting contracts they can sign, and allow them to ask questions. Co-parenting classes help parents work together toward the common goal of protecting their own mental health and that of their children (Braver et al., 2004; Bryan, 2006). Today, 44 states have laws supporting parental education programs in order to protect children from parental conflict, to increase parenting quality, and to ameliorate the negative effects of divorce on children (Bryan, 2006). The programs can educate parents about the legal process and help them find alternatives to litigation. Mental health and legal professionals usually work together

Co-parenting classes
Courses that help parents understand the effects of divorce on children, develop co-parenting contracts they can sign, help parents work together to protect their own mental health and that of their children.

in both live workshops and media presentations for the families. They work to understand the needs of all parties and make rational, objective custody, visitation, and monetary support recommendations to the court.

These programs also try to identify and assist victims of domestic violence, understanding their special needs and vulnerable position during a divorce. The American Psychological Association (1994) suggests that during the divorce, the parents hire only one expert (versus the old system of each parent having his or her own attorney), preferably a mediator, who can be objective and fair to both parties. Keeping the divorce out of the hands of attorneys and litigation reduces animosity between divorcing partners. While many parents struggle to even talk to each other civilly after a divorce, after the first two years, about half of parents are able to effectively co-parent (Forgatch & DeGarmo, 1999; Whiteside, 1998). However, this means that about half are not.

Beyond parents' behaviors, when children are able to keep their same group of friends, stay at the same school, and maintain their hobbies and activities, they are better able to regulate their feelings over the divorce and feel empowered, with higher levels of self-esteem (Pedro-Carroll & Alpert-Gillis, 1997). These findings illustrate the importance of a stable *mesosystem* for children of divorce.

Special masters
Professionals who consult with parents regarding their children's needs before, during, and after divorce.

Parenting coordination office
Locates psychologists to serve as special masters to assist parents in custody problems.

Courts are now aware of much of the research on successful divorce and currently employ professionals to work with families to ease the process of divorce. Many states employ **special masters**, professionals who inform parents about the best practices for maintaining a warm and supportive household for both of their homes when children are around. Other similar professionals include family court advisors, or divorce coordinators. These professionals consult with parents regarding their children's needs before, during, and after the divorce. They make recommendations to both the parents and the court. Employing special masters and mediators instead of lawyers reduces the amount of time families spend in court, increases parents' satisfaction with the divorce process, increases the amount of time non-custodial parents spend with their children, and increases civility between parents. Unfortunately, these practices have yet to lead to improvements in children's mental health or long-term functioning after divorce (Emery, Matthews, & Wyer, 1991; Emery, Sbarra, & Grover, 2005).

In 2009, the first court-established and court-funded **parenting coordination office** opened in Washington DC. It locates psychologists to serve as special masters to assist parents in custody problems. The psychologist and a team of psychology graduate student interns work to improve parental communication and sensitivity to children's needs, and assess children's development academically, psychologically, and socially (Munsey, 2009). They can refer families to family counseling or other services they may need to navigate a more successful divorce. However, program evaluations are limited so the effectiveness of these programs in meeting their goals is currently unknown.

Couples coping enhancement training

One program that has been evaluated for effectiveness on hundreds of families and shows much promise in *preventing* divorce is **Couples coping enhancement training (CCET)**. This program focuses on changing maladaptive thinking patterns, improving interactions between partners, improving

© John McPherson/Distributed by Universal Uclick via CartoonStock.com

Erica hated it when her ex tried to upstage her when he picked up the kids.

FIGURE 12.3 What actions can couples take to minimize the negative psychological effects of their divorce?
© www.CartoonStock.com

stress management techniques, increasing positive communication, improving problem-solving, opening partners' minds to fair and equitable arrangements in their lives, and understanding the obstacles their relationships face (Widmer et al., 2005). Three hundred couples reporting extremely low marital satisfaction were exposed to the treatment and followed longitudinally for one year. They were compared to a matched control group. A year after the treatment, couples in the intervention reported less fighting, more positive feelings and sharing, better communication, and a greater sense of togetherness. Even after two years, marital quality was maintained at higher levels than at pre-test and in comparison to the control group. Improvements were also found in problem-solving and active listening, with decreases in whining and defensiveness. Couples had more empathy for their partners' viewpoints and decreased their hostile attacks on each other. The key to effective therapy is for couples to enroll early rather than later. Widmer et al. (2005) report that up to 50% of couples relapse after therapy because they enroll after their problems grow far too big to tackle.

When divorce cannot be prevented, about two thirds of women and three quarters of divorced men will eventually remarry. Let's take a closer look at those families.

> **Couples coping enhancement training (CCET)**
> Program that focuses on changing maladaptive thinking patterns, improving interactions between partners, improving stress management techniques, increasing positive communication, improving problem-solving, etc., in order to prevent divorce.

REMARRIAGE

- Variables influencing remarriage rates
- Special challenges in stepfamilies
- Different viewpoints on stepfamilies
- Healthy ways to remarry and stepparent

Due to low life expectancy and the lack of medical technology and hygiene in previous centuries, most people had experience with stepparents after one of their natural parents died. Men were usually expected to remarry right away after their first wife's death in order to maintain the productivity of the family and give birth to further children to replace the ones who died (Visher & Visher, 1993).

Today, the word "step" tends to have negative connotations. Lay language often refers to being treated very badly as being treated "like a stepchild." Mythology is also replete with images of the evil stepmother, often witch-like and sadistic, a woman who lives to make the lives of her stepchildren miserable after they had already lost one mother through death. In fact, the origin of the word "step" is the old English "steop," which means "bereaved" or "orphaned." The term "step" evolved over time to refer to the death of a biological parent (Visher & Visher, 1993). Today, most of us are either part of or know someone in a stepfamily, also called a **blended family**, if there were children from each parent's previous life.

> **Blended family**
> A remarried family wherein each partner has children he or she brings to the partnership.

The divorce rate for second marriages is quite high, with estimates ranging from 65% to 75% (Visher & Visher, 1993). It may seem puzzling that people who experienced a painful failure of their first marriage would decide to marry again within four to six years. It may have something to do with our biochemistry. While very few animals are monogamous, humans experience repeated surges of oxytocin (the bonding chemical) and dopamine (the pleasure neurotransmitter) when involved in long-term pair bonding or monogamous relationships (Curtis, Liu, Aragona, & Wang, 2006). It may be in our nature to seek long-term companionship with one person. Combine that with a tenacious drive to succeed, and we see people continuously attempting to form marriages that last. However, not all people have the same likelihood of remarrying. Let's examine some of the factors that influence this choice.

Variables influencing remarriage rates

Remarriage rates vary widely based on variables like divorce initiation status, ethnicity, age, education, and cultural context, showing the impact of each system of the bioecological model on people's decisions to remarry. For example, the person who initiated the divorce is more likely to remarry than the person who was left (Sweeney, 2002). African American and Hispanic people are less likely

TABLE 12.1 Current marital status by age and sex for those ever divorced: 2004.
Source: U.S. Census Bureau, Survey of Income and Program Participation (SIPP), 2004 Panel,
Wave 2 Topical Module.

Age	Men			Women		
	Now divorced (%)	Now married (%)	Now separated (%)	Now divorced (%)	Now married (%)	Now separated (%)
Total, 25 years and over	44.5	52.2	1.5	47.4	43.5	2.4
25 to 29 years	62.7	36.7	0.6	58.8	40.4	0.8
30 to 34 years	50.2	48.8	1.0	53.0	42.9	3.5
35 to 39 years	52.6	46.2	1.0	45.5	49.9	3.8
40 to 44 years	50.1	48.7	1.2	49.7	46.1	2.8
45 to 49 years	47.2	50.2	2.1	47.3	48.6	2.8
50 years and over	39.5	55.8	1.5	46.0	40.3	1.8

to remarry than are European Americans (Sweeney, 2010). Also, older versus younger women tend to wait longer to divorce their first husbands and usually do so only if they feel emotionally prepared to seek out and enter into a new marriage (Sweeney, 2002). See Table 12.1 for the relationships between age and gender and current marital status for previously divorced people.

In the past three decades, women with higher levels of education were less likely to marry and remarry but this trend has reversed. For example, both first marriage and remarriage rates have increased in the past 10 years for college educated women. They view marriage as an emotional partnership and do not have to worry about gaining financial security from the relationship. These women also tend to have higher remarriage satisfaction rates than women with a lower level of education, and are less likely to divorce their second husbands. These patterns of change based on education have not been found for men (Isen & Stevenson, 2010). Cultural context also plays a role in the decision to remarry. For example, if a culture emphasizes the need to keep first marriages together and eschews divorce, people are less likely to divorce and remarry (Meggiolaro & Ongaro, 2010). Remarriage can also vary by region within the same culture. For example, Meggiolaro and Ongaro (2010) found that women living in northern versus southern Italy had quite divergent remarriage patterns.

Special challenges in stepfamilies

While some second marriages are much better than the couple's first marriage and stepchildren come to love their new parents, this usually takes some time. It commonly takes about two or three years to recover from a divorce, and then it takes between five and seven years for a stepfamily to feel like a real family (Hetherington & Stanley-Hagan, 2000). Even for stepfamilies that succeed, it's usually a difficult road and they are much more likely to end in divorce than first marriages. Second marriages are more likely to be characterized by both fewer positive and fewer negative interactions, indicating a withdrawn communication pattern, as compared to first marriages (Sweeney, 2010). Also, remarriages do not exert the same benefits for mental and physical health that first marriages do (Sweeney, 2010). Second marriages tend to allow high levels of autonomy in each partner, from having separate bank accounts, to separate sets of rules for each person's biological children (Sweeney, 2010). Stepchildren have more behavioral problems and psychological adjustment troubles than biological children (Bray, 1999a). Boys in stepfamilies are more likely to run away or drop out of school than other boys (Bray & Kelly, 1998). Some research suggests that if the second marriage does not involve any children, its chances of survival are just as good as those of first marriages. It seems that the adjustment problems involving children put monumental stress on the newly formed union (Preece & DeLongis, 2005).

Why are stepfamilies more conflicted and likely to divorce than first marriage families? They face many challenges with which first families may not have to cope. If the first spouse died, the second marriage may have to deal with the legacy of the dead person, including feelings of longing, grief, and lingering love for that person. The living spouse may feel guilty over marrying a new person and exposing their children to a "replacement" parent. If the first marriage ended in divorce, the partners may struggle with feelings of failure, low self-confidence, and lingering anger, fear of betrayal, and lack of trust. Completely new roles have to be defined for all parties involved (Bray, 1994; Cherlin, 1978). There may be new stepsiblings, and eventually half-siblings, with the accompanying extra sets of grandparents, aunts, uncles, and cousins. Holidays have to be negotiated sometimes between eight different households. The stepparent must struggle with how to approach disciplining children who may have had a different life history than his or her own natural children (Booth & Edwards, 1992).

Stepparents may have unrealistic expectations about how quickly the children should accept them in the parental role and may butt heads with older or more independent children. Because of their previous divorce, stepparents may desire a quick evolution into a real family and may pressure themselves and others, forcing love and intimacy between family members. Bray (1999b) argues that the pervasive belief in the superiority of SNAFs over other family forms may become a self-fulfilling prophecy such that when people enter into a stepfamily they view as flawed, less-than, or not a real family, it is doomed to fail. In stepfamilies, children may compete for the attention of their biological parents and may squabble with stepsiblings over possessions, sleeping arrangements, the enforcement of rules, and so on. The presence of stepsiblings has been shown to impact the well-documented higher levels of academic problems stepchildren experience in school (Tillman, 2008). Sadly, only about 30% of adult stepsiblings think of their stepsiblings as real siblings (Ahrons, 2004), while half-siblings who share one biological parent usually do feel like real siblings, which can lead to conflict, insecurity, and jealousy between half- and stepsiblings (Tillman, 2008).

Adolescent stepsiblings may be confused by feelings of sexual attraction for their new siblings and may be confused about what the boundaries and power dynamics should look like. Stepfamilies overall tend to be more sexually charged than first marriages because the parents are newlyweds and may touch, hug, kiss, and require more time alone or in the bedroom than children were used to with their first families. Adolescent stepchildren may also feel attracted to their stepparent and may flirt or try to get their attention in other ways.

Other challenges arise if the family has to move to a new neighborhood with new schools, stores, churches, co-workers for the parents, and new sets of friends that must be integrated into the fold. In addition, there may be negative feelings or interactions involving ex-spouses. Many children may feel a divided sense of loyalty, not wanting to accept the stepparent because they think that means a rejection of their biological non-custodial parent. Parents may spoil their own biological children in an attempt to assuage their guilt over the divorce. Children may rebel and challenge the new stepparent in order to chase him or her away, in a fantasy attempt to bring their biological parents back together. In this regard, children must be allowed to openly grieve the loss of their former life. It must be acknowledged that it is very difficult to get used to two sets of rules and schedules, ways of doing things, and family dynamics. All parties involved must deal with a sense of their first families being failures and may enter a stepfamily with little faith, much fear, and a sense of holding back their true feelings.

Legal and financial issues

There are legal and financial issues to be negotiated as well. The new couple must arrange their wills differently and think about custody of children, especially if they have children together. Insurance policies, inheritance, bank accounts, and property must all be considered. They may have contrary financial philosophies and may enter into the marriage with debts. They have to reconfigure their retirement policies and college savings for the children, and must decide whether the stepparent will adopt the stepchildren (Nance-Nash, 2004). Step-fathers may feel extremely guilty over leaving their biological children and supporting a new family financially (Visher & Visher, 1993). Nance-Nash (2004) suggests that couples sit down with a financial planner, discuss their financial goals and monitor each others' spending styles and money management techniques for at least one year before deciding to get married.

There is also an issue regarding the legal roles of stepparents. Stepparents are only required by law to financially support their co-residential stepchildren in 15 U.S. states and that responsibility ends with divorce or death of the biological parent (www.stepfamilies.org).

In the absence of a stepparent adopting the stepchildren, the stepparenting role has not been legally formalized. Stepparents really have no rights to their stepchildren after a divorce or death of the children's biological parent, unless there was a legal will specifying such issues. They have no right to visit their stepchildren, who have usually been sent to live with their non-custodial biological parent, even if they raised the children in their own home for years. They also have no obligation to pay child support, even if they had been financially responsible for the children since their infancy (Mason, 2003). Stepchildren are not allowed to sue for the wrongful death of a stepparent and get no inheritance when that person dies. They get no retirement, death, or disability benefits, all of which specifically exclude stepchildren. They may, however, be eligible to receive social security benefits since *federal* law tends to assume a financial commitment to stepchildren.

Challenges for stepmothers vs. stepfathers

Stepparent–stepchild relationships tend to be more conflicted than biological relationships. Stepparents offer stepchildren less in the way of guidance and support, and both step- and biological parents monitor their children's behaviors less after a divorce or remarriage. Stepparents report feeling less connected to and responsible for their stepchildren than their biological children (Tillman, 2008).

Even within stepfamilies, however, there is wide variation in how stepparents function and adjust. For example, because the vast majority of stepfamilies consist of a biological mother and a stepfather, most children have to adjust to a new male in the home instead of a new female. The gender and age of the stepchildren play a role in how well the family adjusts to a new marriage. Younger children adjust more quickly to a stepparent than adolescents do. Also, boys tend to bond more quickly with new stepfathers than girls do (Bray, 1999a). Girls report being very uncomfortable with hugs and affection offered by new stepfathers. Girls, who have often grown extremely close to their mother after a divorce, may resent sharing her with a new husband. The longer the children had lived in a mother-custody family, the more difficult the transition and the more conflictual their relationship with their new stepfather (Montgomery, Anderson, Hetherington, & Clingempeel, 1992). If the mother and stepfather cohabit before the marriage and give the children time to adjust, the children will be better adjusted after the marriage. Children living with stepfathers have more academic and behavioral problems than children living with stepmothers or in single-mother homes (Tillman, 2008).

Interestingly, girls living in remarried stepfather homes begin puberty about a year earlier than girls in other family configurations, influencing early sexual activity. It is suggested that the biochemical response of having a non-genetically related male in the home, in combination with life stress associated with divorce and remarriage, lead a girl's body to trigger the pubertal response sooner, in order to quickly reproduce under threatening circumstances (Tither & Ellis, 2008). Because remarried families tend to monitor children less well, adolescent girls in stepfather families may become more promiscuous and are more likely to get pregnant (Hetherington, 1993), as well as use drugs and alcohol.

While stepfather–stepchild relationships have their own challenges, most research shows that stepmother–stepchild relationships are actually more strained. Because stepfathers usually take a "hands-off" or disengaged approach to parenting stepchildren, they may seem less threatening. Stepmothers often come in and their husbands expect them to immediately take over the mommy role, cooking, cleaning, taking the stepchildren clothes shopping, chauffeuring the children around, and so on. Stepchildren have usually been under the primary physical custody of their biological mother and they feel intense loyalty to her. They may see this new mother as trying to replace the children's biological mother and they may resent her for that (Preece & DeLongis, 2005). Stepmothers routinely report role overload. They are expected to do their stepchildren's laundry, cook more, shop more, and be involved in their stepchildren's homework and activities. Their authority is often challenged and they are routinely told things like "You're not my real mom; I don't have to listen to you!" Stepmothers can feel overworked, under-appreciated, and always under attack.

In contrast, biological fathers are less likely to increase their workloads when their children visit. Instead, they maintain their typical roles and expect their new wives to play the same role their ex-wives played for their biological children. Also, the biological father may over-compensate for his guilt over the divorce by spoiling his own children, buying them gifts, and disciplining them less. If the stepmother also has biological children, this can lead to conflicts over favoritism, inconsistent rules, and confusing expectations for biological versus stepchildren (Preece & DeLongis, 2005). Stepmothers report dealing with conflict and their feelings of being taken advantage of by either confronting people in the home, or by stuffing down their feelings, sulking, and giving people the silent treatment, both of which may lead to higher levels of hostility and conflict in the family (Preece & DeLongis, 2005).

Because non-custodial fathers are less involved in their children's lives, stepfathers may not only be seen as less of a threat than a stepmother, they may be a welcomed addition to the family, providing both emotional and financial support. However, some research suggests that *adolescent* children may have a more difficult time with stepfathers than stepmothers. If their parents divorced when they were young, they may find themselves wanting closure or a deeper relationship with their non-custodial biological father. This may lead them to push their stepfathers away. Bray (1999a) found that about 20% of adolescent children, mostly boys, left their biological mother/stepfather homes and went to live with their biological fathers, even after years of living in the former home, in an attempt to bond with their biological fathers.

It should be evident by now that stepfamilies face some unique challenges. However, all is not negative. Stepfamilies tend to be more flexible, laid back, and open about discussing problems than first marriage families are. They are more

FIGURE 12.4 What specific challenges do remarried families face in comparison to first marriage families?
Photo © UpperCut Images/Alamy.

willing to confront problems head-on and try to work things out. They approach life in a more practical way and tend to be more egalitarian in terms of gender role expectations and work–life balance (Bray & Hetherington, 1993). The challenge, then, is to ensure that more stepfamilies are prepared for the many obstacles that lie ahead for their newly blended family, thereby reducing the divorce rate and other problems they might face. Much of this has to do with the way stepfamilies are viewed, which has implications for their success.

Different viewpoints on stepfamilies

Stranger model
A viewpoint wherein a stepparent is treated like an acquaintance, instead of a family member, in terms of his or her relationship with stepchildren.

Sociobiological perspective
A viewpoint that argues that evolutionarily, we are inclined to care for our biological kin in order to continue our gene pool; we are less likely to love or care for children with whom we share no genes in common.

Most state laws work from a **stranger model**, in that a stepparent is treated like an acquaintance, instead of a family member, in terms of his or her relationship with stepchildren. Stepparents are not allowed to sign permission slips for school, consent to medical treatment for stepchildren, and so on. If the biological parent dies, the child is usually sent to live with a biological non-custodial parent, even if the child doesn't know that person. This model may stem from research done from a **sociobiological perspective** (e.g., Popenoe, 1994). This perspective argues that evolutionarily, we are inclined to care for our biological kin in order to continue our gene pool. Sociobiologists argue that we are less likely to love or care for children with whom we have no genes in common. They cite research showing higher rates of child abuse and child death in stepfamilies versus those with two biological parents. Also, remarried couples are more poorly integrated into their communities and extended families, are less committed and more willing to leave the marriage, tend to have lower socioeconomic status, and exhibit poorer psychological adjustment than people in first marriages (Booth & Edwards, 1992). In a survey of over 2,000 people across four ethnic groups (Latino, African American, Asian American, and European American), people uniformly reported that adult children should help their aging biological parents but not their aging stepparents (Coleman, Ganong, & Rothrauff, 2006).

Despite these findings that may support a sociobiological interpretation, it cannot be denied that millions of adoptive, foster, and stepfamilies love their children as much as biological parents love theirs. MacDonald and DeMaris (1995) found that newly married couples with both step- and biological children had the same levels of conflict as families with only biological children. Moreover, if we examine the absolute numbers of stepchildren with serious behavioral or emotional problems, the rates are about 20–25% in the clinical range, versus about 10–20% in the non-stepchild population (Bray, 1999a). Thus, the majority of both stepchildren and non-stepchildren are well-adjusted. Furthermore, if given the time and support needed to adjust, stepfamilies can evolve over time to be virtually indistinguishable from other families in terms of relationship quality, level of conflict, and emotional and financial dependence.

Dependency model
A viewpoint which assumes that a stepchild was financially dependent on a co-resident stepparent and so stepparents have rights and responsibilities for their stepchildren.

In loco parentis
Laws allowing a stepparent to gain custody of stepchildren if the biological parent dies and it can be proven that the stepparent played an essential parenting role in that child's life.

In contrast to state laws developed from a *stranger model*, federal law usually works from a **dependency model**, which assumes that the stepchild financially relies on a co-resident stepparent (Mason, 2003). These laws, however, are inconsistently implemented and poorly understood by most attorneys and judges. Some states have **in loco parentis** provisions where the stepparent would gain custody of the stepchildren if the biological parent died *and* it could be proven that the stepparent played an essential parenting role in that child's life. This is more easily implemented if the biological non-custodial parent also died or abandoned the family, which isn't always the case. For example, I recently consulted on a child custody case for a boy whose father died in a tragic boating accident. This boy, who was 12 years old, had lived with his father and stepmother for five years. During that five years, his biological mother, who lived 3,000 miles away, kept in touch by mail and visited once or twice a year. After the boy's father died, the biological mother wanted custody of the child and a custody battle ensued. The stepmother also wanted custody, saying she had raised the child every single day for five years. If courts work using *the best interest of the child* standard, what would you decide if you were the judge in this case? What custody situation would be in the best interest of this child? It's not an easy decision to make when a child's future is at stake, and both parents clearly love and want to raise the child.

In an interesting answer to some of these problems, England passed the 1989 Children Act, which provided for three legal parents to be specified for children. If a stepparent has been married to a biological parent for over two years, he or she can petition to be the third legal parent for that child. If accepted, the petition specifies that the stepparent will be responsible for that child until he or she reaches age 16. If the couple divorces, that stepparent also has the right to visitation (Mason, 2003). Having three caring parents can certainly benefit most children.

Healthy ways to remarry and stepparent

The most important strategy people can take after a divorce is serious self-reflection. They need to think about what role they played in the failure of the first marriage and what they need to work on in order to have a successful second marriage. This could include going to counseling or therapy, talking to trusted friends and family members, or just taking time to be alone, reflect, and heal. Making a list of one's own positive qualities and asking supportive people to comment on it, build on it, or point out discrepancies can help one gain self-insight (Anderson & Clandos, 2003). Starting new hobbies, improving skills, building new social networks, and dating without serious expectations can build self-confidence. Before entering into a new serious relationship, the divorced person must understand exactly who he or she is and what he or she wants out of life. If someone is too desperate, rushes into a sexual relationship, compares the new dating partner to the ex, or calls/emails/texts too often, these may be red flags that the person is not ready to be in a healthy new relationship (Anderson & Clandos, 2003).

A person should be happy, positive, joyful, and satisfied being alone in order to make a good partner. If the person engages in excess eating, drinking, or drug use, is depressed and incredibly lonely, withdraws during holidays, and constantly talks about their ex, he or she needs more work before entering into a committed relationship (Anderson & Clandos, 2003).

After a divorced person does decide to remarry, he or she must clearly define expected partner and parenting roles ahead of time, so that children, family, and friends know what to expect in terms of scheduling, rules, boundaries, relationships with exes, and so on. The new couple must put concerted effort into making their relationship a priority and show a united front in parenting all children involved. They must make it clear that manipulation, favoritism, coalitions, or jealousy will not be part of the new family (Everett & Everett, 1994).

A blended family has a better chance of making it if their extended family and community members welcome them, offer to help out with child care or other transitional needs, and all sets of grandparents are open and accepting of the new partners and children. Stepparents should be loving and supportive, discussing their problems behind closed doors and supporting the non-custodial parents as important people who are partners in co-parenting (Hetherington & Stanley-Hagan, 2000).

Marsiglio (2004) found that stepfathers can play crucial roles in helping their stepchildren develop. They can help their stepchildren build their social capital, meaning tapping into their own skills and unique qualities, as well as connecting them to resources in the community, like spiritual leaders, teachers, sports, and neighbors. They can work actively to enhance the quality of the child's life, and part of this includes being an ally to the biological father. While not having to be close friends, the two men can be cordial and communicative, and work together to raise well-adjusted children. Marsiglio's (2004) stepfathers reported that stepfathering allowed them a second chance to be good fathers, and made them re-evaluate what it meant to be a man, including the vital role men play in the lives of women and children. Mason (2003) even argues that if the stepfather makes sufficient income, the family can arrange to reduce the biological father's child support payments and agree to care for the children both financially and emotionally. This gesture can enhance the biological father's feelings of affection and appreciation for the stepfather, and can reduce tension between the exes.

BUILDING YOUR STRENGTHS

Positive stepparenting

1 Do not try to discipline stepchildren until they view you as a parent.

2 Understand stepchildren will always love their non-custodial biological parent and that you will not replace that person.

3 Encourage a positive relationship between all family members and the ex-spouses.

4 Invite the ex-spouses to family events, holiday gatherings, and children's activities, and send them copies of awards children win, letters from teachers, or other noteworthy information.

5 Don't expect the stepchildren to accept you right away. Proceed with caution but in a warm, supportive, friend-like manner.

6 Do not demand love or force children to call you "mom" or "dad." Allow them to develop their feelings gradually and encourage them to express all feelings they have.

7 Work through your feelings of jealousy or resentment over the close bond between your new spouse and his or her biological children.

8 Acknowledge that it's OK if you feel differently about your children and your stepchildren.

9 See the children as individuals with different interests and feelings, and who are at different developmental levels with different needs.

10 Roll with the challenges as a unified group, acknowledging challenges and working together to overcome them.

Source: Matta (2006), p. 40.

In order to build a secure and harmonious stepparent–stepchild relationship, the stepparent must enter into the family first as a friend and confidante. He or she must not attempt to discipline the stepchildren right away, but should focus on disciplining his or her own biological children only (Bray, 1999a). Even when stepparents use authoritative parenting skills and are supportive and warm, they can be ignored or challenged by stepchildren until the children feel they are actually *their* parents.

Bray (1999a) found that after two to three years, most stepchildren responded well to authoritative parenting, including discipline, by stepparents. Parents should communicate openly and honestly with each other on all issues involving the children. They should plan for various eventualities (such as what to do if a child gets into trouble at school) and allow the biological parent to implement the agreed-upon punishments or consequences. Parents should remain united and supportive of each other, even when things get tough. The key to a healthy stepfamily is a strong partnership (Matta, 2006). For more on positive stepparenting, see the *Building Your Strengths* box.

CHAPTER SUMMARY

The U.S. has the highest divorce rates in the industrialized world but the reasons for this are not yet clearly established. For the past 100 years, divorce rates have increased steadily, except for an anomalous dip in the 1940s and 1950s. However, they leveled out in the 1990s, with a steady rate of about 46% of first marriages ending in divorce. Rates for second marriages are higher, at about 66%.

Historically, women had virtually no right to divorce their husbands in many cultures around the world, but husbands could divorce their wives at will. Men usually received custody of children and women were sent away from the family. After industrialization, opinions changed, from viewing men as the responsible parents to seeing women as naturally nurturing, better parents. Thus, divorce and custody proceedings more often went in the direction of the woman's case. However, women still had to prove their husband had done something wrong, such as being unfaithful or deserting the family. In the past few decades, with women's rights movements making headway, women began to fight for their right to divorce more easily without having to prove misdeeds like battering by their husbands. The 1970s brought no-fault divorce laws to many areas, where couples could separate due to "irreconcilable differences," and a person could file for divorce without the consent of the other partner.

The process of divorce is a complex one. People usually stay in unhappy marriages for years, becoming more and more emotionally distant, or conflicted, over time. They weigh the pros and cons of their decisions very carefully, having to consider custody, financial, and family implications, among other things. After they divorce, they have to readjust to a new identity, often facing friends, family, or community members who have an allegiance with their ex-partner. Divorced people have to figure out how to date, engage in sexual relations, and co-parent their children with their ex. There are many different ways divorced people handle these pressures. Some drink, party, and date freely. Others sink into a depression and feel hopeless. Yet others take the opportunity for education or self-betterment, and feel a new lease on life. Men and women experience divorce differently, as do people of differing economic statues, ethnic backgrounds, sexual orientations, and cultures. Divorce also affects people's neurological and immunological functioning, illustrating that all systems of the bioecological model affect and are affected by divorce.

Divorce also affects children differently, depending on their age, gender, the presence of half- and stepsiblings, and the level of conflict present. Some children are devastated, do poorly in school, have behavioral and emotional problems, and so on. Other children learn a lot about relationships, coping, and skill-building. They see the experience as an opportunity to learn, grow, and enhance their self-confidence.

The majority of men and women who divorce eventually remarry. Second marriages have higher levels of conflict, more complications, and higher rates of dissolution than first marriages. Stepmothers often feel overwhelmed by instant childrearing and housekeeping responsibilities as they marry men with children. Stepfathers are much more likely to be seen as a friend instead of a parent and children tend to view stepfathers less negatively than stepmothers.

Stepparents have very few legal rights in terms of caring for stepchildren's medical or educational needs. They are often treated as strangers instead of family members, and if a biological parent dies, stepparents often have no custody or visitation rights, unless the child's other biological parent has also died. Positive adjustment in stepfamilies is possible, however, through open communication, clear financial and childrearing plans, and easing into the role of disciplinarian after building rapport with stepchildren.

KEY TERMS

assortative mating	divorce mill	no-fault divorce
best interests of the child	divorce transition guides	parenting coordination office
blended family	emotionally distant or neutral	pursuer-distancer marriages
competent loners	affective style	seekers
co-parenting classes	emotionally volatile affective style	separation agreement
couples coping enhancement	enhancers	sociobiological perspective
training (CCET)	goodenoughs	special masters
defeated	in loco parentis	stranger model
dependency model	joint legal custody	swingers
disengaged marriages	joint physical custody	
divorce mediation	migratory divorce	

WEBSITES FOR FURTHER EXPLORATION

http://www.divorcesupport.com

A very comprehensive website for all facts related to divorce. It includes information on every state's laws, policies and procedures related to alimony, child support, parental rights, domestic violence, property division, and support for divorcing people. It includes great articles on financial planning and grandparents' rights, and has several books for purchase.

http://www.stepfamilies.info/about.php

The National Stepfamilies Resource Center is a non-profit organization located at Auburn University, which disseminates evidence-based resources for stepfamilies. It helps people find counselors in their area who specialize in work with stepfamilies, has good articles about co-parenting, dealing with difficult exes, handling divorce, interpreting laws, raising teens in divorced families, and so on. They have a research-based training program for professionals who would like to develop specific skills for working with stepfamilies and the training has an additional curriculum for working with Christian families.

http://www.suite101.com/references/adult_kids_of_divorce_akod

A repository for articles on all topics related to families. This specific page has dozens of helpful articles for adult children of divorce. Topics include dealing with new stepparents, step and biological sibling rivalry, dating after divorce, and so on.

CHAPTER 13
GROWING OLDER IN FAMILIES

All older people smell, are forgetful, are slow, they live in the past, they are a burden on the rest of society, and being old is a condition that should be avoided at all costs.

(Stephen Pugh, gerontological social worker, on prejudice against the elderly (2002, p. 163))

LEARNING OBJECTIVES

- To understand historic and contemporary views of aging both in western and non-western cultures

- To get a better understanding of the multidimensional changes that occur with age

- To recognize the factors that are related to healthy aging in multigenerational families

- To understand how seniors interact with their partners, adult children and grandchildren in contemporary families

OVERVIEW: CULTURAL AND HISTORICAL BELIEFS ABOUT AGING

> Historic trends
>
> Contemporary trends around the world

Stephen Pugh's quote above sums up the stereotypes that permeate American society. In a culture obsessed with youth, superficial appearances, and perfection, it's no surprise that older people are less valued, dismissed, and even despised by some. Media images of old, frail, lonely people with hunched backs and bad memories have pervaded our culture and have influenced the common viewpoint that aging is a terrible thing. In this traditional view, people think that those between 60 and 100 years of age play no valuable role. They see seniors as useless people who burden their families as well as social welfare systems. However, this chapter will show that aging in the twenty-first century is a whole new ball game. Most 60-year-olds today are young, active, healthy, and far from considering retirement. They work, love, and play hard. They are vital members of their families and communities. In fact, growing older in contemporary society may be for many people one of the best experiences of their lives.

Life expectancy in western cultures has increased by three decades over the past 100 years. In industrialized nations, there are more old people today than there are young adults (Fisk & Rogers, 2002). In western nations, the proportion of people over 65 is steadily increasing, while low birth rates mean that the proportion of people under 15 is decreasing. In 1900, only 4% of the population was over 65; today, 13% of the population is over 65 (Hirshbein, 2001). In 1900, people in developed countries could expect to live on average about 48 years for men and 51 years for women. Today those ages are 73 for men and 80 for women (Kinsella & Gist, 1998). The longest living women today live in Japan (average life expectancy of 83), with the lowest female life expectancy being in Uganda (average age 43). In 2002, there were still two countries (Qatar and the Maldives) where men outlived women, but no longer. Statistics show female life expectancy surpassing that of men in virtually every country (Barford, Dorling, Smith, & Shaw, 2006).

As a consequence of these trends in life expectancy, four- and five-generation families are becoming more normative now than in any other time in history (Hutter, 1998). Multigenerational bonds are increasingly common as family members live longer. We are more likely now to see grandparents and stepgrandparents playing key roles in the stabilization of families after crises like divorce, death, incarceration, and substance abuse occur in the middle generation.

Today, the SNAF ideal is no longer of much relevance to most western families. In addition to having very few traditional nuclear families, we've changed from a pyramid-shaped population, with lots of young people at the base, and very few at the top in the oldest generation, to a bean-pole-shaped population with fewer people in each generation, but increased verticality, or more generations stacked on top of each other (Bengtson, 2001). Today for the first time in history, 70% of people will enjoy having four grandparents still alive when they reach adulthood.

While macrosystem influences, like the stereotypes of seniors listed in the opening quote, are often negative in the western world, it's important to note that such influences vary markedly around the world. For example, most non-western cultures revere their elders and give them crucial and respected roles to play in the family and community at large. Even in the U.S., in spite of the negative stereotypes, most intergenerational relationships are positive and supportive, with only about 20% of them being high in conflict or estranged (Bengtson, 2001). Let's take a closer look at historical and cultural perspectives on aging.

Historic trends

In previous centuries, older people were a rare commodity. Life was hard and people died young. In ancient Rome, for example, living to the age of 30 was quite a feat. Thus, when people reached old age, others viewed them as wise and treated them with reverence. Older people were often consulted on issues like potential marriages, political decisions, military decisions, and healing practices. It was widely accepted around the world that families cared for their elderly when they became sick or infirm.

In the U.S., before the 1930s, elders were also greatly respected and considered wise. For example, any articles or books written about aging were written by elders themselves and often discussed lessons they had learned or wisdom they desired to share with younger generations. Seniors themselves were considered the experts on aging (Hirshbein, 2001). People were interested in hearing stories about older peoples' past lives, experiences, and accomplishments. They saw elders' lives as teaching significant lessons. People viewed their experiences as heroic. Due to this type of reverence for those who reached old age in those early decades of the twentieth century, the Life Extension Institute (LEI) opened in 1914. Medical professionals there urged people to have preventative health care visits with their doctors in order to find disease or illness in its earliest stages and begin interventions to prolong life (Hirshbein, 2001).

Positive views of seniors slowly began to change after World War I. In fact, a prominent child psychologist of the 1930s, Lillien Jane Martin, even argued that children's behavioral or academic problems could be traced back to poorly adjusted grandparents in their lives (Hirshbein, 2002). She argued that old people needed to be taught how to adjust to old age, and she opened the Old Age Guidance Center for this purpose. Martin argued that it was unreasonable for seniors to expect their family members to listen to their stories or reflect on their memories. She taught old people to forget the past and express an interest in their children's and grandchildren's lives instead.

Other professionals of the 1930s characterized old people as child-like, rambling on about nothing, and argued that they were self-absorbed. They were also thought to suffer from intellectual decline because psychologists found their processing speed decreased, leading to poor performance on traditional intelligence tests, which relied in large part on timed tasks (Hirshbein, 2002). Some scholars argued that 80-year-olds had the same mental functioning as 8-year-olds. Psychologists suggested that elderly men and women should disengage from work and homemaker roles, respectively, and accept their growing irrelevance to modern culture.

During the Great Depression, people viewed older workers as threats, keeping jobs from which younger people could benefit. In the past, most people worked until they were physically incapable of doing so and retirement was an uncommon enterprise. But in 1935, the development of the Social Security program ensured that older people would have funds for basic necessities and so could leave the job market to younger workers. The care of older people was beginning to be viewed as a public duty and nursing homes sprouted up as the field of gerontology emerged in 1942 (Hirshbein, 2001).

With rapid technological advancements and two world wars under our belts, by the 1940s, physicians became the experts on aging and old people's stories were considered irrelevant to fast-paced modern lives. In places where scientific medicine usurped traditional healing practices, people began to view aging as a clinical condition in need of medical intervention (Hirshbein, 2001). Chronological age became associated with rapid decline in cognitive faculties and physical health. This medicalized view of aging led physicians to write about old age in terms of social and medical problems that science must address.

The pathologizing of aging had an impact on all seniors but people of color and sexual minorities suffered particular indignities. For example, gay elders were usually closeted in the early twentieth century, living clandestinely in straight married families or existing as old bachelors or spinster aunts. In Britain, people in the LGBT community invented a new language "Polari," which allowed gay people to communicate to prevent being oppressed, attacked, or jailed (Pugh, 2002). Around the world gay elders attempted to create communities to support each other in their old age. But in the minds of the general public, they were sinners, perverts, or were thought to be asexual and thus were invisible.

With the United States emerging as a world power after World War II, the lives of previous generations seemed quaint, idiosyncratic, and less important to us. The availability of consumer goods that promised to extend the lifespan, bring back youthful features, or improve memory increased. Capitalist endeavors seized on people's new fears of becoming old, unattractive, unwanted, and decrepit. Science and technology spread into people's consciousness as they wanted to look only toward the future and not dwell on the past. Old age and its attendant infirmities were considered a national crisis. With better medical care, social security, and longer lifespans, people in the mid-twentieth century began to wonder what could be done about the impending explosion of the aging population and its negative effects on society. These were topics of much political and media attention. **Disengagement Theory** (Cummings & Henry, 1961), one of the first sociological theories about the aging population, posited that seniors should prepare for death by disengaging from the world around them, isolating themselves from people and activities.

Contemporary trends around the world

Compare the western characterizations of elders to the way other cultures treat elders. Unlike English, most other languages have different words for *you* based on respect for elders. For example, in Spanish people use *usted* to address elders, while *tu* is used for younger people. In Turkey, elders are served meals first, and upon greeting, you kiss their hands and then put them to your forehead (Coles, 2006). Many people in Asian cultures bow when elders enter a room. A 1963 Japanese law mandated that family members love, respect, and care for elders. Korea has a "Respect for Elders" holiday. Most Native American clans have utmost respect for elders. For example, the Sioux call newborn babies "little grandmother" or "little grandfather," to instill in them the goal of being a wise and valuable elder member of the tribe. Denmark provides free home health care for all infirm seniors (Coles, 2006). These examples suggest a radically different contemporary philosophy of aging around the world, one of care, respect, and nurturance of elders. From the bioecological point of view, it becomes apparent that microsystem relationships between elders and their kin, and even individual seniors' biological health and well-being, can be influenced by larger macro- and exosystem forces.

The United States is a diverse country, and there are many differences in the experience of aging within contemporary American culture, depending on one's socioeconomic status, stress level, health care access, and immigration history (Coles, 2006). For example, white seniors are most at risk for poor quality of life, as they are least likely to have a relative care for them due to individualistic values, low birth rates and smaller extended kin networks. Families of color are more likely to live in multigenerational households than white people are. For example, in many Chinese families, sons live with their parents and daughters-in-law care for the elders. African American families are more likely to live in poverty than European Americans and they also experience more chronic health problems. Even with these struggles, however, about 65% of both white and black multigenerational families usually live in the *seniors'* households, suggesting that the seniors are helping to care for the younger generations instead of vice versa. Many white middle-class adult children move back in with older parents after a divorce or college graduation.

Whites have a greater tendency to place seniors in nursing care facilities. About 5% of white seniors live in nursing homes, making up the majority of the institutional care population. Only 11% of nursing home residents are African American (Jones, Sonnenfeld, & Harris-Kojetin, 2004). The majority of African American seniors live at home and are cared for by home health care providers. Asian Americans virtually never use either service but rely solely on family caregivers. Only about 2–3% of all families of color place their seniors in nursing homes (Coles, 2006). This is due to belief systems centered on familialism, but also due to lower socioeconomic status. In addition, families of color tend to live in multigenerational households before an elder becomes impaired, so the family simply continues on with their same way of life.

For cultural minorities or immigrant families, nursing homes may be frightening because they speak English, serve strange food, and practice unfamiliar lifestyle rituals. Luckily, more nursing facilities that cater to specific groups like African American or Latino families are opening up across the western world (Coles, 2006).

Not only is there much diversity across groups of seniors and their families, but within the aging population itself, wide variation exists in how positively or negatively a person will experience growing older.

Disengagement Theory
The outdated idea that seniors should prepare for death by disengaging from the world around them, slowly isolating themselves from people and activities.

MULTIDIMENSIONAL CHANGES WITH AGE

| Physical development |
| Sexual development |
| Cognitive development |
| Socioemotional development |

Multidirectional
The idea that development in old age can be both forward/positive, and backward/negative.

Functional age
The age you appear to be (i.e. how old you feel, how many activities you can still do).

Chronological age
How old you are in years.

Aging is not a uniform phenomenon. Like development at other stages of the lifespan, old people experience complex changes with increased capacities in some areas and decline in others. Aging is therefore, **multidirectional**, meaning we become more positive or well-developed in some areas and more negative or declining in other areas. For example, our ability to understand and remember important information about world events increases, while our ability to remember insignificant facts, like where our car keys are, decreases.

People also have a **functional age**, how old you feel, how many activities you can still do, and so on, and a **chronological age**, how old you are in years (Bedford & Blieszner, 2000). For example, an 80-year-old who runs a marathon has a *chronological age* of 80 but a *functional age* of perhaps 40 or 50.

Development also occurs within a particular historic period and is shaped by particular contexts and social conditions. How people age is related to culturally defined role expectations and societal opportunities given to the elderly person (Bronfenbrenner, 1995). For example, African American elderly people tend to have more chronic health problems than European Americans but they have higher rates of subjective well-being and self-report that they are actually less impaired than whites report themselves to be (Bedford & Blieszner, 2000). This may be due to cultural norms that dictate that family members care for each other so that impaired elders have a strong social and community support network. Older African Americans report that strong sibling relationships are one key to helping and supporting them through their old age.

Some Asian cultures can also be characterized by strong sibling bonds. Brothers provide financial and material support for their sisters and sisters provide emotional support for their brothers. Asian cultures tend to focus on strong family bonds and emphasize children's responsibilities in caring for aging parents. In Hong Kong, an elder is not even allowed to enter a nursing home if he or she has living children. These places are reserved for the childless (Bedford & Blieszner, 2000).

African American elders attribute their relative sense of positive adjustment to their extensive support network. But their relative sense of positive adjustment could also be reflective of a **cohort effect**.

Cohort effect
The idea that how people develop is influenced by the generation they belong to, or the time period in which they were born.

FIGURE 13.1 What do you think this woman's chronological and functional ages are?
Photo © Robert Michael/Corbis.

Quality of life assessment

Instructions: Next to each item, enter a number that best matches your response. Each number you may enter is associated with four possible response choices, based on different types of questions asked. However, enter only one number in each blank, which corresponds to the appropriate response among the four listed.

0 = not satisfied; not at all; poor; no
1 = fairly satisfied; a little; fair; sometimes
2 = very satisfied; a lot; very good; yes

1 How would you rate your quality of life? _____

2 How satisfied are you with your health? _____

3 How much does physical pain prevent you from doing what you want to do?* _____

4 How much do you need medical treatment to function in your daily life?* _____

5 How much do you enjoy life? _____

6 To what extent do you feel your life to be meaningful? _____

7 How well are you able to concentrate? _____

8 How safe do you feel in your daily life? _____

9 How healthy is your physical environment? _____

10 Do you have enough energy for everyday life? _____

11 Are you able to accept your bodily appearance? _____

12 Have you enough money to meet your needs? _____

13 How available to you is the information you need in your daily life? _____

14 To what extent do you have the opportunity for leisure activities? _____

15 How well are you able to get around? _____

16 How satisfied are you with your sleep? _____

17 How satisfied are you with your ability to perform your daily living activities? _____

18 How satisfied are you with your capacity for work? _____

19 How satisfied are you with yourself? _____

20 How satisfied are you with your personal relationships? _____

21 How satisfied are you with your sex life? _____

22 How satisfied are you with the support you get from your friends? _____

23 How satisfied are you with the condition of your residence? _____

24 How satisfied are you with your access to health services?   _____

25 How satisfied are you with your transportation?   _____

26 How often do you have negative feelings such as blue mood, despair, anxiety or depression?*   _____

Scoring: For items 3, 4, and 26 only, the items marked with an asterisk (*), *reverse code* your score. If you had a 0, make it a 2, if you had a 1, keep it, if you had a 2, make it a 0. Then add up all of your points.

Scores between 0 and 13: You are pretty dissatisfied with your life. You might think about making some major changes, getting some psychological counseling, talking to important people who can support you, trying to locate needed services, and then evaluate what else could be done to enhance your quality of life.

14–26: You are fairly satisfied with your life but you may be missing out on some passion and exhilaration, some real joy. Think about new things you'd love to try, changes you'd like to make, ways you can improve your lifestyle, and take some risks to enhance your quality of life. Seeing a counselor and looking for sources of service provision and support may do you good.

27–39: You've got a pretty good thing going; you feel happy about your life. Take time to express gratitude for the things and people that give you such a balanced and wonderful life. And try a few new things to enhance your quality of life even more. Focus on items with low scores.

40–53: Your quality of life is through the roof. Congratulations on making it this far in life with a variety of strong and supportive ecological contexts supporting your development. Think about how you got where you are and how you could perhaps lend a hand to help someone else get what you have. Gratitude and lending a helping hand can only enhance your own quality of life even more.

Source: Adapted From the World Health Organization Quality of Life Group (WHOQOL, 1998b)

Note: *Self-Assessments* are not meant to diagnose, treat, or cure any physical or mental problem; they are for informational purposes only, and are meant to spur discussion.

Cohort effects occur when the way people develop is influenced by the generation they belong to or the time period in which they were born. African Americans living today may see their lives as relatively peaceful and better off than their ancestors had it, so their *cohort* of people—born in the 1930s, for example, compared to blacks born in the 1830s—has a generally positive attitude about life.

Multidimensional
The idea that change occurs in all dimensions of development simultaneously (physical, social, cognitive, emotional, spiritual, sexual).

Taken together, these research findings illustrate that development in old age is **multidimensional**, meaning that change occurs in all dimensions of development simultaneously. Positive aging, or well-being in later life, is characterized by physical, mental, spiritual, and social adjustment, not just a lack of disease or infirmity as we age (Power, 2003). To check out your own sense of personal well-being, see the *Self-Assessment* box "Quality of Life Assessment."

While we may immediately think of gray hair and wrinkles as signs of aging, these characterize only one dimension of development, *physical*. There are also diverse changes that occur in *sexual*, *cognitive*, and *socioemotional* dimensions of development (Steverink, Westerhof, Bode, & Dittman-Kohi, 2001). Even though each dimension changes at the same time across our lifespans, and each dimension intertwines with the others, it may be helpful to examine each dimension separately in order to look at these multidimensional changes in more depth.

Physical development

Physical development is an area that typically declines with age. Starting at about age 30, the body begins to decline from the peak performance experienced in the twenties. We start to see an increase in fat, especially around the middle. The cardiovascular system weakens, lung capacity declines, and bones begin to lose density (Fleg et al., 2005). Eyesight deterioration is almost universal in those over 40. Poor focus, decreases in night vision, and macular degeneration are common problems in those in middle and late adulthood. Much of this decline can be prevented, or at least slowed, through healthy diet and exercise. Consistent exercise and other healthy lifestyle choices have a noticeable impact on preventing or reducing the rate at which various biological systems age. For example, people in their seventies, as well as younger people, benefit from incorporating exercises like weight training into their lives. Resistance training, with weights, with bands, or in water, is a key behavior that prevents bone loss, reduces injuries during exercise, builds muscle strength and resilience, and speeds up metabolism to burn calories more effectively (Layne & Nelson, 1999). This is important for family members' quality of life. The longer seniors can stay strong and active, the more time they will get to stick around and see their children grow up, play with grandchildren, and even experience the birth of great-grandchildren.

Even though physical decline is normative, older people are healthier today than in any previous generation. While our great-grandparents had a life expectancy of 45, today most people consider middle age to *begin* at 40 and continue to about 65 (Berman et al., 2001). Most people are active and healthy, and live longer than ever before. The inescapable fact remains, however, that we will all begin aging at some point. Although researchers aren't exactly sure what makes people physically age, there are many theories, including ideas about free radicals, or rogue oxygen molecules, destroying our cells, as well as theories about simple wear and tear catching up with us over time. Researchers around the world are trying to find the key mechanisms underlying the aging process. If they find what they're looking for, and the aging process can be significantly delayed or slowed down, people would be able to spend a lot more time together as a family, with fewer heartbreaking deaths at younger ages, and the ability to create more memories within multigenerational households.

One of the more promising discoveries has to do with the **Hayflick limit**, which is the maximum number of times a cell can divide. Cells divide throughout our lives and as they do so, our chromosomes wear down. At the end of our chromosomes are DNA caps called **telomeres**. Telomeres are dense repetitive DNA strands, which protect chromosomes from damage. Telomeres get shorter every time a cell divides. There is new research showing that people who experience chronic traumatic stress or many adverse lifetime events have shorter telomeres, suggesting that stressful experiences actually change the genetic structures in our body's cells and lead to a shortened lifespan (Epel, 2009). The stress hormone cortisol and the metabolic chemical insulin are also culprits in shortening telomere length.

Because telomere length is related to longevity, the more quickly telomeres shorten, the less time we have left to live. In addition to stress, obesity and malnutrition can knock off a few telomere lengths (Epel et al., 2004). These findings suggest that we can enhance longevity through increasing both physical and mental health. To enhance longevity, then, we need to protect young people from trauma, ensure proper nutrition, and get sufficient exercise.

Telomeres also seem to be involved in some cancers. Ornish et al. (2008) found that a radical lifestyle-changing intervention for men with prostate cancer was associated with a marked increase in the quantity of *telomerase*. Telomerase, an enzyme that adds DNA to the ends of chromosomes, can counteract the effects of stress on telomere damage. This suggests that dietary and exercise changes can actually alter genetic structures and improve longevity, illustrating the constant interplay between biology and environment.

As discussed previously, adult women live longer than men. They also have longer telomere length than adult men. This correlation merits further investigation. One explanation for the difference in telomere length is that women may have greater levels of social support and work at less stressful careers than men do. Such differences in stress and social support could account for the difference in health and longevity between the sexes. Thus, this biological research has implications for marriages and long-term partnerships. If we might be able to increase male partners' life expectancy by reducing damage to their telomeres, this could have a profound effect on the rate of female widowhood and could ensure couples' more years to spend together. At this point, we just don't know the causal mechanisms behind these trends in aging, but cellular structure appears to be a promising avenue of investigation.

Hayflick limit
The limit placed on the number of times a cell can divide.

Telomeres
Dense repetitive DNA strands at both ends of a chromosome, which protect chromosomes from damage; get shorter every time a cell divides; shorter telomeres are related to higher stress and shortened life expectancy.

Another physical part of development that tends to change as we age is our sexual function. While you may not be interested in hearing about older adults' sex lives, sexuality is a very important part of life, across all phases of adulthood.

Sexual development

Today, the general public may characterize older people of both sexes as not having, needing, or wanting sexual intimacy. Many people cringe at the thought of seniors engaged in sexual relationships. Rest assured, however, that when *you* are old, you may be pleased to know that sexual activity is not only possible, but is completely normative for seniors, and not just those who are married. About 75% of never-married older men and 50% of never-married older women are sexually active.

Older women's sexuality

When women pass middle age, they often feel intense pressure to maintain their beauty and their sex appeal. They may feel afraid that mates will look elsewhere for romance or sexual gratification, due to macrosystem forces that devalue the beauty of older women (Proulx, Caron, & Logue, 2006). However, in recent years, a new phenomenon has piqued the interest of the public and the media: *cougars*. Cougars are described as older women who "stalk their prey": younger, attractive men. Cougars are characterized as sex-starved and aggressive. There isn't any research on whether these stereotypes exist in real people's relationships, but some research suggests that older women are increasingly likely to have intimate relationships with younger men than in the past. For example, Andrew Beveridge, a demographer, was contacted by the *New York Times*, to analyze census data in order to see if the cougar trend was increasing. Beveridge found that from 1960 to 2007, marriage rates have doubled for women five and ten years older than their husbands. Today the number is still quite small but growing steadily (about 1.3% of marriages consist of younger husbands and wives who are 10+ years older) (Kershaw, 2009). In a study conducted for the Association for the Advancement of Retired Persons (AARP) on over 1,000 women aged 40–69, Montenegro (2003) found that 20% of women had dated men at least five years younger than they.

In a qualitative study examining the intimate dynamics between eight couples where the wife was significantly older, husbands said they liked an older wife because she was more mature, had more life experience, and was established in her career (Proulx, Caron, & Logue, 2006). Women reported that their husbands kept them feeling young and energetic. Both parties reported feeling better knowing that they would probably die around the same time, instead of the women being left alone for years, which is common in other marriages. Both partners also reported trouble with stigma from family and friends about their marriage. Men could more easily overlook these challenges but women were more insecure, wondering if they could compete with younger women, or if their husbands would lose interest as they aged. They had more doubts about the future of the relationship than their husbands did. These feelings expressed by couples show the impact of mesosystem, exosystem, and macrosystem forces on the dynamics of their microsystem relationships. As discussed in Chapter 4, sexuality is a multidimensional process, not just a physiological act. It often involves complex dynamics from members of one's families of origin, their grown children, co-workers, and friends. Let's take a little time, however, to examine the biological part of sexuality for older women.

As women age and they are no longer able to reproduce, estrogen levels decrease, and they enter into **menopause**, which is technically marked by the cessation of the menstrual period. However, menopause is a long process, beginning on average in a woman's forties and ending at about age 51, but this varies widely. For some, menopause is extremely stressful, consisting of uncomfortable symptoms like hot flashes and insomnia, but for most women menopause is uneventful and is actually a welcome change (O'dea, Hunter, & Anjos, 1999). While some women experience mood swings or depression, these symptoms are rarely serious for most women. On the plus side, post-menopausal women no longer need to worry about birth control, pregnancy, tampons and

Menopause
The time during which a woman stops menstruating; the process can take years to complete and may be accompanied by uncomfortable physical and mental symptoms.

pads, or being as insecure as they once were. Typically, middle-aged women are more confident in themselves and their bodies, enjoy sexual relations, and are more financially stable.

Some sexual changes that women may experience as they go through menopause include: loss of vaginal elasticity, decreased vaginal lubrication, and lowered libido. Women may experience less blood flow to the genitals, a more difficult time reaching orgasm, and less intense orgasms. Loss of vaginal elasticity can be reduced through regular masturbation and sexual activity, and personal lubricants can help remedy decreased vaginal lubrication. A full medical assessment can inform a woman about whether short-term hormone replacement therapy, or other traditional or alternative medicinal treatments, might alleviate these symptoms (Berman et al., 2001).

It's true that most women experience hormonal decline as they age, but this isn't necessarily correlated with a decline in sexual desire. Instead, many women report being *more* desirous with age and hormonal fluctuations (Levy, 1994). Levy (1994) found that the two best predictors of whether a woman maintained an active sex life in older age were a positive self-image and the availability of a partner. Some older people don't have a partner, which can explain some of the research findings on declines in sexual frequency for seniors. Married and cohabiting people across the adult lifespan have more frequent sex than single people do.

Remember that the brain is one of the most influential organs impacting the quality of our sex lives. Women who are happy with their relationships and highly satisfied with their sex lives actually live longer than those who aren't. Women usually rate satisfaction based on quality of sexual experiences, instead of quantity. Also, satisfaction is not always correlated with achieving orgasm. Kissing, petting, oral sex, and other ways of building intimacy can be just as satisfying for older couples as intercourse (Berman et al., 2001).

In one of the few studies on the **old-old**, people between 80 and 100 years of age, Crooks and Baur (1990) found that 88% of men and 72% of women fantasized and dreamt about sex often. Instead of a general trend for all seniors characterized by a waning sex life, these authors argue that we should focus instead on individual differences. People who enjoyed a robust sex life in their younger years are likely to work harder to maintain that sex life as they age. People who were less interested in sex will probably be so later in life as well. The key to maintaining a healthy sex life as you age is to remain mentally and physically healthy. Good cardiovascular health allows more blood flow and oxygen to the genitals and the brain, which is the most important sexual organ of all. For women especially, frequent masturbation can keep the vaginal walls and uterus firmer and healthier. In terms of sex in the later years, it's a matter of "use it or lose it."

Old-old
The group of seniors between 80 and 100 years of age.

Older men's sexuality

There tends to be a double standard regarding older men compared to older women (Bazzini, McIntosh, Smith, Cook, & Harris, 1997). In western cultures, macrosystem stereotypes often characterize older men as "silver foxes," indicating they are sometimes seen as distinguished and attractive, while older women are judged more harshly for their physical appearance. They can also be "dirty old men," implying that they have continued sexual desire into old age. Viagra, a drug that increases blood flow to the penis, is widely known in society and is accepted as something that might be necessary for older men who want to continue to have sexual intercourse (Berman et al., 2001). People seem more ready to accept sexuality as part of older men's lives but are less accepting about it for women. And unlike the negative connotations associated with the word "cougar," there really isn't a similar derogatory label for older men who date younger women. People much more easily accept a relationship where the man is five to ten years older than the woman compared to the other way around. Men can continue their sexual activity late in life, as well as being able to father children at much older ages than women can have them. However, they also experience some physiological changes in sexuality as they age.

McKinlay and Feldman (1994) examined the changes in sexuality that come with age in a study of over 1,000 men between 40 and 70 years of age. They found that sexual problems like erectile dysfunction were correlated with age. As the participants got older, they reported less frequent intercourse, fewer nocturnal erections, more trouble attaining and maintaining erections, less firm erections, less frequent ejaculation, and fewer ejaculations with masturbation. Some reported an increase in pain with intercourse. They also reported diminished libido, fewer sexual thoughts during the day, and fewer sexual dreams at night. Despite these changes, most of the older men in this study also reported high levels of satisfaction with their sex lives and reported that they were happy with their partners and their partners with them. Those who had experienced prostate surgery had more sexual difficulties (McKinlay & Feldman, 1994). Also, men who were obese, had high levels of anger, or were depressed had less sex, while those in good physical health had more sex and were more satisfied. Men who exercised regularly were less likely to experience erectile dysfunction.

Declining testosterone in older men has been linked to an increase in depression later in life (Morsink et al., 2007). In an interesting study of healthy 70–80-year-old men, the highest levels of depression were found in men with the lowest levels of testosterone. Surprisingly, the link between hormone levels and depressive symptomatology was only present for European American men and did not hold true for African American men. This could be due to black men exhibiting low levels of depression in general, so that hormones have little chance to exert an effect. It could also be related to differential reporting rates of depressive symptoms. Fortunately, testosterone supplements have been shown to improve mood in older depressed men (Morsink et al., 2007).

In a unique set of analyses, frequency of intercourse predicted longevity for men. Studies in Wales, Sweden, and the U.S. showed that mortality was negatively related to the number of orgasms a man had (above two per week). This suggests that, provided couples are capable, having sex two times per week can add two years to a man's life, and sex once per day can add eight years (Berman et al., 2001). Keep in mind, however, the difference between correlation and causation. While it's true that men who have sex regularly live longer, it could also be that men who are more physically healthy both live longer and have more sex. Or it could be that men who live longer have a generally fulfilling life and sex is just one variable influencing this.

I would argue, however, that consensual adult sex is good for anyone. So for those who want it, and are healthy enough to have it, there are no reasons they shouldn't engage in sexual activity, even late in life. And for those who don't have a partner, masturbation is also an option. Research shows that masturbation keeps the sexual organs, including the brain, in tip-top shape as does sex with a partner.

Sexual satisfaction and maintenance in old age depend on many biological, psychological, microsystem, and macrosystem factors. Levy (1994) argues that some sexual problems in older people arise because of cohort effects. Older people today became sexually active at a time when sex before marriage was shunned and there were strict sexual mores against activities like oral sex and masturbation. People of previous generations had little sexual knowledge and virtually no formal education about their bodies or sex in general. They had little access to effective birth control methods, which decreased the frequency of sex for pleasure.

FIGURE 13.2 What would you advise this couple to do in order to maintain a healthy sex life as they age?
Photo © Elena Eliseeva/Stocklib.

Many features of elders' macrosystems affect their sexuality. Older people today may internalize the culture-wide **ageism** that they experience. Ageism includes discrimination, prejudice, and lack of access to information or services due to one's age. Because seniors are thought to be asexual and unattractive and sex between elders is considered disgusting and wrong, they may feel badly about their bodies or insecure about their sexuality. This may be especially true for widows who have had only one sexual partner, their spouse, for decades. Men may even experience **widower's syndrome**, whereby they are impotent in a new marriage without any clear physical cause. Sexual problems may occur most commonly in people who cared for their dying spouse over a long period of time or where sexuality was rare or non-existent in their first marriage (Levy, 1994).

As you can see from the research on sexuality, emotional and cognitive factors can affect physical and sexual development. Thus, multidimensional analyses from a bioecological perspective can really help illuminate explanations for both the positive and negative trends associated with aging.

One of the most feared negative developments associated with aging is memory impairment so let's take a closer look at cognitive development in aging people.

Cognitive development

As discussed earlier, psychologists in the 1930s discovered that people's performance on IQ tests tended to decline with age. However, much of this apparent decline was an artifact of the speeded nature of those early tests. Today we have a more nuanced manner of looking at cognitive development in old age. It appears that some cognitive abilities, like speed of mental processing, do decline with age. This is thought to be related to the brain itself functioning more sluggishly. This type of slow down is referred to as a decline in **fluid intelligence**. You can think about fluid intelligence as part of the "hardware," or neuroanatomy, of the brain itself. In contrast, some other aspects of intelligence actually increase with age. Vocabulary, general knowledge, and skills we practice regularly may increase with age. These aspects of intelligence are called **crystallized intelligence**. Crystallized intelligence is the set of facts, trivia, and information we've learned, or the "software" installed in our brain. Think about it like this: while a senior may become a better piano player with age, understanding complex emotional nuances in the notes, learning more about composers around the world, and cleverly combining different styles over time, he or she may actually play the piano more slowly than when he or she was younger (Kramer & Wills, 2002). This example shows that the hardware is slowing down, but the software is increasing in complexity.

In a clever set of cross-cultural studies examining whether cognitive skill declines are universal, Park and Gutchess (2006) measured younger and older Chinese and American people on several timed cognitive tasks. They found that there were significant cognitive functioning differences between young and old people *within* each culture, with younger people completing timed tasks much faster than older people in both cultures. This means that fluid intelligence decline appears to be associated with aging for everyone, not just Americans. Moreover, there were few differences between the skills of older Chinese and older Americans. This suggests that the decline in *fluid* intelligence is neuroanatomical in nature, and not the result of cultural experiences. However, specific knowledge-based tasks like putting objects into categories did reveal large cultural differences. People *within* cultures answered questions similarly, regardless of age, reinforcing the idea that *crystallized* intelligence involved in tasks like picture categorizing is a learned, or culturally influenced, cognitive skill, which does not decline with age. For example, if shown a picture of a knife, an apple, and a coconut, Americans might categorize the apple and coconut together because they are both fruits or things you eat. People from other cultures might categorize the apple and knife together because the knife cuts the apple. This is crystallized intelligence, and does not decline with age, but varies by culture, suggesting it is learned, and not part of fluid intelligence.

When discussing fluid intelligence decline, Park and Gutchess (2006) suggest that the aging brain is active in trying to compensate for its losses in executive function. For example, when scans of old and young adults' brains are taken using a functional MRI, or fMRI, the scans show that older

Ageism
Discrimination, prejudice, and lack of access to information or services based solely on one's age.

Widower's syndrome
Impotence in a new marriage without any clear physical cause; commonly related to stress or trauma in a first marriage where a spouse died.

Fluid intelligence
Cognitive skills related to the functioning of the neuroanatomy, or the "hardware" of the brain itself.

Crystallized intelligence
Cognitive skills related to information, trivia, or facts we've learned, or the "software" installed on our brain.

people's brains activate areas for specific tasks similar to those in young adults' brains, but those areas show double the activation strength, meaning older people are working harder at the task. In addition, research shows that young people only need one hemisphere of the brain to do some tasks while older adults need both sides (Reuter-Lorenz & Lustig, 2005). With training, older brains might be able develop new synaptic connections to handle some challenging tasks. For example, older adults were taught how to juggle over a three-month period. Then their brains were scanned. The amount of gray matter (the convoluted covering of the brain, or the cortex) in their brains increased in response to the training (Draganski et al., 2004). So, yes, you *can* teach an old dog new tricks!

Older people can improve their cognitive functioning, especially if they practice cognitive and memory skills regularly. Moreover, those who are in good cardiovascular condition and exercise regularly decline less cognitively with age. Physical health means more oxygen and blood flow to the brain, which allows for better executive functioning capabilities for skills like problem-solving, planning, and critical thinking. People who lead less cognitively and physically active lives put themselves at greater risk for serious dementia like that found in **Alzheimer's disease**, a progressive brain disorder wherein the brain slowly dies through the strangulation of its cells. This occurs when the brain fails to metabolize junk proteins or wash them out of the brain through typical metabolic processes. The result is large piles of dead cells, or **plaques**, as well as protein fibers that become wrapped around each other, forming **tangles**. These abnormal brain structures interfere with proper brain cell firing and neurotransmitter levels become altered. Eventually the person experiences memory loss, changes in personality, changes in emotions, and after a few months to several years, death.

There are clear gender differences in both brain anatomy and function in old age. For example, when older men have plaques and tangles in their brains, they do not always show symptoms of dementia on cognitive exams, whereas women are much more likely to (Barnes et al., 2005). Also, when women's brains were examined post-mortem, they had significantly more tangles and neuritic plaques than men's brains. Different brain regions even show varied gender differences. For example, enzyme and protein deficits in the neurons of the hypothalamus were apparent in 90% of older men but in only 9% of older women, while the opposite gender pattern was found for cells in the neocortex (Cahill, 2006). What can explain these gender differences in cognitive decline and brain pathology? Hormones? Genes? Social factors? At this point, we don't know. However, we do know that psychological health and material wealth are contributing factors to almost every single decline we see in the aging population.

Families with access to health care, services, and quality food are more likely to enjoy healthy seniors for longer than families who are poor or unhealthy. Poverty and lack of resources can often take a toll on seniors' physical and mental health, leaving them with a sense of hopelessness over their inability to control their circumstances.

Psychological control

One psychological variable that has been consistently related to the physical and mental health of older people is a sense of control. Eighty percent of Americans believe they can prevent or slow the process of aging through their own actions. However, a sense of control is culturally constructed. Only 50% of people in Japan and 10% of people in Bangladesh believe they can prevent or slow the aging process. Even in the U.S., the sense of control over the aging process declines with age. Among 60–75-year-olds, only 62% continue to believe they can play an active role in preventing the effects of aging (Lachman, 2006).

Those who have strong control beliefs also tend to have a keen sense of life satisfaction. They tend to be healthy, happy, and optimistic, with low rates of depression, health problems, and impairments (Lachman, 2006). You may not be surprised to find out that people living in poverty have lower control beliefs than middle-class people (Lachman, 2006). Interestingly, people's control beliefs can be manipulated experimentally, leading those with a sense of helplessness to feel they actually have some control over their physical health as they age. For example, Lachman (2006) reports on an

---

Alzheimer's disease
A progressive brain disorder wherein the brain slowly dies through a failure of normal brain metabolism of dead cellular material; characterized by dementia, personality, and health changes.

Plaques
Piles of dead protein material sloughed off brain cells; a symptom of Alzheimer's disease.

Tangles
Protein fibers in the brain that become wrapped around each other; a symptom of Alzheimer's disease.

intervention whereby older people with intense fears of falling were taught fall prevention strategies. They were also trained in muscle strength and balance exercises, as well as working on changing their negative beliefs. These older people eventually came to believe they had much control over preventing falling and subsequent serious injury. Thus, much of the experience of physical aging is related to "mind over matter."

The **Lifespan Theory of Control** (Schulz & Heckhausen, 1996) states that people experiencing many health or family problems will increase their sense of well-being if they increase their sense of mastery. The theory differentiates between **primary control** and **secondary control**. Primary control entails changing things in your environment, such as throwing out high-fat foods in order to lose weight and lower cholesterol. Secondary control is related to changing yourself, such as changing your emotional state or motivational levels. For example, a wife may become tired of having the same arguments with her husband and so may decide to adjust her emotional state and not react to him negatively anymore when he annoys her. Thus, she gains secondary control and a sense of mastery over solving the problem.

The Lifespan Theory of Control also calls for disengaging from negative or pessimistic thoughts regarding goals that cannot realistically be met. Wrosch, Schulz, and Heckhausen (2004) conducted interventions based on the idea of disengaging from negative thoughts, which improved the sense of control in a sample of elderly people. The authors helped older people give up a desire for control over things they couldn't change, such as an uneven gait or incontinence that is unresponsive to treatment. Then they helped the seniors focus on things they *could* change, such as stress, pain, or obesity. They worked to develop a set of realistic goals for the seniors to take control over their health. These interventions increased people's sense of control, improved actual health, and decreased depression. This is important because depression is very common in seniors who suffer from chronic conditions like arthritis, Parkinson's disease, or stroke (Wrosch et al., 2004). This research shows that psychological intervention can affect physical health, another example of the multidimensional nature of adult development. When seniors have a strong sense of personal control, they are more likely to join in on family outings, engage in conversations with loved ones, and enjoy family life more.

Socioemotional development

Our interpersonal problem-solving skills, social interactions, emotion regulation abilities, and emotional processing skills all show significant improvement with age. Older people feel less angry when faced with personal conflicts. They tend to take interpersonal problems in stride and exhibit excellent emotional regulatory abilities. They can more easily balance their own feelings with the feelings of others and are efficient at directly solving problems. Their social skills are flexible, mature, and proactive (Blanchard-Fields, 2007).

Labouvie-Vief (2003) posits that people become more aware of their own emotional states as they age. Unconscious or impulsive behavioral patterns of youth become matters of conscious contemplation. Older people more clearly know who they are as individuals, and they are able to coordinate complex layers of their inner lives into a coherent sense of self. Erikson (1961) theorized that in old age we search for a sense of **integrity**, or peace within regarding the paths our lives have taken. The opposite outcome is also possible, in the case of seniors who view the end of life as scary or threatening, and who feel bitter about the way their lives turned out. Those of us who face the end of life with a sense of integrity have a sense of calm acceptance in the knowledge that we've left a good legacy behind, in the form of successful children, contributions to the workplace, benefits to our communities, and so on. Our sense of **generativity**, or giving back, leads us to face death with positive emotions, instead of a sense of fear, regret, or despair. If we have made important contributions to the world during our middle adulthood, and accomplished a sense of generativity, then we do not become stagnated or self-absorbed in our old age. On the negative side, if we have had too many stressors or have been unable to cope with life, we may enter old age with a sense of despair.

Lifespan Theory of Control
The idea that increasing one's sense of mastery over his or her life will increase well-being.

Primary control
Changing one's environment to gain a sense of control over life.

Secondary control
Changing one's self (e.g., emotional state or motivational levels) to gain a sense of control over life.

Integrity
A sense of inner peace at the end of life regarding the paths our lives have taken.

Generativity
A sense of being fulfilled in middle age through having contributed to the next generation and leaving a positive legacy.

Depression and suicide

Negative feelings about life, especially in the form of depression and suicide, are increasing in the older population today. Among women aged 45–54, suicide rates have increased 31% in the past decade (www.cdc.gov/violenceprevention/suicide/). This could be due to more psychotropic medications being prescribed or used improperly, or to reductions in the number of older women taking hormone replacement therapy for menopause; long-term hormone use has been linked to various health problems, so fewer women use this treatment these days. Hormonal fluctuations can increase depressive symptoms, so women may be stuck between a rock and a hard place. It could also be that stressors from economic struggles and family issues are increasing depression rates. For example, compared to surveys in 1985, surveys in 2004 showed that seniors reported a substantial drop in the number of people they felt they could confide in or go to for help. And the number of people who said they had absolutely no one to talk to tripled in that time period (McPherson, Smith-Lovin, & Brashears, 2006). These factors can influence the development of clinical levels of severe depression.

About 15% of people who are clinically depressed eventually kill themselves. Men over 75 years of age have extremely high suicide rates (Gonzalez, 2008). This may be due to them coming from a generation where women took care of their health, meals, and housekeeping, so when their wives die, they are at a loss for how to live without them. It could also be due to depression over chronic health problems or disabilities. If you or someone you know is experiencing suicidal thoughts, please call the suicide prevention hotline at 1–800–273-TALK (8255).

Some African American experiences

Suicide is fairly rare in the African American community but we do see some indicators of *despair* in older black men living in poverty. Newman (2003) studied a large sample of poor, older, African American men. The men reported that they had children but had not kept in contact regularly or were unable to provide for them. Some struggled with substance abuse or illicit criminal behavior and some were incarcerated for a time. In interviews with these men, Newman (2003) found that poor older black men reported feeling "exhausted" and "guilty" over their youth spent posturing around other black men who encouraged sleeping with as many women as possible. They report spending their younger days looking for the next "conquest," and that even if they loved a woman, they felt unable to care for her or the children she had, so they disappeared. They also felt pressure to show their male friends that they had power over women and that they could exhibit risk-taking behaviors like drug use and sales or criminal activity, to prove they were in control. It was only as they aged that these men realized the "collateral damage" they left behind in terms of children and ex-lovers who had needed and loved them.

On the positive side, these men were often in high demand as they settled down and worked steadily in middle age. Because there are so few African American men available for marriage, after middle-aged black women raised their children, they often settled down with these older black men, either marrying or cohabiting. These men usually chose women who had been their friends for many years and they experienced true companionship for the first time in their lives. Many of the men had distanced themselves from family ties early in life. In contrast, older black women have strong kin connections to their children, grandchildren, and their communities at large, so these new partnerships provided senior men with a surrogate family (Newman, 2003).

Some LGBT experiences

Another group of elders who may be lonely or socially isolated are those from LGBT communities. Fokkema and Kuyper (2009) found that older gay Dutch people were much less socially connected and felt far lonelier than heterosexual elders. These elders were more likely to be divorced or childless than straight people. They attended religious and community activities less often. They also spoke to their children and other relatives less often than straight people did. The gay men in this study were more likely to have been "widowed" by the loss of a long-term partner than straight men were. Nineteen percent of the gay men and 14% of the lesbian women were extremely lonely (compared to 2% and 5% of men and women in the straight sample). Similar results were found in the U.S., with 24% of older gay men and

19% of older lesbians in San Francisco living alone, compared to only 3% and 8% of straight men and women, respectively. Also, 72% of gay men and 43% of lesbians had no children to care for them in their old age (compared to 20% of straight people) (Adelman, Gurevitch, de Vries, & Blando, 2006).

Many LGBT people are able to compensate for a lack of long-term partners and children by building families of choice comprised of close friends. Because many older gay and lesbian people grew up in a time where homosexuality was stigmatized and even illegal, they may have never had consistent partnerships, but one study showed that over 90% of them have at least one close friend or confidante, compared to only 39% of straight elders in this study (Shippey, Cantor, & Brennan, 2004). Similarly, Fokkema and Kuyper (2009) found that the LGBT participants in their study were more likely to have close contact with friends and neighbors, as well as volunteering in the community more, and earning higher incomes than older heterosexual people. Moreover, the LGBT participants reported similar levels of self-esteem and life satisfaction as their straight counterparts.

Many LGBT seniors do not feel comfortable venturing into gay-friendly neighborhoods (called gayborhoods), shops, or clubs because these venues often focus on high standards of youth and beauty, especially for gay men (Wierzalis, Barret, Pope, & Rankins, 2006). Gay shops are often geared toward the gay man and the products sold, décor, literature on display, and so on are sexual in nature. There may be loud music, and the décor may be flamboyant (Pugh, 2002). Much of gay male culture rejects its aging members, and older gays feel marginalized from the "youthist" scene. Older gay men may limit their involvement with gay culture and spend more time with close friends. Senior LGBT folks may also not fit in with their heterosexual counterparts, for whom discussions of grandchildren are most prevalent (Galesloot, 2003). Growing up in a heterosexist and homophobic culture can add much stress to the lives of sexual minority persons. They may have developed within a context of oppression, stigma, marginalization, victimization, and ostracism, and these all have an influence on the way they experience their old age.

Gay, lesbian, and bisexual seniors often experience discrimination and even victimization for two or three facets of their identity. Homophobia mixed with ageism can put older LGBT people under *double jeopardy*; if they are women, add sexism for *triple jeopardy*. For gay elders, more liberal laws and social norms did not evolve until they were well into middle age. For most LGBT people around the world today, there is still much personal and institutionalized homophobia. For older people this may take the form of discriminatory home health care, where workers are offended by gay literature, art work, or media in the home. Nursing homes may not allow same-sex couples to room together or exhibit physical affection with each other as they do heterosexual married couples in nursing care (Pugh, 2002). Medical professionals may not take sexual dysfunction in gays and lesbians seriously. What do you think a doctor would say to a gay man who requested Viagra?

Despite these challenges, older people from LGBT communities may actually cope with aging better than some heterosexual people do. They have spent much of their lives coping with the stress of oppression and may have developed competent coping strategies. They tend to be well educated and often make better money than their straight counterparts. Gay men tend to live outside of traditional gender roles when they are young so as they age, retirement may be less of a threat to their identity as it can be for straight men. Thus, the life experiences of sexual minorities vary widely.

Not all LGBT people have had to hide their identity or live in shame or in secret. Many people have been able to live fulfilling lives out in the open (Pugh, 2002). It's not uncommon for gay men and lesbians to "come out" to their families, friends, and co-workers without crisis or emotional turmoil. They are happy to be themselves and have high self-esteem, both of which are related to successful aging (Berger, 1982).

The LGBT people who face old age most successfully tend to have a steady life partner, higher education, and higher income. Older lesbians tend to be educated, middle class, and well employed, and often fit in cohesively with straight culture as well as lesbian subculture, both of which are somewhat less focused on youth and beauty than gay male culture (Pugh, 2002).

Throughout this book, we've seen that intersectional identities including ethnicity, gender, sexual orientation, and socioeconomic status play significant roles in family life. When we try to analyze the family relationships of our seniors we must take these intersectional identities into account.

RETIREMENT

Financial success plays a large role in how people of all background experience the aging process. Some people must work all their lives until they die. Others have the privilege of being able to stop working and enjoy life. For example, the European Union laws of 1979 and 1986 ensure that women and men receive equal pay in unemployment, old age benefits, sickness, disability, and retirement (Cousins, 2005). In developing nations without such benefits, most people live in poverty and work hard until they die. In the U.S., there is a large gap between rich and poor, with many people working hard all their lives and others being able to retire with benefits like pensions. Let's take a closer look at the socioemotional, cognitive, and gendered aspects of retirement to get a clearer picture.

Luborsky and LeBlanc (2003) have found that the idea of "retirement" exists only in countries where there is industrialization, a large middle class, and a Protestant work ethic. These countries tend to have good medical care, a high quality of life, and increased longevity. Their populations are rapidly aging in good health and their birth rates tend to be decreasing. Because of these decreasing birth rates, the government must provide benefits to people to encourage them to have children while continuing to participate in the workforce. Generous pensions are part of this plan. Allowing people to retire in comfort also ensures that there are jobs for younger workers (Luborsky & LeBlanc, 2003).

In most western, industrialized nations, retirement is considered an earned right for people who have worked hard and now are allowed to stop working without being stigmatized as lazy or unproductive. They maintain their status as full citizens. This idea is interesting to people in non-western cultures who have not grown up thinking that people should be allowed to cease performing vital roles as they grow older. Retired persons relinquish key parts of their social identity yet are able to maintain their status as important and respected members of the society, with all the rights of other adult members. They have earned the right to have freedom from responsibility and obligation. These exosystem influences are critically important to the family life and well-being of seniors.

While many cultures may not understand the diminished roles and financial support western nations provide to elders, some non-western cultures also reduce workloads and give new roles to elders. For example, Japan and India have programs similar to the pensioned retirements western nations have (Luborsky & LeBlanc, 2003). In contrast, other cultures completely discount elders. Fulani people in rural South Africa call older adults "socially dead" when their youngest child gets married. These elders' rights as citizens are taken away and they no longer participate in community affairs. They must live ostracized at the outskirts of their village and become completely dependent on their eldest son for support.

People in most non-western cultures, however, simply live subsistence lives and must work hard to survive all of their lives. For example, Hopi Indian elders work until they cannot physically do so. At the same time, they are revered and given more important roles, such as leading rituals. But they do not cease working until they are disabled or die.

Other cultures, such as that in Burma/Myanmar, allow elders to stop laboring to focus on their spiritual lives. Their children care for them while they live a peaceful life of meditation and reflection. They lead religious services and still have great influence on their families and communities (Luborksy & LeBlanc, 2003). Likewise, in traditional Chinese cultures, after the age of 55, adults are considered *lao-nien*, or released from the burden of mundane daily life. They live a life of meditation. Family members come to the *lao-nien* for advice. Even women are allowed this "retirement" privilege and are relieved of their subservient status in relation to men.

In the west, those who adhere to traditional gender roles may have the most difficult time with retirement. Men who have been the breadwinners and have staked their entire identity on being workers may have a very difficult time being home. Their wives may be annoyed with them being under foot all day when they were used to keeping the house the way they wanted it and spending

FIGURE 13.3 What are some of the diverse ways elders are treated in different cultures? A multigenerational Mongolian family.
Photo © Bruno Morandi/Imagebank/Getty Images.

most days as they wish (Barnes & Parry, 2004). For most families, today, however, both men and women work and research suggests that people of both genders who show an intense attachment to work over other roles in their lives may have a difficult time retiring.

The synchrony between each partner's decisions to retire also plays a role in satisfaction with retirement. For example, marital satisfaction is quite low if one partner retires while the other partner continues working, especially if the person still working is the wife. However, after both partners retire and adjust to their new lives (which takes about two years), marital satisfaction then increases (Moen, Kim, & Hofmeister, 2001).

About 30% of people struggle psychologically with trying to adjust to retirement (Back, 1977). However, there are some complex variables at work and more recent research is discovering an interesting pattern of influences on people's adjustment to retirement. Among those with a strong attachment to their worker identity, it's mainly those who have no control over when or how they retire, those who have a low sense of self-regard, and those who have negative expectations about retirement, who adjust most poorly after retirement (van Solinge & Henkins, 2005). Thus, one's personal characteristics interact with the retirement experience to affect adjustment outcomes. Those with high self-esteem, meaningful friendships, whose retirement was voluntary, and who have a good pension, enjoy retirement immensely (Reitzes & Mutran, 2004).

Women, in particular, who have worked their whole adult lives and can afford to retire, find there are innumerable possibilities for new roles to play, from community involvement to helping to raise grandchildren. They tend to have a strong sense of meaning in their lives and feel excited about a new phase of adventure (Price, 2003). Some studies show that connection to a worker identity only affects retirement adjustment in the short term but that being able to control the process and timing of retirement, being in better health, having a higher income, and being married have large influences on retirement (Wong & Earl, 2009). Therefore, having someone to come home to may be an important protective factor in alleviating the adjustment stress of the sometimes radical lifestyle changes retirement brings. Once again, we see the notable importance a sense of control has over how seniors adjust to life after working. If they have both control over their destiny, and a supportive partnership at home, retirement can bring great joys, especially because the research shows that our socioemotional development actually improves with age. This means life in families can be extremely rewarding later in life.

FAMILY LIFE ACROSS GENERATIONS

As you know, divorce rates have increased exponentially over the past 50 years. With so many couples breaking up, remarrying, and forming stepfamilies, can we still assume that it's normal to be in one monogamous relationship for our entire adult lives? We live longer than ever before so while a lifelong marriage in previous generations may have been 20 years, now it can last 60 or 70 years. Are we meant to be with only one person for five decades or more?

Anthropologist Helen Fisher argues that evolution imbued us with the desire to be committed to one person until our offspring are weaned and semi-independent, an average of four years. She suggests that we are really built to be **serial monogamists**, people who move from one long-term committed relationship to another after several years (Fisher, 1988). Fisher states that humans are designed to love more than one person in a lifetime, and that, chemically speaking, it's not unusual at all to feel love and passion for more than one person at any one point in time. Thus, lifetime commitment to one person may be a cultural construction, not an inherent trait among humans. This perspective would argue that the higher divorce rate is reflective of humans' true nature and that people are forced by oppressive laws and mores to stay in culturally defined decades-long relationships. What do you think? Is serial monogamy an acceptable way to carry out one's adult life? Or should we strive for that one enduring partnership that lasts a lifetime?

> **Serial monogamists**
> People who move from one long-term committed relationship to another after several years.

Marriages and committed partnerships in later life

For women, marriage and committed partnerships are much less likely to last a lifetime because of the marked gender differences in longevity. For example, among 60–69-year-olds, there are 115 women for every 100 men. For 80–89-year-olds, there are 180 women per 100 men, and for those over 90, there are 294 women for every 100 men. This means that the *old-old* among women are especially likely to live alone. In fact, 4% of old-old women in any given year are widowed, but only 1% of men are. Fewer men have to face their last years alone, while women are more likely to (Hyde, 2007b).

While it's true that women live longer, they also suffer from more chronic health problems like arthritis, diabetes, high blood pressure, and osteoporosis. They are also more likely to retire to take care of their retired spouse. This means they get less retirement income since they probably took time off from working to care for children. They also probably earned lower wages over their lifetimes than their husbands did (Hyde, 2007a).

Life satisfaction among women

For middle-aged women, life is usually pretty sweet. While there is a stereotype that mothers suffer from **empty nest syndrome**, depression and loneliness that occur after their children leave home, research shows that the primary feeling middle-aged mothers experience is relief (Gorchoff, John, & Helson, 2008). They miss and love their children, but they often relish their new life. In fact, women in their fifties have the highest life satisfaction rates of any age group. They are often in better health than they were in their younger years, they are more financially stable, feel a sense of self-confidence, understand themselves very well, and are ready to take on new hobbies, travel, continue their education, or do whatever strikes their fancy (Hyde, 2007a). They can spend more quality time with their partners and friends, and enjoy more freedom and less responsibility. Marital satisfaction also experiences a sharp rise after children leave home. Only 10% of middle-aged women feel a sense of deep loneliness, despair, or grief after their children leave.

Even women without children experience a greater sense of life satisfaction in middle age. For example, over half of white middle class women aged 55–69 years who had never married had no desire to do so (Mahay & Lewin, 2007). They exhibited much less desire to marry than younger

> **Empty nest syndrome**
> Feelings of depression and loneliness that parents may experience when their children leave home.

cohorts did, and they were happy reaching middle age free to do as they liked. Men in this study who were between 55–69 years of age were even more satisfied than the women. This makes sense in light of the "his" vs. "her" marriage phenomenon discussed earlier in this book.

It's important to keep in mind the many variations in micro-, meso-, and exosystem forces that can influence a person's life satisfaction in middle and old age. For example, the patterns Mahay and Lewin (2007) described may be less true of women living in poverty, who often must continue working and struggle on their own to make ends meet well into old age. Mahay and Lewin (2007) found that those with lower education and incomes desired to marry more often, seeing a benefit to living in a long-term partnership.

Health effects of different personality types

Some fascinating research has found that personality factors can affect the quality of life in old age. For example, men who are very conscientious—detail-oriented, responsible, and planful—have healthier wives later in life. The same works in the reverse as conscientious women have healthier husbands. In contrast, both men and women who are neurotic—emotionally unstable, anxious, moody, and dramatic—have a negative effect on their spouses' health. These findings hold true regardless of the personality traits of the spouse (Roberts, Smith, Jackson, & Edmonds, 2009). The most noteworthy finding from this research is that if a person's spouse is *both* conscientious *and* neurotic, their partner's health is most positively influenced. Neurotic people may experience anxiety and fear over their partner's health and well-being, but because they are also conscientious, they take proactive steps to research health issues and get their partner to seek medical attention or improve their diet and exercise (Roberts et al., 2009). In other words, they don't allow themselves to be overwhelmed by their emotional intensity. Roberts et al. (2009) discuss previous research, which showed that low levels of conscientiousness are related to health problems like strokes, ulcers, and high blood pressure. Moreover, being very conscientious actually slows down HIV disease progression in AIDS patients. In contrast, neuroticism has been linked to immune functioning deficits and even mortality. In sum, two personalities can work together either synchronously or antagonistically to influence the health and longevity of long-term partners.

The research reviewed in this section reinforces the idea that each level of the bioecological model, from biochemical processes, to cultural beliefs, to microsystem dynamics taking place between partners, affects the quality of life as we age.

Unlike for younger couples, some traumatic events like deaths of close friends and widowhood are virtually universal experiences that impact older people's intimate lives in profound ways.

Widowhood

The older people get, the more likely they are to be widowed. However, even young partners can lose a spouse or committed partner. Older widows tend to cope a bit better with the death of a spouse because it is a normative event later in life, they are more financially stable, and don't have the stress of raising young children alone. They also usually have friends who have gone through the same experience and can provide support (Hyde, 2007a). Widows tend to cope better than widowers, who have higher levels of depression, illness, and loneliness after a wife dies. Women are more able to express their grief and reach out for social support. They also tend to be closer to children, siblings, and grandchildren than men are. However, widows are also much more likely to be poor than are widowers. But for both sexes, long-term illnesses before the death of a spouse can drain family finances, including savings and retirement funds. This is especially true for people of color who typically worked for lower wages and had less access to quality preventive health care or retirement funds.

In cases of a slow death resulting from prolonged illness like cancer or Alzheimer's disease, the well spouse often experiences many different emotions. The sick partner tends to garner all the sympathy, attention, and help from loved ones, while kin often fail to realize the well partner is experiencing role strain and burn-out. The well partner has to cope with financial issues, emotional strain, and family and work responsibilities while helping to care for the ill spouse (Kaslow, 2004). Well partners need much support from religious communities, family, and friends.

Advanced directive or living will
Documents that specify exactly what kind of health care or lifesaving measures a person wants if he or she becomes incapacitated.

The process of caring for a spouse with a terminal illness can be easier if people have an **advanced directive** or **living will**. These documents specify exactly what kind of health care a person wants if he or she becomes incapacitated. Life-saving measures can be specified, or a person can make a "do not resuscitate" order (DNR), which alleviates pressure from family members who may be unsure about allowing a person to die in cases of terminal illness. If older people make all health care decisions and funeral arrangements ahead of time, it relieves family members from any responsibility of having to make decisions that can sometimes lead to contentious arguments, family feuds, or estrangement after the person dies. If my own mother had not specified in legal documents that she did not want any heroic measures taken to prolong her life, it would have been much more painful and difficult for us to take her off life support at the end of her life. Because she had expressed her wishes clearly to all of us, it made a difficult process much easier to face. When seniors have advanced directives, living wills, and clear medical instructions in writing, it can make life for their survivors much less stressful.

After a spouse dies, the living partner must be able to express all the feelings he or she has, even if they seem angry or resentful. It's not uncommon for a living partner to resent the years of life taken away while a partner was infirm, or to grieve the loss of a happy life they once shared. They may feel upset that their life savings were used up for health care expenses. They may have a sense of helplessness, fear about the future, or anxiety about how to live life without the caretaking responsibility they had for so long. For most people, these negative feelings last only a few months or a year. Others, especially men, can enter into depression and may even commit suicide; remember that men between 75 and 85 years of age have the highest suicide rates (Kaslow, 2004). The death of a wife is often related to a decline in the quality of remaining father–adult child relationships. This is especially true of father–daughter relationships (Umberson & Slaten, 2000). In comparison to men, most older women maintain strong connections to younger generations and often become even closer to children and grandchildren after the death of a spouse or partner (Logan & Spitze, 1996).

Relationships with adult children

Perma-parenting
The idea that parents play key roles in their children's lives well after they reach adulthood, continuing to financially and emotionally support their children.

While the popular stereotype says that families are disintegrating and becoming estranged, research shows that family is still vitally important to most older people and that maintaining family ties is a priority for most. Over half of elderly parents live within 10 minutes' drive of at least one of their children, and 85% of seniors speak to or see their children weekly (Coles, 2006). **Perma-parenting**, playing key roles in children's lives well after they reach adulthood, remains quite normative. Parents continue to financially and emotionally support their children for many years. Members of the Baby Boom generation, born between 1946 and 1964, are especially close to their children. They have worked hard to form friendships with their kids and welcome their moving back home after college or a divorce (Paul, 2003). With high rents, low wages, an unstable job market and a delay in marriage age, these parents are happy to let their adult children live at home until they can afford a home of their own or until they get married. Fully 61% of white middle-class children with Baby Boomer parents expect to move home after college. But even for other groups, living with parents until marriage or financial independence is quite common. For example, 78% of Latino youth believe one should live at home until married (Paul, 2003).

Most adult children and their parents report feeling true affection, support, and intimacy from each other. They help each other through hard times. Mothers tend to feel more responsible for how adult children are functioning than fathers do, but fathers also hold family in high regard (Umberson & Slaten, 2000). If an adult child goes through a divorce, is widowed, or experiences financial hardships, parents usually provide the support needed. This includes caring for grandchildren. Black families are especially likely to take up the daily care of grandchildren if parents are unable to do so. African Americans also experience more grandchildren caring for their elderly grandparents later in life (Umberson & Slaten, 2000).

Parents also support adult children who are physically or mentally disabled for their entire lives. For example, parents report feeling extreme love and tenderness for their mentally retarded or developmentally delayed adult children. While the caregiving burden is high, they accept it willingly and report that their main fear is what will happen to their children when they are gone (Umberson & Slaten, 2000).

Parents also care for adult children suffering from chronic mental illnesses like schizophrenia, as well as chronic health problems like HIV/AIDS. Fathers tend to take care of the adult child's financial and instrumental needs, while mothers provide daily physical and emotional care. Several studies have examined the dynamics of parental caregivers of adult children with AIDS and have found a distressed group. They may be older or infirm themselves. They may have religious beliefs against homosexuality and so must struggle with their sick child's sexual orientation or substance abuse history. They may suffer in silence because they don't want people to know their child has a stigmatized disease. Therefore, they often lack social support and may experience intense grief and shame. This may be particularly problematic in African American families, who tend to live in a staunchly homophobic culture. It's not uncommon for black grandmothers to care for adult grandchildren dying of AIDS in complete seclusion, without money or social resources for medical or home health care (Umberson & Slater, 2000).

Many older parents who care for an adult child through his or her illness must also take care of or help raise grandchildren. For older adults, grandparenting is one of the key familial roles they play. For example, teenage mothers today are more likely to get two generations of support as they are likely to have parents and healthy and financially stable grandparents available to them (Bengtson, 2001).

Beyond seniors caring for younger generations, the reverse is also quite common.

Adult children as caregivers for elders

Three quarters of seniors live independently and only about 5% live in nursing homes or other care facilities. But 18% live with their children (Hutter, 1998). Those who take care of needy seniors are usually the seniors' own children, and most commonly, their daughters. About 65% of infirm elders are cared for by family members but a growing number will receive professional in-home care.

Women in the "sandwich generation" are caring for both their own children and elderly parents. They have to balance work, marriage, children, and parent care responsibilities. More commonly, though, women move from the mommy track into the daughter track and care for their parents after their children are grown. Most female caregivers spend an average of 18 years caring for elders, the same amount of time they spent raising children (Hutter, 1998). **Caregiving stress**, feelings of depression, loneliness, or being overwhelmed while caring for an elderly parent or infirm partner, is a common experience for these women. Caregiving stress can be reduced if women have the support of siblings and have a husband or long-term partner. Also, those with higher socioeconomic status experience lower levels of caregiving stress.

Research shows that many siblings erupt into conflict over the care of their aging parents. The non-caregivers often criticize their sibling caregivers. Female caregivers tend to be angry at their brothers for not helping out enough, while brothers assume their sisters' lives are more flexible or their work is less important, so they have more freedom to help (Margolies, 2004). Women feel obligated to care for their parents while their brothers often argue for spending the money to pay for professional help. However, it should be emphasized that 48% of men help their elderly mothers and 36% help their fathers, compared to 59% of women helping mothers and 48% helping fathers. Thus, while women bear the brunt of the responsibility, large numbers of men also experience caregiving burdens and role strains (Logan & Spitze, 1996). Men tend to fix things around their parents' houses, make things they need, and spend time with them. Women tend to help with shopping, cleaning, cooking, and providing direct physical care.

People of color are less likely to seek formal medical care, especially if they follow traditional beliefs about illness. They often expect that their children will care for them in their old age. For example, Pueblo Indian women reported a lot of guilt and stress over their inability to care for their elders as they would like, due to the competing demands of work and raising children

Caregiving stress
The overwhelm, depression, or loneliness felt by adult caregivers who must fulfill the needs of elderly or dependent adults; related to higher rates of elder abuse and neglect.

(John, Hennessy, Dyeson, & Garrett, 2000). Because mental illness like anxiety and depression are stigmatized in many cultures, elders may more commonly report that they suffer from somatic complaints like heart palpitations and weight loss. For instance, Mexican people may describe *attaque des nervios*, nervous attacks, which have many physical symptoms, but they may not be willing to get mental health treatment for them.

Hmong people often believe that a spirit world exists alongside the physical world, and they believe they must appease spirits through animal sacrifice in order to relieve illness. If they believe wandering spirits are not appeased and can enter the body and cause illness, they may be less amenable to receiving western medical treatments. If they are not allowed to have a traditional healer sacrifice a goat or a chicken, they may develop extreme fears of dying (Coles, 2006). Because members of Asian cultures tend to be private and work hard not to shame their families, they don't want to share their illnesses with outsiders. Asian Americans tend to be very private and suggesting they get professional medical, mental health, or nursing care may be abhorrent to them. They often don't want others to know that something is wrong with a family member. Thus, it's important that cultural gatekeepers educate family caregivers on proper techniques for toileting, feeding, and giving other types of care to their elders in the privacy of their own homes (Clay, 2009).

Activities of daily living
Things that people become less and less able to do with age, including feeding, dressing, toileting, and taking care of one's own household and medications.

People of color tend to live shorter lives than European Americans but suffer from more chronic conditions. They also have more impairment in **activities of daily living (ADLs)**, which include feeding, dressing, toileting, and taking care of one's own household and medications. Interestingly, black caregivers report far *less* caregiving stress than white caregivers do. This may be because of their strong religious faith and the belief that God has a plan. They may accept illness as just a natural part of life. They also have a more relaxed and flexible caregiving style, along with extensive social support through church and community (Coles, 2006). They tend to take their responsibilities in their stride. However, there may also be cultural sanctions against complaining. At least one study has shown that while African Americans may report lower levels of stress and depression, caregivers' cortisol levels are elevated compared to those of white caregivers (McCallum, Sorocco, & Fritch, 2006).

Whoever is taking care of an infirm elder probably needs some social support and, especially, some time off, even if they never complain or say they are fine. Offering respite care to caregivers is an especially promising way to reduce the caregiving burden. To learn more about one intervention implemented in an attempt to reduce caregiving stress, see the *How Would You Measure That?* box.

Caring for one's aging parents may be stressful, but keep in mind that a lot of caregiving for the elderly is done by their elderly spouses or long-term partners. In a fascinating study of over 3,000 older adults, Brown et al. (2009) found that spouses who cared for their partner for at least 14 hours per week, instead of being stressed out and sick, actually lived longer. Regardless of the severity of the disabled spouse's illness or condition, or his or her cognitive limitations, if his or her spouse did the majority of the caregiving, the caregiving spouse lived longer. These researchers suggest that perhaps caregiving in itself is not stressful. It may be that the grieving over watching someone decline or the fear of a loved one's death is more stressful. Previous research has shown that people who help others are healthier and live longer (Post, 2005). Helping behavior generates surges in the hormone oxytocin, which reduces stress and contributes to improved physical functioning, emotional bonding, and healing (Heaphy & Dutton, 2008). So perhaps caregiving is also beneficial to one's health and longevity, depending on the supports provided in other systems of the bioecological model.

When two seniors are able to care for each other, their emotional bond grows stronger and may enable to them to provide better support and resources to other members of the family, like their grandchildren.

Grandparenting

With better health care and longevity today, most of us will have some experience with our grandparents. In 1900, only 21% of people had even one living grandparent when they reached adulthood (Bengtson, 2001). Today, however, you are more likely to have a grandmother alive

HOW WOULD YOU MEASURE THAT?

Intervention for family caregivers of stroke patients (Shyu, Chen, Chen, Wang, & Shao, 2008)

Many adult children must not only care for their aging parents, but sometimes they must provide specialized care for specific diseases or disorders. If your parent had a stroke, would you know how to care for him or her at home? Yea-Ing Lotus Shyu and colleagues (2008) wanted to test whether a hospital-based educational and supportive intervention could help family members both feel more prepared to care for an elder who had a stroke and reduce their caregiving stress. They examined 158 families of stroke patients in a large hospital in Taiwan. Hospital wards specializing in stroke patients were randomly assigned to receive the intervention or receive the usual discharge procedures, brief instructions and reading material. The researchers saw the need for such an intervention because typical discharges appeared to be handled haphazardly, with some families not getting much information at all.

Their experimental intervention consisted of educational materials customized for each family's needs (for example, for those who were afraid of dropping a patient in the shower, showering procedures were demonstrated). Families were visited four or five times during the stroke victim's average hospital stay of 30 days. They were provided with printed materials, were allowed to ask questions, and spent at least 30 minutes with a nurse. They were also given customized referrals to support groups and other services. Trained nurses administered pre- and post-test surveys about caregiving needs and expectations. They followed up with each family by phone for 20–30-minute checks and question answering. They also completed 60-minute in-home visits two weeks and one month after hospital discharge. In the clients' homes, they watched caregivers implementing care, demonstrated skills with the actual patients, and answered questions. Each nurse was given 6–8 hours of training to participate in the intervention program.

Compared to the treatment-as-usual control group, the intervention group rated themselves and were rated by hospital staff as better prepared to care for their elder upon discharge from the hospital. They also reported their discharge needs were better satisfied one month after discharge. They felt they were better able to balance caregiving with other demands of family life. The experimental group understood their patient's condition better, had mastered the caregiving skills better, and felt more prepared to handle their patients' needs.

These findings illustrate the importance of access to quality medical care and wraparound support services for infirm elders and their family caregivers. With a little extra training and some customized supports, these caregivers were much more prepared and confident in their roles, which made the rest of their family life feel more manageable.

when you turn 18 than people in 1900 were to have their *mothers* alive. Historically, about 35% of those born around 1900 in the U.S. had a grandparent living in another country, so people were often separated from their grandparents. You may be surprised to learn that 25% of Americans today still have grandparents in other countries (Casper & Bianchi, 2002). Today, older adults will likely spend over half of their lives being grandparents. This is longer than they spent caring for their own children (Coles, 2006). Seventy percent of people over the age of 50 are currently grandparents. But with declining birth rates and shrinking family size, most grandparents today have fewer than six grandchildren; compare this to the 12+ grandchildren people in 1900 had.

Factors from all systems of the bioecological model can affect the desires and abilities of grandparents to be part of their grandchildren's lives. To read about how one family views their relationships with their grandparents, see Fernando and Rebecca's story in the *Focus on My Family* box.

FOCUS ON MY FAMILY

Fernando and Rebecca

Like many Mexican American families, our life involves grandparents, aunts and uncles, cousins, parents and children. Being involved in an extended family results in complex relationships, which span generations. In our daily lives, we mainly focus on parent–child relationships. We like to be available to support our children's academic and social development. But beyond daily life, we often play the multiple roles of both parents and children, as we are part of the "sandwich generation." We are raising our children while filling an important role in the lives of our own parents. Being a part of an extended family with many elder relatives means we are constantly providing different forms of social support. We help our parents and their siblings in everything from navigating social security or Medicare to translating modern processes to a more traditional generation. They rely on us to help keep them from being marginalized. This is especially true for those among our parents who are immigrants.

The older generation helps us as well, providing invaluable knowledge. They are the keepers of history and maintain our links to the past. They know the stories of their childhoods and their parents' childhoods. Our elders have wisdom and a calm fortitude for helping us face modern struggles. We can always turn to them in times of stress to ask for advice. My mother, mother-in-law, and aunts are particularly important as we raise our children. For example, if one of the children is sick, they have advice and assistance to offer. There comes a time in one's life when you wish for peace and rest for your older parents. In our own family, our parents are in their late seventies. They have worked hard and struggled for the majority of their lives. Although their own children are adults, they continue to see themselves as parents and are willing to sacrifice their own resources for their children.

There is a constant balancing act when we blend the generations. Adult children and grandchildren attempt to care for their elders while at the same time relying on these same individuals for both social and economic support. It is not always easy to be part of an extended family but the benefits of intergenerational connectedness are immeasurable. We see ourselves as inextricably intertwined with our parents. This interconnectedness is demonstrated in our own children's ability to see themselves as part of a larger whole:

Isabel (age 10): Older people have more wisdom and experience because they grew up in the old days when life was harder. If anything ever happened to my parents, I know I can count on my grandparents to take care of us.

Sofia (age 8): My grandparents care about us. My grandmother comes from far away to help us when someone is sick. She is so smart and can fix anything.

AnaMaria (age 5): They are important because they are going to die soon; they take care of us. Sometimes, they give us toys and invite us over to their houses. I love them because they are important.

Fernando and Rebecca with their children and their parents. Photo reproduced by permission.

TABLE 13.1 Cherlin and Furstenburg's (1985, 1986) grandparenting typology.

	Exchange of services	Discipline and authority	Frequency of contact
Detached (25%)	Low	Low	Low
Passive (29%)	Low	Low	High
Supportive (17%)	High	Low	Low
Authoritative (9%)	Low	High	Low
Influential (19%)	High	High	High

Types of grandparents

Typically, grandmothers have more frequent interaction with their grandchildren, and do more caregiving for them. Grandfathers, on the other hand, do more mentoring and provide advice. Cherlin and Furstenberg (1985, 1986) constructed a typology of grandparents (see Table 13.1). They based their typology on three variables: exchange of services, such as paying for day care, loaning automobiles, and so on; discipline and authority; and frequency of contact. Those who are low on all three are called *detached*; about 25% of grandparents fit into this category. Detached grandparents also live the furthest away from their grandchildren. Those who don't exchange services or provide any discipline, but are in regular contact with grandchildren are called *passive*, and they make up about 29% of grandparents. About 17% of grandparents fit the *supportive* category, whereby they exchange a lot of services but do not discipline or visit much with the grandchildren. *Authoritative* grandparents, about 9% of grandparents, don't exchange services or have much contact, but they are quick to discipline and exert authority over their grandchildren. Finally, grandparents who are high on all three variables, about 19%, are *influential* grandparents. They are extremely active in their grandchildren's lives. Which type do you think best fits your own grandparents? Are your grandparents on each side of the family a different type? What about grandmothers versus grandfathers?

As you can see from these statistics, about 70% of grandparents really don't exert any kind of discipline or authority over their grandchildren. Keep in mind, though, that these typologies are based on studies of American grandparents, who tend to follow the norm of non-interference. Young grandparents are more likely to follow the *influential* style but older grandparents are more likely to be *detached* or *passive*. Therefore, both macrosystem and chronosystem factors may influence the type of grandparent one becomes.

FIGURE 13.4 Out of the five types of grandparents, which do you think is the best one for children's development? Photo © Tom and Dee Ann McCarthy/CORBIS.

African American grandparents tend to see their role as disciplinarian/teacher to their grandchildren, as do Latino and many Asian American grandparents (Casper & Bianchi, 2002). African American grandparents are less involved in recreational activities with grandchildren but are more involved in their religious development and in direct discipline and parenting roles. Grandchildren are also more likely to live with black grandparents than white grandparents. Pacific Islanders and Native Americans also have high rates of grandparents being primary caretakers of their grandchildren. Unfortunately, these groups are also more likely to live in poverty and have little access to quality health care, making family life difficult.

Many states do not provide kinship caregivers with the same support, training, or benefits formal foster parents receive for raising foster children. Grandparents often have to apply for legal custody of their grandchildren in order to be awarded rights and benefits, such as being able to enroll children in school and give consent for medical care, which means their own children must surrender their rights. And because grandparents have few legal rights, if the children's parents decide to remove the child from grandparents' care, they may do so. Sometimes this leads to estrangement and grandparents feel isolated, missing the grandchildren whom they once cared for. These interactions can become stressful and complicated. Each state has different laws regarding how much grandparents can do to fight for custody or visitation rights if their own children refuse to let them see their grandchildren. To see some of the particulars related to the issue of grandparent visitation, see the *FYI* box "Grandparents' Visitation Rights."

FYI

Grandparents' visitation rights

In 2000, the U.S. Supreme Court rejected a Washington state grandparents' visitation rights law because they said the living spouse of a person who committed suicide had the right to decide if the deceased spouse's parents could visit the grandchildren. Since then, however, many grandparents have won visitation rights after their son or daughter's death, especially if they had been in caregiving roles for the children. While each state differs slightly in its law, the law of California is fairly representative. Let's check out Family Code Section 3100–3105:

- Visitation may be granted to grandparents if it is in the best interest of the child, especially if the child's parent is deceased.

- Grandparents have no rights if the child was adopted by anyone other than a stepparent or a grandparent.

- If the grandparent was in a caregiving role, he or she can be ordered to pay child support upon divorce.

- The grandparent's relationship and bond with the child must be balanced with the parents' rights of authority over the child.

- A grandparent may not petition for visitation rights if the parents are still living together or are still married unless one of the parents joins the petition, one parent has abandoned the child, or the parents live apart.

- If the child does not live with either parent, the grandparent may not petition.

- Parents may petition to terminate grandparental visitation rights.

Section 3105 states "The legislature finds and declares that a parent's fundamental right to provide for care, custody, companionship, and management of his or her children, while compelling, is not absolute. Children have a fundamental right to maintain healthy, stable relationships with a person who has served in a significant, judiciously approved parental role."

Source: www.justia.com

Complexities of modern grandparenting

It is increasingly common for people to view grandparents as playing a pivotal role in the lives of their grandchildren. The 2000 census was the first to ask grandparents if they played a parenting role in raising their grandchildren. It was discovered that 22% of Latina single mothers lived with their own parents, as did 18% of black single mothers and 15% of white single mothers, and upwards of 50–70% of single mothers had at one time lived with their own parents for help in raising their children (Casper & Bianchi, 2002).

Grandparents today have more responsibilities for their grandchildren than ever before. Native American grandparents, in particular, have **enculturative responsibilities** for their grandchildren: they are expected to transmit cultural rituals, beliefs, and values to their grandchildren (Robbins, Scherman, Holeman, & Wilson, 2005). They do this through storytelling, costume construction, and the teaching of rituals. Because many elder Indians fear the destruction of their cultures, they involve grandchildren in cultural games, drum circles, dances, preparing traditional food, revering nature, and learning their native language. Indian cultures typically teach respect for elders, pride in one's culture, hard work, and respect for all living things. With much poverty on reservations, however, many Native people are moving to cities to find jobs and children who are acculturated into majority belief systems often see grandparents as irrelevant. Many Native grandparents report feeling under-appreciated by their contemporary families and communities (Robbins et al., 2005).

> **Enculturative responsibilities**
> The duties expected of grandparents of color involving transmitting cultural rituals, beliefs, and values to their grandchildren.

Modern life has made the role of Native American grandmother especially hard. With high rates of drug use, alcoholism, and unemployment in Native communities, grandmothers often take over the role of parent to grandchildren, nieces, nephews, and other children on the reservation. While not all Indians live on reservations, much of the research on Indian grandmothers has been done there. Bahr (1994) interviewed many Apache grandmothers and found that these women expected to play key roles in the upbringing of their grandchildren. In the days before contact with European Americans, Apache mothers and oldest daughters would roam far distances for many days to gather food and firewood. This extended area for family life led to "household" being a fairly flexible term for most Indian families. People "belonged" to extended family and felt close to many generations of kin. These permeable boundaries allowed for all family members to become interdependent and care for each other.

Today, however, this role is largely played by hard-working grandmothers, women who work two or more jobs and have almost total financial and emotional responsibility for the young (Bahr, 1994). These women report demanding jobs, many responsibilities to care for multiple generations of children and adults, as well as being responsible for transmitting culture. They live stressful lives, and Letiecq, Bailey, and Kurtz (2008) found that Native grandparents experienced high levels of depression if they were responsible for the full-time care of their grandchildren, household chores, and cultural responsibilities. In comparison to European American custodial grandparents, Native Americans were more likely to live in poverty and be depressed. However, the Apache women studied by Bahr (1994) also reported being greatly revered and respected by all. They play a very crucial and influential role in their communities, which benefits the whole tribe and life on the reservation in general.

Today, at least 7% of children from all ethnic groups are being raised solely by their grandparents (Goodman & Silverstein, 2002). For divorced families and those with working parents, grandparents provide more relief and support than any other institution (Kemp, 2007). For all ethnic groups today, more and more grandparents are becoming primary caregivers for grandchildren due to parental substance abuse, incarceration, death, violence, military deployment, teen pregnancy, mental or physical illness, or abandonment (Bullock, 2004). Thus grandparents must not only cope with raising young children but also with the sense of failure in raising their own children, and they sometimes consistently worry about or have conflicts with those adult children. Grandparent caregivers have higher rates of depression than grandparent non-caregivers. Those living in rural areas, like many Native Americans, are at even higher risk of experiencing mental health problems, social isolation, financial struggles, ill health, and lack of transportation (Revicki & Mitchell, 1990). Rural communities typically lack proper health care facilities, educational opportunities, well-stocked grocery stores, and job opportunities, making life for both grandparents and their grandchildren very difficult.

Many grandchildren have experienced multiple traumas by the time they reach grandparental care, from in utero exposure to substances, to malnutrition and abuse or neglect. Their grandparents often have little training or knowledge in how to manage children's emotional and behavioral problems. Both grandparents and grandchildren in grandparental caregiving families have higher rates of mental health problems, such as depression or attention deficit disorder, and physical health problems, such as asthma or diabetes. They also experience food insecurity and suffer from poverty at a higher rate than the general population (Casper & Bianchi, 2002).

In spite of the many complexities and problems, the vast majority of both grandparents and grandchildren report that the bonds they share are unbreakable. Grandparents risk everything to keep their grandchildren safe and well cared for. And both children and grandchildren report that their lives are infinitely enriched by intergenerational bonds.

Despite the messages regarding the disintegration of the family, a lack of caring, and epidemic estrangements with which we are bombarded, families continue to interact with and care for their family members across generational lines. Intergenerational relationships are characterized by caring and affection and are essential ingredients to healthy aging. Logan and Spitze (1996, p. 456) state that "the evidence … is that intergenerational ties in adulthood remain strong [today] in spite of social currents that have been expected to disrupt them. These ties are a firm foundation for the family of the future." In the final chapter, I will explore families of the future in greater depth.

CHAPTER SUMMARY

Society's views of older people have changed dramatically over time. In previous centuries, very few people lived into old age, so those who did were revered. Older people were seen as wise, valuable, and important members of families. This view is still held around the world in non-western cultures. Western cultures quickly adopted a medical model as scientific medicine swept through societies. Old age became pathologized and doctors came up with remedies for the infirmities of old age. Old age became a chronic condition people wanted to avoid at all costs. As a result, older people were less valued. Modern families did not want to be burdened with them any longer. In modern times, European Americans are much more likely to put their seniors in nursing homes than are families of color.

Aging is much more complex than popular stereotypes seem to indicate. Growing older occurs in multidimensional ways, with physical, sexual, cognitive, and socioemotional changes occurring throughout the lifespan. Depending on the level of support, education, and psychological control elders experience, they can be more or less satisfied with their marriages and their lives in old age. For example, when seniors feel they have control over choices in their lives regarding where to live, and when to retire, and these choices are supported by family members, they are much more likely to be physically and mentally healthy.

The majority of seniors remain sexually active and interested even though sexual function can decline in numerous ways, from erectile dysfunction in men to loss of vaginal lubrication in women. Sexual intimacy in old age often includes kissing, cuddling, and other acts besides intercourse.

The experience of aging can also be affected by demographic variables such as gender, ethnicity, social class, and sexual orientation. If seniors experience double or triple jeopardy (being an ethnic minority, gay, and poor, for example), they can be marginalized and discriminated against. They also have a higher likelihood of chronic stress and physical ailments as they age. If they have a higher socioeconomic status and are able to retire, however, they can enjoy much leisure time and time with their partners in their latter years.

Many older people in contemporary society are continuing to play vital roles in their families. They maintain financial, emotional, and social support for their grown children through a trend called *perma-parenting*. They also live in multigenerational households with their children and grandchildren, especially if they are seniors of color. Many middle-aged people experience caregiving stress in these households, having to care for older parents and younger children at the same time.

A growing trend is grandparents taking over the parenting role for their grandchildren. There are many types of grandparents, from distant fun grandparents, to authoritative grandparents who discipline grandchildren. Grandparents of color are often responsible for ethnic and religious socialization of many generations of family members.

This chapter illustrated that aging can be a wonderful, happy time of life if seniors are given the right kinds of supports from each of the bioecological systems in their lives.

KEY TERMS

activities of daily living	enculturative responsibilities	old-old
advanced directive or living will	fluid intelligence	perma-parenting
	functional age	plaques
ageism	generativity	primary control
Alzheimer's disease	Hayflick limit	secondary control
caregiving stress	integrity	serial monogamists
chronological age	Lifespan Theory of Control	tangles
cohort effect		telomeres
crystallized intelligence	menopause	widower's syndrome
Disengagement Theory	multidimensional	
empty nest syndrome	multidirectional	

WEBSITES FOR FURTHER EXPLORATION

http://www.graypanthers.org

The Gray Panthers were founded in 1970 by Maggie Kuhn to address common problems faced by seniors. She argued that retired people had free time to make a difference in the world and urged them to become social activists. The Gray Panthers work for social and economic justice and peace for all; they honor maturity and try to unite people across generations for the greater good.

http://www.grandfactsheets.org/state_fact_sheets.cfm

This is a great website with comprehensive fact sheets about all issues facing seniors. Topics include resources for grandparents raising children, foster and kinship care policies, laws, resources, and services listed by state, links to caregiver respite care programs, and census data about the aging population.

http://www.aarp.org

The American Association for Retired Persons is a non-profit, non-partisan group which advocates for people over 50. They aim to improve the quality of life for seniors and create positive social change. They have a speakers bureau, services for seniors, media outlets, magazines, and advocacy services aimed at helping people age with integrity and dignity.

CHAPTER 14
THE EVOLUTION OF FAMILIES IN THE TWENTY-FIRST CENTURY

The future of peace and prosperity that we seek for all the world's peoples needs a foundation of tolerance, security, equality and justice. That foundation is the family. It is only by protecting families, from famine as well as from fragmentation, that they can prosper and contribute to the family of nations that is the United Nations.

(Kofi Annan, seventh UN Secretary General, Nobel Peace Prize winner)

LEARNING OBJECTIVES

- To be able to speak authoritatively about five key ideas for understanding marriages and families

- To understand contemporary trends in diversity in the U.S. and abroad

- To recognize the positive and negative effects of modern trends in globalization

- To decide for yourself whether developed nations have a responsibility to developing nations and/or poor people within their own borders

- To be aware of the controversies surrounding immigration, especially in the U.S.

- To solidify your knowledge of the key strengths that can benefit all families

Marriages and Families in the 21st Century: A Bioecological Approach, First Edition. Tasha R. Howe.
© 2012 Tasha R. Howe. Published 2012 by Blackwell Publishing Ltd.

FIVE KEY IDEAS FOR UNDERSTANDING MARRIAGES AND FAMILIES

- The bioecological model
- Family structure vs. process
- A strengths-based approach
- Intersectional identities
- Diversity as normative

GENERAL TRENDS IN MULTICULTURALISM

- Ethnic changes in the U.S.
- Views in favor of multiculturalism
- Views against multiculturalism

GENDER AND SEXUAL ORIENTATION IN THE TWENTY-FIRST CENTURY

- Women's rights
- LGBT rights
  - Women in Afghanistan

GLOBALIZATION

- Acculturation stress
- Trauma from global violence
- The responsibilities of developed nations

AN IN-DEPTH LOOK AT IMMIGRATION

- Transnational families
- LGBT immigrants
- Undocumented immigrants
- Undocumented children and education

FINAL REFLECTIONS ON THE FUTURE OF FAMILIES

FIVE KEY IDEAS FOR UNDERSTANDING MARRIAGES AND FAMILIES

The bioecological model
Family structure vs. process
A strengths-based approach
Intersectional identities
Diversity as normative

Families, the people in them, and their interrelationships are complex, as you have learned throughout this book. All things that we are and all things that we do are multiply determined. The overarching framework of a bioecological approach makes these fundamental ideas clear and gives us a way to talk about and study them. This is the first, and fundamental, key idea we have discussed in this book: families are affected by influences ranging from neurons, genes, and internal working models, to family members, friends, religion, contexts, and culture. Other keys ideas include: the fact that family processes are more influential than family structures for health and well-being, the necessity of using a strength-based approach to examine families, the impact of intersectional identities, and the fact that diversity has always been normative and continues to affect contemporary family life. Let's review each of these ideas, in turn.

The bioecological model

It is important to realize that we can best understand the functioning of families in the United States and across the globe if we take the time to examine them within the multiple contexts in which they live. The bioecological approach allows us to explore how these multiple contexts interact and intertwine. We are all biological beings, with brains organized to reflect our social and cultural milieu. The inner workings of our nervous systems, hormones, and neurotransmitters are not solely laid down through some genetic blueprint, but are intimately linked to the environments that shape us. Biology and context influence each other reciprocally and impact our family's functioning, whether it be healthy, safe, and stable, or in some way challenged or less than optimal.

Each of us exists within microsystems, which consist of people who have direct and steady interactions with us. Microsystems include our parents, partners, children, teachers, and friends. We also exist within mesosystems, which are comprised of interactions between microsystems. An example would be a situation when your sister discussed a problem with your father and you learned problem-solving skills from that. Exosystems, which are indirect influences filtered through our microsystems, also impact family life. A vital exosystem influence is our parent or our partner's workplace, which can filter down through those members of our microsystems and affect our daily lives. The broadest system of influence, the macrosystem, consists of larger cultural and social factors. Families in the U.S. live in a democratic macrosystem as well as one that includes racism and sexism. Finally, the time period in which we live, or the chronosystem, can affect the way we interact in our families. People who grew up in the 1950s versus the 1990s may have different ideas about "proper" family interactions or about family values. Because each individual, family, and ecological system is unique, there can be no universal family structure that is best for all of us. Diverse family structures evolved to meet varied bioecological demands unique to each family.

Family structure vs. process

Throughout the book it has become evident that stereotyped family forms such as the Standard North American Family (SNAF) are limited in their ability to capture contemporary family life. The SNAF stereotype consists of a working white heterosexual middle-class father, his stay-at-home legal wife, and their small number of biological children. The SNAF stereotype emerged from media images and biased memories of the 1950s, a time that was an anomaly in human history in most ways. Current statistics show that very few people live in SNAFs, and even in the 1950s, few people lived in SNAFs. There is no evidence that the SNAF was ever the norm for most people. And even if a family is a SNAF, knowing only about the family's structure does not reveal much about the happiness or personal adjustment of the family.

This textbook has illuminated the fact that we really cannot understand the health and well-being of a family based only on its structure. There are plenty of SNAF families who are violent, alcoholic, or in other ways dysfunctional. It has also been shown that having a society with diverse family forms is perfectly normative and healthy. The only way to assess family strengths is by looking inside, by moving away from structure and looking at process. What are the processes, the dynamics, and the attachment patterns family members experience? How do they communicate, discipline their children, and cope with loss? Only with a process analysis can we assess whether a family is dysfunctional or has an abundance of strengths that may benefit its members.

A strengths-based approach

Families have evolved and changed continuously since before recorded history, and they will continue to evolve with contemporary challenges and trends. If we view these trends through a strengths-based lens, we see that all family structures have the potential to foster healthy relationships. In addition, as we interact with or learn about diverse types of families, we can build our own strengths through recognition of the many ways healthy families function, which can inform our subsequent attempts to build skills and abilities. Through exposure to diversity, we find varied strengths and recognize that each family, society, and culture has both benefits and disadvantages for family members. This text has presented evidence that any type of family can have strengths. It has also included self-assessments and *Building Your Strengths* exercises so that you can reflect on your own families' strengths and attempt to reinforce them and build on them.

When we focus on the positive attributes of families, we see that most of us have a lot in common. For example, all families include strong emotional attachments, a sense of responsibility and caring, and a desire for children to have better and easier lives than the previous generation. These commonalities tie the human family together and remain true for people from extremely diverse intersectional backgrounds.

Intersectional identities

Each of us lives an intersectional life, carrying with us our sex, gender, sexual orientation, ethnicity, history, "race," social class, age, religion, language, ability and disability status, and biochemical make-up. These many intersectional sources of our identity constitute the fiber of who we are. It's impossible to understand a person or a family by looking at only one or two aspects of their identity. For example, knowing someone is a man or an Asian American doesn't reveal a lot about this person's family dynamics or his approach to interacting with others. If a family member comes out as gay or someone announces an impending divorce, we need to step back and think about how these issues may affect them differently than they would affect us. If we fail to recognize the intersectional nature of each person's identity, we may judge them based on stereotypes or misinformation about people from that group. However, if people different from us live in or marry into our families and we recognize the many layers of their identity, it can help improve tolerance and understanding. When more people comprehend the idea of intersectionality, family interactions may become more harmonious as family members genuinely try to understand each other's diverse perspectives.

Diversity as normative

When people reflect on American history, they often think about many key figures from Western European backgrounds, battles that turned the course of history, or how things were in families in the "good old days." They often refer back to the 1950s as a time of innocent family life, where neighborhoods were safe and families were happier and more secure than they are today. However, this text has presented historical and other research data showing that those ideas are quite Eurocentric because diversity in family life has always been the norm. There have been many ethnic groups in the U.S. since its inception. We read about European historical figures, often forgetting that each of them interacted with diverse others who typically wielded less power and privilege. People of color, women, sexual minorities, and immigrants have always played major roles in American history and shaped important events that affected family life for all of us. They may not have been as prominent in the history books that we read in school, or their roles and importance may have been downplayed, but diverse families have both impacted and been impacted by life in the United States, as well as other countries around the world.

Now we recognize the pervasive impact of diversity on family life because the twenty-first-century family is characterized by interactions with diverse others across the lifespan. Each chapter in this text has shown trends in family life within many groups in the U.S. as well as patterns across the world. In virtually every country today, more and more people are impacted by a global and multicultural perspective. Successful family life in a global community will require that we break out of an ethnocentric world view and make concerted efforts to understand diversity in families.

GENERAL TRENDS IN MULTICULTURALISM

Ethnic changes in the U.S.

Views in favor of multiculturalism

Views against multiculturalism

In the United States, previous generations' ethnic identifications included "Polish," "Italian," and "German." However, after decades of intermarriage with other people from European backgrounds, many of these ethnic identifications have melded into the singular category "White," or "European American." Perhaps 100 years from now, we will have even fewer distinct ethnic categories into which we place people's lives. We can see movement in this direction currently as we meet more and more people whose ethnic background we cannot easily ascertain by the way they look. We see this daily in the celebrities of our time. For example, singer Mariah Carey's father is an African Venezuelan and her mother is third-generation Irish American. Dwayne "The Rock" Johnson, the famous wrestler and actor, has a Samoan mother, an African Canadian father, and he lived for years in New Zealand before becoming an American superstar. Vin Diesel, the action star, is half African American and half Italian American. He calls himself of "ambiguous ethnicity." It often makes people uncomfortable when they can't "place" someone's ethnic background, and people of mixed heritage are often asked "What race are you?"

It's natural for humans to categorize and make blanket judgments or stereotypes about others. Without the ability to quickly judge others, our species would not have survived. But now we live in a vastly more complex and intertwined global culture where all of us are mixing together at rapid rates. Eventually, questions about discrete racial identification may not exist.

Ethnic changes in the U.S.

It is difficult to predict what the ethnic fabric of the United States and other multicultural countries will be like in future decades. Over five million children in American public schools today speak one or more of 150 different languages. In the 2000 U.S. Census, almost seven million people checked the box for "bi-racial," suggesting that a lot of people today identify with more than one ethnic group (Parrillo, 2009). Diverse types of people make up each broad ethnic group category and those diverse people are intermarrying more than ever before. For example, people from similar backgrounds, like "Hispanic" people, are intermarrying at high rates. In the year 2000, over six million people of Hispanic origins married other Hispanic people from countries different from their own. With interracial and interethnic marriages increasing so rapidly, we are seeing more and more people having bi- and tri-racial children.

Today most of us have diverse ethnic mixes in our own family histories, even if we look simply "white" or simply "black." These trends are leading to the "deconstruction of race as we know it," (Parrillo, 2009, p. 199). Parrillo speculates that we will become substantially more melded into one "American" or "European," or "Latin American" or "African" identity as global movement makes the world a smaller place for diverse families. Moreover, Parrillo (2009) estimates that by the year 2025, 84% of the world's population will be from developing nations due to higher birth rates in those countries and lower birth rates in western industrialized nations.

Due to these trends, we are all becoming part of a global village and it is no longer viable to be socially isolated, insular, or ethnocentric. What happens in one corner of the globe now happens to us all. The destruction of environmental ecosystems, dramatic global climate change, mass human migrations, and the tragic events of September 11, 2001 are just four examples illustrating the fact that every family is affected by the actions of unknown family members around the world.

Views in favor of multiculturalism

There are many benefits to multiculturalism. Hong, Wan, No, and Chiu (2007) argue that people with multicultural identities are able to think about the world in a more sophisticated and complex manner. People who travel the world or integrate multiple cultural and linguistic existences into their lives can become cognitively flexible, solving problems and acting in more creative, critical, or innovative ways. When people live insular lives, they are surrounded by those similar to themselves and are deprived of the opportunity to critically examine their own lives, philosophies, and ways of knowing. Thus, multiculturalism leads to cognitive, social, and even spiritual advancement, which can make twenty-first-century families more educated and enlightened than those in previous generations.

Inclusionists (the color blind)
People who appreciate diversity but do not acknowledge the importance and contributions of differences between people; they emphasize our common humanity.

Integrative pluralists
People who believe that all cultures, beliefs, and languages have merit and should be cherished together in one diverse society that appreciates the differences we all bring.

Xenophobia
The intense fear of anything or anyone different or foreign, which often leads to avoidance.

There are two main types of people who appreciate the benefits of a diverse multicultural society, **inclusionists** and **integrative pluralists**. Inclusionists appreciate the diversity that other groups bring to the table but tend to emphasize the humanity that we all have in common. Because inclusionists appreciate diversity, they are sometimes called "color blind." They may say that they don't see color and that everyone is valued for who he or she is inside. They want to ensure that all people are welcome to become citizens and that we focus on what we have in common, not on what makes us different. They would welcome interracial, intercultural, and LGBT members into their families.

Integrative pluralists not only appreciate diversity, but celebrate it, seeing difference as a vital strength in our society, one that should not be downplayed or ignored. They are enthusiastic about learning from other people's cultural backgrounds and value the diverse perspectives, cultural practices, religions, and family values people bring to society. Integrative pluralists see no need for people to assimilate or leave a home culture behind. They emphasize the value of living in a diverse society where people may have bicultural identities, meaning they strongly affiliate with their own history, culture, and language, but also feel affinity for their new homeland, knowing their lives are enriched by living in the new place. People with bicultural identities are able to successfully navigate both worlds and identify as members of both communities (Parrillo, 2009), and integrative pluralists value this flexibility. Integrative pluralists have inclusive and welcoming views of diverse members in their families. They are excited about the prospects of new perspectives and experiences. However, not everyone sees multiculturalism as having benefits for families in the twenty-first century.

Views against multiculturalism

Some people, especially those who think SNAF structures are ideal and see the past as the "good old days," feel threatened or scared by the rapid demographic changes occurring in the world. Much **xenophobia**, a fear of things unfamiliar or foreign, still exists. For example, numerous organizations strive to maintain the integrity of the "white race." The European American Unity and Rights Organization (EURO) states that "we believe that forcing the races together has resulted in a marked decline in educational quality and increased racial tension and violence" (www.whitecivilrights. com). Other groups speak out against immigration. For example, the Federation for American Immigration Reform (FAIR) states that undocumented immigrants cost the United States $113 billion per year over what they contribute in taxes, with almost half of that spent on education, 27% on justice and incarceration, and 21% for medical costs (Martin & Ruark, 2010). However, these numbers are not based on hard data, but on estimates that cannot be confirmed because many schools and agencies serving immigrants do not ask whether they are documented or not. Moreover, because U.S. taxpayers would not identify themselves as undocumented workers, it is unclear how this organization knows how much undocumented immigrants pay in taxes. Nevertheless, many people do feel that immigrants cost more than they contribute to society and want to be sure the country maintains its European American majority and culture. By the year 2010, more than 30 states had passed legislation mandating English as their official language (http://www.okhouse.gov/). The U.S. is particularly divided on this issue, as was seen when Arizona passed a strict immigration law that allowed police officers to check the legal status of any person they stopped whom they suspected might be in the country illegally (http://www.azleg.gov/legtext/49leg/2r/bills/sb1070s.pdf).

People who do not believe in the benefits of multiculturalism are often referred to as **separatists**, also known as **assimilationists**. Separatists emphasize the need for an American culture into which other people's cultures should be melded (Parrillo, 2009). Immigrants' experiences are devalued and they are encouraged to leave their language, culture, and family practices behind, to become assimilated into the American mainstream. This "melting pot" idea is what led millions of immigrants in the nineteenth and early twentieth centuries to change their names and prohibit their own languages and customs to be used at home. Parents didn't teach children about their cultural heritages because they wanted them to assimilate, to blend in and be accepted by American society. Many of my students today wish that their parents had taught them their ancestors' languages or that they could have visited relatives in their country of origin. Living in a multicultural society has led many young people to desire to reconnect with their own cultures.

Multiculturalism usually refers to many cultures living together in one society. Ethnicity and race easily come to mind as examples of this concept. However, many other groups are also experiencing rapid change and are increasingly demanding recognition of their rights by the dominant society. For example, gender and sexual orientation are important aspects of intersectional identities in a multicultural society. Women and those from LGBT communities often feel similar pressures tugging at them as people of color do, finding that they need to navigate the world of people in their own group while also successfully living and working with people from the more powerful majority (that is, men and heterosexuals). With family patterns changing, we have seen women and sexual and gender minorities becoming more powerful, being recognized for their unique strengths, and gaining in human rights around the world. However, women, lesbian, gay, bisexual, and transgender people are still discriminated against, ostracized, and even violently attacked in many parts of the world.

Separatists (assimilationists) People who believe immigrants should adopt their new culture uniformly, assimilating into the culture, practices, beliefs, and language, while leaving their own systems behind.

GENDER AND SEXUAL ORIENTATION IN THE TWENTY-FIRST CENTURY

Women's rights

LGBT rights

In both western and non-western nations alike, women's changing roles have inspired men to question traditional gender role expectations about themselves. Men are beginning to reassess whether they should follow traditional patterns of relating to their families. They may question the power hierarchy they saw in their fathers' relationships with their mothers. They more often see women as their equals than as their property. With their contemporary views on women's equality, the new men's movement is also concerned with enhancing men's health, creating fairness in divorce and custody proceedings, achieving a healthy balance between work and family, and establishing reproductive rights for men, such as having a say in abortion and adoption decisions (Parke & Brott, 1999). The new **masculinist** discourse argues that men also suffer from traditional patriarchy and the pressure to be sole breadwinners, valued only for their earning potential. The masculinist focus stems from a relatively recent men's movement that attempts to release men from the constraints of traditional gender role expectations. Men want more than the pigeonhole they have been allowed, which restricts the definition of masculinity to one of power and control. They want freedom to express their feelings, be intimate in relationships, and find true friendships with other men. They want to be engaged fathers who spend quality time with their sons and daughters (Parke & Brott, 1999). The women's movement has allowed men to reflect on their own position in the family, which is slowly changing in western nations. In developing nations, however, men's and women's roles are still more traditional and women often have very few rights or means for independence.

Masculinist
A relatively recent men's movement that attempts to release men from the constraints of traditional gender role expectations.

Women's rights

Women in developing nations like India are becoming more independent and less willing to limit their career goals. They also want personal freedom to marry whom they wish (Hong et al., 2007). In support of women's right to be independent, western nations are now giving loans of between $100 and $500 to women in African, Asian, and Middle Eastern nations, in a practice called **microfinancing**. Microfinancing refers to lending small amounts to women or families to start their own businesses, in order to become financially independent. Self-sufficiency allows marginalized groups to break free from the oppression they so often suffer. Women who receive microfinancing can often leave abusive husbands and support their children, or make an independent living after being widowed.

Microfinancing
Small loans designed to help impoverished people emerge from poverty by becoming self-sufficient.

Women in Afghanistan

A worldwide movement geared toward educating girls and women in developing nations is the next wave of women's liberation, which will certainly lead to less wasted human potential and a richer social fabric in the global community. For example, the women in Afghanistan, who were brutalized and prohibited from being active members of society under Taliban rule, are now gaining some freedoms, especially in larger cities like Kabul. Under the Taliban, women were not allowed to drive but Kabul issued 180 drivers' licenses to women between 2007 and 2009 (Rubin, 2010). Also, a handful of women are serving in government positions and are working as policewomen. Women are needed in law enforcement because, in this traditional Muslim culture, men are not allowed to frisk female suspects or be alone in a room with a woman to question her. Also, female doctors are needed because men are not allowed to touch women who are not their wives (Rubin, 2010).

Some argue that one key to preventing terrorism and fundamentalism is educating girls and women to play active roles in their societies. When women are oppressed and their voices are not heard, societies are more likely to become unstable. Educated women can help bring prosperity and peace to their regions (Leviton, 2009). Women trained as medical technicians can help reduce infant and maternal mortality rates. Educated women can engage in politics and law and help tribal communities gain recognition and resources. For example, studies show that formal education liberalizes people's political attitudes. This leads to greater acceptance of religious and political diversity among the highly educated (Nilsson, Ekehammar, & Sidanius, 1985). Educated families are more likely to see diverse groups like women, LGBT persons, or those of other ethnicities as their equals (Cote & Erickson, 2009).

Because we don't have the overt form of sexism in western nations that we see in developing nations, we may think that women's battles have been won at home. However, the message from the women who are being brutalized in other nations like Afghanistan is the one that opened this chapter: there can be no peace in the world without peace in families. Here at home, we have rampant

FIGURE 14.1 Zarah, age 19, tried to leave her husband after he beat her for "disobedience." Because she could not leave, she set herself on fire. Self-immolation is one of the only ways Afghan women can speak out against domestic violence. How could ensuring women's rights in Afghanistan also help other families around the world?
Photo © Paula Bronstein/Getty Images.

domestic violence and child abuse. People of color and those from LGBT communities are marginalized, oppressed, and attacked. The extreme cases around the world shed light on the more subtle forms of bias in our own country and show us how far we have to go to bring peace to all families. In western nations, the rights of all people are discussed openly and today, the civil rights movement is focusing more and more the rights of families who have LGBT members.

LGBT rights

Similar to the oppression of women around the world, people from LGBT communities are often seen as inferior or not deserving of civil rights. But with greater acceptance in western nations, gay, lesbian, bisexual, and transgender people around the world are revealing infinite possibilities for gender roles, sexual orientation, and the ability to relate to others in more than just traditionally socially acceptable ways. They are opening businesses and, through the Internet, are able to reach people in developing nations, letting them know they are not alone in their struggles for visibility and acceptance, even if homosexuality is illegal in their country. **Politicized homosexuality** is a social movement wherein people from LGBT communities around the world are using their political and economic power to fight for their civil rights. Politicized homosexuality can be seen anywhere that lesbian and gay families, LGBT business people, and LGBT politicians gain recognition, influence, and acceptance. This is happening, albeit slowly, in regions as unlikely as Peru, Zimbabwe, and Indonesia (Altman, 2002; Petchesky, 2007). The "pink dollar" is creating economic opportunities to build LGBT-friendly workplaces, niche markets, gay publications, travel packages, clothing lines, and Internet services in diverse countries around the globe. There are now huge gay pride events attended by hundreds of thousands of people in Brazil, Australia, and other countries. Today, the International Lesbian and Gay Association has members from over 70 countries. Organizations like this are fighting for freedom for LGBT people to live their lives without discrimination, hatred, and violence. They desire full legal status for marriage, benefits, and opportunities to raise their children.

Politicized homosexuality
A social movement wherein people from LGBT communities around the world are using their political and economic power to fight for their civil rights.

The challenges they continue to face are steep as many developing nations view homosexuality as something that does not exist on their soil; they see it as a "western" evil foisted upon them against their will (Altman, 2002).

LGBT scholars emphasize the need to legitimize lesbian and gay families and acknowledge that they are just as valid and healthy as those of heterosexual families. They encourage people to stop studying LGBT families in comparison to heterosexuals, but as a viable subject of scholarship in its own right (Clarke, 2002). As LGBT voices begin to be heard in the international scholarship literature, as well as in popular media, global trends will support their cause.

GLOBALIZATION

> Acculturation stress
>
> Trauma from global violence
>
> The responsibilities of developed nations

Today, the regions of the world are more interconnected than ever before in history. Cornell and Hartman (2007, p. 252) state that:

> Slavery, colonialism, political upheaval, famine, war, the search for jobs and security—these and other forces have moved people from countryside to city, country to country, and continent to continent in extraordinary numbers, producing a mass redistribution of the world's population in the span of a few centuries and a degree of complexity and mixing unseen before.

Globalization
The development of an increasingly integrated worldwide economy.

Globalization refers to the development of an increasingly integrated worldwide economy. Virtually every location on earth is now accessible for travel, marketing, and communications. Capitalism has spread around the world and has led to one massive interconnected marketplace (Cornell & Hartman, 2007). Evidence for this can be found in the global economic crisis of 2007–2008, which resulted in millions of Americans and workers around the world losing jobs, homes, and benefits such as health care. From the perspective of families, the globalized marketplace failed to look out for our welfare.

The interconnection that caused so much trouble in 2007–2008 may also help pull us out of this mess. Mass media and communications with global impact allow innovative ideas, business plans, educational opportunities, and hiring to occur. Cultural practices, rituals, and ideologies now spread like wildfire. Viral videos on the Internet can get millions of hits in a single day. Globalization can be more than just about economics. It can include a global village of citizens who connect with each other through humanitarian goals and practices. For example, after a spate of suicides by LGBT youth made news throughout the western world in 2010, a global project entitled "It Gets Better" launched, and within weeks, there were thousands of videos uploaded to their site, telling LGBT youth that life gets better and that they are worth saving. Everyone is connected today, so we're all in it together, be it good or bad.

In this interconnected world, it is unlikely that the United States and Western Europe will hold the same prominence and sway that they had in the past century. The global competition for jobs has led many American and European companies to outsource their work to cheaper labor forces, especially in Asia and Latin America. Many of these workers are highly educated yet willing to work for less than their American and European counterparts. For the United States to compete, we need to raise generations of citizens with high motivation, advanced education, and a willingness to work hard. We need innovation, creativity, critical thinking, and better science and technology education. Highly qualified math and science teachers are dwindling as are research dollars allocated to basic science that generates new knowledge (Augustine, 2007).

Our customary lifestyles may change as the U.S. loses its economic supremacy in the world. The World Economic Forum has placed the United States seventh in a list of nations prepared to take advantage of rapid technological advances; we used to be ranked #1. The United States spends three times less money on research than it does on court costs surrounding litigation (Augustine, 2007).

President George W. Bush attempted to remedy this by signing the COMPETES plan to improve math and science education and research in the U.S. Likewise, Exxon Mobil has allocated $125 million to improving K–12 education in math and science.

Augustine (2007) notes that in the sixteenth century, Spain was the leading world power, in the seventeenth century, it was France, and in the nineteenth century it was Britain. If the United States dominated the twentieth century, perhaps our time is over now. He says "no nation has a monopoly on greatness" (p. 77). We are entering the first generation of Americans that will have a lower standard of living than the previous generation. Being born American does not carry the same economic weight and universal privilege that it used to. More and more mainstream Americans will have to make an effort to understand other ways of life, as well as political and religious viewpoints. They will have to work with people from many nations and will see the effects of globalization and acculturation first hand.

Acculturation stress

The continuous changes occurring due to mass globalization will affect us all. Today 185 million people live in a country other than the one they were born in (Hong et al., 2007). Ten percent of people in developed nations today are immigrants from developing nations. The United States and Germany host the most immigrants, with Canada and Australia not far behind. While most immigrants adjust to their new countries well, they also often experience a sense of culture shock. They may not immediately know how to speak the language and may face racism and discrimination. They may be separated from their families if they immigrated to find work. **Acculturation stress** refers to the pressure and strain immigrants experience as they try to adapt to a new environment.

Acculturation stress
The pressure and strain immigrants experience as they try to adapt to a new environment.

Acculturation stress can be acute or chronic, leading people to feel depressed, isolated, and confused about which identity they want to take on. For example, Mexicans emigrating to the United States face prejudice, discrimination, and hatred, not only from the dominant culture, but even from U.S. born Chicanos (Niemann, Romero, Arredono, & Rodriguez, 1999). Similarly, Japanese Brazilians are discriminated against and disliked by native Japanese when they immigrate to Japan for work, while being seen as Japanese outsiders by the dominant Brazilian citizens in their home country of Brazil (Tsuda, 2003).

As people struggle to define themselves and adapt to new identity structures, they may have to fight to maintain their home cultures. For example, Inglehart and Baker (2000) studied 65 societies and found that, as capitalism spread, citizens began to endorse western values like secularism, assertiveness, and rational thought over their own cultures' values of familialism, collectivism, and religious devotion.

Acculturation stress and lack of community connectedness may increase as people migrate around the world to new locations to find work. As you have learned throughout this text, chronic stress affects both mental and physical health. Neurological and physiological changes occur when a person faces daily discrimination, racism, or the struggle to rise out of poverty. Exposure to stress hormones like cortisol over a long period of time can impair cognitive functioning, hamper memory, and lead to depression and anxiety. The hippocampus region of the brain, which consolidates memory, can atrophy. When the HPA axis is chronically activated in response to threat, the immune system can shut down and people can develop disorders and diseases such as diabetes and respiratory infections (Reagan, Grillo, & Piroli, 2008).

Reagan et al. (2008) discovered that similar neurochemical processes related to HPA axis functioning are at work in both diabetes and depression, suggesting that the brain's ability to metabolize stress hormones may contribute to both the poorer mental and poorer physical health we see in people of color and immigrants. For example, stress hormones influence the development of insulin resistance in the brain, thereby influencing diabetes (Reagan et al., 2008). The brain's memory centers and emotion-processing structures are negatively affected by this process, which can contribute to high rates of acculturation stress, anxiety, and depression. Moreover, these authors remind us of the important link between chronic stress and cardiovascular dysfunction. These findings support the bioecological model because environmental experiences change people's biological functioning and people's neurochemical functioning shapes their further interactions within the multiple contexts of their lives. In the case of acculturation stress, if the environment becomes too taxing, such stress can develop into a clinical diagnosis of post-traumatic stress disorder (PTSD).

Trauma from global violence

Research suggests that over 30% of children living in violent urban neighborhoods in the U.S. have PTSD symptoms (Foster et al., 2004). The results of Reagan et al.'s (2008) research described above helps explain the high rates of cognitive failure these vulnerable inner city children, who live in virtual war zones, experience. They drop out of school, can't pay attention, react emotionally without forethought, and suffer headaches, anxiety, obesity, and malnutrition at high rates (Tucker, 2007). Tucker reports that Senator Darrell Steinberg of California asked inner city kindergarteners about their lives and found that 90% had a friend or relative in jail and 75% knew someone who had been injured or killed from gun violence. We rarely think of children in wealthy western nations struggling with mental and physical health problems caused by violence, but it is clear that exposure to trauma is a leading contributor to youth violence and declining academic performance in the U.S. as well as abroad.

Millions of children around the world are affected by violence. Ethnic conflict and ethnic cleansing, tribal warfare, and the wars in Bosnia, Rwanda, Sudan, Iraq, and Afghanistan have left in their wake a generation of traumatized children. In a study of Bosnian children, almost half had clinical levels of depression and one quarter had clinical rates of anxiety and PTSD (Papageorgiou et al., 2000). During the war in Bosnia-Herzegovina in the 1990s, over 1,000 children were killed and 15,000 injured (Miller, Langhans, Schaller, & Zecevic, 1996). Likewise, Lebanese children have been exposed to shelling, separation from their parents, and war trauma like being victims and witnesses of violent atrocities, which led many of them to develop mental health problems (Macksoud & Aber, 1996). Also, Kuwaiti children from the first Gulf War witnessed deaths and injuries and saw mutilated bodies on TV every day. Seventy percent of the Kuwaiti children examined had symptoms of PTSD

FIGURE 14.2 How does exposure to violence affect children's development?
Photo © Abid Katib/Getty Images.

HOW WOULD YOU MEASURE THAT?

Moral reasoning in Bosnian children after the War (Garrod et al., 2003)

In studies of moral reasoning, researchers typically find two key moral orientations. In the first, people reason about moral dilemmas (like stealing, lying, and so on) by reflecting on the *fairness* or *justice* of the act. In the second, people reflect on moral dilemmas from a *care and compassion* perspective, focusing on how the action affects others. For example, if there was a drug that could cure a man's wife's cancer but he could not afford it, would it be acceptable for him to steal the drug? A *justice* perspective might reflect on whether stealing was fair or whether keeping expensive drugs from dying people was just. A *care* perspective might reflect on the man's desire to help his wife, or on his desire to maintain harmony in the community by not stealing. Garrod et al. (2003) wondered whether children exposed to intense warfare, trauma, relocation, and chronic stress might respond to moral dilemmas in a different manner than other children. War could make them depressed, angry, and aggressive. However, it could also heighten their awareness of the fragility of life and increase their care and compassion for others. Garrod et al. (2003) examined several samples of Muslim Bosniak, Catholic Croat, and Orthodox Serbian children, all of whom had been affected by the 1991–1995 war between ethnic factions in the former Yugoslavia.

Villages that once housed one ethnic group were "cleansed" through forced resettlement, imprisonment, and murder. In the Herzegovinian city of Mostar, the war between the Serbs, Croats, and Bosniaks inflicted intense damage. Children ages 6–11 in Mostar were interviewed for this study. Children of all ethnic backgrounds were examined using moral dilemmas read to them in their native languages. These dilemmas involved animals. For example, in one scenario, a family of moles is living in their underground den when a prickly hedgehog comes and decides to live there. The children were asked what should be done and why. The scenarios resembled dilemmas the children may have faced with relocation and conflict between other ethnic groups during the war.

The researchers found that the children responded to most dilemmas with a *care and compassion* orientation. They expressed concern for the animals

and tried to come up with solutions that could benefit both parties. These results were similar to results found with children in regions unaffected by war. What surprised the researchers, however, was that the children in Bosnia brought up many issues about size, strength, power, and domination of one group over another. They often talked about the inability of two species to get along and be friends. Whether they used a justice or a care perspective, they focused on power, control, and domination, whereas children from peaceful areas never brought up these issues. For example, one boy said the moles should leave their home because the hedgehog is stronger. He emphasized the hedgehog's sharp needles. When the researcher said that it was the moles' home, so why shouldn't the hedgehog leave, the boy replied that they can't do anything to fight the hedgehog and that he would scratch them, so they had no choice but to leave. Other children talked about the moles being afraid to be sent out into the forest at night.

The children's responses illuminated their attempts to process what had happened in their communities in a war that displaced over two million families. Today, the schools in Bosnia and Herzegovina are segregated by ethnicity, leaving little opportunity for children to interact with diverse others and heal their fear of and disdain for the other groups. This study shows that even if exposure to war does not make children violent and aggressive, it changes the way they process information. It also suggests that in the aftermath of war, adult decisions can play a crucial role in children's perceptions of both their own safety and their views of the previous enemy.

Psychologists recommend that professionals base interventions for children and families involved in armed conflict, refugee struggles, and other social ills on a comprehensive understanding of their cultural contexts. Researchers and clinicians must thoroughly study the conflict, understand the various sides and family members' perceptions of what happened, and respect the families' descriptions of what happened to them. Members of the culture must be on board with treatment teams so that culturally specific manifestations of anxiety, depression, or trauma reactions can be better understood (Saltzman, Layne, Steinberg, Arslanagic, & Pynoos, 2003). Educators must train local professionals and para-professionals to conduct assessments and treatments so that they may sustain the recovery process on their own without outside interventions becoming permanent. When this type of treatment is conducted, we see significant reductions in PTSD symptoms, depression, anxiety, and extended grief reactions (Saltzman et al., 2003).

(Nader, Pynoos, Fairbanks, Al-Ajeel, & Al-Asfour, 1993). Israeli and Palestinian children also evidence high levels of PTSD symptomatology (Diamond et al., 2010; Thabet & Vostanis, 1999).

To learn how the Bosnian conflict may have affected schoolchildren's moral reasoning, read the *How Would You Measure That?* box.

The women's minister in Iraq, Nawal al-Samarraie, resigned in 2009 because she could not get aid for the thousands of unemployed widows she was trying to help deal with their intense grief, trauma, poverty, and health problems. She reported that there were three million war widows in Iraq in 2009, most of whom were uneducated and had relied on their husbands for sustenance. Today, women make up almost 70% of the Iraqi population. Al-Samarraie reports extremely high levels of domestic violence in families where traumatized men have returned home, plus rampant homelessness and military detention of Iraqi women (Gamel, 2009).

Ethnopolitical conflict, foreign occupation, and widespread poverty, sickness, and death traumatize entire families in conflicts around the world. To see how one family dealt with the ethnopolitical conflict on the island nation of Cyprus, and what happened when they immigrated to England, read Refia's story in the *Focus on My Family* Box.

The responsibilities of developed nations

Globalization, the interactions between diverse nations and peoples, carries with it both extremely positive outcomes and horrific outcomes. Interacting with people from different backgrounds can enrich people's lives and lead them to learn and grow. However, many of the conflicts discussed earlier are related to people from different backgrounds fighting for scarce resources or exploiting each other for greater power or recognition. Many people feel that it is the responsibility of wealthy nations with high standards of living to invest in developing nations in order to raise their standard of living and thus ensure their families' mental and physical health. When a country's standard of living increases, its citizens make larger incomes and more people are educated and healthy. As a consequence, they may have less inclination to leave their country and emigrate elsewhere. They may also be less inclined to take desperate measures such as committing crimes or joining extremist groups. There are many complex reasons for civil strife, oppression, war, and terrorism. Improving the standard of living for people around the world will not solve all of these issues (Wade, 2004), but scholars feel that ensuring a minimum standard for quality of life is a major first step (Engle et al., 2007).

The U.S. Institute of Medicine has published several opinion papers on these matters. They argue that the U.S. has a key role to play in ensuring the health of our global neighbors. The Committee on the U.S. Commitment to Global Health (CUSCGH) (2009) argues that wealthy industrialized nations must share the knowledge and technology they acquire with the developing world. Their Executive Summary (2009, p. 1) states:

> U.S. leadership in global health reflects many motives: the national interest of protecting U.S. residents from threats to their health; the humanitarian obligation to enable healthy individuals, families, and communities everywhere to live more productive and fulfilling lives; and the broader mission of U.S. foreign policy to reduce poverty, build stronger economies, promote peace, increase national security, and strengthen the image of the United States in the world.

FOCUS ON MY FAMILY

Refia's story

I am a Turkish Cypriot, from Cyprus, in the eastern Mediterranean. In 1963, I was 9 years old, living near the border between Greek and Turkish communities. On New Year's Eve 1963, heavy fighting began between the two communities and we had to flee. We were taken to an elementary school within the ancient walled city of Nicosia where we shared a classroom with three families for two months. Then we had to go back to our house because my mother's family had to evacuate their village and had nowhere to go. My brother, sister, parents, grandparents, uncle, aunt, cousins and I lived together for many years in our house.

At 19, I married and went to England. I was away from my family for the first time. It took many months to adjust to being married as well as being in a new country with a different culture and values. I would wait for my husband to sleep so I could cry freely, saying *I want my family*. In England, people wanted to know if I had a family. I found the question puzzling, thinking, *Of course I have a family; how could I exist if I did not have a family?* When I inquired, they replied, "We mean a family of your own." Did they mean my mother, father, brother, sister, grandparents, uncles, and aunties were not my family? I realized westerners' concept of "family" consisted only of one's own children. I did not have any children so I was without a family.

When I did have a "family," we decided to return to Cyprus after the 1974 conflict between Turks and Greeks ended. When you are away from your country, you have an illusion that when you go back things will be the same, but things change. I found that when I came back, even I had changed. Living abroad made me independent. I started to miss our British life, where we could make our own decisions without interference.

In Cyprus, our families had a say in all of our choices, like how we raised our children. Because we had always lived in a segregated community, surrounded by Greeks, our only pastime was being with family. It may be hard to believe but I was living on an island yet could not go to the sea for years because we had to go through checkpoints, waiting for hours to be searched. After the 1974 conflict, though, and with new checkpoints opening, we can now travel more freely.

This freedom has affected young Turkish Cypriots' viewpoints as well. Now they can go for education, holidays or to work abroad and interact with new people, cultures, and values. This changes their individuality through entering the big melting pot of globalization. The young prefer to spend their time according to their plans, which often do not include the family if it's not their "own family." My experience shows that international relations have both benefits and harsh realities for families.

Refia's family.
Photo reproduced by permission.

The CUSCGH makes clear connections between the physical health of global populations and their emergence from poverty and subsistence living into a technologically and educationally advanced world. The Committee emphasizes that western nations may put programs in place and support start-up clinics and modern health practices, but that ultimately, each country must make citizen health and well-being a top priority for their own legislation and policy development.

Our historic practice of giving monetary and material aid to developing nations has not helped them become self-sufficient. Many developing nations have become dependent on the western world for their survival. What they need is small microfinancing loans like the ones discussed earlier, to help individuals develop small businesses, skilled craft markets, or farms (Wood & Gough, 2006). People need training and support to be able to sustain themselves, their families, and their villages and towns. They need to understand basic preventive health practices such as good hygiene, family planning, and the use of condoms to prevent disease and pregnancy.

In this regard, the United Nations implemented a plan to achieve **Millennium Development Goals** by the year 2015. These goals include reducing infant and maternal mortality, combating HIV/AIDS, malaria, and other diseases, and reducing chronic and severe poverty around the world (CUSCGH, 2009). Sub-Saharan Africa and South Asia are particular targets of UN efforts to reduce poverty and improve the health and well-being of all citizens. To learn more about the Millennium Development Goals and see how frequent infant mortality is in various countries, check out Figures 14.3 and 14.4.

A global approach to health care is imperative because with two billion people traveling by air every year, infectious diseases can spread rapidly, as was seen with the 2010 H1N1 (swine flu) outbreak that affected 20 countries in only three weeks. The U.S. has begun to address these needs by committing extensive resources to the fight against global health crises. In May, 2009, President Barack Obama requested $63 billion dollars for global health initiatives. And between 2004 and 2008, President George W. Bush had begun to make record commitments to global health with the U.S. Agency for International Development (USAID) increasing U.S. commitments to global health programs by 350 percent (http://www.usaid.gov/). Much of this funding is focused on AIDS, tuberculosis, and malaria (CUSCGH, 2009). Even with these increases, however, the U.S. does not spend as much per capita on global health as other wealthy nations, indicating that even more can be done with American technology, medical advances, scientific knowledge, equipment, training, and direct service provision for people around the world. When we safeguard the health of those in developing poor and middle income countries, we ensure our own health through reducing worldwide epidemics, reducing crime and violence, and enabling people to remain in their countries with their own families, instead of emigrating to find work and better mental and physical health care away from home.

What do you think? Is it the responsibility of western industrialized nations to look after poorer countries? The issue is an important one because many Americans feel that wealthier people should not be responsible for the health and well-being of poor people, even those within our own borders.

In addition to addressing issues of global health and welfare, we need to tackle many salient social issues, including immigration in our own communities. Let's take a closer look at current immigration rates, issues immigrant people face, and how their lives in their new countries take shape.

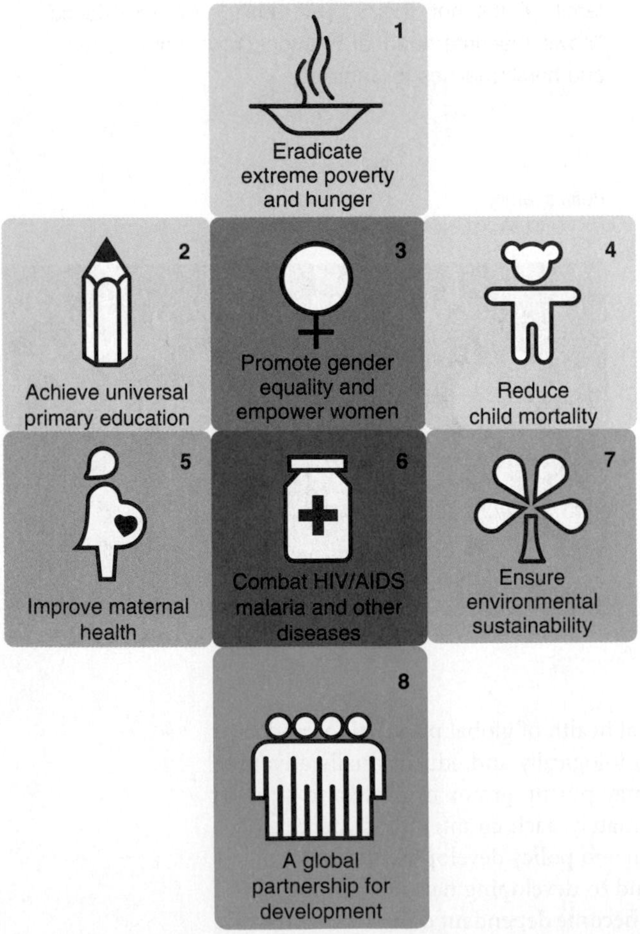

Millennium Development Goals A set of goals the United Nations has set forth, which they hope to accomplish by the year 2015; these goals include the eradication of extreme poverty, great reductions in HIV/AIDS, and improvement in infant and maternal health around the world.

FIGURE 14.3 United Nations Millennium Development Goals.
Source: http://www.un.org/millenniumgoals/poverty.shtml

FIGURE 14.4 Infant mortality rates by country.
Source: http://www.un.org/millenniumgoals/poverty.shtml

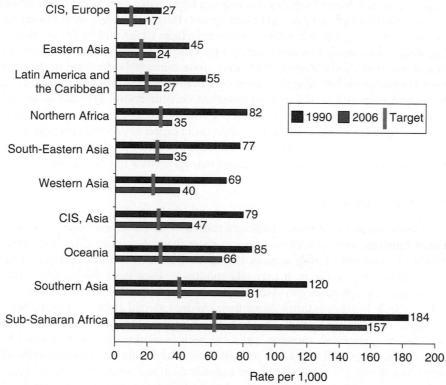

Deaths of children under 5 per 1,000 live births (1990, 2006, and 2015 target).

AN IN-DEPTH LOOK AT IMMIGRATION

- Transnational families
- LGBT immigrants
- Undocumented immigrants
- Undocumented children and education

For the first time in U.S. history, non-European immigrants are now the majority of new entrants into the country. This means that white Americans will soon be in the statistical minority and we will have a **minority majority**. Minority majority refers to a situation where an ethnic minority group increases in number to surpass the numbers of people in the original majority group. Keep in mind that this is a statistical majority. This doesn't mean they necessarily gain in prestige or positions of power over the original majority group. For example, in the state of California, European Americans make up slightly less than half of the population, making them a minority majority, but they are still more prominent in political and business leadership positions.

The changing demographics of the United States and other western nations like Australia, Canada, and Britain, mean that the previous power elite will potentially lose some of its clout over time. Fully 25% of children in the United States today are children of immigrants. Almost 80% of children born to immigrant parents were born in the U.S., making them American citizens. These children have the same rights and privileges as any other child, yet they face discrimination, lack of access to health care and other services, and high levels of poverty. Today's aging population of Baby Boomers will rely greatly on these children to take care of them through service work and through their contributions

Minority majority
An ethnic minority group increases in number to surpass the numbers of people in the original majority group.

to the tax base and programs like social security. Thus, it serves all of our interests to ensure a positive life for immigrants so that continued marginalization in our society does not cause them to fail to live up to their potential. When immigrant people are highly educated, healthy, and economically well-off, the benefits to society at large will be widespread (Hernandez, Denton, & Macartney, 2008).

Many of the new immigrants from Asia (for example, from China and India) are already highly educated professionals coming to a new country with valuable skills to offer. But others have little education and few skills. Today low-skilled workers have a much harder time finding work than earlier waves of immigrants had when low levels of education were acceptable. A person could then make a living and support a family without advanced skills or knowledge. Not so anymore. The world we live in is rapidly increasing in complexity and technological sophistication. In previous generations, immigrants with little skill or education could expect to become upwardly mobile, or at least they could expect such for their children. With today's downward spiraling economy and global competition in virtually all fields, such expectations may go unfulfilled (Pyke, 2004).

Transnational families

Many immigrants are aware of these challenges and come to their new country alone, forming **transnational families**, families with members in more than one country. Transnational families usually consist of one or more family member immigrating to a new country, having to leave the rest of the family in the home country. It may take months or even years for the immigrant family member(s) to earn enough money to return home or sponsor their relatives to emigrate as well. Many wealthy people in other countries send their children abroad alone to reap the benefits of a college education or graduate/medical schooling. These transnational trends lead to the separation of families who are often from countries that value both familialism and a clear social hierarchy. When family members go it alone in a new western/developed nation, they often experience internal and external struggle with the western values of individualism and gender equality (Pyke, 2004).

Transnational families
Families who live in different countries due to work possibilities abroad.

Today, the majority of new immigrants are women who are the primary breadwinners for their families either in the new country or by sending money back home. Many of these women speak little or no English. Seventy-nine percent of Latina, 73% of Vietnamese, 70% of Korean, and 63% of Chinese new immigrants report speaking very little English. Two thirds of these people live below the poverty line and struggle every day to keep their families together. Most of them have no health insurance. However, unlike the stereotype of immigrants not wanting to learn English or assimilate into the culture, two thirds of immigrant women have attended English-language classes and over 90% of Vietnamese, Arab, and Latino immigrants report wanting to become U.S. citizens (Pyke, 2004).

Studies on adolescent offspring of immigrants show that these teenagers feel extreme stress and anxiety, especially if they serve as cultural brokers or gatekeepers (intermediaries between their immigrant parents and the dominant culture). They report higher rates of poor health, stomach aches, headaches, and illnesses (Almgren, Magarati, & Mogford, 2009). Both students and parents who come to a new country alone feel isolated and desperate, being away from their families for long periods of time. They also report experiencing racism, discrimination, and disdain from local citizens (Pereda, 2009). Part of the stress they feel comes from the immigration process itself. For example, there is bias in the naturalization process, with Asians being allowed to bring in more relatives and have their cases processed more quickly than other groups. Moreover, the massive amount of paperwork required and the exorbitant fees, which few immigrants can afford, are also sources of distress for immigrants (Pereda, 2009).

LGBT immigrants

When immigrants are sexual minorities, they face even more challenges. While heterosexual immigrants who arrive alone can meet, fall in love, and marry citizens of their new country, ensuring them future citizenship, same-sex couples have no such privilege. Lesbian, gay, and transgender immigrants are often escaping cultures of oppression, hatred, and even violence. For example, gay men from Mexico are often called *joto*, meaning "faggot," or *mariposa*, a derogatory slant on the word "butterfly." Similarly, gay men from Guatemala face routine callous killings by local police forces. They immigrate to western nations where attitudes toward LGBT people are more progressive, yet they live in constant fear of deportation. If they are successful in traveling to the U.S., they face more challenges as the Immigration and Naturalization Service does not recognize same-sex domestic partnerships as legitimate. Even if same-sex couples were legally married in a state like Massachusetts, they cannot become citizens through marriage like heterosexual couples can, because federal law does not recognize such unions. LGBT persons can apply for political asylum if they can convince authorities that they face threats of bodily harm or death upon their return to their home country, but having their application approved is never a certainty (Henneman, 2006).

Undocumented immigrants

Even when immigrant families fit the SNAF structure, they often live with constant fear and intimidation. Several years ago, U.S. Immigration and Customs Enforcement (ICE) began massive sweeps of workplaces and even individual homes looking for undocumented immigrants (Thronson, 2008). They began placing entire families in detention facilities that were once prisons or psychiatric hospitals. The American Civil Liberties Union (ACLU) and other human rights organizations protested the treatment of hard-working people who were thrown into prison-like circumstances, often experiencing traumatic separation from their children. Women who were nursing were often separated from their infants for long periods of time if their workplaces were raided and they were incarcerated. No attempts were made to locate children in day care centers or schools as their parents were being hauled away. Many of the parents caught in raids were instantly deported, leaving minor children (most of whom are U.S. citizens) to fend for themselves (Hernandez et al., 2008). Through the efforts of organizations like the Women's Refugee Commission and Texans United for Families, the conditions at these detention centers have improved greatly. For example, nursing women are allowed to stay with their infants, nutritious food and hygiene products are more readily available, and privacy curtains were installed around toilets. Children are allowed to wear street clothes instead of prison uniforms, access to educational services has improved, and guards cannot threaten to punish children by breaking up their families (http://www.aclu.org).

The largest groups of undocumented immigrants detained in these sweeps are from Latin American countries. Hispanics are the fastest growing group of immigrants. In 1970, they made up 5% of new immigrants, and by the year 2000, they made up 13%. It is estimated that between 11% and 30% of Hispanic immigrants are undocumented, or living in the country illegally (Hernandez et al., 2008).

Undocumented children and education

Perhaps one of the most complex examples of struggles faced by children of immigrants involves the case of higher education. Education is the ticket out of poverty for many people. If we can educate children, regardless of their documented or undocumented status, they can reach their developmental and economic potentials, which benefits all of us through a more highly skilled workforce, reduced crime, and reduced use of public services.

Children whose parents moved to the United States illegally when the children were very young face unique challenges. Even if they attended U.S. schools their entire lives and only speak English, they are often denied access to American universities. They also cannot legally work in the U.S. (Gonzales, 2008). For an adolescent who has grown up in the U.S., the prospect of being deported to a country that is completely unfamiliar is frightening. Children have no say and no initiative in the immigration process. If their parents chose to bring them into a country illegally, and the children grow up there, what choice do they have? Many of them take full advantage of their educational opportunities and excel in school in the new country. They want nothing more than to attend university. While many universities do not check on immigration documentation and even welcome undocumented students, these students are not eligible for financial aid. Thus, their attempts to use education to rise above the poverty line are often thwarted. People fear that allowing these students into American universities will result in American citizens losing available student slots in universities. However, studies following the 10 states that allow undocumented students who graduated from U.S. high schools to attend college have not found a huge influx of immigrants trying to take university slots meant for U.S. citizens (Gonzales, 2008).

In 2010, Congress was considering a bill, the Development, Relief, and Education for Alien Minors, or DREAM, Act, which would allow undocumented students who have lived in the U.S. for several years to apply for permanent resident status if they graduate from high school and enter college or military service. This program would allow over 300,000 undocumented high school graduates to legally work and become educated in colleges and universities (Gonzales, 2008). This would benefit the students because currently they are forced to pay out-of-state tuition if they are allowed to attend and cannot receive financial aid or legally work to help defray costs. California has implemented Assembly Bill AB 540, which allows any student who graduated from a California high school to pay in-state tuition. This bypasses the issue of undocumented status because all students, regardless of immigration status, can qualify to pay in-state tuition if they graduated from a California high school.

Similar bills have not been passed around the country, though, which has left thousands of adolescents without the opportunity to attend college or work legally (Gonzales, 2008). This creates a Catch-22 because federal law states that we may not discriminate against children in K–12 education based on their immigration status. All immigrants, documented or not, are allowed free public education in the United States. But when they graduate, they are denied the same opportunities for higher education that their classmates are given. The current situation means that our laws are perpetuating the problem of immigrants and their children being trapped in a cycle of poverty and low achievement, when education and work opportunities for people would benefit not only their families but society at large.

Research shows that educating immigrants adds about 10% to public educational budgets, but these costs are more than offset by the benefits an educated populace provides for society. In addition, universities receive tuition dollars from students who would not ordinarily be in college. A college educated immigrant will contribute over $5,000 more in taxes to the government per year and will consume almost $4,000 less of public services like welfare and health care than a high school dropout would (Gonzales, 2008). This means a $9,000 surplus for the government per child educated. Because these students are usually bilingual and bicultural, educating them will also result in a talented and highly valuable workforce for the new global economy.

FINAL REFLECTIONS ON THE FUTURE OF FAMILIES

Instead of focusing on families' deficits and problems, this textbook has encouraged you to think about ways that diverse families can reach health and competence. Family well-being depends on focusing on solutions to social problems, not detailing the deficits we see in families that may be unlike our own. A punitive approach or a series of judgments will never encourage families to strive to reach their emotional and psychological potentials. This strengths-based approach focuses on prevention over intervention and support over punishment. For example, in most western nations, modern welfare states are seeking new ways to compensate for the rapid drop in birth rates. There are not currently enough children being born to replace retired workers in most western nations. Thus, industrialized nations are implementing generous social welfare programs and benefits packages, including high-quality health care and child care available to all, in order to entice people to both work and have children (Cousins, 2005). For more on this idea, and to compare the traditional deficits-based approach to a strengths-based approach, look at Figure 14.5.

This new strengths-based conceptualization must include family-friendly policies such as flex-time and work sharing. Research spanning 27 European countries shows clearly that child and family well-being (both physical and emotional) are greatest in countries with the highest levels of spending on publicly funded family benefits and services (Bradshaw & Richardson, 2009). Thus, part of building family strengths rests on government responsibility for supporting families. A policy of rugged individualism will not work to raise family well-being. Only with a widespread, preventative, and governmentally supported focus will families around the world be elevated to higher levels of happiness, mental health, productivity, and security, which are needed in a global economy (Silverstein & Auerbach, 2005).

In order to help more families become happy and healthy, the National Research Council (1997) suggested that public policy must focus on raising people out of poverty. Related to that goal is a global alteration in consciousness, led by a preventive (versus intervention or crisis-focused) approach, such as ensuring that all pregnancies become planned and that all children are wanted, revered, and conscientiously raised. This would lead to massive reductions in child abuse and neglect around the world. Ensuring a living wage and minimum standard of living for everyone ultimately

FIGURE 14.5 Comparing a deficits-based approach to a strengths-based approach.
Source: Braver et al., 2004.

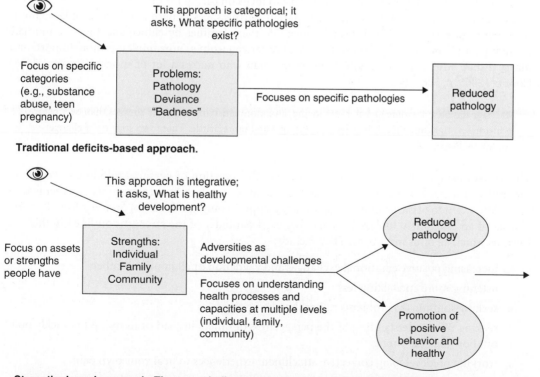

Traditional deficits-based approach.

Strengths-based approach. The arrow indicates the process is ongoing and dynamic.

FIGURE 14.6 What advantages and challenges do you think this couple experiences in their twenty-first-century relationship?
Photo © Koichi Kamoshida/Getty Images.

benefits us all. When we divide the world into the haves and the have-nots, we hesitate to share valuable resources. Modern families must work to focus on caring for others.

Modern families are evolving into egalitarian partnerships between diverse people, many of whom are not related by blood. People enter into these families by choice and they are mutually satisfying for all members. For example, 80% of American women now think it is more important to marry a man who can share his feelings than a man who makes a lot of money (Coontz, 2005). Coontz (2005, p. 306) states:

> Marriage has become more joyful, more loving, and more satisfying for more couples than ever before in history. At the same time, it has become optional and more brittle. These two strands of change cannot be disentangled.

Thus, relationships are moving more and more in the direction of personal fulfillment. People see the frailty of life all around them, with global starvation, warfare, and environmental emergencies. They don't want to waste precious time being unhappy. In our final focus on *Building Your Strengths*, instead of an assessment tool or box, here is a brief reminder of the strengths outlined in this text, towards which all of us may strive. They include:

- increasing positive emotional exchanges and validation of all family members
- listening more and talking less
- seeking solutions to problems rather than being right
- seeking true understanding of the perspectives of others instead of jumping to quickly point out how they are wrong
- working on developing corrective attachment experiences to heal your own pain
- caring for your own mind, body, and spirit, so that you may care for others.

The Global Oneness Project (www.globalonenessproject.org) asks that people strive for a new global identity, where we all see each other as members of the same tribe. No person, family, group, country, or religion is revered over any other. They ask you to envision what the world would be like if *all* families were valued.

CHAPTER SUMMARY

This chapter summarized the key themes of the book and outlined major challenges and trends occurring in families around the world. The five themes of the book include: the necessity of using the bioecological approach to studying families, the importance of examining family processes over structures to understand family well-being, the need to focus on family strengths and building on them, the fact that intersectional identities affect interactions between people in all families, and the idea that diversity has always been the norm in family life.

Western nations are becoming more and more diverse as travel, communication, and the distribution of economic capital are now common across cultures. Globalization has led to diverse people engaging in relationships and business ventures around the world. It can also affect marginalization and exploitation of people who have little power, as there are many nations today who are desperately poor and are experiencing war and hunger. Women and sexual minorities are particularly at risk of oppression, violence, and a lack of civil rights.

Many scholars feel it is the responsibility of western nations to spread their wealth and help ensure the well-being of people from developing nations. The United Nations has developed several Millennium Development Goals meant to increase family health and longevity. Microfinancing loaned to people in developing countries improves health and reduces violence, malnutrition, and maternal and infant mortality. With millions of people, particularly children, exposed to violence and trauma, rates of post-traumatic stress disorder are alarming and in need of attention. Of particular interest is the education of girls and women to bring their families out of poverty and increase the viability of their cultures in the twenty-first century.

With globalization comes increasing focus on immigration, especially in western nations, which receive large numbers of immigrants seeking asylum or a better livelihood for their families. The U.S. struggles with immigration issues because in many areas, ethnic minorities are becoming a statistical majority and people question whether immigrants cost more than they contribute to society. Issues regarding immigrant labor, crime, and education were discussed as challenges facing the U.S. in the twenty-first century.

KEY TERMS

acculturation stress
globalization
inclusionists (the color blind)
integrative pluralists

masculinist
microfinancing
Millennium Development Goals
minority majority

politicized homosexuality
separatists (assimilationists)
transnational families
xenophobia

WEBSITES FOR FURTHER EXPLORATION

http://www.globalization101.org/index.html

Globalization 101 is a project of the Levin Institute at the State University of New York. It covers the advantages and disadvantages of a globalized world. It has blogs and "Ask the experts" sections for students to learn everything they want to know about other regions of the world. There are constantly updated articles on topics like Iraqi elections, Haiti, jihadist teachings, international law, women's and human rights, the global media, and so on.

http://www.immigrationvoice.org/index.php

Immigration Voice is a non-profit, non-partisan group that serves as an intermediary between highly educated and skilled legal immigrants and the U.S. government. They advocate for fairness and justice and attempt to alleviate barriers to citizenship. They work for the over 150,000 highly skilled legal immigrants who run into constant roadblocks due to onerous green card procedures, immigration country quotas, and quotas on certain professions. They have links to lawyers and a really cool link to track and analyze the progress of green card applications.

http://www.who.int/hac/crises/en/

The World Health Organization's crisis page. This page lists political, warfare, disease, and hunger crises country by country. You can track the health and nutrition of citizens in every country. The most amazing section covers their "photo stories," which are photo essays taken in dozens of countries that document the plight of displaced and struggling people around the world.

GLOSSARY OF KEY TERMS

Accomplishment of natural growth A parenting style used by working class or poor parents to allow their children to develop naturally within strict power hierarchies and expectations for obedience.

Acculturation stress The pressure and strain immigrants experience as they try to adapt to a new environment.

Active engagement Initiating constructive ways to handle one's partner's problems.

Activities of daily living Things that people become less and less able to do with age, including feeding, dressing, toileting, and taking care of one's own household and medications.

Advanced directive or living will Documents that specify exactly what kind of health care or lifesaving measures a person wants if he or she becomes incapacitated.

Affective reactivity The extent to which a person reacts with limbic arousal (like the secretion of stress hormones) when potential intimacy threats arise.

Affinal family A family where the marital relationship is given priority and extended family is expected to be secondary.

Agape One of Lee's typologies; similar to Sternberg's consummate love, in that the couple is completely devoted to each other. They care for the very "soul" of the other person, always wanting to ensure their partner's welfare. They are selfless in their pursuit to make the other one happy; includes true intimacy, passion, and commitment.

Ageism Discrimination, prejudice, and lack of access to information or services based solely on one's age.

Allostasis A homeostatic balance between the demands of the environment and one's neurophysiological systems.

Allostatic load Increasing pressure on the nervous system, which prevents internal balance or equilibrium; leads to stress reactions.

Aloof fathers Dads who follow traditional gender stereotypes and expect to contribute to their family mainly by providing material goods.

Alzheimer's disease A progressive brain disorder wherein the brain slowly dies through a failure of normal brain metabolism of dead cellular material; characterized by dementia, personality, and health changes.

Ambivalents Involuntary singles who feel unsure about their singlehood, seeing some positive and some negative aspects to their lives.

Analog A research method that resembles real-life situations but is artificially manipulated in the lab.

Androcentrism A world view that holds men and male perspectives as the norm by which women are measured and compared.

Androgynous People who are characteristically both highly feminine and highly masculine; they score high on traits like assertiveness and strength as well as on sensitivity and nurturing; they do not conform rigidly to traditional gender roles.

Androgynous love The modern idea that both men and women should work on tenderness, empathy, and expressing their love to each other (in contrast to the idea that women are responsible for maintaining love).

Animal hoarding A form of animal abuse wherein the person attempts to help animals but has neither the money nor skill to do so; excessive numbers of animals are held in deplorable conditions.

Anti-miscegenation laws Laws that outlaw interracial marriage.

Antisocial/violent (cobra) batterers A type of batterer who is cold, callous, and calculating; they see their victims as objects and feel no love for them or remorse for their battering.

Anxious, preoccupied, ambivalent attachments Insecure attachments which lead people to fear abandonment, cling onto partners, or alternatively want closeness and then distance.

Arousal problems Sexual dysfunctions wherein women may have deficient lubrication, and men or women may experience a lack of tissue engorgement or sensation.

Arranged marriage A marriage wherein partners are chosen by family members, religious leaders, or cultural leaders, and not by the bride and groom.

Marriages and Families in the 21st Century: A Bioecological Approach, First Edition. Tasha R. Howe.
© 2012 Tasha R. Howe. Published 2012 by Blackwell Publishing Ltd.

Artificial insemination The introduction of sperm into the vagina to aid in fertilization.

Assimilationists People in favor of the legalization of same-sex marriage who argue that granting this privilege will allow same-sex couples to assimilate their lifestyles into the larger population; gay people who want to be recognized in the eyes of God and the community, and be given the same benefits that heterosexual spouses share through marriage.

Assisted reproductive technologies New scientific approaches that help people have babies.

Assortative mating A theory that says people with similar challenges in personality, antisocial behavior, impulsivity, and poor relationship skills find each other and marry, increasing the risk for both divorce and poor outcomes in their children.

Attachment The third phase involved in the neurochemistry of attraction; characterized by a sense of calm, security, and emotional intimacy. Oxytocin is circulating in higher amounts in the brain, as is vasopressin, which constricts the blood vessels and influences feelings of bonding. Attachment also refers to the emotional bonds between children and their caregivers or romantic partners.

Attachment Theory John Bowlby's theory stressing the importance of early caregiving relationships for shaping the way people process information and their social and emotional adjustment in adulthood.

Attraction The second phase involved in the neurochemistry of attraction; characterized by increases in the neurotransmitter dopamine. It also involves increases in norepinephrine (popularly known as adrenalin) and decreases in serotonin (the mood stabilizing neurotransmitter). Attraction involves heightened energy with attention focused specifically on one person. There is a sense of romantic or passionate love, feelings of exhilaration and intrusive thoughts about the person.

Attrition The rate at which participants leave a study through drop-out, death, relocation, or refusal to participate.

Authoritarian parenting A parenting style that is low on warmth/responsiveness but high on control/demandingness; emphasizes conformity and obedience.

Authoritative parenting A parenting style that is high on warmth/responsiveness and also high on control/demandingness; the style related to the best child outcomes in western cultures.

Authority ranking One of four elements of intimate relationships, characterized by deciding on power sharing and control issues.

Baby blues A general feeling of malaise or sadness after one has a baby; usually lasts a week or two.

Baseline assessment A manipulation check to assess the participants on key variables before the experiment has taken place.

Benevolent sexism Covert words or behaviors that express a denigration of women and ensure their continued inferiority; these acts or words may appear kind and positive but they represent a sense that women are helpless or weak.

Benevolent sexism Positive gender bias which paints women as weak or fragile (in need of protection) so that their inferiority at work is ensured.

Best interests of the child The contemporary legal standard whereby all decisions made in divorces and custody rulings include individualized decisions regarding what would benefit the children most.

Bicultural identity The ability of marginalized people (i.e. people of color, sexual minorities) to identify strongly with their own group and at the same time function well in the larger society.

Bigamy The crime of marrying someone while still being married to someone else.

Bioecological Theory The organizing framework of this book, which assumes that individuals exist within multiple complex systems of influence, from biological to cultural, all of which interact with each other to shape family functioning.

Biopsychosocial model of orgasm Mah and Binik's (2001) model which states that orgasms include a sensory, evaluative (cognitive), and affective (emotional) component.

Blastocyst A fluid-filled ball of layered cells, which develops by the fourth day after fertilization and travels down the fallopian tubes to implant in the lining of the uterus.

Blended family A remarried family wherein each partner has children he or she brings to the partnership.

Brain stem/reptilian brain The most primitive part of the triune brain that controls reflexes and basic behaviors like blood pressure and quick reactions.

Caregiving stress The overwhelming, depression, or loneliness felt by adult caregivers who must fulfill the needs of elderly or dependent adults; related to higher rates of elder abuse and neglect.

Causality A definitive statement about one variable causing changes in another variable.

Cesarean section A surgical procedure that removes a baby from its mother's womb by cutting directly into the uterus.

Chronological age How old you are in years.

Chronosystem Time period effects on development.

Civil unions A legal status for unmarried couples that grants them the same rights and responsibilities as married partners.

Clitoral orgasms Female orgasms that are thought to originate from clitoral stimulation.

Clitoridectomy A method of female genital mutilation where the glans and oftentimes the clitoral shaft are removed to keep a woman from feeling sexual pleasure.

Clitoris A hard bulb of nerve tissue that responds sensitively to sexual stimulation and assists in the female orgasmic response; located above the vagina and protected by a hood of tissue; includes a base with a shaft that continues into the body.

Cognitive reframing Helping one's partner think about a situation from another perspective.

Cohort effect The idea that how people develop is influenced by the generation they belong to, or the time period in which they were born.

Commitment A term Marcia (1980) used to describe the process of identity solidification; after a period of intense exploration in early adulthood, one will eventually commit to a set of values, goals, and personal identities.

Common law marriage A marriage recognized in some states and countries where a couple is given all the rights, privileges, and responsibilities of marriage because they've been together a long time, not because they have gone through a formal marriage ritual.

Communal sharing One of four elements of intimate relationships, characterized by being open and intimate with a partner.

Communism An analysis of capitalist societies that claims the rich will always exploit the labor of the poor and eventually the poor will revolt to reap the fruits of their own labor; it emphasizes the need for a communal way of life where all workers benefit equally from shared work.

Community development Collective efforts by all public agencies to provide goods and services that support all parents in helping their children meet their developmental potentials.

Community of care model A model of caring for families and children in order to prevent or intervene in family violence; includes multi-agency culturally sensitive practices such as involving tribal elders or adhering to cultural customs in making care plans.

Compadrazgo A belief common in Hispanic/Latino families where many men and women are thought of as co-parents for children (in other words, all "aunties" care for all children in the family).

Companionate love A type of love that usually exists in long-term relationships where sexual passion may have declined but intimacy, commitment, and a sense of security are high.

Comparable worth legislation Laws that mandate equal pay and benefits for men and women when they have comparable experience, skills, and education.

Competent loners Post-divorce, these people are independent, happy, and self-confident; have successful careers and many friends.

Concerted cultivation A parenting style used by middle-class parents to cultivate their children's individuality, self-confidence, and independent thinking.

Conflict Theory Argues that conflict is a normal and natural part of family life; people can use conflicts to help relationships mature and grow through renegotiating power relationships.

Conflicted marriage A mostly unsatisfying marriage that is less likely to lead to divorce than a devitalized marriage because the couple has many friends and other interests outside of the relationship that make them happy.

Consanguineal relationships A family where extended family and blood kin are more important and their needs are catered to more than those of the married couple.

Constructionists People who think sex and gender differences are socially constructed.

Control group The group of participants that does not receive the independent variable manipulation; can receive another similar manipulation if a no-treatment control group is also employed.

Cooperative traditional arranged marriages The family and the young person have equal abilities to bring in potential spouses, and the final choice is agreed upon jointly.

Co-parenting classes Courses that help parents understand the effects of divorce on children, develop co-parenting contracts they can sign, help parents work together to protect their own mental health and that of their children.

Co-provider family A family where both partners must work to sustain family livelihood.

Correlated In research terms, a statistical finding that two variables, or things measured, are in some way related to each other; we cannot assume one variable caused the other, however.

Correlational study A study that examines links, associations, or relationships between variables but cannot assess causal influences due to a lack of experimental controls.

Couples coping enhancement training (CCET) Program that focuses on changing maladaptive thinking patterns, improving interactions between partners, improving stress management techniques, increasing positive communication, improving problem-solving, etc., in order to prevent divorce.

Courtship The process whereby people select each other as mates and decide to make a committed partnership with each other, such as in the case of marriage.

Couvade syndrome Male "sympathy pregnancy" symptoms like weight gain and back ache.

Covenant marriage Marriages that restrict a couple's ability to divorce by having them enroll in premarital counseling, endure a long waiting period for divorce, make every attempt to reconcile during pre-divorce counseling, and divorce only in extreme circumstances such as domestic violence, abandonment, and adultery; often include more traditional attitudes about religion and gender roles.

Crisis A term Marcia (1980) used to describe the Eriksonian search for identity, which includes meeting diverse people, traveling, trying new things, and basically experimenting with life.

Critical thinking The ability to use reason to find accurate information, to think logically and skeptically, and not be gullible to ideas that have no supporting evidence.

Cross-sectional A study design where one or more groups of people are measured at one point in time.

Crystallized intelligence Cognitive skills related to information, trivia, or facts we've learned, or the "software" installed on our brain.

Cultural assimilation A process whereby a person decides to dress, act, speak, and practice daily rituals like those in the new host country.

Cultural brokers or gatekeepers Children who serve as liaisons between their home culture and the larger dominant culture, providing key services for their families and often taking on adult-like responsibilities.

Cultural relativism The idea that each culture's beliefs and practices hold equal value and that one culture should not judge another culture as inferior, wrong, or unhealthy for its members.

Cycle of violence A repetitive pattern of domestic violence escalation, cooling off, and re-escalation; violence is often followed by apologies, forgiveness, happiness, and then escalation back into violence.

Daddy track A negative stereotype of working fathers that believes they are less committed to their jobs if they are committed to their children; results in fewer promotions or raises.

Dating Early stage romantic excursions that serve as a foundation for building a potentially committed relationship.

Defeated Post-divorce, these people have low self-concepts and high rates of depression and antisocial behavior; tend to drink and use drugs, get into trouble with the law, and have health problems.

Deinstitutionalized A radical change in the "institution" of marriage, which was once comprised of a set of rules for how, when, and why people should marry; today, the social controls which influenced people's behaviors are weakening and marriage rates have decreased.

Delegated dyadic coping One partner takes over the other's responsibilities when the first partner is feeling stressed.

Demand characteristics Characteristics of the researchers or research setting that influence the behavior or thoughts of participants.

Dependency model A viewpoint which assumes that a stepchild was financially dependent on a co-resident stepparent and so stepparents have rights and responsibilities for their stepchildren.

Dependent variable The variable that is measured at the end of a research study.

Devitalized marriage A marriage that is wholly unsatisfying and likely to lead to divorce; the couples are often young, with low income and large numbers of children, as well as having divorce in their families of origin.

Disengaged marriages Couples live independent lives in the same house; have few interests in common and different sets of friends; don't fight but don't engage in positive ways.

Disengagement Theory The outdated idea that seniors should prepare for death by disengaging from the world around them, slowly isolating themselves from people and activities.

Disillusionment model A model explaining that people often put on false fronts during dating relationships so that when they commit to a relationship, they become disillusioned to find out the flaws in their partners. They feel unhappy that the person has "changed."

Dismissing avoidant attachment An insecure attachment style where people don't value intimacy with others and keep a cold distance in relationships.

Divorce mediation A trained professional (attorney, psychologist) helps a couple devise an amicable agreement on custody, dividing up property, child visitation, child support and alimony, scheduling activities, etc.

Divorce mills States or regions in the nineteenth century where people came to get easy divorces.

Divorce transition guides Trained professionals (social workers, psychologists) who consult with families in order to minimize conflict and counsel parents on the best way to talk to their children about divorce, as well as co-parent after divorce.

Divorced same-sex families Gay or lesbian families that contain children who were born into previous heterosexual unions; these children have experienced divorce and a parent's "coming out."

Domestic partnerships Policies available for non-married heterosexual or homosexual couples, which give them the same rights and responsibilities as married people.

Doulas Professionally trained birthing assistants who support women giving birth.

Duluth Model The most commonly used model of batterer treatments; the focus is on rehabilitation of the batterer and support for the survivor, without a focus on maintaining their relationship; includes all community agencies working together to prevent further violence.

Dyadic stress A stressor that causes grief for both partners simultaneously, with which they must cope dyadically (meaning two people together) within a given time frame.

Dyspareunia Pain during intercourse.

Dysphoric/borderline batterers A type of batterer who feels he is not responsible for his actions, blames his partner, and often suffers from mental illnesses like depression and personality disorders.

Eclectic approach An approach to research that capitalizes on the strengths of many different theories.

Educated partners Young adults who, by age 24, go to college and are in committed partnerships or marriages.

Educated singles Young adults who are highly educated by age 24, are in steady dating relationships, have no children, and live either with their parents or in their own apartments.

Embracing singlehood A strategy to cope with being single in a couples-oriented world; adjusting one's attitude to see all the advantages of such a lifestyle.

Embryo The name for the baby after it implants into the uterus about two weeks after conception.

Embryonic stage The stage of prenatal development after the embryo is implanted into the uterus (from approximately 14 days and lasting until nine weeks after fertilization); the embryo's organs begin to form.

Emerging adulthood The stage of life from approximately ages 18 to 25 when, in western cultures, young people spend time on improving themselves through education and experimentation (in contrast to getting married right away).

Emic An "insider's" approach to research, looking at a topic from the perspective of the research participants.

Emotional neglect Not meeting a child or dependent adult's need for love, affection, and validation of who they are.

Emotionally distant or neutral affective style Emotional disengagement from one's romantic partner.

Emotionally volatile affective style Continuous engagement in an attack–defend pattern and emotions (both positive and negative) run high.

Emotion-focused couples therapy (EFCT) An evidence-based practice for improving love relationships which focuses on unraveling the tender emotions underlying harsh emotions like anger.

Empty love One of Sternberg's categories of love, where commitment is high but passion and intimacy are low.

Empty nest syndrome Feelings of depression and loneliness that parents may experience when their children leave home.

Enculturative responsibilities The duties expected of grandparents of color involving transmitting cultural rituals, beliefs, and values to their grandchildren.

Endogamy A set of beliefs, practices, or mandates regarding people within one's own group who are considered to be one's only viable marriage partners.

Endogenous opiates Internal chemicals like endorphins that make a person feel less pain and give one a sense of euphoria.

Enforceable trust The idea that a formal, legal marriage creates a legal "trust," which reduces the chances of divorce because the public ceremony makes the couple's vows to each other harder to break.

Enhancers Post-divorce, these people are successful in employment, relationships with their children, and physical and mental well-being.

Epididymis A narrow, tightly coiled tube connecting the rear of the testicle to its vas deferens; sperm mature here so they are able to travel during ejaculation.

Episiotomy A surgical procedure that snips a birthing mother's perineum in a vertical line to allow for easier extraction of the baby.

Equality matching One of four elements of intimate relationships, characterized by finding partners with similarities to oneself.

Erectile dysfunction The inability of a penis to become erect or maintain erections.

Erogenous zones Areas of the body that are sensitive to stimulation and increase sexual arousal.

Eros One of Lee's typologies; like Sternberg's passionate/romantic love, in that people experiencing it want intense intimacy and commitment from their partner. This style can be healthy, especially in the beginning of a match.

Escalation Part of the cycle of violence, which occurs after the honeymoon period and is characterized by increasing tension and foreshadowing of violence to come.

Essentialist People who think sex and gender differences are biological, essential, or natural.

Essentialized When traits or behaviors of a specific gender are believed to be "essential," or natural/biologically determined.

Ethnicity A categorical grouping of people based on their cultural group membership, shared historical experiences, language, rituals, and food.

Ethnocentrism Viewing one's own ethnicity as normative and others' as deficient or foreign; privileging one ethnic group's perspective over that of others.

Ethnography A research study conducted on a group of people from their own perspective, often after the researcher lives within the society for a length of time; usually qualitative.

Etic An "outsider's" approach to research, looking at a topic from the perspective of the researcher.

Eugenics movement A movement stemming from Social Darwinist ideas, which advocated for sterilization of any people considered genetically "unfit." This movement influenced Nazi genocide methods.

Exogamy A set of beliefs, practices, or mandates regarding people who should be excluded as possible marriage partners. People outside of one's own group are often excluded as marriage partners.

Exosystem Indirect influences on development, affecting people through their microsystems.

Expectancy Value Theory A theory of mate selection which states that people evaluate potential partners based on perceived attractiveness, compatibility, similarity, and whether the person has the attributes and the potential to play roles we consider to be vital characteristics of an "ideal" mate.

Experiment A research method employing strict controls and random assignment of subjects; the only method that allows one to make causal statements.

Experimental group The group of participants that receives the independent variable manipulation.

Exploratory/curiosity animal abuse A child plays with animals (usually invertebrates) to see what will happen if they alter or dismember them in some way; easy to stop with education and good role modeling.

External locus of control The belief that one's life is outside of one's own control.

Familism A belief common in Hispanic/Latino families (as well as others) wherein the needs and goals of the family, especially elders, take precedence over the needs and goals of any given individual.

Family A group of two or more people connected by blood, adoption, marriage, or choice, who may rely on each other for social, emotional, and/or financial support.

Family of origin The family you grew up in.

Family of procreation The family you form as an adult and often have children in.

Family only (pit bull) batterers A type of batterer who reacts to conflict with violence but usually feels guilty and apologizes; can respond well to treatment and often loves their partners greatly.

Family planning The act of conscientiously controlling one's own fertility and planning for the timing and number of births.

Family process model of economic hardship A model showing that when families experience economic or job stress, it spills over into marital/couple, and parent–child relationships.

Family Systems Theory A theoretical approach stemming from Structural-Functionalism, which examines role and power dynamics present in families, emphasizing that every individual exists within a complex relationship system; the whole is greater than the sum of the parts.

Fast starters Young adults who, by age 24, have already embarked upon all the adult roles and are on their way to financial stability. They have children, spouses, and jobs.

Fearful avoidant attachment An insecure attachment style where people fear being hurt and so avoid intimacy altogether.

Female deficit perspective The traditional research approach that interpreted gender differences as due to female inferiority, instead of appreciating findings about women as normal in their own right.

Feminist marriages Characterized by open criticism of inequality both inside and outside the home, with constant self-reflection and active strategizing to ensure that women have the same rights, roles, and responsibilities as their husbands.

Feminist Theory A broad umbrella term for the many theoretical perspectives espousing the equality of men and women; feminist scholars examine women from their own perspective, often using qualitative research methods, without comparing women to men. This perspective often engenders social activism.

Feminized love The idea that women are naturally skilled at love, are good at empathy and tenderness, and that women's ways of loving are ideal compared to those of men.

Fetal stage The last stage of prenatal development when no new structures form; growth and refinement of existing structures take place; begins about nine weeks after fertilization.

Fiduciary abuse specialist team A multi-disciplinary team comprised of accountants, FBI agents, insurance professionals, and others who investigate and bring charges against perpetrators of financial elder abuse.

Filter Theory A theory which states that people have various cognitive filters through which they sift the pool of eligibles in order to create a perfect soulmate in their minds; the filters usually contain preconceived ideas about what a future mate must be like.

Financial infidelity Keeping bank accounts, credit cards, or debts outside of the awareness of one's spouse; people may hide income or purchases.

Financial/material abuse/exploitation A form of elder abuse where the senior is taken advantage of and made to write checks, change wills, or otherwise give money to the perpetrator.

Flex time A family-friendly work policy that allows people to create their own schedules that fit in with their family lives.

Fluid intelligence Cognitive skills related to the functioning of the neuroanatomy, or the "hardware" of the brain itself.

Four stage sexual response cycle Masters and Johnson's (1966) discovery that most people go through consistent stages of sexual response: excitement, plateau, orgasm, and resolution.

Friends with benefits Engaging in sexual activities with friends or acquaintances without expecting the development of a committed partnership.

Functional age The age you appear to be (i.e. how old you feel, how many activities you can still do).

Gender The socially constructed aspects of what makes a person male or female.

Gender aschematic A way of thinking wherein children's gender schemas are comprised of diverse ideas about gender; thinking is very flexible and children find it easy to imagine and accept people who cross traditional gender lines.

Gender identity A person's sense of being either male or female.

Gender roles Socially prescribed actions, behaviors and traits expected of men and women.

Gender Schema Theory A theory of gender role development that focuses on children's changing gender schemas and the desire to perform socially accepted roles for their gender.

Gender schematic A way of thinking wherein children's gender schemas are comprised of stereotypical ideas about gender; thinking is inflexible regarding what is appropriate for boys and girls or men and women.

Gender schemas Mental representations or cognitive templates that comprise a person's ideas about gender roles.

Gender similarity hypothesis The idea that men and women are actually more similar than they are different and that gender differences are largely overstated.

Gender symmetry hypothesis The idea that men and women are equally likely to perpetrate domestic violence.

Generalizability The degree to which research results can be applied to larger populations based on the sample results found in a study.

Generalized physiological arousal One of Bancroft's (2005) four aspects of sexual motivation; this refers to excitement, nervousness, or tingling in body parts outside of the genital region.

Generativity A sense of being fulfilled in middle age through having contributed to the next generation and leaving a positive legacy.

Genital response One of Bancroft's (2005) four aspects of sexual motivation; this refers to excitement, arousal, or tingling in the genital region.

Glass ceiling A hypothetical barrier women face when trying to reach the top of their careers; often due to sexism or discrimination in the workplace.

Glass escalator A hypothetical pathway to the top of the career ladder, which is often "ridden" by men who engage in traditionally feminine careers.

Globalization The development of an increasingly integrated worldwide economy.

Good provider role A traditional male gender ideology where men gain most of their identity from working and providing material goods for their families.

Goodenoughs Post-divorce, these people do fairly well but do not exhibit the kind of drive to achieve a higher quality of life that the enhancers do; their new lives resemble their old lives.

Grooming The process sexual abusers use to gain the trust of a victim and proceed slowly to sexual interactions without fear of violence.

Harmonious marriage Couples are generally very happy and get along well but may have conflicts over parenting and sexual relations. In African Americans, they mainly struggle over parenting and their sexual lives are satisfying.

Hayflick limit The limit placed on the number of times a cell can divide.

Hegemonic masculinity A definition of masculinity that centers on power, control, dominance, and achievement.

Heteronormativity A belief that heterosexuality is normal and right and other sexual orientations are abnormal or inferior to heterosexuality.

Heterosexism Viewing heterosexual orientation as normative and others' orientation as deficient or foreign; privileging heterosexuality over other orientations.

Homophily A liking for people like ourselves.

Honeymoon period Part of the cycle of violence, which occurs after violent episodes; the batterer has apologized and things are calm and happy for a while.

Hooking up Casual sexual experiences with strangers or acquaintances (kissing, oral sex, intercourse) without the expectation of any further contact after the fact.

Hostile attribution bias A cognitive style of interpreting ambiguous social stimuli as negative or hostile in nature; often leads to aggressive or violent reactions.

Hostile masculinity A male ideology comprised of negative attitudes about women and an acceptance of violence against women.

Hostile sexism Negative gender bias which often involves anger and combativeness directed at women.

HOX genes The set of 39 genes that determine the order in which a baby's body structures develop in the womb.

Hypothesis A concrete, testable statement employed in research studies.

Identity achievement The positive outcome of the search for identity, combining a prolonged search with a strong commitment to identity; those who reach identity achievement are considered to be mature and psychologically balanced. They have a clear sense of their vocational, spiritual, social, emotional, and cognitive identities.

Identity versus role confusion and intimacy versus isolation Erik Erikson's psychosocial stages for late adolescence and early adulthood (Erikson, 1969). Healthy people will search far and wide for diverse experiences and then decide upon an integrated identity, which will help them build intimacy skills with others. Negative solutions to these states include a feeling of confusion over identity and a sense of social isolation.

Illouz's four symbolic assessments Four ways to examine the rituals cultures engage in to enhance love experiences. They consist of temporal, spatial, emotional, and artifactual assessments.

In loco parentis Laws allowing a stepparent to gain custody of stepchildren if the biological parent dies and it can be proven that the stepparent played an essential parenting role in that child's life.

In vitro fertilization The introduction of a zygote or blastocyst into the uterus to increase the chances of pregnancy.

Incentive motivation One of Bancroft's (2005) four aspects of sexual motivation; this refers to a mental process whereby one considers possible incentives or rewards for their actions.

Inclusionists (the color blind) People who appreciate diversity but do not acknowledge the importance and contributions of differences between people; they emphasize our common humanity.

Independent variable The variable that is manipulated in a research study.

Infatuation One of Sternberg's (1986) categories of love, where passion is high but commitment and intimacy are low.

Infibulation A method of female genital mutilation where the entire external female genitalia are removed and the vaginal opening may be sewn shut, in order to ensure virginity at marriage and no sexual pleasure for the woman.

Information processing One of Bancroft's (2005) four aspects of sexual motivation; this refers to how people judge incoming information regarding possible sexual opportunities.

Inorgasmia The inability to have an orgasm, or having unsatisfactory orgasms.

Integrative pluralists People who believe that all cultures, beliefs, and languages have merit and should be cherished together in one diverse society that appreciates the differences we all bring.

Integrity A sense of inner peace at the end of life regarding the paths our lives have taken.

Internal locus of control The belief that one's life is within one's own control.

Internal working model Unconscious mental representations or cognitive templates shaped through interactions with early caregivers; according to Attachment Theory, these models of ourselves and other people guide our thinking and behavior in adult relationships.

International adoptions Adoptions conducted across country lines; usually western parents adopting children from developing nations.

Intersectional identities The idea that every person is affected by multiple identities stemming from his or her sex, gender, sexual orientation, race, religion, ethnicity, and social class.

Intersex Characteristics that make a person less clearly distinctly male or female; often includes ambiguous genitalia.

Intersexed A person who is not clearly male or female and may have ambiguous genitalia.

Intimacy The ability to be completely open and honest with another person, merging your lives together without losing your own identity.

Intimate fathers Calm, peaceful dads who believe in gender equality; they desire intimacy in their families.

Intimate partner violence (IPV) The preferred term used today for "domestic violence," which is more inclusive of all types of couples and does not have the conceptualization of "domestic," or "home-like" associated with it.

Intimate terrorism A form of intimate partner violence where one partner wields complete control over the other and uses power tactics to isolate him or her from family and friends; the victim often feels worthless and helpless to leave; can results in severe injury and death and is almost always perpetrated by men.

Involuntary stable singles Those who do not want to be single but do not foresee finding a partner.

Involuntary temporary singles People who wish they were coupled and see that potentially happening in the future.

Job sharing A family-friendly work policy that allows more than one employee to share a job so that they have time to spend with family.

Joint legal custody A legal ruling allowing both divorced parents to have equal access to and responsibility for their children.

Joint physical custody The actual practice of both divorced parents spending equal amounts of time and taking equal responsibility for their children.

Kinship care Foster care provided to children by their biological relatives.

Kinship work The work done in families (usually by women) that maintains strong blood ties; activities include writing letters and sending cards, buying gifts, and organizing parties and gatherings.

Labia majora The external folds of skin, or "lips" of the vagina.

Labia minora The internal folds of skin, or "lips" of the vagina.

Lamaze birth A natural form of birth where parents use visualization, breathing exercises, supportive partners, and knowledge about the physiology of labor to reduce pain and the length of labor.

Learned helplessness A psychological state where victims of IPV feel so beaten down and unskilled that they could never leave the batterer or succeed on their own.

Lee's styles of love A typology of love that examines the dynamics of health and well-being with different configurations of relationships (Lee, 1973).

Lifespan Theory of Control The idea that increasing one's sense of mastery over his or her life will increase well-being.

Limbic brain The second level of the triune brain which comprises the emotion regulation centers of the brain which are involved in emotional reactions and attachment strategies.

Limbic co-regulation The idea that two people who live together or are involved in a romantic bond can affect the functioning of each others' limbic brains.

Longitudinal A study design that follows the same people over long periods of time.

Love The subjective feeling of emotional connection with another person, often accompanied by intense desire to be near, care for, protect, and/or share one's life with that person.

Love stories Sternberg's (1986) idea that we form templates in our childhood based on interactions in our families and exposure to media images of what characteristics should be present in ideal love relationships.

Low sexual desire A sexual dysfunction where men or women have little interest in sex.

Ludus One of Lee's typologies (Lee, 1973); love is taken less seriously. It's seen as an endeavor undertaken for fun or enjoyable pursuit one can share with many different partners. It's treated almost like a game. Like Sternberg's infatuation, this approach has little intimacy or commitment. It thrives on passion; related to poor relationship quality and unhappiness.

Lust The first phase involved in the neurochemistry of attraction; characterized by high libido or sex drive. Sex hormones like estrogens and androgens are peaking. This is thought to reflect the evolutionary desire to reproduce.

Macrosystem Large cultural and societal influences on development.

Male entitlement The belief that men have certain inherent rights, roles, and responsibilities that are greater and more valuable than those of women.

Managed interactions A strategy to cope with being single in a couples-oriented world; thinking of polite ways to decline invitations to non-single-friendly events as well as how to respond to "singlist" comments.

Mandatory arrest Laws whereby police officers must arrest perpetrators of domestic violence, regardless of whether the partner wants them to; these laws take the responsibility for having to press charges against partners away from victims.

Mania One of Lee's typologies (Lee, 1973); obsessive and insecure love often characterized by emotional drama. Partners are not happy, satisfied, or fulfilled; similar to the anxious/preoccupied/enmeshed attachment style.

Marital assimilation A process whereby immigrants intermarry with those from the new culture.

Marital rape Any act of psychological coercion, or physical force, used to induce a female partner or wife to engage in sexual activities for which she has no desire.

Market pricing One of four elements of intimate relationships, characterized by a cost/benefit analysis of the worth of a specific partner.

Masculinist A relatively recent men's movement that attempts to release men from the constraints of traditional gender role expectations.

Matriarchal A social system where women hold power and influence in the clan or family.

Matrifocal A social system where men marry into their wives' families or clans and often live with them.

Matrilineal A social system where goods and property are inherited or passed down through the maternal line.

Medical/educational neglect Not providing adequate preventive medical or dental care; denying access to education.

Menarche The beginning of a woman's menstrual cycle; a woman's first menstrual period.

Menopause The time during which a woman stops menstruating; the process can take years to complete and may be accompanied by uncomfortable physical and mental symptoms.

Mere exposure effect The idea that the more we are exposed to a person, the more likely we are to engage in a relationship with him/her.

Mesosystem Interactions between microsystems which provide a new level of influence on development, separate from the influence of individual microsystem effects.

Meta-analysis A research technique where the results of multiple studies can be analyzed together to assess the overall magnitude of effects for a given topic.

Microfinancing Small loans designed to help impoverished people emerge from poverty by becoming self-sufficient.

Microsort sperm sorting An optional procedure occurring during in vitro fertilization where chromosomes are marked with dye so that gender selection of babies can take place before implantation.

Microsystem Immediate, direct influences on development (e.g., parents and peers).

Migratory divorce The trend where couples move to other cities, states, or even countries to obtain divorces that are illegal in their area.

Millennium Development Goals A set of goals the United Nations has set forth, which they hope to accomplish by the year 2015; these goals include the eradication of extreme poverty, great reductions in HIV/AIDS, and improvement in infant and maternal health around the world.

Minority majority An ethnic minority group increases in number to surpass the numbers of people in the original majority group.

Model minority A belief that a specific ethnic group is characterized by positive traits such as fastidiousness, intelligence, and financial success.

Modern family A family where both adult partners work outside the home but the female partner still completes the majority of the housework and child care.

Modified traditional arranged marriage Family and community members may choose several potential spouses and the young person is allowed to make the final choice.

Mommy/caring tax Loss of wages or benefits for employees, usually women, who take time off from work to care for children or elderly parents.

Mommy track A negative stereotype of working mothers that believes they are less committed to their jobs if they are committed to their children; results in fewer promotions or raises.

Multidimensional The idea that change occurs in all dimensions of development simultaneously (physical, social, cognitive, emotional, spiritual, sexual).

Multidirectional The idea that development in old age can be both forward/positive, and backward/negative.

Multiple primary partners structure A polyamorous family configuration where there can be multiple primary partners; each partner is committed to every other partner to the same degree.

Natural prepared birth Dr. Dick-Read's method of educating parents about the physiology of labor as well as working on relaxation and stress management.

Natural/quasi experiment A group comparison research design where groups are not randomly assigned but are naturally occurring.

Negative dyadic coping A partner pretends to care but rarely listens or only responds superficially or sarcastically.

Neglect The failure of caregivers to provide for the needs of children or dependent adults; neglect can take many forms, like not providing food, shelter, clothing, health care, or emotional support.

Neglectful parenting A completely uninvolved parenting style, low on both warmth/responsiveness and control/demandingness.

Neocortex The third level of the triune brain, which controls rational decision-making, executive functions, planning, and analysis.

Neural plasticity The ability for children's brain cells to respond to environmental stimulation; makes the brain malleable and able to adapt to its specific environment.

No-fault divorce A contemporary trend where no one has to prove fault or wrong-doing for a divorce; divorce can occur unilaterally, or without the consent of a second party, and possessions one owned before the marriage remain his/hers.

Non-normative singles Older singles (usually over age 35) who will face more discrimination and negative judgments than those who are single but are still within the normative age range for committed partnerships and marriage.

Normative life cycle model A SNAF ideology which suggests that all people will form romantic relationships, settle down into coupledom (usually heterosexual marriage) and have children, in that order. The assumption is that all adults wish to be in committed partnerships and that no one would really want to be "single by choice."

No-treatment control group A group of participants that receives no level of the independent variable manipulation.

Nuclear family A small family consisting of parents and children, without extended kin present.

Old-old The group of seniors between 80 and 100 years of age.

Oocyte Female germ cells, or eggs.

Open model structure A polyamorous family configuration where the primary partnership is open to other sexual and romantic liaisons.

Operational definition A concrete, extremely clear definition of research variables which allows others scientists to easily replicate the work.

Over-commitment An extreme form of career striving where people have an intense need for approval and a hard time coping with workplace stress; they commit too much energy to work at the expense of family relationships.

Ovum A female germ cell ("egg").

Paraphilias Unusual sexual preferences that include objects, behaviors, or other people; paraphilias become diagnosable mental conditions if a person cannot be sexually satisfied without the object or behavior, he or she feels extreme distress over the object or behavior, or the sexual practices interfere with life functioning.

Parenting coordination office Locates psychologists to serve as special masters to assist parents in custody problems. The psychologist and a team of student interns work to improve parental communication and sensitivity to children's needs, and actually assess children's development academically and psychologically.

Parents without careers Young adults (mainly women) who, by age 24, had children early but do not engage in work roles.

Pathological animal abuse Severe or frequent harm of animals in an attempt to cause them pain or gain sadistic pleasure; includes injuries to warm-blooded vertebrates; often a sign of emotional disturbance or family violence and a warning sign for violence against humans.

Patriarchal A social system where men hold power and influence in the clan or family.

Peer marriages These couples see child care, housework, earning money, and power as things to be shared equally; they are peers without domination or control over their partners.

Pelvic floor orgasms Female orgasms that are thought to originate from the G-spot inside the vagina being stimulated in conjunction with the clitoris.

Perceived support A subjective sense that someone cares, listens, and is there for a given person.

Perma-parenting The idea that parents play key roles in their children's lives well after they reach adulthood, continuing to financially and emotionally support their children.

Permissive/indulgent parenting A parenting style that is high on warmth/responsiveness but low on control/demandingness; few rules or expectations are placed on children.

Personalismo A practice common in Hispanic/Latino families, where goods and services are exchanged in a face-to-face, or personal manner; people prefer to deal with those in their own community on a personal level.

Philematology The scientific study of kissing.

Physical abuse Physical harm of a family member in the form of hitting, slapping, kicking, choking, or other physical acts.

Physical neglect Not meeting a child or dependent adult's need for food, shelter, clothing, or hygiene.

Placenta A vascularly rich organ that attaches to the uterus and provides a baby with nutrients while protecting it from waste and toxins.

Planned same-sex families Gay or lesbian families that planned to have children together in their union.

Plaques Piles of dead protein material sloughed off brain cells; a symptom of Alzheimer's disease.

Politicized homosexuality A social movement wherein people from LGBT communities around the world are using their political and economic power to fight for their civil rights.

Polyamory Loving more than one person.

Polyandry The practice of one woman taking more than one husband.

Polygamy The practice of one man taking more than one wife; also known as polygyny.

Pool of eligibles The available group of people who could be potential mates for us.

Post-adoption depressive syndrome Similar to post-partum depression but occurring in adoptive parents who are disenchanted, sad, or overwhelmed by their new parenting duties.

Post-modern family A family where at least one element, such as a working mother or same-sex partners, of the SNAF is deconstructed or transformed.

Post-partum depression A serious clinical disorder arising after childbirth where parents feel sad, anxious, overwhelmed, and may even think of harming themselves or their babies.

Power and control The two key elements in the cycle of violence, which explain many of the interpersonal dynamics found in violent relationships; these tactics are used to continue to perpetrate violence against a partner without fear of him or her leaving.

Pragma One of Lee's typologies (Lee, 1973); people seek out a rational choice, a logical mate, instead of relying on their passions during mate selection. The person chosen must logically fit into one's lifestyle and family configuration; practical contentment that does not necessarily include feelings of personal happiness or sexual passion.

Preimplantation genetic diagnosis An optional procedure occurring during in vitro fertilization where genetic disorders are screened out and only healthy embryos implanted.

Premarital counseling a brief form of therapy that helps couples outline their goals and align their expectations before getting married, in order to prevent divorce.

Premature ejaculation Male ejaculation which occurs directly upon arousal, or earlier than preferred.

Primary control Changing one's environment to gain a sense of control over life.

Primary/secondary structure A polyamorous family configuration where the initial couple takes precedence over any subsequent partners.

Private adoptions Adoptions conducted through private agencies, usually working with birth mothers in order to obtain a newborn or infant; babies are usually European American.

Processes Interactional variables like caring, sharing, and communicating, which are not always easily visible; we cannot determine how well a child will turn out, or how successful or content a family will be based solely on its external structure.

Propinquity In close proximity; people are more likely to date those who are nearby.

Prostate gland A walnut-sized gland lying directly between the anus and the base of the penis, manufactures seminal fluid which protects the sperm and delivers it during ejaculation.

Prostate orgasm A male orgasm which originates through stimulation of the prostate gland.

Protective buffering An attempt to minimize the stress one's partner feels.

Psychological/emotional abuse Humiliation, put-downs, criticisms, and threats that attack the core character of the person and make him or her feel worthless.

Public adoptions Adoptions conducted through the foster care system; more often these children are older or children of color.

Pure relationship A relationship based on the happiness of each partner; it is entered into for the sole purpose of satisfaction of the couple.

Purging The attempt to rid oneself of a transgendered identity by acting as stereotypically male or female as one can; these acts are an attempt to confirm that one's gender identity is the same as his or her biological sex.

Pursuer–distancer marriages Marriages involve nagging, hostility, and back-biting by wives; husbands then retreat and withdraw; couples have intense angry conflicts.

Qualitative Data that occur in narrative form, as is found in open-ended interviews.

Quantitative Data that occur in numerical form, as is found in questionnaires or surveys.

Queer Theory A theory that was developed to counterbalance the traditional theories of gender and sexuality which privileged heteronormativity and traditional gender roles. Queer Theory seeks to bring marginalized groups to the forefront of scientific study and to recognize the intersectional identities of all people being studied.

Race A socially constructed concept referring to different colors of people thought to stem from diverse genetic lines in human history; in reality there are no true races of people.

Radical argument A view against same-sex marriages often proffered by feminists and those in LGBT communities, which states that same-sex marriage reinforces heteronormativity and oppression of other lifestyles; they argue that legalizing same-sex marriage will further oppress those who don't or cannot get married.

Random assignment A technique used in experiments whereby participants are assigned to groups in a random, versus systematic, manner; increases validity of conclusions made from results.

Received support The objective number of people available to support a given person; does not mean the given person feels supported.

Regretfuls Those who live a lifetime of regret over having led a single life.

Replication Doing a research study again to confirm that results are valid.

Representative sample A sample of participants that closely resembles the larger group to whom research results are meant to generalize.

Reproductive surrogacy The use of a "donor" womb to carry one's child.

Resistant thinking A strategy to cope with being single in a couples-oriented world; working hard to not fall prey to the social pressure saying that every person should be in a committed relationship to be "normal" or "whole."

Resolveds Involuntary singles who have accepted their single life as meaningful even if lived without a partner.

Role strain A feeling of stress or pressure experienced by being torn between work, relationships, and parenting roles.

Role-scarcity hypothesis The idea that a person only has so much energy for each role in life so that physical and mental resources devoted to one role necessarily mean less available for another role.

Romantic/passionate love A type of love that usually exists with newer relationships, where sexual excitement and intrusive thoughts of the person are common.

Sandwich generation Adults who are responsible for caring for both elderly parents and young children at the same time; a source of caregiving stress.

Scientific method A series of steps taken to conduct accurate research.

Second shift The work shift that occurs once a person gets home from work, including cooking, cleaning, and child care.

Secondary control Changing one's self (e.g., emotional state or motivational levels) to gain a sense of control over life.

Seekers Post-divorce, these people anxiously seek a new partner to marry right away; tend to have low self-concepts and are highly emotional.

Self-Expansion Theory Aron and Aron's (1986) theory that true love stems from one's wish to expand one's self; one's partner fills in the gaps, balances out their partner's traits, and each partner helps the other become a better version of the self they once were.

Self-neglect The most common form of elder abuse, wherein a senior fails to care for his or her own basic needs.

Seminiferous tubules Located in the testes, these tubes aid in creating sperm cells and helping them travel during ejaculation.

Separation agreement A document that outlines custody, visitation, and bill-paying schedules, among other things.

Separatists (assimilationists) People who believe immigrants should adopt their new culture uniformly, assimilating into the culture, practices, beliefs, and language, while leaving their own systems behind.

Serial monogamists People who move from one long-term committed relationship to another after several years.

Sex A person's biological characteristics that make him or her male or female.

Sexism Any discriminatory or differential treatment based on gender.

Sexual abuse Any act of a sexual nature that is perpetrated against the will or without the knowledge or consent of the victim; includes fondling, rape, exposing one's self and sexual exploitation.

Sexual antagonistic selection A term used by evolutionary theorists to indicate that homosexuality has not been weeded out of the gene pool over the eons of human evolution because females in families of gay males have higher than average fertility rates.

Sexual aversion disorder A diagnosable mental condition wherein people are afraid of or repulsed by sexual behavior.

Sexual double standard (SDS) The idea that sex is normal and expected for men and disapproved of for women.

Sexual orientation The sexual attraction one has toward people of a specific gender or genders.

Similarity-attraction effect The idea that instead of opposites attracting, most of us actually choose mates very similar to ourselves in attractiveness, personality, and social standing.

Singles pride movement A civil rights movement which advocates for the rights and protections of singles.

Singles strain A process whereby people may feel stressed over stigmatization, a less active social life, lack of intimacy with a romantic partner, a future old age that may be more difficult, a lack of caretakers available when one needs help, or an isolated daily life.

Singlism Prejudice, stereotyping, and discrimination against single people.

Situational couples violence The most common form of violence in community samples and young western couples; mutual slapping, pushing, or other forms of less severe violence which rarely result in injury and are often initiated by women.

Slow starters The worse adjusted group of singles, who by age 24 show no signs of successfully negotiating the roles of adulthood; they have minimal education, poor job prospects, usually live at home, and are unsuccessful in

relationships; many are already parents at age 24 yet they engage in fairly high rates of illegal behavior (drunk driving, stealing, taking drugs, etc.).

Social class One's level of income or socioeconomic status.

Social Cognitive Theory A theory of gender role development that emphasizes children's modeling of adult role models and imitating the gender behaviors they see; gender roles are socialized through reinforcing gender appropriate and punishing gender inappropriate behaviors and traits.

Social Constructionism The idea that humans construct their own reality, and those constructions affect behaviors in families.

Social Darwinism The idea that evolution will take its natural course over time, weeding out genetically "unfit" people so that eventually a master human race will emerge through "survival of the fittest"; this theory was used to justify political attitudes against social welfare programs and in favor of the eugenics movement.

Social dominance orientation A person's viewpoint that groups are not equal and that dominance and hierarchy should be maintained.

Social Dominance Theory A structural-functionalist idea that people naturally form in-group privileging social hierarchies which are validated by policies, laws, and practices in their culture.

Social Exchange Theory A theory arguing that people make a deliberate tally of costs and benefits during decision-making and behaviors they perform in families.

Social marriages A marriage where there is no legal process, no licenses, no fees, but simple vows or gifts are exchanged.

Socialization goals The ideologies that drive parents' plans for their children's future, and influence the parenting tactics they implement.

Sociobiological perspective A viewpoint that argues that evolutionarily, we are inclined to care for our biological kin in order to continue our gene pool; we are less likely to love or care for children with whom we share no genes in common.

Solution focused therapy One type of premarital counseling which focuses on the couple's strengths, cultural beliefs, and goals; the counselor helps the couple identify possible problems and proactively implement positive strategies for change.

Special masters Professionals who consult with parents regarding their children's needs before, during, and after divorce; can inform parents about best practices for maintaining a warm and supportive household for both homes; make recommendations to parents and court.

Sperm A male germ cell.

Spermatozoa Male germ cells, or sperm.

Standard North American Family (SNAF) The concept articulated by sociologist Dorothy Smith, which consists of a homemaker mother, a breadwinning father, and their children; usually envisioned as white and middle class.

Stereotype A standardized belief about a group of people where all members are thought to be similar to each other in specific ways; these beliefs are often oversimplifications and can include prejudiced attitudes.

Stereotype threat The process of a person performing poorly on tasks because of the pressure felt by knowing the negative stereotypes that abound about his or her own group.

Sternberg's Triangular Theory of Love One typology of love characterized by three parts, passion, intimacy, or commitment (Sternberg, 1986).

Storge One of Lee's typologies (Lee, 1973); like Sternberg's companionate love (Sternberg, 1986), it involves maintaining a healthy egalitarian relationship with someone who is your best friend; couples are happy and satisfied because they are each concerned with the well-being of the other person and enjoy sharing their lives with each other.

Stranger model A viewpoint wherein a stepparent is treated like an acquaintance, instead of a family member, in terms of his or her relationship with stepchildren. Stepparents are not allowed to sign permission slips for school, consent to medical treatment for stepchildren, etc.

Structural assimilation A process whereby a person adopts the educational, employment, and political values of the host country.

Structural-Functionalism Stems from Communist Theory; Emphasizes maintaining the status quo of a society or family, with specific structures remaining in place to ensure the system works as it should, with specific people in power; each person plays a crucial role in keeping the family functioning as it always has.

Structure A family's composition, how many members it has, whether people are married, their ages, and other demographic variables.

Survivors The preferred term for "victims" of IPV; refers to people who use their protective factors and coping skills to get themselves out of a dangerous situation. This term implies active attempts to help one's self and reach out for support.

Swingers Post-divorce, these people spend a lot of time in bars and clubs, take more drugs, have more sex, and engage in more antisocial behavior than most divorced adults; also rate high on depression.

Tangles Protein fibers in the brain that become wrapped around each other; a symptom of Alzheimer's disease.

Telecommuting A family-friendly work policy that allows people to work from home and attend meetings by videophone, etc.

Telomeres Dense repetitive DNA strands at both ends of a chromosome, which protect chromosomes from damage; get shorter every time a cell divides; shorter telomeres are related to higher stress and shortened life expectancy.

Teratogens Any substance that can cross the placental barrier and negatively affect a developing embryo or fetus.

Theory An organizing set of principles used to guide thinking and predict research outcomes.

Tokenism The practice of hiring or promoting a single woman or person of color in order to suggest a lack of bias in the workplace.

Traditional arranged marriages Parents, elders, and/or religious leaders have complete control over marriage matches.

Traditional marriage A couple with strong religious beliefs and ties to extended kin; they often have poor communication and conflict resolution skills; partners, especially women, are mostly unsatisfied with the relationship.

Transgender A person whose gender identity does not match his or her biological sex.

Transnational families Families who live in different countries due to work possibilities abroad.

Transudation A physiological process during female sexual arousal in which vaginal tissues swell with blood and fluid droplets seep out of the vaginal lining to aid in lubrication.

Triune brain The depiction of the brain as consisting of three parts, from an older more primitive part to a newer, sophisticated part.

Type A personality A personality style involving extreme hostility, competitiveness, and a drive to succeed; often related to health problems.

Type B personality A personality style involving a laid back, happy, carefree approach to life.

Unbiased The attempt to keep personal beliefs out of the research process.

Underemployed The group of people who want to work full time but cannot find full-time work; they are counted as "employed" in government statistics.

Urethra The opening through which urine passes. In women it is situated above the vagina and may be stimulated during sexual activity.

Vagina A canal leading from the uterus to the external genitalia; a female sexual organ.

Vaginismus Involuntary vaginal spasms which prevent intercourse.

Vas deferens Tubes that transport sperm from the epididymis in anticipation of ejaculation; contractions in these organs propel sperm forward.

Violent resistance Violence used by victims of intimate partner violence to fight back against their abusers.

Vitalized marriage A happy marriage with very satisfied partners who have strong internal and external sources of support; they tend to be highly educated and have good problem-solving skills. African Americans are more satisfied than whites and less likely to consider divorce.

Voluntary stable singles People who choose to stay single over the long-term.

Voluntary temporary singles People who choose to be single temporarily, e.g., to take a break from relationships or figure themselves out.

Vulva The entire external female genital area.

Widower's syndrome Impotence in a new marriage without any clear physical cause; commonly related to stress or trauma in a first marriage where a spouse died.

Wishfuls Involuntary singles who want desperately to find a partner but have not.

Workaholism A condition where people work too much and cannot enforce proper boundaries between work and home life; they are often disconnected from family and work to avoid intimacy.

Working singles Young singles (usually men) who, by age 24, have some college or technical training, have begun their careers and are in either good jobs with room for advancement; good success with dating relationships but most still live with their parents.

Xenophobia The intense fear of anything or anyone different or foreign, which often leads to avoidance.

Zygote The newly created being that is formed when sperm meets egg.

REFERENCES

Abel, E. (1999). *Comparing the social service utilization, exposure to violence, and trauma symptomology of domestic violence victims and female batterers*. Paper presented at the Seventh International Family Violence Research Conference, University of New Hampshire.

Abell, S., & Dauphin, B. (2009). The perpetuation of patriarchy: The hidden factor of gender bias in the diagnosis and treatment of children. *Clinical Child Psychology and Psychiatry, 14*(1), 117–133.

Adams, M. (2006). The consequences of witnessing family violence on children and implications for family counselors. *The Family Journal: Counseling and Therapy for Couples and Families, 14*(4), 334–341.

Adams, M., & Coltrane, S. (2003). Boys and men in families. In S. Coltrane (Ed.), *Families and society* (pp. 189–198). Belmont, CA: Wadsworth/Thompson Learning.

Adams, R. E., Laursen, B., & Wilder, D. (2001). Characteristics of closeness in adolescent romantic relationships. *Journal of Adolescence, 24*, 353–363.

Adelman, M. B., & Bankoff, E. A. (1990). Lifespan concerns: Implications for mid-life adult singles. In H. Giles, M. Coupland, & J. M. Wiemann (Eds.), *Communication, health, and the elderly* (pp. 64–91). Manchester, U.K.: Manchester University Press.

Adelman, M., Gurevitch, J., de Vries, B., & Blando, J. A. (2006). Openhouse: Community building and research in the LGBT aging population. In D. Kimmel, T. Rose, & S. David (Eds.), *Lesbian, gay, bisexual, and transgender aging: Research and clinical perspective* (pp. 247–264). New York: Columbia University Press.

Adelman, M. B., & Kil, S. H. (2007). Dating conflicts: Rethinking dating violence and youth conflict. *Violence Against Women, 13*(12), 1296–1318.

Ahmed-Ghosh, H. (2003). A history of women in Afghanistan: Lessons learnt for the future: Women in Afghanistan. *Journal of International Women's Studies, 4*(3), 1–14.

Ahrons, C. (2004). *We're still family: What grown children have to say about their parents' divorce*. New York: HarperCollins.

Alesina, A., & Glaeser, E. L. (2004). *Fighting poverty in the US and Europe: A world of difference*. Oxford: Oxford University Press.

Ali, L., & Miller, L. (2004, July 12). The secret lives of wives. *Newsweek*, 47–54.

Al-Krenawi, A., Lev-Wiesel, R., & Sehwail Mahmud, A. (2007). Psychological symptomatology among Palestinian adolescents living with political violence. *Child and Adolescent Mental Health 12 (1)*: 27–31. doi: 10.1111/j.1475–3588.2006.00416.x.

Allen, D. W., & Gallagher, M. (2007). *Does divorce law affect the divorce rate? A review of empirical research, 1995–2006*. Manassas, VA: Institute for Marriage and Public Policy.

Allen, K. R. (2007). Ambiguous loss after lesbian couples with children break up: A case for same-sex divorce. *Family Relationships, 56*, 175–183.

Allen, P. G. (1986). Who is your mother? Red roots of white feminism. In C. Lemert (Ed.), *Social theory: The multicultural and classical readings* (pp. 209–221). Boulder, CO: Westview Press.

Allen, W. D., & Olson, D. H. (2001). Five types of African American marriages. *Journal of Marital and Family Therapy, 27*(3), 301–314.

Allgeier, E. R., & Wiederman, M. W. (1991). Love and mate selection in the 1990s. *Free Inquiry, 11*(3), 25–27.

Almgren, G., Magarati, M., & Mogford, L. (2009). Examining the influences of gender, race, ethnicity, and social capital on the subjective health of adolescents. *Journal of Adolescence, 32*, 109–133.

Alquist, A. (2008). Comment: The migration of same-sex marriage from Canada to the U.S.: An incremental approach. *University of LaVerne Law Review, 30*, 200–203.

Altman, D. (2002). Globalization and the international gay/lesbian movement. In D. Richardson & S. Seidman (Eds.), *Handbook of lesbian and gay studies* (pp. 415–426). Thousand Oaks, CA: Sage.

Amato, P. R. (2000). Diversity within single-parent families. In D. H. Demo, L. R. Allen, & M. A. Fine (Eds.), *Handbook of family diversity* (pp. 149–172). New York: Oxford University Press.

Amato, P. R. (2001). The consequences of divorce for adults and children. In R. M. Milardo (Ed.), *Understanding families in the new millennium: A decade in review* (pp. 488–506). Minneapolis: National Council on Family Relations.

Amato, P. R., & Afifi, T. D. (2006). Feeling caught between parents: Adult children's relations with parents and subjective well-being. *Journal of Marriage and Family, 68,* 222–235.

Amato, P. R., & DeBoer, D. D. (2001). The transmission of marital instability across generations: Relationships skills or commitment to marriage. *Journal of Marriage and Family, 63,* 1038–1051.

Amato, P. R., & Gilbreth, J. G. (1999). Nonresident fathers and children's well-being: A meta-analysis. *Journal of Marriage and the Family, 61,* 557–573.

Amato, P. R., & Keith, B. (1991a). Consequences of parental divorce for the wellbeing of children: A meta-analysis. *Psychological Bulletin, 110,* 26–46.

Amato, P. R., & Keith, C. (1991b). Parental divorce and adult well-being: A meta-analysis. *Journal of Marriage and the Family, 53,* 43–58.

Amato, P. R., Loomis, L. S., & Booth, A. (1995). Parental divorce, marital conflict, and offspring well-being during early adulthood. *Social Forces, 73,* 895–915.

American Academy of Pediatrics. (2010). Policy statement: Media education. *Pediatrics, 126*(5), 1012–1017. doi: 10.1542/peds.2010–1636.

American Anthropological Association. (1998, May 17). Statement on "race." Retrieved from http://www.aaanet.org/stmts/racepp.htm.

American Psychiatric Association. (1987). *Diagnostic and statistical manual of mental disorders* (3rd ed., rev.) (*DSM–III–R*). Washington, DC: Author.

American Psychiatric Association. (2000). *Diagnostic and statistical manual of mental disorders* (4th ed., text rev.) (*DSM–IV–TR*). Washington, DC: Author.

American Psychological Association. (1994). Guidelines for child custody evaluations in divorce proceedings. *American Psychologist, 49,* 677–680.

Amram, D. W. (2009). *The Jewish law of divorce.* Charleston, SC: BiblioLife LLC.

Anderson, D. (1987). Family and peer relations of gay adolescents. *Adolescent Psychiatry, 14,* 162–178.

Anderson, D. A., & Clandos, R. (2003, January/February). Dating after divorce. *Psychology Today,* 46–56.

Andoh, E., & Bogden, J. (2009). *Resilience in LGBTQ African American adolescents.* Washington, DC: American Psychological Association.

Archer, J. (2000). Sex differences in aggression between heterosexual partners: A meta-analysis review. *Psychological Bulletin, 126,* 651–680.

Archer, J. (2006). Cross-cultural differences in physical aggression between partners: A social-role analysis. *Personality and Social Psychology Review, 10*(2), 133–153.

Arditti, J. A. (1999). Rethinking relationships between divorced mothers and their children: Capitalizing on family strengths. *Family Relations, 48,* 109–119.

Arendell, T. (1992). The social self as gendered: A masculinist discourse of divorce. *Symbolic Interactions, 15*(2), 151–181.

Arnett, J. J. (2000). Emerging adulthood: A theory of development from the late teens through the twenties. *American Psychologist, 55,* 469–480.

Aron, A., & Aron, E. (1986). *Love and the expansion of self: Understanding attraction and satisfaction.* New York: Hemisphere.

Ascione, F. R. (1993). Children who are cruel to animals: A review of research and implications for developmental psychology. *Anthrozoos, 6*(4), 226–247.

Ascione, F. R. (1997). Battered women's reports of their partners' and their children's cruelty to animals. *Journal of Emotional Abuse, 1,* 119–133.

Ascione, F. R. (2000). *Save havens for pets: Guidelines for programs sheltering pets for women who are battered.* Retrieved from http://www.vachss.com/guest_dispatches/ascione_safe_havens.pdf

Ascione, F. R. (2005). Children, animal abuse, and family violence: The multiple intersections of animal abuse, child victimization, and domestic violence. In K. A. Kendall-Tackett & S. Giacomoni (Eds.), *Child victimization* (pp. 3.1–3.36). Kingston, NJ: Civic Research Institute.

Ascione, F. R., Weber, C. V., Thompson, T. M., Heath, J., Maruyama, M., & Hayashi, K. (2007). Battered pets and domestic violence: Animal abuse reported by women experiencing intimate violence and by nonabused women. *Violence Against Women, 13*(4), 354–373.

Ashton, R. (2010). Practitioner review: Beyond shaken baby syndrome: What influences the outcome for infants following traumatic brain injury? *Journal of Child Psychology and Psychiatry, 51,* 967–980.

Astin, H., & Leland, C. (1991). *Women of influence, women of vision: A cross-generational study of leaders and social change.* San Francisco, CA: Jossey-Bass.

Astone, N. M., Constance, A. N., Schoen, R., & Kim, Y. J. (1999). Family demography, social theory, and investment in social capital. *Population and Development Review, 25*(1), 1–31.

Augustine, N. R. (2007). *Is America falling off the flat earth?* Washington, DC: The National Academies Press.

Aumann, K., & Galinski, E. (2009). *The state of health in the American workforce: Does having an effective workplace matter?* Families and Work Institute 2008 National Study of the Changing Workforce. Retrieved from http://familiesandwork.org/site/research/reports/HealthReport.pdf.

Babcock, J. C., Jacobson, N. S., Gottman, J. M., & Yerington, T. P. (2000). Attachment, emotional regulation, and the function of marital violence: Differences between secure, preoccupied, and dismissing violent and nonviolent husbands. *Journal of Family Violence, 15*(4), 391–406.

Baca Zinn, M., & Thornton Dill, B. (1994). *Women of color in U.S. society.* Philadelphia, PA: Temple University Press.

Bachu, A., & O'Connell, M. (1998). *Fertility of American women* (Technical Report). Washington, DC: U.S. Census Bureau.

Back, K. W. (1977). The ambiguity of retirement. In E. W. Busse & E. Pfeiffer (Eds.), *Behavior and adaptation in late life* (pp. 79–98). Boston, MA: Little, Brown.

Bagley, D., Character, C., & Shelton, L. (2003). Eating disorders among urban and rural African American and European American women. In M. E. Banks, & E. Kaschack (Eds.), *Women with visible and invisible disabilities* (pp. 57–79). New York: Haworth Press.

Bahr, K. S. (1994). The strengths of Apache grandmothers: Observations on commitment, culture, and caretaking. *Journal of Comparative Female Studies, 25*(2), 233–248.

Bailey, B. (1988). *From front porch to back seat.* Baltimore: Johns Hopkins University Press.

Bailey, J. M., & Pillard, R. C. (1991). A genetic study of male sexual orientation. *Archives of General Psychiatry, 48*(12), 1089–1096.

Baird, R. M., & Rosenbaum, S. R. (1997). *Same-sex marriage: The moral and legal debate.* Amherst, NY: Prometheus Books.

Baker, E. H., Sanchez, L. A., Nock, S. L., & Wright, J. D. (2009). Covenant marriage and the sanctification of gendered marriage roles. *Journal of Family Issues, 30*, 147–178.

Bakker, A. B., Demerouti, E., & Burke, R. (2009). Workaholism and relationship quality: A spillover–crossover perspective. *Journal of Occupational Health Psychology, 14*(1), 23–33.

Bales, K. L., vanWesterhuyzen, J. A., Lewis, A. D., Grotte, N. D., Lanter, J. A., & Carter, C. S. (2007). Oxytocin has dose-dependent developmental effects on pair-bonding and alloparental care in female prairie voles. *Hormones and Behavior, 52*, 274–279.

Bancroft, J. (2005). The endocrinology of sexual arousal. *Journal of Endocrinology, 186*, 411–427.

Bandura, A. (1989). Self-regulation of motivation and action through internal standards and goal systems. In L. A. Pervin (Ed.), *Goal concepts in personality and social psychology* (pp. 19–85). Hillsdale, NJ: Lawrence Erlbaum Associates.

Banyard, V. L., Moynihan, M. M., & Plante, E. G. (2007). Sexual violence prevention through bystander education: An experimental evaluation. *Journal of Community Psychology, 35*, 463–481.

Barber, N. (1995). The evolutionary psychology of physical attractiveness: Sexual selection and human morphology. *Ethnology and Sociobiology, 16*(5), 395–424.

Barford, A., Dorling, D., Smith, G. D., & Shaw, M. (2006). Life expectancy: Women now top men everywhere. *British Medical Journal, 332*, 808. doi: 10.1136/bmj.332.7545.808.

Bargh, J. A., & Raymond, P. (1995). The naive misuse of power: Nonconscious sources of sexual harassment. *Journal of Social Issues, 26*, 168–185.

Barnes, H., & Parry, J. (2004). Renegotiating identity and relationships: Men and women's adjustments to retirement. *Age and Society, 24*, 213–233.

Barnes, L. L., Wilson, R. S., Bienias, J. L., Schneider, J. A., Evans, D. A., & Bennett, D. A. (2005). Sex differences in the clinical manifestations of Alzheimer disease pathology. *Archives of General Psychiatry, 62*, 685–691.

Barnett, O., Miller-Perrin, C. L., & Perrin, R. D. (2004). *Family violence across the lifespan* (2nd ed.). New York: Sage.

Barnett, R. C., & Brennan, R. C. (1997, May 21). Flexing it in the workplace. *Boston Globe*, A24.

Barnett, R. C., & Hyde, J. S. (2001). Women, men, work, and family. An expansionist theory. *American Psychologist, 56*(10), 781–796.

Barnett, R. C., & Marshall, N. L. (1993). Men, family-role quality, job-role quality, and physical health. *Health Psychology, 12*, 48–55.

Baron-Cohen, S. (2002). The extreme male brain theory of autism. *Trends in Cognitive Sciences, 6*, 248–354.

Bartels, A., & Zeki, S. (2000). The neural basis of romantic love. *Neuroreport, 11*(17), 3829–3834.

Bartholomew, K., & Horowitz, L. M. (1991). Attachment styles among young adults: A test of a four-category model. *Journal of Personality and Social Psychology, 61*, 226–244.

Basile, K. C. (1999). Rape by acquiescence: The ways in which women "give in" to unwanted sex with their husbands. *Violence Against Women, 5*, 1036–1058.

Basile, K. C. (2002). Prevalence of wife rape and other intimate partner sexual coercion in a nationally representative sample of women. *Violence and Victims, 17*, 511–524.

Bateman, A. J. (1948). Intra-sexual selection in drosophila. *Heredity, 2*, 349–368.

Baumbusch, J. (2004). Unclaimed treasures: Older women's reflections on lifelong singlehood. *Journal of Women and Aging, 16*, 105–121.

Baumeister, R. F. (2000). Gender differences in erotic plasticity: The female sex drive as socially flexible and responsive. *Psychological Bulletin, 126*(3), 347–374.

Baumeister, R. F., & Leary, M. R. (1995). The need to belong: Desire for interpersonal attachments as a fundamental human motivation. *Psychological Bulletin, 117*, 497–529.

Baumeister, R. F., & Vohs, K. D. (2004). Sexual economics: Sex as female resource for social exchange in heterosexual interactions. *Personality and Social Psychology Review, 8*, 339–363.

Baumrind, D. (1967). Child care practices anteceding three patterns of preschool behavior. *Genetic Psychology Monographs, 75*, 43–88.

Bauserman, R., & Rind, B. (1997). Psychological correlates of male child and adolescent sexual experience with adults: A review of non-clinical literature. *Archives of Sexual Behavior, 26*, 105–141.

Bazzini, D. G., McIntosh, W., Smith, S., Cook, S., & Harris, C. (1997). The aging woman in popular film: Underrepresented, unattractive, unfriendly, and unintelligent. *Sex Roles, 36*, 531–543.

Beale, C. R. (1994). *Boys and girls: The development of gender roles.* New York: McGraw-Hill.

Bean, F. D., & Tienda, M. (1987). *The Hispanic population of the United States*. New York: Russell Sage.

Becatoros, E. (2008, October 5). Tradition of "sworn virgins" dying out in Albania. *Associated Press*.

Becerra, R. M. (1998). The Mexican-American family. In C. H. Mindel, R. W. Habersein, & R. Wright, Jr. (Eds.), *Ethnic families in America: Patterns and variations* (pp. 153–171). Upper Saddle River, NJ: Prentice Hall.

Bedford, V. H., & Blieszner, R. (2000). Older adults and their families. In D. H. Demo, K. R. Allen, and M. A. Fine (Eds.), *Handbook of family diversity* (pp. 216–231). New York: Oxford University Press.

Behson, S. J. (2008). Work, family, and sports: When even millionaire athletes need employer help to balance work and family. *Journal of Diversity Management, 3*, 23–31.

Bekemeier, B. (1995). Public health nurses and the prevention of and intervention in family violence. *Public Health Nursing, 12*(4), 222–227.

Bell-Kaplan, E. (1996). Black teenage mothers and their mothers: The impact of adolescent childbearing on daughters' relations with mothers. *Social Problems, 43*(4), 427–443.

Bellah, R., Madsen, R., Sullivan, W., Swidler, A., & Tipton, S. (1985). *Habits of the heart*. Berkeley, CA: University of California Press.

Bellotti, E. (2008). What are friends for? Elective communities of single people. *Social Networks, 30*, 318–329.

Belsky, J. (2001). Emanuel Miller Lecture: Developmental risks (still) associated with early child care. *Journal of Child Psychology and Psychiatry, 47*, 845–849.

Bem, S. L. (1974). The measurement of psychological androgyny. *Journal of Consulting and Clinical Psychology, 42*(2), 155–162.

Bem, S. L. (1977). On the utility of alternative procedures for assessing psychological androgyny. *Journal of Consulting and Clinical Psychology, 45*(2), 196–205.

Bem, S. L. (1981). Gender schema theory: A cognitive account of sex typing. *Psychological Review, 88*, 354–364.

Bem, S. L. (1983). Gender schema theory and its implications for child development: Raising gender-aschematic children in a gender-schematic society. *Signs, 8*(4), 598–616.

Bem, S. L. (1995). Dismantling gender polarization and compulsory heterosexuality: Should we turn the volume down or up? *Journal of Sex Research, 32*(4), 329–334.

Bengtson, V. L. (2001). Beyond the nuclear family: The increasing importance of multigenerational bonds. *Journal of Marriage and Family, 63*, 1–16.

Bengtson, V. L., Biblarz, T. J., & Roberts, E. L. R. (2002). *How families still matter: A longitudinal study of youth in two generations*. New York: Cambridge University Press.

Benjamin, L. T. (1975). The pioneering work of Leta Hollingworth in the psychology of women. *Nebraska History, 56*, 493–505.

Bennice, J. A., & Resick, P. A. (2003). Marital rape: History, research, and practice. *Trauma, Violence, and Abuse, 4*, 228–246.

Benokraitis, N. V. (Ed.). (2000). *Feuds about families: Conservative, centrist, liberal, and feminist perspectives*. Upper Saddle River, NJ: Prentice Hall.

Berenbaum, S. A. (2005). Hormones in human behaviour [Review of *Prenatal testosterone in mind: Amniotic fluid studies* by S. Baron-Cohen, S. Lutchmaya, & R. Knickmeyer]. *The Lancet Neurology, 4*, 339.

Berenbaum, S. A., & Bailey, M. (2003). Effects on gender identity of prenatal androgens and genital appearance: Evidence from girls with congenital adrenal hyperplasia. *Journal of Clinical Endocrinology and Metabolism, 88*, 1102–1106.

Berenbaum, S. A., & Korman-Bryk, K. L. (2008). Biological contributions to gendered occupational outcome: Prenatal androgen effects on predictors of outcomes. In H. M. G. Watt & J. S. Eccles (Eds.), *Gender and occupational outcomes: Longitudinal assessment of individual, social, and cultural influences* (pp. 235–264). Washington, DC: American Psychological Association.

Berg, S. J., & Wynne-Edwards, K. E. (2001). Changes in testosterone, cortisol, and estradiol levels in men becoming fathers. *Mayo Clinic Proceedings, 76*, 582–592.

Berger, P. L., & Luckmann, T. (1967). *The social construction of reality: A treatise in the sociology of knowledge*. Garden City, NY: Doubleday.

Berger, R. M. (1982). The unseen minority: Older gays and lesbians. *Social Work, 27*(3), 236–242.

Berkowitz, A., & Padavia, I. (1999). Getting a man or getting ahead: A comparison of white and black sororities. *Journal of Contemporary Ethnography, 27*(4), 530–557.

Berman, J., Berman, L., & Bumiller, E. (2001). *For women only: A revolutionary guide to overcoming sexual dysfunction and reclaiming your sex life*. New York: Henry Holt Company.

Bernard, J. (1982). *The future of marriage*. New Haven, CT: Yale University Press.

Berscheid, E., & Walster, E. H. (1978). *Interpersonal attraction*. Reading, MA: Addison-Wesley.

Berthier, N. E., DeBlois, S., Poirier, C. R., Novak, M. A., & Clifton, R. K. (2000). Where's the ball? Two- and three year-olds' reasoning about unseen events. *Developmental Psychology, 36*, 394–401.

Bialystock, E., Craik, F. I., Klein, R., & Viswanathan, M. (2004). Bilingualism, aging, and cognitive control: Evidence from the Simon task. *Psychology and Aging, 19*(2), 290–303.

Bianchi, S. M. (2000). Maternal employment and time with children: Dramatic change or surprising continuity? *Demography, 37*, 401–414.

Bianchi, S. M., Milkie, M. S., Sayer, L. C., & Robinson, J. P. (2000). Is anyone doing the housework? Trends in gender division of household labor. *Social Forces, 79*, 191–228.

Bianchi, S. M., Robinson, J. P., & Milkie, M. A. (2006) *Changing rhythms of American family life*. New York: Russell Sage Foundation.

Biddulph, S. (2008). *Raising boys: Why boys are different*. Berkeley, CA: Celestial Arts Publishing.

Bigler, R. S., Averhart, C. J., & Liben, L. S. (2003). Race and the workforce: Occupational status, aspirations, and stereotyping among African American children. *Developmental Psychology, 39,* 572–580.

Bigner, J. J., & Jacobsen, R. B. (1989). Parenting behaviors of homosexual and heterosexual fathers. *Journal of Homosexuality, 18,* 173–186.

Biller, H. B. (1974). *Parental deprivation.* Lexington, MA: Heath.

Birkhead, T. R., & Moller, A. P. (1998). *Sperm competition and sexual selection.* New York: Academic Press.

Blair-Loy, M., & Wharton, A. (2004). Organizational commitment and constraints on work–family policy use. *Sociological Perspectives, 47,* 243–267.

Blaisure, K. R., & Allen, K. R. (1995). Feminism and the ideology and practice of marital equality. *Journal of Marriage and the Family, 57,* 5–19.

Blanchard-Fields, F. (2007). Everyday problem solving and emotion: An adult developmental perspective. *Association for Psychological Science, 16*(1), 26–31.

Blee, K. M., & Tickamyer, A. R. (1995). Racial differences in men's attitudes about women's gender roles. *Journal of Marriage and Family, 57,* 21–30.

Bleeker, M. M., & Jacobs, J. E. (2004). Achievement in math and science: Do mothers' beliefs matter 12 years later? *Journal of Educational Psychology, 96,* 97–109.

Blumstein, P., & Schwartz, P. (1983). *American couples.* New York: William Morrow.

Bockting, W. O., & Coleman, E. (1992). *Gender dysphoria: Interdisciplinary approaches to clinical management.* New York: Haworth Press.

Bodenmann, G. (2005). Dyadic coping and its significance for marital functioning. In T. A. Revenson, K. Kayser, & G. Bodenmann (Eds.), *Couples coping with stress: Emerging perspectives on dyadic coping* (pp. 33–49). Washington, DC: American Psychological Association.

Bohan, J. S. (1993). Regarding gender: Essentialism, constructionism, and feminist psychology. *Psychology of Women Quarterly, 17*(1), 5–21.

Bohannon, P. (1970). *Divorce and after.* New York: Doubleday.

Bohner, G., Jarvis, C. I., Eyssel, F., & Siebler, F. (2005) The causal impact of rape myth acceptance on men's rape proclivity: Comparing sexually coercive and noncoercive men. *European Journal of Social Psychology, 35,* 819–828.

Boldizar, J. P. (1991). Assessing sex typing and androgyny in children: The Children's Sex Role Inventory. *Developmental Psychology, 27,* 505–515.

Bond, J. T., Galinsky, E., & Swanberg, J. E. (1998). *The 1997 national study of the changing workforce.* New York: Families and Work Institute.

Boone, J. L. (1988). Parental investment, social subordination, and population processes among the fifteenth- and sixteenth-century Portuguese nobility. In L. Betzig, M. Borgerhoff Mulder, & P. Turke, (Eds.), *Human reproductive behavior: A Darwinian perspective* (pp. 201–219). Cambridge, U.K.: Cambridge University Press.

Booth, A., & Edwards, J. (1992). Starting over: Why remarriages are more unstable. *Journal of Family Issues, 13,* 179–194.

Bornstein, K. (1994). *Gender outlaw: On men, women and the rest of us.* New York: Routledge.

Bos, H. M. W., van Balen, F., & van den Boom, D. C. (2005). Lesbian families and family functioning: An overview. *Patient Education and Counseling, 59,* 263–275.

Bouvier, J. (1856). *A law dictionary* (8th ed.). Philadelphia, PA: G. W. Childs.

Bowen, M. (1978). *Family therapy in clinical therapy.* New York: J. Aronson.

Bowlby, J. (1978). Attachment theory and its therapeutic implications. *Adolescent Psychiatry: Developmental and Clinical Studies, 6,* 5–33.

Bowlby, J. (1980). *Attachment and loss.* New York: Basic Books.

Bowlby, J. (1988). *A secure base: Parent–child attachment and healthy human development.* New York: Basic Books.

Bowles, H. R., & Gelfand, M. (2009). Status and the evaluation of workplace deviance. *Psychological Science, 20,* 1–6; doi: 10.1177/0956797609356509.

Bradshaw, J., & Richardson, D. (2009). An index of child well-being in Europe. *Child Indicators Research.* doi: 10.1007/s12187–009–9037–7.

Braithwaite, R. L., & Taylor, S. E. (Eds.). (2001). *Health issues in the black community* (2nd ed.). San Francisco, CA: Jossey-Bass.

Braver, S. L., Hipke, K. N., Ellman, I. N., Sandler, I. N. (2004). Strengths-building public policy for children of divorce. In K. I. Maton, C. J. Schellenbach, B. J. Leadbeater, & A. J. Solarz (Eds.), *Investing in children, youth, families, and communities: Strengths-based research and policy* (pp. 53–72). Washington, DC: American Psychological Association.

Bray, J. H. (1990). Impact of divorce on the family. In R. E. Rakel (Ed.), *Textbook of family practice* (4th ed., pp. 111–122). Philadelphia, PA: Saunders.

Bray, J. H. (1994). What does a typical stepfamily look life? *Family Journal: Counseling and Therapy for Couples and Families, 2,* 66–69.

Bray, J. H. (1999a). From marriage to remarriage and beyond: Findings from the developmental issues in stepfamilies research project. In E. M. Hetherington (Ed.), *Coping with divorce, single-parenting and remarriage: A risk and resiliency perspective* (pp. 253–271). Hillsdale, NJ: Erlbaum.

Bray, J. (1999b). Stepfamilies: The intersection of culture, context, and biology. *Monographs of the Society for Research in Child Development, 64,* 210–218.

Bray, J. H., & Hetherington, E. M. (1993). Families in transition: Introduction and overview. *Journal of Family Psychology, 7,* 3–8.

Bray, J. H., & Kelly, J. (1998). *Stepfamilies: Love, marriage, and parenting in the first decade.* New York: Broadway Books.

Brewaeys, A., Devroey, P., Helmerhorst, F. M., van Hall, E. V., & Ponjaert, I. (1995). Lesbian mothers who conceived after donor insemination: A follow-up study. *Human Reproduction, 10,* 2731–2735.

Bronfenbrenner, U. (1994). Ecological models of human development. In T. Husen & T. N. Postlethwaite (Eds.), *The international encyclopedia of education* (2nd ed., pp. 1643–1647). New York: Elsevier Science.

Bronfenbrenner, U. (1995). The bioecological model from a life course perspective: Reflections of a participant observer. In P. Moen, G. H. Elder Jr., & K. Luscher (Eds.), *Examining lives in context: Perspectives on the ecology of human development* (pp. 599–618). Washington, DC: American Psychological Association.

Bronfenbrenner, U. (2004). *Making human beings human: Bioecological perspectives on human development.* Thousand Oaks, CA: Sage.

Bronfenbrenner, U., & Ceci, S. J. (1993). Heredity, environment, and the question "How?": A first approximation. In R. Plomin & G. E. McClearn (Eds.), *Nature, nurture, and psychology* (pp. 313–324). Washington, DC: American Psychological Association.

Bronfenbrenner, U., & Ceci, S. J. (1994). Nature–nurture reconceptualized: A bioecological model. *Psychological Review, 101,* 568–586.

Bronfenbrenner, U., & Morris, P. A. (1998). The ecology of developmental processes. In W. Damon & R. M. Lerner (Eds.), *Handbook of child psychology: vol. 1. Theoretical models of human development* (5th ed., pp. 993–1028). New York: John Wiley.

Bronfenbrenner, U., & Morris, P. A. (2006). The bioecological model of human development. In R. M. Lerner (Ed.). *Handbook of child psychology: vol. 1. Theoretical models of human development* (6th ed., pp. 793–828). Hoboken, NJ: Wiley.

Brookes, M., & Zietman, A. (1998). *Clinical embryology: A colour atlas and text.* Boca Raton, FL: CRC Press.

Brooks, A. C. (2008). *Gross national happiness: Why happiness matters for America— and how we can get more of it.* New York: Basic Books.

Brooks-Gunn, J., Han, W.-J., & Waldfogel, J. (2002). Maternal employment and child cognitive outcomes in the first three years of life: The NICHD study of early child care. *Child Development, 73*(4), 1052–1072.

Brown, A., Williams, K. R., & Dutton, D. G. (1999). Homicide between intimate partners: A 20-year review. In M. D. Smith & M. A. Zhan (Eds.), *Homicide: A sourcebook of social research* (pp. 149–164). Thousand Oaks, CA: Sage.

Brown, M. J., & Groscup, J. L. (2008, December). Breaking up is hard to do: Challenges of same-sex divorce. *Judicial Notebook,* 17–27.

Brown, S. L., Smith, D. M., Schulz, R., Kabeto, M. U., Ubel, P. A., Poulin, M., … Langa, K. M. (2009). Caregiving behavior is associated with decreased mortality risk. *Psychological Science, 20*(4), 488–494.

Browne, A., & Bassuk, S. (1997). Intimate violence in the lives of homeless and poor housed women. *American Journal of Orthopsychiatry, 67*(2), 261–278.

Browning, C. (1987). Therapeutic issues and intervention strategies with young adult lesbian clients: A developmental approach. *Journal of Homosexuality, 14,* 45–52.

Bryan, P. E. (2006). *Constructive divorce. Procedural justice and sociolegal reform.* Washington, DC: American Psychological Association.

Budig, M. J., & England, P. (2001). The wage penalty for motherhood. *American Sociological Review, 66,* 204–225.

Buehler, C., Krishnakumar, A., Stone, G., Anthony, C., Pemberton, S., Gerard, J., & Barber, B. K. (1998). Interparental conflict styles and youth problem behaviors: A two-sample replication study. *Journal of Marriage and the Family, 60,* 119–132.

Bulcroft, K., & O'Connor, M. (1986). The importance of dating relationships on quality of life for older persons. *Family Relations, 35,* 397–401.

Bulcroft, R. A., & Bulcroft, K. A. (1991). The nature and functioning of dating in later life. *Research on Aging, 13,* 244–260.

Bullock, K. (2004). The changing role of grandparents in rural families: The results of an exploratory study in southeastern North Carolina. *Families in Society, 85*(1), 45–54.

Bumpass, L. L., & Lu, H. (1999). Trends in cohabitation and implications for children's family contexts in the U.S. *Population Studies, 54,* 29–41.

Bumpass, L., & Sweet, J. (1989). National estimates of cohabitation. *Demography, 26*(4), 615–625.

Bumroongsook, S. (1992). *Conventions of mate selection in twentieth-century central Thailand* (Unpublished masters thesis). Department of History, University of Hawaii, Honolulu.

Bureau of Justice Statistics (1995). *Violence against women: Estimates from the redesigned survey.* Washington, DC: Office of Justice Programs, U.S. Department of Justice.

Burgess, N. J. (1995). Looking back, looking forward: African American families in sociohistorical perspective. In B. B. Ingoldsby & S. Smith (Eds.), *Families in multicultural perspective* (pp. 321–334). New York: Guilford.

Buriel, R. (1993). Acculturation, respect for cultural differences and biculturalism among three generations of Mexican American and Euro-American school children. *Journal of Genetic Psychology, 154,* 531–543.

Buriel, R., Perez, W., DeMent, T. L., Chavez, D. V. & Moran, V. R. (1998). The relationship of language brokering to academic performance, biculturalism, and self-efficacy among Latino adolescents. *Hispanic Journal of the Behavioral Sciences, 20,* 283–297.

Burke, R. J. (2000). Workaholism and extra-work satisfactions. *International Journal of Organizational Analysis, 7,* 352–364.

Buss, D. M. (2000). *The dangerous passion: Why jealousy is as nessary as love and sex.* New York: Free Press.

Buss, D. M., Shackelford, T. K., Kirkpatrick, L. A., & Larsen, R. J. (2001). A half century of mate preferences: The cultural evolution of values. *Journal of Marriage and the Family, 63,* 491–503.

Butler, J. (1990). *Gender trouble: Feminism and the subversion of identity*. New York: Routledge.

Butler, J. R., & Barton, L. M. (1990). Rethinking teenage childbearing: Is sexual abuse a missing link? *Family Relations, 38*(1), 73–80.

Byrne, A., & Carr, D. (2005). Caught in the cultural lag: The stigma of singlehood. *Psychological Inquiry, 16*, 84–141.

Cahill, L. (2006). Why sex matters for neuroscience. *Nature Reviews Neuroscience, 7*, 477–484. doi: 10.1038/nrn/909.

Cameron, G., & Freymond, N. (2006). Understanding international comparisons of child protection, family service, and community caring systems of child and family welfare. In N. Freymond & G. Cameron (Eds.), *Towards positive systems of child and family welfare: International comparisons of child protection, family service, and community caring systems* (pp. 3–25). Toronto: University of Toronto Press.

Camperio-Ciani, A., Cermelli, P., & Zanzotti, G. (2008). Sexual antagonistic selection in human male homosexuals. *PLoS ONE, 3*, e2282; doi: 10.1371/journal.pone.000.2282.

Cancian, F. M. (1987). *Love in America: Gender and self-development*. Cambridge, U.K.: Cambridge University Press.

Carbarino, R. (2006). Family foster care: Voices from around the world. *Families in Society, 87*(4), 467–468.

Carden, S. E., & Hofer, M. A. (1990). The effects of opioid and benzodiazepine antagonists on dam-induced reductions in rat pup solitary distress. *Developmental Psychobiology, 23*, 797–808.

Carlisle-Frank, P., Frank, J. M., & Nielson, L. (2004). Selective battering of the family pet. *Anthrozoos, 17*, 26–42.

Carr, D. (2004). The desire to date and remarry among older widows and widowers. *Journal of Marriage and Family, 66*, 1051–1068.

Carrere, S., Buehlman, K. T., Gottman, J. M., Coan, J. A., & Ruckstuhl, L. (2000). Predicting marital stability and divorce in newlywed couples. *Journal of Family Psychology, 14*(1), 42–58.

Carrington, C. (1999). *No place like home: Relationships and family life among lesbians and gay men*. Chicago, IL: University of Chicago Press.

Carroll, J. S., Padilla-Walker, L. M., Nelson, L. J., Olsen, C. D., Barry, C. M., & Madsen, S. D. (2008). Generation XXX: Pornography acceptance and use among emerging adults. *Journal of Adolescent Research, 23*, 6–30.

Carson, J., Burks, V., & Parke, R. D. (1993). Parent–child physical play: Determinants and consequences. In K. MacDonald (Ed.), *Parent–Child Play* (pp. 197–220). Albany, NY: State University of New York Press.

Carter, C. S., DeVries, A. C., & Getz, L. L. (1995). Physiological substrates of mammalian monogamy: The prairie vole model. *Neuroscience and Biobehavioral Reviews, 19*, 303–314.

Casper, L. M., & Bianchi, S. M. (2002). *Continuity and change in the American family*. Thousand Oaks, CA: Sage.

Casper, W. J., Weltman, D., & Kwesiga, E. (2007). Beyond family-friendly: The construct and measurement of singles-friendly work culture. *Journal of Vocational Behavior, 70*(3), 478–501.

Caspi, A., McClay, J., Moffitt, T. E., Mill, J., Martin, J., Craig, I. W., . . . & Poulton, R. (2002). Role of genotype in the cycle of violence in maltreated children. *Science, 297*(5582), 851–854.

Caspi, A., Williams, B., Kim-Cohen, J., Craig, J. W., Milne, B. J., Poulton, R., . . . Moffitt, T. E. (2007). Moderation of breastfeeding effects on the IQ by genetic variation in fatty acid metabolism. *Proceedings of the National Academy of Sciences, 104*(47), 18860–18865.

Castro Martin, T., & Bumpass, L. (1989). Recent trends in marital disruption. *Demography, 26*(1), 37–51.

Catalano, S., Smith, E., Snyder, H., & Rand, M. (2009). *Female victims of violence*. U.S. Department of Justice Office of Justice Programs, Bureau of Justice Statistics. Retrieved on April 15, 2011 from http://bjs.ojp.usdoj.gov/content/pub/pdf/fvv.pdf.

Catalyst (2004). *The bottom line: Connecting corporate performance and gender diversity*. Retrieved from http://www.catalyst.org/publication/82/the-bottom-line-connecting-corporate-performance-and-gender-diversity.

Catalyst (2006). *2005 Catalyst census of women board directors of the Fortune 500*. Retrieved from http://www.catalyst.org/publication/19/2005-catalyst-census-of-women-board-directors-of-the-fortune-500.

Catalyst (2007). *The bottom line: Connecting corporate performance and gender diversity*. New York: Catalyst.

Catalyst (2008). *Women and minorities on Fortune 100 boards*. Retrieved from http://www.catalyst.org/publication/185/women-and-minorities-on-fortune-100-boards.

Catalyst (2011). *Women CEOs of the Fortune 1000*. Retrieved from http://www.catalyst.org/publication/322/women-ceos-of-the-fortune-1000.

Center for Disease Control and Prevention (2010). Health disparities in HIV/AIDS, viral hepatitis, STDs, and TB. Retrieved from http://www.cdc.gov/nchhstp/healthdisparities/Hispanics.html

Chabrol, H., Teissedre, F., Saint-Jean, M., Teisseyre, N., Rogé, B., & Mullet, E. (2002). Prevention and treatment of postpartum depression: a controlled randomized study on women at risk. *Psychological Medicine, 32*(6), 1039–1047.

Chan, R. W., Raboy, B., & Patterson, C. J. (1998). Psychosocial adjustment among children conceived via donor insemination by lesbian and hereosexual mothers. *Child Development, 69*, 443–457.

Chan, S. (1991). *Asian Americans: An interpretive history*. Boston, MA: Twayne.

Chao, R. (1994). Beyond parental control and authoritarian parenting style: Understanding Chinese parenting through the cultural notion of training. *Child Development, 65*, 1111–1119.

Charney, D. S. (2004). Psychobiological mechanisms of resilience and vulnerability: Implications for successful adaptation to extreme stress. *American Journal of Psychiatry, 161*(2), 195–216.

Chasteen, A. L. (1994). The world around me: The environment of single women. *Sex Roles, 31*, 309–328.

Chege, J. N., Askew, I., & Liku, J. (2001). *An assessment of the alternative rites approach for encouraging abandonment of female genital mutilation in Kenya.* Frontiers in Reproductive Health. Washington, DC: Population Council.

Cherlin, A. (1978). Remarriage as an incomplete institution. *American Journal of Sociology, 84*, 634–650.

Cherlin, A. J. (1992). *Marriage, divorce and remarriage.* Cambridge, MA: Harvard University Press.

Cherlin, A. J. (2004). The deinstitutionalization of American marriage. *Journal of Marriage and Family 66*, 848–861.

Cherlin, A. J. (Ed.). (2008). *Public and private families: A reader* (5th ed.). New York: McGraw Hill.

Cherlin, A. J., Burton, L. M., Hurt, T. R., & Purvin, D. M. (2004). The influence of physical and sexual abuse on marriage and cohabitation. *American Sociological Review, 69*, 768–789.

Cherlin, A. J., & Furstenberg, F. F. (1985). Styles and strategies of grandparenting. In V. K. Bengtson & J. F. Roberston (Eds.), *Grandparenthood* (pp. 97–116). Beverly Hills, CA: Sage.

Cherlin, A. J., & Furstenberg, F. F. (1986). *The new American grandparent: A place in the family, a life apart.* New York: Basic Books.

Cherlin, A. J. and Furstenberg, F. F. (1994). Stepfamilies in the United States: a reconsideration. *Annual Review of Sociology, 20*, 359–381

Cherlin, A. J., Kiernan, K. E., & Chase-Lansdale, P. L. (1995). Parental divorce in childhood and demographic outcomes in young adulthood. *Demography, 32*, 299–318.

Chhin, C. S., Bleeker, M. M., & Jacobs, J. E. (2008). Gender-typed occupational choices: The long-term impact of parents' beliefs and expectations. In H. M. G. Watt & J. S. Eccles (Eds.), *Gender and occupational outcomes: Longitudinal assessment of individual, social, and cultural influences* (pp. 215–234). Washington, DC: American Psychological Association.

Child Abuse Prevention and Treatment Act. 42 USC 5101 *et seq.* (1996).

Chinitz, J. G., & Brown, R. A. (2001). Religious homogamy, marital conflict, and stability in same-faith and interfaith Jewish marriages. *Journal of the Scientific Study of Religion, 40*, 723–733.

Chira, S. (1998). *A mother's place.* New York: HarperCollins.

Chiu, L. H. (1987). Child-rearing attitudes of Chinese, Chinese-American, and Anglo-American mothers. *International Journal of Psychology, 22*, 409–419.

Chivers, M. L., & Bailey, M. J. (2005). A sex difference in features that elicit genital response. *Biological Psychology, 70*, 115–120.

Chivers, M. L., Rieger, G., Latty, E., & Bailey, J. M. (2004). A sex difference in the specificity of sexual arousal. *Psychological Science, 15*, 736–744.

Cho, W., & Cross, S. (1995). Taiwanese love styles and their association with self-esteem and realistic quality. *Genetic, Social and General Psychology Monographs, 121*, 283–309.

Choi, N. G. (1999). Living arrangements and household compositions of elderly couples and singles: A comparison of Hispanics and Blacks. *Journal of Gerontological Social Work, 31*(1–2), 41–61.

Chrisler, J. C., & McCreary, D. R. (2010). *Handbook of gender research in psychology: vol. 1. Gender research in general and experimental psychology.* New York: Springer.

Christiansen, S., & Palkovitz, R. (2001). Providing as a form of paternal involvement: Why the good provider role still matters. *Journal of Family Issues, 22*, 84–106.

Christopher, F. S., & Sprecher, S. (2000). Sexuality in marriage, dating, and other relationships: A decade review. *Journal of Marriage and the Family, 62*, 999–1017.

Chunkath, S. R., & Athreya, V. B. (1997). Female infanticide in Tamil Nadu: Some evidence. *Economic and Political Weekly, 32*(17), 21–28.

Cicchetti, D., & Lynch, M. (1993). Toward an ecological/transactional model of community violence and child maltreatment: Consequences for child development. *Psychiatry: Interpersonal and Biological Processes, 56*, 96–118.

Cikara, M., & Fiske, S. T. (2009). Warmth, competence, and ambivalent sexism: Vertical assault and collateral damage. In M. Barreto, M. Ryan, & M. Schmitt (Eds.), *Barriers to diversity: The glass ceiling 20 years on* (pp. 73–96). Washington, DC: American Psychological Association.

Clark, L. S. (1998). Dating on the net: Teens and the rise of "pure relationships." In S. G. Jones (Ed.), *Cyberspace 2.0: Revisiting computer-mediated communication and community* (pp. 159–183). Thousand Oaks, CA: Sage.

Clark, M. A., Bonacore, L., Wright, S. J., Armstrong, G., & Rakowski, W. (2004). The Cancer Screening Project for Women: Experiences of women who partner with women and women who partner with men. *Women and Health, 38*(2), 19–34.

Clarke, V. (2002). Resistance and normalization in the construction of lesbian and gay families: A discursive analysis. In A. Coyle & C. Kitzinger (Eds.), *Lesbian and gay psychology: New perspectives* (pp. 98–116). Malden, MA: Blackwell Publishers.

Clarke, V., & Peel, E. (2007). *Out in psychology: Lesbian, gay, bisexual, trans, and queer perspectives.* Chichester, U.K.: Wiley.

Clatterbaugh, K. (1997). *Comtemporary perspectives on masculinity: Men, women, and politics in modern society.* Boulder, CO: Westview.

Clay, R. A. (2009, February). Caring for caregivers. *Monitor on Psychology*, 50–53.

Cogan, J. C., Bhalla, S. K., Sefa-Dedeh, A., & Rothblum, E. D. (1996). A comparison study of United States and African students on perceptions of obesity and thinness. *Journal of Cross-Cultural Psychology, 27*, 98–113.

Cohen, D. (2007). Methods in cultural psychology. In S. Kitayama & D. Cohen (Eds.), *Handbook of cultural psychology* (pp. 196–236). New York: Guilford Press.

Coleman, M., Ganong, L. H., & Rothrauff, T. C. (2006). Racial and ethnic similarities and differences in beliefs about intergenerational assistance to older adults after divorce and remarriage. *Family Relations, 55,* 576–587.

Coleman, T. F. (2007, September 17). Ranks of unmarried adults reach 100 million mark. Unmarried America. Retrieved from http://www.unmarriedamerica.org/column-one/09–17–07-census-report.htm

Coles, R. L. (2006). *Race and family: A structural approach.* Thousands Oaks, CA: Sage.

Collins, W. A. (2003). More than myth: The developmental significance of romantic relationships during adolescence. *Journal of Research on Adolescence, 13,* 1–24.

Collins, W. A., Welsh, D. P., & Furman, W. (2009). Adolescent romantic relationships. *Annual Review of Psychology, 60,* 631–652.

Coltrane, S. (1998). *Gender and families.* Thousand Oaks, CA: Pine Forge Press.

Coltrane, S. (2004). Fathering paradoxes, contradictions, and dilemmas. In M. Coleman & L. H. Ganong (Eds.), *Handbook of contemporary families* (pp. 224–243). Thousand Oaks, CA: Sage.

Coltrane, S., & Adams, M. (2008). *Gender and Families.* Lanham, MD: Rowman & Littlefield Publishers.

Committee on the U.S. Commitment to Global Health. (2009). *The U.S. commitment to global health: Recommendations for the public and private sectors.* Washington, DC: The National Academies Press.

Condit, C. M. (2008). Feminist biologies: Revising feminist strategies and biological science. *Sex Roles, 59,* 492–503.

Conduct Problems Prevention Research Group. (2002). Evaluation of the first three years of the Fast Track Prevention Trial with children at high risk of adolescent conduct problems. *Journal of Abnormal Child Psychology, 30,* 19–35.

Conger, R. D., Conger, K. J., Elder, G. H., Lorenz, F. O., Simons, R. L., & Whitbeck, L. B. (2010). A family process model of economic hardship and the adjustment of adolescent boys. *Child Development, 63,* 526–541; doi: 10.1111/j.1467–8624.1992.

Conkle, A. (2010). Scientific insights from twenty-first-century dating. *The Observer of the Association for Psychological Science, 23,* 12–15.

Connell, R. W. (1993). Disruptions: Improper masculinities and schooling. In L. Weis & M. Fine (Eds.), *Beyond silenced voices: Class, race and gender in United States schools* (pp. 191–208). Albany, NY: State University of New York Press.

Conniff, R. (2003). Go ahead, kiss you cousin: Heck, marry her if you want to. *Discover,* 60–64.

Consolacion, T. B., Russell, S. T., & Sue, S. (2004). Sex, race/ethnicity, and romantic attractions: Nultiple minority status adolescents and mental health. *Cultural Diversity and Ethnic Minority Psychology, 10,* 200–214.

Contreras, R., Hendrick, S. S., & Hendrick, C. (1996). Perspectives on marital love and satisfaction in Mexican American and Anglo couples. *Journal of Counseling and Development, 74,* 408–415.

Cook, P. W. (1997). *Abused men.* Westport, CT: Praeger.

Cook, S. L., Woolard, J. L., & McCollum, H. C. (2004). The strengths, competence, and resilience of women facing domestic violence: How can research and policy support them? In K. I. Maton, C. J. Schellenbach, B. J. Leadbeater, & A. L. Solarz (Eds.), *Investing in children, youth, families, and communities: Strengths-based research and policy.* Washington, DC: American Psychological Association.

Coontz, S. (1992). *The way we never were: American families and the nostalgia trap.* New York: Basic Books.

Coontz, S. (1997). *The way we really are: Coming to terms with America's changing families.* New York: Basic Books.

Coontz, S. (2000). Historical perspectives on family diversity. In D. H. Demo, K. R. Allen, & M. A. Fine (Eds.), *The handbook of family diversity* (pp. 15–31). New York: Oxford University Press.

Coontz, S. (2004). The world historical transformation of marriage. *Journal of Marriage and Family, 66,* 974–979.

Coontz, S. (2005). *Marriage, a history: From obedience to intimacy, or how love conquered marriage.* New York: Viking Press.

Cooper, J., & Weaver, K. D. (2003). *Gender and computers: Understanding the digital divide.* Mahwah, NJ: Lawrence Erlbaum Associates, Inc.

Cornell, S., & Hartman, D. (2007). *Ethnicity and race: Making identities in a changing world* (2nd. ed.). Thousand Oaks, CA: Pine Forge Press.

Costello, C. B., Wight, V. R., & Stone, A. J. (2003). *The American woman 2003 to 2004: Daughters of a revolution: young women today.* New York: Palgrave Macmillan.

Cote, R. C., & Erickson, B. H. (2009). Untangling roots of tolerance: How forms of social capital shape attitudes toward ethnic minorities and immigrants. *American Behavioral Scientist, 52,* 1664–1689.

Courtenay, W. H. (2000). Constructions of masculinity and their influence on men's well-being: A theory of gender and health. *Social Science and Medicine, 50,* 1385–1401.

Cousins, M. (2005). *European welfare states: Comparative perspectives.* Thousand Oaks, CA: Sage Publications.

Cowan, C. P., & Cowan, P. A. (1992). *When partners become parents: The big life change for couples.* New York: Harper Collins.

Cowan, C., & Cowan, P. (1995). Interventions to ease the transition to parenthood: Why they are needed and what they can do. *Family Relations, 44,* 412–414.

Cox, M. J., Paley, B., & Harter, K. (2001). Interpersonal conflict and parent–child relationships. In J. Grych & F. Fincham (Eds.), *Child development and interparental conflict* (pp. 249–272). Cambridge, U.K.: Cambridge University Press.

Coyne, J. C., Rohrbaugh, M. J., Shoham, V., Sonnega, J. S., Nicklas, J. M., & Cranford, J. A. (2001). Prognostic importance of marital quality for survival of congestive heart failure. *American Journal of Cardiology, 88*(5), 526–529.

Craig, I. W., Harper, E., & Loat, C. S. (2004). The genetic basis for sex differences in human behaviour: Role of the sex chromosomes. *Annals of Human Genetics, 68,* 269–284.

Crawford, I., Allison, K. W., Zamboni, B. D., & Soto, T. (2002). The influence of dual-identity development on the psychosocial functioning of African-American gay and bisexual men. *Journal Sex Research, 39,* 179–89.

Crenshaw, K. (1994). Mapping the margins: Intersectionality, identity politics, and violence against women of color. In M. Fineman & R. Mykitiuk (Eds.), *The public nature of private violence* (pp. 93–118). New York: Routledge.

Crick, N. R., & Dodge, K. A. (1994). A review and reformulation of social information-processing mechanisms in children's social adjustment. *Psychological Bulletin, 115,* 74–101.

Crittenden, A. (2001). *The price of motherhood.* New York: Henry Holt and Company.

Crockett, L. J., Eggebeen, D. J., & Hawkins, A. J. (1993). Fathers' presence and young children's behavioral and cognitive adjustment. *Journal of Family Issues, 14,* 355–377.

Crook, J., & Osmaston, H. (1994). *Himalayan Buddhist villages: Environment, resources, society, and religious life in Zangskar, Ladakh.* Bristol, U.K.: University of Bristol.

Crooks, R., & Baur, K. (1990). *Our sexuality.* Redwood City, CA: Cummings.

Crosby, F. J., & Jaskar, K. L. (1993). Women and men at home and at work: Realities and illusions. In S. Oskamp & M. Costanzia (Eds.), *Gender issues in contemporary society* (pp. 143–171). Newbury Park, CA: Sage.

Crouch, J. (2007). No-fault divorce laws and divorce rates in the U.S. and Europe: Variations and correlations. In A. Loveless & T. B. Holman (Eds.), *The family in the new millennium: World voices supporting the natural clan* (pp. 306–331). New York: Praeger.

Csikszentmihalyi, M. (1999). If we are so rich, why aren't we happy? *The American Psychologist, 54,* 821–827.

Csikszentmihalyi, M., & Hunter, L. (2003). Happiness in everyday life: The uses of experience sampling. *Journal of Happiness Studies, 4,* 185–199.

Csikszentmihalyi, M., & Schneider, B. (2000). *Becoming adult: How teenagers prepare for the world of work.* New York: Basic Books.

Cui, M., Fincham, F. F., & Pasley, K. (2008). Young adult romantic relationships: The role of parents' marital problems and relationship efficacy. *Personality and Social Psychology Bulletin, 34,* 1226–1235.

Cumming, E., & Henry, W. (1961). *Growing old.* New York: Basic Books.

Cunningham, M., & Thornton, A. (2006). The influence of parents' marital quality on adult children's attitudes toward marriage and its alternatives: Main and moderating effects. *Demography, 43,* 659–672.

Cunradi, C. B., Todd, M., Duke, M., & Ames, G. (2009). Problem drinking, unemployment, and intimate partner violence among a sample of construction industry workers and their partners. *Journal of Family Violence, 2,* 63–74. doi: 10.1007/s10896–008–9209–0.

Currie, C. L. (2006). Animal cruelty by children exposed to domestic violence. *Child Abuse and Neglect, 30,* 425–435.

Curtis, J. T., Liu, Y., Aragona, B. J., & Wang, Z. (2006). Dopamine and monogamy. *Brain Research, 1126*(1), 76–90.

D'Augelli, A. R. (1991). Gay men in college: Identity processes and adaptations. *Journal of College Student Development, 32,* 140–146.

Dahrendorf, R. (1959). *Class and class conflict in industrial society.* Stanford, CA: Stanford University Press.

Daley, S. (2000, April 18). French couples take plunge that falls short of marriage. *New York Times,* A1–A4.

Dalton, S. E., & Bielby, D. D. (2000). That's our kind of constellation. Lesbian mothers negotiate institutionalized understandings of gender within the family. *Gender and Society, 14*(1), 36–61.

Daly, M., & Wilson, M. I. (1983). *Sex, evolution and behavior: Adaptations for reproduction.* (2nd ed.). Boston, MA: Willard Grant Press.

Danet, B. (1998). Text as mask: Gender and identity on the Internet. In S. Jones (Ed.), *Cybersociety 2.0* (pp. 129–158). Thousand Oaks, CA: Sage.

Darrington, J., Piercy, K., & Niehuis, S. (2005). The social and cultural construction of singlehood among young, single Mormons. *The Qualitative Report, 10*(4), 639–661.

Davies, L. (2003). Singlehood: Transitions within a gendered world. *Canadian Journal on Aging, 22,* 343–352.

Davies, L., Avison, W. R., & McAlpine, D. D. (1997). Significant life experiences and depression among single and married mothers. *Journal of Marriage and the Family, 59,* 294–308.

Davies, P. T., Sturge-Apple, M. L., Cicchetti, D., & Cummings, E. M. (2008). Adrenocortical underpinnings of children's psychological reactivity to interparental conflict. *Child Development, 79*(6), 1693–1706.

Davies, P. T., Winter, M. A., & Cicchetti, D. (2006). The implications of emotional security theory for understanding and treating childhood psychopathology. *Development and Psychopathology, 18,* 707–735.

Davis, D. A., & Davis, S. S. (1995). Possessed by love: gender and romance in Morocco. In William Jankowiak (Ed.), *Romantic passion: A universal experience?* (pp. 219–238). New York: Columbia University Press.

Davis, E. C., & Friel, L. V. (2001). Adolescent sex: Disentangling effects of family structure and family context. *Journal of Marriage and Families, 63,* 669–681.

Day, R. D., & Hook, D. (1987). A short history of divorce: Jumping the broom and back again. *Journal of Divorce, 10*(3/4), 57–73.

Deadbeat Parents Punishment Act. Pub. L. No. 105–187 § 112 Stat. (1998).

de Beauvoir, S. (1952). *The second sex.* New York: Knopf.

De Jong, J. T. V. M., Komproe, I. H., Van Ommeren, M., Masri, M., Araya, M., Khaled, N., van de Put, W., & Somasundaram, D. (2001). Lifetime events and posttraumatic stress disorder in four postconflict settings, *Journal of the American Medical Association, 286,* 555–562.

Deady, D. K., Smith, M. J. L., Kent, J. P., & Dunbar, R. I. M. (2006). Is priesthood an adaptive strategy? Evidence from a historical Irish population. *Human Nature. Special Issue on Human Fertility, 17*(4), 393–404.

DeBellis, M. D. (2005). The psychobiology of neglect. *Child Maltreatment, 10,* 150–172.

DeBellis, M. D., Chrousos, G. P., Dorn, L. D., Burke, L., Helmers, K., Kling, M. A., . . . Putnam, F. W. (1994). Hypothalamic-pituitary-adrenal axis dysregulation in sexually abused girls. *Journal of Clinical Endocrinology and Metabolism, 78*(2), 249–255.

DeBellis, M. D., & Putnam, F. W. (1994). The psychobiology of childhood maltreatment. *Child and Adolescent Psychiatric Clinics of North America, 3,* 663–677.

Demos, J. (1970). *A little commonwealth: Family life in Plymouth Colony.* New York: Oxford University Press.

Denizet-Lewis, B. (2009, September 27). Coming out in middle school. *New York Times.*

Dennis, W. (1973). *Children of the crèche.* East Norwalk, CT: Appleton-Century-Crofts.

Denny, D., & Pittman, C. (2007). Gender identity: From dualism to diversity. In M. S. Tepper & A. F. Owens (Eds.), *Sexual health: Psychological foundations* (pp. 205–227). Westport, CT: Praeger.

Department of Justice, Canada (2009). *Fact sheet: Reference to the Supreme Court of Canada on civil marriage and the legal recognition of same-sex unions.* Retrieved from http://www.justice.gc.ca/eng/news-nouv/fs-fi/2004/doc_31110.html

DePaulo, B. (2006). *Singled out: How singles are stereotyped, stigmatized, and ignored, and still live happily ever after.* New York: St Martin's Press.

DePaulo, B. M., & Morris, W. L. (2005). Singles in society and in science. *Psychological Inquiry, 16*(2–3), 57–83.

DePaulo, B. M., & Morris, W. L. (2006). The unrecognized stereotyping and discrimination against singles. *Current Directions in Psychological Science, 15*(5), 251–254.

Dessaulles, A., Johnson, S. M., & Denton, W. H. (2003). Emotion-focused therapy for couples in the treatment of depression: A pilot study. *American Journal of Family Therapy, 31,* 345–353.

Deutsch, F. (1999). Equality works. In F. Deutsch, *Having it all: How equally shared parenting works* (pp. 225–233). Cambridge, MA: Harvard University Press.

DeVault, M. L. (1991). Feeing as women's work. In M. L. DeVault (Ed.), *Feeding the family: The social organization of caring as gendered work* (pp. 95–119). Chicago, IL: University of Chicago Press.

Devita-Raeburn, E. (2006, Jan./Feb.). Lust for the long haul. *Psychology Today.*

Di Leonardo, M. (1987). The female world of cards and holidays: Women, families, and the work of kinship. *Signs: Journal of Women in Culture and Society, 12,* 440–453.

Diamond, G. M., Lipsitz, J. D., Fajerman, Z., & Rozenblat, O. (2010). Ongoing trauma: Stress responses in Sderot, Israel. *Professional Psychology: Research and Practice, 41,* 19–25.

Diaz, R. M. (1998). *Latino gay men and HIV: Culture, sexuality, and risk behavior.* New York: Routledge.

Dicker, S., & Gordon, E. (2001). Early intervention and early childhood programs: Essential tools for child advocacy. *Journal of Poverty Law and Policy, 34,* 727–743.

Dicker, S., Gordon, E., & Knitzer, J. (2001). *Improving the odds for the health development of young children in foster care.* New York: National Center for Children in Poverty.

Dickson, F. C., Hughes, P. C., & Walker, K. L. (2005). An exploratory investigation into dating among later-life women. *Western Journal of Communication, 69,* 67–82.

Diemer, M. A. (2002). Constructions of provider role identity among African American men: An exploratory study. *Cultural Diversity and Ethnic Minority Psychology, 8*(1), 30–40.

Dieter, J. N., Field, T., Hernandez-Reif, M., Emory, E. K., & Redzepi, M. (2003). Stable preterm infants gain more weight and sleep less following five days of massage therapy. *Journal of Pediatric Psychology, 28*(6), 403–411.

Dobash, R. E., & Dobash, R. P. (1979). *Violence against wives.* New York: The Free Press.

Dobash, R. P., Dobash, R. E., Wilson, M., & Daly, M. (1992). The myth of sexual symmetry in marital violence. *Social Problems, 39*(1), 71–91.

Domar, A. D. (2004, September 27). A new fertility factor: Stress is just one of many obstacles to pregnancy, but it's one you can control. *Newsweek,* 72–74.

Dore, M. M., & Mullin, D. (2006). Treatment family foster care: Its history and current role in the foster care continuum. *Families in Society, 87*(4), 475–480.

Draganski, B., Gaser, C., Busch, V., Schuierer, G., Bogdahn, U., & May, A. (2004). Changes in grey matter induced by training. *Nature, 427,* 311–312.

Droes, M. I., & vanLamoen, C. R. (2010). Did unilateral divorce laws raise divorce rates? Comment. *Tjalling C. Koopman's Research Institute Discussion Paper 10–11.* Retrieved from http://www.uu.nl/rebo/economie/discussionpapers.

Duncan, A., Thomas, J. C., & Miller, C. (2005). Significance of family risk factors in development of childhood animal cruely in adolescent boys with conduct problems. *Journal of Family Violence, 20,* 235–239.

Duncan, G., & Brooks-Gunn, J. (1997). *Growing up poor.* New York: Russell Sage Foundation.

Dunn, J., Deater-Deckard, K., Pickering, K., & O'Connor, T. G. (1998). Children's adjustment and prosocial behaviour in step-, single-parent, and on-stepfamily setting: Findings from community study. *Journal of Child Psychology and Psychiatry, 39,* 1083–1095.

Eaton, W. O., & Yu, A. P. (1989). Are sex difference in child motor activity level a function of sex differences in maturational status? *Child Development, 60*(4), 1005–1011.

Eby, L. T., Allen, T. D., Noble, C. L., & Lockwood, A. L. (2004). Perceptions of singles and single parents: A laboratory experiment. *Journal of Applied Social Psychology, 34*(7), 1329–1352.

Eccles, J. S., Freedman-Doan, C., Frome, P., Jacobs, J., & Yoon, K. S. (2000). Gender role socialization in the family: A longitudinal approach. In T. Eckes & H. M. Trautner (Eds.), *The development of social psychology of gender* (pp. 333–360). Mahwah, NJ: Lawrence Erlbaum Associates.

Eckes, T. (2002). Paternalistic and envious gender stereotypes: Testing predictions from the stereotype content model. *Sex Roles, 47*, 99–114.

The Economist (December, 30, 2009). Count their blessings.

Edin, K., Kefalas, M. J., & Reed, J. M. (2004). A peek inside the black box: What marriage means for poor unmarried parents. *Journal of Marriage and the Family, 66*, 1007–1014.

Edin, K., & Lein, L. (1997). *Making ends meet: How single mothers survive welfare and low-wage work*. New York: Russell Sage Foundation.

Edwards, M. (1981). *The challenge of being single*. New York: Signet.

Egeland, B., Jacobvitz, D., & Sroufe, L. A. (1988). Breaking the cycle of abuse. *Child Development, 59*, 1080–1088.

Eisele, J. A., Kegler, S. R., Trent, R. B., & Coronado, V. G. (2006). Nonfatal traumatic brain injury-related hospitalization in very young children—15 states, 1999. *Journal of Head Trauma Rehabilitation, 21*, 537–543.

Eisenberg, M. E., & Resnick, M. D. (2006). Suicidality among gay, lesbian, and bisexual youth: The role of protective factors. *Journal of Adolescent Health, 39*, 662–668.

Eisikovits, Z., Winterstein, T., & Lowenstein, A. (2004). *The national survey on elder abuse and neglect in Israel*, Haifa: Haifa University and ESHEL.

Elkin, T. (2009). *Is divorce becoming a luxury?* Retrieved from http://www.yourtango.com

Ellis, B. H., MacDonald, H. Z., Lincoln, A. K., & Cabral, H. J. (2008). Mental health of Somali adolescent refugees: The role of trauma, stress, and perceived discrimination. *Journal of Consulting and Clinical Psychology, 76*(2), 184–193.

Ellis, B. J., Bates, J. E., Dodge, K. A., Ferguson, D. M., Horwood, L. J., Pettit, G. S., & Woodward, L. (2003). Does father absence place daughters at special risk for early sexuality and teen pregnancy. *Child Development, 74*, 801–821.

Ellsberg, M. C., Peña, R., Herrera, A., Liljestrand, J., & Winkvist, A. (1996). *Confites en el infierno. Prevalencia y características de la violencia conyugal hacia las mujeres en Nicaragua*. Managua, Nicaragua: Departamento de Medicina Preventiva, UNAM-León.

Elrod, L. D., & Dale, M. D. (2008). Paradigm shifts and pendulum swings in child custody. *Family Law Quarterly, 42*, 381–418.

Emery, R. E., Matthews, S. G., & Wyer, M. M. (1991). Child custody mediation and litigation: Further evidence on the differing views of mothers and fathers. *Journal of Consulting and Clinical Psychology, 59*, 410–418.

Emery, R. E., Sbarra, D., & Grover, T. (2005). Divorce mediation: Research and reflections. *Family Court Review, 43*, 22–37.

Emslie, C., & Hunt, K. (2009). Live to work or work to live? A qualitative study of gender and work–life balance among men and women in mid-life. *Gender, Work And Organization, 16*(1), 151–172.

England, P., Garcia-Beaulieu, C., & Ross, M. (2004). Women's employment among blacks, whites, and three groups of Latinas. Do more privileged women have higher employment? *Gender and Society, 18*, 494–509.

Engle, P. L., Black, M. M., Behrman, J. R., Cabral de Mello, M., Gertler, P. J., Kapiriri, L., . . . Young, M. E. (2007). Strategies to avoid the loss of developmental potential in more than two-hundred million children in the developing world. *The Lancet, 369*, 229–242.

Epel, E. S. (2009). Telomeres in a life-span perspective: A new psychobiomarker. *Current Directions in Psychological Science, 18*(1), 6–10.

Epel, E. S., Blackburn, E. H., Lin, J., Dhabhar, F. S., Adler, N. E., Morrow, J. D., & Cawthon, R. M. (2004). Accelerated telomere shortening in response to life stress. *Proceedings of the National Academies of Sciences, 101*, 17312–17315.

Epstein, C. F. (2007). Great divides: The cultural, cognitive, and social bases of the global subordination of women. *American Sociological Review, 73*, 1–22.

Epstein, M., Calzo, J. P., Smiler, A. P., & Ward, L. M. (2009). "Anything from making out to having sex": Men's negotiations of hooking up and friends with benefits scripts. *Journal of Sex Research, 46*, 414–424.

Erikson, E. (1961). *Childhood and society*. New York: W. W. Norton.

Erikson, E. (1969). *Gandhi's truth*. New York: W. W. Norton

Esch, T., & Stefano, G. B. (2007). The neurobiology of love. *Activitas Nervosa Superior, 49*, 1–18.

Eskenazi, B., Kidd, S. A., Marks, A. R., Sloter, E., Block, G., & Wyrobek, A. J. (2005). Antioxidant intake is associated with semen quality in healthy men. *Human Reproduction, 20*(4), 1006–1012.

Espelage, D. L., & Holt, M. K. (2007). Dating violence and sexual harassment across the bully–victim continuum among middle and high school students. *Journal of Youth and Adolescence, 36*, 799–811.

Everett, C., & Everett, S. V. (1994). *Healthy divorce*. San Francisco, CA: Jossey-Bass Publishers.

Facione, P. A. (2009). *Critical thinking: What it is and why it counts*. Millbrae, CA: Measured Reasons and the California Academic Press. Retrieved from http://www.insightassessment.com/pdf_files/what&why2009.pdf

Fagot, B. I. (1985). A cautionary note: Parents' socialization of boys and girls. *Sex Roles, 12*, 471–476.

Faludi, S. (1999). *Stiffed: The betrayal of the American man*. New York: HarperCollins.

Fang, C. Y., Sidanius, J., & Pratto, F. (1998). Romance across the social status continuum: Interracial marriage and the ideological asymmetry effect. *Journal of Cross-Cultural Psychology, 29*(2), 290–305.

Farkas, A., Chertin, B., & Hadas-Halpren, I. (2001). One-stage feminizing genitoplasty: Eight years of experience with 49 cases. *Journal of Urology, 165*, 2341–2346.

Farrell, B. (1999). *Family*. New York: Westview Press.

Fausto-Sterling, A., & Balaban, E. (1993). Genetics and male sexual orientation. *Science, 261*(5126), 1257.

Faver, C. A., & Strand, E. B. (2003) To leave or to stay? Battered women's concern for vulnerable pets. *Journal of Interpersonal Violence, 18*(12), 1367–1377.

Feder, L. (1997). Domestic violence and police response in a pro-arrest jurisdiction. *Women and Criminal Justice, 8*, 79–98.

Feingold, A. (1988). Matching for attractiveness in romantic partners and same-sex friends: A meta-analysis and theoretical critique. *Psychological Bulletin, 104*, 226–235

Feiring, C., & Lewis, M. (1987). The child's social network: Sex difference from three to six years. *Sex Roles, 17*(11–12), 621–636.

Felitti, V. J., Anda, R. F., Nordenberg, D., Williamson, D. F., Spitz, A. M., Edwards, V. … Marks, J. S. (1998). Relationships of childhood abuse and household dysfunction to many of the leading causes of death in adults. *American Journal of Preventive Medicine, 14*(4), 245–258.

Ferguson, S. J. (2007). *Shifting the center: Understanding contemporary families* (3rd ed.). New York: McGraw-Hill.

Festinger, L., Schacter, S., & Back, K. (1950). *Social pressures in informal groups: A study of human factors in housing.* Stanford, CA: Stanford University Press.

Fielder, R. L., & Carey, M. P. (2010). Predictors and consequences of sexual "hookups" among college students: A short-term prospective study. *Archives of Sexual Behavior, 39*, 1105–1119.

Fields, J., & Casper, L. M. (2001). *America's families and living arrangements. Current Population Report, 20–537.* Washington, DC: U.S. Census Bureau.

Fisher, B., & Alberti, R. (2006). *Rebuilding: When your relationship ends* (3rd ed.). Atascadero, CA: Impact Publishers.

Fisher, H. E. (1988). Evolution of human serial pairbonding. *American Journal of Physical Anthropology, 78*, 331–354. doi: 10.1002/ajpa.1330780303.

Fisher, H. E. (1998). Lust, attraction and attachment in mammalian reproduction. *Human Nature, 9*, 23–52.

Fisher, H. E. (1999). *The first sex: The natural talents of women and how they are changing the world*. New York: Random House.

Fisher, H., Aron, A., & Brown, L. L. (2005). Romantic love: An fMRI study of a neural mechanism for mate choice. *Journal of Comparative Neurology, 493*(1), 58–62.

Fisher, H. E., Aron, A., Mashek, D., Haifang L., & Brown, L. L. (2002). Defining the brain systems of lust, romantic attraction, and attachment. *Archives of Sexual Behavior, 31*(5), 413–419.

Fisher, H. E., Aron, A., Mashek, D., Li, H., Strong, G., & Brown, L. L. (2002). The neural mechanisms of mate choice: A hypothesis. *Neuroendocrine Letters Special Issue, 23*, 92–97.

Fisher, H. E., & Thomson, J. A. (2007). Lust, romance, and attachment: Do the side effects of serotonin enhancing antidepressants jeopardize romance, love, marriage, and fertility? In S. M. Platek, J. P. Keenan & T. K. Shakelford (Eds.), *Evolutionary Cognitive Neuroscience* (pp. 245–283). Cambridge, MA: MIT Press.

Fisher, K., Egerton, M., Gershuny, J. I., & Robinson, J. P. (2006). Gender convergence in the American Heritage Time Use Study (AHTUS). *Social Indicators Research, 82*(1), 1–33.

Fisher, T. D. (2007). Sex of experimenter and social norm effects on reports of sexual behavior in young men and women. *Archives of Sexual Behavior, 36*, 89–100.

Fisk, A. D., & Roger, W. A. (2002). Psychology and aging: Enhancing the lives of an aging population. *Association for Psychological Science, 11*(3), 107–110.

Fiske, A. P. (1991). The four elementary forms of sociality: Framework for a unified theory of social relations. *Psychological Review, 99*, 689–723.

Fitzgerald, B. (1999). Children of lesbian and gay parents: A review of the literature. *Marriage and Family Review, 29*(1), 57–75.

Fitzpatrick, J., Sharp, E. A., & Reifman, A. (2009). Midlife singles' willingness to date partners with heterogeneous characteristics. *Family Relations, 59*(1), 121–133.

Flanders, S. (1996). Conservative: The benefits of marriage. *The Public Interest, 124*, 80–86.

Fleg, J. L., Morrell, C. H., Bos, A. G., Brant, L. J., Talbot, L. A., Wright, J. G., & Lakota, E. G. (2005). Accelerated longitudinal decline of aerobic capacity in healthy older adults. *Circulation, 112*, 674–682. doi: 10.1161/circulationha.105.54549.

Flinn, M. V., & Low, B. S. (1986). Resource distribution, social competition, and mating patterns in human societies. In D. Rubenstein & R. Wrangham (Eds.), *Ecological aspects of social evolution* (pp. 217–243). Princeton, NJ: Princeton University Press.

Flynn, C. P. (2000). Why family professionals can no longer ignore violence toward animals. *Family Relations, 49*(1), 87–95.

Fokkema, T., & Kuyper, L. (2009). The relation between social embeddedness and loneliness among older lesbian, gay, and bisexual adults in the Netherlands. *Archives of Sexual Behavior, 38*, 264–275.

Ford, D. (2001). *Spiritual divorce: Divorce as a catalyst for an extraordinary life.* New York: Harper Collins.

Forgatch, M. S., & DeGarmo, D. S. (1999). Parenting through change: An effective prevention program for singles mothers. *Journal of Consulting and Clinical Psychology, 67*, 711–724.

Foster, H., Brooks-Gunn, J., & Martin, A. (2007). Poverty, socioeconomic status, and exposure to violence in the lives of children and adolescents. In D. Flannery, A. T. Vazsonyi, and I. D. Waldman (Eds.), *The Cambridge handbook of violent behavior and aggression* (pp. 664–687). New York: Cambridge University Press.

Foster, J. D., Kuperminc, G. P., & Price, A. W. (2004). Gender differences in post-traumatic stress and related symptoms in African American inner city youth exposed to community violence. *Journal of Youth and Adolescence, 33,* 59–69.

Fowers, B. J., & Olson, D. H. (1993). ENRICH marital satisfaction scale: A reliability and validity study. *Journal of Family Psychology, 7,* 176–185.

Franklin, D. L. (1997). *Ensuring inequality: The structural transformation of the African-American family.* New York: Oxford University Press.

Frazier, P., Arikian, N., Benson, S., Losoff, A., & Maurer, S. (1996). Desire for marriage and life satisfaction among unmarried heterosexual adults. *Journal of Social and Personal Relationships, 13,* 225–239.

Freudenberg, N. (2004). Community capacity for environmental health promotion: Determinants and implications for practice. *Health Education and Behavior, 31,* 472–490.

Frick, P. J., Cornell, A. H., Barry, C. T., Bodin, S. D., & Dane, H. A. (2003). Callous-unemotional traits and conduct problems in the prediction of conduct problem severity, aggression, and self-report of delinquency. *Journal of Abnormal Child Psychology, 31,* 457–470.

Friedlander, L. J., Connolly, J. A., Pepler, D. J., & Craig, W. M. (2007). Biological, family, and peer influences on dating of early adolescents. *Archives of Sexual Behavior, 36,* 821–830.

Frome, P. M., Alfeld, C. J., Eccles, J. S., & Barber, B. L. (2008). Is the desire for a family-flexible job keeping young women out of male-dominated occupations? In H. M. G. Watt & J. S. Eccles (Eds.), *Gender and occupational outcomes: Longitudinal assessments of individual, social, and cultural influences* (pp. 195–214). Washington, DC: American Psychological Association.

Fu, X., Tora, J., & Kendall, H. (2001). Marital happiness and inter-racial marriage: A study in a multi-ethnic community in Hawaii. *Journal of Comparative Family Studies, 32*(1), 47–50.

Furstenberg, F. F., & Teitler, J. O. (1994). Reconsidering the effects of marital disruption. *Journal of Family Issues, 15,* 173–190.

Galesloot, H. (2003). *Visible and invisible pink elderly: A report of the conference "Pink Wrinkles 2" about the position of gay and lesbian elderly.* Amsterdam: Schorerstichting, Kenniscentrum homoseksualiteit en gezondeid.

Gallagher, M. (1996). *The abolition of marriage: How we destroy lasting love.* Washington, DC: Regnery.

Gamel, K. (2009, February 8). Iraqi women's minister resigns in protest. *Associated Press.*

Garcia, A. (1989). The development of Chicana feminist discourse. *Gender and Society, 3,* 217–238.

Gardner, M. (2003, May 28). For better or worse: Couples confront unemployment. *Christian Science Monitor,* 19–20.

Garrod, A., Beal, C. R., Jaeger, W., Thomas, J., Davis, J., Leiser, N., & Hodzic, A. (2003). Culture, ethnic conflict and moral orientation in Bosnian children. *Journal of Moral Education, 32*(2), 131–150.

Geary, D. C. (1998). Sexual selection, the division of labor, and the evolution of sex differences. *Behavioral and Brain Sciences, 21*(3), 444–448.

Gerressu, M., & Stephenson, J. M. (2008). Sexual behavior in young people. *Current Opinion in Infectious Diseases, 21,* 37–41.

Gershoff, E. T. (2002). Parental corporal punishment and associated child behaviors and experiences: A meta-analytic and theoretical review. *Psychological Bulletin, 128,* 539–579.

Gerson, J. M., & Peiss, K. (1985). Boundaries, negotiation, consciousness: Reconceptualizing gender relations. *Social Problems, 32*(4), 317–331.

Gibson-Davis, C. M., Edin, K., & McLanahan, S. (2005). High hopes but even greater expectations: The retreat from marriage among low income couples. *Journal of Marriage and the Family, 67,* 1301–1312.

Giddens, A. (1991). *Modernity and self-identity.* Stanford, CA: Stanford University Press.

Giedd, J. N. (2004). Structural magnetic resonance imaging of the adolescent brain. *Annals of the New York Academy of Sciences, 1021,* 77–85.

Gilbert, D. T. (2006). *Stumbling on happiness.* London: Harper Perennial.

Gilbert, L. A. (1993). *Two careers/one family.* Newbury Park, CA: Sage.

Gilder, G. (1986). *Men and marriage.* Gretna, LA: Pelican.

Gillis, J. (1996). *A world of their own making.* New York: Basic Books.

Gilman, J., Schneider, D., & Shulak, R. (2005). Children's ability to cope post-divorce: The effects of Kids' Turn intervention program on 7 to 9 year olds. *Journal of Divorce and Remarriage, 42,* 109–126.

Glauber, R. (2007). Marriage and the motherhood wage penalty among African-Americans, Hispanics, and Whites. *Journal of Marriage and the Family, 69,* 951–961.

Glick, P., & Fiske, S. T. (2001). An ambivalent alliance: Hostile and benevolent sexism as complementary justifications for gender inequality. *American Psychologist, 56*(2), 109–118.

Glick, P., Fiske, S. T., Mladinic, A., Saiz, J. L., Abrams, D., Masser, B. … Lopéz Lopéz, W. (2000). Beyond prejudice as simple antipathy: Hostile and benevolent sexism across cultures. *Journal of Personality and Social Psychology, 79,* 763–775.

Gmelch, G., & San Antonio, P. M. (2001). Baseball wives: Gender and the work of baseball. *Journal of Contemporary Ethnography, 30,* 335–356.

Gohm, C. L., Oishi, S., Darlington, J., & Diener, E. (1998). Culture, parental conflict, parental marital status, and the subjective well-being of young adults. *Journal of Marriage and the Family, 60*(2), 319–334.

Goldberg, W. A., & Keller, M. A. (2007). Co-sleeping during infancy and early childhood: Key findings and future directions. *Infant and Child Development, 16,* 447–469.

Goldman, R. N., & Greenberg, L. S. (2006). Promoting emotional expression and emotion regulation in couples. In D. K. Snyder, J. A. Simpson, & J. N. Hughes (Eds.), *Emotion regulation in couples and families: Pathways to dysfunction and health* (pp. 231–248). Washington, DC: American Psychological Association.

Gonzales, J. L., Jr. (1998). *Racial and ethnic families in America* (3rd ed.). Dubuque, IA: Kendall/Hunt.

Gonzales, R. G. (2008, April). Young lives on hold: The college dreams of undocumented students. *College Board Advocacy.* Retrieved from www.collegeboard.com/advocacy

Gonzalez, N. (2008). *When mid-life becomes end of life: Suicide in middle age.* Retrieved from http://community.ncfr.org/blog/Lists/Posts/Post.aspx?ID=44

Goode, E. (1996). Gender and courtship entitlement: Responses to personal ads. *Sex Roles, 34*(3–4), 141–169.

Goode, W. J. (1959). The theoretical importance of love. *American Sociological Review, 24,* 38–47.

Goode, W. J. (1982). *The family* (2nd ed.). Englewood Cliffs, NJ: Prentice-Hall.

Goodkind, D. (1997). The Vietnamese double marriage squeeze. *International Migration Review, 31*(1), 108–127.

Goodman, C., & Silverstein, M. (2002). Grandmothers raising grandchildren: Family structure and well-being in culturally diverse families. *The Gerontologist, 28,* 66–72.

Goodrum, S., Umberson, D., & Anderson, K. L. (2001). The batterer's view of the self and others in domestic violence. *Sociological Inquiry, 71*(2), 221–240.

Goodyear-Smith, F. A., & Laidlaw, T. M. (1998). Can tampon use cause hymen changes in girls who have not had sexual intercourse? A review of the research. *Forensic Science International, 94,* 147–153.

Gorchoff, S. M., John, O. P., & Helson, R. (2008). Contexualizing change in marital satisfaction during middle age: An 18-year longitudinal study. *Psychological Science, 19*(11), 1194–1200.

Gordon, M. M. (1964). *Assimilation in American life.* New York: Oxford University Press.

Gottman, J. M. (1994). *What predicts divorce.* Mahwah, NJ: Lawrence Erlbaum Associates.

Gottman, J. M., Driver, J., Yashimoto, D., & Rushe, R. (2002). Approaches to the study of power in violent and nonviolent marriages, and in gay male and lesbian cohabiting relationships. In P. Noller (Ed.), *Understanding marriage* (pp. 323–346). Cambridge, U.K.: Cambridge University Press.

Gottman, J. M., & Levenson, R. W. (2002). A two-factor model for predicting when a couple will divorce: Exploratory analyses using 14-year longitudinal data. *Family Process, 41*(1), 83–97.

Gottman, J.M., Levenson, R.W., Gross, J., Frederickson, B.L., McCoy, K., Rosenthal, L., . . . & Yoshimoto, D. (2003). Correlates of gay and lesbian couples' relationship satisfaction and relationship dissolution. *Journal of Homosexuality, 45,* 23–43.

Gottman, J. M., & Schwartz-Gottman, J. (2007). *And baby makes three: The six-step plan for preserving marital intimacy and rekindling romance after baby arrives.* New York: Crown Publishing.

Gottman, J. M., Schwartz-Gottman, J., & DeClaire, J. (2006). *Ten lessons to transform your marriage.* New York: Crown Publishers.

Gowan, M., & Trevino, M. (1998). An examination of gender differences in Mexican-American attitudes toward family and career roles. *Sex Roles, 38*(11–12), 1079–1093.

Grace, D. M., David, B. J., & Ryan, M. K. (2008). Investigating preschoolers' categorical thinking about gender through imitation, attention, and the use of self-categories. *Child Development, 79*(6), 1928–1941.

Graham, C. A., Bancroft, J., Doll, H. A., Greco, T., & Tanner, A. (2007). Does oral contraceptive-induced reduction in free testosterone adversely affect the sex and mood of women? *Psychoneuroendocrinology, 32*(3), 246–255. doi: 10.1016/j.psyneuen.2006.12.011.

Grall, T. (2007). Custodial mothers and fathers and their child support: 2005. *Current Population Reports P 60–234.* Washington, DC: U.S. Census Bureau.

Granqvist, P., & Hagekull, B. (2000). Religiosity, adult attachment, and why "singles" are more religious. *International Journal for the Psychology of Religion, 10*(2), 111–123.

Green, W. M. (1988). *Rape: The evidential examination and management and the adult female victim.* Lexington, MA: Lexington Books/D. C. Heath.

Greenglass, E. R., Schwarzer, R., & Taubert, S. (1999). The proactive coping inventory (PCI): A multidimensional research instrument. Retrieved from http://userpage.fu-berlin.de/~health/greenpci.htm

Greenhaus, J. H., & Parasuraman, S. (1993). Job performance attributions and career advancement prospects: An examination of gender and race effects. *Organizational Behavior and Human Decision Processes, 55,* 273–297.

Grossman, K. E., Grossman, K., & Waters, E. (Eds.) (2005). *Attachment from infancy to adulthood.* New York: Guilford.

Grossman, S. E., & Lundy, M. (2003). Use of domestic violence services across race and ethnicity by women aged 55 and older. *Violence against Women, 9,* 1442–1452.

Grotenhermen, F., & Russo, E. (Eds.) (2002). *Cannabis and cannabinoids. Pharmacology, toxicology, and therapeutic potential.* Binghamton, NY: Haworth Press.

Gruenbaum, E. (2006). Sexuality issues in the movement to abolish female genital cutting in Sudan. *Medical Anthropology Quarterly, 20,* 121.

Gubrium, J. F. (1974). Victimization in old age: Available evidence and three hypotheses. *Crime and Delinquency, 20,* 245–250.

Guralnik, J. M., Butterworth, S., Patel, K., Mishra, G., & Kuh, D. (2009). Reduced midlife physical functioning among never married and childless men: Evidence from the 1946 British birth cohort study. *Aging Clinical and Experimental Research, 21,* 174–181.

Gutek, B. A. (2001). Women and paid work. *Psychology of Women Quarterly, 25*(4), 379–393.

Gutman, H. G. (1976). *The black family in slavery and freedom, 1750–1925*. New York: Pantheon.

Guttman, M., & Mowder, B. A. (2005). The ACT training programs: The future of violence prevention aimed at young children and their caregivers. *Journal of Early Childhood and Infant Psychology, 1*, 25–36.

Haddix, K. (2001). Leaving your wife and brothers: When polyandrous marriages fall apart. *Evolution and Human Behavior, 22*(1), 47–61.

Hage, W. E., Griebel, G., & Belzung, C. (2006). Long-term impaired memory following predatory stress in mice. *Physiology and Behavior, 87*, 45–50.

Haight, W. (2002). *African American children at church: A sociocultural perspective*. Cambridge, U.K.: Cambridge University Press.

Halpern, C. T., Campbell, B., Agnew, C. R., Thompson, V., & Udry, J. R. (2002). Associations between stress reactivity and sexual and nonsexual risk taking in young adult human males. *Hormones and Behavior, 42*, 387–398.

Halpern, C. T., Kaesle, C. E., Guo, G., & Hallfors, D. D. (2007). Gene–environment contributions to youth adults' sexual partnering. *Archives of Sexual Behavior, 36*, 543–554.

Hamer, D. H. (2002). Genetics of sexual behavior. In J. Benjamin, R. Ebstein, and R. Belmaker (Eds.), *Molecular genetics and the human personality* (pp. 257–272). Washington, DC: American Psychiatric Publishing.

Hamer, D. H., Hu, S., Magnuson, V. L., Hu, N., & Pattattucci, A. M. L. (1993). A linkage between DNA markers on the X chromosome and male sexual orientation. *Science, 261*, 321–327.

Hamer, J. (2001). *What it means to be daddy*. New York: Columbia University Press.

Hammersley, M. (2000). *Taking sides in social research: Essays on partisanship and bias*. London: Routledge.

Hancock, T. U., & Siu, K. (2009). A culturally sensitive intervention with domestically violent Latino immigrant men. *Journal of Family Violence, 24*, 123–132.

Hanna, B., Jarman, H., & Savage, S. (2004). The clinical application of three screening tools for recognizing post-partum depression. *International Journal of Nursing Practice, 10*, 72–79.

Hansard, P., & McLean, C. (2001, December 17). The grandparent as parent. *Newsmagazine*.

Hardy, L. (2009, June). The changing face of homelessness. *American School Board Journal*, 18–20.

Harjo, S. S. (1993). The American Indian experience. In H. P. McAddo (Ed.), *Family ethnicity* (pp. 199–207). Newbury Park, CA: Sage.

Harlow, H. F. (1962). The heterosexual affectional system in monkeys. *American Psychologist, 17*(1), 1–9.

Harlow, H. F. (1963). The maternal affectational system. In B. M. Foss (Ed.), *Determinants of infant behaviour II* (pp. 3–33). London: Methuen.

Harter, J. K., & Schmidt, F. L. (2000). *Validation of a performance-related and actionable management tool: A meta-analysis and utility analysis* [Gallup Technical Report]. Lincoln, NE: Gallup Organization.

Hartmann, K., Viswanathan, M., Palmieri, R., Gartlehner, G., Thorp, J., & Lohr, K. N. (2005). Outcomes of routine episiotomy: A systematic review. *Journal of the American Medical Association, 293*, 2141–2148.

Hartung, C. M., & Widiger, T. A. (1998). Gender differences in the diagnosis of mental disorders: Conclusions and controversies of the DSM-IV. *Psychological Bulletin, 123*, 260–278.

Harvey, E. (1999). Short-term and long-term effects of early parental employment on children in the National Longitudinal Survey of Youth. *Developmental Psychology, 35*, 445–459.

Hassebrauck, M., & Aron, A. (2001). Prototype matching in close relationships. *Personality and Social Psychology Bulletin, 27*(9), 1111–1122.

Hatfield, E., & Rapson, R. L. (1996). Stress and passionate love. In C. D. Spielberger & I. G. Sarason (Eds.), *Stress and emotion: Anxiety, anger, and curiosity* (pp. 29–50). Washington, DC: Taylor & Francis.

Hatfield, E., Rapson, R. L., & Martel, L. D. (2007). Passionate love and sexual desire. In S. Kitayama, & D. Cohen (Eds.), *Handbook of cultural psychology* (pp. 760–779). New York: Guilford Press.

Hatfield, E., & Sprecher, S. (1995). Men's and women's preferences in marital partner in the United States, Russia, and Japan. *Journal of Cross-Cultural Psychology, 26*(6), 728–750.

Hays, S. (2003). *Flat broke with children: Women in the age of welfare reform*. Oxford, U.K.: Oxford University Press.

Hayward, C., & Sanborn, K. (2002). Puberty and the emergence of gender differences in psychopathology. *Journal of Adolescent Health, 30*, 49–58.

Heaphy, E. D., & Dutton, J. (2008). Positive social interactions and the human body at work: Linking organizations and physiology. *Academy of Management Review, 33*(1), 137–162.

Heine, S. J. (2008). *Cultural psychology*. New York: W. W. Norton and Company.

Heise, L. (1998). Violence against women: An integrated, ecological framework. *Violence Against Women, 4*(3), 262–283.

Heise, L., Moore, K., & Toubia, N. (1995). *Sexual coercion and women's reproductive health: A focus on research*. New York: Population Council.

Hendrick, C., & Hendrick, S. S. (2003). Romantic love: Measuring cupid's arrow. In S. J. Lopez & C. R. Snyder (Eds.), *Positive psychological assessment: A handbook of models and measures* (pp. 235–249). Washington, DC: American Psychological Association.

Hendrick, C., Hendrick, S. S., & Dicke, A. (1998). The Love Attitudes Scale: Short form. *Journal of Social and Personal Relationships, 15*, 147–159.

Henneman, T. (2006, June 6). We too are immigrants. *The Advocate*, 29–32.

Henwood, K., & Proctor, J. (2003). The "good father": Reading men's accounts of paternal involvement during the transition to first-time fatherhood. *British Journal of Social Psychology, 42*, 337–355.

Herdt, G. (1993). *Third sex, third gender: Beyond sexual dimorphism in culture and history.* New York: Zone Books.

Hernandez, D. J., Denton, N. A., & Macartney, S. E. (2008). Children in immigrant families: Looking to America's future. *Social Policy Report, 22*(3), 3–11.

Hernandez, G. (2006, June). Big gay love. *The Advocate Magazine.*

Hesketh, T., Lu, L., & Xing, Z. W. (2005). The effect of China's one-child family policy after 25 years. *New England Journal of Medicine, 353*(11), 1171–1176.

Hetherington, E. M. (1992). Coping with marital transitions: A family systems perspective. *Monographs of the Society for Research in Child Development, 227*(2–3), 1–14.

Hetherington, E. M. (1998). What matters? What does not? Five perspectives on the association between marital transitions and children's adjustment. *American Psychologist, 53*, 167–184.

Hetheringon, E. M. (2003). Intimate pathways: Channing patterns in close personal relationships across time. *Family Relations, 52*, 318–331.

Hetherington, E. M., & Elmore, A. M. (2003). Risk and resilience in children coping with their parents' divorce and remarriage. In S. S. Luthar (Ed.), *Resilience and vulnerability: Adaptation in the context of childhood adversities* (pp. 182–212). New York: Cambridge University Press.

Hetherington, E. M., & Kelly, J. (2002). *For better or for worse: Divorce reconsidered.* New York: W. W. Norton.

Hetherington, E. M., & Stanley-Hagen, M. (2000). Diversity among stepfamilies. In D. H. Demo, K. R. Allen, & M. A. Fine (Eds.), *Handbook of family diversity* (pp. 173–196). New York: Oxford University Press.

Higgenbotham, E., & Weber, L. (1992). Moving up with kin and community: Upward social mobility for black and white women. *Gender and Society, 6*, 416–440.

Higgins, D., & McCabe, M. (2003). Maltreatment and family dysfuntion in childhood and the subsequent adjustment of children and adults. *Journal of Family Violence, 18*(2), 107–120.

Higgins, L. T., Zheng, M., Liu, Y., & Sun, C. H. (2002). Attitudes to marriage and sexual behaviours: A survey of gender and culture differences in China and the United Kingdom. *Sex Roles: A Journal of Research, 46*(3/4), 75–89.

Hill, J. E., Jackson, A. D., & Martinengo, G. (2006). Twenty years of work and family at IBM Corporation. *American Behavioral Scientist, 49*, 1165–1183.

Hill, S. (2005). *Black intimacies: A gender perspective on families and relationships.* Walnut Creek, CA: AltaMira Press.

Hill, W., Wilson, C. A., & Lebovitz, E. E. (2009). *Kissing chemicals: Hormonal changes in response to kissing.* Paper presented at the American Association for the Advancement of Science Annual Meeting, Chicago.

Hill-Collins, P. (1986). Learning from the outside within: The sociological significance of black feminist thought. *Social Problems, 33*, S14–S32.

Hill-Collins, P. (1994). Shifting the center: Race, class, and feminist theorizing about motherhood. In E. N. Glenn, G. Chang, & L. Forcey (Eds.), *Mothering: Ideology, experience and agency* (pp. 45–65). New York: Routledge

Hilton, Z. N. (1992). Battered women's concerns about their children witnessing wife assault. *Journal of Interpersonal Violence, 7*(1), 77–86.

Hipwell, A. E., Goossens, F. A., Melhuish, E. C., & Kumar, R. (2000). Severe maternal psychopathology and infant–mother attachment. *Development and Psychopathology, 12*, 157–175.

Hirshbein, L. D. (2001). Popular views of old age in America, 1900–1950. *Journal of the American Geriatrics Society, 49*, 1555–1560.

Hirshbein, L. D. (2002). The senile mind: Psychology and old age in the 1930s and 1940s. *Journal of the History of the Behavioral Sciences, 38*(1), 43–56.

Hobara, M. (2003). Predictors of transitional objects in young children in Tokyo and New York. *Infant Mental Health Journal, 24*, 174–191. doi: 10.1002/imhj.10046.

Hoch, C. C., Reynolds, C. F., Kupfer, D. J., Houck, P. R., Berman, S. R., & Stack, J. A. (1987). The superior sleep of healthy elderly nuns. *International Journal of Aging and Human Development, 25*(1), 1–9.

Hochschild, A. (1989). *The second shift.* New York: Viking.

Hofer, M. A. (1987). Shaping forces within early social relationships. In N. A. Krasnegor, E. M. Blass, & M. A. Hofer, *Perinatal development: A psychobiological perspective. Behavioral biology* (pp. 251–264). San Diego, CA: Academic Press.

Hofferth, S. (2003). Race/ethnic differences in father involvement in two-parent families. *Journal of Family Issues, 24*, 185–216.

Hofferth, S., Phillips, D., & Cabrera, N. (2001). Public policy and family and child well-being. In A. Thornton (Ed.), *The well-being of children and families* (pp. 384–408). Ann Arbor, MI: University of Michigan Press.

Hollingworth, L. (1916). Social devices for impelling women to bear and rear children. *American Journal of Sociology, 22*(1), 19–29.

Holloway, R. L., Anderson, P. J., Defendini, R. & Harper, C. (1993). Sexual dimorphism of the human corpus callosum from three independent samples: Relative size of the corpus callosum. *American Journal of Physical Anthropology, 92*, 481–498.

Holmbeck, G. N., Paikoff, R. L., & Brooks-Gunn, J. (1995). Parenting adolescents. In M. Bornstein (Ed.), *Handbook of Parenting* (vol. 1, pp. 91–118). Hillsdale, NJ: Lawrence Erlbaum Associates.

Holtzworth-Monroe, A., & Stuart, G. L. (1994). Typologies of male batterers: Three subtypes and the differences among them. *Psychological Bulletin, 116*, 476–497.

Homans, G. C. (1958). Social behavior as exchange. *American Journal of Sociology, 63*(6), 597–606.

Hondagneu-Sotelo, P., & Avila, E. (1997). "I'm here, but I'm there": The meanings of Latina transnational motherhood. *Gender and Society, 11*(5), 548–571.

Hong, Y. Y., Wan, C., No, S., & Chiu, C. Y. (2007). Multicultural identities. In S. Kitayama & D. Cohen (Eds.), *Handbook of cultural psychology* (pp. 323–345). New York: Guilford Press.

Hortacsu, N. (1997). Family- and couple-initiated marriages in Turkey. *Genetic, Social, and General Psychology Monographs, 123*(3), 325–342.

Hostetler, A. J. (2009). Single by choice? Assessing and understanding voluntary singlehood among mature gay men. *Journal of Homosexuality, 56*, 499–531.

Howard, D. E., Qi Wang, M., & Yan, F. (2008). Psychosocial factors associated with reports of physical dating violence victimization among U.S. adolescent males. *Adolescence, 43*(171), 449–460.

Hrdy, S. B. (1981). *The woman that never evolved.* Cambridge, MA: Harvard University Press.

Huguet, P., & Regner, J. (2007). Stereotype threat among schoolgirls in quasi-ordinary classroom circumstances. *Journal of Educational Psychology, 99*(3), 545–560.

Hunt, L., Laroche, G., Blake-Beard, S., Chin, E., Arroyave, M., & Scully, M. (2009). Cross-cultural connections: Leveraging social networks for women's advancement. In M. da Costa Barreto, M. K. Ryan, & M. T. Schmitt (Eds.), *The glass ceiling in the twenty-first century* (pp. 227–255). Washington, DC: American Psychological Association.

Hunt, M. (1996). *The middling sort: Commerce, gender, and the family in England, 1680–1780.* Berkeley, CA: University of California Press.

Hurtado, A. (1996). *The color of privilege: Three blasphemies on race and feminism.* Ann Arbor: University of Michigan Press.

Huston, T. L., Caughlin, J. P., Houts, R. M., Smith, S. E., & George, L. J. (2001). The connubial crucible: Newlywed years as predictors of marital delight, distress, and divorce. *Journal of Personality and Social Psychology, 80*(2), 237–252.

Hutchison, J. B. (1997). Gender-specific steroid metabolism in neural differentiation. *Cellular and Molecular Neurobiology, 17*(6), 603–626.

Hutter, M. (1998). *Intimate strangers: The elderly and home-care worker relationships.* Paper presented at Couch/Stone Society for the Study of Symbolic Interaction Symposium, Houston, TX.

Hvistendahl, M. (2009). Demography: Making every baby count. *Science, 323*, 1164–1166.

Hyde, J. S. (2006). Gender similarities still rule. *American Psychologist, 61*(6), 641–642.

Hyde, J. S. (2007a). *Half the human experience* (7th ed.). Boston, MA: Houghton Mifflin Company.

Hyde, J. S. (2007b). New directions in the study of gender similarities and differences. *Current Directions in Psychological Science, 16*, 259–263.

Hyde, J. S & Grabe, S. (2008). Meta-analysis in the psychology of women. In F. L. Denmark and M. A. Paludi (Eds.), *Psychology of women: A handbook of issues and theories* (2nd ed., pp. 142–173). Westport, CT: Praeger Publishers/ Greenwood Publishing Group.

Hyde, J. S. and Linn, M. C. (1988). Gender differences in verbal ability: A meta-analysis. *Psychological Bulletin, 104*(1), 53–69.

Iemmola, F., & Camperio-Ciani, A. (2009). New evidence of genetic factors influencing sexual orientation in men: Female fecundity increase in the maternal line. *Archives of Sexual Behavior, 38*, 393–399.

Illouz, E. (1997). *Consuming the romantic Utopia: Love and cultural contradictions of capitalism.* Berkeley: University of California Press.

Inglehart, R., & Baker, W. E. (2000). Modernization, cultural change, and the persistence of traditional values. *American Sociological Review, 65*, 19–51.

Insight Center for Community Economic Development (2010). Executive summary. *Lifting as we climb: Women of color, wealth, and America's future.* Oakland, CA: Insight Center for Community Economic Development.

International Monetary Fund (2010). *World economic outlook (WEO).* Washington, DC: IMF.

Irons, J. (2009). *Economic scarring: The long-term impacts of the recession* [Economic Policy Institute Briefing Paper #243]. Retrieved from http://www.epi.org/publications/entry/ bb2431

Isay, R. A. (1989). *Being homosexual: Gay men and their development.* New York: Avon.

Isen, A., & Stevenson, B. (2010). *Women's education and family behavior: Trends in marriage, divorce, and fertility* [Working Paper No. 15725]. Cambridge, MA: National Bureau of Economic Research.

Jablonski, N. G. and Chaplin, G. (2000). The evolution of human skin coloration. *Journal of Human Evolution, 39*, 57–106.

Jacobs, J., & Gerson, K. (2004). *The time divide: Work, family, and gender inequality.* Cambridge, MA: Harvard University Press.

Jacobson, J. L., Jacobson, S. W., Sokol, R. J., Martier, S. S., Ager, J. W., & Kaplan-Estrin, M. G. (1993). Teratogenic effects of alcohol on infant development. *Alcoholism: Clinical and Experimental Research, 17*, 174–183.

Jacobson, N., & Gottman, J. (1998). *Why men batter women.* New York: Simon and Schuster.

Jaffe, P., Wolfe, D., & Wilson, S. (1990). *Children of battered women.* Newbury Park, CA: Sage.

James, S. M., & Busia, A. P. A. (Eds.) (1993). *Theorizing black feminisms: The visionary pragmatism of black women.* New York: Routledge.

Jankowiak, W., & Fisher, E. (1992). Romantic love: A cross-cultural perspective. *Ethnology, 31*, 149–156.

Jefferson, D. (2006, May). How AIDS changed America. *Newsweek*, 36–41.

Jensen, T. K., Bonde, J. P., & Joffe, M. (2006). The influence of exposure on male reproductive function. *Occupational Medicine, 56*, 544–553.

Jiang, J., Yan, X., & Li, Z. (2004). The influence of Type A personality and locus of control upon job satisfaction and mental health among medical staff. *Chinese Journal of Clinical Psychology, 12*(4), 359–361.

John, R. (1998). Native American families. In C. H. Mindel, R. W. Haberstein, & R. Wright, Jr. (Eds.), *Ethnic families in America: Patterns and variations* (pp. 382–420). Upper Saddle River, NJ: Prentice Hall.

John, R., Hennessy, C. H., Dyeson, T. B., & Garrett, M. D. (2000). Toward the conceptualization and measurement of caregiver burden among Pueblo Indian family caregivers. *The Gerontologist, 41*(2), 210–219.

Johnson, M. P. (1996). Patriarchal terrorism and common couple violence: Two forms of violence against women. *Journal of Marriage and the Family, 57*(2), 283–294.

Johnson, M. P. (2001). Conflict and control: Symmetry and asymmetry in domestic violence. In A. Booth, A. C. Crouter, & M. Clements (Eds.), *Couples in conflict* (pp. 95–104). Mahwah, NJ: Lawrence Erlbaum.

Johnson, S. (2008). *Hold me tight: Seven conversations for a lifetime of love.* Boston, MA: Little, Brown and Company.

Jonason, P. K. (2007). A mediation hypothesis to account for the sex difference in reported number of sexual partners: An intrasexual competition approach. *International Journal of Sexual Health, 19*, 41–49.

Jonason, P. K., & Marks, M. J. (2009). Common vs. uncommon sexual acts: Evidence for the sexual double standard. *Sex Roles, 60*, 357–365.

Jones, A. L., Sonnenfield, N. L., & Harris-Kojetin, L. D. (2004). *Racial differences in functioning among elderly nursing home residents* [National Center for Health Statistics Data Brief # 25]. Hyattsville, MD: National Center for Health Statistics.

Jones, D. (1995). Sexual selection, physical attractiveness, and facial neoteny. *Current Anthropology, 36*, 723–748.

Jones, J. (2002). *Who adopts? Characteristics of women and men who have adopted children.* Atlanta, GA: Centers for Disease Control and Prevention.

Julien, D., Chartrand, E., Simard, M. C., Bouthillier, D., & Begin, J. (2003). Conflict, social support, and relationship quality: An observational study of heterosexual, gay male, and lesbian couple communication. *Journal of Family Psychology, 17*, 419–428.

Just the Facts Coalition (2008). *Just the facts about sexual orientation and youth: A primer for principals, educators, and school personnel.* Washington, DC: American Psychological Association. Retrieved from www.apa.org/pi/lgbc/publications/justthefacts.html

Kadlec, D. (2003, May 26). Where did my raise go? *Time Magazine*, 27–31.

Kaiser, C. R., & Kashy, D. A. (2005). The contextual nature and function of singlism. *Psychological Inquiry, 16*(2/3), 122–126.

Kalb, C. (2004, January 26). Brave new babies. *Newsweek*, 45–53.

Kamerman, S. B. (2000). Early childhood education and care (ECEC): An overview of developments in OECD countries. *International Journal of Education, 33*, 7–29.

Kandoian, E. (1986). Cohabitation, common law marriage, and the possibility of a shared moral life. *Georgetown Law Journal, 75*, 1829–1840.

Karney, B. R. (2010, February). Keeping marriages healthy, and why it's so difficult. *Psychological Science Agenda*, 1–3.

Kaslow, F. W. (2004). Death of one's partner: The anticipation and the reality. *Professional Psychology: Research and Practice, 35*(3), 227–233.

Kass, L. R. (1997). The end of courtship. *The Public Interest, 126*, 39–63.

Katz, S. N. (1994). Historical perspective and current trends in the legal process of divorce. *Future of Children, 4*, 44–62.

Kaufman, M. (1998). The construction of masculinity and the triad of men's violence. In M. Kimmel & M. Messner (Eds.), *Men's lives* (pp. 4–16). Boston, MA: Allyn & Bacon.

Kawakami, N., & Haratani, T. (1999). Epidemiology of job stress and health in Japan: Review of current evidence and future directions. *Industrial Health, 37*, 174–186.

Kazdin, A., & Benjet, C. (2003). Spanking children: Evidence and issues. *Current Directions in Psychological Science, 12*(3), 99–103.

Kelly, J. B. (2007). Children's living arrangements following separation and divorce: Insights from empirical and clinical research. *Family Process, 46*, 35–52.

Kelly, P. J., Lesser, J., & Smoots, A. (2005). Tailoring STI and HIV prevention programs for teens. *American Journal of Maternal Child Nursing, 30*(4), 237–242.

Kemp, C. (2007). Grandparent–grandchild ties: Reflections on continuity and change across the generations. *Journal of Family Issues, 28*(7), 855–881.

Kennedy, R. (2002, December). Interracial intimacy. *Atlantic Monthly*, 102–110.

Kenrick, D. T., Gabrielidis, C., Keefe, R. C., & Cornelius, J. (1996). Adolescents' age preferences for dating partners: Support for an evolutionary model of life-history strategies. *Child Development, 67*, 1499–1511.

Kenrick, D. T., Groth, G. E., Trost, M. R., & Sadalla, E. K. (1993). Integrating evolutionary and social-exchange perspectives on relationships: Effects of sex, self-appraisal, and involvement level on mate selection criteria. *Journal of Personality and Social Psychology, 64*, 951–969.

Kerckhoff, A. C., & Davis, K. E. (1962). Value consensus and need complementarity in mate selection. *American Sociological Review, 27*(3), 295–303.

Kershaw, S. (2009, October 14). Rethinking the older-woman–younger-man relationship. *New York Times*.

Keskes-Ammar, L., Feki-Chakroun, N., Rebai, T., Sahnoun, Z., Ghozzi, H., Hammami, S. ... Bahloul, A. (2003). Sperm oxidative stress and the effect of oral vitamin E and selenium supplementation on semen quality in male infertility. *Systems Biology in Reproductive Medicine, 49*, 83–94.

Keyes, C. L. M., & Lopez, S. J. (2002). Toward a science of mental health: Positive directions in diagnosis and intervention. In C. R.. Snyder & S. J. Lopez (Eds.), *Handbook of positive psychology* (pp. 26–44). New York: Oxford University Press.

Keyes, C. L. M., & Magyar-Moe, J. L. (2003). The measurement and utility of adult subjective well-being. In S. J. Lopez & C. R. Snyder (Eds.), *Positive psychological assessment: A handbook of models and measures* (pp. 411–426). Washington, DC: American Psychological Association.

Kiecolt-Glaser, J. K., Bane, C., Glaser, R., & Malarkey, R. (2003). Love, marriage, and divorce: Newlyweds' stress hormones foreshadow relationship changes. *Journal of Consulting and Clinical Psychology, 71*(1), 176–188.

Kiecolt-Glaser, J. K., Fisher, L. D., Ogrocki, P., Stout, J. C., Speicher, C. E., & Glaser, R. (1987). Marital quality, marital disruption, and immune function. *Psychosomatic Medicine 49*(1), 13–34.

Kiecolt-Glaser, J. K., & Newton, T. K. (2001). Marriage and health: His and hers. *Psychological Bulletin, 127*(4), 472–503.

Kiernan, K. (2002). Cohabitation in western Europe: Trends, issues, and implications. In A. Booth & A. C. Crouter (Eds.), *Just living together: Implications of cohabitation on families, children, and social policy* (pp. 3–31). Mahwah, NJ: Lawrence Erlbaum Associates.

Kiernan, K. (2004). Changing European families: Trends and issues. In J. Scott, J. Treas, & M. Richards (Eds.), *The Blackwell companion to the sociology of families* (pp. 17–33). Malden, MA: Blackwell.

Kim, J. Y., Park, S. K., & Emery, C. R. (2009). The incidence and impact of family violence on mental health among South Korean women: Results of a national survey. *Journal of Family Violence, 24*(3), 193–202.

Kimmel, D. C. (2000). Including sexual orientation in life span developmental psychology. In B. Greene, & G. L. Croom (Eds.), *Education, research, and practice in lesbian, gay, bisexual, and transgendered psychology: A resource manual* (pp. 59–73). Thousand Oaks, CA: Sage.

Kimmel, M. S. (1986). *The "crisis" of masculinity in historical perspective.* Paper presented at the meeting of the American Sociological Association.

Kimmel, P. L., Peterson, R. A., Weihs, K. L., Shidler, N., Simmens, S. J., Alleyne, S. … Phillips, T. M. (2000). Dyadic relationship conflict, gender, and mortality in urban hemodialysis patients. *Journal of the American Society of Nephrology, 11*, 1518–1525.

Kimura, D. (1993). Sex differences in the brain. In *Mind and brain: Readings from* Scientific American *magazine* (pp. 32–37). New York: W. H. Freeman.

Kinsella, K., & Gist, Y. J. (1998). *International brief: Gender and aging.* Washington, DC: U.S. Census Bureau.

Kirby, D., Short, L., Collins, J., Rugg, D., Kolbe, L., Howard, M. … Zabin, L. S. (1994). School-based programs to reduce sexual risk behaviors: A review of effectiveness. *Public Health Reports, 109*(3), 339–360.

Kirkwood, M. K., & Cecil, D. K. (2001). Marital rape: A student assessment of rape laws and the marital rape exemption. *Violence Against Women, 7*, 1234–1253.

Kisilevsky, B. S., Hains, S. M. J., Brown, C. A., Lee, C. T., Cowperthwaite, B., Stutzman, S. S. … Wang, Z. (2009). Fetal sensitivity to properties of maternal speech and language. *Infant Behavior and Development, 32*(1), 59–71.

Kitano, K. J., & Kitano, H. H. L. (1998). The Japanese-American family. In C. H. Mindel, R. W. Haberstein, & R. Wright, Jr. (Eds.), *Ethnic families in America: Patterns and variations* (pp. 311–330). Upper Saddle River, NJ: Prentice Hall.

Klaus, M. H., & Kennel, J. H. (1976). *Maternal–infant bonding: The impact of early separation of loss on family development.* St Louis, MO: C. V. Mosby Company.

Klaus, H. M., & Kennel J. H. (1982). *Parent–infant bonding* (2nd ed.). St Louis: C. V. Mosby Company.

Klaus, H. M., & Kennel J. H. (1997). The doula: An essential ingredient of childbirth rediscovered. *Acta Paediatrica, 86*(10), 1034–1036.

Klawitter, M. M. (2002). Gays and lesbians as workers and consumers in the economy. In D. Richardson & S. Seidman (Eds.), *Handbook of lesbian and gay studies* (pp. 329–338). New York: Sage.

Kline, M., Tschann, J. M., Johnson, J. R., & Wallerstein, J. S. (1989). Children's adjustment in joint and sole physical custody families. *Developmental Psychology, 25*, 430–438.

Knox, D., Daniels, V., Sturdivant, L., & Zusman, M. E. (2001). College student use of the internet for mate selection. *College Student Journal, 35*(1), 158–160.

Knudson, E. (2006). *National Scientific Council on the Developing Child, perspectives: Early influences on brain architecture.* Retrieved from http://www.developingchild.net

Kohn, M. L. (1969). *Class and conformity: A study in values.* Oxford, U.K.: Dorsey.

Koniak-Griffin, D., Logsdon, M. C., Hines-Martin, V., & Turner, C. C. (2006). Contemporary mothering in a diverse society. *Journal of Obstetric, Gynecologic, and Neonatal Nursing, 35*(5), 671–678.

Koomen, W., & Dijker, A. J. M. (1997). Ingroup and outgroup stereotypes and selective processing. *European Journal of Social Psychology, 27*, 589–601.

Koss, M. P., Heise, L., & Russo, N. F. (1994). The global health burden of rape. *Psychology of Women Quarterly, 18*, 499–527.

Kossek, E. E., & Nichol, V. (1992). The effects of on-site child care on employee attitudes. *Personnel Psychology, 45*, 485–510.

Kozol, J. (1992). *Savage inequalities: Children in American schools.* New York: Harper Perennial.

Kramer, A. F., & Willis, S. J. (2002). Enhancing the cognitive vitality of older adults. *Association for Psychological Science, 11*(5), 173–177.

Krishnan, S. P., Baig-Amin, M., Gilbert, L., El-Bassel, N., & Waters, A. (1998). Lifting the veil of secrecy: Domestic violence against South Asian women in the United States. In S. Das Dasgupta (Ed.), *A patchwork shawl: Chronicles of South Asian women in America* (pp. 145–159). New Brunswick, NJ: Rutgers University Press.

Krugman, R. D. (1996). Child abuse and neglect: A worldwide problem. In F. Mak and C. C. Nadelson (Eds.), *International Review of Psychiatry* (Vol. 2, pp. 367–377). Washington, DC: American Psychiatric Association.

Krugman, S. (1995). Male development and the transformation of shame. In R. L. Levant and W. S. Pollack (Eds.), *A new psychology of men* (pp. 91–126). New York: Basic Books.

Kulikoff, A. (1986). *Tobacco and slaves: The development of southern cultures in the Chesapeake, 1680–1800.* Chapel Hill: University of North Carolina Press.

Kuper, H., Singh-Manoux, A., Siegrist, J., & Marmot, M. (2002). When reciprocity fails: Effort–rewards imbalance in relation to coronary heart disease and health functioning within the Whitehall II study. *Occupational and Environmental Medicine, 59*(11), 777–784.

Kurdek, L. A. (1995). Lesbian and gay couples. In A. R. D'Augelli & C. J. Patterson (Eds.), *Lesbian, gay, and bisexual identities over the lifespan: Psychological perspectives* (pp. 243–261). New York: Oxford University Press.

Kurdek, L. A. (1998). The nature and predictors of the trajectory of change in marital quality for husbands and wives over the first 10 years of marriage. *Developmental Psychology, 35*(5), 1283–1296.

Kurz, D. (1995). Why women seek divorce. In D. Kurz, *For richer, for poorer: Mothers confront divorce* (pp. 46–62). New York: Routledge.

L'Abate, L., & L'Abate, B. L. (1981). Marriage: The dream and the reality. *Family Relations, 30,* 131–136.

Labouvie-Vief, G. (2003). Dynamic integration: Affect, cognition, and the self in adulthood. *Association for Psychological Science, 12*(6), 201–206.

Labriola, K. (2006). Are you open to an alternative lifestyle? Retrieved from http://www.polyorlando.org.html/non-monogamy.htm

Lachman, M. E. (2006). Perceived control over aging-related declines: Adaptive beliefs and behaviors. *Association for Psychological Science, 13*(1), 17–20.

Lachs, M. S., & Pillemer, K. (2004). Elder abuse. *The Lancet, 364,* 1263–1273.

Ladas, A., Whipple, B., & Perry, J. (2005). *The G-spot and other discoveries about human sexuality.* New York: Henry Holt.

LaFramboise, T. D., Choney, S. B., James, A., & Running Wolf, P. R. (1995). American Indian women and psychology. In H. Landrine (Ed.), *Bringing cultural diversity to feminist psychology: Theory, research, and practice* (pp. 197–239). Washington, DC: American Psychological Association.

Lahikainen, A. R., Tolonen, K., & Kraav, I. (2008). Young children's subjective well-being and family discontents in a changing cultural context. *Child in Research, 1,* 64–85.

Lamaze International (2007). *Position paper: Lamaze for the twenty-first century.* Retrieved from http://www.lamaze.org/Portals/0/Policies/3_Lamaze21st Century.pdf

Lamborn, S. D., Mounts, N. S., Steinberg, L., & Dornbusch, S. M. (1991). Patterns of competence and adjustment among adolescents from authoritative, authoritarian, indulgent, and neglectful families. *Child Development, 62,* 1049–1065.

Laner, M. R. (1995). *Dating: Delights, discontents, and dilemmas.* Salem, WI: Sheffield Publishing Company.

Lansford, J. E. (2009). Parental divorce and children's adjustment. *Perspectives on Psychological Science, 4*(2), 140–152.

Lansford, J. E., Ceballo, R., Abbey, A., & Stewart, A. J. (2001). Does family structure matter? A comparison of adoptive, two parent biological, single mother, stepfather, and stepmother households. *Journal of Marriage and the Family, 63,* 840–851.

Lansford, J. E., Malone, P. S., Castellino, D. R., Doge, K. A., Pettit, G. S., & Bates, J. E. (2006). Trajectories of internalizing, externalizing, and grades for children who have and have not experienced their parents' divorce. *Journal of Family Psychology, 20,* 292–301.

Lareau, A. (2002). Invisible inequality: Social class and childrearing in black families and white families. *American Sociological Review, 67*(5), 747–776.

Larrain, S. (1993). *Estudio de frecuencia de la violencia intrafamiliar y la condición de la mujer en Chile.* Santiago, Chile: Panamerican Health Organization.

Lateiner, D. (2009, February 14). *Kissing among the Greeks and Romans.* Lecture given to the American Academy for the Advancement of Science Annual Meeting, Chicago. Retrieved from http://go.owu.edu/~dglatein/lectures.html

Laumann, E. O. (2004). *The social organization of sexuality: Sexual practices in the United States.* Chicago, IL: University of Chicago Press.

Lavee, Y., & Olson, D. H. (1993). Seven types of marriage: Empirical typology based on ENRICH. *Journal of Marital and Family Therapy, 19*(4), 325–340.

Lawrence, D., & Fitzgerald, A. (2011, February 22). America last among peers with no paid federal maternity leave. *Bloomberg.* Retrieved from http://www.bloomberg.com/news/2011–02–22/america-last-among-peers-with-no-paid-federal-maternity-leave.html

Lawson, E. J., & Thompson, A. (1999). Divorce and fatherhood. In E. J. Lawson & A. Thompson (Eds.), *Black men and divorce* (pp. 184–201). New York: Sage Publications.

Lawson, H. M., & Leck, K. (2006). Dynamics of internet dating. *Social Science Computer Review, 24,* 189–208.

Layne, J. E., & Nelson, M. E. (1999). The effects of progressive resistance training on bone density: A review. *Medicine and Science in Sports and Exercise, B1,* 25–30.

Le, C. N. (2011). Interracial dating and marriage: U.S.-raised Asian Americans. In *Asian-Nation: The Landscape of Asian America.* Retrieved from http://www.asian-nation.org/interracial2.shtml

Leaper, C., & Ayres, M. M. (2007). A meta-analytic review of gender variations in adults' language use: Talkativeness, affiliative speech, and assertive speech. *Personality and Social Psychology Review, 11*(4), 328–363.

Lederman, C. S., & Osofsky, J. D. (2004). Infant mental health interventions in juvenile court. *Psychology of Public Policy and Law, 10*(1), 162–177.

Lederman, C. S., Osofsky, J. D., & Katz, L. (2001). When the bough breaks, the cradle will fall: Promoting the healthy development of infants and toddlers in juvenile court. *Juvenile and Family Court Journal*, 33–38.

Lee, J. A. (1973). *The colours of love:An exploration of the ways of loving*. Toronto: New Press.

Lempers, J. D., Clark-Lempers, D., & Simons, R. L. (1989). Economic hardship, parenting, and distress in adolescence. *Child Development, 60*, 25–39.

Lerner, R. M., Sparks, E. E., & McCubbin, L. D. (2000). Family diversity and family policy. In D. H. Demo, K. R. Allen, & M. A. Fine (Eds.), *Handbook of family diversity* (pp. 380–401). New York: Oxford University Press.

Lessinger, J. (1995). *From the Ganges to the Hudson: Indian immigrants in New York City*. New York: Allyn & Bacon.

Letiecq, B. L., Bailey, S. J., & Kurtz, M. A. (2008). Depression among rural Native American and European American grandparents rearing their grandchildren. *Journal of Family Issues, 29*(3), 334–356.

Levant, R. F. (1997). The masculinity crisis. *Journal of Men's Studies, 5*, 221–231.

Levant, R. F., Majors, R. G., & Kelley, M. L. (1998). Masculinity ideology among young African American and European American women and men in different regions of the United States. *Cultural Diversity and Ethnic Minority Psychology, 4*(3), 227–236.

LeVay, S. (1996). *Queer science: The use and abuse of research into homosexuality*. Cambridge, MA: MIT Press.

Levin, I. (2004). Living apart together: A new family form. *Current Sociology, 52*(2), 223–240.

Levine, R., Sato, S., Hashimoto, T., & Verma, J. (1990). Love and marriage in eleven cultures. *Journal of Cross-Cultural Psychology, 26*(5), 554–571.

Levinson, D. (1989). *Family violence in cross-cultural perspective*. Newbury Park, CA: Sage Publications.

Leviton, D. (2009). Potential untapped: Health education and health promotion as a means to peace. In J. M. Black, S. Furney, H. M. Graf, and A. E. Nolte (Eds.), *Philosophical foundations of health education* (pp. 275–296). New York: John Wiley & Sons.

Levy, J. A. (1994). Sex and sexuality in later life stages. In A. S. Rossi (Ed.), *Sexuality across the life course* (pp. 287–309). Chicago, IL: University of Chicago Press.

Lewin, E. (1998). *Recognizing ourselves: Ceremonies of lesbian and gay commitment*. New York: Columbia University Press.

Lewis, K. G., & Moon, S. (1997). Always single and single again women: A qualitative study. *Journal of Marital and Family Therapy, 23*, 115–134.

Lewis, T., Amini, F., & Lannon, R. (2000). *A general theory of love*. New York: Random House.

Lichter, D. T., & Qian, Z. (2008). Serial cohabitation and the marital life course. *Journal of Marriage and the Family, 70*, 861–878.

Liu, H. (2009). Till death do us part: Marital status and mortality trends, 1986–2000. *Journal of Marriage and Family, 71*, 1158–1173.

Livi-Bacci, M. (1971). *A century of Portuguese fertility*. Princeton, NJ: Princeton University Press.

Liz Claiborne, Inc. (2006, April 25). *New survey of American teens reveals shocking levels of teen dating abuse and violence*. Retrieved from http://www.loveisnotabuse.com/pressreleases.htm

Loeb, T. B., Williams, J. K., Carmona, J. V., Rivkin, I., Wyatt, G. E., Chin, D., & Asuan-O'Brien, A. (2002). Child sexual abuse: Associations with the sexual functioning of adolescents and adults. *Annual Review of Sex Research, 13*, 307–345.

Loftus, M. (2004, November 1). Till debt do us part. *Psychology Today*, 44–52.

Logan, J., & Spitze, G. (1996). *Family ties: Enduring relations between parents and their grown children*. Philadelphia, PA: Temple University Press.

Lohr, J. M., Hamberger, L. K., & Parker, L. A. (2006). Scientific evidence for domestic violence treatment. In J. Fishers & W. O'Donohue (Eds.), *Practitioners guide to evidence-based practice* (pp. 258–265). New York: Kluwer Publishers.

Lomawaima, K. T. (1994). *They called it prairie light: The story of Chilocco Indian school*. Lincoln: University of Nebraska Press.

Lombardo, P. A. (1983). Involuntary sterilization in Virginia: From *Buck v. Bell* to *Poe v. Lynchburg*. *Developments in Mental Health Law, 3*(3), 13–21.

Lopez, S. J., & Snyder, C. R. (Eds.) (2003). *Positive psychological assessment: A handbook of models and measures*. Washington, DC: American Psychological Association.

Lopman, B. A., Nyamukapa, C., Hallett, T. B., Mushati, P., Spark-du, P. N., Kurwa, F. ... Gregson, S. (2009). Role of widows in the heterosexual transmission of HIV of Manicaland, Zimbabwe, 1998–2003. *Sexual Transmitted Infection, 85*, 41–48.

Lorenz, K. (1935). The companion in the bird's world. The fellow-member of the species as releasing factor of social behavior. *Journal of Ornithology, 83*, 137–213.

Loscocco, I. C. (1990). Reactions of blue-collar work. *Work and Organization, 17*(2), 152–177.

Luborsky, M. R., & LeBlanc, I. M. (2003). Cross-cultural perspectives on the concept of retirement: An analytic redefinition. *Journal of Cross-Cultural Gerontology, 18*, 251–271.

Lum, D. (1986). *Social work practice and people of color: A process-stage approach*. Monterey, CA: Brooks/Cole.

Luthar, S. S. (2003). The culture of affluence: Psychological costs of material wealth. *Child Development, 74*(6), 1581–1593.

Luthar, S. S., & Becker, B. E. (2002). Privileged but pressured: A study of affluent youth. *Child Development, 73*, 1593–1610.

Luthar, S. S., & D'Avanzo, K. (1999). Contextual factors in substance use: A study of suburban and inner-city adolescents. *Development and Psychopathology, 11*, 845–867.

Lyall, S. (Feburary 15, 2004). In Europe, lovers now propose: Marry me a little. *New York Times*, A3.

Lydon, J. E., Jamieson, D. W., & Zanna, M. P. (1988). Interpersonal similarity and the social and intellectual dimension of first impressions. *Social Cognition, 6*, 269–286.

MacCallum, F., & Golombok, S. (2004). Children raised in fatherless families from infancy: A follow-up of children of lesbian and single heterosexual mothers at early adolescence. *Journal of Child Psychology and Psychiatry, 45*, 1407–1419.

Maccoby, E. E. (1995). The two sexes and their social systems. In P. Moen, G. Eider Jr., & J. Luscher (Eds.), *Examining lives in context* (pp. 347–364). Washington, DC: American Psychological Association.

Maccoby, E. E., Depner, C. E., & Mnookin, R. H. (1990). Coparenting in the second year after divorce. *Journal of Marriage and the Family, 52*, 141–155.

MacDonald, W., & Demaris, A. (1995). Remarriage, stepchildren, and marital conflict: Challenges to the incomplete institutionalization hypothesis. *Journal of Marriage and the Family, 57*, 387–398.

Macksoud, M. S., & Aber, L. (1996). The war experiences and psychosocial development of children in Lebanon. *Child Development, 67*, 70–88. doi:10.1111/j.1467–8624.1996. tb01720.x.

MacLachlin, P. (1985). *Sarah plain and tall*. New York: HarperCollins.

Madathil, J., & Benshoff, J. M. (2008). The importance of marital characteristics and marital satisfaction: A comparison of Asian Indians in arranged marriages and Americans in marriages of choice. *The Family Journal, 16*, 222–230.

Madden, M., & Lenhart, A. (2006, March 5). *Online dating*. Pew Internet & American Life Project. Retrieved from http://www.pewinternet.org/Reports/2006/Online-Dating. aspx

Magoke-Mhoja, M. E. (2008). *Child-widows silenced and unheard: Human rights sufferers in Tanzania*. Milton Keynes, U.K.: AuthorHouse.

Maguire, E. A., Gadian, D. G., Johnsrude, I. S., Good, C. D., Ashburner, J., Frackowiak, R. S., & Frith, C. D. (2000). Navigation-related structural change in the hippocampi of taxi drivers. *Proceedings of the National Academy of Sciences, 97*(8), 4398–4403.

Mah, K., & Binik, Y. M. (2001). The nature of human orgasm: A critical review of major trends. *Clinical Psychology Review, 21*(6), 823–856.

Mahalingam, R. (2003). Essentialism, culture, and beliefs about gender among the Aravanis of Tamil Nadu, India. *Sex Roles, 49*(9–10), 489–496.

Mahay, J., & Lewin, A. C. (2007). Age and the desire to marry. *Journal of Family Issues, 28*(5), 706–723.

Maikovich-Fong, A. K., & Jaffee, S. R. (2010). Sex differences in child sex abuse characteristics and victims' emotional and behavioral problems. *Child Abuse and Neglect, 34*, 429–437.

Maines, R. P. (2001). *The technology of orgasm: "Hysteria," the vibrator, and women's sexual satisfaction*. Baltimore, MD: Johns Hopkins University Press.

Mainiero, L. A., & Sullivan, S. E. (2006). *The Opt-out revolt*. Mountain View, CA: Davies-Black Publishers.

Major, B., Quinton, W. J., & McCoy, S. K. (2002). Antecedents and consequences of attributions to discrimination: Theoretical and empirical advances. In M. P. Zanna (Ed.), *Advances in experimental social psychology* (pp. 251–330). San Diego. CA: Academic Press.

Majors, R., & Billson, J. M. (1992). *Cool pose: The dilemmas of black manhood in America*. New York: Lexington Books.

Malamuth, N. M. (2003). Criminal and noncriminal sexual aggressors: Integrating psychopathology in a hierarchical-meditational confluence model. In R. A. Prentky, E. S. Janus, & M. C. Seto (Eds.), *Sexually coercive behavior: Understanding and management* (pp. 33–58). New York: Annals of the New York Academy of Sciences.

Malo, C. (1994). Ex-partners, families, friends, and other relationships: Their role within the social network of long-term single mothers. *Journal of Applied Social Psychology, 24*, 60–81.

Mannis, V. S. (1999). Single mothers by choice. *Family Relations, 48*, 121–128.

Marazziti, D., Akiskal, H. S., Rossi, A., & Cassano, G. B. (1999). Alteration of the platelet serotonin transporter in romantic love. *Psychological Medicine, 29*, 741–745.

Marazziti, D., Rucci, P., Di Nasso, E., Masala, I., Baroni, S., Rossi, A. … Lucacchini, A. (2003). Jealousy and subthreshold psychopathology: A serotonergic link. *Neuropsychobiology, 47*, 12–16.

Marcia, J. (1980). Identity in adolescence. In J. Adelson (Ed.), *Handbook of adolescent psychology* (pp. 159–187). New York: Wiley.

Margolies, L. (2004). *My mother's hip: Lessons for the world of eldercare*. Philadelphia, PA: Temple University Press.

Marin, B. V., & Gomez, C. A. (1997). Latino culture and sex: Implications for HIV prevention. In J. Garcia & M. Zea (Eds.), *Psychological interventions and research with Latino populations* (pp. 73–93). Boston, MA: Allyn & Bacon.

Marsiglio, W. (2004). When stepfathers claim stepchildren: A conceptual analysis. *Journal of Marriage and Family, 66*, 22–39.

Marston, C., & King, E. (2006). Factors that shape young people's sexual behaviour: A systematic review. *The Lancet, 368*(9547), 1581–1586.

Marston, M., Slaymaker, E., Cremin, I., Floyd, S., McGrath, N., Kasamba, I., … Zaba, B. (2009). Trends in marriage and time spent single in sub-Saharan Africa: A comparative analysis of six population-based cohort studies and nine demographic and health surveys. *Sexually Transmitted Infection, 85*(Suppl. I), i64–i71.

Martin, A. (1996, November/December). Why get married? *The Utne Reader*, 17–18.

Martin, A. D. & Hetrick, E. S. (1988). The stigmatization of the gay and lesbian adolescent. *Journal of Homosexuality, 15*, 163–184.

Martin, C. L., & Halverson, C. F. (1983). The effects of sex typing schemas on young children's memory. *Child Development, 54*, 563–574.

Martin, E. K., Taft, C. T., & Resick, P. A. (2007). A review of marital rape. *Aggression and Violent Behavior, 12*, 329–347.

Martin, J., & Ruark, E. A. (2010). The fiscal burden of illegal immigration on U.S. taxpayers. Retrieved from http://www.fairusa.org.

Martin, J. A., Hamilton, B. E., Sutton, P. D., Ventura, S. J., Menacker, F., & Munson, M. L. (2003). *Births: Final data for 2002* [National Vital Statistics Reports, 52(10)]. Washington, DC: Government Printing Office.

Martin-DuPan, R. C., Bischof, P., Campana, A., & Morabia, A. (1997). Relationship between etiological factors and total motile sperm count in 350 infertile patients. *Archives of Andrology, 39*, 197–210.

Martineau, H. (1837). Marriage. *Society in America, 3*, 107–151.

Mason, M. A. (2003). The modern American stepfamily: Problems and possibilities. In M. A. Mason, A. Skolnik, & S. D. Sugarman (Eds.), *All our families* (pp. 96–97, 102–116). New York: Oxford University Press.

Massey, D. (1996). The age of extremes: Concentrated poverty and affluence in the twenty-first century. *Demography, 33*(4), 395–412.

Masten, A. S., & Coatsworth, J. D. (1998). The development of competence in favorable and unfavorable environments: Lessons from research on successful children. *American Psychologist, 53*(2), 205–220.

Masters, W. H., & Johnson, V. E. (1966). *Human sexual response.* Boston, MA: Little, Brown.

Masters, W. H., Johnson, V. E., & Kolodny, R. (1988). *On sex and human loving.* Little, Brown.

Matta, W. J. (2006). *Relationship sabotage: Unconscious factors that destroy couples, marriages, and family.* Westport, CT: Praeger Publishes/Greenwood Publishing Group.

Mattingly, M. J., & Bianchi, S. M. (2003). Gender differences in the quantity and quality of free time: The U.S. experience. *Social Forces, 81*, 999–1030.

Maurer, T. W., & Pleck, J. H. (2006). Fathers' caregiving and breadwinning: A gender congruence analysis. *Psychology of Men and Masculinity, 7*, 101–112.

McAdoo, H. P. (1993). Ethnic families: Strengths that are found in diversity. In H. P. McAdoo (Ed.), *Ethnic families: Strength in diversity* (pp. 3–14). Newbury Park, CA: Sage.

McAdoo, H. P. (1998). African-American families. In C. H. Mindel, R. W. Haberstein, & R. Wright, Jr. (Eds.), *Ethnic families in America: Patterns and variations* (pp. 361–381). Upper Saddle River, NJ: Prentice Hall.

McCallum, T. J., Sorocco, K. H., & Fristch, T. (2006). Mental health and diurnal salivary cortisol patterns among African American and European American female dementia family caregivers. *American Journal of Geriatric Psychiatry, 14*(8), 684–693.

McCarthy, J. (2009, June 18). Job losses hurting child support. *USA Today.*

McElhany, L. J. (1992). Dating and courtship in the later years. *Generations, 16*, 21–23.

McEwan, B. S., & Seeman, T. (1999). Protective and damaging effects of mediators of stress: Elaborating and testing the concepts of allostasis and allostatic load. *Annals of the New York Academy of Sciences, 896*, 30–47.

McHugh, P. (2004). Surgical sex. *First Things, 147*, 34–38.

McKinlay, J. B., & Feldman, H. A. (1994). Age-related variation in sexual activity and interest in normal men: Results from the Massachusetts male aging study. In A. S. Rossi (Ed.), *Sexuality across the life course* (pp. 261–285). Chicago, IL: University of Chicago Press.

McKinnon, J. (2003). *The black population in the United States: March 2002* [Current Population Reports. Series P20-S41]. Washington, DC: U.S. Census Bureau.

McLanahan, S. (1999). Father absence and the welfare of chidren. In E. M. Hetherington (Ed.), *Coping with civorce, Single parenting and remarriage: A risk and resiliency perspective* (pp. 117–146). Mahwah, NJ: Lawrence Erlbaum Associates.

McLanahan, S. (2002). Life without father: What happens to the children? *Contexts, 1*(1), 35–44.

McLanahan, S. S., & Sandefur, D. (1994). *Growing up with a single parent: What hurts, what helps?* Cambridge, MA: Harvard University Press.

McLaughlin, F. J., Altemeier, W. A., Christensen, W. A., Sherrod, K. B., Dietrich, M. S., & Stern, D. T. (1992). Randomized clinical trial of comprehensive prenatal care for low income women: Effect on infant birth weight. *Pediatrics, 89*, 128–132.

McLemore, S. D., Romo, H. D., & Baker, S. G. (2001). *Racial and ethnic relations in America* (6th ed.). Boston, MA: Allyn & Bacon.

McMillan, M. A. C. (1993). International adoption: A step toward a uniform process. *Pace International Law Review, 5*, 137–164.

McPhedran, S. (2009). Animal abuse, family violence, and child wellbeing: A review. *Journal of Family Violence, 24*, 41–52.

McPherson, D. (1993). *Gay parenting couples: Parenting arragements, arrangement satisfaction, and relationship satisfaction.* Unpublished doctoral disseration, California School of Professional Psychology, San Francisco.

McPherson, M., Smith-Lovin, L., & Brashears, M. E. (2006). Social isolation in America: Changes in core discussion networks over two decades. *American Sociological Review, 71*, 353–375.

McPherson, M., Smith-Lovin, L., & Cook, J. M. (2001). Birds of a feather: Homophily in social networks. *Annual Review of Sociology, 27*, 415–444.

Medora, N. P., Larson, J. H., Hortacsu, N., & Dave, P. (2002). Perceived attitudes towards romanticism: A cross-cultural study of American, Asian-Indian, and Turkish young adults. *Journal of Comparative Family Studies, 33*(2), 155–178.

Meggiolaro, S., & Ongaro, F. (2010). The implications of marital instability for a woman's fertility: Empirical evidence from Italy. *Demographic Research, 23*, 963–996.

Meinlschmidt, G., & Heim, C. (2005). Decreased cortisol awakening response after early loss experience. *Psychoneuroendocrinology, 30*, 568–576.

Merz-Perez, L., Heide, K. M., & Silverman, I. J. (2001). Childhood cruelty to animals and subsequent violence against humans. *International Journal of Offender Therapy and Comparative Criminology, 45*(5), 556–573.

Mignon, S. I., Larson, C. J., & Holmes, W. M. (2002). *Family abuse: consequences, theories, and responses.* Boston, MA: Pearson Education

Miguel, J. J., & Howe, T. R. (2006). Implementing and evaluating a national early violence prevention program at the local level: Lessons from ACT (adults and children together) against violence. *Journal of Early Child and Infant Psychology, 2*, 16–37.

Mikulincer, M. (1998). Attachment working models and the sense of trust: An exploration of interaction goals and affect regulation. *Journal of Personality and Social Psychology, 74*, 1209–1224.

Miller, L., Langhans, N., Schaller, J., & Zecevic, E. (1996). Effects of war on the health care of Bosnian children. *Journal of the American Medical Association, 276*, 370–371.

Miller-Perrin, C.L., & Perrin, R.D. (2007). *Child maltreatment.* Thousand Oaks, CA: Sage.

Mills, A. (1993). Helping male victims of sexual abuse. *Nursing Standard, 7*, 36–39.

Mintz, S., & Kellogg, S. (1988). *Domestic relations: A social history of American family life.* New York: Free Press.

Minuchin, P. (1985). Families and individual development: Provocations from the field of family therapy. *Family Development, 56*, 289–302.

Mistry, R. S., Vandewater, E. A., Huston, A. C., & McLoyd, V. C. (2002). Economic well-being and children's social adjustment: The role of family process in an ethnically diverse low-income sample. *Child Development, 73*(3), 935–951.

Modell, J. (1989). Dating becomes the way of American youth. In L. P. Moch, and G. Stark (Eds.), *Essays on the family and historical change.* College Station: Texas A&M University Press.

Moen, P., Kim, J. E., & Hofmeister, H. (2001). Couples' work/retirement transitions: Gender and marriage quality. *Social Psychology Quarterly, 64*, 55–71.

Molidor, C., & Tolman, R. M. (1998). Gender and contextual factors in adolescent dating violence. *Violence Against Women, 4*(2), 180–194.

Molloy, B. L., & Herzberger, S. D. (1998). Body image and self-esteem: A comparison of African-American and Caucasian women. *Sex Roles, 38*, 631–643.

Montagu, A. (1986). *Touching: The human significance of skin.* New York: Harper and Row.

Montenegro, X. (2003, September). Lifestyles, dating, and romance: A study of midlife singles. *AARP The Magazine*, 1–16.

Montgomery, M. J., Anderson, E. R., Hetherington, E. M., & Clingempeel, W. G. (1992). Patterns of courtship for remarriage: Implications for child adjustment and family relations. *Journal of Marriage and the Family, 54*, 686–698.

Moore, M. L. (2006). Adolescent pregnancy rates in three European countries: Lessons to be learned? *Journal of Obstetric, Gynecological, and Neonatal Nursing, 29*, 355–362.

Morelli, G., & Rothbaum, F. (2007). Situating the child in context: Attachment relationships and self-regulation in different cultures. In S. Kitayama & D. Cohen (Eds.), *Handbook of cultural psychology* (pp. 500–527). New York: Guilford.

Morris, W. L., Sinclair, S., & DePaulo, B. M. (2007). No shelter for singles: The perceived legitimacy of marital status discrimination. *Group Processes and Intergroup Relations, 19*(4), 457–470.

Morrow, J. (2004, November 1). A place for one. *American Demographics*.

Morsink, L. F. J., Vogelzangs, N., Nicklas, B. J., Beekman, A. T. F., Satterfield, S., Rubin, S. M. … Penninx, B. W. J. H. (2007). Associations between sex steroid hormone levels and depressive symptoms in elderly men and women: Results from the health ABC study. *Psychoneuroendocrinology, 32*, 8–10.

Mossakowski, K. N. (2009). The influence of past unemployment duration on symptoms of depression among young women and men in the U.S. *American Journal of Public Health, 99*, 1826–1832.

Muecke, M. (2004). Female sexuality in Thai discourses about *maechii* ("lay nuns"). *Culture, Health, and Sexuality, 6*(3), 221–238.

Mullender, A., Hague, G., Imam, U. F., Kelly, L., Malos, E., & Regan, L. (2002). *Children's perspectives on domestic violence.* London: Sage.

Mullings, L. (1986). Anthropological perspectives on the Afro-American family. *American Journal of Social Psychiatry, 6*(1), 11–16.

Munsey, C. (2009, February). For the first time, a court directly supports psychology's role in lessening conflict in family breakups through parenting coordination. *Monitor on Psychology, 27*.

Murdock, G. P. (1981). *Atlas of world cultures.* Pittsburgh, PA: University of Pittsburgh Press.

Murray, C. E., & Murray, T. L. (2004). Solution-focused premarital counseling: Helping couples build a vision for their marriage. *Journal of Marital and Family Therapy, 30*, 349–358.

Murray, L., & Cooper, P. (2003). Intergenerational transmission of affective and cognitive processes associated with depression: Infancy and the preschool years. In I. Goodyer (Ed.), *Unipolar depression: A lifespan perspective* (pp. 17–46). Oxford, U.K.: Oxford University Press.

Murray, L., Cooper, P. J., Wilson, A., & Romaniuk, H. (2003). Controlled trial of the short- and long-term effect of psychological treatment of post-partum depression. *Journal of Psychiatry, 182,* 420–427.

Murstein, B. I. (1970). On exchange theory, androcentrism, and sex stereotypy. *Psychological Reports, 81*(3, Pt 2), 1151–1162.

Murstein, B. I. (1976). *Who will marry whom? Theories and research in marital choice.* New York: Springer Publishing Company.

Nader, K., Pynoos, R., Fairbanks, L., Al-Ajeel, M., & Al-Asfour, A. (1993). A preliminary study of PTSD and grief among the children of Kuwait following the Gulf crisis. *British Journal of Clinical Psychology, 32,* 407–416.

Nance-Nash, S. (2004, February 1). Managing a blended family. *Black Enterprise.*

Nash, J. M. (2002, November 11). Inside the womb. *Time Magazine,* 68–78.

National Center for Injury Prevention and Control (2003). *Costs of intimate partner violence against women in the United States.* Atlanta, GA: Centers for Disease Control and Prevention.

National Clearing House for Marital and Date Rape (2005). State law chart. Retrieved from http://www.ncmdr.org

National Research Council. (1997). *The new American economic, demographic, and fiscal effects of immigration.* Washington, DC: National Academy Press.

Neff, L. J., Sargent, R. G., McKeown, R. E., & Jackson, K. L. (1997). Black–white differences in body size perceptions and weight management practices among adolescent females. *Journal of Adolescent Health, 20,* 459–465.

Nelson, C. A. (2001). The development and neural bases of face recognition. *Infant Child Development, 10,* 3–18.

Nelson, C. A., Furtado, E. A., Fox, N. A., & Zeanah, C. H. (2009). The deprived human brain. *American Scientists, 97,* 222–229.

Neto, F., & Barros, J. (2003). Predictors of loneliness among students and nuns in Angola and Portugal. *Journal of Psychology: Interdisciplinary and Applied, 137*(4), 351–362.

Neuman, M. G. (1998). *Helping your kids cope with divorce the sandcastles way.* New York: Random House.

New Hampshire Research Division of the Office of Legislative Services (2010). *State Putative Father Registries.* Retrieved from http://www.courts.state.nh.us/probate/registrylist.pdf

Newman, K. S. (2003). *A different shade of grey: Midlife and beyond in the inner city.* New York: The New Press.

Niehuis, S., Huston, T. L., & Rosenband, R. (2006). From courtship into marriage: A new developmental model and methodological critique. *Journal of Family Communication, 6*(1), 23–47.

Niemann, Y. F., Romero, A. J., Arredono, J., & Rodriguez, V. (1999). What does it mean to be "Mexican"? Social construction of an ethnicity identity. *Hispanic Journal of Behavioral Sciences, 21,* 47–60.

Nilsson, I., Ekehammar, B., & Sidanius, J. (1985). Education and sociopolitical attitudes. *Scandinavian Journal of Educational Research, 29,* 1–15.

Nussbaum, J. F., Pecchioni, L., & Croswell, T. (2001). The older patient–health care provider relationship in a managed care environment. In M. L. Hummert & J. F. Nussbaum (Eds.), *Aging, communication, and health: Linking research and practice for successful aging* (pp. 23–42). Mahwah, NJ: Lawrence Erlbaum Associates.

Nussbaum, J. F., Pecchioni, L. L., Robinson, J. D., & Thompson, T. (2000). *Communication and aging* (2nd ed.). Mahwah, NJ: Lawrence Erlbaum Associates.

Nyrop, R. F. (1985). *India: A country study.* Washington, DC: American University.

Obi, S. N., & Ozumba, B. C. (2008). Cervical cancer: Socioeconomic implications of management in a developing nation. *Journal of Obstetrics and Gynecology, 28*(5), 526–528.

O'Connell, L., Betz, M., & Kurth, S. (1989). Plans for balancing work and family life: Do women pursuing nontraditional and traditional occupations differ? *Sex Roles, 20*(1), 35–45.

O'dea, I., Hunter, M. S., & Anjos, S. (1999). Life satisfaction and health-related quality of life of middle aged men and women. *Climacteric, 2,* 131–140.

OECD (2005). *Employment outlook.* Paris: OECD

Oettel, M., & Mukhopadhyay, A. K. (2004). Progesterone: The forgotten hormone in men? *Aging Male, 7,* 236–257.

Ogg, J., & Bennet, G. (1992). Elder abuse in Britain. *British Medical Journal, 305,* 998–999.

O'Keeffe, M., Hills, A., Doyle, M., McCreadie, C., Scholes, S., Constantine, R. … Erens, B. (2007). *UK study of abuse and neglect of older people: Prevalence survey report.* London: National Centre for Social Research and King's College London.

Olds, D., Henderson, C. R., Cole, R., Eckenrode, J., Kitzman, H., Luckey, D., … Powers, J. (1998). Long-term effects of nurse home visitation on children's criminal and antisocial behavior: 15-year follow-up of a randomized trial. *Journal of the American Medical Association, 280*(14), 1238–1244.

Olson, D. H., Fournier, D. G., & Druckman, J. M. (1985). ENRICH. In D. H. Olson, H. I. McCubbin, H. Barnes, A. Larsen, M. Muxen, & M. Wilson (Eds.), *Family inventories* (pp. 68–77). St Paul, MN: University of Minnesota Press.

Opinion Research Corporationn (2009). Single parents survey for eharmony. Retrieved from http://www.eharmony.com/press/release/21

Orecklin, M. (2004, August 23). Stress and the superdad. *Time Magazine.*

Ornish, D., Lin, J., Daubenmier, J., Weidner, G., Epel, E. S., Kemp, C. … Blackburn, E. H. (2008). Increased telomerase activity in a pilot study of comprehensive lifestyle changes. *Lancet Oncology, 9,* 1048–1057.

Osgood, D. W., Ruth, G., Eccles, J. S., Jacobs, K. E., & Barber, B. L. (2005). Six paths to adulthood: Fast starters, parents without careers, educated partners, educated singles, working singles, and slow starters. In R. A. Settersten Jr., F. F. Furstenberf Jr., & R. G. Rumbaut (Eds.), *On the frontier of adulthood: Theory, research, and public policy.* (pp. 320–355). Chicago, IL: University of Chicago Press.

Overall, N. C., Fletcher, G. J., & Simpson, J. A. (2006). Regulation processes in intimate relationships: The role of ideal standards. *Journal of Personality and Social Psychology, 91*(4), 662–685.

Owen, J. J., Rhoades, G. K., Stanley, S. M., & Fincham, F. D. (2010). "Hooking up" among college students: Demographic and psychological correlates. *Archives of Sexual Behavior, 39*, 653–663.

Page, S. (2003, July/August). After the bliss: For many adoptive moms, post-baby depression is a real and painful ordeal. *Adoptive Families*, 36–38.

Panel on Research on Child Abuse and Neglect, National Research Council. (1993). *Understanding child abuse and neglect*. Washington, DC: National Academy Press.

Papageorgiou, V., Frangou-Garunovic, A., Iordanidou, R., Yule, W., Smith, P., & Vostanis, P. (2000). War trauma and psychopathology in Bosnian refugee children. *European Child and Adolescent Psychology, 9*, 84–90.

Paradis, H., Montes, G., Szilagyi, P. G. (2008, May 4). *A national perspective on parents' knowledge of child development, its relation to parent–child interaction, and associated parenting characteristics*. Paper presented at Pediatric Academic Societies, Honolulu, Hawai'i.

Pardo, M. (1990). Mexican American women grassroots community activists: Mothers of East Los Angeles. *Frontiers: A Journal of Women's Studies, 11*, 1–7.

Park, D., & Gutchess, A. (2006). The cognitive neuroscience of aging and culture. *Association for Psychological Science, 15*(3), 105–108.

Parke, R. D. (1996). *Fatherhood*. Cambridge, MA: Harvard University Press.

Parke, R. D., & Brott, A. A. (1999). *Throwaway dads: The myths and barriers that keep men from being the fathers they want to be*. New York: Houghton Mifflin Company.

Parke, R. D., & Buriel, R. (1998). Socialization in the family: Ethnic and ecological perspectives. In W. Damon and N. Eisenberg (Eds.), *Handbook of child psychology* (pp. 463–552). New York: Wiley.

Parke, R., & Buriel, R. (2006). Socialization in the family: Ethnic and ecological perspectives. In N. Eisenberg (Ed.). *The handbook of child psychology: Social, emotional, and personality development* (6th ed., vol. 3, pp. 429–504). New York: Wiley.

Parks, M. R. (2007). *Personal relationships and personal networks*. Mahwah, NJ: Lawrence Erlbaum Associates.

Parra-Cardona, J. R., Meyer, E., Schiamberg, L., & Post, L. (2007). Elder abuse and neglect in Latino families: An ecological and culturally relevant theoretical framework for clinical practice. *Family Process, 46*(4), 451–467.

Parrillo, V. N. (2009). *Diversity in America* (3rd ed.). Los Angeles: Pine Forge Press.

Parsons, T. (1951). *The social system*. New York: Free Press.

Parsons, T., & Bales, R. F. (1955). *Family, socialization, and interaction process*. Glencoe, IL: Free Press.

Pascoe, P. (1991). Race, gender, and intercultural relationships: The case of interracial marriage. *Frontiers: A Journal of Women's Studies, 12*, 5–18.

Pascoe, P. (1996). Miscegenation law, court cases, and ideologies of "race" in twentieth-century America. *Journal of American History, 83*, 44–69.

Pasztor, E. M., & McFadden, E. J. (2006). Foster parent associations: Advocacy, support, and empowerment. *Families in Society, 87*(4), 483–487.

Patterson, C. J. (1995). Families of the lesbian baby boom: Parents' division of labor and children's adjustment. *Development Psychology, 31*, 115–123.

Patterson, C. J. (2009). Children of lesbian and gay parents: Psychology, law, and policy. *American Psychologist, 64*, 727–736.

Patterson, C. L. (2006). Children of lesbian and gay parents. *Current Directions in Psychological Science, 15*, 241–244.

Paul, P. (2003, September/October). The perma parent trap. *Psychology Today*, 40–53.

Paulesu, E., McCrory, E., Fazio, F., Menoncello, L., Brunswick, N., Cappa, S. F. … Frith, U. (2000). A cultural effect on brain function. *Nature Neuroscience, 3*, 91–96.

Pedersen, W., & Blekesaune, M. (2003). Sexual satisfaction in young adulthood: Cohabitation, committed dating, or unattached life? *Acta Sociologica, 46*, 179–195.

Pederson, F. A. (1991). Secular trends in human sex ratios: their influence on individual and family behavior. *Human Nature, 2*, 271–291.

Pedro-Carroll, J. L., & Alpert-Gillis, L. J. (1997). Preventive interventions for children of divorce: A developmental model for 5 and 6 year old children. *Journal of Primary Prevention, 18*, 5–23.

Peisner-Feinberg, E., Murchinal, M., Clifford, R., Culkin, M., Howes, C., & Kagan, S. L. (1999). The children of the cost, quality, and outcomes study go to school. Retrieved from www.fpg.unc.edu

Penhale, B. (2003). Older women, domestic violence, and elder abuse: A review of commonalities, differences, and shared approaches. *Journal of Elder Abuse and Neglect, 15*(3–4), 163–183.

Peplau, L. A., Veniegas, R. C., & Campbell, S. M. (1996). Gay and lesbian relationships. In R. C. Savin-Williams & K. M. Cohen (Eds.), *The lives of lesbians, gays, and bisexuals: Children to adults* (pp. 250–273). Fort Worth, TX: Harcourt Brace.

Pereda, C. F. (2009, May 18). Immigrant women changing America … and themselves. Retrieved from www.alternet.org/story/140090

Perfect, D. and Hurrell, K. (2003). *Pay and income. Women and men in Britain*. Manchester, U.K.: Equal Opportunities Commission.

Perkins, D. D., Crim, B., Silberman, P., & Brown, B. B. (2004). Community development as a response to community-level adversity: Ecological theory and research and strengths-based policy. In K. I. Maton, C. J. Schellenbach, B. J. Leadbeater, & A. L. Solarz (Eds.), *Investing in children, youth, families, and communities: Strength-based research and policy* (pp. 117–136). Washington, DC: American Psychological Association.

Perry, B. D. (2004). *Maltreated children: Experience, brain development, and the next generation*. New York: W. W. Norton.

Perry, B. D. (2005). *Maltreatment and the developing child: How early childhood experience shapes child and culture*. London, ON: Centre for Children and Families in the Justice System.

Petchesky, R. (2007). Sexual rights policies across countries and cultures: Conceptual frameworks and minefields. In R. Parker, R. Petchesky, and R. Sember (Eds.), *Sexpolitics: Reports from the frontlines* (pp. 9–26). New York: Sexuality Policy Watch. Retrieved from http://www.sxpolitics.org/frontlines/book/pdf/sexpolitics.pdf

Peter, K., & Horn, L. (2005). *Gender differences in participation and completion of undergraduate education and how they have changed over time*. Washington, DC: National Center for Education Statistics, U.S. Department of Education, Institute of Education Sciences. Retrieved from http://nces.ed.gov/pubs2005/2005169.pdf

Peterson, G. W., Bodman, D. A., Bush, K. R., & Madden, D. A. (2000). Gender and parent–child relationships. In D. H. Demo, K. R. Allen, & M. A. Fine (Eds.), *The handbook of family diversity* (pp. 82–104). New York: Oxford University Press.

Pettit, G. S., Lansford, J. E., Malone, P. S., Dodge, K. A., & Bates, J. E. (2010). Domain-specificity in relationship history, social information processing, and violent behavior in early adolescence. *Journal of Personality and Social Psychology, 98*, 190–200.

Pham, P. N., Weinstein, H. M., & Longman, T. (2004). Trauma and PTSD symptoms in Rwanda: Implications for attitudes towards justice and reconciliation. *Journal of the American Medical Association, 292*, 602–612.

Phelan, M. B., Hamberger, L. K., Guse, C. E., Edwards, S., Walczak, S., & Zosel, A. (2005). Domestic violence among male and female patients seeking emergency medical services. *Violence and Victims, 20*, 187–206.

Phillips, J. A., & Sweeney, M. M. (2005). Premarital cohabitation and marital disruption among white, black, and Mexican-American women. *Journal of Marriage and the Family, 67*, 296–314.

Phillips, J. A., & Sweeney, M. M. (2006). Can differential exposure to risk factors explain recent racial and ethnic variations in marital disruption? *Social Science Research, 35*, 409–434.

Phinney, V. G., Jensen, L. C., Olsen, J. A., & Cundrick, B. (1990). The relationship between early development and psychosexual behaviors in adolescent females. *Adolescence, 25*(98), 321–332.

Pierce, C. A. (1996). Body height and romantic attraction: A meta-analytic test of the male-taller norm. *Social Behavior and Personality, 24*(2), 143–149.

Pietromonaco, P. R., Barrett, L. F., & Powers, S. I. (2006). Adult attachment theory and affective reactivity and regulation. In D. K. Snyder, J. Simpson, & J. N. Hughes (Eds.), *Emotion regulation in couples and families: Pathways to dysfunction and health* (pp. 57–74). Washington, DC: American Psychological Association.

Pietromonaco, P. R., Greenwood, D., & Feldman, B. L. (2004). Conflict in adult close relationships: An attachment perspective. In W. S. Rholes & J. A. Simpson (Eds.), *Adult attachment: New directions and emerging issues* (pp. 267–299). New York: Guilford Press.

Pillemer K., & Finkelhor, D. (1988), The prevalence of elder abuse: A random sample survey. *Gerontologist 28*(1), 51–57.

Piotrowski, C., & Vodanovich, S. J. (2006). The interface between workaholism and work–family conflict. *Organization Development Journal, 24*(4), 84–90.

Plante, T. G., Aldridge, A., & Louie, C. (2005). Are successful applicants to the priesthood psychologically healthy? *Pastoral Psychology, 54*(1), 81–91.

Plante, T. G., Manuel, G., & Tandez, J. (1996). Personality characteristics of successful applicants to the priesthood. *Pastoral Psychology, 45*(1), 29–40.

Pleck, J. H. (1981). *The myth of masculinity*. Cambridge, MA: MIT Press.

Pleck, J. H., Sonenstein, F. L., & Ku, L. C. (1991). Adolescent men's condom use: Relationships between perceived cost-benefits and consistency of use. *Journal of Marriage and the Family, 53*, 735–745.

Podnieks, E. (1990). *National survey on abuse of the elderly in Canada*. Toronto: Ryerson Polytechnical Institute.

Polomeno, V. (2000). The Polomeno Family Intervention Framework for perinatal education: Preparing couples for the transition to parenthood. *Journal of Perinatal Education, 9*, 31–48.

Popenoe, D. (1994). The evolution of marriage and the problem of stepfamilies: A biosocial perspective. In A. Booth & J. Dunn (Eds.), *Stepfamilies* (pp. 3–27). Hillsdale, NJ: Lawrence Erlbaum Associates.

Popenoe, D. (2006, May/June). Marriage and family in the Scandinavian experience. *Society*, 68–72.

Porter, B., & Howe, T. R. (2008). Pilot evaluation of the "ACT parents raising safe kids" violence prevention program. *Journal of Child and Adolescent Trauma, 1*, 193–206.

Post, S. G. (2005). Altruism, happiness, and health: It's good to be good. *International Journal of Behavioral Medicine, 12*, 66–77.

Power, M. J. (2003). Quality of life. In S. J. Lopez & C. R. Snyder (Eds.), *Positive psychological assessment: Handbook of models and measures* (pp. 427–442). Washington, DC: American Psychological Association.

Powers, S., Pietromonaco, P., Gunlicks, M., & Sayer, A. (2006). Dating couples' attachment styles and patterns of cortisol reactivity and recovery in response to a relationship conflict. *Journal of Personality and Social Psychology*, 90, 613–628.

Powers, V. (2004). Keeping work and life in balance. *American Society of Training and Development, 58*, 32–35.

Preece, M., & DeLongis, A. (2005). A contextual examination of stress and coping processes in stepfamilies. In T. A. Revenson, K. Kayser, & G. Bodenmann (Eds.), *Couples coping with stress: Emerging perspectives on dyadic coping* (pp. 159–174). Washington, DC: American Psychological Association.

Price, C. A. (2003). Professional women's retirement adjustment: The experience of reestablishing order. *Journal of Aging Studies, 17*(3), 341–355.

Prinstein, M. J., Meade, C. S., & Cohen, G. L. (2003). Adolescent oral sex, peer popularity, and perceptions of best friends' sexual behavior. *Journal of Pediatric Psychology, 28*, 243–249.

Proulx, N., Caron, S. L., & Logue, M. E. (2006). A look at the implications of age differences in marriage. *Journal of Couple and Relationship Therapy, 5*, 43–64.

Pruett, M. K., Insabella, G. M., & Gustafson, K. (2005). The Collaborative Divorce Project: A court-based intervention for separating parents with young children. *Family Court Review, 43*, 38–51.

Pudrovska, T., Schieman, S., & Carr, D. (2006). Strains of singlehood in later life: Do race and gender really matter? *Journal of Gerontology: Social Science, 61B*(6), S315–S322.

Pugh, S. (2002). The forgotten: A community without a generation—older lesbians and gay men. In D. Richardson & S. Seidman (Eds.), *Handbook of lesbian and gay studies* (pp. 161–182). Thousand Oaks, CA: Sage.

Pyke, K. D. (2004). Immigrant families in the U.S. In J. L. Scott, J. Treas, & M. P. M. Richards (Eds.), *The Blackwell companion to the sociology of the family*. (pp. 253–269). New York: Blackwell.

Qian, Z. (2005). Breaking the last taboo: Interracial marriage in America. *Contexts, 4*, 33–37.

Raffaelli, M., & Ontai, L. L. (2001). She's sixteen years old and there's boys calling over to the house. An exploratory study of sexual socialization in Latino families. *Culture, Health, and Sexuality, 3*, 295–310.

Rahman, Q., Collins, A., Morrison, M., Orrells, J. C., Cadinouche, K., Greenfield, S., & Begum, S. (2008). Maternal inheritance and familial fecundity factors in male homosexuality. *Archives of Sexual Behavior, 37*(6), 962–969.

Rainwater, L., & Smeeding, T. M. (2003). Doing poorly: U.S. child poverty in cross-national context. *Children, Youth, and Environments, 13*(2), np.

Raley, R. K. (1999). *Then comes marriage? Recent changes in women's response to nonmarital pregnancy.* Presented at the annual meeting of the Population Assocation of America, New York.

Raman, J. D., & Schlegel, P. N. (2002). Aromatase inhibitors for male infertility. *Journal of Urology, 167*, 624–629.

Ramey, C. T., & Ramey, S. L. (1998). Early intervention and early experience. *American Psychologist, 53*, 109–120.

Rank, M. R. (2000). Poverty and economic hardship in families. In D. H. Demo, K. R. Allen, & M. A. Fine (Eds.), *Handbook of family diversity* (pp. 293–315). New York: Oxford University Press.

Rank, M. R. (2003). As American as apple pie: Poverty and welfare. *Contexts, 2*(3), 41–49.

Rayburn, C. A. (1991). Counseling depressed female religious professionals: Nuns and clergywomen. *Counseling and Values. Special Issue: Depression and Religion, 352*, 136–148.

Reagan, L. P., Grillo, C. A., & Piroli, G. G. (2008). The As and Ds of stress: Metabolic, morphological and behavioral consequences. *European Journal of Pharmacology, 1*(6), 65–75.

Regan, P. C., & Joshi, A. (2003). Ideal partner preferences among adolescents. *Social Behavior and Personality, 31*(1), 13–20.

Reiner, W. G., & Gearheart, J. P. (2004). Discordant sexual identity in some genetic males with cloacal exstrophy assigned to female sex at birth. *New England Journal of Medicine, 350*(4), 333–41.

Reiss, I. L. (1960). *Premarital sexual standards in America.* New York: The Free Press.

Reitzes, D. C., & Mutran, E. J. (2004). The transition to retirement: Stages and factors that influence retirement adjustment. *International Journal of Aging and Human Development, 59*, 63–84.

Remafedi, G. (1987). Male homosexuality: The adolescent's perspective. *Pediatrics, 79*, 326–330.

Remafedi, G. (1990). Fundamental issues in the care of homosexual youth. *Adolescent Medicine, 74*, 1169–1179.

Rennison, R. R., & Welchans, S. (2000). Intimate partner violence [Electronic version]. Retrieved from the U.S. Department of Justice, Bureau of Justice Statistics Special Report at http://www.ojp.usdoj.gov/bjs/pub/pdf/ipv.pdf

Renzetti, C. M. (1992). *Violent betrayal: Partner abuse in lesbian relationships.* New York: Sage.

Repetti, R. L. (1994). Short-term and long-term processes linking job stressors to father–child interaction. *Social Development, 3*, 1–15.

Reuter-Lorenz, P. A., & Lustig, C. (2005). Brain aging: Reorganizing discoveries about the aging mind. *Current Opinion in Neurobiology, 15*, 245–251.

Revicki, D. A., & Mitchell, J. P. (1990). Strain, social support, and mental health in rural elderly individuals. *Applied Psychological Measurement, 1*, 385–401.

Reynolds, T. (1997). Studies suggest fathers who smoke may increase children's future cancer risk. *Journal of the National Cancer Institute, 89*, 348–349.

Rhodes, G., Lee, K., Palermo, R., Weiss, M., Yoshikawa, S., Clissa, P. ... Jeffery, L. (2005). Attractiveness of own-race, other-race, and mixed-race faces. *Perception, 34*, 319–340.

Rhodes, G., Zebrowitz, L. A., Clark, A., Kalick, S. M., Hightower, A., & McKay, R. (2001). Do facial averageness and symmetry signal health? *Evolution and Human Behavior, 22*, 31–46.

Richardson, J. T. E. (2000). *Clinical and neuropsychological aspects of closed head injury* (2nd ed.). Hove, U.K.: Psychology Press.

Richters, J., & Martinez, P. (1993). The NIMH Community Violence Project: Children as victims and witnesses to violence. *Psychiatry, 56*, 7–21.

Riggs, D. (2007). Queer theory and its future in psychology: Exploring issues of race privilege. *Social and Personality Psychology Compass, 1*, 39–52.

Riley, G. (1991). *Divorce: An American tradition*. New York: Oxford University Press.

Rivara, F. P. (1994). Epidemiology and prevention of pediatric traumatic brain injury. *Pediatric Annals, 23*, 12–17.

Robbins, R., Scherman, A., Holeman, H., & Wilson, J. (2005). Roles of American Indian grandparents in times of cultural crisis. *Journal of Cultural Diversity, 12*(2), 62–68.

Roberts, S. L., Bushnell, J. A., Collings, S. C., & Purdie, G. L. (2006). Psychological health of men with partners who have post-partum depression. *Australian and New Zealand Journal of Psychiatry, 40*(8), 704–711.

Roberts, W. R., Smith, J., Jackson, J. J., & Edmonds, G. (2009). Compensatory conscientiousness and health in older couples. *Psychological Science, 20*(5), 553–559.

Robinson, B. E., Flowers, C., & Carroll, J. (2001). Work stress and marriage: A theoretical model examining the relationship between workaholism and marital cohesion. *International Journal of Stress Management, 8*, 165–175.

Robinson, B. E., & Kelley, L. (1998). Adult children of workaholics: Self-concept, anxiety, depression, and locus of control. *American Journal of Family Therapy, 26*, 35–50.

Robinson, B. E., Flowers, C., & Ng, K. M. (2006). The relationship between workaholism and marital disaffection: Husbands' perspective. *The Family Journal, 14*(3), 213–220.

Robles, T. F., & Kiecolt-Glaser, J. K. (2003). The physiology of marriage: Pathways to health. *Physiology and Behavior, 79*, 409–416.

Roediger, D. (1988). *The wages of whiteness: Race and the making of the American working class*. London: Verso.

Roisman, G. I., Clausell, E., Holland, A., Fortuna, K., & Elieff, C. (2008). Adult romantic relationships as contexts of human development: A multimethod comparison of same-sex couples with opposite-sex dating, engaged, and married dyads. *Developmental Psychology, 44*, 91–101.

Roscoe, W. (2000). *Changing ones: Third and fourth genders in Native North America*. London: Macmillan.

Roselli, C. E., & Stormshak, F. (2009). Prenatal programming of sexual partner preference: The ram model. *Journal of Neuroendocrinology, 21*(4), 359–364.

Rosen, C. (2004, Winter). New technologies and our feelings: Romance on the internet. *The New Atlantis*, 3–16.

Rosenbaum, J. E. (2009). Patient teenagers? A comparison of the sexual behavior of virginity pledgers and matched nonpledgers. *Pediatrics, 123*(1), 110–120.

Rostosky, S. S., Riggle, E. D. B., Horne, S. G., & Miller, A. D. (2009). Marriage amendments and psychological distress in lesbian, gay and bisexual (LGB) adults. *Journal of Counseling Psychology, 56*, 56–66.

Rothbart, M. (2002). Category dynamics and the modification of outgroup stereotypes. In R. Brown and S. Gaertner (Eds.), *Blackwell handbook of social psychology: Intergroup processes*. Malden, MA; Wiley-Blackwell.

Rubin, E. (2010, December). Veiled rebellion. *National Geographic*.

Rubin, L. (1995). *Families and society*. New York: HarperCollins.

Ruggles, S. (1994). The origins of African-American Indian family: State of the art. In J. Red Horse, A. Shattuck, & F. Hoffman (Eds.), *The American Indian family: Strengths and stress* (pp. 25–43). Isleta, NM: American Indian Social Research and Development Associates.

Rupp, H. A., & Wallen, K. (2008). Sex differences in response to visual sexual stimuli: A review. *Archives of Sexual Behavior, 37*, 206–218.

Russell, S. (2004). The economic burden of illness for households in developing countries: A review of studies focusing on malaria, tuberculosis, and human immunodeficiency virus/acquired immunodeficiency syndrome. *American Journal of Tropical Medicine and Hygiene. 71*(2), 147–155.

Russell, S. T., & Consolacion, T. B. (2003). Adolescent romance and emotional health in the United States: Beyond binaries. *Journal of Clinical Child and Adolescent Psychology, 32*, 499–509.

Russell-Hochschild, A. (1997, April 20). There's no place like work. *New York Magazine*, 51–54, 81, 84.

Ryan, K. M., Weikel, K., & Sprechini, G. (2008). Gender differences in narcissism and courtship violence in dating couples. *Sex Roles, 58*(11–12), 802–813.

Rygaard, N. P. (2006). *Severe attachment disorder in childhood: A guide to practical therapy*. New York: Springer Science and Business Media.

Sabattini, L., & Crosby, F. J. (2009). Ceilings and walls: Work–life and family friendly policies. In M. da Costa Barreto, M. K. Ryan, & M. T. Schmitt (Eds.), *The glass ceiling in the twenty-first century* (pp. 201–223). Washington, DC: American Psychological Association.

Sacks, O. (2008). Unchained by melody. *Neurology Now, 4*, 16–19.

Sagarin, B. J. Cutler, B., Lawler-Sagarin, K. A., & Matuszewich, L. (2009). Hormonal changes and couple bonding in consensual sadomasochistic activity. *Archives of Sexual Behavior, 38*, 186–200.

Saltzman, K. M., Holden, G. W., & Holahan, C. J. (2002). The psychobiology of children exposed to marital violence. *Journal of Clinical Child and Adolescent Psychology, 24*(1), 129–139.

Saltzman, W. R., Layne, C., M., Steinberg, A. M., Arslanagic, B., & Pynoos, R. S. (2003). Developing a culturally and ecologically sound intervention program for youth exposed to war and terrorism. *Child Adolescent Psychiatric Clinics, 12*, 319–342.

Samuels, P. A., & Lester, D. (1985). A preliminary investigation of emotions experienced toward God by Catholic nuns and priests. *Psychological Reports, 56*(3), 706.

Sandman, C. A. (2009). Efficacy of opioid antagonists in attenuating self-injurious behavior. In R. Dean, E. Bilsky, & S. Negus (Eds.), *Opiate receptors and antagonists: From bench to clinic* (pp. 457–472). New York: Humana Press.

Sastry, J. (1999). Household structure, satisfaction and distress in India and the United States: A comparative cultural examination. *Journal of Comparative Family Studies, 30*(1), 135–152.

Savin-Williams, R. C. (1990). *Gay and lesbian youth: Expressions of identity.* Washington, DC: Hemisphere Publishing Corp.

Savin-Williams, R. C. (1996). Self-labeling and disclosure among lesbian, gay, and bisexual youths. In J. Laird & R. J. Green (Eds.), *Lesbians and gays in couples and families: A handbook for therapists* (pp. 153–182). San Francisco: Jossey-Bass.

Savin-Williams, R. C., & Esterberg, K. G. (2000). Lesbian, gay, and bisexual families. In D. H. Demo, K. R. Allen, & M. A. Fine (Eds.), *Handbook of family diversity* (pp. 197–215). New York: Oxford University Press.

Savitz, D. A., Brett, K. M., Dole, N., & Tse, C. J. (1997). Male and female occupation in relation to miscarriage and preterm delivery in central North Carolina. *Annals of Epidemiology, 7*, 509–516.

Schaefer, R. T. (2004). *Racial and ethnic groups* (9th ed.). Upper Saddle River, NJ: Prentice Hall.

Scharf, M., & Mayseless, O. (2008). Late adolescent girls' relationships with parents and romantic partners: The distinctive roles of mothers and fathers. *Journal of Adolescence, 31*, 837–855.

Schmitt, D. P. (2005). Fundamentals of human mating strategies. In D. M. Buss (Ed.), *The handbook of evolutionary psychology* (pp. 258–291). Hoboken, NJ: Wiley.

Schmitt, M. T., Spoor, J. R., Danaher, K., & Branscombe, N. R. (2009). Rose-colored glasses: How tokenism and comparisons with the past reduce the visibility of gender inequality. In M. Barreto, M. Ryan, & M. Schmitt (Eds.), *Barriers to diversity: The glass ceiling 20 years on* (pp. 49–71). Washington, DC: American Psychological Association.

Schnurr, M. P., & Lohman, B. J. (2008). How much does school matter? An examination of adolescent dating violence perpetration. *Journal of Youth and Adolescence, 37*(3), 266–283.

Schoen, R., & Canudas-Romo, V. (2006). Timing effects on divorce: Twentieth-century experiences in the U.S. *Journal of Marriage and the Family, 68*, 749–758.

Schroeder, E. (2008). *Taking sides. Clashing views in family and personal relationships.* (7th ed.). Dubuque, IA: McGraw-Hill Contemporary Learning Series.

Schulz, R., & Heckhausen, J. (1996). A life span model of successful aging. *American Psychologist, 51*, 702–714.

Schwartz, P. (1994). *Love between equals.* New York: The Free Press.

Schwartz, P., & Rutter, V. (1998). *The gender of sexuality: Sexual possibilities.* Thousand Oaks, CA: Pine Forge Press.

Sears, J. T. (1991). *Growing up gay in the South: Race, gender, and journeys of the spirit.* New York: Harrington Park Press.

Serbin, L. A., Poulin-Dubois, D., Colburne, K. A., Sen, M. G., & Eichstedt, I. (2001). Gender stereotyping in infancy: Visual preferences for and knowledge of gender-stereotyped toys in the second year. *International Journal of Behavioral Development, 25*, 7–15.

Shackelford, T. K., & Larsen, R. J. (1997). Facial asymmetry as an indicator of psychological, emotional, and physiological distress. *Journal of Personality and Social Psychology, 72*, 456–466.

Shapiro, A. F., Gottman, J. M., & Carrere, S. (2000). The baby and the marriage: Identifying factors that buffer against decline in marital satisfaction after the first baby arrives. *Journal of Family Psychology, 14*(1), 59–70.

Shaver, P. R., Morgan, H. J., & Wu, S. (1996). Is love a "basic" emotion. *Personal Relationships, 3*(1), 81–96.

Shepard, D. S. (2002). A negative state of mind: Patterns of depressive symptoms among men with high gender role conflict. *Psychology of Men and Masculinity, 3*, 3–8.

Shippy, R. A., Cantor, M. H., & Brennan, M. (2004). Social networks of aging gay men. *Journal of Men's Studies, 13*, 45–66.

Shonkoff, J., & Phillips (2000). *From neurons to neighborhoods: The science of early childhood development.* Washington, DC: National Academy Press.

Shore, A. N. (2001). Effects of a secure attachment relationship on right brain development, affect regulation, and infant mental health. *Infant Mental Health Journal, 22*(1–2), 7–66.

Shostak, A. B. (1987). Singlehood. In M. B. Sussman and S. K. Steinmetz (Eds.), *Handbook of marriage and the family* (pp. 355–367). New York: Plenum Press.

Shulman, P. (2004, March/April). Great expectations. *Psychology Today, 33*–34, 37–38, 41–42.

Shyu, Y. L., Chen, M. C., Chen, S. T., Wang, H. P., & Shao, J. H. (2008). A family caregiver oriented discharge planning program for older stroke patients and their family caregivers. *Journal of Clinical Nursing, 17*, 2498–2508.

Silva, J. M., & Randall, A. (2005). Giving psychology away: Educating adults to ACT against early childhood violence. *Journal of Early Childhood and Infant Psychology, 1*, 37–43.

Silverman, I., & Eals, M. (1992). Sex differences in spatial abilities: Evolutionary theory and data. In J. H. Barkow and L. Cosmides (Eds.), *The adapted mind: Evolutionary psychology and the generation of culture* (pp. 533–549). New York: Oxford University Press.

Silverstein, L. B., & Auerbach, C. F. (2005). Post-modern families. In J. P. Roopnarine & U. P. Gielen (Eds.), *Families in global perspective* (pp. 33–47). New York: Allyn & Bacon.

Simon, R. W. (2005). Clarifying the relationship between parenthood and depression. *Journal of Health and Social Behavior, 46*, 341–358.

Simon, V. A., Aikins, J. W., & Prinstein, M. J. (2008). Romantic partner selection and socialization during early adolescence. *Child Development, 79*(6), 1676–1692.

Singer, I. (1987). *The nature of love: Vol. 3. The modern world.* Chicago, IL: University of Chicago Press.

Singh, D., & Luis, S. (1995). Ethnic and gender consensus for the effect of waist-to-hip ratio on judgment of women's attractiveness. *Human Nature, 6*(1), 51–65.

Singley, S., & Hynes, K. (2005). Transitions to parenthood: Work–family policies, gender, and the couple context. *Gender and Society, 19*, 376–397.

Skeels, H. M. (1966). Adult status of children with contrasting early life experiences. *Monographs of the Society for Research in Child Development, 31*(3).

Skolnick, A. (1991). *Embattled paradise: The American family in an age of uncertainty.* New York: Basic Books.

Skolnick, A. (1994). *The life course revolution. Family in transition.* New York: HarperCollins.

Slep, A. M., & O'Leary, S. G. (2005). Parent and partner violence in families with young children: Rates, patterns, and connections. *Journal of Consulting and Clinical Psychology, 73*(3), 435–444.

Smart, C., Neale, B., & Wade, A. (2001). *The changing experience of childhood: Families and divorce.* Cambridge, U.K.: Polity Press.

Smiler, A. P. (2008). "I wanted to get to know her better": Adolescent boys' dating motives, masculinity ideology, and sexual behavior. *Journal of Adolescence, 31*(1), 17–32.

Smith, D. (1993). The Standard North American Family. *Journal of Family Issues, 14*(1), 50–65.

Smith, D. S., & Hindus, M. (1975). Premarital pregnancy in America 1640–1971: An overview and interpretation. *Journal of Interdisciplinary History, 4*, 537–570.

Smith, T. W., Uchino, B. N., Berg, C. A., Florsheim, P., Pearce, G., Hawkins, M. … Olsen-Cerny, C. (2009). Conflict and collaboration in middle-aged and older couples: Cardiovascular reactivity during marital interaction. *Psychology and Aging, 24*, 274–286.

Smock, P. (2000). Cohabitation in the United States. *Annual Review of Sociology, 26*, 1–20.

Smock, P. J., & Gupta, S. (2002). Cohabitation in contemporary North America. In A. Booth and A. C. Crouter (Eds.), *Just living together: Implications of cohabitation on families, children, and social policy* (pp. 53–84). Mahwah, NJ: Lawrence Erlbaum Associates.

Snir, R., & Harpaz, I. (2006). The workaholism phenomenon: A cross-national perspective. *Career Development International, 11*(5), 374–393.

Solomon, J. C., & Marx, J. (1995). To grandmother's house we go: Health and school adjustment of children raised solely by grandparents. *The Gerontologist, 35*, 386–394.

Soule, S. A. (2004). Going to the chapel? Same-sex marriage bans in the U.S., 1973–2000. *Social Problems, 51*, 453–477. doi: 10.1525/sp. 2004.51.4.453

Span, P. (2003, February 23). Marriage at first sight. *Washington Post*, W16.

Spector, P. E. (1997). *Job satisfaction: Application, assessment, cause, and consequences.* Thousand Oaks, CA: Sage.

Spencer, H. (1857). Progress: Its law and causes. *Westminster Review, 67*, 445–465.

Spencer, M. B. (2006). Phenomenology and ecological systems theory: Development of diverse groups. In W. Damon and R. Lerner (Eds.), *Handbook of child psychology: vol. 1:*

Theoretical models of human development (6th ed., pp. 829–893). New York: Wiley.

Spitz, R. A. (1955). The primal cavity: A contribution to the genesis of perception and its role for psychoanalytic theory. *The Psychoanalytic Study of the Child, 10*, 215–240.

Spoor, J. R., & Schmitt, M. T. (2011). "Things are getting better" isn't always better: Considering women's progress affects perceptions of and reactions to contemporary gender inequality. *Basic and Applied Psychology, 33*(1), 24–36. doi: 10.1080/01973533.2010.539948

Sprecher, S., & Chandak, R. (1992). Attitudes about arranged marriages and dating among men and women from India. *Free Inquiry in Creative Sociology, 20*, 59–69.

Sprecher, S., Aron, A., Hatfield, E., Cortese, A., Potapova, E., & Levitskaya, A. (1994). Love: American style, Russian style, and Japanese style. *Personal Relationships, 1*, 349–369.

St. George, D. (January 19, 2010). More wives are the higher-income spouse, Pew report says. *Washington Post*.

Stacey, J. and Davenport, E. (2002) Queer families quack back. In D. Richardson & S. Seidman (Eds.), *Handbook of lesbian and gay studies* (pp. 355–374). London: Sage Publications.

Stanton, M. E. (1995). Patterns of kinship and residence. In B. B. Ingoldsby & S. Smith (Eds.), *Families in multicultural perspective* (pp. 97–116). New York: Guilford.

Steckel, A. (1987). *Separation-individuation in children of lesbian and heterosexual couples.* Unpublished doctoral dissertation, the Wright Institute Graduate School, Berkeley, CA.

Steele, C. M., & Aronson, J. (1995). Stereotype threat and the intellectual test performance of African Americans. *Journal of Social and Personality Psychology, 69*, 797–811.

Stein, P. J. (1978). The lifestyles and life-chances of the never-married. *Marriage and Family Review, 1*, 2–11.

Steinberg, L., & Silk, J. (2002). Parenting adolescents. In M. Bornstein (Ed.), *Handbook of parenting: vol. 1. Children and parenting* (pp. 103–134). Mahwah, NJ: Lawrence Erlbaum Associates.

Stephenson, P. A., Bakoula, C., Hemminki, E., Knudsen, L., Levasseur, M., Schenker, J. … Lomas, J. (1993). Patterns of use of obstetrical interventions in 12 countries. *Paediatric and Perinatal Epidemiology, 7*, 45–54.

Steptoe, A., Siegrist, J., Kirschbaum, M., & Marmot, M. (2004). Effort–reward imbalance, over commitment, and measures of cortical and blood pressure over the working day. *Psychosomatic Medicine, 65*, 461–470.

Sterling, P., & Eyer, J. (1988). Allostasis: A new paradigm to explain arousal pathology. In S. Fisher & J. Reason (Eds.), *Handbook of life stress, cognition, and health* (pp. 629–649). New York: John Wiley.

Sternberg, R. J. (1986). A triangular theory of love. *Psychological Review, 93*(2), 119–135.

Sternberg, R. J. (2007, Spring). Stories we love by. *Tufts Magazine*.

Sternberg, R. J., & Barnes, M. L. (1988). *The psychology of love.* New Haven, CT: Yale University Press.

Stets, J. E., & Straus, M. A. (1990). The marriage license as a hitting license: A comparison of assaults in dating, co-habiting, and married couples. In M. A. Straus & R. J. Gelles (Eds.), *Physical violence in American families: Risk factors and adaptations to violence in 8,145 families* (pp. 227–244). New Brunswick, NJ: Transaction.

Stevens-Simon, C., & McAnarney, E. R. (1994). Childhood victimization: Relationship to adolescent pregnancy outcome. *Child Abuse and Neglect, 18*(7), 569–575.

Stevenson, B. E. (1995). Black family structure in colonial and antebellum Virginia: Amending the revisionist perspective. In M. B. Tucker & C. Mitchell-Kernan (Eds.), *The decline in marriage among African Americans: Causes, consequences and policy implications* (pp. 27–56). New York: Russell Sage.

Steverink, N., Westerhof, G. J., Bode, C., & Dittman-Kohi, F. (2001). The personal experience of aging: Individual resources and subjective well-being. *Journal of Gerontology, 56*, 364–373. doi: 10.1093./geronb/56.6.p364.

Stiers, G. A. (1999). *From this day forward: Commitment, marriage, and family in lesbian and gay relationships.* New York: St. Martin's Press.

Stockard, J. E. (2002). *Marriage in culture: Practice and meaning across diverse societies.* New York: Harcourt College.

Stone, E. A., Shakelford, T. K., & Buss, D. M. (2007). Sex ratio and mate preferences: A cross-cultural investigation. *European Journal of Social Psychology, 37*(2), 288–296.

Stopes-Roe, M., & Cochrane, R. (1990). *Citizens of this country: The Asian British.* Clevedon, U.K.: Multilingual Matters.

Storey, A. E., Walsh, C. J., Quinton, R. L., & Wynne-Edwards, K. E. (2000). Hormonal correlates of paternal responsiveness in new and expectant fathers. *Evolution and Human Behavior, 21*, 79–95.

Straus, M. A., & Stewart, J. H. (1999). Corporal punishment by American parents: National data on prevalence, chronicity, severity, and duration, in relation to child, and family characteristics. *Clinical Child and Family Psychology Review, 2*(2), 55–70.

Strober, M. H. (2004, Fall). Children as public good. *Dissent,* 57–61.

Strong, B., & DeVault, C. (1994). *Human sexuality.* Mountain View, CA: Mayfield.

Stuart, P. (1987). *Nations within a nation: Historical statistics of American Indians.* Westport, CT: Greenwood Press.

Sturge-Apple, M. L., Davies, P. T., & Cummings, E. M. (2006). Impact of hostility and withdrawal in interparental conflict on parental emotional unavailability and children's adjustment difficulties. *Child Development, 77*(6), 1623–1641.

Suarez, Z. (1998). The Cuban-American family. In C. H. Mindel, R. W. Haberstein, & R. Wright, Jr. (Eds.), *Ethnic families in America: Patterns and variations* (pp. 172–198). Upper Saddle River, NJ: Prentice Hall.

Subrahmanyam, K., Smahel, D., & Greenfield, P. (2006). Connecting developmental constructions to the internet: Identity presentations and sexual exploration in online teen chat rooms. *Developmental Psychology, 42*, 395–406.

Sugarman, S. D. (2004). Single-parent families. In S. Coltrane (Ed.), *Families and society* (pp. 365–288). Belmont, CA: Wadsworth/Thompson Learning.

Suina, J. H., & Smolkin, L. B. (1994). From natal culture to school culture to dominant society culture: Supporting transitions for Pueblo Indian students. In P. M. Greenfield & R. R. Cocking (Eds.), *Cross-cultural roots of minority child development* (pp. 115–130). Hillsdale. NJ: Lawrence Erlbaum Associates.

Sun, Y., & Li, Y. (2001). Marital disruption, parental investment, and children's academic achievement: A prospective analysis. *Journal of Family Issues, 22*, 27–62.

Surbey, M. K. (1990). Family composition, stress, and the timing of human menarche. In T. E. Ziegler (Ed.), *Socioendocrinology of primate reproduction. Monographs in primatology* (pp. 11–32). New York: Wiley-Liss.

Swaab, D. F. (2007). Sexual differentiation of the brain and behavior. *Best Practice and Research: Clinical Endocrinology and Metabolism, 21*(3), 431–444.

Swain, J. E., Tasgin, E., Mayes, L. C., Feldman, R., Constable, R. T., & Leckman, J. F. (2008). Maternal brain response to own baby-cry is affected by cesarean section delivery. *Journal of Child Psychology and Psychiatry, 49*(10), 1042–1052. doi: 10.1111/j.1469–7610.2008.01963.x.

Sweeney, M. M. (2002). Remarriage and the nature of divorce: Does it matter which spouse chooses to leave? *Journal of Family Issues, 23*, 410–440.

Sweeney, M. M. (2010). Remarriage and step-families: Strategic sites for family scholarship in the twenty-first century. *Journal of Marriage and the Family, 72*, 667–684.

Sweezy, K., & Tiefenthaler, J. (1996). Do state-level variables affect divorce rates? *Review of Social Economy, 54*, 47–65.

Swim, J. K., Aikin, K. J., Hall, W. S., & Hunter, B. A. (1995). Sexism and racism: Old-fashioned and modern prejudices. *Journal of Personality and Social Psychology, 68*, 199–214.

Tang, C. S.-K., & Yan, E. (2001). Prevalence and psychological impact of Chinese elder abuse. *Journal of Interpersonal Violence, 16*, 158–174.

Tang, C.-Y., & Wadsworth, S. M. (2010). *2008 National Study of the Changing Workforce: Time and workplace flexibility.* New York: Families and Work Institute. Retrieved from http://www.familiesandwork.org/site/research/reports/time_work_flex.pdf

Tasker, F. (2002). Lesbian and gay parenting. In A. Coyle and C. Kitzinger (Eds.), *Lesbian and gay psychology: New perspectives* (pp. 81–97). Oxford, U.K.: Blackwell Publishers.

Tavris, C. (1992). *The mismeasure of woman.* New York: Touchstone.

Taylor, N., Donovan, W., & Leavitt, L. (2008). Consistency in infant sleeping arrangements and mother–infant interaction. *Infant Mental Health Journal, 29*(2), 77–94.

Taylor, S. E., Saphire-Bernstein, S., & Seeman, T. E. (2009). Are plasma oxytocin in women and plasma vasopressin in men biomarkers of distressed pair-bond relationships? *Psychological Science, 20*, 1–5.

Teachman, J. D. (2000). Diversity of family structure: Economic and social influence. In D. H. Demo, K. R. Allen, & M. A. Fine (Eds.), *Handbook of family diversity* (pp. 32–58). New York: Oxford University Press.

Teachman, J., Tedrow, L., & Crowder, K. (2000). The changing demography of America's families. *Journal of Marriage and the Family, 62,* 1234–1246.

Teaster, P. B. (2003). *A response to the abuse of vulnerable adults: The 2000 survey of adult protective services.* Washington, DC: National Center on Elder Abuse.

Teaster, P. B., Dugar, T. D., Mendiondo, M. S., Abner, E., Cecil, K. A., & Otto, J. M. (2007). *The 2004 survey of state adult protective services: Abuse of adults 60 years of age and older.* Washington, DC: National Center on Elder Abuse.

Teich, M. (2006). Love but don't touch. *Psychology Today, 39*(2), 80–86.

Teicher, M. H. (2002). Scars that won't heal: The neurobiology of child abuse. *Scientific American, 286,* 68–75.

Thabet, A. A., Tawahina, A. A., Sarraj, E. E., & Vostanis, P. (2008). Exposure to war trauma and PTSD among parents and children in the Gaza strip. *European Child Adolescent Psychiatry, 17,* 191–199.

Thabet, A. A., & Vostanis, P. (1999). Post-traumatic stress reactions in children of war: A longitudinal study. *Child Abuse and Neglect, 24*(2), 291–298.

Thai, H. C. (2002). Clashing dreams: Highly educated overseas brides and low-wage U.S. husbands. In B. Ehrenreich and A. R. Hochschild (Eds.), *Global woman: Nannies, maids, and sex workers* (pp. 175–184). New York: Metropolitan Books.

Thornton-Dill, B. (1988). Our mothers' grief: Racial ethnic women. *Journal of Family History, 13*(4), 418–429.

Thronson, D. B. (2008). Creating crisis: Immigration raids and the destabilization of immigrant families. *Wake Forest Law Review, 43,* 391–396.

Tillman, K. H. (2008). Non-traditional siblings and the academic outcomes of adolescents. *Social Science Research, 37,* 88–108.

Tither, J. M., & Ellis, B. J. (2008). Impact of fathers on daughters' age at menarche: A genetic and environmental comparison sibling study. *Developmental Psychology, 44,* 1409–1420.

Tjaden, P., & Thoennes, N. (1998, November). *Prevalence, incidence, and consequences of violence against women: Findings from the National Violence Against Women Survey.* Washington. DC: National Institute of Justice and the Centers for Disease Control and Prevention Research Brief.

Tjaden, P., & Thoennes, N. (2000). *Extent, nature, and consequences of intimate partner violence* [Research report; electronic version]. Washington, DC: National Institute of Justice and the Centers for Disease Control and Prevention. Retrieved from http://www.ncjrs/pdffiles1/nij/181867.pdf

Toscano, S. F. (2006). Sex parties: Female teen sexual experiences. *Journal of School Nursing, 22,* 285–289.

Toubia, N. F., & Sharief, E. H. (2003). Female genital mutilation: Have we made progress? *International Journal of Gynecology and Obstetrics, 82*(3), 251–261.

Townsend, N. W. (2002). *The package deal: Marriage, work, and fatherhood in men's lives.* Philadelphia, PA: Temple University Press.

Trejos-Castillo, E., & Vazsonyi, A. T. (2009). Risky sexual behaviors in first and second generation Hispanic immigrant youth. *Journal of Youth Adolescence, 38,* 719–731.

Trickett, P. K., Kurtz, D. A., & Noll, J. G. (2005). The consequences of child sexual abuse for female development. In D. J. Bell, S. L. Foster, & E. J. Mash, *Handbook of behavioral and emotional problems in girls* (pp. 357–379). New York: Kluwer Academic/Plenum Publishers.

Trimble, J. E., & Medicine, B. (1993). Diversification of American Indians: Forming an indigenous perspective. In U. Kim & J. W. Berry (Eds.), *Indigenous psychologies* (pp. 133–151). Newbury Park, CA: Sage.

Trivers, R. L. (1972). Parental investment and sexual selection. In B. Campbell (Ed.), *Sexual selection and the descent of man 1871–1971* (pp. 136–179). Chicago, IL: Aldine Publishing.

Tsapelas, I., Aron, A., & Orbuch, T. (2009). Marital boredom now predicts less satisfaction nine years later. *Psychological Science, 20*(5), 543–545.

Tsuda, T. (2003). *Strangers in the ethnic homeland: Japanese Brazilian return migration in transnational perspective.* New York: Columbia University Press.

Tucker, J. (2007, August 28). With spotlight on PTSD in urban youth, officials vow cooperation. *SF Gate.*

Turnage, B. F. (2004). Influences on adolescent African American females' global self-esteem: Body image and ethnic identity. *Journal of Ethnic and Cultural Diversity in Social Work, 13*(4), 27–45.

Tuschen-Caffier, B., Florin, I., Krause, W., & Pook, M. (1999). Cognitive behavioral therapy for idiopathic infertile couples. *Psychotherapy and Psychosomatics, 68,* 15–21.

Tynes, B., Reynolds, L., & Greenfield, P. M. (2004). Adolescent race and ethnicity on the internet: A comparison of discourse in monitored and unmonitored chat rooms. *Journal of Applied Developmental Psychology, 25,* 667–684.

Uchino, B. N. (2009). Understanding the links between social support and physical health. *Perspectives on Psychological Science, 4*(3), 236–255.

Udry, J. R., & Chantala, K. (2004). Masculinity–femininity guides sexual union formation in adolescents. *Personality and Social Psychology Bulletin, 30*(1), 44–55.

Umberson, D., & Slaten, E. (2000). Gender and intergenerational relationships. In D. H. Demo, K. R. Allen, & M. A. Fine (Eds.), *Handbook of family diversity* (pp. 105–127). New York: Oxford University Press.

Umberson, D., Wortman, C. B., & Kessler, R. C. (1992). Widowhood and depression: Explaining gender differences in vulnerability. *Journal of Health and Social Behavior, 33,* 10–24.

United Nations Population Fund (2009). *Mutilation/cutting: Promoting gender equality.* Retreived from http://www.unfpa.org/gender/practices2.htm

U.S. Bureau of Labor Statistics (2002). Rankings of full time occupations by earnings, 2000. *Monthly Labor Review Onlin, 125*(3). Retrieved from http://www.bls.gov/opub/mlr/2002/03/ressum.htm

U.S. Bureau of Labor Statistics (2009). Household data annual averages. *Current Population Survey Tables*. Washington, DC: U.S. Bureau of Labor Statistics.

U.S. Census Bureau (1998). *Marital status and living arrangements: March 1998*. Washington, DC: U.S. Government Printing Office.

U.S. Census Bureau (2000a). *Households and families*: 2000. [Electronic version]. Retrieved from Census 2000 Summary File 2 (SF-2) QT-P10 at http://factfinder.census.gov

U.S. Census Bureau (2000b). *Living together, living alone: Families and living arrangements*. Washington, DC: U.S. Government Printing Office.

U.S. Census Bureau (2002) *The Asian population 2000: Census 2000 brief*. Washington, DC: U.S. Government Printing Office.

U.S. Census Bureau (2003). *American community survey*. Washington, DC: U.S. Government Printing Office.

U.S. Census Bureau (2004). *Fertility and family statistics detailed tables*. Washington, DC: U.S. Government Printing Office.

U.S. Census Bureau (2005). *Historical income tables: Income equality*. Retrieved from http://www.census.gov/hhes/www/income/histinc/p60no231_tablea3.pdf

U.S. Census Bureau (2006). *Income, earnings, and poverty data from the 2006 American community survey*. Washington, DC: U.S. Government Printing Office.

U.S. Census Bureau (2007). *Population and housing narrative profile: 2005–2007*. Washington, DC: U.S. Government Printing Office.

U.S. Census Bureau (2008). *Marriage and divorce*. Washington, DC: U.S. Government Printing Office.

U.S. Department of Health and Human Services (1999). *America's children*. Retrieved from http://www.childstats.gov/ac1999.asp

U.S. Department of Health and Human Services. (2007). *Child maltreatment*. Washington, DC: Administration on Children, Youth and Families.

U.S. Department of Health and Human Services (2008). Administration on children, youth and families. *Child maltreatment 2006*. Washington, DC: U.S. Government Printing Office.

U.S. Department of Health and Human Services (2009). Poverty rates. *Federal Register, 74*, 4199–4201. Retrieved from http://www.aspe.hhs.gov

U.S. General Accounting Office (1992). *Child support enforcement: Opportunity to reduce federal and state costs*. (No. GAO/HRD-92–39FS). Washington, DC: U.S. General Accounting Office. Retrieved from http://archive.gao.gov/t2pbat1/154467.pdf

U.S. General Accounting Office (1997). *Defense of Marriage Act*. (No. GAO/OGC-97–16). Washington, DC: U.S. General Accounting Office.

Valiente, C., & Eisenberg, N. (2006). Parenting and children's adjustment: The role of children's emotion regulation. In D. K. Snyder, J. A. Simpson, and J. N. Hughes (Eds.), *Emotion regulation in couples and families: Pathways to dysfunction and health* (pp. 123–142). Washington, DC: American Psychological Association.

Van der Kolk, B. A., Perry, J. C., & Herman, J. L. (1991). Childhood origins of self-destructive behavior. *American Journal of Psychiatry, 148*, 1665–1671.

Van Rossem, R., & Gage, A. J. (2009). The effects of female genital mutilation on the onset of sexual activity and marriage in Guinea. *Archives of Sexual Behavior, 38*, 178–185.

Van Solinge, H., & Henkins, K. (2005). Couples' adjustment to retirement: A multi-actor panel study. *Journals of Gerontology B: Psychology Sciences and Social Sciences, 60*, 11–20.

Vander Ven, T. M., Cullen, F. T., Carrozza, M. A., & Wright, J. P. (2001). Home alone: The impact of maternal employment on delinquency. *Social Problems, 48*(2), 236–257.

Vannoy, D. (1991). Social differentiation, contemporary marriage, and human development. *Journal of Family Issues, 12*, 251–267.

Vasey, P. L., & VanderLaan, D. P. (2007). Birth order and male androphilia in Samoan fa'afafine. *Proceedings of the Royal Society of London, Series B: Biological Sciences, 274*, 1437–1442.

Vestal, C. (2008, May 16). California gay marriage ruling sparks new debate. Retrieved from http://www.stateline.org/live/details/story?contentId=310206

Vinovskis, M. A. (2011). Historical perspectives on parent–child interactions. In J. B. Lancaster, J. Altman, A. S. Rossi and L. R. Sherrod, *Parenting across the life-span* (pp. 295–314). New York: De Gruyter.

Violence Policy Center (2006). *American roulette: Murder-suicide in the United States*. Washington, DC: Violence Policy Center. Retrieved from http://www.vpc.org/studies/amroul2006.pdf

Visher, E. B., & Visher, J. S. (1993). *Stepfamilies: Myths and realities*. New York: Carol Publishing.

Vishwanath, R. (2003). Artificial insemination: The state of the art. *Theriogenology, 59*, 571–584.

Voller, E. K., Long, P. J., Aosved, A. C. (2009). Attraction to sexual violence towards women, sexual abuse of children, and non-sexual criminal behavior: Testing the specialist vs. generalist models in male college students. *Archives of Sexual Behavior, 38*, 235–243.

Wachholtz, A. B., Pearce, M. J., & Koenig, H. (2008). Exploring the relationship between spirituality, coping, and pain. *Spirituality and Health International, 9*, 161–173.

Wachs, T. D. (2000). *Necessary but not sufficient: The respective roles of single and multiple influences on individual development*. Washington, DC: American Psychological Association.

Wade, R. H. (2004). Is globalization reducing poverty and inequality? *World Development, 32*, 567–589.

Waite, L. J., & Gallagher, M. (2000). *The case for marriage*. New York: Boradway Books.

Walker-Bynum, C. (1983). *Jesus as mother: Studies in the spirituality of the high Middle Ages*. Berkeley, CA: University of California Press.

Walker, S., Spohn, C., & DeLone, M. (2007). *The color of justice: Race, ethnicity, and crime in America* (4th ed.). Belmont, CA: Wadsworth.

Wallen, K. (2001). Sex and context: Hormones and primate sexual motivation. *Hormones and Behavior, 40*(2), 339–357.

Wallen, K., & Hassett, J. M. (2009). Sexual differentiation of behavior in monkeys: Role of prenatal hormones. *Journal of Neuroendcrinology, 21*(4), 421–426.

Wallerstein, J. S. (1983). Children of divorce: Stress and developmental tasks. In N. Garmeyzy & M. Rutter (Eds.), *Stress, coping, and development in children* (pp. 265–302). New York: McGraw-Hill.

Wallerstein, J. S. (2005). Growing up in the divorced family. *Clinical Social Work Journal, 33*(4), 401–417.

Wang, H., & Amato, P. R. (2000). Predictors of divorce adjustment: Stressors, resources, and definitions. *Journal of Marriage and the Family, 62*, 655–668.

Wang, Z., Yu, G., Gascio, C., Liu, Y., Gingrich, B., & Insel, T. R. (1999). Dopamine D2 receptor-mediated regulation of partner preferences in female prairie voles (Microtus ochrogaster): A common mechanism for pair bonding? *Behavioral Neuroscience, 113*, 602–611.

Ward, R. A. (1981). The never-married in later life. In P. J. Stein (Ed.), *Single life: Unmarried adults in social context* (pp. 342–356). New York: St. Martin's Press.

Ward-Gailey, C. (2004). Adoptive families in the United States. In S. Coltrane (Ed.), *Families and society* (pp. 365–288). Belmont, CA: Wadsworth/Thompson Learning.

Warehime, M. N., & Bass, L. E. (2008). Breaking singles up: Sexual satisfaction among men and women. *International Journal of Sexual Health, 20*(4), 247–261.

Waskul, D., & Lust, M. (2004). Role-playing and playing roles: The person, player, and persona in fantasy role-playing. *Symbolic Interaction, 27*(3), 333–356.

Wayment, H. A., & Peplau, L. A. (1995). Social support and well-being among lesbian and heterosexual women: A structural modeling approach. *Personality and Social Psychology Bulletin, 21*, 1189–1199.

Weidenholzer, J., & Aspalter, C. (2008). The American and European social dream: The competition of welfare regimes. *Journal of Comparative Social Welfare, 24*(1), 3–11.

Weil, E. (2006, July/August). Breeder reaction: Does everybody have the right to have a baby? And who should pay when nature alone doesn't work? *Mother Jones*, 33–37.

Weinberg, D. H. (2007, July/August). Earnings by gender: Evidence from Census 2000. *Monthly Labor Review, 130*. Retrieved from http://www.bls.gov/opub/mlr/2007/07/art3full.abs

Weinraub, M., Horvath, D. L., & Gringlas, M. B. (2002). Single parenthood. In M. H. Bornstein (Ed.), *Handbook of parenting* (vol. 3, pp. 109–139). Hillsdale, NJ: Lawrence Erlbaum Associates.

Weinstock, M. (2007). Gender differences in the effects of prenatal stress on brain development and behaviour. *Neurochemical Research, 32*(10), 1730–1740.

Weiss, G. (1995). Sex-selective abortion: A relational approach. *Hypatia, 10*(1), 202–217.

Wellings, K., Collumbien, M., & Slaymaker, E. (2006). Sexual behaviour in context: A global perspective. *The Lancet, 368*, 1706–1728.

Wen, M., Browning, C. R., & Cagney, K. A. (2003). Poverty, affluence, and income inequality: Neighborhood economic structure and its implications for health. *Social Science and Medicine, 57*, 843–860.

Werner, E. E., & Smith, R. S. (2001). *Journeys from childhood to midlife: Risk, resilience, and recovery*. Ithaca, NY: Cornell University Press.

West's encyclopedia of American law (1998). (2nd ed.). Eagan, MN: West Publishing Group.

Wethington, H. R., Hahn, R. A., Fuqua-Whitley, D. S., Sipe, T. A., Crosby, A. E., Johnson, R. L. … Chattopadhyay, S. K. (2008). The effectiveness of interventions to reduce psychological harm from traumatic events among children and adolescents: A systematic review. *American Journal of Preventative Medicine, 35*(3), 287–313.

Whipple, B., Ogden, G., & Komisaruk, K. (1992). Quantification of the perceptual and physiological correlates of imagery-induced orgasms in women. In W. Bezemer (Ed.), *Sex Matters* (pp. 9–12). Amsterdam: Elsevier Science.

White, L., & Keith, B. (1990). The effect of shift work on the quality and stability of marital relationships. *Journal of Marriage and the Family, 52*, 453–462.

White, L., & Rogers, S. J. (2000). Economic circumstances and family outcomes: A review of the 1990s. *Journal of Marriage and the Family, 62*, 1035–1051.

Whiteside, M. F. (1998). The parental alliance following divorce: An overview. *Journal of Marital and Family Therapy, 24*, 3–24.

Whitney, P., & Davis, L. (1999). Child abuse and domestic violence in Massachusetts: Can practice be integrated in a public child welfare setting? *Child Maltreatment, 4*, 158–166.

Whitton, S. W., Rhoades, G. K., Stanley, S. M., & Markman, H. J. (2008). Effects of parental divorce on marital commitment and confidence. *Journal of Family Psychology, 22*(5), 789–793.

WHO (2005). *WHO multi-country study on women's health and domestic violence against women: Summary report*. Geneva: World Health Organization.

WHO (2008). *A global response to elder abuse and neglect*. Retrieved from http://www.who.int/ageing/publications/ELDER_DocAugust08.pdf

Whyte, M. K. (1992). Choosing mates—the American way. *Society, 29*(3), 71–77.

Widmer, K., Cina, A., Charvoz, L., Shantinath, S., & Bodenmann, G. (2005). A model dyadic-coping intervention. In T. A. Revenson, K. Kayser, & G. Bodenmann (Eds.), *Couples coping with stress: Emerging perspectives on dyadic coping* (pp. 159–174). Washington, DC: American Psychological Association.

Wienke, C. (2009). Does the "marriage benefit" extend to partnered gay and lesbian relationships? Evidence from a random sample of sexually active adults. *Journal of Family Issues, 30,* 259–289.

Wierson, M., Long, P. J., & Forehand, R. L. (1993). Toward a new understanding of early menarche: The role of environmental stress in pubertal timing. *Adolescence, 28*(112), 913–924.

Wierzalis, E. A., Barret, B., Pope, M., & Rankins, M. (2006). Gay men and aging: Sex and intimacy. In D. Kimmel, T. Rose, & S. David (Eds.), *Lesbian, gay, bisexual, and transgender aging: Research and clinical perspectives* (pp. 91–109). New York: Columbia University Press.

Wilkins, R. G. (2003). The constitutionality of legal preferences for heterosexual marriage. *Regent University Law Review, 16,* 121–126.

Williams, C. L. (1998). Food for thought: Brain, genes, and nutrition. *Brain Research, 27,* 1–4.

Williams, J. E., & Best, D. L. (1990). *Measuring sex stereotypes: A multination study* (rev. ed.). Newbury Park, CA: Sage.

Williamson, J. (1995). *New people: Miscegenation and mulattoes in the United States.* Baton Rouge: Louisiana State University Press.

Wilson, G., & Roscigno, V. J. (2010). Race and downward mobility from privileged occupations. *Social Science Research, 39,* 67–77.

Wineberg, H. (1994). Marital reconciliation in the U.S.: White couples are successful? *Journal of Marriage and the Family, 56,* 80–88.

Winkielman, P., & Cacioppo, J. T. (2001). Mind at ease puts a smile on the face: Psychophysiological evidence that processing facilitation elicits positive affect. *Journal of Personality and Social Psychology, 81,* 989–1000.

Wirtz, P. H., Siegrist, J., Rimmele, U., & Ehlert, U. (2007). Higher over-commitment to work is associated with lower norepinephrine secretion before and after acute psychosocial stress in men. *Psychoneuroendcrinology, 33*(1), 92–99.

Wise, R. A. (1996) Neurobiology of addiction. *Current Opinion in Neurobiology, 6,* 243–251.

Wismer-Fries, A. B., Shirtcliff, E. A., & Pollak, S. D. (2008). Neuroendocrine dysregulation following early social deprivation in children. *Developmental Psychobiology, 50,* 588–599.

Wolfe, D. A., Crooks, C. C., Chiodo, D., & Jaffe, P. (2009). Child maltreatment, bullying, gender-based harassment and adolescent dating violence: Making the connections. *Psychology of Women Quarterly, 33,* 21–24.

Wolfers, J. (2006). Did unilateral divorce laws raise divorce rates? *American Economic Review, 96,* 1802–1820.

Wolfers, J., & Stevenson, B. (2006). Bargaining in the shadow of the law: Divorce laws and family distress. *Quarterly Journal of Economics, 121,* 1–15.

Wolin, S. J., Bennett, L. A., & Jacobs, J. S. (1998). Assessing family rituals. In E. Imber-Black, J. Roberts, & R. Whiting (Eds.), *Rituals and family therapy* (pp. 230–256). New York: Norton.

Wong, J. W., & Earl, J. K. (2009). Towards an integrated model of individual, psychosocial, and organizational predictors of retirement adjustment. *Journal of Vocational Behavior, 75,* 1–13.

Wong, M. G. (1998). The Chinese-American family. In C. H. Mindel, R. W. Haberstein, & R. Wright, Jr. (Eds.), *Ethnic families in America: Patterns and variations* (pp. 284–310). Upper Saddle River, NJ: Prentice Hall.

Wood, G., & Gough, I. (2006). A comparative welfare regime approach to global social policy. *World Development, 34,* 1696–1712.

Wood, P. (2003, September 23). Sex and consequences. *The American Conservative.*

World Health Organization. (2000, June). *Female genital mutilation* (Fact Sheet No. 241). Geneva: World Health Organization.

Wright, C. (1999). Female singlehood and urban space in Lesotho. *Review of Southern African Studies, 3*(2), 75–102.

Wright, T. A., & Cropanzano, R. (2000). Psychological well-being and job satisfaction as predictors of job performance. *Journal of Occupational Health Psychology, 5,* 84–94.

Wrigley, E. A., & Schofield, R. S. (1989). *The population history of England 1541–1871.* Cambridge, U.K.: Cambridge University Press.

Wrosch, C. Schulz, R., & Heckhausen, J. (2004). Health stresses and depressive symptomatology in the elderly: A control-process approach. *Association for Psychological Science, 13*(1), 17–20.

Xie, X., Dzindolet, M., & Meredith, W. (1999). Marriage and family life attitude: Comparison of Chinese and American students. *International Journal of Sociology of the Family, 29*(1), 53–66.

Yan, E., & Tang, C. S. (2001). Prevalence and psychological impact of Chinese elder abuse. *Journal of Interpersonal Violence, 16*(11), 1158–1174.

Yan, E., Tang, C. S., & Yeung, D. (2002). No safe haven: A review on elder abuse in Chinese families. *Trauma, Violence, and Abuse, 3*(3), 167–180.

Yanagisako, S. J. (1985). *Transforming the past: Tradition and kinship among Japanese Americans.* Palo Alto, CA: Stanford University Press.

Yang, J. (2009). Just what are the same-sex benefits? Retrieved from http://firstread.msnbc.msn.com/archive/2009/06/17/1968225.aspx

Yep, G. A., Lovaas, K. E., & Elia, J. P. (2003). A critical appraisal of assimilationist and radical ideologies underlying same-sex marriage in LGBT communities in the United States. *Journal of Homosexuality, 45*(1), 45–64.

Yllo, K. A. (2005). Through a feminist lens: Gender, diversity and violence: Extending the feminist framework. In D. R. Loseke, R. J. Gelles, & M. M. Cavanaugh (Eds.), *Current controversies on family violence* (pp. 611–622). New York: Sage.

Yodanis, C. (2005). Divorce culture and marital gender equality: A cross-national study. *Gender and Society, 19*(5), 644–659.

Zabin, L. S., Emerson, M. R., & Rowland, D. L. (2005). Childhood sexual abuse and early menarche: The direction of their relationship and its implications. *Journal of Adolescent Health, 36,* 93–400.

Zaidi, A. U., & Shuraydi, M. (2002). Perceptions of arranged marriages by young Pakistani Muslim women living in a western society. *Journal of Comparative Family Studies, 33*(4), 495–514.

Zajicek, A. M., & Koski, P. R. (2003). Strategies of resistance to stigmatization among white middle-class singles. *Sociological Spectrum, 23*(3), 377–403.

Zajonc, R. B. (2005). *Preferences.* Invited address at the 6th Convention of the Society for Personality and Social Psychology, New Orleans.

Zamboni, B. D., & Crawford, I. (2007). Minority stress and sexual problems among African-American gay and bisexual men. *Archives of Sexual Behavior, 36,* 569–578.

Zambrano, E., Martínez-Samayoa, P. M., Bautista, C. J., Deás, M., Guillén, L., Rodríguez-González, G. L., … Nathanielsz, P. W. (2005). Sex differences in transgenerational alterations of growth and metabolism in progeny (F_2) of female offspring (F_1) of rats fed a low protein diet during pregnancy and lactation. *Journal of Physiology, 566,* 225–236.

Zawacki, T., Abbey, A., Buck, P. O., McAuslan, P., & Clinton-Sherrod, A. M. (2003). Perpetrators of alcohol-involved sexual assaults: How do they differ from other sexual assault perpetrators and nonperpetrators? *Aggressive Behavior, 29,* 366–380.

Zayas, V., Shuda, Y., Mischel, W., Osterhout, L. & Takahashi, M. (2009). Neural responses to partner rejection cues. *Psychological Science, 20,* 813. doi: 10.1111/j.1467–9280.2009.02373.x

Zhang, S., & Kline, S. L. (2009). Can I make my own decision? A cross-cultural study of perceived social network influence in mate selection. *Journal of Cross-Cultural Psychology, 40,* 3–23.

Zhou, Q., Eisenberg, N., Wang, Y., & Reiser, M. (2004). Chinese children's effortful control and dispositional anger/frustration: relations to parenting styles and children's social functioning. *Developmental Psychology, 40*(3), 352–366.

INDEX

Marriages and Families in the 21st Century: A Bioecological Approach, First Edition. Tasha R. Howe.
© 2012 Tasha R. Howe. Published 2012 by Blackwell Publishing Ltd.